Eileen Southern

PROFESSOR OF MUSIC, YORK COLLEGE
OF THE CITY UNIVERSITY OF NEW YORK

Black Americans:
A History

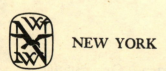
NEW YORK

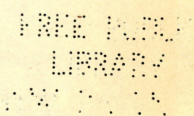

Published simultaneously in Canada
by George J. McLeod Limited, Toronto

Maps by Theodore R. Miller

PRINTED IN THE UNITED STATES OF AMERICA

7 8 9 0

To my husband, Joseph

ALSO BY EILEEN SOUTHERN

Readings in Black American Music

Contents

Part I   Song in a Strange Land, 1619–1775

Part II   Let My People Go, 1776–1866

Part IV   Lift Every Voice, 1920–

Illustrations and Plates

Plates *between pages 282 and 283*

XVII. W. C. Handy and Duke Ellington • World War II jam
session • Leontyne Price • George Shirley
XVIII. Arthur Cunningham • Hale Smith • William Grant Still

Preface

A history of the musical activities of black Americans in the United States is long overdue. The black musician has created an entirely new music—in a style peculiarly Afro-American—that today spreads its influence over the entire world. And ever since his arrival in the New World, he has enriched with his contributions the European-based musical traditions of the nation. The present work concerns itself with these dual aspects of his musical activity and is intended to fulfill a twofold purpose: first, to serve as an introduction and guide to those who wish to become better informed about the history of black American music makers; second, to serve as a much-needed textbook for college courses that treat the subject of Afro-American music. I have traced the course of this music from the colonial period to modern times, with conscious concern for its relationship to the general traditions of western music. I have been equally concerned with the social, political, and economic forces in American history that helped to shape the development of Negro music and to determine the course it took.

The facts that have emerged during the course of my investigation, many of them never before collected into a single source, present a colorful and fascinating history. Because of the great time span involved, it was necessary to omit some material; only the most important events could be described and only the most significant persons or groups discussed. Musical practices in West Africa, the place of origin for the ancestors of most black Americans, have been documented to the extent necessary for understanding the musical heritage that the black man brought with him to the New World. My discussion of colonial music is centered on practices in the English colonies, which later became the United States. The music of black men in Spanish- and French-speaking areas belongs to a different tradition and, consequently, calls for its own special treatment. It is not to be assumed that the history of Afro-American music as presented here is necessarily complete. Much research yet needs to be done in all areas of musical activity, particularly in the earlier periods. Perhaps the present study will stimulate such general research and investigation into special aspects of black American music.

The chief emphasis in my discussion has been placed on the creators of music, whether they were anonymous slaves of the ante-bellum period, ballad writers of the Gay Nineties, jazzmen of the early twentieth century, or composers of symphonic music in recent decades. But I have also given considerable attention to a number of musicians who were primarily performers, particularly the pioneers who broke down barriers of race prejudice and discrimination and made it easier for those who came after to succeed. Whenever possible, I have tried to let the individuals who were on the scene or who were directly involved with the making of the music tell its history—the travelers and diarists, the local historians, and above all, the black music makers themselves. With regard to developments in recent times, especially in the field of jazz, I have taken a deliberately cautious approach. We are yet too close in time to this music to be able to view it in proper perspective.

Since the immediate purpose of the present work is to record the facts of history, which must precede esthetic and stylistic evaluation, I have not tried to make explicit a definition of black American music. My concern has been with all music created by Afro-Americans. By gathering together the strands that have made up the fabric of this music in the United States—the folksongs, popular, vocal and dance music, religious, theatrical, and concert music—I have tried to provide a solid and useful basis for discussion of the question of its definition.

It is to be hoped that my experience in teaching courses in Afro-American music at New York University and at York College of the City University of New York reflects itself in the organization of the contents of this book. Care has been taken to present technical concepts in terms easily grasped by the layman. Analyses of a selected number of characteristic musical forms have been included in order to make for a better understanding of the music on the part of the listener. The majority of the folksongs used as musical examples are complete and, therefore, can—and should—be sung by the reader. Afro-American music is primarily a vocal music. To appreciate this fact leads to an increase in the understanding of the instrumental music.

It would be impossible to name all of the persons from whom I have received help in carrying out this project. Some obligations stand out, however, above all others. I am especially indebted, for example, to the staffs of some libraries and institutions for kind assistance in procuring information and materials; among them, the American Antiquarian Society; the American Society of Composers, Authors, and Publishers; Broadcast Music, Inc.; the York College Library of the City University of New York; the Cleveland Hall Library in Chicago; the Library of Congress; the Metropolitan Opera Association Archives; the Moreland Library at Howard University; the Newport Historical Society; the Philadelphia Library Company and the Pennsylvania Historical Society; and the New York Public Library —particularly the Rare Book Division, the Lincoln Center Americana Collection, and, above all, the Schomburg Collection.

It is a pleasure to acknowledge the generosity of colleagues Jan LaRue (New York University) and Barry Brook (City University of New York) for giving active encouragement to my project in its early stages. Other colleagues, friends, and relatives who assisted either by interviewing musicians or by obtaining data include Stella Hall, Roy Hill (Rutgers University), Marion Lathrop (formerly, Brooklyn College), Dominique-René de Lerma (Indiana University), Angela McLinn, Eliza Tapp, and Elizabeth Wiggins. Jean Leach, Thomas Leach, and April Southern Reilly read parts of the manuscript and made useful suggestions. My son, Edward, helped with the proofreading. Special thanks are due my mother, Mrs. Lilla Rose, who patiently cut clippings from news sources over a period of many months. Bibliophiles Clarence Holte and Gertrude McBrown graciously allowed me access to their large personal Negro collections. David Hamilton, music editor at W. W. Norton & Company, contributed valuable suggestions with regard to numerous aspects of the text, and Carol Flechner, also of Norton, kept a close watch on many important details. My participation as an adjunct professor in the experimental Urban Preceptorial Program at New York University (1969–70) made it possible for me to explore the activity of Negro musicians in New York City in greater depth than otherwise would have been possible.

I reserve a special measure of gratitude for my fellow Negro musicians, who responded graciously to my requests for biographical information, pictures, and other kinds of data, often for other musicians as well as for themselves. Especially helpful in this way were Jewelle Anderson, Andrew Frierson, Leonard Goines, and George Shirley. My long conversations with Eubie Blake, Eva Jessye, Hall Johnson, and William Grant Still among the older composers and with Thomas J. Anderson, Hale Smith, and Olly Wilson among the young composers helped me immeasurably as a musicologist to gain insight into the composer's world and to form conclusions about the music. I was rewarded in a similar way by my direct or indirect contacts with Marion Cumbo; James Reese Europe, Jr.; Fannie Howard Douglass (Mrs. Joseph Douglass, granddaughter-in-law of Frederick Douglass); John Matheus; and Portia Washington Pittman (daughter of Booker T. Washington). Finally, it is not likely that I would have been able to begin or to complete this work without the active assistance, unflagging encouragement, and patient cooperation of my husband, Joseph.

EILEEN SOUTHERN
May, 1970

The Music of Black Americans: A History

I

Song in a Strange Land

1619-1775

IMPORTANT EVENTS

1619 First arrival of Africans in the English colonies: James-
      town, Va.
1620 Landing of the Pilgrims: Plymouth, Mass.
1626 Founding of New Amsterdam. Eleven Africans
      brought in as indentured servants.
1630 Founding of Boston, Mass. Cultural center and larg-
      est city in the colonies as late as 1743.
1638 Beginning of the New England slave trade with the
      arrival of the first blacks on the ship *Desire:* Bos-
      ton, Mass.
1640 Publication of the first book in the English colonies,
      the *Bay Psalm Book:* Boston, Mass.
1641 Earliest record of a slave baptized and taken into the
      church: Dorchester, Mass.
      Enactment of the famous "Body of Liberties" laws in
      Mass., giving tacit approval to the institution of
      slavery.
1644 Earliest record of the manumission of slaves: New
      Amsterdam, N. Y.

1646   Earliest mention of manumission in New England: New Haven, Conn.

1661   First of the so-called Black Codes giving statutory recognition to the institution of slavery: Va.

1664   New Amsterdam taken over by the British; renamed New York.

1667   Law passed by the Virginia Assembly stating that the baptism of slaves did not exempt them from bondage.

1670   Founding of Charles Town, S. C., only "city" in the South during the colonial period.

1681   Founding of Philadelphia, cultural center and largest city in the colonies on the eve of the American Revolution.

1688   Germantown protest; pioneer attack on the institution of slavery by the Quakers: Germantown, Pa.

1693   Organization by the Reverend Cotton Mather, of the "Society of Negroes," pioneer effort to provide instruction for slaves: Boston, Mass.

1704   Establishment of one of the earliest schools for slaves by Elias Neau: Trinity Episcopal Church, New York, N. Y.

1707   Publication of *Hymns and Spiritual Songs* by Isaac Watts, which influenced the development of black American hymnody: London (American edition, Boston, 1739).

1712   New York City slave insurrection.

1717   Publishing of *The Psalms of David, Imitated . . .* by Isaac Watts: London (first American edition, Philadelphia, 1728).

1723   Earliest record of a black army musician—Nero Benson, trumpeter: Framingham, Mass.

1731   First public concert in the colonies: Boston, Mass.

1735   Five slaves baptized by the Reverend Jonathan Edwards at the Northampton, Mass. revival of the "Great Awakening" movement.

1739   Slave uprising, the "Stono Conspiracy," near Charles Town, S. C.

1741   Founding of the first permanent Moravian settlement, with black men among the first settlers: Bethlehem, Pa.
       New York City slave conspiracy.

1743   "Negro School House" opened by Alexander Garden, with two educated slaves as teachers (until 1764): Charles Town, S. C.

1756   French and Indian War (until 1763).

1760   Beginning of Methodism in the colonies: New York, N. Y.

CHAPTER I

The African Heritage

End (African music)

"About the last of August came a Dutch man-of-warre that sold us twenty Negars." This statement, dated 1619, in the *Generall Historie of Virginia* by Captain John Smith, refers to the first arrival of black men in the English colonies on the mainland (i.e. the eastern seaboard of the present United States). They were to continue to come for more than two hundred years, brought at first in small groups (called "parcels"), then later by the shiploads, clamped in irons and wedged into foul vessels so closely together that there was hardly enough room for movement. The Africans came for the most part from the west coast of Africa—from the area now occupied by the lands of Senegal, Guinea, Gambia, Sierra Leone, Liberia, Ivory Coast, Ghana, Togo, Dahomey, Nigeria, Cameroon, Gabon, and part of the Congo republics. Before the arrival of the white man on Africa's west coast, the area was dominated by such empires as Ghana, Mali, Songhay, Kanem-Bornu, and the Mossi, Hausa, and other states. With the collapse of some of the older empires, new ones came into existence. During the period of the Atlantic slave trade, the powerful kingdoms, states, and city-states included Ashanti, Benin, Dahomey, the Delta states, Gambia, Oyo, and Senegal.

Olaudah Equiano, one of the first Africans to write a book in the English language, described the area from which slaves were taken in his autobiography, *The Interesting Narrative of the Life of Olaudah Equiano, or Gustavus Vassa the African. Written by Himself* (1789):

That part of Africa, known by the name of Guinea, to which the trade for slaves is carried on, extends along the coast about 3400 miles, from Senegal to Angola, and includes a variety of kingdoms.

White traders gave to the region such names as the Gold Coast, the Ivory Coast, and the Slave Coast. The first white travelers in the region found a wide variety of political organizations: some were highly organized, with kings, governors, and noblemen (for example, the palace chiefs and town chiefs of Benin); others were loosely formed into clans, tribes, or similar kinship groups. Regardless of the political make-up of West Africa, however, the most important divisions were the ancient ones that separated peoples into groups according to their clans, or their villages of origin, or their descent from common ancestors. Thus the various peoples included such tribes as the Fon, Yoruba, Ibo, Fanti, Fulani, Ashanti, Jolof, Mandingo, and Baoulé.

MUSIC IN WEST AFRICA

It is impossible to know all of the facts about the music of the past in West Africa because of the lack of indigenous written records. We can learn a great deal, however, from two major sources of historical information: the oral traditions of the land and the books written by European travelers and traders. Some of these chronicles provide surprisingly rich details about one or more aspects of West African music and occasionally include examples of the music itself. Possibly the earliest account written in English is the chronicle of Richard Jobson, an English captain who visited Gambia during the years 1620 through 1621. Upon his return to London in 1623, Jobson published a book entitled *The Golden Trade or a Discovery of the River Gambra [Gambia] and the Golden Trade of the Aethiopians*. Early in his travels, Jobson observed the importance of music in the African way of life:

> There is without doubt, no people on the earth more naturally affected to the sound of musicke than these people; which the principall persons [that is, the kings and chiefs] do hold as an ornament of their state, so as when wee come to see them their musicke will seldome be wanting.

At another point in his book Jobson observed, "If at any time the Kings or principall persons come unto us trading in the River, they will have their musicke playing before them." A statement made by Equiano reveals how the Africans themselves regarded music:

We are almost a nation of dancers, musicians, and poets. Thus every great event . . . is celebrated in public dances which are accompanied with songs and music suited to the occasion.

In other accounts of the period there is similar testimony to the primacy of music in the lives of the African peoples. The Englishman James Houstoun wrote, for example, in 1725: "I visited King Conny in his Castle, who received me very kindly with the usual ceremonies of their Country, Musick, Drums, and Horns." A traveler to Dahomey in the late eighteenth century, Robert Noris, noted the importance of music and the dance in his book *Memoirs of the Reign of Bossa Ahadee, King of Dahomy* (1789). And Mungo Park, a Scottish surgeon sent in 1795 by the African Association of England to explore the region of the Niger River, and land of the Mandingos and the Malinkes, devoted several pages to music and dancing in his chronicle *Travels in the Interior Districts of Africa* . . . (1800). One of the most detailed accounts of musical practices in Africa during the slavery period is found in the book of Thomas Edward Bowdich, *Mission from Cape Coast Castle to Ashantee* (1819). Bowdich was a member of a four-man delegation sent by the African Committee of London in 1817 to explore the realm of the king of Ashanti and to bring back information about the interior of black Africa. In his book Bowdich not only fully relates the events which occurred on the occasions when he heard music, but also gives graphic descriptions of musical instruments and, even more important, records a number of pieces in music notation.

For every "custom" (the term used in Africa with reference to public ceremonies, rites, festivals, and similar events) and for almost every activity among the Africans, there was an appropriate music. Ceremonial music composed the largest part of the musical repertory of a village or a people. Music accompanied religious ceremonies and rites associated with birth, initiation, marriage, healing, going to war, and death. Bowdich observed, for example, that the Ashanti thought it "absurd" to worship God in any way other than with chanting or singing. All sources report on the performances of the African bards on public occasions, who sang of the "historical events" of the people and of the kings and rulers, "enumerating their titles and proclaiming their grandeur and actions in terms of the most fulsome adulation."

Bowdich gives a fascinating account of the ceremonial music performed on his mission's arrival at Kumasi, the capitol of Ashanti:

> Upwards of 5000 people, the greater part warriors, met us with awful bursts of martial music, discordant only in its mixture; for horns, drums, rattles, and gong-gongs were all exerted with a zeal bordering on phrenzy. . . . We were halted whilst the captains performed their Pyrrhic dance in the centre of a circle formed by their warriors.

The dance lasted for about a half hour, after which the Englishmen were escorted by the warriors through the streets of the town to an open square near the palace. They were totally unprepared for the "magnificence and novelty" of the scene that lay before them.

> The king, his tributaries, and captains, were resplendent in the distance, surrounded by attendants of every description. . . . The sun was reflected, with a glare scarcely more supportable than the heat, from the massy gold ornaments, which glistened in every direction. More than a hundred bands burst at once on our arrival, [all playing] the peculiar airs of their several chiefs; the horns flourished their defiances [i.e. fanfare melodies], with the beating of innumerable drums and metal instruments, and then yielded for a while to the soft breathings of their long flutes, which were truly harmonious; and a pleasing instrument, like a bagpipe without the drone, was happily blended. At least a hundred large umbrellas, or canopies, which could shelter thirty persons, were sprung up and down by the bearers with brilliant effect, being made of scarlet, yellow, and the most shewy [i.e. showy] cloths and silks. . . .

Bowdich made several references to the fact that each band had its own special "theme music," which it performed during parades associated with various festivals and public celebrations. On one occasion, the drummers threw their "white-washed drums" into the air and caught them again, "with much agility and grimace," as they walked along.

One of the special functions of African bards was to accompany warriors to battle, singing of the glorious deeds of the past in order to arouse the fighters to emulation of their ancestors. The music performed during preparations for major hunting expeditions was also of a ceremonial nature and similar in function to that performed in connection with war. A special kind of music was called for at victory celebrations, of course, whether in commemoration of the defeat of the enemy or a successful hunt. Special festivals of the year—such as the "Yam Customs" of the Ashanti or the "Annual Customs" of the Dahomans—also called for special instrumental and vocal music. Among some tribes of Angola (now the western Congo) there was a tradition for litigation music. In presenting their cases to the chief-judge in a village court, the litigants chanted or sang their arguments to the accompaniment of drums and occasional singing of the assembled villagers.

Among all Africans, one of the most important ceremonies was the occasion when local rulers and minor chiefs went to the capital of a country to pay homage to the king, particularly upon his installation. Bowdich's account of the events of one such occasion in Ashanti (not an installation, however) is reminiscent of the reception given to his mission upon its arrival in the capital city. We know from other sources that the crowds who filled the city at such times were composed not only of the chiefs and their followers who had come to pay their respects, but also envoys and merchants from other kingdoms and states, traders from within the country, and villagers from miles around. The court musicians played on instruments plated or tipped with gold, in both seated and standing positions and protected from the glare of the sun by huge canopies. Bowdich was so impressed by the scene that he painted a picture of it, feeling that words could not adequately describe what he saw and heard (see Plates IV–V).

African music of a nonceremonial type included worksongs

of all kinds, hunting songs, instructional songs, social-commentary songs (including gossip and satirical songs), and entertainment music. Boat songs, in particular, were found everywhere, for waterways provided the chief means of transportation in West Africa. As an agricultural people, the Africans had many varieties of worksongs associated with their planting and harvesting, cattle raising, preparation of food, and similar activities.

As has been noted, music and dance were the chief forms of entertainment. Festivals customarily lasted many days in succession—the "Annual Customs" of Dahomey, for instance, for several weeks—and the dancing that took place lasted for many hours at a time. Jobson described a typical dance as follows:

> Both day and night, more especially all the night the people continue dancing, until he that plays be quite tyred out . . . the standers-by seeme to grace the dancer, by clapping their hands together after the manner of keeping time.

Park, too, remarked that "at all their dances and concerts, clapping of hands appears to constitute a necessary part of the chorus." An eyewitness to a Dahoman festival observed that a "numerous crowd of people" danced to the music of trumpets, flutes, bells, and drums of various sizes. When one band of musicians grew tired of playing during the all-night dancing, another took its place.

MUSICAL INSTRUMENTS AND PERFORMANCE PRACTICES

The written sources provide much useful information about instruments and orchestras or bands. Equiano mentions the instruments in common use among his people:

> We have many musical instruments, particularly drums of different kinds, a piece of music which resembles a guitar, and another much like a stickado. These last are chiefly used by betrothed virgins, who play on them on all grand festivals.

Jobson supplies rich details about instruments and performance

practices. After remarking that "they have little varieties of instruments," he continues, describing those used most frequently:

> That which is most common in use, is made of a great gourd,
> and a necke thereunto fastened, resembling in some sort, our
> Bandora; but they have no manner of fret, and the strings they
> are such as the place yeeldes or their invention can attaine to
> make. . . .

The "bandora" (or pandora) to which Jobson referred was a
European instrument of the Renaissance, a plucked string instrument similar to the lute but with the flat back of the guitar. It
was further distinguished by a body with sides curved in a
scalloplike manner and a large number of strings—from ten to
fourteen strings tuned in five to seven courses at the unison or
the octave. Of English origin, the bandora would naturally come
to the mind of the Englishman Jobson when he encountered
an African instrument of similar construction. The African instrument obviously belonged to the plucked-string family (as
distinguished from the bowed-string type), since Jobson compared it to a bandora. He says nothing about the tuning of the
strings, except that the music of the instrument was "unapt" to
be "sweete and musicall" (i.e. to the ears of a European).
  Sometimes the string instrument was performed "in consort-
ship with a little drumme." The drummer held his drum under
the left arm and beat it with his left-hand fingers and at the
same time with a little stick held in his right hand. Mungo Park
refers to three major kinds of string instruments among the
Mandingos: the *koonting,* a three-string plucked instrument; the
korro, a large eighteen-string harp; and the *simbing,* a small
seven-string harp. An instrument called a *bow-string* by Park
evidently is the prototype for the ubiquitous musical bow of
modern Africa. Bowdich encountered a similar type of Ashanti,
called the *bentwa:*

> [It] is a stick bent in the form of a bow, and across it, is fastened
> a very thin piece of split cane, which is held between the lips [of
> the player] at one end, and struck with a small stick; whilst at
> the other [end] it is occasionally stopped, or rather buffed, by a
> thick one [i.e. piece of split cane]. . . .

In Ashanti, there were two principal string-instrument types. The *sanko* was a zither type made of a narrow box, the open top of which was covered with an alligator or antelope skin. The eight strings of the *sanko* were sometimes tuned to sound like the diatonic major scale of European music from middle C to its octave (i.e. C D E F G A B C), but Bowdich noted that players on the *sanko* often tuned the strings at random to any pitches within the octave. The other string instrument belonged to the violin family. Its body was made of a calabash, covered on top with deerskin punctured by two holes "for the sound to escape." The strings and bow were made of cow's hair.

In the land of Gabon, Bowdich saw a five-string mandolin type and heard an African play on a harp

> . . . formed of wood, except that part emitting the sound, which was covered with goat skin, perforated at the bottom. The bow to which the eight strings were fixed, was considerably curved, and there was no upright; the figure head, which was well carved, was placed at the top of the body [of the harp], the strings were twisted round long pegs, which easily turned when they wanted [i.e. needed] tuning, and, being made of the fibrous roots of palm wine tree, were very tough and not apt to slip. The tone was full, harmonious, and deep.

The major instrument of black Africa was, of course, the drum. Without exception contemporary writers commented upon the "multitude of drums in various sizes" seen and heard in Africa. From a book written by James Hawkins, *A History of a Voyage to the Coast of Africa* (1797), comes a description of two kinds of drums found among the Ibo peoples. A medium-sized drum, about a foot in diameter and eighteen inches high, was made from a hollow log, the bark being pulled off and the knotty parts sanded down until smooth. After a square hole was cut in the side, pieces of dried sheepskin were drawn tightly over the opening and over both ends of the log. A smaller drum was made by cutting a gourd or calabash in half and drawing a skin tightly over the opening. Both instruments were played by striking the skin with the palms of the hands or the fingers. Mungo Park refers to a drum called a *tang tang* that was open at the lower end.

Drums ranged in length from as small as twelve inches to as long as six or seven feet and in diameter from two or three inches to several feet. Two or more drums were customarily played together, each producing different pitches and rhythms. Bowdich observed that drums were most often made of

> . . . hollow'd trunks of trees, frequently carved with much nicety, mostly open at one end, and of many sizes: those with heads of common skin (that is, of any other than Leopard skin) are beaten with sticks in the form of a crotchet rest [i.e. ⅂]; the largest are borne on the head of a man, and struck by one or more followers; the smaller are slung round the neck, or stand on the ground.

Like Jobson, Bowdich noticed that the Africans sometimes used the fingers in striking drums, particularly those drums with heads of leopard skin. The drums standing upright on the ground, including kettledrums, were sometimes struck with the palm of the hand instead of sticks. The wrists of the players on the kettledrums "were hung with bells and curiously-shaped pieces of iron," which made loud, jingling noises as the drummers beat their drums.

Among the other instruments described in contemporary sources are small flutes; three-hole flutes made of long hollow reeds; bagpipe types with very soft drones; horns made of elephant tusks; clarinet types made of wood, called *dududen;* trumpets made of wood and ivory; and an endless variety of pipes, bells, castanets and gong-gongs made of iron, and rattles. Like the drum, keyboard instruments were found in different varieties. Equiano and Bowdich both refer to a small keyboard type, Equiano calling it a *stickado* and Bowdich comparing it to a *staccado* but calling it an *oompoochwa.* The latter's description is as follows:

> [It] is a box, one end of which is left open; two flat bridges are fastened across the top, and five pieces of thin curved stick, scraped very smooth, are attached to them, and (their ends being raised,) are struck with some force by the thumb.

This instrument is common in present-day Africa, generally known as a *sansa* or thumb-piano.

References to large keyboard types are found in several sources. Park describes an instrument, the *balafou*, as being composed of twenty pieces of hard wood of different lengths, underneath which were hung gourds to increase the sound. Jobson's description of the instrument he heard is more detailed. Called a *ballards*, it consisted of seventeen wooden keys arranged on a board about a "foot about the ground." The player, sitting on the ground, struck the keys with two sticks, one in each hand. Attached to the end of each twelve-inch stick was a ball "covered withe some soft stuffe, to avoyd the clattering noyse the bare stickes would make." On his arms the player had large iron rings, to which were attached horizontally extending iron bars that had "upon them smaller rings and juggling toyes." When the player struck the instrument, the small iron rings and "juggling toyes" made "a kinde of musicall sound agreeing to their barbarous content." What impressed Jobson most of all was the ingenious method of resonance. From each key hung two gourds, "like bottles," which received the sound and resonated it with an "extraordinary loudness." The sound of the instrument and its player's iron rings could be heard for the distance of a "good English mile."

The most common form of musical performance involved an ensemble (as distinguished from solo performers) including instrumentalists, singers, and dancers. Generally, only males played musical instruments; the women joined in on the singing and dancing. Onlookers participated in the activity by clapping the hands, as we have seen, or by tapping the feet. According to tradition, onlookers also shouted words of encouragement to the performers (or disapproval, if they wished). Essentially, then, there was no audience; all persons were actively involved in the music-dance performance in one way or another. This illustrates one of the basic characteristics of the African tradition in music and dance—its emphasis on communal activity. A successful celebration was one in which there was general participation by all, in which the interaction among the dancers, musicians, and onlookers contributed to the perfect whole. To be sure, African performance allowed for the exhibition of professional skill by the master drummer or the village bard, but it was as members of a performing group rather than as individuals that professionals made their greatest contribution to the performance.

The exceptions to the all-male instrumental groups seem to have been associated with the music performed in connection with rites of birth, marriage, and death. As has been observed, however, Equiano the African states that young women played upon the thumb-piano at grand festivals in his country, the land of Benin. Moreover, a slave trader who published his memoirs in 1854, *Captain Canot: Or Twenty Years of an African Slaver*, gives an account of a young woman playing entertainment music on another kind of African piano. The instrument consisted of a board about two feet square,

> . . . bordered by a light frame at two ends, across which a couple of cane strings were tightly stretched. On these [strings] strips of nicely trimmed bamboo, gradually diminishing in size from left to right, were placed; while beneath them, seven gourds, also gradually decreasing [in size], were securely fastened to mellow the sound. The instrument was carried by a strap [hung] round the player's neck, and was struck by two small wooden hammers softened by some delicate substance.

After singing and playing for the white visitors, the musician danced. "Small silvery bells" attached to her feet, ankles, knees, hands, wrists, and elbows made a pleasing, tinkling sound as she moved about.

Unaccompanied singing apparently was rare. Singers preferred to sing with accompaniment and, when accompanying themselves, showed a predilection for stroked, bowed, or plucked string instruments. When others accompanied the singer, a variety of instruments was drawn upon, including drums. In discussing the kinds of musical performance associated with chief instruments of the Ashanti, Bowdich points out that only lively music was played, for example, on the *sanko* and the thumb-piano. Players maintained a strict regard for the contrasts between loud and soft passages in their music. They had "a method of stopping the strings with the finger, so as to produce a very soft and pleasing effect." In Gabon, performers recited long stories to the accompaniment of the five-string *enchambee* on moonlit evenings. Harps also were customarily employed in the accompaniment for long narrative songs. Horns and trumpets were associated with military occasions and civic celebrations.

The African system of communicating over long distances by the use of drums (i.e. the "talking drums") is not a musical practice and is therefore beyond the scope of the present survey. It may be pointed out, however, that such communication is possible because of the characteristic pitch structure of the West African languages. In sending out messages, the drummers reproduce the speech-tone inflections and the rhythms of spoken sentences. To a lesser extent, horns and xylophones were used in the same way. Bowdich gives an example of a horn "flourish" (fanfare melody) that stated, "O saï, great king! I laud thee every where!"

The singing style employed by the Africans was characterized by high intensity and use of such special effects as falsetto, shouting, and guttural tones. Few of the white contemporary writers liked the sound of the African voice. To them, it was too loud, high-pitched, and harsh. Jobson wrote, for example, about a male singer:

> . . . with his mouth gaping open, [he] makes a rude noyse, resembling much the manner and countenance of those kinde of distressed people which amongst us are called changelings. . . .

In 1638 John Josselyn, a traveler in the colony of Massachusetts, commented similarly in an adverse manner upon the tone quality of the African female voice:

> Mr. Maverick's Negro woman came to my Chamber window and in her own countrey language and tune sang very loud and shril.

And Bowdich pointed out that the men who sang to the accompaniment of the native violin employed a "strong nasal sound."

THE PROFESSIONAL MUSICIAN

Every village had one or two bards whose duties were to teach as well as to entertain. As we have seen, the bard was responsible for remembering the history of the people and transmitting the knowledge to other members of the tribe. Jobson compares African bards to the bards of Great Britain:

> . . . they have a perfect resemblance to the Irish Rimer [i.e. poet], sitting in the same manner as they [i.e. the Irish bards] doe upon the ground, somewhat remote from the company; and as they use [as do the Irish] [the] singing of Songs unto their musicke, the ground and effect whereof is the rehearsall of the ancient stock of the King, exhalting his antientry, and recounting over all the worthy and famous acts by him or them [i.e. the people, that] hath been achieved.

Park calls the bards "singing men" or *jillikea*. Bards did not limit their singing to praises of chiefs and other noblemen; they were willing to sing in honor of anyone who, in the words of Park, was willing to give "solid pudding for empty praise." On several occasions bards accompanied him in his travels, using their considerable talents to "divert the fatigue" of his party or to obtain for them "a welcome from strangers." Another class of professional singers included the itinerant minstrels who wandered from village to village, participating in ceremonies of the people. Park refers to these men as

> devotees of the Mahomedan faith, who travel about the country, singing devout hymns, and performing religious ceremonies, to conciliate the favour of the Almighty, either in averting calamity, or in insuring success to any enterprize.

Not always did the wanderers confine themselves to participation in religious ceremonies, however; other sources indicate that some were equally active in social and recreational ceremonies.

Instrumentalists seem to have had a higher status than singers. All important rulers maintained court bands or orchestras, and the master of the band was one of the chief personages of the ruler's household. The master drummer and the royal horn-blower enjoyed equally high status. In some places the drum—the large drum in particular—was associated with the power and prestige of the chief, who alone had the honor of playing upon it. Members of bands shared in some of the "esteem" given to the music leaders, as did also song leaders, to be sure. Jobson notes, for example, that at the end of a dance, the dancers always gave something to the musicians, and Park observes that "very liberal contributions" were made to bards.

MUSIC AND POETIC FORMS

The most constant feature of African songs was the alternation of improvised lines and fixed refrains. This form allowed for both innovative and conservative procedures at the same time: the extemporization of verses to suit the specific occasion and the retention of traditional words in the refrains; the participation of the soloist in the verses and of the group in singing the refrains; improvisation or embellishment upon the solo melody and reinforcement of the traditional tune in the refrains. Without exception, contemporary writers marveled at the skill of the African musician—and even the ordinary villager—in composing tunes and texts without prior preparation. Actually, the musical procedure involved more an embellishing of a traditional melody than the composing of a new tune. But, as Bowdich pointed out, the performers applied their embellishing melodic motives to the original melody in such profusion that one could hardly hear any trace of the original tones. During the course of a performance a tune was repeated again and again, each time with different embellishments. Moreover, performers were very free in the way they handled repetitions of the music:

> sometimes between each beginning they introduce a few chords, sometimes they leave out a bar, sometimes they return to the middle [of the piece], so entirely is it left to the fancy of the performer.

The earliest example of an African song text written down in a European language is found in Mungo Park's book. The song was composed under unusual circumstances. Park had been compelled to seek shelter in a small village, but was unsuccessful in finding someone who would take him in, and so consequently had to spend the entire day sitting under a tree without food. Toward evening, as thunderclouds threatened and Park began to give up hope of finding a place for the night, a woman passing

by took pity on him and invited him into her home. She gave
him supper and directed him to a mat where he could sleep.
The woman and her companions spent the greater part of the
night spinning cotton; as they worked, they lightened their
labors with songs, one of which was extemporized on the subject
of Park himself. Park listened carefully, observing that the song
"was sung by one of the young women, the rest joining in a
sort of chorus." The following is Park's literal translation of the
spinners' song:

> The winds roared, and the rains fell;
> The poor white man, faint and weary,
> Came and sat under our tree.
> He has no mother to bring him milk,
> No wife to grind his corn.
>
> *Chorus:* Let us pity the white man.
> No mother has he to bring him milk,
> No wife to grind his corn.

The song of the spinners represents a typical African poetic
form—the alternation of stanza and chorus, with the quite common feature of the reappearance of the stanza refrain as part
of the chorus.

An early example of a more common poetic form, the
alternation of verse lines and refrain, was recorded in a source
of 1826, *Narrative of Travels and Discoveries in Northern and
Central Africa*. The authors of the book, Clapperton, Denham,
and Oudney, heard the song in the land of Bornu.

> Give flesh to the hyenas at daybreak,
>   Oh, the broad spears!
> The spear of the Sultan is the broadest,
>   Oh, the broad spears!
> I behold thee now—I desire to see none other,
>   Oh, the broad spears!
> My horse is as tall as a high wall,
>   Oh, the broad spears!
> He will fight against ten—he fears nothing,
>   Oh, the broad spears!

He has slain ten; the guns are yet behind,
   Oh, the broad spears!
The elephant of the forest brings me what I want,
   Oh, the broad spears!
Like unto thee, so is the Sultan,
   Oh, the broad spears! . . .

Modern scholars often use the term "call and response" to describe the responsorial or antiphonal nature of African song performance—i.e. the alternation of solo passages and choral refrains or of two different choral passages. Typically, a song consisted of the continuous repetition of a single melody, sung alternately by the song leader and the group, or alternately by two groups. The importance of the song leader cannot be over-stressed: it was he who chose the song to be sung, who embellished the basic melody and improvised appropriate verses to fit the occasion, and who brought the performance to an end. As we have seen, melodic embellishment of, or improvisation on, the basic melody was quite extensive, often to the point that the original tune was no longer identifiable. Bowdich points out that some of the embellishing figures used by professional musicians were passed down from father to son—evidently in the same way as craftsmen passed secrets of their trade to their sons or apprentices—and other figures were improvised on the spot.

Because of the great complexity of African embellished melodies, Bowdich made no attempt to write down songs as the Africans sang them. Instead, he persuaded an excellent *sanko* player to play some of the traditional tunes of the country on his instrument—without embellishments. In recording the songs, Bowdich was careful to write the notes exactly as he heard them. He observed:

> To have attempted any thing like arrangement . . . would have altered [the melodies], and destroyed the intention of making them known in their original character. I have not even dared to insert a flat or a sharp.

The following song was ancient even at the time Bowdich recorded it in 1817. Its notes represent simply a melodic skeleton to which a performer added extra ornamenting tones, called "graces" by Bowdich, in performance:

Ex. I.1 "A very old Ashantee Air"

Aganka oshoom noofa Oboibee oshoom noofa Aganka oshoom noofa wekirree wekirree

oimiyow wekirree   wekirree wekirree oimiyow

The short tune of the Gabon song below fills only three measures. By comparing the repetition (mm. 4–6) with the original, we can obtain some notion of how performers applied embellishment to the original:

Ex. I.2 Song of Gabon

Andantino

MELODY, RHYTHM, AND MUSICAL TEXTURE

We must rely on Bowdich for first-hand information about melody and rhythm, for the other contemporary writers said little about such matters. To be sure, Park observed that the song improvised in his honor had a "sweet and plaintive air," but he did not, or probably could not, explain why this was so. As we have seen, the eight-string *sanko* was capable of producing a melody whose compass extended over eight tones, the lowest of which was middle C. The following *sanko* melody, however, uses only the top notes of the compass:

Ex. I.3   Ashanti Air

Melody types included one-, two-, and three-note tunes as well as those which extended over wider ranges. Judging from the evidence available, pentatonic (or five-note) melodies were common. (The sound of the pentatonic scale can be obtained by striking five successive black keys on the piano.) The melody of Example I.2 is pentatonic, as is also the following melody for musical bow, although it uses only the first four tones of that scale:

Ex. I.4   Ashanti Air

A long *sanko* melody draws upon the full range of the diatonic scale and, moreover, has passages with harmonic intervals (cf. the successions of thirds in mm. 3, 7, 10–13, 15–16):

Ex. I.5   "The Oldest Ashanti and Warsaw Air"

The African song was basically melodic in musical texture, consisting of a succession of single tones. But often when a performance involved two or more persons or melody instruments, some parts of a piece were performed in unison (i.e. with all performers producing the same melody) and other parts in thirds or fifths, as in Example I.1 or in the following song of the Fanti people:

Ex. I.6   Fanti Air

According to Bowdich, a group of performers playing or singing "in concert" often produced tones of the "common chords" (i.e. with three tones sounding simultaneously). Musical tradition offers support for this assertion; songs of many West African peoples include short passages in chordal texture. Sometimes the chordal sounds result when the group that is singing a choral refrain begins to sing before the soloist has finished his tune, thus producing an overlapping of solo and refrain.

It is relevant to mention here some comments of the American music critic and scholar Henry E. Krehbiel, who heard the music of the Dahomans and watched their dancing at the World's Columbian Exposition in 1893 at Chicago. Predictably, the instruments used to accompany the dances included a large drum made from a hollow log, a variety of small drums (beaten with the fingers), and bells made of iron. Especially worthy of note is Krehbiel's statement that the eight-string harp, which was used to accompany some songs, was tuned so that its first five tones had the sound of a pentatonic scale (such as C D E G A B C D).

Krehbiel also discusses rhythmic characteristics of Dahoman music in his book *Afro-American Folksongs*. The harp player produced a rhythmically complex melody on the two highest strings with his left hand, while with the right hand he played over and over again a descending melodic motive with an equally complex rhythmic pattern. The complexity was even more pronounced in the dance performances. The song accompaniments for the dances used duple meters and the instrumental accompaniment employed triple meters. Moreover, the drummers and bell players played very intricate rhythms, including syncopations, while the chief drummer maintained a rigid adherence to the basic one-two-three beat.

The only pointed discussion of rhythm in our contemporary sources is found in Bowdich's book, where he remarks that despite the elaborate ornamentation and fast tempos of pieces played on the *sanko*, the performers maintained strict time (i.e. concern for the basic pulse or beat). Moreover, he adds:

> The observation made on the time [i.e. rhythm] of the Sanko [pieces] may be extended to almost every other instrument, but it is always perfect, and the children will move their heads and limbs, whilst on their mother's backs, in exact unison with the tune which is playing.

Rhythm is the most pronounced feature of African folk music today, and obviously it was equally important in music of the slave-trade period. As the above examples illustrate, even the melodic skeletons of the simple pieces recorded by Bowdich display rhythmic complexities. How much more complicated must have been the rhythms in actual performance! All of the sources indicate, either directly or indirectly, that the performance of two or more rhythms simultaneously represented the norm, each rhythmic pattern being associated with a different instrument—most often, drums of different sizes.

POETRY AND THE DANCE

In West Africa, as Equiano stated, poetry and the dance were inextricably associated with music. Generally, the languages of the West African peoples were "full of figures [of speech], hyperbolical, and picturesque," to quote Bowdich. From the evidence it seems that poetic rhyme was uncommon. Bowdich gives, however, an example of a rhymed poem of the Fanti people to indicate that the concept of rhyme at least was known, though not used. As we have stated, the African bard was both poet and musician. In a similar way, music making and dancing were typically merged into one entity in performance. Numerous kinds of dances are discussed in the writings of travelers to West Africa, too many to enumerate here. Like ceremonial music, there were dances associated with war, marriage, initiation, death, religion, fertility rites, and other important events of human activity.

The character of the dancing observed depended upon the context of the dance, the people involved, and the sex of the dancers. Generally, men used large body movements, including jumping and leaping. Jobson describes an active dance, for example, in which the men used "swords naked in their hands." Women's dances were characterized by smaller movements and much use of a "shuffle step," the body in a bent position with "crooked knees." Everywhere the circle dance predominated, sometimes with solo dancers or musicians in the center, sometimes with a couple or a single dancer in the center. The ecstatic seizure was an essential element of ceremonial dancing, both religious and secular. At the height of a wild, furious dance participants often fell to the ground in an unconscious state, after having worked themselves up into an uncontrollable frenzy of movement. Musicians, too, exhibited a propensity for becoming so involved in their music making, particularly drumming, as to be totally oblivious of anything else.

SLAVERY IN THE COLONIES

According to reliable estimates there were 1,980 colonists on the mainland of America in 1625—180 in the Plymouth Colony and 1,800 in Virginia. The records do not indicate the number of blacks included in the population figures for Virginia at that time; it is not likely that Plymouth had any at all. By 1649, Virginia's population had increased to 15,000 whites and 300 blacks. In 1626 the Dutch West India Company brought eleven black men from Angola into New Amsterdam, a settlement at the mouth of the Hudson River, to work as the "Company's Negroes" about the village as builders, domestics, and farm hands. Two years later three black women were brought in from Angola. Sometime before 1638 New England saw its first black men, and by the middle of the century black folk on the streets of colonial America were common.

The earliest African arrivals in the colonies had the status of indentured servants, as did many whites and Indians of the period. Already by 1644 Governor Kieft of New Amsterdam had manumitted (released from bondage) the original eleven men of Angola and their wives for "long and faithful service"; and the records show that black indentured servants in Virginia began to secure their freedom in the 1650s, having served out their time. During the second half of the seventeenth century, the importation of Africans into the colonies increased. More and more black captives were given contracts that made them "servants for life" instead of "servants for a time." Eventually they received no indentures at all.

It was during this period that black slavery became established, at first by custom, then by law. From North to South the colonists began to enact laws insuring that the incoming blacks would be held in lifetime servitude. Although a Massachusetts law of 1641 prohibited the enslavement of men except for "lawful Captives taken in just warres, and such strangers as willingly sell themselves or are sold to us," it was easy to evade the law. Slave traders had only to see to it that the Africans they imported were captured in wars—or skirmishes—or sold to them by "others." During the 1660s the codes of the colonies giving statutory recognition to black slavery came swiftly: Virginia in 1661, Maryland in 1663, New York and New Jersey in 1664. Later the colonies of Pennsylvania, Delaware, New England, and the Carolinas followed suit. By 1700 the "peculiar institution" of slavery was a reality throughout the thirteen colonies.

CHAPTER II

New England and the Middle Colonies

Whether they were gentlemen adventurers in Virginia, religious dissenters in New England, wealthy merchants in the Hudson Valley, or black and white indentured servants, the first settlers landing on the shores of the Atlantic seaboard were confronted with the tremendous task of clearing the "hideous and desolate wilderness" and building a place in which to live. During the first decades of the colonial experience, the cultural and social life of the people was necessarily that of a frontier community, and there was little time for the cultivation of the arts. To be sure, back in the countries from which they emigrated the settlers had participated in the musical life characteristic of the seventeenth century. The white settlers brought their psalm books to the New World and later imported musical instruments. The black folk were brought in chains, stripped to the skin, but they retained memories of the rich music and dance traditions of Africa. Together the settlers, black and white, were to lay the foundation for a phenomenal subsequent development of music in America.

MUSIC IN THE COLONIES

Colonial society in the seventeenth century was basically a rural society, and its music was primarily a vocal music, organized in relation to the needs of the meetinghouse (or church), the home, and the community. For the majority of the settlers the meetinghouse provided not only religious guidance but also social diversion. In the town it was the tavern or "ordinary" that served as the chief social institution for all classes of society— the "better sort," "the middling sort," and the "inferior classes." At the beginning of the eighteenth century, however, town dwellers constituted only about 8 per cent of the population. In 1720, they were concentrated in Boston (with a population of 12,000), Newport (3,800), New York (7,000), Philadelphia (10,000), and Charles Town (3,500).

Undoubtedly it was the lack of organized recreational activities that stimulated so great an interest in dancing among the colonists, for dancing was the favorite form of social entertainment everywhere—from Boston in New England to Charles Town in the South—and with everyone, white settlers and black. The favorite instrument for dance music was the violin, played by white and black fiddlers. Except for the fife, trumpet, and drum music of the militia, dance music was the chief type of instrumental music performed in the colonies during the early years.

Vocal music remained dominant throughout most of the eighteenth century. The rapidly developing cities, however, soon began to stimulate the production of a wider variety of music, a music for the "concert room" and the "ballroom" as well as for the meetinghouse and the tavern. It became evident, as Benjamin Franklin wrote in 1743, that the "first drudgery of settling new colonies, which confines the attention of people to mere necessaries," was just about over and that there were many persons "in every province in circumstances that set them at ease." The colonists could afford to cultivate the fine arts. They purchased instruments for use in their homes: "vialls" (viols) of all sizes, the more popular violins, virginals (small harpsichords), "hautboys" (oboes), "guittars," flutes, "fortepianos," and "harmonicas" (mechanically controlled musical glasses invented by Benjamin Franklin). In 1714 the first permanent church organ, the "Brattle organ," was installed in King's Chapel in Boston. In 1731 the first public concert held in the colonies took place in Boston, a "Concert of Musick on Sundry Instruments."

Music schools and dancing schools sprang up in the towns, and in the rural areas intinerant music and dancing masters provided instruction, particularly south of the Delaware River, where the plantation was the chief unit of settlement. The musicians of colonial America came from all classes: there were professional emigrants from Europe, native professionals, "gentlemen amateurs" and amateurs among the lower classes, and musician-domestics—both indentured servants and slaves, both black and white.

SOURCES OF INFORMATION
ABOUT BLACK MUSICIANS

Understandably, the black man of colonial America left few written records of his cultural activities. After recovering from the initial shock of being uprooted from his ancestral home and forcibly integrated into an alien society, he had to learn to adjust —first, to the traumatic experience of slavery itself, then to the master group's language, culture, and way of life. Invariably the black man had to do these things without help. Indeed, most frequently there was strong opposition to his acquiring any knowledge or skill that did not relate directly to his value as a servant. In order to piece together the history of the black musician we must turn to documents of the master group—to their colonial newspapers, town and court records, legislative journals, and to the various diaries, letters, personal narratives, missionary reports, journals, and fiction of white colonists and travelers to the New World.

THE COLONIAL NEWSPAPER

The colonial newspaper provides a rich source of information about slave musicians. From the beginning, the advertising columns in newspapers (the *Boston News-Letter*, established in 1704, was the first permanent one) regularly carried listings of slaves "for sale" or "for hire." Numerous listings included references to the possession of musical skills by slaves, for their market value was thereby greatly increased. In March, 1766, for example, the *Virginia Gazette* advertised:

TO BE SOLD. A young healthy Negro fellow who has been

used to wait on a Gentlemen and plays extremely well on the French horn.

On August 6, 1767, a prospective slave buyer reading the *Virginia Gazette* was offered yet a bigger bargain:

> TO BE SOLD a valuable young handsome Negro Fellow about 18 or 20 years of age; has every qualification of a genteel and sensible servant and has been in many different parts of the world. . . . He . . . plays on the French horn. . . . He lately came from London, and has with him two suits of new clothes, and his French horn, which the purchaser may have with him.

Judging from the evidence, slave musicians most frequently were fiddlers. Numerous examples, such as the following one from the *New York Gazette-Post-Boy*, can be cited to illustrate this:

> TO BE SOLD. A Negro Indian Man slave, about forty years of age, well known in town, being a fiddler.   [June 21, 1748]

Similar advertisements appeared in other newspapers of the time:

> . . . he plays remarkably well on the violin.
> . . . a Virginia-born Negro . . . can play upon the violin.
> . . . a Negro Man slave, about 38 years old . . . can read and play on the Fiddle.

"Runaway" listings invariably gave more information about slaves than did "for sale" advertisements. The slaveholders omitted no details of personal appearance or habits that would help to identify the fugitives; for example, the clothing worn (generally made of "Negro cloth"), the color of the skin (ranging from black to "whitish"), the tools or other articles taken away (sometimes a gun), and the presence of identifying marks on the body (frequently the owner's initials branded on the cheeks). The possession of musical skills was considered to be noteworthy, as the following examples indicate:

> RUN AWAY . . . a Negro Man about 46 years of age . . . plays on the Violin and is a Sawyer. [*Virginia Gazette*, April 24, 1746]

RUN AWAY . . . a likely Negro Man named Damon . . . was born in the West Indies, beats the drum tolerably well, which he is very fond of.   [*Virginia Gazette*, April 17, 1766]

CAESAR: Absented himself from my Plantation . . . plays well on the French horn.   [*South Carolina Gazette*, April 19, 1770]

A slave fugitive of Poughkeepsie, New York, could play two instruments:

RUN AWAY: Negro man named Zack . . . speaks good English, plays on the fife and German flute, had a fife with him.

[*Poughkeepsie Journal*, 1791]

A South Carolinian could whistle and also fiddle:

RUN AWAY: Dick, a mulatto fellow . . . a remarkable whistler and plays on the Violin.   [*South Carolina Gazette*, June 4, 1772]

Were the matter not so grim, one might be inclined to smile at the phrasing of some of the listings:

RUNAWAY . . . a Negro Man named Derby, about 25 years of age, a slim black Fellow, and plays on the Fiddle with his Left Hand, which he took with him. [*Virginia Gazette*, May 14, 1772]

RUN AWAY: a Negro fellow named Peter, about 44 years of age . . . he carried away a fiddle, which he is much delighted in when he gets any strong drink. [*Virginia Gazette*, May 4, 1769]

RUN AWAY: a Mulatto fellow named John Jones, about 26 years old . . . is a mighty singer.

[*Maryland Gazette*, April 14, 1745]

RUN AWAY: Negro man named Robert . . . speaks good English, is a fiddler and took his fiddle with him.

[*New York Packet & American Advertiser*, September 2, 1779]

Of a girl it was related that she was "fond of Liquor and apt to sing indecent and Sailors' songs" when intoxicated. Other examples, too numerous to cite here, could be drawn from colonial newspapers attesting to the prevalence of musical abilities among the slaves.

OTHER PRIMARY SOURCES

A second type of primary source is represented by town and court records and assembly journals of the time, which frequently reveal items of musical interest among the dry lists of facts. Thus we learn, for example, that the slave Nero Benson served as a trumpeter in the company of Captain Isaac Clark in 1723 in Framingham, Massachusetts. On October 5, 1765, the two young drummers who marched through the streets of Philadelphia beating "crepe-festooned" drums to call the citizenry to a town meeting on the State House grounds were black boys. The trial records of the New York City slave revolt in 1741 show that one of the slaves involved was a fiddler: a man named Jamaica, a slave of Ellis, who was "frequently at Hughson's [tavern] with his fiddle."

Most informative of all, of course, are the various kinds of personal writing, nonfiction and fiction, that have come down from the colonial period. The traveler who remarked on a slave's song or the instrument he played, the local historian who cited the names of black musicians in his village or town or described slave festivals, the diarist who jotted down notes about his musically inclined servants, the novelist who recreated scenes of slave merrymaking—all represent valuable sources of information about the musical activities of the colonial blacks.

Of the writings of white colonists, the most useful is the diary kept over a span of fifty-five years (1674–1729) by the Puritan judge Samuel Sewall of Boston. Sewall was very fond of music and, moreover, was the precentor (or deacon) in his church, one of his duties being to lead congregational singing. Because of his talent he was frequently called upon to lead group singing on the many and varied occasions in the Puritan way of life that called for psalm singing: religious services on weekdays, weddings, funerals, meetings of the town council, holiday celebrations, and social gatherings in the home. Sewall's diary is of value, then, for two reasons: it throws light on musical practices of his time; and it reveals the extent to which black people participated in community life. Consequently, we learn indirectly from Sewall about the musical activities of the blacks.

CONGREGATIONAL SINGING
AT WORSHIP SERVICES

In New England, where Sabbath services were held mornings and evenings, Negroes joined in the singing from the special pews where they sat separately from the whites (sometimes the pews were marked "BW" for black women and "BM" for black men). Along with other members of the congregation they waited for the precentor to "line out" the psalm and "set the tune" according to traditional procedures. The Reverend John Cotton provided explicit instructions in a treatise of 1647:

> it will be a necessary helpe, that the lines of the Psalme, be openly read beforehand, line after line, or two lines together, that so they who want either books or skill to reade, may know what is to be sung, and joyne with the rest in the dutie of singing.

In the colony of New York it was the Dutch Reformed Church that ordered, in a church law of 1645, the precentor or *voorzanger* to "tune the psalm" for congregational singing. The procedure consisted in the precentor's chanting one line (or two lines) at a time, ending on a definite pitch, and the congregation following with the singing of the same line, generally with some elaboration of the tune. (This practice, called "lining out," later became a characteristic feature of hymn singing in Negro churches and still lingers on in some places.) It was the precentor's responsibility not only to start the psalm tune on the right pitch, but also to sing loudly and clearly enough to lead the congregation in the singing.

People learned to sing psalm tunes by rote, in the same way they learned folksongs, and inevitably they altered the tunes a little each time they sang. The most popular of the early psalters, called the *Bay Psalm Book*, contained no music at all in its first edition (1640) but only suggested the names of appropriate tunes to which the psalm texts could be fitted. This psalter was the first book printed in the English colonies. A 1698 edition of the psalter included thirteen tunes: *Oxford, Litchfield, Low Dutch, York, Windsor, Cambridge Short, St. David's, Martyrs, Hackney, 119 Psalm, 100 Psalm, 115 Psalm,* and *148*

Psalm. The explanations given for use of the tunes pointed out that "any psalm could be sung to a variety of tunes, the choice being restricted by the need to match the metrical system of psalm and tune."[1]

Ex. II.1   Comparison of a scriptural psalm and a related metrical psalm: (a) Psalm 19, Verses 1–6 [King James Version]

> The heavens declare the glory of God;
>   and the firmament sheweth his handywork.
> Day unto day uttereth speech,
>   and night unto night sheweth knowledge.
> There is no speech nor language,
>   where their voice is not heard.
> Their line is gone out through all the earth,
>   and their words to the end of the world.
>   In them hath he set a tabernacle for the sun,
> Which is as a bridegroom coming out of his chamber,
>   and rejoiceth as a strong man to run a race.
> His going forth is from the end of the heaven,
>   and his circuit unto the ends of it:
>   and there is nothing hid from the heat thereof.

(b) Metrical version of Psalm 19, from the *Bay Psalm Book; York Tune*

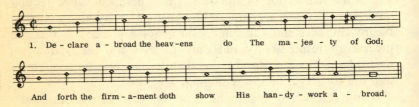

1. De - clare a - broad the heav - ens   do   The ma - jes - ty of God;
And   forth the   firm - a - ment doth   show   His han - dy - work a - broad.

> 2. Day speaks to day, night hath likewise
>   Knowledge to night declared;
>   There neither speech nor language is
>   Where their voice is not heard.

[1] That is, common-meter tunes were to be used when psalms had alternating lines of eight and six syllables; long-meter tunes, when psalms had all eight-syllable lines; short-meter tunes, when psalms had all six-syllable lines, etc. See further in Zoltán Haraszti, *The Enigma of the Bay Psalm Book* (Chicago, 1956).

The small repertory of melodies in general use increased the probability of most members of the community being willing and able to learn to sing psalms, whether or not they could read or had access to psalters. Among the other psalm collections (some of them containing tunes) available to the early settlers were Thomas Ravenscroft's *Whole Booke of Psalmes*, the popular Ainsworth Psalter (mentioned by Longfellow in *The Courtship of Miles Standish*), the Sternhold and Hopkins, the Tate and Brady, and the Allison Psalters.

At Judge Sewall's church on October 25, 1691, the black folk in the attic gallery would have joined with the whites in the singing of psalm texts to the *Windsor Tune* before the sermon, to the *Low Dutch Tune* after the Lord's Supper, and to *Litchfield* at the evening service. On the cold Sabbath in December, 1711 when "Two persons were taken into church . . . Mrs. Francis Bromfield and Marshall's Negro woman," the black folk would have sung with special enthusiasm.

PSALM SINGING IN THE HOME
AND THE COMMUNITY

We know from contemporary sources that the singing of psalms was not confined to the meetinghouse. Black servants sang with their masters on special occasions, as on October 3, 1688, at Sewall's house: "Have a Day of Prayer at our House: One Principal reason as to particular, about my going to England. . . . Sung *Cambridge Short Tune*, which I set"; and at weekly prayer meetings, such as the one held at Sewall's house on January 1, 1718: "Privat Meeting at our House . . . Sung clauses out of the 143rd Psalm."

Psalm singing was as essential at the wedding ceremony as at the funeral service. Sewall took personal charge of the wedding of "Mr. John Wait's Bastian and Mrs. Thair's Negro Jane" in January, 1701. Although Sewall did not describe this wedding, he described many others in his diary, so that it is easy to recreate events at the servants' wedding. After the brief ceremony held in the "Hall" of his house, Sewall would have set the psalm tune—perhaps *York* or *Low Dutch*—"in a very good key, which made the singing with a good number of voices very agreeable." For wedding refreshments "cake and sack-posset" would have been served.

When the community gathered for public ceremonies such as the King's Birthday or Election Day, psalm singing was again in order. Sewall described a typical ceremony that took place on May 20, 1691: "Election Day [was] very fair and comfortable weather. Led the South Company into the Common, there prayed with them. . . . The 122nd Psalm was sung. Mr. Allen got me to set the Tune, which was *Windsor*."

The singing of psalms by the colonists, black and white, was not confined to formal occasions. Like their contemporaries in Europe, they believed that

> The first and chief Use of Musick is for the Service and Praise of God, whose gift it is. The second Use is for the Solace of Men, which as it is agreeable unto Nature, so it is allow'd by God, as a temporal Blessing to recreate and cheer men after long study and weary labor in their Vocations.[2]

An evening spent in fellowship with friends inevitably ended with a little music, especially when a music lover like Sewall was among the company, as on December 21, 1691. "Went . . . to the House of Joshua Gardner, where came [six other friends]. . . . Had a very good dinner. Sung the 23rd Psalm."

RELIGIOUS INSTRUCTION AND PSALM SINGING

In New England the white population was of predominantly English stock and belonged, for the most part, to the Congregational Church. The middle colonies, on the other hand, were settled by a variety of ethnic and religious groups: Dutch settlements were clustered around the Hudson and Delaware Rivers, Germans were in Pennsylvania, Swedes and Finns on the lower Delaware, and the English everywhere. Among the religious groups most interested in the plight of the black man were the Quakers first and foremost; the Moravians; the Congregation-

2 John Playford, *Brief Introduction to the Skill of Musick* (London, 1687 ed.), Preface ("Of Music in General and of Its Divine and Civil Uses"), p. 3.

alists to some extent; the Catholics; and the Methodists (beginning about the middle of the eighteenth century).

Throughout the region slavery assumed a milder form than in the southern colonies, although in some places the harsh and severe treatment of blacks provoked more than one rebellious uprising. Generally, slavery tended to be paternalistic, slaves being regarded as part of the family. They were listed as members of the family (usually taking the family's surname) on the "household baptism plan"; they lived in the home and worked alongside their masters in the field, the shop, or the kitchen. The attitude of the Puritan Cotton Mather toward his black servants was shared by many of his contemporaries, not only in Massachusetts but in the other colonies:

> I would always remember that my servants are in some sence [sic] my children, and by taking care that they want nothing which may be good for them, I would make them as my children. . . . Nor will I leave them ignorant of anything, wherein I may instruct them to be useful. . . .

One of the major concerns of clergymen was the matter of converting the so-called heathen of the New World, the blacks and the Indians, to Christianity. As early as 1648 a Massachusetts law was passed that instructed "all masters of families doe once a week do catechize their children and servants in the grounds and principles of Religion." When the colonial family gathered for prayer services in the home, the light of the blazing fire generally "glowed on the dark shining faces intermixed familiarly with the master's children." Religious instruction always included psalm singing, and blacks were frequently given the rudiments of reading and writing as well. The earliest slave baptism in the colonies seems to have taken place in 1641 when "a Negro woman belonging to Rev. Stoughton of Dorchester . . . being well approved . . . for sound knowledge and true godliness was received into the Church and baptized." It was axiomatic that the woman's "sound knowledge" should include familiarity with psalms.

Several leading clergymen took steps early to provide instruction for slaves that included learning to sing psalms; among them John Eliot, beginning in 1674, and Cotton Mather, who organized in 1693 a "Society of Negroes" and set up rules for its operation. Among other things, the slaves were to meet regularly at his house on Sunday evenings to listen to sermons, pray, be catechized, and sing psalms. In New Amsterdam as early as 1638 a petition was made to Dominie Bogardus, pastor of the Dutch Reformed Church, for a "schoolmaster to teach and train the youth of both Dutch and blacks in the knowledge of Jesus Christ." As in New England, the teaching included psalm singing. A New York teacher's contract of 1682, for example, included among its articles of agreement: "School shall begin with the Lord's prayer, and close by singing a Psalm."

Psalm singing was equally important among the other religious groups that concerned themselves with educating the slaves, except for the Quakers. George Fox, founder of the Society of Friends (the Quakers), was violently opposed to music. He wrote in 1649, "I was moved also to cry against all sorts of music and against the montebanks playing tricks on their stages, for they burdened the pure life, and stirred up people's minds to vanity." In Philadelphia, at the Friends' Yearly Meeting in 1716, Friends were advised against "going to or being in any way concerned in plays, games, lotteries, music, and dancing." But the Quakers were exceptional; the rest of colonial America sang psalms in the eighteenth century.

In New York a missionary society of the Established Church of England, the Society for the Propagation of the Gospel (hereafter referred to as SPG), which was founded in 1701, made great strides in its work among the slaves. Elias Neau maintained in 1704 a school for slaves in an upper room of Trinity Church and of course included psalm singing in his instruction. In 1726 the rector and vestry of Trinity observed that "upwards of a hundred English and Negro servants" attended the catechism on Sundays and sang psalms at the close of instruction. In the same church the Reverend Richard Charlton reported to his superior in 1741 that forty-three Negroes were studying psalmody with the church organist, Mr. Clemn. In 1745 Charlton wrote, "I have got our Clark to raise a Psalm when their instruction is over, and I can scarce express the satisfaction I have in seeing 200 Negroes and White Persons with heart and voice glorifying their Maker." In 1751 Joseph Hildreth reported that about twenty Negroes came to him regularly in the evenings for instruction in singing psalms.

There was yet another religious group in the northern colonies that concerned itself with teaching the slaves to sing—the Associates of Doctor Bray. The records show that in 1760 slaves received training in psalmody regularly from the master of the society's charity school. The study of psalmody by the blacks involved more than just learning psalm tunes by rote—they could, after all, do that in religious-instruction classes or at church. In psalmody classes they were taught how to read music according to one of the several methods in vogue during the time. The first music-instruction books published in the colonies were written by two young ministers: *An Introduction to the Singing of Psalm-Tunes, In a plain & easy Method* (ca. 1726), by the Reverend John Tufts, and *The Grounds and Rules of Musick Explained, or an Introduction to the Art of Singing by Note* (Boston, 1721), by the Reverend Thomas Walter. It is probable that the slaves mentioned above were taught according to the methods advanced by Tufts or Walter.

When schoolmasters began in the eighteenth century to operate schools independently of the church, they retained psalm singing in the curriculum as a matter of course. We may be sure, for example, that psalmody was studied by the blacks attending the school operated by Nathaniel Pigott in Boston, which announced in a newspaper advertisement (1728) that it was opened for the "Instruction of Negroes in Reading, Catechizing & Writing." The same would have been true in Samuel Keimer's school in Philadelphia, although his objective, as stated in a newspaper advertisement (1723), was simply to teach the slaves to "read the Holy Writ in a very uncommon, expeditious and delightful manner."

CONGREGATIONAL SINGING AND THE REFORM MOVEMENT

The traditional way of singing psalms, without recourse to music and without the aid of instrumental accompaniment, inevitably led to the development of undesirable practices with regard to congregational singing. People forgot the psalm tunes or changed the tunes slightly as they sang. Had there been instrumental accompaniment for the singing, it would have sufficed to keep the congregation on pitch, but the use of instruments in the meetinghouse was frowned upon in most places and absolutely forbidden in Puritan churches. The precentor could not always be depended upon to provide good leadership; sometimes he himself forgot the tune, or set the pitch too high, or embellished the melody so freely that the singers following his leadership became confused.

Deacon Sewall experienced several embarrassing moments, for example, during his years as leader of congregational singing. The blacks in attendance at church on those occasions contributed as much to the confusion, no doubt, as did the white worshipers. On October 25, 1691, Sewall wrote:

> In the morning I set *York Tune* and in the second going over, the gallery carried it irrestibly to *St. David's* which discouraged me very much.

Later, the same thing happened again:

> I set *York Tune* and the Congregation went out of it into *St. David's* in the very 2nd going over. They did the same three weeks before.

At another time Sewall realized that he himself was to blame:

> He spake to me to set the tune. I intended *Windsor* and fell into *High Dutch,* and then essaying to set another tune went into a Key much to [*sic*] high. So I pray'd to Mr. White to set it which he did well. *Litchfield Tune.* The Lord humble me and Instruct me that I should be the occasion of any interruption in the worship of God.

The occurrences in Sewall's church were not unusual; similar ones were taking place in churches all over the land. Some learned clergymen began to agitate for the improvement of psalm singing in the church, making such allegations as:

> Tunes are now miserably tortured, and twisted, and quavered in some Churches, into an horrid Medley of confused and discordant Noises . . . and besides no two men in the Congregation quaver-

ing alike, or together, which sounds in the Ears of a Good Judge like five hundred different tunes roared out at the Same Time.

or:

the same person who sets the Tune and guides the Congregation in Singing, commonly reads the Psalm, which is a task so few are capable of performing well, that in Singing two or three staves the Congregation falls from a cheerful Pitch to downright Grumbling. . . .[3]

By the 1720s a movement was definitely under way to improve the quality of congregational singing.

The conventional approach to the singing of the psalms, called the "common way," was "grave and serious." Tunes were sung in a very slow tempo with much ornamentation of the melodic lines. The reformers wanted to replace the old style with a new one, called "regular singing," which emphasized singing by rules, in a strict tempo, and with exact pitches. The ordinary people clung to their old ways for as long as they could, for they liked the slow melodies with flourishes and shakes on the notes, but the reformers eventually won out. Singing schools, and later singing societies, were organized where people could receive instruction in "correct singing"—that is, could learn to read music. Organs were brought into the church to accompany the congregational singing and to keep the singing on pitch, and trained singers were organized into church choirs that took over the responsibility for performing difficult religious music—for example, the anthems—and leading the congregation in its singing. Psalters and hymnals containing tunes were gradually used more and more, so that people could follow the music as they sang.

THE GROWTH OF HYMNODY

During the 1730s a new religious movement swept the colonies, the so-called "Great Awakening," bringing with it a demand for

[3] The two statements are quoted in Gilbert Chase, *America's Music* (New York, 1955), pp. 26, 33. The first is from Thomas Walter, *The Grounds and Rules of Musick Explained* . . . (Boston, 1721); the second is from an article that appeared in the *New England Courant* in 1724.

the use of livelier music in the worship service. The "new" songs
of the movement were *hymns;* for texts they employed religious
poems instead of the scriptural psalms. In 1707 Dr. Isaac Watts,
an English minister and physician, published a book, *Hymns and
Spiritual Songs,* that became immensely popular in the colonies,
especially among the black folk, because of the freshness and
vitality of the words. In 1717 he published another collection
of his attractive hymns, entitled *The Psalms of David, Imitated
in the Language of the New Testament and Apply'd to the
Christian State and Worship.* Before long, people began to neglect the psalms, preferring to sing hymns instead, especially
since the latter were fitted to lively tunes. Slowly, the various
Protestant denominations in the colonies, one after the other,
adopted the hymns of Watts. The "Era of Watts" in the history
of American religious music had begun. The following example
shows a Watts hymn based on the same scriptural psalm as
Example II.1 (see p. 32).

Ex. II.2   *A Morning Hymn,* Isaac Watts, based on
Psalm 19; *Old Hundredth Tune*

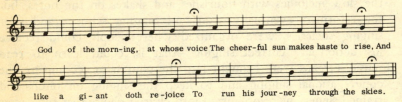

God   of the morn-ing, at whose voice The cheer-ful sun makes haste to rise, And
like   a   gi-ant   doth re-joice To   run his jour-ney   through the skies.

2. From the fair chambers of the east
   The circuit of his race begins,
   And without weariness or rest
   Round the whole earth he flys and shines.

In Charles Town, South Carolina, a hymnal was published in
1737 by the Reverend John Wesley (who with his brother
Charles had founded the Methodist Church in 1729), George
Whitefield, and other students at Oxford University. The book,
A Collection of Psalms and Hymns, launched John Wesley's
career as a hymnal compiler and, as well, became the first of a
long series of official Methodist hymnbooks. The collection of

seventy hymns included thirty-five hymns of Dr. Watts, the remainder being contributed by a number of other men, among them Wesley's father and brother. Wesley had been influenced in his decision to compile a hymnal by the music of the Moravians, members of a religious sect of German origin, who came to the colonies in 1735 on the same ship as the Wesley brothers. The deeply moving hymns sung by the Moravians while on shipboard impressed the Wesleys and, consequently, affected considerably the development of Methodist hymnody—and thus, as we shall see, indirectly affected Negro hymnody as well.

MUSICAL ACTIVITIES AMONG THE MORAVIANS

The Moravians settled first in Georgia, then permanently at Bethlehem, Pennsylvania, in 1741. One of the members of the first Moravian settlement at Bethlehem, the "Sea Congregation," was Andrew the Negro (Andreas der Mohr). Andrew participated in the special activities assigned to the "single men," one of which was the Saturday-evening twilight serenade, a gathering of all the single men together to sing hymns outside the buildings on the settlement grounds. Single and married persons alike took part in the evening prayer services, generally in the form of song services. The entire congregation also celebrated "love feasts"—that is, services with emphasis on the taking of communion and the singing of psalms, hymns, and other spiritual songs.

The records do not indicate whether Andrew played an instrument in one of the Moravian ensembles, such as the *Collegium musicum* or the trombone choir. Members of the settlement took part in musical activities to the extent of their capabilities. Whether singer or instrumentalist, Andrew would have received excellent instruction in music from the musical leader of the settlement, Prylaeus, who was a demanding taskmaster. By 1747, at least four other blacks had joined the congregation: another Andrew, Maria Magdalena, Johannes, and Jupiter. The extraordinary musical activity of the Moravians far surpassed that of other contemporary settlements; Bethlehem in particular became a musical center where visitors came from near and far to hear impressive performances of choral and instrumental music.

HOLIDAY CELEBRATIONS AND MUSIC

For the most part the colonists in New England and the middle colonies observed the same holidays: New Year's Day, Easter, Pentecost or Whitsunday, Election Day, Militia or Muster Day, Guy Fawkes Day (November 5), Thanksgiving Day, and Christmas. The Puritans, to be sure, had fewer holidays than others; in 1699 a contemporary complained, "Election, Commencement and Training Days are their only Holy Days." The observance of Christmas was especially avoided among the Puritans. The special gala days of the "middling and inferior sort" were the annual fairs held in many towns and villages. For the gentry, celebrations of the birthdays of "prince and proprietary" or military events provided not only the public ceremonies which they shared with their fellow citizens, but also exclusive formal dances, assemblies, and other kinds of special "Entertainments." Sewall wrote about a typical celebration of the King's Birthday on October 14, 1685:

> Many Guns fired, and at night a Bonfire on Noodles Island in remembrance of the King's Birthday. Some marched through the streets with Viols and Drums, playing and beating by turns.

Sewall did not identify the musicians as black or white, but contemporary sources attest to the fact that blacks generally joined the boisterous crowds that roamed the streets on holidays, some among them playing their fiddles, drums, and trumpets. Sometimes the town rowdies in Boston, black and white, celebrated for no particular reason at all, as on a Saturday night in October, 1685: "Many Guns, Drums and Trumpets going."

Militia Day, also called Training or Muster Day, never failed to attract a large gathering of bystanders, including slaves. More than likely, many a black fifer "picked up" the skill of playing his instrument on these occasions. In the early years all servants, including "Negars" and Indians, were compelled to undergo military training. Every company had at least one fifer (or trumpeter) and one drummer. During the 1650s colonial fears of Negro and Indian uprisings led to counteracting laws exempting the nonwhites from military service. In later years they were allowed to enroll for service only as drummers, fifers, trumpeters, or pioneers. In times of emergency, to be sure, the colonists conveniently forgot their laws and pressed black men into service as fighters, particularly during the French and Indian War.

Records of the pre-revolutionary period do not often identify musicians of the armed services by race, but there are enough scattered references to black musicians to suggest that they were not uncommon. It has been noted that Nero Benson was a trumpeter in a Massachusetts regiment. In 1744 a report on a Philadelphia parade by Dr. Alexander Hamilton, "gentleman traveler" from Maryland, refers to another black musician, although not exactly in complimentary terms:

> The procession was led by about thirty flags and ensigns taken from privateer vessels. . . . They were followed by 8 or 10 drums that made a confounded martial noise, but all the Instrumental Musick they had was a pitiful scraping Negro Fiddle, which followed the drums and could not be heard for the noise and clamour of the people and the rattle of the drums.

New Year's Day was an occasion for merrymaking everywhere. In some places men went from house to house firing gun salutes, finally gathering on the village green for a day of riotous fun. In Boston, trumpets instead of guns were used for New Year's Day saluting. In 1705 the trumpeter who gave a New Year's salute to Judge Sewall was a black musician:

> Colonel Hobbey's Negro came about 8 or 9 mane and sends in by David to have leave to give me a Levit [trumpet blast] and wish me a merry new year. I admitted it: gave him 3 Reals. Sounded very well.

SOCIAL DIVERSIONS AND MUSIC

A variety of informal social activities were available to colonial villagers, participated in by white and black alike: church and house raisings, maple sugarings, cornhuskings, etc., most of these generally followed by dancing to the music of the fiddle. When there was no special activity taking place, people gathered together in taverns, where they danced and sang "wanton ditties." By the beginning of the third decade of the eighteenth century, people living in towns could listen to concerts performed in concert rooms, in taverns, or in homes. Dancing, however, was more popular. During the 1730s and 1740s, dancing assemblies were organized in Newport, New York, Philadelphia, and some smaller towns, with membership limited, for the most part, to the aristocracy. The Philadelphia Assembly floundered at times because of the combined influence of the staid Quakers and George Whitefield's "Great Awakening" movement, but eventually gained a reputation for being one of the most brilliant and exclusive assemblies in the colonies.

Black musicians provided much of the dance music for the colonists of all classes; they played for country dances, balls in the towns, and frequently for dancing schools, too. One of the best-known fiddlers in New England was Sampson, slave of Colonel Archelaus Moore. For many years Sampson "afforded fine fun for frolicsome fellows in Concord [Massachusetts] with his fiddle on Election Days." The fiddler Polydor Gardiner of Narragansett was in great demand for parties and dances, as were also Caesar, slave fiddler of East Guilford, and Zelah, black fiddler of Groton. In Wallingford, Connecticut, Colonel Barker's slave Cato "ranked high as a fiddler in the community" and provided music "for balls on the nights preceding the annual Thanksgiving and other occasions when dancing was expected." Of another slave in the area, Robert Prim, it was said that he and his violin were "indispensable requisites at every party or merrymaking." Although few other names of black dance musicians have been preserved for posterity, most of the colonial villages and towns had access to some fiddler on whom they could rely to furnish music for their dances, and very often that fiddler was a black man, slave or free.

Slave musicians also played in some of the dancing schools that were established in the towns to prepare the socially minded citizens for the great amount of dancing that took place. After all, slaves were reliable, skilled enough, affable, and cheap. An anecdote of old New York reports on the slave Caesar, who drove the coach that took the young ladies to the dancing school, played for the dancing, and then served as a waiter during refreshment time. The dancing began at one o'clock in the afternoon. "Caesar, on their arrival, tuned his three-string fiddle, the gentlemen appeared . . . and at it they went, dancing and skipping for dear life until 8 o'clock."

What kind of music did the colonists have for their dancing? Contemporary accounts mention most often the music of violins. It is probable that for gala occasions oboes and transverse flutes were added to the string ensembles. The fact that the dance tunes in a popular collection, *Thompson's Compleat Collection of 200 Favourite Country Dances Performed at Court . . .* , were arranged or "Set for the Violin, German flute & Hautboy" suggests such a probability. Moreover, the contemporary references to slave musicians point out that most often they were violinists and flutists, a phenomenon obviously to be attributed more to the demands of the white colonists for dance musicians than to mere coincidence or to any preference for these instruments among the black people.

Colonial dance musicians had available to them several excellent sources of dance music, the two best-known collections of which were published in England. In addition to the Thompson collection, there was one even better known and more popular, *The English Dancing Master or Plaine and Easie Rules for the Dancing of Country Dances with the Tune to Each Dance*, by John Playford, author of several other music manuals. These two books contained a varied repertory of traditional ballad tunes, country dance tunes, and the more formal court-dance melodies. Consequently, dance musicians could provide music for all of the colonists' favorite dances; for example, *Pea Straw*, *Faithful Shepherd*, *Arcadian Nuptials*, *Lady Hancock*, and *Boston's Delight*. Some of the tunes in the Playford collection, such as *Greensleeves* or *Sellinger's Round* or *Paul's Steeple*, were the "hit tunes" of the period.

THE DEVELOPMENT OF MUSICAL SKILLS AMONG THE SLAVES

One persistent question, for which there seems to be no satisfactory answer, is how the slave, lacking personal possessions and control of his time, developed instrumental skills. Although the African heritage gave him a natural talent for and inclination toward making music, he came to the New World empty-handed, and upon arrival had to acquaint himself with strange instruments and different ways of handling them. To be sure, some of the white man's instruments were similar to those the African had known in his own country, but the instruments were not identical. In music—as in language, religion, and customs—the African had to adjust to the ways of his white masters.

Only tentative answers, based on the meager evidence available, can be offered to the question. With regard to the acquiring of instruments, it is obvious that many slave musicians must have fashioned their own instruments from whatever materials were at hand. In some instances slave owners purchased instruments for their slaves. The following excerpt from a letter written in 1719 by a Philadelphian Quaker supports both these suppositions:

> Thou knowest Negro Peter's Ingenuity In making for himself and playing on a fiddle without any assistance. As the thing in them [i.e. the musical impulse] is Innocent and diverting and may keep them from worse Employment, I have to Encourage [him] in my Service promist him one from England. Therefore buy and bring a good strong well-made Violin with 2 or 3 Sets of spare Gut for the Suitable Strings. Get somebody of skill to Chuse and by [buy] it. . . .

How widely the practice of buying musical instruments for slaves was followed during the colonial period is a question that cannot be satisfactorily answered until more evidence comes to light.

With regard to the development of skill in playing an instrument, we may assume that most slaves taught themselves to play. There is documentary evidence for such an assumption in the case of nineteenth-century slave musicians. It is thus logical to accept the notion that colonial slaves also might have taught themselves, especially since they were closer to the African tradition, and would have remembered the musical activities they pursued before coming to the New World. The curious phrasing in a newspaper "runaway" advertisement throws considerable light on the question of how other slaves might have learned to play musical instruments:

Whereas Cambridge, a Negro Man belonging to James Oliver of Boston doth absent himself sometimes from his Master: said Negro plays well upon a flute, and not so well on a Violin. This is to desire all Masters and Heads of Families not to suffer said Negro to come into their Houses to teach their Prentices or Servants to play, nor on any other Accounts. All Masters of Vessels are also forbid to have anything to do with him on any Account, as they may answer it in the Law. N. B. Said Negro is to be sold: Enquire of said Oliver.

[*Boston Evening Post,* October 24, 1743]

This advertisement suggests that in Boston, at least, slaveholders followed the practice of engaging slave musicians to teach their slaves and, as well, their apprenticed white servants. (Slaves are commonly referred to as servants in colonial sources.) Who taught the slave music-teachers? Did they "pick up" their skills, or were they apprenticed out to white professional musicians? Undoubtedly both questions should be answered in the affirmative.

At any rate, there is nothing in the available evidence to suggest that slaves as a group were given instrumental lessons—that is, in the same way as they were taught to read music in psalmody classes. Under the circumstances, then, the musical instruments favored by the slaves would have had to fulfill three conditions: first, the instruments had to offer a minimum of technical difficulties in the learning process, so that they could be learned with little or no professional help; second, the instruments had to be easily available and so easily handled that the slaves could carry them around and practice them at odd times of the day or night, whenever there were a few extra minutes to spare; third, the instruments had to be useful, so that once the slaves had learned to play them they would have opportunities to perform for others.

A genuine musician, to be sure, would get a great deal of pleasure from playing to himself. But that kind of performance, according to the African tradition, was not the most desirable; music was meant to be shared with others, and the most successful musical experience involved dancing and singing. Consequently, the black musician was happiest when playing for the dancing and singing of others, whether black or white.

SOCIAL SONGS

None of the white colonists in the North, not even the Puritans, limited themselves exclusively to the singing of psalms. They sang the old ballads brought with them from Europe, and they called upon various kinds of worksongs—sea chanties, weavers' songs, sugar-making songs, etc.—to ease their labors. As early as the seventeenth century, some clergymen began to speak out against the people's excessive attention to secular music. But even the son of the influential Reverend John Cotton, Seaborn Cotton, who later became a minister himself, found time to copy words of popular ballads into his "commonplace book" while he was a student at Harvard. Some of the songs he copied were among those most widely disseminated during the period and mentioned again and again in contemporary accounts; for example, *Two Faithful Lovers*, *The Last Lamentation of the Languishing Squire*, and *The Love-Sick Maid*.

Some of the "idle, foolish ballads" sung by the settlers were Yankee versions of English ballads; for example, *Barb'ry Ellen* (*Barbara Allen*) or *Dirante, My Son* (*Lord Randall, My Son*). When ballad makers needed tunes for topical songs they drew upon the melodies of old favorites, such as the tune *Derry Down, Down, Down* (*The Three Ravens*) for a text about the notorious Kitty Crow in 1765, or the *Boston Come All Ye* tune for a satirical text entitled *The Paxton Expedition* (ca. 1764). One of the most popular songs of all was the *Yankee Song:*

> Corn stalks twist your hair off,
> Cart-wheel frolic round you.
> Old fiery dragon carry you off,
> And mortar pessel pound you.

The song with different words became better known as *Yankee Doodle*.

In singing schools the colonists could learn to sing not only psalms, but also secular songs, "catches, glees, [and] canons . . . with sobriety and ease." Consequently, what was not picked up in the tavern or on the street could be learned from a singing master. The black man sang all kinds of songs at all times. He sang psalms along with the white settlers and turned to hymns in the eighteenth century along with everyone else. He sang the old African songs as long as he could remember them —especially on the occasions of special slave festivals, as we shall see. In the taverns and on the streets he sang the white man's ballads and ribald songs. And when he tired of singing those or he exhausted his repertory, the black man made up his own songs, stumbling a bit over the unfamiliar English or Dutch or Swedish or German or French words (depending upon where he lived), but managing, nevertheless, to express his ideas in the alien tongues.

SLAVE FESTIVALS AND
THE AFRICAN TRADITION

Black men in the English colonies found ways to carry on some of their traditional African practices despite the bonds of slavery. Perhaps the most spectacular of these practices occurred in the slave gatherings and festivals that took place throughout the colonial period in northern cities where there were large concentrations of blacks. Although the slaves that were brought into the colonies originally came from a wide area of West Africa (and parts of East Africa) and represented many different tribes, they shared enough traditions of music and dancing in common to enable them to participate in collective dances with ease. Moreover, slaves who spoke different African languages were generally able to communicate with each other, as Equiano pointed out in his book: "I understood them, though they were from a distant part of Africa."

Special Holiday Sprees. A colonial holiday observed solely by black folk was "Lection Day." On this occasion the blacks elected their own "governors" (or "kings" in New Hampshire), in elaborate ceremonies that paralleled those of Election Day for the white population. The custom seems to have originated in Connecticut about 1750 and lasted, in some New England towns, as late as the 1850s. Depending upon the place, the holiday was observed in May or June. Generally, slaves were given the vacation period from Wednesday to the following Sunday in which to elect their rulers and to celebrate.

First in the order of events would be the election parade. A parade in Hartford, Connecticut, often involved as many as one hundred slaves, either mounted on horseback or marching, two by two, on foot. The procession of slaves, each dressed in his finest apparel, would advance with colors flying to the music of fifes, fiddles, "clarionets," and drums. But the Hartford parades were unusually elaborate affairs. In most places, the processions marched or rode to the music of fifers and drummers. To be sure, only the best musicians were given the honor of playing for an election parade. It was said, for example, that King Caesar of Wallingford, Connecticut, was always escorted by an "indefatigable drummer and a fifer of eminence."

After the election ceremony came the merrymaking, consisting of games, wrestling, jumping, singing, and dancing to the music of fiddles. To white observers the singing was quite exotic:

> Every voice in its highest key, in all the various languages of Africa, mixed with broken and ludicrous English, filled the air, accompanied with the music of the fiddle, tambourine, banjo and drum.

One writer reported on the kind of dancing that took place, noting that the slaves "shuffled and tripped" to the sounds of the fiddles. It is noteworthy that although black folk in the North were fairly well integrated into community activities— at least, to the extent possible for a servant class—they nevertheless preferred their own African style of merrymaking.

Pinkster Celebrations. "Pinkster Day," the name given to Pentecost Sunday (or Whitsunday, in the Anglican Church), was originally a principal holiday of the Dutch in the Netherlands settlements. Later it was adopted by the English in New York, in parts of Pennsylvania, and in Maryland. It seems that the earliest reference to the popular name of the holiday occurred in a Sermon Book of 1667 by Adrian Fischer, "Story of the Descent of the Holy Ghost on the Apostles on 'Pinckster Dagh.'" After the first day or so of Pinkster—the celebration was often prolonged for as much as the full week after Pentecost—the blacks took over completely with their Congo dances, dancing as they had danced back in Africa. The festivals attracted large crowds of white spectators from both city and rural sections. Local historians wrote about "Pinkster, the Carnival of the Africans," and novelists incorporated scenes from the "great Saturnalia of the New York Blacks" in their fictional works, just as writers were to describe the exotic dancing of the blacks in the Place Congo of New Orleans at the beginning of the nineteenth century.

One of the most vivid descriptions appears in an account written by Dr. James Eights of Albany, who was an eyewitness on more than one occasion. He tells us that the Pinkster grounds were laid out in the form of an "oblong square," on a hill that is now the site of the state capitol. Along the perimeter of the square were erected stalls, booths, and tents that featured exhibitions of wild animals, rope dancing, bareback riding, and other attractions common to a fair. The center was left clear for dancing. Few blacks were to be seen on the Monday after Pentecost, for it was considered "ungenteel for the colored nobility to make their appearance on the commencing day." But on the second day, about ten o'clock in the morning, a "deputation [from the assembled multitude] . . . anxiously desirous to pay all proper homage to his majesty their king," would gather to wait upon the leading spirit of the festival, Old King Charley, the venerable sovereign of the blacks.

At this time Charley, who had been brought from Angola and was said to have been a prince back in Africa, was over seventy years old, tall, thin, and extremely agile. He customarily wore the costume of a "British brigadier of the olden times," and made a very colorful appearance as he slowly advanced toward the center of the square, dressed in a scarlet coat ornamented with tracings of golden lace, his "small clothes" of new yellow buckskin, his black shoes with silver buckles, and a tricornered cocked hat upon his head.

> The greetings were at length over, and the hour of twelve having arrived, peace and tranquility had once more been partially restored to the multitude; his majesty, the king, was in the midst of his assembled friends and subjects, and the accomplished master of the ceremonies, with his efficient aids were busily employed in making the necessary arrangements to commence the festivities

with zeal and earnestness; partners were then selected and let out upon the green, and the dancing [began]. . . .

New couples joined the performance from time to time as fatigued dancers dropped out, forced to stop from exhaustion. The principal instrument for the dance music was a drum made from a wooden eel-pot with a cleanly dressed sheepskin drawn tightly over its wide end:

> Astride this rude utensil sat Jackey Quackenboss, then in his prime of life and well known energy, beating lustily with his naked hands upon its loudly sounding head, successively repeating the ever wild, though euphonic cry of *Hi-a-bomba, bomba, bomba,* in full harmony with the thumping sounds. These vocal sounds were readily taken up and as oft repeated by the female portion of the spectators not otherwise engaged in the exercises [that is, dances] of the scene, accompanied by the beating of time with their ungloved hands, in strict accordance with the eel-pot melody.

The dancing grew more rapid and furious as the day wore on:

> Briskly twirled the lads and lasses over the well trampled green sward; loud and more quickly swelled the sounds of music to the ear, as the excited movements increased in energy and action; rapid and furious became their motions . . . and still the dance went on with all its accustomed energy and might; but the eye at length, becoming weary in gazing on this wild and intricate maze, would oftimes turn and seek relief by searching for the king, amid the dingy mass; and there, enclosed within their midst, was his stately form beheld, moving along with all the simple grace and elastic action of his youthful days, now with a partner here, and then with another there, and sometimes displaying some of his many amusing antics, to the delight and wonderment of the surrounding crowd.

On the next day the occurrence was repeated, and the next day, and the next. By the end of the week all the celebrants, black and white, must have welcomed the Sabbath, which became quite literally a day of rest, and the "ancient city was at length again left to its usual quietude."

In a later account of the Albany festival, Old King Charley

was described as being well over one hundred years old, but still the ruler of the festival. No longer did he dance; instead he took over the drum beating, using a drum made from a box with a sheepskin head, and was accompanied by the singing of "some queer African airs." After Charley's death, the celebration was observed with less enthusiasm, but continued, nevertheless, until in 1811 the town council of Albany prohibited further erection of stalls on "Pinkster Hill."

In Manhattan the favorite gathering place for Pinkster celebrations was the site now known as City Hall Park. The blacks "collected in thousands in those fields," coming into the city from as far away as thirty or forty miles. Although the festival lasted only three days in Manhattan and "was not celebrated with as much vivacity as at Albany," it nevertheless was a time of great excitement for both white spectators and black participators. Hundreds upon hundreds of people watched the blacks sing African songs, strum banjos, and dance to the music of drums constructed by drawing skins over the ends of hollow logs.

OTHER SLAVE GATHERINGS

The Revolutionary War brought an end to the Manhattan slave festivals, but after the war the tradition of public slave dances was revived in a different form. On holidays, and particularly for Pinkster celebrations, the slaves would come in from Long Island and New Jersey to the city markets—and as well from the city itself—to engage in friendly dancing contests. Butchers of the markets and other bystanders would toss in a little money so that prizes could be offered to the best dancers. Music for the dancing, which consisted of jigs and breakdowns, was provided in a novel manner: the slaves produced a kind of percussion music by beating their hands on their thighs and stomping their heels. Over the years these practices resulted in the development of some "excellent dancers." Catherine Market, near the Bowery, was the favorite gathering place for the slave-dance competitions, but there was also dancing at Bear Market in Maiden Lane.

Contemporary accounts refer to yet another colonial town

where whites gathered to watch the slaves perform traditional African dances and songs. In Philadelphia, where semiannual fairs were held until the time of the revolution, the last days of the fairs were given over to the slaves for their own "jubilees." The dancing on these occasions was similar to that of the New York slaves. Blacks danced in Potter's Field (now Washington Square), divided into small groups according to their "nations" or tribes. The dancing of the slaves lasted for many hours at a time:

> . . . the Blacks joyful above, while the sleeping dead reposed below. In that field could be seen at once more than one thousand of both sexes, divided into numerous little squads, dancing and singing, each in their own tongue, after the customs of their several nations in Africa.[4]

In Boston the slaves and free blacks congregated about the wharves in an area called "New Guinea," but there is no evidence that group dancing ever took place there.

During colonial times, slave festivals were held only in the North. Such gatherings were possible in places where slavery was relatively benign, where indulgent owners allowed their slaves time off for frolics, where town authorities were not afraid to let huge masses of slaves assemble, where black leaders were respected as much by the local white townspeople as by their own people—and none of these conditions existed in the southern colonies. The next site of African festivals in the United States was to be in nineteenth-century New Orleans, where the mingling of diverse cultures—Spanish, French, British, German, and African—encouraged the development and the flowering of music and dance to an extent previously unknown in the New World.

It is quite evident that the festivals described above represent African survivals among blacks in the English colonies, despite the pressures exerted upon them by the slavery experience to accommodate to the folk ways and customs of the dominant culture. The prevailing "myth of the Negro past"—that enslavement caused the blacks to lose their every vestige of the

---

[4] John Fanning Watson, *Annals of Philadelphia* (Philadelphia, 1850), II, p. 265.

African heritage—is nowhere more firmly refuted than in the areas of music and dance and, more specifically, than by the occurrence of the slave festivals. An equally significant, though less dramatic, survival of "Africanisms" is represented by the storytelling and singing of black women in New England who, in their own way, kept alive the African traditions. For example, Lucy Terry of Deerfield and Senegambia of Narragansett, Rhode Island, won wide recognition for their gifts in this regard. Lucy, who called herself Luce Bijah, married a free black man, Abijah Prince. After gaining her own freedom, she made her home a gathering place for slaves and freedmen of the community, a place where they could listen to tales and songs of old Africa. Indeed, American literature contains numerous references to female slaves of colonial times who kept young audiences spellbound, and adults, too, with their ancient tales.

CHAPTER III

The Southern Colonies

With its large plantations the South resembled rural England, and the wealthy planters, many of them originally members of English nobility or landed gentry, led lives similar in some ways to those of English country gentlemen. The isolation of the plantation necessarily encouraged the development of considerable self-sufficiency on the part of the master family and the slaves. One of the richest and most powerful of the southern aristocrats, William Byrd II of Westover, Virginia, wrote in 1726:

> I have my flocks and my birds, my bond-men and bond-women, and every soart of trade among my own servants, so that I live in a kind of independence on everyone but providence.

The isolation of the plantation also gave the master unusual power over his family and slaves. He interpreted the slave codes and unwritten traditions as he willed; he made of the institution of slavery either the brutal experience that it was for most blacks or something better, which at times and in certain places approximated the relatively humane condition of slavery in New England.

CHARLES TOWN AND OTHER TOWNS

As was indicated earlier, Charles Town (Charleston), South Carolina, was the only town in the South worthy of the title. Just before the American Revolution its population was estimated at 10,887, of which 5,030 were white, 5,833 were slaves, and 24 were free black men. As the metropolis of the South, Charles Town was a cultural center, particularly with regard to music. Thought of by some historians as the musical center of the entire eastern seaboard during the first half of the eighteenth century, Charles Town was the port of entry for most professionals coming from Europe to perform or teach music in the New World. The first performance of an opera in America took place there in 1735; the work, *Flora: Or Hob in the Well*, was a one-act ballad opera that had been extremely popular in London. In Charles Town was also organized the first society devoted exclusively to music, the St. Cecilia Society, in 1762. Concerts in honor of St. Cecilia, the patron saint of music, were given there as early as 1735.

As an urban center, Charles Town offered opportunity for the "better sort" to live as did their counterparts in cities of the North and in European capitals—to attend concerts, plays, balls, assemblies, and other sophisticated entertainments. There were singing schools and dancing schools, which attracted men as well as women. Any young gentleman was "presumed to be acquainted with Dancing, Boxing, playing the Fiddle, & Small-Sword, & Cards." In Charles Town, because of the tremendous demand for skilled and unskilled labor, the slaves were able to develop their talents and skills to a greater extent than in any other colonial town. Black men worked at all trades, crafts, and arts. They seriously competed with white laborers and actually took over some trades—to such an extent that in 1744 some white artisans petitioned the commons house for relief from the ruinous competition.

In addition to Charles Town, the villages of Annapolis in Maryland, and Richmond and Williamsburg (called Middle Plantation from 1633 to 1699) in Virginia provided social and cultural activities for the southern colonists, some of whom maintained townhouses in the villages in addition to their plantation residences. Wherever there were dancing and music, there was apt to be a slave musician playing the fiddle or flute or French horn for the dancers, whether in the town or on the plantation. It may be assumed that black musicians occasionally participated in more formal musical activity as well. In 1752, for example, the president of the Tuesday Club in Annapolis—a club whose motto was "fiddlers, fools and farces" but whose chief activity seems to have been composing music—complained that the members' musical compositions were of low quality, that "only the ditties of a visiting Negro boy showed talent." From the same town comes evidence that black fiddlers played overtures in one of the theaters.

RELIGIOUS INSTRUCTION
FOR THE SLAVES

In the South as in the North, various religious groups were concerned about the souls of the slaves and consequently made efforts to convert them. For the colonial black man, religious instruction provided the chief opportunity for self-improvement and for participation in the life of the community. Though the slaves might find themselves sitting on the floors of the churches at the Sabbath services or listening to the sermon through open windows from outside the churches, they were at least involved in an experience that allowed them to forget for the moment their state of degradation. Sometimes slaveholders arranged for ministers to preach to slave congregations in separate services or brought ministers to the plantations to preach. The Established Church of England exerted a strong and widespread influence on southerners, white as well as black, especially through its missionary society, the SPG. Each parish was provided with a minister-schoolmaster, who had to make periodic reports to the bishop of London or his representative in the colonies on the religious and educational conditions in his parish.

There are extant a number of documents attesting to the activities of colonial clergymen among the slaves, stating how many adults were taken into the church, how many infants baptized, how many slaves given religious instruction, and how many taught the basic rudiments of reading and writing. Religious instruction, moreover, always included the teaching of psalms and hymns. The slaves preferred the musical activities of the religious experience above all else. In 1755 the Presbyterian Reverend Samuel Davies (later president of Nassau Hall = Princeton University) commented upon this phenomenon in a letter to his superiors:

The Negroes . . . have an Ear for Musick, and a kind of extatic Delight in *Psalmody;* and there are no Books they learn so soon or take so much pleasure in, as those used in that heavenly Part of divine Worship.

In the next decade another missionary, the Reverend Mr. Wright, wrote in a similar vein:

My landlord tells me, when he waited on the colonel at his county-seat two or three days, they heard the Slaves at worship in their lodge, singing Psalms and Hymns in the evening, and again in the morning, long before break of day. They are excellent singers, and long to get some of Dr. Watts' Psalms and Hymns, which I encouraged them to hope for.

The psalms and hymns of Dr. Watts, so beloved by the slaves, were published in colonial editions as early as 1729 (*Psalms of David, Imitated,* in Philadelphia) and 1739 (*Hymns and Spiritual Songs,* in Boston). The missionaries acknowledged the preference on the part of black folk for the hymns of Dr. Watts and requested Watts' song books along with Bibles in their orders sent to London. The Reverend Mr. Hutson wrote in 1758:

This is accompanied with the warmest gratitude for the late parcel of Books received from the Society, to distribute among the poor with us. . . . I was extremely glad of the Books for their sakes, especially the Bibles, Dr. Watts' Psalms and Hymns, and the Compassionate Address.

In 1760 the Reverend Mr. Todd lamented that he had been "obliged to turn sundry empty away who have come to me for Watts Psalms and Hymns."

Not all clergymen were conscientious about their responsibilities for the souls of the slaves. In 1758 Davies wrote that "thousands of Negroes are neglected or instructed just according to the character of the established clergy in their several parishes." Ultimately, the amount of religious training given to the slaves depended upon their masters, however diligent the clergymen. Even slaveholders who were inclined toward humane treatment of their slaves hesitated to allow religious instruction and baptism for them, at first because of the widely circulated idea that slaves who were received into the church would automatically achieve freedom. To refute this, the Virginia Assembly passed a law in 1667 specifically stating that the baptism of slaves did not exempt them from bondage and urging the masters to encourage their slaves to accept Christianity. Maryland passed a similar law in 1671.

The slave owners were reluctant to allow their slaves to be converted, however, for additional reasons. The Reverend Hugh Jones pointed out in his book *The Present State of Virginia from Whence Is Inferred a Short View of Maryland and North Carolina* (1724): "As for baptising Indians and Negroes, several of the people disapprove of it; because they say it often makes them proud, and not as good servants." There was yet an even more compelling reason. Unlike in the North, where the black population reached early a relatively stable level, throughout the colonial period large numbers of Africans were still being imported into the southern colonies. This continuous influx, resulting in ever increasing numbers of blacks in the South, contributed to the development among the slaveholders of well-founded fears of slave conspiracies and uprisings. As a consequence, the South paid a great deal of attention to laws and other possible means for keeping the slaves under firm control. To allow the slaves to congregate together, for whatever reason, was simply not considered wise under the circumstances. Governor Spotswood of Virginia stated plainly in 1710 his objections to any kind of slave assemblage:

> We are not to depend on either their stupidity, or that babel of languages among them; freedom wears a cap, which can without a tongue call together all those who long to shake off the fetters of slavery.

In no way did religious instruction for black folk in the South attain the level that it did in the North; at no time did it reach an equivalent proportion of the black population. Indeed, during the colonial period most blacks were hardly touched by efforts of the missionaries. They lived in their separate quarters on the plantations and farms away from the whites, and used their holiday Sundays "to dig up their small lots of ground allowed by their Master for potatoes, peas, etc." and to divert themselves in dancing or watching cock fights. In many places slaves were made to work on Sundays, despite the colonial laws requiring slaveholders to set aside Sundays as free days.

SABBATH ACTIVITIES

Many a white clergyman protested against the way the Sabbath was observed by the slaves "in frolicking, dancing, and other profane courses." As early as 1709 Dr. LeJau, one of the first SPG missionaries, complained: "It has been customary among them to have their feasts, dances, and merry meetings upon the Lord's Day." The planters, however, generally accepted the fact that the slaves, having no other free time during the week and not being admitted into the church for one reason or another, should use Sundays as a day of rest and diversion. An English traveler in Maryland, Nicholas Cresswell, wrote in his journal in 1774:

> Mr. Bayley and I went to see a Negro Ball. Sundays being the only days these poor creatures have to themselves, they generally meet together and amuse themselves with Dancing to the Banjo. . . . They all appear to be exceedingly happy at these merry-makings and seem if they had forgot or were not sensible of their miserable condition.

As a matter of fact, the attitude of the slaves toward the Sabbath was not very different from that of their white counterparts. An entry in the diary of the New Englander Philip Vickers Fithian reveals his surprise at the lax attitude taken by the southerners toward observance of the Sabbath:

> A Sunday in Virginia dont seem to wear the same Dress as our Sundays to the Northward. Generally here by five o'clock on Saturday every face (especially the Negroes) looks festive and cheerful. All the lower class of people, & the Servants, & the slaves, consider it a Day of Pleasure and Amusement & spend it in such Diversions as they severally choose.

OPPORTUNITIES FOR
DEVELOPING MUSICAL SKILLS

Despite the limitations of the social structure in the South, the slaves managed to find ways to develop their musical skills. Those fortunate enough to live on the great plantations or in homes of wealthy townsmen were generally exposed to a high level of cultural activity. Fithian's journal and letters are valuable for the information they contain about life in the South. The young Princeton graduate, who spent two years (1773–1774) as a "Plantation Tutor of the Old Dominion" to the children of the aristocrat Robert Carter, gives a vivid description of the mode of life for the wealthy and, as well, for indentured servants, white and black. Fithian's employer had a large collection of musical instruments on his plantation, Nomini Hall: "a Harpsichord, Forte Piano, Harmonica, Guittar, Violin, & German Flutes . . . & at Williamsburg [the site of his townhouse] a good Organ." Almost every evening in the Carter home the members of the family played chamber music. The slaves, who moved freely about the house and among the members of the family, listened to the music along with their masters and, perhaps, "picked out" pieces on the musical instruments whenever they found opportunities to do so.

To teach the sons and daughters of the wealthy colonists, itinerant music masters traveled from plantation to plantation, staying several days at each place, depending upon the number of persons to be given musical instruction. Mr. Stadley, the German music master who taught the Carter children, generally remained three or four days each time he came to Nomini Hall, chiefly to instruct the young women in the art of playing the violin and "Forte Piano." With Mr. Stadley in the house, the evenings provided occasions for the playing of more demanding chamber music and singing, to which the addition of a professional added a great deal of zest. It was inevitable that musically inclined slaves should benefit from the periodic visits of music masters to the plantations. Those who worked about the house would have been able to listen to the instruction of the music masters and to observe how passages could be executed on various instruments. Frequently, young people of slaveholding families taught the slaves to play flutes and violins themselves. Fithian, tor example, commented more than once upon the close relationship existing between "several Negroes, & Ben & Harry [the Carter boys]." More than once, the young Carters were chased from the schoolroom where they had been dancing with some slaves to the music of fiddles. Finally, in some instances, slaveholders arranged for blacks to be given lessons; such a practice equipped the slave with sufficient musical skill to play for plantation dances or to entertain visiting guests.

Students took their slaves with them to the College of William and Mary in Williamsburg (established in 1693). Some contemporaries thought it unfortunate that there were not special quarters for the blacks, similar to the "apartment" for the Indians. "There is very great occasion for a quarter for the Negroes and inferior servants belonging to the college," wrote Hugh Jones in 1724. For the slaves, however, the circumstance was fortunate; they lived in the rooms of their young masters and undoubtedly attended classes with them on various occasions. More than likely, many a slave at the college learned to "play very well on the Violin" or to "play extremely well on the French horn" from attending music classes at the college, which were taught by "masters from the town" rather than by members of the regular faculty.

The evidence suggests that some slaves in Charles Town and other urban centers of the South must have been taught to play by professional musicians, just as slaves were trained in bricklaying, carpentry, soldering, etc. Despite the laws against the teaching of blacks, intrepid southerners taught their slaves any number of skills and trades. In 1743 a member of the Associates of Doctor Bray, Commissary Alexander Garden, opened a "Negro School House," using as teachers two young slaves that he himself had educated. The course of study included psalmody, along with reading, writing, and catechizm. Another school for slaves in Charles Town was maintained by a Mr. Boulson, who in 1740 made his dancing school and concert hall over into a school for slaves after he was converted by the evangelist George Whitefield. The records fail to indicate the subjects taught by Mr. Boulson to his fifty-three black students, but it is improbable that the former music master would neglect singing.

There are numerous entries in southern colonial newspapers attesting to the southern slaves' possession of musical skills. In the *Virginia Gazette* alone, the advertisement sections contained more than sixty references to black musicians during the years 1736–80, forty-five of which were to black violinists or fiddlers. It is noteworthy that some references were made to fiddle *makers,* as distinguished from performers:

> RUN AWAY . . . a black Virginia born Negro fellow named Sambo, about 6 ft. high, about 32 years old. He makes fiddles, and can play upon the fiddle, and work at the carpenter's trade.
>
> [August 18, 1768]

BLACK DANCE MUSICIANS

All over the South slaves played for the dancing of their masters at balls, assemblies, and special "Entertainments" in the taverns, plantation ballrooms, and "palaces" of the colonial governors. Splendid affairs were given by the royal governor in Williamsburg, for example, where the colonists danced country dances, minuets, and reels, including their favorite *Sir Roger de Coverley* or the *Virginia Reel.* Interestingly enough, colonists were also fond of a special type of lively jig called by some the "Negro Jig." Nicholas Cresswell referred to one of these in 1774:

> 37 Ladies dressed and powdered to life. All of them fond of dancing. . . . Betwixt the country dances they have what I call everlasting Jigs. A couple gets up and begins to cut a jig (to some Negro tune). Others come and cut them out, and these dances always last as long as the Fiddler can play.

This reference to a "Negro tune" may well represent the earliest record of the influence of slave music on the white colonists. Fithian, too, writes about whites dancing "giggs," but does not identify the music to which such dancing was done. There is a *Negro Jig* in a dance collection of 1782, *A Selection of Scotch,*

English, Irish and Foreign Airs, published by James Aird in Scotland. There is no way of knowing whether this piece was of slave origin, or whether it was composed in imitation of a slave dance tune. The implication is clear, however, that the colonists were developing an awareness of the distinctive qualities of so-called "Negro music" and using this music for dancing.

Few names of black dance musicians in the South have come down to us from the colonial period. Generally, the records simply indicate that some slaves were especially valued for their musical skills; for example, the "accomplished black fiddler" on the plantation of Richard Bailey in Acomorack County, Virginia. We do know, however, that the young slave fiddler belonging to Charles Carrol of Annapolis was named John Stokes and that Sy Gilliat, the slave violinist owned by Baron Botetourt of Williamsburg (royal governor of Virginia), was reputed to be very skilled.

Slaves frequently were used as fiddlers for dancing in the home and for dancing classes. Many were the nights at Nomini Hall, for example, when "John the Waiting Man played" and the young ladies spent the evening "merrily in dancing." Just as there were itinerant music masters for young southerners, so were there itinerant dancing masters. The dancing teachers held classes in rotation at the plantation homes of their scholars, giving instruction at each place for several days in succession. Their pupils traveled with them from one plantation to the other, remaining as guests in the house where the dancing classes were being held.

Fithian's diary recounts in detail the events of the dancing-school sessions. Francis Christian, the dancing master for the Tidewater area where Nomini Hall was located, brought his own musician with him to the plantation. During the days he taught the young people to dance in the dancing room, "several hours before and several hours after dinner." In the evenings candles were lit and there was informal dancing. Presumably, the same dance musician played during both the day and the evening. Generally Mr. Christian retired about seven thirty, but the dancers continued on for several more hours. On one occasion the weather was so bad that Mr. Christian was delayed in arriving for his classes at Nomini Hall, but since all the pupils had come they proceeded without the dancing master: "Mr.

Carter's Man played and the Dance [went] on with great Spirit and Neatness."

RECREATIONAL MUSIC OF THE SLAVES

Twice a year, at Christmas and at Easter, the slaves were given a respite of several days from work to celebrate their jubilees. Christmas was the most joyous festival of the year. Fithian wrote about one Christmas Eve: "Guns are fired this Evening in the Neighborhood and the Negroes seem to be inspired with new life." The days following Christmas were spent in merry-making and dancing to the music of the fiddle or banjo—most often the fiddle. On Easter Sunday, people dressed in their finest and went to church—"all the Parish seemed to meet together, High, low, black, white, all came out." Afterward, the slaves were "disbanded till the [following] Wednesday morning." Their chief mode of diverting themselves during the Easter vacation was dancing to fiddle music. But then the favorite form of entertainment for their masters, too, was dancing!

The records of the colonial South contain few references to exclusively black musical activities. Chroniclers of southern life in the eighteenth century were generally unconcerned about what happened in the slave quarters, and visitors to the planta-tions were not curious enough—in those times—to spy. The colonists, of course, were aware that a great deal of dancing went on to the music of fiddles, most of them homemade. In Maryland the Englishman Cresswell noticed that the slaves were playing a different kind of string instrument and described it:

> This instrument (if it may be so called) is made of a Gourd some-thing in the imitation of a Guitar, with only four strings and played with the fingers in the same manner.

Cresswell noted further that the music of the banjo was ac-companied by the singing of "very droll music indeed," the slaves singing about their masters and mistresses "in a very satirical manner."

Cresswell's description of a banjo (1774) is apparently the earliest such reference in colonial writings, although these instruments may have been found among the slaves even in the seventeenth century.[1] Obviously, however, they were not common during colonial times. The singing at Cresswell's "Negro Ball" reflects the African propensity for musical improvisation. The singers vied with one another in poking fun at their masters —a practice reported again and again by chroniclers—making up their verses as they sang and each trying to outdo the previous singer. The white observer noted that the "poetry [was] like the music—rude and uncultivated." The music was evidently African, for no other kind would have been appropriate for the slaves' dancing, which to Cresswell was "so irregular and grotesque" that he was "not able to describe it."

Slaves in the colonial South apparently danced and sang in the traditional African ways, as did their northern counterparts when gathered together for diversion. But with the exception of Cresswell, the slaveholders did not record any such activities, and the blacks obviously could not keep records because they had not been allowed to learn how to write. There is just one eyewitness account of an occasion in the South where African music might have been performed. In 1739 there was a slave uprising on a plantation in Stono, near Charles Town. The "Angola Negroes" who began the revolt were joined by other slaves, and all proceeded down the road toward St. Augustine, burning and killing as they went. Along the way they stopped in a field "and set to dancing, singing and beating Drums by way of triumph." [2]

By the time of the American Revolution, the black man was an integral part of colonial society. Comprising over 20 per cent of the population, black men performed most of the labor in the colonies, both in towns and on plantations. With regard to music, the black man participated in the musical activities of the colonies to whatever extent he was allowed. In the meetinghouse he sang psalms and hymns along with the white wor-

[1] The oft-quoted statement of Thomas Jefferson about the "banjar" of the slaves appears in his *Notes on the State of Virginia* (1803), ed. William Peden (paperback ed., Chapel Hill, N. C.).

[2] See further in Edwin Clifford Holland, *A Refutation of the Calumnies Circulated Against the Southern and Western States, Respecting the Institution and Existence of Slavery Among Them* (Charleston, 1822), pp. 68–69, 81.

shipers. Some were impressed by the beauty of the slaves' sing-ing—for example, Samuel Davies, who wrote:

> I can hardly express the pleasure it affords me to turn to that part of the Gallery where they [the slaves] sit, and see so many of them with their Psalm or Hymn Books, turning to the part then sung, and assisting their fellows who are beginners, to find the place; and then all breaking out in a torrent of sacred har-mony, enough to bear away the whole congregation to heaven.

And the colonists grew to depend upon the services of the slave fiddler. About 1760 the gentleman-farmer Hector St. John de Crèvecoeur, who had immigrated from France and settled in Orange County, New York, wrote, "If we have not the gorgeous balls, the harmonious concerts, the shrill horn of Europe, yet we dilate our hearts as well with the simple Negro fiddle." [3]

[3] Hector St. John de Crèvecoeur, *Letters from an American Farmer: Sketches of Eighteenth-Century America*, eds. Henri Bourdin, Ralph Gabriel, Stanley Williams (New Haven, 1925; paperback ed., New York), p. 96.

II

Let My People Go

1776-1866

IMPORTANT EVENTS

1775–83   The American Revolution.
1775   The Dunmore Proclamation, promising freedom to
          all slaves who joined the British army; caused lib-
          eralizing of colonial laws that prohibited the enlist-
          ment of Negroes as servicemen.
          Organization of first anti-slavery society by the Quak-
          ers: Philadelphia, Pa.
          Fifteen Negroes initiated into a British army lodge of
          freemasons: Boston, Mass.
1776   The Declaration of Independence; Philadelphia, Pa.
          Possibly the earliest establishment of a Negro Baptist
          Church: Petersburg, Va.
1778   First enactment of laws offering freedom to slaves
          who should serve in the army for a number of
          years.
1781   Philadelphia selected as the capitol of the United
          States (until 1800).
1782   Publication of *Selection of Scotch, English, Irish and
          Foreign Airs* by James Aird, which included first
          known printing of *Yankee Doodle* and a *Negro Jig*:
          Glasgow, Scotland.

1783   Slavery abolished by law in Massachusetts, followed by similar laws in other New England states.
Northwest Territory ceded to the United States.

1784   First black men, Richard Allen and Absalom Jones, granted licenses to preach (by the Methodists): Old St. George's Methodist Episcopal Church, Philadelphia, Pa.

1787   Pioneer protest by black men against discrimination; Richard Allen, Absalom Jones, and William White walk out of Old St. George's Methodist Episcopal Church because of discriminatory treatment: Philadelphia, Pa.
Founding of the Free African Society by Allen and Jones: Philadelphia, Pa.
Beginning of Negro freemasonry with the establishment of African Lodge No. 459 by Prince Hall under warrant from the Grand Lodge of England (American freemasons had rejected the application of the Negroes): Boston, Mass. Other benevolent and fraternal organizations organized later.
Slavery prohibited in the Northwest Territory, but provision made for the return of fugitive slaves.
Establishment of the New York Free African School by the New York Manumission Society: New York, N. Y.

1789   Publication of *The Interesting Narrative of the Life of Olaudah Equiano, or Gustavus Vassa the African. Written by Himself:* London, England.

1790   First census taken in the United States; black population more than three-quarters of a million, including 59,000 free blacks.

1792   First law passed by Congress authorizing the formation of military bands (other than fife and drum corps); law amended in 1803.

1794   Organization of the first independent black church in the United States by Richard Allen: the Bethel African Methodist Episcopal Church, Philadelphia, Pa.

1796   Organization of the second independent Negro church in the United States, by black men who walked out in protest from the John Street Methodist Episcopal Church of New York City: the African Methodist Episcopal Zion Church, New York, N. Y.

1800   Gabriel Prosser slave revolt: Richmond, Va.
Beginning of the "Second Awakening" or the "Great Revival" (until ca. 1830). First camp meeting held in Logan County, Ky.

1801   Publication of first hymnal designed for the exclusive use by black folk, *A Collection of Hymns and Spiritual Songs from Various Authors, by Richard Allen, Minister of the African Methodist Episcopal Church* (two editions): Philadelphia, Pa.

1803   Louisiana Purchase.

1804   Founding of pioneer school for slaves and free blacks by the African Free Society: New York, N. Y.

1808   Congressional Act abolishing the slave trade (1807); went into effect on January 1.

1812–15   War of 1812.

1816   Organization of the American Colonization Society, whose aim was to repatriate black men in Africa.

1819   Spanish Cession (Florida Territory).

1820   Earliest record of an all-black military band: Philadelphia, Pa.

1821   Establishment of the American colony of Liberia on the west coast of Africa with 130 American blacks.
Establishment of the African Grove Theatre at New York City (until 1828).

1822   Denmark Vesey insurrection, the most elaborate conspiracy of the times, involved as many as 9,000 slaves: Charleston, S. C.

1827   Publication of the first Negro newspaper, *Freedom's Journal:* New York, N. Y.

1831   Nat Turner slave revolt: Southampton County, Va.
First publication of the *Liberator,* voice of militant anti-slavery sentiment, by William Lloyd Garrison.

1833   Organization of the American Anti-Slavery Society: Philadelphia, Pa.

1841–42   First introduction of choral singing into the A. M. E. Church, causing great controversy among members: Mother Bethel Church, Philadelphia, Pa.

1842   Founding of the New York Philharmonic Society.
Heyday of Dickens' Place in "Five Points" area of New York (Pete Williams, black proprietor), where all-black shows were presented.

1843   First organized white minstrel show, the Virginia Minstrels: the Bowery Amphitheatre, New York, N. Y.

1845   Annexation of Texas Territory.

1846   Annexation of Oregon Territory.

1848   Mexican Cession (New Mexico and California Territories).
The "Gold Rush" to California.

1852   Publication of *Uncle Tom's Cabin* by Harriet Beecher Stowe.

1853   Aborted slave revolt in New Orleans; involved 2,500 slaves.

Publication of *Twelve Years a Slave* . . . by Solomon Northup, black violinist.

1856   Establishment of the first Negro college, Wilberforce University, by the Cincinnati Conference of the Methodist Episcopal Church: Wilberforce, Ohio.

1857   Dred Scott decision of the Supreme Court, affirming that a slave could not be recognized as a citizen of the United States.

1860   Census indicated 4,880,009 Negroes in the United States, including 488,070 free Negroes.

1861–65   Civil War.

1861   Lincoln inaugurated as sixteenth president of the United States.

1863   The Emancipation Proclamation issued by Lincoln became effective on January 1, stating that "all persons held as slaves within any State or designated part of the State, the people whereof shall be in rebellion against the United States, shall be then, thenceforward, and forever free." (Slaves freed only in confederate states.)

The Draft Riots (Negro homes and businesses burned, including Negro Orphanage): New York, N. Y.

1865   Thirteenth Amendment, which abolished slavery throughout the United States.

Establishment of the Bureau of Refugees, Freemen and Abandoned Lands (called Freedmen's Bureau), which aided the newly freed slaves and established schools for them.

Beginning of the establishment of independent black churches in the South.

First large migration of blacks to urban areas.

Organization of the first all-black minstrel group to receive international acclaim, the Georgia Minstrels under the leadership of George Hicks, a Negro.

Establishment of Oberlin Conservatory of Music, which attracted black students: Oberlin, Ohio.

1866   Civil Rights Act, which gave citizenship to black men and guaranteed them equal treatment under the law.

CHAPTER IV

Two Wars and the New Nation

During the first half of the eighteenth century, England was too preoccupied in her struggle with France to pay much attention to the American colonies. But with the attainment of victory in the Seven Year's War in Europe and the French and Indian War in the New World (both wars, 1756–63), England began to enforce a policy regarded by the colonists as threatening to their political and economic freedom. Their vigorous protests against the new imperial policy included denunciation not only of the series of intolerable Acts passed by England, but also of the slave trade. Some of the colonists, in affirming their right to freedom from England, began to realize that the same right of freedom might apply as well to black men. And the slaves themselves began to agitate for their freedom in the courts and legislative assemblies as early as 1766. In 1773, for example, a "Grate number of Blacks" sent a petition to the governor and General Court of Massachusetts asking for freedom from the "state of slavery."

BLACK MUSICIANS IN THE WARS

Extant military records often fail to list the race of servicemen in the American wars of the eighteenth and early nineteenth centuries, and town and other civic records—which are the chief sources of information about black servicemen—are often incomplete. To be sure, meager bits of information about black servicemen may sometimes be obtained from local histories.

When army rolls do refer to race, the lists often include such enigmatic entries as "A Negro Man" or "A Negro, name not known." Only occasionally will an entry give a full citation of name, race, and classification—such as "Negro Bob, drummer." For all these reasons, few names of black army musicians have come down to us. We know, however, that a typical assignment for a black was that of drummer. Indeed, a Virginia Act of 1776 specifically stated that blacks "shall be employed as drummers, fifers, or pioneers."

THE REVOLUTIONARY WAR

The first blood shed in the colonists' struggle for freedom was that of a runaway slave, Crispus Attucks, in the Boston Massacre of 1770. More than one American historian has commented upon the significance of this occurrence, that a fugitive slave should have been willing to risk his life in a fight for the freedom of his country when he himself was not free. But Attucks was not the only black man to join the War for Independence, he was merely the first. More than 5,000 blacks fought in the seven-year war against England. Since some blacks had fought in the French and Indian War despite laws excluding them from military service, there were precedents for their entrance into the Revolutionary War. Among the black soldiers who fought in the Battle of Bunker Hill in the Spring of 1775 was Barzillai Lew, a drummer and fifer of Chelmsford, Massachusetts. Lew had also fought in the French and Indian War.

However in November, 1775, General Washington issued orders prohibiting the further recruitment of Negroes. About the same time, and unknown to Washington, the royal governor of Virginia, Lord Dunmore, issued a proclamation that promised freedom to all slaves and indentured servants who should join His Majesty's troops. Hundreds of slaves responded to the call, some to join the British lines, others simply to seek freedom as best they could. The colonies were forced to liberalize their policy in view of the Dunmore Proclamation, and eventually black men were actively recruited (except in Georgia and South Carolina), generally with the understanding that their services would automatically grant them freedom. Most blacks fought in integrated units in both the North and the South. In New England, however, there were all-black companies attached to regiments of Connecticut, Rhode Island, and Massachusetts. One black battalion of Massachusetts, called the "Bucks of America," was under the command of a black leader, Colonel Middleton.

Among the extant names of black army musicians are Jazeb Jolly, drummer in the Seventh Massachusetts Regiment; William Nickens, a drummer in a Virginia company; "Negro Tom," a drummer in Captain Benjamin Egbert's Orangetown, New York, regiment; and "Negro Bob, drummer," of the First Company of Rangers in South Carolina. The fifer Barzillai Lew, mentioned above, served throughout the war. Another fifer was Richard Cozzens of a Rhode Island regiment. There are many references in contemporary sources to anonymous black army musicians. Each of the black detachments of New England, for instance, had a drummer and a fifer. The typical composition of a Negro company is indicated in a proposal made to the General Assembly of Massachusetts by one Thomas Kench, an officer in an artillery regiment stationed at Castle Island in Boston Harbor. According to Kench, the command should be white and consist of the regular officers and an orderly sergeant. The black soldiers should include three sergeants, four corporals, two drummers and fifers, and eighty-four rank and file. The Bucks, of course, represented a typical black company; incidentally, its leader, Colonel Middleton, was a fiddler. Only one name of a navy musician seems to have been preserved from anonymity, that of Nimrod Perkins of Virginia, drummer on the galley the *Diligence*.

The martial music of the Revolutionary War period emanated primarily from fifes and drums; occasionally, trumpets were used. According to the Orderly Book of a Virginia general, each regiment was allowed a "Fifer-Major" and a "Drummer-Major," whose duties were "to practice the young fifers and drummers between the hours of eleven and one o'clock every day, and to take care that they perform their several duties with as much exactness as possible." It was not until 1792 that the first laws were passed by Congress for the formation and regulation of true military bands (as distinguished from fife-and-drum corps). The duties of service musicians in the War for Independence included performing at ceremonies of an official nature as well as sounding calls, and more than likely, they were required to provide entertainment at times. We may be sure that fiddles were brought forth at such times, particularly where black soldiers were present.

The armed-services musicians played spirited marches in the field for their comrades-at-arms and on parade before their countrymen. A large body of war songs developed during the war, many of them using familiar tunes for verses of topical interest—about the defeat of a British general, about the Boston Tea Party, about "Liberty's call" or "the American hero." One popular hymn, *Chester*, represented the contribution to the war effort of the renowned composer William Billings of Massachusetts. According to some, this hymn tune, fitted with a special patriotic text, was so well liked that it became the theme song of the revolution. But it could not compete with an older song (composer unknown) that served as a rallying point for the whole country—the infectious *Yankee Doodle*. Hundreds of verses were sung to the lively melody, and it was quoted in one of the new nation's first overtures, Benjamin Carr's *Federal Overture* (1794).

Black servicemen apparently sang the same songs as did their fellows; they seem not to have developed special musical traditions as blacks were to do in later wars. Undoubtedly there was much improvisatory singing among the black soldiers as they sat around the campfires at night or worked at their tasks during the day. Just as they had satirized their masters, mistresses, and fellow slaves in their songs back home, so must they have extemporized songs about the white officers and soldiers, their new mode of life, their army adventures, and the civilians they encountered. But no one bothered to record the music of the black servicemen, and so it is lost, as are most of the names of those who sang and played it.

THE WAR OF 1812

The number of black men who served in the War of 1812 was small by comparison with the roll of Revolutionary War black servicemen, although here again, the records rarely refer to race. Most Negroes seemed to have entered the navy, undoubtedly because at the beginning of the war they were excluded from joining the army. History preserves the names of three navy musicians: George Brown, a bugler on the *Chesapeake;* Cyrus Tiffany, a fifer on the *Alliance*, who fought in the Battle of Lake Erie; and Jessie Wall, a fifer on the frigate *Niagara*.

In 1814 General Jackson issued a proclamation allowing blacks to enlist in the army, and later they fought in some of the strategic battles of the war, especially in Louisiana. Throughout the period of the war, as during the revolution, slaves went over in considerable numbers to the British lines in response to promises of freedom.

There is very little on record in regard to black army musicians in the War of 1812. A contemporary newspaper of New Orleans carried an item referring to Jordan B. Noble of the Seventh Regiment of Infantry as a "matchless drummer." In another source, a drummer named Jordan Little is praised for having drummed the Americans into line at the Battle of New Orleans. It was said that the "colored Creoles" of Louisiana who fought in the Battle of New Orleans had their own special war song, *En Avan' Grenadié* ("Go forward, grenadiers; he who is dead requires no ration"), which they sang along with *La Marseillaise* and other songs. And that is all!

We know, however, that more black musicians must have been active during the war because of the number of all-black brass bands that began to appear soon after the war—especially in New Orleans, Philadelphia, New York, and sections of New England. After the war, for example, the Third Company of Washington Guards (Philadelphia) organized a Negro band under the leadership of Frank Johnson that was destined to become internationally famous. Johnson, a Negro, earned for himself a reputation as "one of the best performers on the bugle and French horn in the United States." The black musicians who composed the military bands of the early nineteenth century undoubtedly acquired their training—as well as their instruments—during the War of 1812.

THE POST–REVOLUTIONARY PERIOD

During the 1780s the southern states suffered a severe depression, chiefly because of the decline in prices of their main crops—tobacco, rice, and indigo. For a while it seemed that "the peculiar institution" of slavery itself might go into a decline. But the invention in 1793 of the cotton gin by a Yankee schoolteacher, Eli Whitney, effected a complete reversal of the situation and ushered in a period of economic prosperity for the southern planters. Partly because of the Industrial Revolution, there had been created a great market for cotton goods and, consequently, for cotton fiber wherever it could be produced. With the invention of Whitney's machine, which separated the cotton seed from the fiber, southern planters were able to employ their slave labor solely in the cultivation of the crop. The growing of cotton became extremely profitable, and most of the planters switched over from the cultivation of tobacco and rice to that of cotton. Now there was an increased demand for slaves! Consequently, the beginning of the nineteenth century saw a renewed flourishing of the slave trade, with New England's ships taking the lead in supplying southern planters with the human cargo.

Meanwhile, anti-slavery groups, which had begun to appear even before the War for Independence, pressed for legislation against the slave trade. Finally, on March 2, 1807, Congress passed a law prohibiting the importation of African slaves into the States after January 1, 1808. The law was openly flouted for many years, however, and slavery became more firmly established in the South than ever before. In the North slavery slowly died away. Beginning as early as 1780 in Pennsylvania, laws were passed that provided for the gradual abolition of slavery. In 1787 Congress prohibited slavery in the newly acquired Northwest Territory (ceded by Great Britain to the United States in 1783), although at the same time it provided for the obligatory return of fugitive slaves to their owners. By 1783 complete emancipation had come for the blacks of Massachusetts, the first to be freed; by 1830 slavery was eradicated in all of the northern states.

MUSICAL ACTIVITIES IN THE NEW NATION

After the war the musical life of the States resumed at the point where it had stopped earlier: concerts, plays, and operas began to flourish again, singing and dancing schools reopened, and the people returned with gusto to their singing of hymns and ballads. Professional musicians continued to come to the States in increasing numbers, particularly from England. The activity of these foreign musicians combined with that of the natives to stimulate a flourishing of the arts that evoked admiration from travelers unprepared for such vigorous cultural activity in so young a republic. The foreign musicians settled chiefly in the larger cities—Boston, New York, Philadelphia, Charleston, and New Orleans in the French-owned Louisiana Territory—where they gave lessons "on the pianoforte, harpsichord and violin"; joined orchestras or organized them where none existed; inaugurated concert series; established music publishing houses and opened music stores; founded music societies, and collaborated with theatrical companies in presenting plays and operas to the public. Philadelphia early established itself as the chief center of music publishing, with a prolific output of psalm and hymn collections, instruction books, and collections of the "newest country dances" and "latest songs." New Orleans took the lead in producing operas; it was the first city to have a permanent opera company.

Both native and foreign musicians responded to the great demand emanating from the vigorous musical activity of the land; they wrote hymn tunes and arrangements, anthems, marches, ballads, dances, and incidental music for plays. Moreover, they wrote "instructors" for their students or incorporated such material in their song collections. In a typical collection, five to ten pages were given over to a discussion of music theory, entitled perhaps "A Plain and Concise Introduction to Music" or "Easy Introduction to the Grounds of Music" and covering such subjects as "the gamut," staves and clefs, note values, musical signs, sol-fa syllables and "transposition of the mi," time and key signatures, intervals, and syncopation. If music students of the period did not learn theory, it was through no fault of the professional musicians.

There is evidence that in several places Negroes were included among the students taught by established musicians. The Englishman William Tuckey, for example, who had come to the colonies before the war, became the organist and choirmaster at Trinity Church in New York and taught music to the pupils of the church's charity school, some of them blacks. It was Tuckey's church choir that in 1770 presented the first performance of music from Handel's *Messiah* heard in the United States. In New Orleans, some of the French, German, and Italian musicians who were associated with opera companies and orchestras taught Negro students—who themselves became music teachers, composers and conductors. The Congregational minister and musician Andrew Law (1748–1821), was associated with two of the earliest black music teachers in the North.

BLACK SINGING–SCHOOL MASTERS

One of the first black music teachers in the new nation was Newport Gardner (1746–1826?). Nothing is known of his early childhood, for he was fourteen years old when he was sold to Caleb Gardner, a prominent merchant of Newport. The African lad showed a great interest in music, and Mrs. Gardner arranged for him to study with "a singing master named Law [who] occasionally came to Newport to give lessons." Since Andrew Law (mentioned above) conducted a singing school in Newport during the year 1783, it seems likely that he was the teacher in question, and we have some indication of what Gardner learned, for Law published several books including *Select Harmony* (1778), the *Art of Singing* (1780), and the *Rudiments of Music* (1785). In his books Law discusses "toning and tuning the voice," articulation and pronunciation, music theory (that is, "voice parts, cliffs [i.e. clefs], sharps and flats"), accent, "The swell of soft and Loud," time, and mode.

It was said of Gardner that he "read and wrote music with ease" and "possessed a voice remarkably strong and clear." A contemporary writer, John Ferguson, stated the matter even more emphatically in a book published in 1830:

Newport Gardner . . . early discovered to his owner very superior powers of mind. He taught himself to read, after receiving a few lessons on the elements of written language. He taught himself to sing, after receiving a very trivial initiation into the rudiments of music. He became so well acquainted with the science and art of music, that he composed a large number of tunes, some of which have been highly approved by musical amateurs, and was for a long time the teacher of a very numerously-attended singing school in Newport.

Gardner was enabled in 1791 to purchase freedom for himself and some of his family. He rented the "upper chamber" of a house on High Street in Newport for his music school and included among his students his former mistress, Mrs. Sarah Ann Gardner. Gardner became a deacon in the First Congregational Church in Newport and a protégé of its minister, the Reverend Samuel Hopkins. After the death of Hopkins, Gardner organized the Newport Colored Union Church and Society. In 1826 he went to Africa as a missionary. It is possible that the song *Crooked Shanks*, attributed to Gardner in the collection *A Number of Original Airs, Duettos and Trios* (1803), is one of the "large number of tunes" he composed. One of his anthems was performed in a Boston concert in 1825.

An early black singing-school master of New York is identified only as Frank the Negro in a letter written by Andrew Law, Frank's former teacher. "About 40 scholars" were in attendance at Frank's school in 1786. In Philadelphia, one of the first black music teachers was John Cromwell, who was active during the 1820s.

THE EMERGENCE OF
INDEPENDENT NEGRO CHURCHES

Throughout the colonial period black folk, free and slave, had worshiped in churches alongside the whites, although in most places they had been assigned to segregated pews. Black and white churchgoers sang the same psalms and hymns, and it may be assumed that they shared in common a basic repertory of religious music. Although the compilers of psalters and hymnals were typically ministers of a particular denomination, the psalms and hymns they published were "collected from various authors" and "designed for the use of Christians of all denominations." The full title of the official hymnal of the Methodists, for example, was *A Pocket Hymn Book, Designed as a Constant Companion for the Pious of All Denominations. Collected from*

Various Authors. It was not until the nineteenth century that hymnals designed for the use of a specific denomination or for a special kind of religious gathering began to appear in large numbers.

Toward the end of the eighteenth century a movement for the establishment of separate black congregations gradually gained momentum, primarily because of the growing impatience of blacks with the discrimination they encountered in white churches. In some places white congregations encouraged the organization of all-black congregations; in other places they bitterly opposed such groups. For the most part, however, the white churches were too preoccupied with their own problems—those involved in setting up their independence from the European mother churches—to be overly concerned with the problems of their black members. The American church that in 1800 had the largest black membership of all—the Methodist Church—did not itself become independent until 1784, the year of its organizational General Conference in Baltimore, Maryland.

THE EARLIEST BLACK CONGREGATIONS

George Leile, slave of a Baptist deacon in Kiokee, Georgia, apparently was the first black man to be granted a license to preach in the United States. As early as 1774, he traveled up and down the Savannah River, preaching to slaves on the plantations bordering the river. Sometime between 1779 and 1782, Leile helped to organize at Savannah, Georgia, the first Negro congregation in the country, the African Baptist Church. During the last three decades of the century, other black Baptist congregations were established in Virginia (Petersburg, Richmond, and Williamsburg), and after 1800 separate black groups appeared in Boston (1809), Philadelphia (1808), and New York (1808).

Beginning in 1787, groups of dissident Negroes began to withdraw from Methodist churches—first at Philadelphia, later at New York. At this time Negroes constituted almost one-fifth of the American Methodist Church, for their membership had been encouraged from the earliest period of that church's establishment. Indeed, two Negroes, Richard Allen and Black Harry Hoosier, were present at the first General Conference in

Baltimore, and one of the first converts of the local Baltimore church was Aunt Annie, a slave of the Sweitzer family. Both Allen and Hoosier served as itinerant Methodist preachers, traveling the New York-Baltimore-Philadelphia circuit armed with Bible and hymnbook and preaching to both whites and Negroes. Methodism made a special appeal to the lowly, and Negroes found its preachments and practices especially suited to their needs.

In 1786 Allen was sent to Old St. George's Methodist Episcopal Church in Philadelphia, where he was assigned to preach at the 5:00 A.M. and 5:00 P.M. services. When Allen first arrived there were only five black members; in less than a year, under his leadership, the number of blacks had increased to forty-two. Some of the whites became alarmed at so large an attendance of blacks and wanted them "removed from their original seats and placed around the wall." One Sunday morning when Allen and three others arrived for service they were sent to find seats in the gallery. Later, Allen wrote about that morning:

> We expected to take the seats over the ones we formerly occupied below, not knowing any better, we took those seats. . . . Just as we got to the seats, the elder said, "Let us pray." We had not been long upon our knees before I heard considerable scuffling and low talking. I raised my head and saw one of the trustees, H . . . M . . . , having hold of the Rev. Absalom Jones, pulling him up off his knees, and saying, "You must get up, you must not kneel here." Mr. Jones replied, "Wait until prayer is over." Mr. H. M. said, "No, you must get up now, or I will call for aid and force you away." Mr. Jones said, "Wait until prayer is over and I will get up and trouble you no more." With that he [the trustee] beckoned to one of the other trustees, William White, to pull him up. By this time prayer was over, and we all went out of the church in a body, and they were no more plagued with us in the Church.

Allen and his followers resolved from that day to establish their own organization, although they

had subscribed largely towards finishing St. George's Church, in building the gallery and laying floors, and just as the house was made comfortable . . . were turned out from enjoying the comforts of worshipping therein.

THE FIRST INDEPENDENT
BLACK DENOMINATIONS

The first act of the ousted blacks was to organize the Free African Society (1787). From that organization came two Negro congregations: Absalom Jones's African Episcopal Church, which affiliated with the white Protestant Episcopal denomination, and Richard Allen's African Methodist Episcopal Church (hereafter, A. M. E.), which eventually severed all relationships with the white Methodist sect. The A. M. E. Church, consequently, became the first independent Negro church in the United States. Allen's church, called Mother Bethel, was dedicated on July 29, 1794. By 1813 the A. M. E. Church had 1,272 members among its various congregations. The denomination grew rapidly, establishing branches in the neighboring states and as far south as Charleston, South Carolina. In 1816 an organizing General Conference was held in Baltimore, which formally bound the different branches together into one denomination, electing Richard Allen the first black bishop of America. By 1826 the A. M. E. Church had 7,937 members. The strategic centers of the denomination during the early decades of the nineteenth century were Philadelphia, New York, Baltimore, and Charleston.

At New York in 1796 a second independent black denomination was established. The black members withdrew from the John Street Methodist Episcopal Church and organized the A. M. E. Zion Church, for the same reasons that had led the black Methodists to withdraw in Philadelphia. Among the first black congregations of other major denominations that were established during the nineteenth century were the Presbyterians in Philadelphia (1807), and the Roman Catholics in New York.

The Negro church did more than just provide religious experiences for its congregations. For black folk—who were denied participation in the social, economic, and political life of the white American community—the church was at once a religious temple, a school for children and adults, a social center, a training ground for potential leaders of the race and, like the Catholic

Church of early Europe, a patron of the arts—particularly music. Significantly, since their beginnings in the eighteenth century, Negro churches have occupied an important place in the lives of black folk; many black leaders have been ministers, and many black musicians have begun their careers in church choirs.

RICHARD ALLEN'S HYMNBOOK

Richard Allen (1760–1831) was born a slave into the family of an eminent Philadelphia lawyer, Benjamin Chew. During Allen's formative years, he was exposed to the conversation of some of the leading intellectuals in the country, for Philadelphia was the capital of the new nation, and Chew's residences—both the town-house and Clivenden, the country estate—were the gathering places for important people. Indelible impressions must have been left upon the mind of the young slave through his incidental contacts with these people in the Chew home. In 1767 the Allen family was sold to the Stokely plantation near Dover, Delaware. It was there that Richard was converted, at the age of seventeen, to Methodism, and there also that he saved enough money from doing "hired out" jobs to purchase his freedom. Allen received his most impressive religious experiences in the Methodist "class meetings" that he attended, which were under the leadership of a black man. The meetings were often held secretly, deep in the forest near Dover, for slaves were not allowed to assemble without the presence of a white man. The slave custom of hold-ing secret religious meetings at night in a woods was by no means restricted to the Delaware area or to the members of any one sect. The practice was common among slaves wherever formal religious services were conducted solely under the leader-ship of white ministers, or where religious services were forbid-den outright.

Although Allen was not an educated man, he was extremely intelligent and highly articulate. At the time he organized the first congregation of the A. M. E. Church, he had had extensive experience as both an itinerant and a resident minister. Because he knew and appreciated the importance of music to his people, one of his first official acts as an A. M. E. minister was to publish a hymnal for the exclusive use of his congregation. The importance of this first hymnal designed exclusively for an all-black congregation cannot be overemphasized; whereas Allen might have used the official Methodist hymnal—and, as a good Methodist, should have done so—instead he consciously set about to collect hymns that would have a special appeal to the members of his congregation, hymns that undoubtedly were long-time favorites of American Negroes. Thus the hymnal provides an index to the hymns popular among black congregations (the A. M. E. in particular) of the new nation. These hymns represent the black worshipers' own choices, not the choices of white missionaries and ministers.

Allen's hymnal, entitled *A Collection of Spiritual Songs and Hymns Selected from Various Authors by Richard Allen, African Minister*, appeared in 1801; it was printed by John Ormrod, who had the previous year printed for Allen *The Articles of Association of the AME Church of the City of Philadelphia*. The collection consists of fifty-four hymn texts, without tunes, drawn chiefly from the collections of Dr. Watts, the Wesleys, and other hymn writers favored by the Methodists of that period, but also including hymns popular with the Baptists. Within the same year an enlarged second edition of the hymnbook was printed by T. L. Plowman, with the title page this time reading *A Collection of Hymns and Spiritual Songs from Various Authors, by Richard Allen, Minister of the African Methodist Episcopal Church*. Ten additional hymns were added to the collection, making a total of sixty-four, and a few changes were made in some texts of the original corpus. As was customary at the time, Allen neither provided authors' names nor indicated appropriate melodies for his hymns. We can identify the authors, however, by finding concordances for the hymns in the original Watts collections and in the few eighteenth-century hymnals that contain authors' names. (We shall take up the question of the hymn tunes later.)

The wording of the title chosen by Allen was not novel for the time; indeed, it was rather common, its earliest use dating back to a revised edition of the *Bay Psalm Book* printed in 1651 with the title *The Psalms, Hymns and Spiritual Songs of the Old and New Testaments*. The original inspiration for the title was the Scriptural passage:

Let the word of Christ dwell in you richly in all wisdom teaching and admonishing one another in Psalms and Hymns and Spiritual Songs, singing with grace in your hearts unto the Lord.

[Col. 3:16]

How and where did the self-educated ex-slave minister find the hymns for his collection? Hymnbook compilers typically gathered their hymns from the large number of hymnals already in print. Augustus Toplady, for example, wrote in the preface to his collection of 1776 that a few of the hymns were of his own authorship and the remainder he had selected after examining "between forty and fifty volumes." It is not probable, however, that Richard Allen would have had access to any large number of hymnals, nor would he have had the time for examining hymnals had he been able to consult them. In addition to his responsibilities as minister to the fledgling church, Allen had to earn a living; at various times in his life he was a teamster, brickyard worker, woodcutter, shoemaker, and day laborer. It may be assumed, therefore, that some of the hymns Allen used must have been selected from the hymnals to which he had access as an itinerant preacher traveling the Pennsylvania-Delaware circuit and as an assistant minister at Old St. George's Methodist Episcopal Church. Other hymns in his collection may have been in oral circulation among Methodists and Baptists of the area—in the same way that folksongs circulated. Finally, it seems clear that Allen himself must have written some of the hymns.

There are several bases for assuming that Allen wrote hymn texts. From time to time he published sermons, doggerel verses, tracts, and other kinds of writings. Eventually, he wrote a brief autobiography, *The Life Experience and Gospel Labours of the Right Reverend Richard Allen, Written by Himself and Published by His Request* (publ. 1887). Allen, always practical-minded, was very much aware of the needs of his flock, most of whom were ex-slaves. He had withdrawn from the Free African Society because he felt that the "emotional natures" of his people should not be swallowed up in a cold intellectual ritual:

I was confident that no religious sect or denomination would suit the capacity of the colored people so well as the Methodists, for the plain simple gospel suits best for any people, for the unlearned can understand, and the learned are sure to understand.

The primacy of music was also clear to Allen. He realized the power of a Watts hymn, such as *There Is a Land of Pure Delight* (Hymn No. 27), to help his people believe that their wretched existence on earth would be followed by a happier one in heaven:

> There is a land of pure delight,
> Where saints immortal reign.
> Infinite day excludes the night,
> And pleasures banish pain.
>
> There everlasting Spring abides.
> And never-with'ring flowe'rs:
> Death, like a narrow sea divides
> This heav'nly land from ours.
>
> Sweet fields beyond the swelling flood,
> Stand dress'd in living green;
> So, to the Jews, old Canaan stood,
> While Jordan roll'd between.

But he also knew that his people needed courage to face the problems on earth and so he taught them to sing such songs as the following one (Hymn No. 11):

> What poor despised company
> Of travellers are these,
> That's walking yonder narrow way,
> Along that rugged maze?
>
> Why they are of a royal line,
> They're children of a King;
> Heirs of immortal crown divine,
> And loud for joy they sing.
>
> Why do they then appear so mean,
> And why so much despis'd,
> Because of their rich robes unseen
> The world is not appriz'd.
>
> Why some of them seem poor distress'd
> And lacking daily bread;
> Heirs of immortal wealth possess'd
> With hidden Manna fed.

In addition to writing hymns especially for the 1801 collection, Allen (or one of his associates) made alterations or introduced supplementary lines into some of the orthodox hymns that he included. In some instances sophisticated words or phrases were replaced by simpler ones that would have more meaning for the illiterate worshippers in the Bethel congregation. More important, refrain lines or choruses were added to the orthodox stanza forms—this, at a time when the hymn-with-chorus was not yet admitted into the repertory of official Protestant hymnody. For example, the very first hymn of the book employs a stanza-chorus form:

[*Stanza:*]   The voice of Free Grace cries, escape to the mountain,
             For Adam's lost race Christ hath open'd a fountain,
             For sin and transgression, and every pollution,
             His blood it flows freely in plenteous redemption.

[*Chorus:*]   Hallelujah to the Lord who purchas'd our pardon,
             We'll praise him again when we pass over Jordan.

The Bethel congregation evidently liked this chorus, for it appears again as an appendage to Hymn No. 50, *From Regions of Love*. In Hymn No. 4, *Oh, God, My Heart with Love Aflame*, the single line "Glory, Hallelujah" is added as the ninth line to a rather elegantly phrased eight-line stanza.

It is improbable that each hymn in Allen's collection had its own tune. It is more likely that a limited number of tunes were drawn upon, any of which would have been appropriate for the singing of a hymn as long as the metrical patterns of tune and hymn matched. A four-line hymn with eight syllables to a line could be sung, for example, to any "long meter" tune with its eight tones to the line or phrase. Similarly, a hymn with six-syllable lines would call for a "short meter" tune. There is no way of knowing which tunes actually were used by Allen's congregation, but we can make some logical assumptions based on current practices during the period when the Bethel A. M. E. Church was in its infancy—that is, during the years 1794–1830.

In the first place, it may be assumed that the tunes consistently linked with specific hymns in other hymnals of the period probably were sung with those hymns at Allen's church. For example, the tune *Newark* is associated with the hymn *Now*

Begins the Heav'nly Theme (No. 31) in more than one of the
sources published during the years 1776–1805. On the other hand,
a hymn such as *Come All Ye Weary Trav'lers* (No. 64) is associated with three different tunes in as many different hymnals
of the period, and consequently, we cannot be sure which tune
was employed in Allen's church, or even if any one of the three
tunes was used. Compilers of collections that included both
hymns and their tunes generally threw in a few extra tunes for
good measure, as, for example, Andrew Adgate did in his *Philadelphia Harmony . . .* (1788) or Nehemiah Shumway in *The
American Harmony* (1793).

A second assumption possible with regard to tunes for some
of the Allen hymns is that folksongs and popular songs were
used. This was a common practice of the period among some
sects, and indeed, had been a common practice since the beginning of Protestantism—some of Martin Luther's best chorale
melodies were borrowed from German folk music. There is
direct evidence about the black Methodists following such practices in a book by John F. Watson entitled *Methodist Error or
Friendly Christian Advice to Those Methodists Who Indulge in
Extravagant Religious Emotions and Bodily Exercises* (1819).
Watson's advice was directed to all Methodists of the Philadelphia
Conference (which included both New Jersey and Pennsylvania), for they had a reputation for being "noisy" and excessively
exuberant in their worship services, but he singled out the blacks
for special censure:

> We have too, a growing evil, in the practice of singing in our
> places of public and society worship, *merry* airs, adapted from
> old *songs*, to hymns of our composing: often miserable as poetry,
> and senseless as matter. . . . Most frequently [these hymns are]
> composed and first sung by the illiterate *blacks* of the society.

Since Allen's A. M. E. Church was the only independent black
group in the Philadelphia Conference in 1819, it follows that
Watson must have been directing his criticism to that group.
These black Methodists, being free to develop their own style
of worship, apparently preferred lively tunes to the sober, traditional hymn tunes, particularly for the singing of hymns composed by their minister, Richard Allen.

Our third assumption is that some of the hymns were probably sung to melodies composed by Allen himself or by members of his congregation. Here again Watson is a witness, speaking of the blacks singing "for hours together" and actually composing the songs as they sang. Another witness is the Methodist elder William Colbert, who visited Allen's church in the company of others in 1804 and later wrote in his diary about the experience. Some of his companions made satirical remarks about the singing of the black Methodists, he wrote, not so much with regard to the actual sound of the singing as to the kinds of songs that were sung. Presumably the blacks were singing their own composed songs in the worship service instead of official Methodist hymns. At any rate, original tunes would certainly have been used for the singing of the choruses and refrains that were added to orthodox hymns.

Visitors to Philadelphia rarely failed to visit the Methodist churches, which were reputed to have unusual customs of worship, and the black A. M. E. Church was a special attraction. In his *Annals of Philadelphia*, Watson wrote:

> It was the forte and the purposed system of the Methodists to have very superior and attractive singing—always of such popular cast and spirit as would easiest please the ear and enchain the attention; and it well succeeded with all those who were unsophisticated. . . . The Methodist church had a quicker and more animated style of singing at all times than prevailed in the slower heavier cadence of the other churches of the city. It was not uncommon to find many persons who went purposely to Methodist churches to hear the singing.

A Russian traveler, Paul Svinin, visited Bethel Church in 1811. Accustomed to the restrained style of the Greek Orthodox worship service, he found Bethel's service much too unusual for his taste. However, his account of the singing is of special value because of the information it provides about musical practices. When Svinin and his friend arrived at the church, the minister was reading from the psalms.

> . . . At the end of every psalm the entire congregation, men and women alike, sang verses in a loud, shrill monotone. This lasted about half an hour. When the preacher ceased reading, all turned toward the door, fell on their knees, bowed their heads to the

ground and set up an agonizing, heart-rending moaning. After-
wards, the minister resumed the reading of the psalter and when
he had finished sat down on a chair; then all rose and began chanting psalms in chorus, the men and women alternating, a procedure
which lasted some twenty minutes. . . .

Two features of this part of the service are worthy of note:
the choral response given by the congregation to the reading of
each psalm, and the singing of the psalms in alternation by the
men and the women. Both procedures point back to the traditional African predilection for antiphonal singing. The loudness of the singing and the "heart-rending moaning" are also
typically in the African tradition—the singers singing with all
their might and becoming totally involved in the experience.

Richard Allen's hymnbook undoubtedly was widely disseminated among black Methodist groups, for it was the only A. M. E.
hymnal until 1818, when the A. M. E. Church issued another
official hymnal, "a collection of hymns designed to supersede
all others hitherto made use of in that Church." The compilers
of the new hymnal used only eighteen hymns from Allen's 1801
collection, dropping many of the homely, practical hymns that

Ex. IV.1   A spiritual, *Give Up the World*, related to
Psalm 19, from Allen, Ware, and Garrison, *Slave Songs
of the United States*

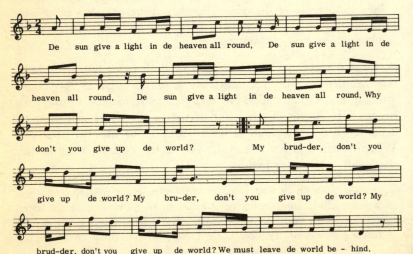

we believe to have been written by Allen himself. Not all of the hymns discarded by the compilers were forgotten, however; some remained alive in oral tradition among black Methodists and Baptists. Moreover, as we shall see, verses taken from these hymn texts reappeared in the people's own music, their "spirituals." The above example of a spiritual seems to point back to the same scriptural psalm as do Examples II.1 and II.2 (see pp. 32 and 40).

THE CAMP MEETING

The camp meeting was an American phenomenon that evolved during the "Second Awakening," a revival movement dominating the religious life of America's frontier communities during the period 1780 to 1830. Its participants were the common people, black and white, of all the Protestant denominations; its format, that of a continuous religious service spread out over several days, often an entire week. Religious services took place in a forest or woods, the members of the huge temporary congregations worshiping in large tents and living in small tents. The historic first camp meeting was held in Logan County, Kentucky, in July, 1800, and drew thousands of participants. A Presbyterian minister, the Reverend James McGready, was the leading spirit in organizing the meeting, but various denominations were represented among the several preachers involved in the conduct of the services and the handling of the large crowds. Eventually the camp-meeting movement came to be dominated by Methodist ministers, who taught their own Methodist hymns to the campers in the early years. From Kentucky the idea of camp meetings traveled in all directions—northeast into West Virginia, Maryland, Delaware, Pennsylvania, and up to the northern states; east into Virginia and on into the Carolinas; south into Tennessee and down into the Deep South.

The camp meeting was an interracial institution; indeed, sometimes there were more black worshipers present than white. Foreign visitors to the States were greatly impressed by what they saw and heard at camp meetings, there being no European prototypes for the vast assemblages in forest groves. The visitors filled their diaries and travel journals with detailed descriptions of the people attending these meetings, of the sermons, of the procedures, and, above all, of the singing—especially the songs of the blacks. Ex-slaves, too, provided descriptions of camp meetings in their writings.

At night the scene of a meeting was an awesome sight. Huge campfires burned everywhere, so that it seemed as if the "whole woods stood in flames." From three to five thousand persons or more were assembled in the huge main tent, called a *tabernacle*, to listen to the preacher-for-the-evening address them from an elevated stand. On benches below the elevation sat the other preachers. Then there were rows of seats for the people—according to some reports, one side for the Negroes and the other side for the white congregation. Other accounts state, however, that the black folk had to *stand*, not sit, in a narrow space reserved for them behind the preachers' elevation; undoubtedly, practices varied from place to place. Robert Todd, a Methodist historian who was active in the Pennsylvania-Maryland-Delaware-Virginia area, says that "a portion of the circle to the rear of the preacher's stand [was] invariably set apart for the occupancy and use of the colored people."

Occasionally black ministers preached to camp-meeting assemblies. Precedents for blacks addressing white or interracial congregations had been set by the Methodists in their early "itinerating" practices, which sent ministers to preach in rural areas, hunting up all those who "dwelt in the wilderness." The first of the English Methodist missionaries to come to America (and, later, the first bishop of the American Methodist Church), the Reverend Francis Asbury, generally was accompanied by Black Harry Hoosier in his travels, estimated to have totaled over 270,000 miles. On some occasions Black Harry substituted for Asbury and was well received. Daniel Coker, a black minister of Baltimore and a leading figure at the organizational Conference of the A. M. E. Church in 1816, noted in his journal that he had addressed a gathering of 5,000 at a camp meeting in Maryland.

SINGING IN THE CAMP MEETING

To both participants and observers, the singing was one of the most impressive aspects of camp meetings. When the people sang their hymns and spirituals, they instantaneously formed a "superb choir." After attending a camp meeting in Georgia, the Swedish novelist Fredrika Bremer wrote:

> A magnificent choir! Most likely the sound proceeded from the black portion of the assembly, as their number was three times that of the whites, and their voices are naturally beautiful and pure.

According to a report on a camp meeting held in Pennsylvania in 1838, where there were seven thousand in attendance, the Negroes sang louder than any others, although they were greatly outnumbered:

> Their shouts and singing were so very boisterous that the singing of the white congregation was often completely drowned in the echoes and reverberations of the colored people's tumultuous strains.

The blacks customarily continued singing in their segregated quarters long after the whites had retired to their tents for the night, and sometimes sang all night long. More than a dozen contemporary writers commented upon this unusual practice. Fredrika Bremer observed that although the meeting she attended had lasted long past midnight, the blacks did not go to sleep afterward:

> On the black side [of the camp] . . . the tents were still full of religious exaltation, each separate tent presenting some new phasis. . . . In one [tent] . . . a song of the spiritual Canaan was being sung excellently. . . . At half-past five [the next morn] . . . the hymns of the Negroes . . . were still to be heard on all sides.

Black campers made their influence felt in the camp-meeting movement in yet another way—much to the discomfiture of the church fathers. Watson observed this in his discussion of the "errors" made by Methodists of the time:

> Here ought to be considered too, a most exceptional error, which has the tolerance at least of the rulers of our camp meetings. In the *blacks'* quarter, the coloured people get together, and sing for hours together, short scraps of disjointed affirmations, pledges,

or prayers, lengthened out with long repetition *choruses*. These are all sung in the merry chorus-manner of the southern harvest field, or husking-frolic method, of the slave blacks. . . .

Such practices he condemned, pointing out that

. . . the example has already visibly affected the religious manners of some whites. From this cause, I have known in some camp meetings, from 50 to 60 people croud into one tent, after the public devotions had closed, and there continue the whole night, singing tune after tune, (though with occasional episodes of prayer) scarce one of which were in our hymn books.

Let us examine the practices of the blacks which affected camp-meeting singing to such an extent that churchmen were moved to protest. First, the blacks were holding songfests away from proper supervision, and this was undesirable in the eyes of the church fathers. They were singing songs of their own composing, which was even worse in the eyes of the officials. The texts of the composed songs were not lyric poems in the hallowed tradition of Watts, but a stringing together of isolated lines from prayers, the Scriptures, and orthodox hymns, the whole made longer by the addition of choruses or the injecting of refrains between verses. Finally, for their composed religious songs the blacks used tunes that were dangerously near to being dance tunes in the style of slave jubilee melodies. None of this was acceptable to the orthodox. Nevertheless, from such practices emerged a new kind of religious song that became the distinctive badge of the camp-meeting movement.

THE CAMP–MEETING SPIRITUAL

Just as the "Great Awakening" movement in the eighteenth century had stimulated a revolt among the common people against the staid psalmody of the religious establishment and had ushered in the livelier hymnody, so the "Second Awakening" of the early nineteenth century brought a reaction against the now antiquated hymns. In the noisy, folksy atmosphere of the camp meeting, songs of a different kind were demanded. There were no hymnbooks in the early years of the movement; the campers had either to sing from memory or to learn songs in the meetings. Most of the congregation was illiterate and, at any rate, it would have been difficult to read by the light of flickering campfires or torches. As a result the same kind of procedures were developed at camp meetings as had been practiced among Negroes. Song leaders added choruses and refrains to the official hymns so that the people could join in with the singing. They introduced new songs with repetitive phrases and catchy tunes. Spontaneous songs were composed on the spot, often started by some excited preacher and developed by the crowds who shouted "Hallelujah" and similar praise words or phrases between the preacher's lines. The new songs were called "spiritual songs," as distinguished from the hymns and psalms. True, the term "spiritual song" had been in use for over a century, but now it acquired a different meaning, being used to designate the camp-meeting hymn. According to modern authorities, the first collection of songs to be directly inspired by camp-meeting revivalism was published in Philadelphia in 1803, John Scott's *Hymns and Spiritual Songs for the Use of Christians, Including a Number Never Before Published*. Within the same decade appeared a number of similiar collections; among them, *The Christian Harmony or Songster's Companion* (1805) by Jeremiah Ingalls, and *A Collection of the Most Admired Hymns and Spiritual Songs with the Choruses Affixed as Usually Sung at Camp Meetings* (1809) by Joseph Totten.

The distinctive features of the camp-meeting spiritual song were the chorus, the folksong-style melodies, and the rough and irregular couplets that referred to scriptural concepts and to everyday experiences. Frequently, as we have seen, choruses and refrains originally belonging to one song were attached to other songs. Eventually there developed a body of such "wandering verses," which became immensely popular with camp-meeting congregations. It is worthy of note that some of the verses that were to become most popular with campers appeared in print for the first time in Richard Allen's collection of 1801— for example:

> Hallelujah to the Lamb,
> Who has purchased our pardon;

We will praise him again
When we pass over Jordan.

[Chorus sung with Hymns Nos. 1 and 50]

There's glory, glory in my soul;
Come, mourners, see salvation roll.

[Couplet in Hymn No. 14]

Firm united let us be,
In the bonds of charity;
As a band of brothers join'd,
Loving God and all mankind.

[Chorus of Hymns Nos. 45 and 56]

There were at least two other favorite camp-meeting verses that belonged to the Negro tradition, according to contemporary sources:

Roll, Jordan, roll

and

Shout, shout, we are gaining ground;
Glory, Hallelujah.

In his book *Methodist Error*, Watson discussed the latter along with several other verses "composed and first sung by Blacks."

SHOUTS IN THE CAMP MEETING

Watson reported on a curious activity of the Negroes that took place while they were singing in their quarters after the all-camp services were ended. To him it seemed that the singers were almost dancing, and indeed they were:

With every word so sung, they have a sinking of one or [the] other leg of the body alternately; producing an audible sound of the feet at every step, and as manifest as the steps of actual Negro dancing in Virginia, etc. If some, in the meantime, sit, they strike the sounds alternately on each thigh.

This is the earliest account of a religious dance ceremony of

African origin, the "ring shout," that was to be described many, many times in nineteenth- and twentieth-century American literature. Watson apparently did not take note of the circle formation of the dancers, but he did observe the thigh slapping. As we have seen, the slaves who danced in the markets of New York City accompanied themselves with percussive sounds produced in this manner. And during the period when Watson was writing, the slaves in New Orleans were drawing crowds of whites to the Place Congo on Sunday afternoons to watch a similar form of dancing. (This point will be discussed in a later chapter.)

There was another camp-meeting practice that allowed the blacks to indulge in their traditional "shuffle step" dancing—the "farewell march around the encampment." Robert Todd reported on a typical occurrence in a northern slave state:

> Usually the tide of enthusiasm on the colored side of the encampment arose and intensified as the days and nights rolled by; and reached the climatic point on the last night of the meeting. By general consent, it was understood that, as to the colored people, the rules requiring quiet after a certain hour, were, on this last night, to be suspended; and great billows of sound from the tornado of praise and singing rolled over the encampment, and was echoed back from hill and wood for miles away, until the morrow's dawning.

With the sunrise, the blacks would begin knocking down the plank partitions that separated the white quarters from those of the blacks. Then they would begin the "grand march round de campment,"

> accompanied with leaping, shuffling, and dancing, after the order of David before the ark when his wife thought he was crazy; accompanied by a song appropriate to the exciting occasion. . . . The sound of the hammer aforesaid became the signal for a general arising all around the camp; and, in a few moments, curtains were parted; tents thrown open; and multitudes of faces peered out into the early dawning to witness the wierd spectacle. Sometimes the voices of the masters and veterans among the white people would echo back, in happy response, the jubilant shout of the rejoicing slaves.

ETHIOPIAN MINSTRELSY

Blackface minstrelsy was a form of theatrical performance that emerged during the 1820s and reached its zenith during the years 1850–70. Essentially it consisted of an exploitation of the slave's style of music and dancing by white men, who blackened their faces with burnt cork and went on the stage to sing "Negro songs" (also called "Ethiopian songs"), to perform dances derived from those of the slaves, and to tell jokes based on slave life. Two basic types of slave impersonations were developed: one in caricature of the plantation slave with his ragged clothes and thick dialect; the other portraying the city slave, the dandy dressed in the latest fashion, who boasted of his exploits among the ladies. The former was referred to as Jim Crow and the latter, as Zip Coon.

ANTECEDENTS OF THE MINSTREL SONGS

So-called "Negro songs" had been in circulation in England as early as the mid-eighteenth century; they were performed on the concert stage and published in song collections. In the United States contemporary sources report the singing of "Negro songs" as early as 1769, the year when Lewis Hallam the Younger sang *Dear Heart! What a Terrible Life I Am Led* in Bickerstaffe's play *The Padlock* at a New York theater. Negro songs were also sung in New York concerts by a Mr. Tyler, a Mr. Dibdin, and by Mrs. Hallam during the years 1798–1800, and a "Negro Dance" was performed in 1796 by M. Francisque, choreographer of the Old American Company, an actors' group. Among the best known of the songs—all of them published in American collections and all generally portraying the black man sympathetically as either a tragic or pitiful figure—were *Negro Philosophy*, *Poor Black Boy*, *An African Love Song*, *The Negro Boy* (also entitled *I Sold a Guiltless Negro Boy*), *The Desponding Negro*, and *The Negro's Humanity* (also entitled *A Negro Song*).

The last of these was a versified arrangement of the genuine African song recorded by Mungo Park in the eighteenth century (see p. 17). Park had sent the original words to his friend, the Duchess of Devonshire, who "versified" the text—that is, changed the verses so that they would rhyme and altered some of the phrasing that to her was crude. She, in turn, arranged for the new text to be set to music by an "eminent composer," Giacomo Gotifredo Ferrari. The song was later set to music by other composers, both in its original form and in the Devonshire version, and became extremely popular on both sides of the Atlantic.

> The loud wind roar'd, the rain fell fast,
> The white man yielded to the blast;
> He sat down, beneath our tree,
> For weary, sad, and faint was he,
> And ah, no wife, or mother's care.

Chorus:
> For him, the milk or corn prepare,
> The white man shall our pity share;
> Alas, no wife, or mother's care,
> For him, the milk or corn prepare.

> The storm is o'er, the tempest past,
> And mercy's voice has hush'd the blast;
> The wind is heard in whispers low,
> The White Man, far away must go,
> But ever in his heart will bear
> Remembrance of the Negro's care.

Repeat Chorus

GROWTH OF THE "ETHIOPIAN" TRADITION

Beginning in the second decade of the nineteenth century, song writers and entertainers began to treat the black man as a comic figure, as in the songs *The Negro and Buckra Man* (1816) and *The Guinea Boy* (1816), and in the play *Obi, or Three-Fingered Jack* (1812). Later on, blackface acts were included in theatrical performances, where dances and songs were typically performed between the acts of plays. From these beginnings emerged the minstrel show, which caught on with the public and developed into an American institution. The first organized full-length minstrel show was produced in 1843 in New York by Daniel Decatur Emmett and his Virginia Minstrels. Among the most successful of the blackface entertainers, all of them white men, were George Washington Dixon, Thomas Nichols, Dartmouth Rice—called the "father of American minstrelsy"— Daniel Emmett, and E. P. Christy.

To obtain materials for their shows, the white minstrels visited plantations, then attempted to recreate plantation scenes on the stage. They listened to the songs of the black man as he sang at work in the cotton and sugar cane fields, on the steamboats and river docks, and in the tobacco factories. The melodies they heard served as bases for minstrel songs, and they adapted the dances they saw to their needs. The musical instruments originally associated with plantation "frolics" became "Ethiopian instruments"—banjos, tambourines, fiddles, and bone castanets. In its established form, the minstrel show consisted of two parts: the first contained songs and jokes; the second comprised a variety of acts and ensemble numbers. Typically, the performance concluded with a "walk around," an act in which some of the performers sang and danced up front (on the stage) and the remainder of the company gave support from the back. Essentially, as the famous minstrel E. P. Christy pointed out, white minstrels tried "to reproduce the life of the plantation darky" and to imitate the "Negro peculiarities of song."

It was common knowledge that one of the most famous of the minstrel songs, *Jump Jim Crow*, stemmed originally from an old, deformed, black stable-worker of Louisville, Kentucky. Thomas Rice, a white actor who had been playing bit parts at the Louisville Theatre during the 1820s, heard the old man singing a funny little song as he went about his work in a stable near the theater and noticed that he moved with a curious shuffle step, made almost ludicrous because of his deformity and because every so often, at a certain point in his song, he would give a little jump into the air. Rice decided to impersonate the old black worker on the stage—song, dance, old clothes, and all. The act went over big, and Rice's future was made; he became Jim Crow Rice. Many other nameless black men contributed songs in a similar way to the "Ethiopian" vogue that swept over the United States.

"Respectable voices" were raised in criticism of "Ethiopian music." It was proclaimed to be representative of the "lowest dregs of music," and composers were admonished to write more refined music—such as the sentimental ballads and elegant salon pieces preferred in polite society circles. But the American public clamored for the "Ethiopian melodies," and the minstrel-song writers gave it such songs as *Old Dan Tucker*, *Zip Coon*, *Dixie*, *Jim Along Josey*, *Coal-Black Rose*, and *Clare de Kitchen*. Everybody sang these melodies; the music became a part of American musical tradition. Little of the black man's folk music was left in the finished product. Elements of Scotch and Irish folk music, in particular, were to be found in these songs and, of course, there was the stamp of the composer's own musical identity. But few forgot that the black man was behind it all. A contributor to the staid *Knickerbocker Magazine* in 1845, J. Kennard, summarized the matter in this manner:

> Who are our true rulers? The Negro poets, to be sure. Do they not set the fashion, and give laws to the public taste? Let one of them, in the swamps of Carolina, compose a new song, and it no sooner reaches the ear of a white amateur, than it is written down, amended (that is, almost spoilt), printed, and then put upon a course of rapid dissemination, to cease only with the utmost bounds of Anglo-Saxondom, perhaps with the world. Meanwhile, the poor author digs away with his hoe, utterly ignorant of his greatness.

The greatest of the white minstrel composers was Stephen Foster, "America's Troubadour" (1826–64). As a child Foster early came into contact with the music of black folk, for a family servant, Olivia Pise, regularly took him to Negro church services. When he began to compose "Ethiopian songs" in 1845, he consciously based some of his songs on tunes that he had heard sung by black folk—particularly *Oh, Boys, Carry Me Along* and *Hard Times Come No More*. In later years Foster had other opportunities to hear the singing of blacks, especially black stevedores on the wharfs of Pittsburgh and black boatmen on the steamboat *James Milligan* when he took a trip to New Orleans. The songs of these workers remained with him, exerting their influence on his best-known minstrel songs: *Old Black Joe*, *Camptown Races*, *My Old Kentucky Home*, *Old Folks at Home*, and *Massa's in de Cold, Cold Ground*.

Black folk sang the minstrel songs just as did the whites. Here was a curious kind of interaction. The minstrel songs, originally inspired by genuine slave songs, were altered and adapted by white minstrels to the taste of white America in the nineteenth century, and then were taken back again by black folk for further adaptation to Negro musical taste. Thus the songs passed back into the folk tradition from which they had come. Contemporary records reveal that the slaves had their own favorites among the minstrel songs: *Old Rosin the Beau, Rosa Lee, Dearest May*, and many of the Stephen Foster songs. By all accounts the slaves sang these songs with the same "touching pathos" that they sang their own songs. There was, however, an obvious difference between the two kinds of songs that observers could not help but note. H. G. Spaulding wrote in the *Continental Monthly* (1863):

. . . a tinge of sadness pervades all their melodies, which bear as little resemblance to the popular Ethiopian melodies of the day as twilight to noonday.[1]

And W. H. Russell commented in *My Diary, North and South:*

The oarsmen, as they bent to their task, beguiled the way singing in unison a real Negro melody, which was unlike the works of the Ethiopian Serenaders as anything in song could be unlike another.[2]

The practices of white minstrels in the nineteenth century established unfortunate stereotypes of black men—as shiftless, irresponsible, thieving, happy-go-lucky "plantation darkies"—that persisted into the twentieth century on the vaudeville stage, in musical comedy, on the movie screen, radio, and television. And yet, blackface minstrelsy was a tribute to the black man's music and dance, in that the leading figures of the entertainment world spent the better part of the nineteenth century imitating his style.

[1] Henry George Spaulding, "Under the Palmetto," in the *Continental Monthly* (August, 1863), p. 200.

[2] See William Francis Allen, Charles Ware, and Lucy McKim Garrison, *Slave Songs of the United States* (New York, 1867) p. 19. (Modern paperback ed. with arrangements by Irving Schlein, New York, 1965.)

CHAPTER V

The Ante-Bellum Period: Urban Life

In 1800 the federal census classified as Negro slightly more than a million persons in the United States; by 1840 the number had increased to almost three million; and by 1860, the date of the last census enumeration before the Civil War, there were 4,441,830, of whom 3,953,760 were slaves and 488,070 freedmen. In 1800 almost 19 per cent of the black population was free; by 1860, less than 13 per cent was free. Although the black population doubled in size during the first half of the nineteenth century, the proportion of free men remained the same, and during the years 1840–60 it fell considerably.

At the beginning of the nineteenth century, about 10 per cent of the black population of the United States lived in urban communities. In the North all blacks, whether living in urban or rural areas, would be free by 1827, the year the last of the manumission laws became effective. In the South there were large communities of free Negroes in the cities of Baltimore, Maryland; Washington, D. C.; Charleston, South Carolina; Mobile, Alabama; and New Orleans, Louisiana. Their presence there exerted a considerable influence upon urban life, and the character of urban life, in turn, brought about a greater relaxation of the strict disciplines of slavery than was possible on isolated plantations and farms. Although the majority of free black men in cities were employed in personal services or common labor occupations, there were many with skills of various kinds who followed the trades. Moreover, there were black men who operated small businesses and practiced such professions as law, medicine, dentistry, teaching, ministry, and music.

A considerable number of urban slaves worked as artisans, some for their own masters, others for townspeople to whom they had been "hired out." Alexander Newton, an ex-slave of North Carolina, explained in his autobiography how a slave might learn a trade:

> As the result of slavery, many young men were apprenticed, as in my case, to some good workman for at least four years or more. At the end of that time they were efficient, practical workmen who, if free, could command good wages.

Slaves were used in factories, in construction, and particularly on boats and in waterfront occupations as firemen, roustabouts, and stevedores.

BLACK MUSICIANS AND THE GENERAL STATE OF MUSIC

What kinds of music did black folk produce in the nineteenth century before the Civil War? As during the colonial period, slave musicians continued to serve their masters by providing music for entertainment and dancing. Among themselves the slaves sang their own folksongs—about their work, their places of abode, their loves, their frolics and jubilees, their religion, political events—about whatever was closest to their hearts or minds. Early in the nineteenth century, some free black men began to establish themselves as professional musicians. It was no easy thing to do. As we have noted, European musicians were in firm control of music making in America: they filled the important posts in theaters and churches; they gave the concerts and directed the musical institutions, which they, for the most part, had organized. Native-born white musicians, who had achieved recognition in the eighteenth century for their psalms, hymns, and anthems, added popular music to the list in the nineteenth century.

It was a time of impressive beginnings in the new nation. In Boston a Philharmonic Society was organized in 1810 that gave public concerts for fourteen years, the Handel and Haydn

Society was formed in 1815, and the Boston Academy of Music was established in 1832. In New York the Philharmonic Society was founded in 1842 (making it the oldest symphony orchestra in the country). In Philadelphia a Musical Fund Society was started.

At first glance, it would seem that America had no place for black musicians in the scheme of things. But several ameliorating factors entered into the picture. First, black musicians had established the tradition of providing dance music for white America, and it was to be some time before they were seriously challenged in that field. Second, there was a tremendous demand for other kinds of music from the steadily expanding and increasingly prosperous population, which could afford to pay for the things it demanded. America wanted to hear band music, for example, and was sometimes willing to listen to the music of black bandsmen as long as the music was well played. America wanted music teachers, and in some places the color of a man's skin was less important than his ability to impart instruction. America needed music to which it could dance—quadrilles, cotillions, jigs, and quicksteps—sentimental ballads to sing, lively tunes to whistle, and salon pieces to play on the "fortepianos." Finally, America was curious about the black concert artist, so recently removed from the bonds of slavery. The public often attended the concerts of black performers out of mere curiosity, but remained to acclaim the sound of a beautiful voice or the exhibition of extraordinary technique.

There is ample data for the study of the musical activities of black folk during the ante-bellum period. A considerable number of published autobiographies and narratives of former slaves provide first-hand information about the quality of life for black men during these years. White Americans wrote letters, local histories, fiction, travel narratives, diaries, and miscellaneous nonfiction works in which they referred to the music of black men. At the same time the country was flooded with visitors from abroad who also kept diaries, wrote letters back to Europe, and published accounts of their travels in the States. To these visitors the activities of Indians and black men—and especially the music of the latter—were among the more exotic attractions of the New World. Other sources of information are newspapers, of which there were many more in the nineteenth century than in the preceding one, and periodicals, which sprang up for the first time during these years. Certain kinds of knowledge can be obtained, of course, from various types of official records—military, legislative, court, and civic.

With regard to the documentation of the actual music, the picture is not so bright. Black composers wrote a considerable quantity of art music, some of which was published by such established houses as J. L. Peters in New York, John Church in Cincinnati, and Oliver Ditson in Boston. Much more of this music, however, remains unpublished—some of it in manuscript form in various libraries, a great deal of it apparently lost. As for the music of the common people and the slaves, even less is extant. A few songs were written down in personal narratives and periodicals, but it was not until 1867 that the first collection of slave songs was published in book form, *Slave Songs of the United States,* collected and compiled by William Allen, Charles Ware, and Lucy McKim Garrison.

The turn of the century was for black men in the North a period of transition from slavery to freedom and, therefore, a time of difficult adjustments. Blacks struggled not only to improve their economic condition, but also to gain a measure of respect from a hostile white society convinced of their inferiority. Black writers and their white sympathizers repeatedly pointed out the accomplishments of distinguished Negroes as proof that "the powers of the mind are disconnected with the color of the skin" and that "black men are not naturally inferior to the whites, and unsusceptible of attainments in arts and sciences." They pointed to Benjamin Banneker (1731–1806), the gifted mathematician and astronomer; to James Derham (1762–?), the first black physician in the nation; to the Reverend Prince Hall (1735–1807), founder of Negro freemasonry; to the poets Phillis Wheatley (1753–94) and Jupiter Hammon (1717–87); and to the writer Olaudah Equiano (Gustavus Vassa, 1745–1801). Predictably, some of the intense pursuit of respectability by the emerging black middle class reflected itself in their cultural activities. For those Negroes who managed to attain various levels of affluence, the most acceptable modes of social diversion were literary-society meetings, concerts, and musical evenings in the home.

URBAN MUSIC IN THE NORTH: PHILADELPHIA

At the beginning of the nineteenth century Philadelphia was populous, wealthy, and the foremost cultural center in the United States. A monograph published anonymously in 1841, *Sketches of the Higher Classes of Colored Society in Philadelphia. By a Southerner*, provides interesting glimpses into the social life of economically secure Negroes at that time. Judging from contemporary evidence, free middle-class Negroes lived in much the same way in other large cities of the nation. The anonymous author defines his use of the term "upper class" to mean "those whose incomes enable them to maintain the position of house holder and their families in comparative ease and comfort." He points out that "among no people is the pursuit of knowledge more honored," and cites as evidence the establishment in 1833 of the Philadelphia Library Company of Colored Persons (the first institution of its kind), which not only served as a book repository, but also sponsored concerts, lectures, debating societies, and trained young men in public speaking.

More relevant to the present discussion is the author's statement that "Music is made a prominent part of the amusements on all occasions of social meeting together of friends." Almost every parlor contained a pianoforte; young ladies were expected to exhibit skill in piano playing, singing, and painting, as well as in the traditional literary and culinary arts. Like their white fellow-citizens, middle-class Negroes filled their houses with stuffed furniture and bric-a-brac and their cultural life with musical soirées and parlor parties. Our anonymous author wrote:

It is rarely that the Visitor in the different families where there are 2 or 3 ladies will not find one or more of them competent to perform on the pianoforte, guitar or some other appropriate musical instrument; and these, with singing and conversation on whatever suitable topics that may offer, constitute the amusements of their evenings at home. The love of music is universal; it is cultivated to some extent—vocal or instrumental—by all.

The kind of music cultivated in the homes of middle-class blacks was the trite and rather superficial music favored by white society during this period of America's growth. The music historian Gilbert Chase has used the phrase "music in the genteel tradition" to apply to this type of music, which was

> . . . characterized by the cult of the fashionable, the worship of the conventional, the emulation of the elegant, the cultivation of the trite and artificial, the indulgence of sentimentality, and the predominance of superficiality.[1]

The musical taste of the new nation was in a formative stage and, influenced by the foreign musicians who poured into the country from the politically restless countries of Europe, the public strained after what it considered to be aristocratic. Much of the music heard at the fashionable recitals held in the cities was frivolous; the singing was intended to draw tears or induce chills, the instrumental performances were meant only to dazzle with their brilliance. The nineteenth century was the time of the sentimental ballad and the salon piece full of endless runs, arpeggios, and trills. Travelers to the United States lamented the "great, too great uniformity" among the Americans and protested that no matter where they traveled they heard "the same questions about Jenny Lind . . . and the same 'Last Thoughts of Weber' on the piano."

In 1818, according to an article by William C. Bolivar in the *North American*, Philadelphia had an all-Negro marching band under the direction of Matt Black. One of the bandsmen, Frank Johnson, was destined for later fame. Visitors to the city in 1826 saw four black musicians in the theater orchestra of the Walnut Street Theater: the two Appo brothers, William and Joseph, and the two Newton brothers. In 1841 the Colored Choral Society of 150 members, accompanied by Frank Johnson's fifty-piece orchestra, sang an oratorio at the African Presbyterian Church on Seventh Street and at a white church on New Market and Callowhill Streets.

A survey made in 1856 indicated that there were fifteen black professional musicians in the city. Of the fifteen, six were performers, five were music teachers, and four were teacher-per-

[1] Chase, *America's Music*, p. 165.

formers. There were, to be sure, many more black musicians—part-time musicians, who combined music making with working at their trades. There were barber-musicians, boot- and shoe-maker-musicians, brick-maker-musicians, and tanner-musicians. These men, most of them self-taught, followed in a hallowed American tradition; the renowned William Billings himself (see p. 76) and many other native white composers were self-taught artisan-musicians. One energetic black musician was obviously very talented and very busy, if we may credit his description of himself as "Portrait Sign and Ornamental Painter, Daguerreo-typist, Teacher of Photography, the Guitar and Singing."

On the Concert Stage.   To Elizabeth Taylor Greenfield (1809–76), a soprano, was given the sobriquet "The Black Swan" by the critics for her "remarkably sweet tones and wide vocal compass." Born a slave in Natchez, Mississippi, she was taken to Philadelphia as an infant, where she was adopted by a Quaker, Mrs. Greenfield. Elizabeth's guardian arranged for her to study music as a child, despite the Society of Friends' ban on musical pursuits, and allowed her to sing at private parties. Elizabeth made her debut in 1851, singing before the Buffalo Musical Association and thereby establishing her reputation as an artist. A concert tour of the northern states followed during the years 1851–53; a tour of England in 1854 was climaxed by a command performance at Buckingham Palace for Queen Victoria. Miss Greenfield was the best-known black concert artist of her time. An excerpt from press notices of the period follows:

Any one who went to the concert of Miss Greenfield on Thursday last, expecting to find that he had been deceived by the puffs of the American newspapers, must have found himself most agreeably disappointed. . . .

After he [the pianist] had retired, there was a general hush of expectation to see the entrance of the vocalist of the evening; and presently there appeared a lady of a decidedly dark color, rather inclined to an embonpoint, and with African formation of face. . . . The amazing power of the voice, the flexibility, and the ease of execution took the hearers by surprise. . . . The higher passages of the air were given with clearness and fullness, indicating a soprano voice of great power. . . . She can, in fact, go as low as Lablache, and as high as Jenny Lind,—a power of voice perfectly astonishing. It is said she can strike thirty-one full, clear notes; and we could readily believe it.

[*Globe*, Toronto, May 12–15, 1852]

After a brief concert career, during which she received much acclaim from the critics but little support from the American public, Greenfield retired and opened a voice studio in Philadelphia.

One of Elizabeth Taylor Greenfield's younger contemporaries was Thomas Bowers (1836–85?), who rose to the level of a "first-rank tenor" in his musical career. As a child he studied piano and organ; as a young adult he served as organist in the St. Thomas African Episcopal Church. His debut in 1854 was followed by a tour of the northern states and Canada. The critics hailed his appearances everywhere, calling him "The American Mario" or the "The Colored Mario" (after a renowned Italian tenor of the period, Conte di Candia Mario). Bowers' programs consisted primarily of standard arias from operas and oratorios, but like his white counterparts on the concert stage he also sang ballads.

"The Leader of the Band." "The leader of the band," wrote Robert Waln in 1819, "is a descendant of Africa [who] possesses a most respectable share of musical talents." Waln's reference was to Frank Johnson (1792–1844), who built for himself an enviable reputation during the early decades of the nineteenth century as a fiddler, bugler, and horn player, bandmaster, orchestra leader, and composer. During the 1820s and 30s his band was employed by the State Fencibles and Philadelphia Grays, both white organizations of Philadelphia. In 1838 Johnson toured with his band in England, and at a command performance for Queen Victoria at Buckingham Palace he was presented with a silver bugle. With regard to racial incidents, his career was not uneventful; on more than one occasion white bands refused to march in the same parade with his band.

Johnson's band was primarily a woodwind band, consisting of flutes, clarinets, and bassoons, to which were added one or two French horns, a serpent, cymbals, triangles, bells, and a bass drum. During parades a drummer and a fifer played at intervals to give the regular bandsmen periods of rest. The band was nationally acclaimed for its excellence. A British traveler to the States who heard the Johnson band at a Fourth of July celebration in Albany, New York, wrote:

> The only military bands I ever remember to have heard superior to it was the royal band that attends at the Palace of St. James in London and the band of the National Guards in Paris.[2]

When playing for dances, Johnson added string instruments to his band, producing an orchestra that became a favorite of the fashionable people in cities and resorts all along the Atlantic seaboard. Waln noted that in Philadelphia, "Among other follies of our young ladies, it is quite a fashionable one, to be 'enchanted' with this fiddler." As far south as Richmond, Virginia, Frank Johnson's Colored Band was highly regarded. One planter, James Avirett, in reminiscing about the "Great Balls" when all of Virginia society would come out in full force, wrote:

> Old Frank Johnson's (Negro) String Band furnished the music and who ever heard better dance music than this? It is said that, as the night wore away, this remarkably gifted [fiddler] has often been known to lose consciousness and go to sleep, yet go on calling figures and never make a mistake.

Johnson's duties as orchestra leader, of course, included calling the figures for the dancing as well as playing. In addition, he composed most of the music that he played. In short, his duties were all-inclusive, as Waln pointed out:

> In fine, he is leader of the band at all balls, public and private; sole director of all serenades . . . inventor-general of cotillions; to which add, a remarkable taste in distorting a sentimental, simple, and beautiful song, into a reel, jig, or country-dance.

Undoubtedly, it was Johnson's "taste in distorting" songs into reels that contributed to his great popularity—in other words, his ability to "jazz" the music—although the word "jazz," of course, had not yet been invented.

Johnson composed a considerable quantity of music, some of which was published as early as 1818. A number of unpublished

[2] Joel Munsell, *Annals of Albany* (Albany, 1871) IX, p. 309.

manuscripts are deposited in the Free Library Company of Philadelphia. The published music includes twelve collections of cotillions and marches, among them the *Recognition March on the Independence of Hayti* (ca. 1825) and a march especially written in 1824 for performance at the "Grand Ball given in the New Theatre in honor of [the] illustrious guest, General La Fayette."

Other black composers active in the Philadelphia area during the years ca. 1820–60 include William Brady, A. J. R. Connor, John T. Douglass, James Hemenway, and Henry Williams. The music composed by these men was the kind in vogue during the period: dances (such as minuets and cotillions), marches, anthems, overtures, and sentimental ballads. Richard Milburn, a barber-guitarist, won a reputation as a professional whistler. The popularity of one of his tunes, *Listen to the Mocking Bird*, has lasted up to the present day. The song was first published in 1855 with Milburn's name on the title page along with that of Alice Hawthorne (pseudonym for Septimus Winter), the person who transcribed and arranged the melody (see p. 115). Later printings of this best-selling song of the 50s dropped the name of Milburn, and America soon forgot that a black man had composed the melody.

Street Vendors. On the streets of large cities, a familiar sight was that of street vendors and hucksters, calling out their wares or offering their services. Their cries, although typically more song fragments than true songs, are nevertheless a part of the musical tradition of blacks in the United States. As a class the street vendors remained anonymous, but a few became legendary figures in their communities because of their unusual voices or because they peddled their wares over so long a period of time. One such man was "The Hominy Man" in Philadelphia, who was well-known during the 1820s for his strong resonant voice. His cry was a simple one:

> Hominy man come out today
> For to sell his homi*nay*.

or

> Hominy man is on his way
> For to sell his homi*nay*.

To Aaron R. Dutcher.

Sentimental

ETHIOPIAN BALLAD

LISTEN TO THE

Mocking Bird

MELODY

By

RICHARD MILBURN

Written and arranged by

Alice Hawthorne

Piano.   Price 25 Cts.   Guitar.

Philad. Published by WINNER & SHUSTER. 110 North Eighth St.
Washington D.C. HILBUS & HITZ   A.E. JONES & CO. Indianapolis.   FAULDS, STONE & MORSE. Louisville.
Entered according to Act of Congress in the Year 1855 by Winner & Shuster in the Clerks Office of the District Court of the Eastern District of Pa
P. M. Gow Eng.

Title page of Richard Milburn's *Listen to the Mocking Bird*, 1855. *(Courtesy New York Public Library, Schomburg Collection.)*

NEW YORK

In the United States census returns of 1850, twenty-four black men were listed as professional musicians in New York, more than in any other city in the nation. New York was ahead in yet another respect: from 1821 to 1828 the Negroes there maintained their own theater, the African Grove, where ballets and plays were presented with black actors and where, ironically, a special gallery was reserved for white spectators. New York at this time was the theatrical capital of the country. It was remarkable that any city in so young a nation as the United States should have been able to maintain four flourishing theaters, and it was particularly remarkable that one of the theaters should have been operated by blacks. Visitors to the city invariably found their way to the African Grove. A traveler from Scotland, Peter Neilson, wrote in his journal:

> One of the theaters is for the black people of the city; it is really worth one's while to go there for a few nights for the novelty of the thing.

Information about events at the African Grove Theatre is recorded in newspaper items (e.g. in the *National Advocate* in 1821), old playbills, and reports made by visitors. Simon Snipe, man about town, described his visit to the theater on Mercer Street in two tiny pamphlets, both entitled *Sports of New York* (1823, 1824). Despite his supercilious tone, Snipe's description permits a glimpse of theater life for blacks.

In accordance with the custom of the period, music and dancing were performed between the acts of the plays. An evening's program in October, 1821, featured a ballad opera, described as an "Opera," before the play of the night. The presentation was typical of the times, consisting primarily of sentimental ballads interspersed with folksongs and comic songs. James Hewlett, the principal actor, sang seven songs, including *Behold in His Soft, Expressive Face*, *Scots Wha' Ha'e in Wallace Bled*, *Robin Adair*, *Maid of the Mill*, and *Is There a Heart That Never Loved*. The latter seems to have been a favorite with the acting company

FOR THE BENEFIT OF
Mr. HEWLET.

Mr. BROWN has spared neither time or expense in rendering this Entertainment agreeable to the Ladies and Gentlemen of Colour, being the third attempt of this kind in this City, by persons of Colour.

AN OPERA

Will take place corner of Mercer and Bleecker-st.
On MONDAY EVENING, Oct. 1st.

SONGS.

" Behold in his soft expressive face,"	Mr. Hewlet.
The Light House,	Hutchington.
"Scots wha' hae' wi Wallace bled,"	Hewlet.
Corporal Casey,	Thompson.
" Is there a heart that never loved,"	Hewlet.
"I knew by the smoke that so gracefully curl'd,"	Hutchington.
" My Deary,"	Hewlet.
Maid of the Mill,	Hewlet.
Robin Adair,	Hewlet.
The Hunter's Horn,	Hewlet.

After which will be performed, for the last time
this Season, the TRAGEDY of

Richard the Third.

KING HENRY,	Mr. Hutchington.
PRINCE OF WALES,	Miss S. Welsh.
RICHARD,	Mr. Hewlett.
BUCKINGHAM,	Hutchington.
LORD STANLEY,	J. Hutchington.
RICHMOND,	Mathews.
LADY ANN,	Miss Welsh.
QUEEN ELIZABETH,	J. Welsh.

PANTOMIME ASAMA.

ASAMA,	Mr. Hewlet.
ASANA,	S. Welsh.

The BALLET got up under the direction of Mr. Hewlet, being received on Monday evening, Sept. 24, with unbounded applause, will be repeated again
on Monday Evening, October 1st, 1821.

Columbine,	Miss S. Welsh.	Old Man,	Thompson.
Daphas,	Mr. Hewlet.	Servant,	Master Geib.

ADMITTANCE 50 CENTS.

A playbill of the African Grove Theatre, 1821.

for it was presented on several occasions. Obviously, the singing of this song, and similar ones, brought tears to the eyes of the listeners:

> Is there a heart that never loved
> Or felt soft woman sigh?
> Is there a man can mark unmoved
> Dear woman's tearful eye?
> Oh, hear that man to some distant shore
> Or solitary cell,
> Where none but savages roam,
> Where love doth never dwell.

Sometimes the songs came at the end of the evening's program, as on August 3, 1821, when "some fashionable songs were sung at the conclusion"; among them, *Eveleen's Bower* by the leading lady. On the night of Snipe's visit in 1823, the featured play was *Othello*, which was followed by songs and dances, and then by another play, *The Poor Soldier*. A three-piece ensemble, consisting of violin, clarinet, and bass fiddle, played "a lively tune" as an overture before the curtain rose. After *Othello*, a male trio sang some comic songs, followed by a soloist singing *Is There a Heart*. Two solo dances were performed, including a hornpipe danced by the woman who had played Desdemona in the Shakespeare play. After the final curtain of the evening the ensemble struck up another lively number, this time a march.

The most renowned actor at the Grove was Ira Aldridge (1807–67), the Shakespearean tragedian who made a name for himself in Europe playing Othello to Edmund Kean's Iago, then went on to play roles in other dramas in vogue during the time. Aldridge was noted for his singing of "Negro Songs," especially one that apparently was of genuine slave origin, *Opossum Up a Gum Stump*. On the night that the English actor Charles Mathews visited the theater in 1822, the noisy audience stopped the tragedian in the middle of the play with a demand for this song. Aldridge "came forward and informed them that he would sing their favorite melody with great pleasure" and proceeded with:

> Opossum him creep softly,
> Raccoon him lay mum;
> Pull him by the long tail,
> Down opossum come.

Jin kum, jan kum, beangash,
Twist 'em, twist 'em, run;
Oh, the poor opossum,
Oh, the sly raccoon.

The Grove was closed by city authorities in 1828. It was the "inroad of whites coming for a lark and bringing disorder and wanton mischief [that] led to the closing." More than seventy years were to elapse before Negroes again appeared on a stage in New York City in a show produced, directed, and performed by themselves.

Emancipation Day.   An act passed in 1817 by the New York State Legislature provided that all slaves in the state should be free after July 4, 1827. All over the state there were celebrations among the blacks on July 5, 1827 (July 4 fell on a Sunday), particularly in New York City. One celebrant wrote:

[There was] a real, full-souled, full-voiced shouting for joy, and marching through the crowded streets, with feet jubilant to songs of freedom. . . .[3]

In Albany, a formal parade began at 11 A.M. The African Band, accompanied by three marshals, led the procession, which wound its way "through numerous streets," according to the *Albany Argus and Daily City Gazette*. Banners were on display at the Second Baptist Church, where the special services were to be held. After the performance of "appropriate music," an oration was delivered by the church's minister.

The "Five Points" Neighborhood.   It was inevitable that many of the newly freed slaves in New York City should find themselves unprepared to cope with the bitter competition of the free market, especially those who were without skills and had no experience in taking care of their own affairs. The government gave them no such aid as it had given, for example, to the refugees of the Haitian Revolution who poured into New York City in the early 1800s, and some ex-slaves gravitated toward a life of crime and idleness. One of the neighborhoods in Manhattan inhabited by such ex-slaves and working-class whites, the

[3] James McCune Smith, Introduction to Rev. Henry Highland Garnet, *A Memorial Discourse* (Philadelphia, 1865), p. 24.

so-called "Five Points" area, earned for itself the unsavory reputation of being one of the worst slums in the United States. But
it also won a measure of fame when Charles Dickens visited there
in 1842 and wrote about his experience in his book, *Notes on
America.*

Each dance hall in the area had its own fiddler who played for
the dancing. Almack's, called Dickens' Place after the English author had visited there, was "the assembly room of the Five Point
fashionables." Pete Williams, its black owner, was an amateur
actor and a drama enthusiast, who occasionally presented shows
for his patrons. For the most part the performances were staged
by the waitresses, who doubled as singers and dancers. On Saturday nights the musicians sitting in the orchestra, a "shammy
platform with a trembling railing," generally included a trumpeter and drummer as well as the fiddler. A visitor, George Foster, found the music to be "of no ordinary kind":

> . . . that red-faced trumpeter . . . looks precisely as if he were
> blowing glass, which needles [of sound] penetrating the tympa-
> num, pierce through and through your brain without remorse.
> . . . the bass-drummer . . . sweats and deals his blows on every
> side, in all violation of the laws of rhythm.

This was assuredly "hot music," played long before such words
as "jazz" or "ragtime" had entered the vocabulary of popular
music cognoscenti. One of the favorite pieces of the dancers
was *Cooney in de Holler*, a variant of the popular *Opossum Up
a Gum Stump*. From all evidence, the following melody was
associated with the song during this period.

Ex. V.1   *Cooney in de Holler*

On the night that Dickens visited Almack's a "corpulent black fiddler" was joined by "his friend who plays the tambourine." The English author was particularly impressed by the dancing of a "lively young Negro, wit of the assembly and the greatest dancer known." This was undoubtedly the world-renowned black dancer known as "Juba" (William Henry Lane, ca. 1825–53). The dancer performed the "single shuffle, double shuffle, cut and cross cut . . . spinning about on his toes and heels like nothing but the man's fingers on the tambourine." Though neither Dickens nor Juba himself may have been aware of it, the shuffle steps of the dancing and the drumming accompaniment on the tambourine were in the African tradition.

Master Juba, who was commonly regarded as the "greatest of all dancers" in the first half of the nineteenth century, toured with white minstrels in both the United States and Europe. He learned his techniques from Uncle Jim Lowe, a black jig-and-reel dancer of unusual talent who was well-known in tenderloin districts [4] of northern and southern cities. Juba's contribution to white minstrelsy was himself and his style of dancing. One of the few black men permitted to perform on the stage alongside whites, Juba was a link between the white minstrel world and authentic Negro source material; his dancing contributed to the preservation of integrity in blackface minstrel dances. A critic in the *Illustrated London News* found another praiseworthy talent of Juba that deserved mention:

Juba is a musician as well as a dancer. To him the intricate management of the nigger tambourine is confined, and from it he produces marvellous harmonies. We almost question where, upon a great emergency, he could not play a fugue upon it. . . . The great Boy [a reference to Dickens] immortalized him; and he deserved the glory thus conferred.

[August 5, 1848]

The dance halls of "Five Points" are regarded by some as the antecedents of Harlem's famous "black-and-tan cabarets" of the 1920s. The dance musicians who played in "Five Points" were musical illiterates, but they "beat out hot music" that

[4] The sections of cities devoted to institutionalized vice and prostitution; also known as "red-light districts."

stimulated the dancers to wild and frenzied dancing. And like the Harlem cabarets were to do in later years, some of the dance halls—Dickens' Place, for example—catered to the so-called "quality trade" of wealthy whites.

OTHER NORTHERN CITIES

Peter O'Fake (1820–?), of Newark, New Jersey, achieved a reputation as a flutist and violinist. In and near Newark, O'Fake performed with various music ensembles, once going to New York City to play with the celebrated Jullien Society, a white ensemble. In 1848 O'Fake made musical history by conducting the Newark Theatre Orchestra for an evening's performance—unprecedented for a black man. During the 1850s, O'Fake played with the band of Frank Johnson, which was then under the leadership of Connor. Later he organized his own orchestra, which played for the society circles of Newark, and composed some of the music it played. One of his best-known compositions was a quadrille, *The Sleigh Ride,* which was said to be so realistic that dancers imagined themselves actually "in the enjoyment of a veritable sleighride." This versatile man also directed a choir in one of the city's Episcopal churches.

In Baltimore, Maryland, during the 1840s the violinist William Appo was regarded by some as "the most learned musician of the race." Among his many activities there, Appo conducted a small string ensemble. Early in his career Appo played in a theater orchestra in Philadelphia, as we have seen, and later he performed in Frank Johnson's band. He combined performance with teaching in both Philadelphia and Baltimore, and later in New York, where he settled permanently.

Justin Holland (1819–86) wrote two instruction manuals for the guitar that made his name a household word to guitarists of the nineteenth century. He was born in Virginia, but left at the age of fourteen for New England, where he settled first in Boston, then later in Chelsea, Massachusetts. Holland first took up the study of the guitar for his own amusement, eventually becoming a "correct and brilliant" performer. He went to Oberlin College in 1841 for further study. In 1845 he settled in Cleveland, Ohio, where he established himself as a guitar instructor.

Beginning about 1848 he began to publish arrangements for the guitar, and later, his *Holland's Comprehensive Method for the Guitar* (1874) and *Holland's Modern Method for the Guitar* (1876). Before 1845 Holland had published a book entitled *Choral Reform.* In addition to adapting standard works for guitar performance, Holland composed pieces for that instrument and also for piano and flute, two other instruments that he played proficiently.

Horace Weston (1825–90) was a banjoist whose fame among banjo players has lasted into the twentieth century. As recently as March, 1969, his composition *Minor Jig* was performed at a recital in New York City. Weston was born in Derby, Connecticut, into a musical family. His father, Jube Weston, was a music and dancing teacher. Horace had earned his reputation as a skilled banjoist and composer by the 1850s. After the Civil War he toured Europe twice, once with minstrel groups and later independently.

One of the leading black musicians in Boston was Henry F. Williams (1813–89?), instrumentalist and composer, who was born in Boston and studied music there as a child. Early in his career he played with Frank Johnson's band in Philadelphia. Later he returned to Boston, devoting his time to teaching, arranging and composing, and performing with bands and orchestras. Williams was frequently called upon to arrange music for the celebrated band of the Irish bandmaster, Patrick Sarsfield Gilmore. A highlight of his career came in 1872 when he and another Negro violinist played in the orchestra of 2,000 performers that Gilmore conducted at the World's Peace Jubilee. Best known of his compositions were a dance suite, *Parisien Waltzes* (1854), and four songs: *Lauriette* (1840), *Come, Love, and List Awhile* (1842), *It Was by Chance We Met* (1866), and *I Would I'd Never Met Thee* (1876).

Part-Time Musicians and Itinerants.   For each black musician who achieved a national reputation during ante-bellum period, there were hundreds of humble part-time musicians who followed their trades and picked up extra money by playing for dances at night, on week ends, and during holidays. An English traveler, John Maude, encountered one of these Jacks-of-all-trades on the sloop *Nancy,* on which Maude was traveling. The black man, Nicholas, who had purchased his own freedom and that of his wife, performed "well on the violin" and was "very smart." When the boat reached its destination Maude and his party arranged for Nicholas to play for some dancing, about which he wrote in his diary:

> Went on shore; took with us Nicholas and his violin, the fiddle soon got the girls together; we kicked up a dance and kept it up till midnight.[5]

Black fiddlers also invaded college campuses. At Princeton University in 1789, for example, an observer was shocked when he came across some undergraduates

> . . . dancing up and down the entry as a Negro played upon a violin with twenty students hallooing and tearing about.[6]

One of the best-known black itinerant musicians of the nineteenth century was Solomon Northup of Saratoga Springs, New York, who became even better known for the "slave narrative" he wrote than for his fiddling. His book, *Twelve Years a Slave . . .* , presents a vivid account of how he, a free man, was kidnapped by slave raiders, sold into slavery in Louisiana, then rescued twelve years later. One of many ex-slave narratives that appeared in the mid-nineteenth century, Northup's book is highly regarded by scholars for its reliability and historical value. Northup's experiences before his abduction may be taken as typical for black violinists in the North trying to earn a livelihood with music. He tells us that he had "numerous calls to play upon the violin," and that "throughout the surrounding villages [his] fiddling was notorious [*sic*]." In the Summer he worked at the United States Hotel in Saratoga Springs; in the Winter he relied upon his violin playing. As a matter of fact, Northup's fiddle was his undoing. When two men offered him a job playing with a show, he followed them to Washington, D. C., where he was drugged and kidnapped. He had been promised one dollar for each day's work, three dollars for each night's playing, and the cost of his travel expenses back to Saratoga Springs. We know from other sources that the three-

[5] Joel Munsell, III, pp. 58–59.
[6] Joseph Marks, *America Learns to Dance* (New York, 1957), p. 57.

dollars-a-night payment for dance musicians was common. (We shall return later to Northup as a slave on a southern plantation.)

Black Musical Organizations. A number of places in the North supported Negro brass bands or orchestras, though none achieved the national fame of Frank Johnson's band, which continued its activity under the leadership of Joseph Anderson after its founder's death. Another band that included some of Johnson's men was led by A. J. Connor. There was also in Philadelphia a Negro band called Hazzard's Band. At Newburgh, New York, according to William White in *A History of Military Music in America:*

> A colored band, consisting of men of average talent known as Dixon's Brass Band, was organized in 1827 with Samuel Dixon as the leader. They were uniformed in yellow pants and red coats and were quite popular.

During the decade of the 1850s three bands of Ohio won statewide recognition: the Scioto Valley Brass Band (1855), the Roberts Band (1857), and the Union Valley Brass Band (1859).

The Luca family troupe of Connecticut was organized at a time when "singing family" troupes, generally composed of from four to as many as twelve singers and often including instrumentalists as well, were much in vogue in the United States. They toured the nation, singing songs that appealed to the public—for the most part, ballads. Alexander Luca, the father (1805–?), organized his wife and three sons into a vocal ensemble in 1853, using his youngest son, Cleveland, as a pianist. The group's first appearance in 1853 was successful, and they were encouraged to undertake tours of the northern states. During one tour, in 1859, the Lucas joined with a white troupe, the Hutchinsons, to present some concerts in Ohio, generally to favorable press notices:

> The Hutchinsons and Lucas sang to quite a full audience at West's Hall last evening. The performance could not, coming from troupes possessing talent varied and of the higher order, be otherwise than good. These bands, when they united, made a palpable hit. Their combined concerts are almost invariably successes.
>
> [Sandusky (Ohio) paper, March 1, 1859]

To be sure, not all communities welcomed interracial concerts, as the following excerpt from a newspaper of Fremont, Ohio, indicates:

> The Hutchinsons,—Asa B., Lizzie C., and little Freddy,—accompanied by the Luca family, gave a concert at Birchard Hall on last Wednesday evening. The house was not more than a paying one. When we went to the concert, we anticipated a rare treat; but alas! how woefully were we disappointed! . . . We have, perhaps, a stronger feeling of prejudice than we should have felt under other circumstances, had their abolition proclivities been less startling; but to see respectable white persons (we presume they are such) travelling hand in hand with a party of negroes, and eating at the same table with them, is rather too strong a pill to be gulped down by a democratic community.
>
> [February 25, 1859]

THE ANTI–SLAVERY MOVEMENT

Abolitionists in the North were not satisfied with emancipating the black folk in their own region; they would settle for nothing less than complete freedom for all slaves in the United States. The anti-slavery movement, which had its beginnings in the colonial period, increased in numbers and became very militant. As early as 1817 publications began to appear vigorously denouncing slavery. In 1831 the New England Anti-Slavery Society was formed, followed in 1833 by the organization of the American Anti-Slavery Society; periodicals were published, pamphlets distributed, and lecturers sent out into the field. Black men fought alongside the whites against "the peculiar institution" of slavery, many blacks serving as full-time agents and orators; among them, Frederick Douglass (ca. 1817–95), William Wells Brown (1816–84), and a woman given at birth the name of Isabella, which she later changed to Sojourner Truth (1797–1885).

Anti-Slavery Songs. At a typical anti-slavery meeting the lecture platform was shared by speakers (one or two of them black) and singers—or, at least, a song leader. Songs were an indis-

Ex. V.2   Anti-slavery song, *The Sweets of Liberty*
(to the tune, *Is There a Heart That Never Loved*),
Braham

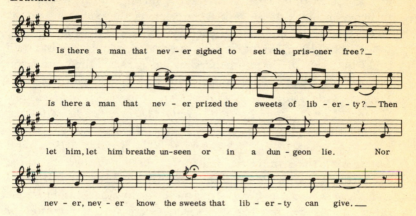

Is there a man that nev-er sighed to set the pris-oner free?_

Is there a man that nev-er prized the sweets of lib-er-ty?_Then

let him, let him breathe un-seen or in a dun-geon lie.   Nor

nev-er, nev-er know the sweets that lib-er-ty can give.__

    2. Is there a heart so cold in Man
         Can galling fetters crave?
         Is there a wretch so truly low,
         Can stoop to be a slave?
         O, let him, then, in chains be bound,
         In chains and bondage live;
         Nor never, never know the sweets
         That liberty can give.

    3. Is there a breast so chilled in life,
         Can nurse the coward's sigh?
         Is there a creature so debased,
         Would not for freedom die?
         O, let him, then, be doomed to crawl
         Where only reptiles live;
         Nor never, never know the sweets
         That liberty can give.

pensable part of the program, being used to "put fire" into the
meetings. Frequently the platform singers had composed their
own song texts; Sojourner Truth was acclaimed, for example,
both for her oratory and her original songs, which often were
deeply religious in nature. In 1849 William Wells Brown published some of the most popular anti-slavery songs in a collec-

tion, *The Anti-Slavery Harp*. In accordance with the common practice of the time, only song texts were included, but there are references to suitable tunes.

The list of tunes suggested for the singing of Brown's songs provides an index of songs in vogue among the common people, black and white, at the mid-century. Since the words of these songs were all-important, it was essential that only well-known tunes be used, so that audiences would give all their attention to the texts. Predictably, songs from the British Isles dominate the list: *Auld Lang Syne, Flow Gently Sweet Afton, Kathleen O'More, Long, Long Ago*, and *Gaily the Troubadour* (the last two by the English song writer Thomas Haines Bayly). There are three minstrel songs, *O Susannah, Old Rosin the Beau*, and *Dandy Jim;* the sentimental ballad, *Is There a Heart;* and three hymn tunes, *Lenox, My Faith Looks Up to Thee*, and *When I Can Read My Title Clear*. It is noteworthy that among these other tunes suggested for use, several were special favorites of black folk; for example, *Old Rosin the Beau, Is There a Heart*, and *When I Can Read My Title Clear*. Example V.2, an anti-slavery song, uses the tune *Is There a Heart* (see p. 127).

The white "singing family" troupe, the Hutchinson family, became so closely associated with the movement, touring with the abolitionists and contributing a number of original songs, that its members were sometimes referred to as "the minne-singers of American freedom." The Hutchinsons also toured independently, beginning in 1842, and carried anti-slavery songs (as well as popular ballads, temperance songs, and women's suffrage songs) to audiences all over America and the British Isles. The black Luca family troupe of Connecticut also sang for anti-slavery meetings, its first professional appearance taking place before an Anti-Slavery Society meeting held at the Tabernacle in New York.

The Underground Railroad. One of the earliest activities of the abolitionists was the Underground Railroad, which was not a railroad at all but a loosely knit organization existing for the sole purpose of helping fugitive slaves to escape. As early as the eighteenth century there had been people who came to the assistance of fugitive slaves, especially among the Quakers. At the beginning of the nineteenth century various persons began to develop ways of giving systematic aid to fugitives, and so secret pathways of "underground roads" were planned, with "stations," "conductors," and sometimes even travel vehicles. Most of the traveling was done at night, the fugitives moving on foot, guided by the North Star or following along well-known water routes. During the day, they hid out at the "stations," where they received food, rest, and directions for continuing the journey.

All "lines" led North, from southern plantations to "stations" in Ohio, Pennsylvania, New Jersey, New York, and eventually to Canada—especially after the passage of the Fugitive Slave Law in 1850. The slaves often had to disguise themselves, mulattos posing as white persons, women posing as men and vice versa. Elaborate codes were worked out, so that messages could be sent from station to station, via the "grapevine telegraph," when fugitives were on the way. The story of the Underground Railroad is fascinating, full of hair-raising, breathtaking adventures that cannot be recounted here. Some of the scenes in Harriet Beecher Stowe's novel, *Uncle Tom's Cabin* (1852), vividly recreate aspects of the journey along the Railroad.

Songs played a significant role in the activities of the Underground Railroad. An essential part of the operation was the preliminary planning; prospective travelers had to be informed first of the possibility of escaping, then given specific instructions for departure. Frederick Douglass, whose first plans for escape in 1835 failed, later wrote about the songs he and his fellow slaves sang during the period they were plotting the escape:

> We were, at times, remarkably bouyant, singing hymns and making joyous exclamations, almost as triumphant in their tone as if we had reached a land of freedom and safety. A keen observer might had detected in our repeated singing of
>
> > "O Canaan, sweet Canaan,
> > I am bound for the land of Canaan,"
>
> something more than a hope of reaching heaven. We meant to reach the *north*—and the north was our Canaan.

Douglass wrote also about another song that inspired him to escape from slavery:

"I thought I heard them say,
There were lions in the way,
I don't expect to stay
   Much longer here.
Run to Jesus—shun the danger—
I don't expect to stay
   Much longer here."

was a favorite air, and had a double meaning. In the lips of some, it meant the expectation of a speedy summons to a world of spirits; but in the lips of *our* company, it simply meant, a speedy pilgrimage toward a free state, and deliverance from all the evils and dangers of slavery.

The purpose of some songs was to alert the slaves that a "conductor" was on the way. Many conductors made trip after trip into the South to personally lead caravans of slaves off the plantations, the white operators posing as slaveholders, slave traders, peddlers, or anyone else they thought could gain the confidence of slaveowners. One of the leading conductors of the organization was the ex-slave Harriet Tubman (1820?–1913), called the "black Moses of her race." After escaping from slavery herself, she made innumerable trips back into the South to help others to escape. It is said that she always used a special song to disclose her presence to the slaves:

Dark and thorny is de pathway
Where de pilgrim makes his ways;
But beyond dis vale of sorrow
Lie de fields of endless days.

When the slaves heard this song, whether or not they could see the singer, they knew that their "Moses" had come after them, and they would begin to make preparations for leaving.

Those who were left behind would have been consoled by such songs as *Bound to Go* or *Members, Don't Get Weary*. Many of the old songs that the slaves had been singing for years must have been sung with special meaning when an escape plot was in the air. Such songs as *Steal Away to Jesus; Swing Low, Sweet Chariot; Brother Moses Gone to de Promised Land; I Hear from Heaven To-Day; Good News, de Chariot's Coming; Oh, Sinner, You'd Better Get Ready;* and numbers of others with similar texts undoubtedly served as "alerting" songs. Then there were songs that served as "maps," the best known of which was *Follow the Drinkin' Gourd*, which directed the fugitives to always travel in the direction of the Big Dipper.

Ex. V.3 *Follow the Drinkin' Gourd*, Traditional

It is possible that when an escape plot was in the air, traditional songs were provided with parody verses specifically stating meeting places and departure times. No such versions survive, however. Most of the records of Underground Railroad activities were systematically and carefully destroyed, and understandably so, for the penalties of discovery were too great to risk taking chances.

THE NEGRO CHURCH AND MUSIC

Several black church historians of the nineteenth century published accounts of the organization and growth of their churches, but most of these tells us little about musical practices. The A. M. E. bishop, Daniel Alexander Payne (1811–93), however, provides a wealth of information in his book *Recollections of Seventy Years* (1888) about both religious and secular musical practices encountered in his travels about the country. It is fair to assume that what Payne wrote about the A. M. E. practices applies as well to other independent black denominations of the time. Born of free parents in Charleston, South Carolina, Payne received his early education in that city, but left at the age of twenty-three to live in the North. There he studied for the ministry at a Lutheran seminary in Pennsylvania, and after completing his studies, served as a pastor to a Presbyterian church in East Troy, New York. In 1841, however, he joined the A. M. E. Church and devoted the remainder of his life to service in that church—at various times he was a minister, historian, bishop, and college president (of the A. M. E. Wilberforce University, founded 1856). At the time he wrote his memoirs, Payne was very proud of the state of music in A. M. E. churches. He observed:

> In a musical direction what progress has been made within the last forty years! There is not a Church of ours in any of the great cities of the republic that can afford to buy an instrument which is without one; and there are but few towns or villages where our Connection exists that are without an instrument to accompany the choir.

To be sure, many bitter controversies had to be resolved before musical standards in the A. M. E. churches reached the high level boasted of by Payne in the 1870s. It will be recalled that at the first "Mother Bethel" Church in Philadelphia the elder lined-out the psalms and hymns for the congregation, just as the deacons of white Protestant sects had been compelled to do for their congregations in the eighteenth century. And just as the common people in the eighteenth century had rebelled against the introduction of new kinds of musical practices (see Chapter II), so in the nineteenth century black Methodist old-timers fought similar battles in their independent churches. The first conflict arose when forward-looking forces in the church attempted to bring in trained choirs to join the congregation in the singing during worship services. What an uproar! Payne remembered:

The first introduction of choral singing into the A. M. E. Church took place in Bethel, Philadelphia, Pa., between 1841 and 1842. It gave great offense to the older members, especially those who had professed personal sanctification. Said they: "You have brought the devil into the Church, and therefore we will go out." So, suiting the action to the word, many went out of Bethel, and never returned.

The split in Bethel's congregation failed, however, to solve the dispute. Although Payne had only recently become associated with the A. M. E. Church, he was drawn into the fray:

So great was the excitement and irritation produced by the introduction of the choir into Bethel Church that I, then a local preacher and school-master, was requested by the leader of the choir and other prominent members in it to preach a special sermon on sacred music. This I did as best I could. In my researches I used a small monograph on music written by Mr. Wesley [founder of the white English Methodist Church], but drew my information chiefly from the word of God. The immediate effect of that discourse was to check the excitement, soothe the irritation, and set the most intelligent to reading as they had never done before.

Payne observed that similar "excitements" and "irritations" occurred when choirs were introduced into other churches of the sect, "not only in the cities but also in the large towns and villages." Conservative members withdrew from churches in many places, with the result that large congregations were supplanted by smaller ones. In Chicago the minister, the Reverend Elisha Weaver, actually was impeached by his congregation in 1857 for introducing vocal and instrumental music into the church. From the vantage point of the present time, the parallels are obvious between the development of white Protestant musical traditions in the colonial period and the growth of similar traditions in the independent black churches of the nineteenth century.

The first use of musical instruments in the church also caused conflict among black Methodists, although not to the same extent as the introduction of choral singing. The earliest performance of instrumental music in an A. M. E. church took place in Baltimore in 1848, the occasion being a concert of sacred music presented under the direction of James Fleet of Washington, D. C. In a second concert of sacred music given in the same year, William Appo directed a seven-piece string ensemble. It was not long before black congregations everywhere began to develop great pride in their choirs, their organs, and the concerts presented in their churches.

Ring Shouts and Bush Meetings.   It was inevitable that Payne should come into contact with some practices that he did not condone. He disapproved, for example, of the singing of "spiritual songs" in the worship services, dismissing such songs as mere "cornfield ditties." He also protested against the custom prevailing in some churches whereby members of the congregation remained after the sermon to participate in "praying and singing bands." Payne thought the church members were acting "in a most ridiculous and heathenish way" when they formed a circle, then sang songs, clapped their hands, and stomped their feet as they moved slowly around in the circle. At camp meetings and bush meetings (meetings held in wooded areas without the use of tents), the "bands" were even more common. When Payne remonstrated with one of the leaders about such practices, the man answered:

> The Spirit of God works upon people in different ways. At camp-meeting there must be a ring here, a ring there, a ring over yonder, or sinners will not get converted.

This traditional ritual dance was one of the most persistent of the African customs that survived in the New World. Despite the efforts of ministers such as Payne to "modify these extravagances in worship," the masses regarded the rituals as the "essence of religion" and refused to desist from their practices.

URBAN MUSIC IN THE SOUTH:
NEW ORLEANS

In the early nineteenth century, New Orleans was undoubtedly the most musical city in the land. Sometimes as many as three opera companies were playing at the same time; there were plays and concerts and balls and street parades and, most stirring of all, the yearly celebrations of Carnival or Mardi gras. Thomas Ashe, a traveler to the city in 1806, stated that among the French residents "the concert, dance promenade and *petit souper* [were] conducted with as much attention as at Paris or Rome."

New Orleans was certainly the most exotic city in the land. In 1803, the year of the Louisiana Purchase, its Spanish, French, African, English, Irish, and German traditions were fusing into something that was new and different, into a truly American culture. Its Negro population, the largest of any American city, constituted more than one-third of the city's total, numbering over 12,000 persons. Peculiar to the city's social structure was a rigid caste system, which distinguished between whites, blacks (who were mostly slaves), and so-called "creoles of color" (who were generally free mulattos, quadroons, or octoroons). To a greater extent than in any other city, the caste class distinctions were reflected in the social and cultural activities of the citizens, particularly those of the Negroes.

Dancing in the Place Congo.   One of the most exotic sights of old New Orleans was the slave dancing that took place in the Place Congo (now Beauregard Square). The slaves' custom of assembling on Sundays and church holy days to dance in public squares must have begun before 1786, for in that year a local ordinance was passed forbidding such dancing until after the close of religious services. In 1799 a traveler saw "vast numbers of slaves" assembled together on the levee and "dancing in large rings." The most detailed contemporary description of dancing in the Place Congo is found in the journal of Benjamin Henry B. Latrobe, the famous architect, who spent some time in New Orleans during the years 1818–20. "Accidentally stumbling upon an assembly of Negroes" who met on Sunday afternoons to dance in the Place, Latrobe counted five or six hundred dancers gathered there, all of them "formed into circular groups." From the narrative of William Wells Brown, *My Southern Home*, we learn that "not less than two or three thousand people would congregate to see the dusky dancers," who represented six different African tribes: "Kraels, Minahs, Congos and Mandringas, Gangas, Hiboas, and Fulas."

At about three o'clock in the afternoon the dancers would

begin to gather, each tribe assembling in a different part of the square. There were no trees or grass, for over the years the ground had been worn hard by the feet of the dancers. Each group had its own orchestra, consisting generally of drums in several sizes (made of "gum stumps" that had been "dug out" and covered with sheepskin heads), banjos (made of Louisiana gourds), and rattles (made from the jawbones of horses). The dancing would build up in excitement, becoming wilder and more frenzied as the afternoon wore on, until men and women would fall fainting to the ground. Their places were quickly taken, however, by other couples. By nine o'clock the dancing would have come to an end, the spectators gone home, and the square deserted.

Latrobe "crowded near enough" to observe the performance of several groups at close range and later wrote in his diary about the instruments and the dance steps:

> The music consisted of two drums and a stringed instrument . . . , [one of which was] a cylindrical drum, about a foot in diameter. . . . The other drum was an open-staved thing held between the knees. . . . They made an incredible noise. The most curious instrument, however, was a stringed instrument, which no doubt was imported from Africa. On the top of the finger board was the rude figure of a man in a sitting posture, and two pegs behind him to which the strings were fastened. The body was a calabash. It was played upon by a very little old man, apparently eighty or ninety years old.

The instruments used in another dancing ring were of a different construction:

> One which from the color of the wood seemed new, consisted of a block cut into something of the form of a cricket bat, with a long and deep mortise down the center. This thing made a considerable noise, being beaten lustily on the side by a short stick. In the same orchestra was a square drum, looking like a stool, which made an abominable, loud noise; also a calabash with a round hole in it, the hole studded with brass nails, which was beaten by a woman with two short sticks.

The largest of the rings formed by the dancers was not over ten feet in diameter. In some instances the ring of dancers

"walked, by way of dancing, round the music in the center."
Here the walking movements must have involved the kind of
shuffle step characteristic of West African dancing. In one instance two dancers, both women, were in the center of the ring.
"They held each a coarse handkerchief extended by the corners
in their hands and set to each other in a miserably dull & slow
figure, hardly moving their feet or bodies." Again, here is a
reference to the shuffle step. As noted above, the dances began
slowly, but gradually quickened, building up into wild, frenzied
movements. The vocal music accompanying the dances obviously comprised chants rather than genuine songs, and these
were repeated over and over again for as long as five or six
hours. As much as fatigue, it was the combination of the in-
cessant chanting and the exciting music that sent the dancers into
a state of ecstacy and eventually caused them "to fall fainting
to the ground."

Latrobe noticed that the singing resembled in some ways
what he had heard in cities on the eastern seaboard:

> The women squalled out a burden to the playing, at intervals, con-
> sisting of two notes, as the negroes working in our cities respond
> to the song of their leader.

For another group of dancers, "a man sung an uncouth song . . .
which I suppose was in some African language, for it was not
French, and the women screamed a detestable burden on one
single note." Latrobe, whose standards were derived from white
concert music, found the dancing too dull for his taste and the
singing monotonous and too loud.

Obviously, the entire performance of the Place Congo dance
was in the same African tradition as the Pinkster dances in New
York and the jubilees in Philadelphia. The instruments and the
performance practices were like those described by witnesses
of the eighteenth-century slave festivals in the North and, moreover, like those reported by travelers to Africa during the
eighteenth and nineteenth centuries. The jubilees of Philadelphia
came to a halt with the beginning of the Revolutionary War;
the Pinkster celebrations in Albany were halted by city authorities in 1811, and had been in decline for several years previously

in other sections of the state; the Place Congo dances of New Orleans were terminated by city officials in 1843. Thus it would appear that this special tradition of African dancing died out in the United States under the pressures of an indifferent and unconcerned society. The tradition was too strong among the slaves, however, to be completely suppressed. The circle dance, the shuffle steps, the monotonous chants all reappeared in only slightly disguised form in the "ring shout" of black Protestant groups.

European-Style Bands and Orchestras. Not all slave dancing in New Orleans was in the African tradition; jigs, fandangos, and Virginia breakdowns were also danced on the Place to the accompaniment of fifes and fiddles. In the taverns where slaves gathered for diversion, they danced to the music of fiddles, flutes, clarinets, triangles, tambourines, and drums. Negro orchestras played for much of the dancing that took place in New Orleans, whether the dances were for whites, slaves, or colored creoles. To have a white dance-orchestra play for an affair was a novelty. In 1834, for example, the promoter of a great ball made a special appeal to the snobbish by promising the performance of a "new band, fresh from Europe"—obviously a white group.

At a large affair the dance orchestra might be composed of from five to eight players; typically, "a clarionet, three fiddles, two tambourines, and a bass drum." It was the job of one of the players to call out the dance figures. Latrobe's comment about the caller he heard at a *Grand Bal* during Carnival time (that is, Mardi gras) in 1819 is colored by his bias, but is nevertheless worth quoting because of the first-hand details it provides:

> . . . a tall, ill-dressed black, in the music gallery who played the tambourine standing up, and in a forced and vile voice called the [dance] figures as they changed.

The slave orchestras that played for parties held in town mansions or on the plantations near New Orleans were generally small ensembles, sometimes simply fiddle, flute, and fife, or perhaps two fiddles, flute, triangle, and tambourine. It was not uncommon to find dance music being provided by a single fiddler. Dance fiddlers were in great demand, and a good one, such as Massa Quamba, could charge as much as three dollars per night for his services.

At white balls, sections were often set aside for blacks, where they could listen to the music but could not dance. The so-called "Quadroon Balls" were, like the Place Congo dances, an exotic New Orleans tradition. The special attractions of these balls were the beautiful, colored creole girls—the quadroons and octoroons—and only white males were admitted as guests. Ironically, the music for these balls was provided by orchestras composed of male "creoles of color."

New Orleans had a great fondness for brass bands, shared by the black and white populations alike. Any event was used as a pretext for a parade, and the same musicians who played in the dance orchestras at night could be found parading the streets during the day. A newspaper item in the *New Orleans Picayune* (1838) called it "a real mania for horn and trumpet playing." Negroes had their own brass bands, the members recruited from among free blacks or colored creoles, who took their musical activities very seriously. They studied music with the players associated with the French Opera House and the city orchestras; some of them went to Paris to complete their studies. As a result, the Negro bands and orchestras of New Orleans maintained high levels of musicianship. It was not always necessary for a talented Negro to obtain his own musical instruction; the demand for bandsmen was so great that often a patron could be found who was willing to advance a Negro's music education. In 1820, for example, the New Orleans Independent Rifle Company advertised for "two young men of color," offering not only to teach them to play but also to provide them with keyed bugles, uniforms, and a monthly salary.

Vocal Music and Entertainers.   Although the Negroes of New Orleans concentrated their attention on instrumental music, vocal music was hardly neglected. At the opera houses, sections were reserved for free Negroes and for slaves. Visitors to the city were surprised to note that even the slaves hummed operatic arias as they walked through the streets. In the cathedrals, visitors noted that the blacks added both warmth and volume to the singing during Mass. Women made up the larger part of the congregations. In 1842 the first convent for colored women in the United States was established—the Convent of the Holy Family.

Some of the most moving ceremonies of the year occurred in the convent during Passion Week—on Good Friday, Holy Saturday, and Easter Sunday. An early established tradition was the singing of a French chant by the nuns in the "Way of the Cross" procession on Good Friday:

Vive Jésus, vive sa croix,	Long live Jesus, long live his cross,
O, qu'il est bien juste qu'on l'aime,	Oh, how fitting it is that we love him,
Puisqu'en expirant sur ce bois,	For, in dying on that cross,
Il nous aima plus que lui-même.	He loved us more than himself.
Dissons donc, tous à haute voix,	Let us, then, all say loudly,
Vive Jésus, vive sa croix.	Long live Jesus, long live his cross.

[Translation by E. Epel]

A white visitor to the services, Julie Bishop, wrote in a magazine article about the singing on Easter:

Kyrie eleison, they sing *Kyrie, Kyrie, Kyrie eleison.* All the singers are women and they have brought to the song service the rich quality of the Negro voice, musical in its wildest state, and now trained to the most perfect melody. But the voices have also brought with them that pathetic touch which lingers around the gayest notes and which training has never been able to remove and even the Gloria in Excelsis which presently arises thrills to the heart with its grand and lofty melancholy.

It was in New Orleans in 1837 that a Negro singer appeared on the stage of a white theater, the St. Charles, for the first time in the United States. The entertainer, popularly called Signor Cornmeali, "was warmly received by the public" and acclaimed by the press for his "novel manner" of singing and the wide compass of his voice. Originally a street vendor of corn meal, the Signor always featured first his own song, *Fresh Corn Meal,* then followed with such popular songs as *My Long Tail Blue, Such a Gettin' Up Stairs,* and *Old Rosin the Beau.* It was said that this vendor was known and loved by all New Orleans, and upon his death the entire city mourned.

Another famous entertainer of New Orleans was Picayune Butler, the banjo virtuoso. He began his musical career during the 1820s. By 1857 he was so skilled that he was able to participate in a national banjo competition held at New York City and would have won, according to eyewitnesses, had he not been indisposed. Even though he broke two of his banjo strings, he plucked through the required waltz, reel, schottische, polka, and jig with obvious skill. Butler was reputed to have given many a white minstrel his original songs for use on the stage. A peripatetic entertainer, Butler was known all along "the river" from Cincinnati to New Orleans. Someone—probably a minstrel—wrote a special song in his honor, *Picayune Butler's Come to Town*, which was printed in a collection of 1858.

A Symphony Orchestra, Composers, and Music Teachers. During the 1830s the Negroes of New Orleans organized a Negro Philharmonic Society that was composed of more than one hundred members. In addition to presenting concerts, the society arranged for performances by visiting artists. Some of the players also provided music at the *Théâtre de la Renaissance*, a theater for "the free colored," under the direction of Constantin Debarque, a black violinist, music teacher, and sometime-conductor. Richard Lambert, a noted music teacher, and Debarque were among the permanent directors of the symphony orchestra. Often professional white musicians of the city played with the orchestra when works calling for special instrumentation were performed.

Richard Lambert was the patriarch of a family that produced four professional male musicians and two talented females. The eldest son, Lucien, won a reputation as a young man for his fine pianistic abilities. Later he went to Paris, where he continued his musical education and studied composition. Discouraged by the color bar which stopped him at every turn in New Orleans, he finally settled in Brazil and became associated with a company that manufactured pianos. Among his best-known compositions were *La Juive*, *Le Départ du Conscrit*, *Le Niabara*, *Cloches et Clochettes*, *Etude Mazurka*, and *Au Clair de la Lune*, with variations. A second son, Sidney, also achieved recognition as a pianist and a composer. In addition to his compositions, he wrote a piano manual that won him a merit award from the king of

Portugal. He settled in Paris, earning his living as a music teacher. Two younger sons developed skills as instrumentalists and played in brass bands of the city. One of the Lamberts became the leader of the St. Bernard Brass Band.

There were yet other natives of New Orleans who won wide recognition for their talents. Edmund Dédé (1829–1903) studied clarinet as a child with Debarque and later took up study of the violin with Gabici, one-time white director of the St. Charles Theatre Orchestra. Dédé developed into a good violinist and composer, author of works such as *Le Sement de l'Arabe*, *Vaillant Belle Rose Quadrille*, and *Le Palmier Overture*. In 1857 he went to Paris for further study, and finally settled in Bordeaux, France, where he became director of the orchestra of L'Alcazar. Samuel Snaer (1833–?) was highly regarded in the city as a pianist, music teacher, and composer of ballads, instrumental works, dance suites, and a Mass. One of the most popular music teachers in New Orleans was Thomas Martin, who taught piano, guitar, and violin. Martin was a great favorite in white aristocratic society circles.

In the music of Negroes in New Orleans, two equally strong traditions developed side by side during the nineteenth century. On the one hand was the music of the cultured, highly trained free blacks and "colored creoles," who for generations provided dance and parade music for all levels of New Orleans society and who performed European art music with skill. In complete contrast was the emotional, strongly rhythmical African music of the Place Congo slaves who, after the suppression of the Place dances, were driven underground with their music into taverns, cabarets, and low-life rendezvous spots. After the Civil War the two traditions were to merge, producing a new music that first would astonish the whole world with its new sounds and its profound relevance to modern life, and then go on to conquer the realm of popular music and penetrate so deeply into that of art music as to drastically change its course.

OTHER SOUTHERN CITIES

For most black folk in the South outside New Orleans, the pleasures of city life were limited, centering around their homes, the churches, the shops and taverns, and the occasional public dances given by various societies or institutions in the larger cities. In some places, slaves were allowed to find their own housing as well as their employment, a circumstance that frequently resulted in the formation of ghetto areas inhabited chiefly by blacks. As a consequence, however, slaves gained the opportunity to mingle with other slaves, with free Negroes, and with working-class whites. In their efforts to achieve economic security, free blacks often managed to overcome almost insurmountable obstacles, including discriminatory legislation and the hostility of white laborers. City slaves saw about them the possibility for a better life, and many of them took advantage of it. They learned to read and write, despite the laws everywhere that prohibited the instruction of slaves; they developed skills that enabled them to compete for jobs; and they saved money to purchase their freedom. They discovered, as did the ex-slave Frederick Douglass, that "a city slave is almost a freeman, compared with a slave on the plantation."

Recreational Activities. While the occasional balls that took place in cities such as Baltimore, Charleston, Louisville, and, of course, New Orleans provided only brief respite for the slaves from the frustrations of daily life, it seems that some were quite elaborate affairs. For example, when the Falls City Hotel in Louisville gave a New Year's Eve Ball in 1856 for the slaves it owned or hired, the affair was described with extravagant phrases in the local newspaper. Readers were assured that the hotel owners "exerted themselves to render their colored guests comfortable and their entertainment agreeable." Black musicians, of course, provided the music for dancing.

More typically, however, black musicians played in taverns and on the streets for their fellow slaves and freedmen. A visitor to Richmond in 1799, Thomas Fairfax, remarked about one of these street troubadours:

After going to bed I was entertained with an agreeable serenade by a black man, who had taken his stand near the Tavern, and for the amusement of those of his Colour, sung and played on the Banjoe. . . . This African instrument is certainly capable of Conveying much to the musical ear. Its wild notes of melody seem to correspond to the State of Civilization of the Country where this Species of music originated.[7]

Richmond had its own Negro band, the Richmond Blues, which was composed of free men.

Black Fiddlers and White Dancers.   As before the revolution, music for the dances of white society in the nineteenth century was generally provided by slaves. More frequently than in earlier times, the dance orchestras consisted of two or three musicians and were occasionally interracial. The traveler Thomas Ashe noticed in 1806, for instance, that the orchestra for a ball held in Wheeling, West Virginia, was composed of two black banjo players and a white lutenist. In Richmond, the black fiddler-slave Sy Gilliat of colonial fame was still active in the 1800s. The leading figure at the city's balls, he appeared at dances wearing the same kind of court dress as he had worn for years, complete with brown wig, and his manners remained as courtly as ever. The most exciting event in Richmond of those days was the annual Race Ball, which took place at the end of a week of horse racing. It customarily opened with a dignified *minuet de la cour*, but after this bow to convention the dancers "commenced the reel, like a storm after a calm." The music of "Sy Gilliat's fiddle and the flute or clarionet of his blacker comrade, London Briggs" was quite "fast and furious," and the dancers cut "all sorts of capers" to it, dancing not only reels, but contradances, congos, hornpipes, and jigs. After Gilliat's death, his place as a leading dance musician was taken by the violinist George Walker. A newspaper advertisement acclaimed Walker as "the best leader of a band in all eastern and middle Virginia":

FOR HIRE: either for the remainder of the year or by the month, week or job, the celebrated musician and fiddler, George Walker. All persons desiring the services of George Walker are notified that they must contract for them with us, and in no case pay to him or any other person the amount of his hire without a written order from us. George Walker is admitted by common consent, to be the best leader of a band in all eastern and middle Virginia.

[*Richmond Daily Enquirer*, June 27, 1853]

[7] Julian Mates, *The American Musical Stage Before 1800* (New Brunswick, New Jersey, 1962), p. 80.

Music and the Church.   For the first decades of the nineteenth century, the Negro churches provided not only religious guidance but also the greatest opportunities for fellowship and education among black folk. After 1820, however, the enactment in most southern states of stringent laws designed to control the movement of blacks more closely sharply curtailed religious and other group activities. Southerners had been greatly upset by the Gabriel Prosser conspiracy in 1800 at Richmond, Virginia, and the Denmark Vesey revolt in 1822 at Charleston, South Carolina. When the next decade brought about an even larger and more destructive insurrection, the Nat Turner revolt of 1831 in Virginia, the South was thrown into a panic. Black Codes were strengthened everywhere, and an unprecedented period of harassment began for blacks.

Since some whites believed Negro Methodists to have had a hand in the Vesey plot, the brunt of the attack on black institutions fell upon the A. M. E. Church, which found continuation of its work impossible; many of its preachers moved North. Bishop Daniel Payne, for example, had been teaching at a school for free blacks in Charleston, but was forced to leave that city in 1834. Particularly affected by the move was Charleston, a stronghold of independent black Methodism. Black preachers of other denominations were either discouraged from preaching or forbidden outright. The formal religious life of the southern blacks in cities came under the control of whites, who generally handled it indifferently. Sometimes Negroes were allowed to sit in segregated pews or on the floors of white churches; sometimes special services were held for them, before or after the regular services for whites. Most often, Negroes did not go to church at all.

These practices continued until after the Civil War. In many southern urban areas the blacks took refuge in secret meetings. While there is no direct evidence as to the effect of all of this on the religious music of the Negro in the South, there can be little doubt that in their secret religious meetings the blacks turned away from Protestant psalms and hymns, in favor of music more responsive to their special needs—that is, to songs of their own creation. More than one preacher, black and white, felt it necessary to reprove the blacks for their "outlandish" religious practices.

Music Instruction in Sabbath Schools. Because of the laws that prohibited the teaching of blacks, Sabbath schools provided one of the few opportunities for blacks of all ages to meet together in educational pursuits. In some urban churches Negroes were taught hymns and psalms; in exceptional instances they actually studied psalmody. There was, to be sure, great danger in all of this; a Charleston law of 1800, for example, gave the police authority to "break down gates or windows" in dispersing groups gathered together "for the purpose of mental instruction of the blacks." Nevertheless, such instruction continued, even after Negro church activities were curtailed by the authorities. Frederick Douglass, like other Negro leaders, held Sabbath school classes in the home of a free black man in Baltimore, Maryland, with the express purpose of teaching his forty scholars of all ages to read.

The white minister, Charles Colcock Jones of Savannah, Georgia, had very strong convictions about the importance of music in religious instruction for blacks and devoted several passages to the subject in his book *The Religious Instruction of the Negroes in the United States* (1842). He stated that not only should scholars be taught psalms and hymns, but they should be taught "how to sing them." Jones recommended highly some of the hymns of Dr. Watts; for example, *There Is a God Who Reigns Above, I'm Not Ashamed to Own My Lord*, and *When I Can Read My Title Clear*. Included among the hymns written by other writers he recommended was the popular *Blow Ye the Trumpet, Blow*.

Significantly, Jones wanted the blacks to learn psalms and hymns so that they would desist from singing songs of their own creation:

> One great advantage in teaching them good psalms and hymns, is that they are thereby induced to lay aside the extravagant and nonsensical chants, and catches and hallelujah songs of their own composing; and when they sing, which is very often while about their business or of an evening in their houses, they will have something profitable to sing.

Jones's attitude corresponded with that of most white preachers and missionaries during the nineteenth century—and of some black preachers too. Negroes were reproved for their love of music and dancing, to the degree that when they joined the church they gave up dancing and "fiddle-sings," singing only psalms and hymns. When the Swedish traveler Fredrika Bremer asked some slaves in South Carolina to sing their own folksongs for her, she was informed that they " 'dwelt with the Lord,' and sang only hymns."

Many a traveler and local historian commented upon the psalm and hymn singing of city slaves in the South. In Richmond, for example, the singing of the slaves who worked in the tobacco factories was a special attraction of the city. Samuel Mordecai, a local historian, observed:

> Many of the negroes, male and female, employed in the factories, have acquired such skill in psalmody and have generally such fine voices, that it is a pleasure to listen to the sacred music with which they beguile the hours of labour. Besides the naturally fine voice and ear for music which seems to have been given to the black race . . . many of the slaves in Richmond have acquired some knowledge of music by note, and may be seen, even in the factories, with their books of psalmody open on the work-bench.

BLACK WATERMEN

As a group, the most musical black folk of the ante-bellum period may well have been the men working on the waters and waterfronts of the United States—on the eastern seaboard, the Gulf Coast, the Mississippi River and its two big tributaries, the Missouri and the Ohio. Negroes were employed as stevedores on the wharfs and on the levees; they worked as firemen and laborers and in food services on the boats that plied back and forth between waterfront cities. In many instances they also served as entertainers, providing shows of the vaudeville type for the boat passengers at the end of the day's labor and music for dancing afterward. Stevedores always sang as they worked. A black writer, Martin Delany, commented upon their songs in *Blake: or the Huts of America* (1859):

> In the distance, on the levee and in the harbor among the steamers, the songs of the boatmen were incessant. Every few hours land-ing, loading and unloading, the glee of these men of sorrow was touchingly appropriate and impressive. . . . If there is any class of men anywhere to be found whose sentiments of song and words

of lament are made to reach the sympathies of others, the black slave-boatmen are that class . . . they are seemingly contented by soothing their sorrows with songs apparently cheerful, but in reality wailing lamentations.[8]

Black watermen carried their special worksongs, along with other kinds of Negro folksongs, up and down the rivers—from Wheeling, West Virginia, and Cincinnati on the Ohio River, from Omaha, Nebraska, Kansas City and St. Louis on the Missouri River, to the towns on the Mississippi itself, Cairo, Illinois, Memphis, Tennessee, and finally, to New Orleans. The same songs or similar ones could be heard on the Gulf Coast in Mobile, Alabama, and on the Atlantic coast in Savannah, Georgia; Charleston, South Carolina; Norfolk, Virginia; and in northern ports. The watermen were truly itinerant musicians, and may have been responsible, more than any other single force, for the spread of Negro folksongs from one community to another, white as well as black.

On shore the stevedores and boatmen found amusement and comradeship in waterfront shacks, dives, and "dance halls" where the music was similar to that heard in the "Five Points" cafés of New York City. Although few chroniclers seem to have ventured into these waterfront hangouts until after the Civil War, the curious who began to explore such spots in the 1870s and 1880s found well-established traditions of "hot music."

Nineteenth-century literature is replete with anecdotes about the singing of black boatmen. Beginning in the 1770s song collectors began to record the songs, just as other song collectors were writing down the spirituals. Accounts written before the war, however, typically include only descriptions of performance practices and song texts. Fredrika Bremer was particularly impressed, for example, by the singing of black firemen on board the Mississippi River steamer *Belle Key*. As the firemen flung wood into the engine fires:

> . . . the Negro up aloft on the pile of fire-wood began immediately an improvised song in stanzas, and at the close of each [stanza] the Negroes down below joined in vigorous chorus. . . . They, amid their . . . fantastic song, keeping time most exquisitely, hurled one piece of fire-wood after another into the yawning fiery gulf.

[8] Quoted in Maude Cuney-Hare, *Negro Musicians and Their Music* (Washington, D. C., 1936), p. 88.

CHAPTER VI

The Ante-Bellum Period: Rural Life

At the beginning of the nineteenth century the vast majority of slaves in the United States lived on plantations in the South. The slave population had increased rapidly since the time of the first United States census enumeration in 1790 from somewhat fewer than 700,000 to almost four million in 1860. Although slaves were generally concentrated in the lower southern states on plantations where such crops as cotton and rice were produced on a large scale, they were not equally distributed among the white population in these states. Only about one quarter of the whites in the South were slaveholders. Of this group fewer than 15 per cent owned plantations with more than twenty slaves. In essence, the majority of slaves belonged to small planters and lived on plantations where their numbers ranged from two or three to about fifteen.

CONTEMPORARY SOURCES OF INFORMATION

A number of contemporary accounts of plantation life are extant, some written by the slaves themselves, some by sympathetic whites, and some by slaveholders. Obviously the point of view taken in any of the accounts depended upon whether the writer was white or black, and if he were white, whether he was pro-slavery or anti-slavery. About the basic features of plantation life, however, there is surprisingly little disagreement among sources, despite variations in the routine of daily existence that occurred from one plantation to another, from one state to another, and from one region of the South to another.

Among those sources that reveal most about the musical practices of the slaves are the journals of Frances Anne Kemble, an English actress, and Fredrika Bremer, the Swedish novelist. Kemble published her diary as *Journal of a Residence on a Georgian Plantation in 1838–1839.* Bremer traveled in the United States in 1849 and after returning home wrote a two-volume work, *Homes of the New World,* based on the notes she had taken. The narrative of Lewis Paine, *Six Years in a Georgia Prison* (1851), is perhaps unique for its time. Neither a slaveholder nor an ardent abolitionist, Paine was nevertheless sympathetic to the tragic plight of the slaves and was imprisoned for aiding a slave to escape. His observations throw much light on slave life and customs. The introductory material in the 1867 collection, *Slave Songs of the United States* (compiled by Allen, Ware, and Garrison), is also useful as a source of information about plantation life.

The accounts of ex-slaves are especially valuable because they reveal "inside information" about the musical activities of the slaves. The narratives of Solomon Northup, William Wells Brown, and Frederick Douglass are as pertinent to plantation life as to urban life. So too is the autobiography of Isaac Williams, *Sunshine and Shadow of Slave Life* (1885), and the material contained in the Slave Narrative Collection of the Library of Congress, which preserves the comments of ex-slaves.

Of the books written by slaveholders the most useful musical descriptions are found in James Hungerford's *The Old Plantation and What I Gathered There in an Autumn Month* [*of 1832*] (published in 1859), James Avirett's *The Old Plantation . . . 1817–1869* (published in 1901), and R. Q. Mallard's *Plantation Life Before Emancipation* (1892). The many other journals, narratives, magazine articles, and fictional works that were published during the ante-bellum period generally support the evidence furnished by the basic sources, and in a few instances provide additional information about a particular aspect of slave music.

DAILY LIFE ON THE PLANTATION

On large plantations there were two classes of slaves—the house slaves and the field hands. For the former, life was similar in many ways to that of typical household servants at any time or place; their tasks revolved around the activities of the slave-holding family, and their daily periods of relaxation occurred at times when the cleaning, cooking, and laundering were completed. As we have observed, however, most plantations were small and maintained few slaves. On these plantations, work in the fields took precedence over any other tasks, and the house-work was assigned chiefly to older women and children. And since on the large plantations most of the slaves were field hands, it was a fact of rural life in ante-bellum days that the vast majority of slaves followed the rigorous routines of field hands rather than the relatively relaxed schedules of house servants. For most slaves, whether working on cotton, rice, sugar cane, or tobacco plantations, life was as an anonymous white writer described it in his article entitled "Manner of Living of the Inhabitants of Virginia" (1787):

> The Negro is called up about daybreak, and is seldom allowed time enough to swallow three mouthfuls of homminy, or hoe-cake, but is driven out immediately to the field of hard labor . . . the noon meal . . . [consists of] homminy and salt and, if his master be a man of humanity, he has a little fat, skimmed milk, rusty bacon or salt herring to relish his homminy or hoecake. . . . They then return to severe labour . . . until dusk in the evening, when they repair to the tobacco-houses, where each has his task in stripping alloted him, which employs him some hours. . . . It is late at night before he returns to his second scanty meal.

The food allowance of slaves varied from state to state, of course, but on many plantations it was insufficient. In Georgia, for example, a typical ration consisted of a peck of meal and sometimes two or three pounds of salt pork per week; on rice plantations slaves were given a peck of rice per week; on other plantations, a peck of corn. Slaves supplemented their meager and monotonous diet by hunting and fishing whenever possible (it was unlawful in most places) and by growing vegetables in tiny plots about their cabins. Rare were the opportunities to "filch" more appetizing edibles from the "big house" (that is, the slaveowner's house), for "ole missus" kept the food stores locked, carrying the keys around on her person.

On most plantations, slaves worked in "gangs," supervised by overseers or "drivers" on the larger units and by the planters themselves on small farms. The other work system commonly used was the "task" assignment, where the individual slave had to complete a certain amount of work each day—as, for example, on rice plantations or in tobacco-curing barns. Under both systems, the lash was heavily used to get as much work as possible from the slaves, even under the most lenient of masters. The lash did not distinguish between men and women, old and young, sick and well, healthy adolescents and pregnant middle-aged mothers; it provided the answers to most of the slaveholders' problems. And if, in the process of the whipping, a slave was beaten to death—as happened over and over again —there were always other slaves to replace the dead one.

The slave system itself generally protected owners from prosecution. Even though brutal beatings were frequently administered in the presence of others—the slaves, members of the slaveholding family, and sometimes visitors—in most instances no charges were made. Who was there to press charges? The testimony of black men against whites was not accepted in courts. After freedom came, the slaves exulted in the knowledge that all these things had been wiped out and they sang:

> No more peck of corn for me,
> No more, no more;
> No more peck of corn for me,
> Many thousands gone.

> No more driver's lash for me,
> No more, no more;
> No more driver's lash for me,
> Many thousands gone.

> No more pint of salt for me,
> No more, no more;
> No more pint of salt for me,
> Many thousands gone.

No more hundred lash for me,
No more, no more;
No more hundred lash for me,
Many thousands gone.

No more mistress' call for me,
No more, no more;
No more mistress' call for me,
Many thousands gone.

No more auction block for me,
No more, no more;
No more auction block for me,
Many thousands gone.

Singing accompanied all kinds of work, whether it consisted of picking cotton, threshing rice, stripping tobacco, harvesting sugar cane, or doing the endless small jobs on the plantation, such as clearing away underbrush or repairing fences. The music served the double function of alleviating the monotony of the work and, at the same time, of spurring the workers on to fresh efforts. If work activity called for changes in movements—for example, the need for occasional sudden and united pulls—then the worksong's rhythm included sharply defined accents, such as:

Oh, this is the day to roll and go,
Hill-up boys, hilo;
Oh, this is the day to roll and go,
Hill-up boys, hilo.

The importance of the song leader in affecting the amount of work to be obtained from a gang was well recognized by plantation owners. Frequently these leaders were excused from labor so that they could devote their entire energies to leading the singing, or they were given extra rewards as incentives.

A different type of song was that of the lone worker as he went about his assignment of mending a fence or building a barn or cooking a meal. With no necessity for coordinating his work movements with others, his song took on the nature of a deeply personal utterance. Tempo, text, melody—all these things were manipulated by the worker to fit his mood of the moment.

If he were gay, his fingers flew and his worksong cheered all who might be listening; if he were melancholy, the same song might be sung so mournfully as to slow up his activity and to depress all within hearing.

The slaves often sang together as they returned from the fields to their quarters at the end of the day, particularly on plantations where the gang system was in use and all of the workers would have stopped work at the same time. The songs were carried through the gathering dusk to the ears of the white residents in the big house, conveying a message of hopelessness and despair, even though the words of the songs were unintelligible at so great a distance. Again at night, such songs could be heard coming up from the slave quarters, sung by the tired workers as they sat on their cabin doorsteps or by their cabin fires before going to bed.

On the plantation, as in the city, it was the songs of the boatmen that seemed most frequently to excite the interest of visitors (and residents too). Travel by boat was a common form of transportation in the South, and few travelers or native Americans missed the experience of sitting behind black boatmen at one time or another. Kemble noticed during her first few days on the Georgia plantation that the slave oarsmen kept "time and tune to their oars with extemporaneous chants" as they rowed down the plantation streams. She wrote:

> My daily voyages up and down the river have introduced me to a great variety of new musical performances of our boatmen. . . . When the rowing is not too hard, they accompany the stroke of their oars with the sound of their voices. . . . The chorus strikes in with the burden [i.e. the refrain], between each phrase of the melody, [which is] chanted by a single voice.

THE PATROL SYSTEM

Another fact of daily plantation life was the supervision of patrolmen—"patty-rollers" was the slave's name for them. The patrol system in the South was especially organized to enforce the Black Codes, which were enlarged and strengthened after each major slave insurrection. Composed of local whites, patrols had the authority to challenge slaves (and free black men, too, in some places) caught without passes and to break up unlawful assemblages of Negroes. Needless to say, the patrol system did not prevent the slaves from moving about without permission; it only caused them to move with greater caution. They became familiar with all the crosscuts and bypaths in the areas surrounding their plantations and learned how to use the stars as a guide at night, the time of their greatest wanderings. Thus, the intrepid among the slaves found ways to attend their religious gatherings and "frolics" in the woods or to visit friends on neighboring plantations. Of course, the very daring among the slaves escaped to freedom, especially from the upper South.

The slaves were afraid of patrolmen, nevertheless, and they sang about their transportation problems. If they could get passes, all was fine:

> Hurrah for good old massa,
> He give me the pass to go to the city;
> Hurrah for good old missus,
> She boil the pot and give me the licker [that is, the juices];
> Hurrah, I'm going to the city.

If passes were not forthcoming, then one had to watch sharply for the patrols. Two of the most widely dispersed patty-roller songs were:

> The day is done, night comes down,
> You are a long ways from home;
> Oh, run, nigger, run,
> Patty-roller get you.

> Yellow gal look and tryin' to keep you overtime;
> The bell done rung, overseer hollering loud;
> Oh, run, nigger, run,
> Patty-roller get you.

> Run, nigger, run, the patty-roller catch you,
> Run, nigger, run, for it's almost day;
> Massa was kind and Missus was true,
> But if you don't mind, the patty-roller catch you.

ACTIVITIES OF FREE TIME

All over the South, Sundays were generally given to the slaves as free days. Although there are numerous records of slaves having to work on their legal holidays, this does not seem to have been the rule. Slaves spent their Sundays in various ways—tending their vegetable plots, making merry, going to religious services, caring for their clothes—in short, going about all the activities for which they had no time during the week. It was the general custom in many places to pay slaves if they had to work on Sundays. Many a slave earned enough money thereby to purchase necessities and even small luxuries such as violins, for example. More important, industrious slaves were often able to accumulate enough money over the years to purchase their freedom, particularly in such border states as Maryland, Virginia, and Kentucky. As has been observed, Richard Allen, founder of the A. M. E. Church, obtained his freedom in this way.

On Sundays, musicians would have had time to play their violins, either for themselves or for the dancing of their fellows. Solomon Northup, for example, could not conceive of having to endure the "weariness, and fear, and suffering, and unremitting labor" of bondage without his violin. He wrote:

> It was my companion—the friend of my bosom—triumphing loudly when I was joyful, and uttering its soft, melodious consolations when I was sad. Often, at midnight, when sleep had fled affrighted from the cabin, and my soul was disturbed and troubled with the contemplation of my fate, it would sing me a song of peace. On holy Sabbath days, when an hour or two of leisure was allowed, it would accompany me to some quiet place on the bayou bank, and, lifting up its voice, discourse kindly and pleasantly indeed.

Other slaves also reported slipping away into the woods or sitting on the doorsteps of cabins and playing their violins, particularly on warm summer evenings.

No slave quarter was complete without the sounds of fiddle dance music during "free time." Some slave masters themselves purchased violins for distribution to the fiddlers among the slaves.

In an article that appeared in *De Bow's Review* (1851), "Management of Negroes upon Southern Estates," a planter set forth the ideal conditions, as he saw them, with regard to slave music:

> I have a good fiddler, and keep him well supplied with catgut, and I make it his duty to play for the Negroes every Saturday night until twelve o'clock. . . . Charley's fiddle is always accompanied with Ihurod on the triangle and Sam to "pat." . . . I also employ a good preacher, who regularly preaches to them on the Sabbath Day. . . . Father Garritt regularly calls on Brother Abraham . . . [who] gives out and sings his hymn with much unction.

Frequently the slaves purchased their own violins with the money earned from working on Sundays. The ex-slave Isaac Williams earned money to buy his violin by catching "over a hundred muskrat skins and selling them." Most of the slaves, however, had to be content with homemade instruments.

Depending upon the place and custom, various kinds of materials were used for the fiddles and banjos. Given a good pocket-knife, some pine boards, and gut from a slaughtered cow that had been carefully cut into strips, dried, and treated, a skilled craftsman could produce a fairly good fiddle. In some places, fiddles were made of gourds and the strings and bows were made of horsehair. A banjo might be made from half of a fruit with a very hard rind, such as a calabash or gourd, by stretching a thin skin or piece of bladder over the opening, adding two or three strings made from gut, and raising the strings on a bridge. Banjos were also constructed by stretching the tanned hide of a ground hog or woodchuck over a piece of timber fashioned like a cheesebox. In Louisiana a jawbone and key were used musically, the key being rubbed against the bone. In summary, the slaves employed any and every type of material that could be forced to produce musical sounds—old pieces of iron, ribs of a sheep, jawbones of a cow, various kinds of wood.

Rare are the references to drums and horns in contemporary records of plantation life. Paine states that a Georgia law expressly forbade the slaves "using and keeping drums, horns or other loud instruments, which may call together, or give sign or notice to one another," and other states of the deep South had similar laws. There is a reference in a Virginia source, however, to a Negro dance accompanied by music played on a "banjor" (a large, hollow instrument with three strings) and a "quaqua" (somewhat resembling a drum). It was in Virginia also that R. Q. Mallard remembered Sundays on the plantation to have "resounded with the sounds of jollity—the merry strains of the fiddle, the measured beats of the 'quaw sticks' and the rhythmical shuffling and patting of the feet in the Ethiopian jig." Obviously the "quaw sticks" were rhythm instruments. For the most part, however, the slaves on plantations during the ante-bellum period played fiddles (or occasionally banjos).

RELIGIOUS SERVICES

As we have noted, it was customary for slaves in the South to attend the churches of the whites. Although the black worshipers frequently outnumbered the whites, the latter nevertheless maintained control, so that black men had no such opportunities for developing leadership skills as they found in the black churches of the North.

In regard to religious services for slaves in the South, some of the observations of ex-slaves that are preserved in the Slave Narrative Collection are illuminating. One slave noted that in the special afternoon services customarily held for blacks on his plantation the only message ever delivered by the preacher was, "Sarvants, obey yo' Massas. Dat's de Lawd's will." Another man provided more details:

Us servants stayed outside, and set down on de logs close by. . . . When de preacher get all warmed up and had de white folks inside thinking on what they ought to know and on de way to glory, he stick his head out de window and then exhort us servants: "You cullud people out there—listen at me. De way to make good slaves is to obey your Massa and Missis. You hear that? Obey 'em constant." Then he stick his head back in and preach till he had some mo' words for us all.

Although there were stringent laws in the South forbidding slaves to assemble without the presence of whites, in some places the slaves managed, nevertheless, to congregate for religious meetings. In Mississippi, for example, a favorite time for secret worship services was at sunrise on Sundays. Slaveholding families customarily slept late on Sunday mornings, and the patrols, after having been on duty all night, retired at dawn. Consequently, the slaves could worship as they pleased without interference. Another popular meeting time for secret services was midnight, after the whites had gone to bed. On plantations where masters were interested in the religious development of their slaves or were inclined to be lenient, mid-week prayer meetings and Sunday evening meetings were not uncommon.

Whether whites were present or not, the slaves generally adhered to conventional forms of worship in their formal services. Such services might be held in the cabin of the preacher or the "exhorter," in a "cotton house," or even in a special "praise house" set aside for the slaves. If the leader of the service —either the preacher or the exhorter—were able to read, he read a chapter from the Bible. Another slave read a psalm and lined it out for congregational singing, and the leader followed this with a prayer. If the leader could not read, he delivered a brief "exhortation" based on a passage of the Bible that he had memorized. The congregation then sang a psalm or hymn from memory, and the service closed with prayer. Amazingly, there usually was someone on the plantation who could read the Bible and who taught others to do so—this, despite laws in all of the southern states prohibiting the teaching of slaves to read and write.

Almost as important as the exhorter was the song leader. An ex-slave explained it in this way:

I was the singing man. I led the hymns. I learned them all by heart, and lined them off for the people to follow.

A white listener commented thus:

One hears the elder "deaconing" a hymn-book hymn, which is sung two lines at a time, and whose wailing cadences, borne on the night air, are indescribably melancholy.

The slaves, led by the singing man, sang the old hymns as slowly as the American colonists had sung psalms a century earlier. Long-meter and common-meter hymns were most common.

Sometimes the song leader was an older woman. She might have been the same person who attended the small children during the day while their parents worked, who taught them to "say their prayers, repeat a little catechism and sing a few hymns." Judging from the evidence, the singing of religious folksongs was not encouraged in formal services. Mallard, who became a minister in later life, seemed to be proud of the fact that sometimes, when in a generous mood, he would let the slaves sing "their own improvised spiritual" at church services:

> My brother, you promised Jesus,
> My brother, you promised Jesus,
> My brother, you promised Jesus
> To either fight or die.
>
> Oh, I wish I was there
> To hear my Jesus's orders,
> Oh, I wish I was there
> To wear my starry crown.

THE SHOUT

After the regular service there frequently was held in the same room a special service, purely African in form and tradition. The most detailed account of this rite in any nineteenth-century source is given in the 1867 collection, but numerous other sources also describe it.

The true "shout" takes place on Sundays or on "praise" nights through the week, and either in the praise-house or in some cabin in which a regular religious meeting has been held. Very likely more than half the population of the plantation is gathered together. . . . The benches are pushed back to the wall when the formal meeting is over, and old and young, men and women . . . all stand up in the middle of the floor, and when the "sperichil" [spiritual] is struck up, begin first walking and by-and-by shuffling round, one after the other, in a ring. The foot is hardly taken from the floor, and the progression is mainly due to a jerking, hitching motion, which agitates the entire shouter, and soon brings out streams of perspiration.

Generally, the gathering divided itself into two groups, shouters (that is, dancers) and singers. The latter, "composed of some of the best singers and of tired shouters stand at the side of the room to 'base' the others, singing the body of the song and clapping their hands together or on the knees." The dancers participated in the singing according to how they felt. Sometimes they danced silently; sometimes they sang only refrains of the song; sometimes they sang the entire song along with the singers. The descriptive passage concludes:

> Song and dance are alike extremely energetic, and often, when the shout lasts into the middle of the night, the monotonous thud, thud of feet prevents sleep within half a mile of the praise-house.

For the participants the shout was not under any circumstances to be construed as a dance, and strictly observed rules insured that the line between "shouting" and dancing was firmly drawn. Only songs of a religious nature were sung, and the feet must never be crossed (as would happen in the dance). Among strict devotees, the feet must not even be lifted from the ground. Presumably, any song could function as a shout song or "running spiritual." In practice, however, the slaves preferred some songs to the exclusion of others, and a special body of these songs was developed among them (see Chapter VII).

In performance, a ring spiritual was repeated over and over as the shouters moved around in a circle, often for as long as four and five successive hours. The song thus took on the character of a chant, a "wild monotonous chant," and its text became the "repetition of an incoherent cry." Although the ring of shouters moved slowly at the beginning, the tempo of the music and the pace of the circling gradually quickened so that the performance eventually displayed "signs of frenzy." The religious fervor of the participants and the loud monotony of the music combined to produce a state of ecstasy in all present, and shouters often fell to the ground in a state of complete exhaustion. Their places were quickly taken by others, however, and the ring dance continued.

It can readily be seen that this religious performance belongs to the same tradition as the eighteenth-century "jubilees" and Pinkster dances, the Place Congo dancing in New Orleans, the circle dances at camp meetings, and the "Methodist praying bands" in urban areas. Here were the same ring formations, the loud chanting, the shuffling movements, the intense concentration of the participants, and the gradual build-up of the performance to a wild and frenzied state. The only missing element was the instrumental music of drums and string instruments, and to a certain extent this was compensated for by the hand clapping of the singers. Some nineteenth-century writers thought that only the Baptists had shouts. The editors of *Slave Songs* thought that the shout was "confined to South Carolina and the States south of it." From the vantage point of the present we can see, however, that the shout belonged to no one denomination nor to any one region. It simply represented the survival of an African tradition in the New World.

There were in existence more elaborate versions of the ring shout, called by some the "drama shout." A "good sister" would stand in the center of the ring. As the shouters circled around her, she would slowly lower herself, inch by inch, to her knees, and then lower yet, until her head touched the floor. Just as slowly she rose, inch by inch. Two favorite songs used to accompany this feat were *Where Is Adam?* and *Going Down to the Mire.* Those persons who could demonstrate such skill, while all the time in a state of religious ecstasy, were held in high regard by the slaves. But if a person should become too intoxicated with the excitement of the performance and jump from the ground or let his feet "cross over," he was "thrown out of the church."

It will be of interest to explore briefly the nature of the relationship between the religious "ring shout" of the black Protestants and the secular ring dances of the black Catholics. The African prototype of the ritual may have had religious overtones, for in Africa the dance was an integral part of religious activity. In the European Protestant tradition, however, dancing was regarded as sinful, and slaves who were admitted into the church were compelled to "put away sinful things," such as profane songs and dancing. Obviously the ring dance was too strong a tradition to be discarded in the process of the African's acculturation to Anglo-Saxon traditions, and so the dance was sublimated into a religious ritual. On the other hand, the Catholics in the New World did not take so harsh a position on dancing, and it was unnecessary for the blacks to give up an activity essential to their very existence. Consequently, ring dances were performed in social context. In the West Indies, where African traditions are stronger than in the United States, the ring-dance tradition is still very much alive.

MUSIC ON THE AUCTION BLOCK

Rare was the slave dealer or slaveholder, no matter how cruel, who prohibited the singing of his slaves. Indeed, a more common practice was to force slaves to sing and dance under the most tragic of circumstances. On the slave ships loaded with human cargo, captured Africans were frequently made to dance and sing during their "airings" on deck, the reluctant ones among them being stimulated by the sting of a whip. In the slave pens of the States, slaves were often forced to sing and dance prior to being put up for sale on the auction block.

There was usually a slave fiddler available to play for such dancing—often one of the slaves who, himself, was up for sale. Solomon Northup, for example, was forced to play on such an occasion. He described his experience as follows:

[The] keeper of the slave pen in New-Orleans, was out among his animals early in the morning. With an occasional kick of the older men and women, and many a sharp crack of the whip about the ears of the younger slaves, it was not long before they were all astir, and wide awake. . . . In the first place we were required to wash thoroughly, and those with beards, to shave. We were then furnished with a new suit each, cheap, but clean. . . . During the day he exercised us in the art of "looking smart," and of moving to our places with exact precision.

After being fed, in the afternoon, we were again paraded and made to dance. Bob, a colored boy, who had some time belonged to Freeman, played on the violin. Standing near him, I made bold to inquire if he could play the "Virginia Reel." He answered he could not, and asked me if I could play. Replying in the affirmative he handed me the violin. I struck up a tune, and finished it. Freeman ordered me to continue playing, and seemed well pleased, telling Bob that I far excelled him—a remark that seemed to grieve my musical companion very much.

The slave traders relied on such activities to "liven up" their human stock and to enable them to obtain better prices. Little did it matter that slave auctions invariably separated members of families—brother from sister, husband from wife, mother from child. If the unfortunate slaves could not rise above their personal tragedies to make a good appearance before a prospective buyer, there was always the lash to encourage them.

Music making occasionally was demanded of slaves during the lengthy journeys from one slave-trading center to another. Gathered together into large groups, called "coffles," that numbered in the hundreds, they were handcuffed and moved along the road, two by two. Running down the center of the double file was a long chain, to which each slave was joined. The slaves were accompanied on these trips by men on horseback, who wielded long whips to goad the "reluctant and weary," and by the driver of the supplies wagon. Fiddlers among the slaves were encouraged to bring out their instruments, and so the grim procession would take on the bizarre aspect of a nightmarish parade (see Plate VII).

Often the slaves in these mournful processions sang of their own accord. The traveler George Tucker described the singing of a coffle in a letter written to a friend in 1816:

I took the boat this morning, and crossed the ferry over to Portsmouth, the small town which I told you lies opposite to this place. Here I rambled about for some time thro' the vacant streets, as my fancy led me, till I came to the court-house. It was court day, and a large crowd of people was gathered about the door. I had hardly got upon the steps to look in, when my ears were assailed by the voice of singing, and turning around to discover from what quarter it came, I saw a group of about thirty negroes, of different ages and sizes, following a rough looking white man, who sat carelessly lolling in his sulkey. They had just turned around the corner, and were coming up the main street to pass by the spot where I stood, on their way out of town. As they came nearer, I saw some of them loaded with chains to prevent their escape; while others had hold of each others hands, strongly grasped, as if to support themselves in their affliction. . . . They came along singing a little wild hymn of sweet and mournful melody; flying, by a divine instinct of the heart, to the consolation of religion, the last refuge of the unhappy, to support them in their distress. . . .

"My dear sir," said I, to one who stood next to me, "can you tell me what these poor people have been doing? What is their crime? And what is to be their punishment?" "O," said he, "it's nothing at all but a parcel of negroes sold to Carolina and that man is their driver, who has bought them."

Slavery was brutal; its system "bred indecency in human relations," not only between black and white, but also between white and white—between man and wife, father and son, master and overseer. For the slave, music was one of the chief avenues of escape from a life that held little dignity and meaning. The slaveholders, realizing the power of music, encouraged its use, not only as a means of increasing the work output of the slaves, but more important, as a means of preventing depression and suicidal impulses.

However, the planters frequently misunderstood the singing of the slaves. Too often they saw the blacks on their plantations as "a large flock of cheerful and contented slaves . . . ever merry and ever working with a song." On one occasion a slave, when questioned by Fredrika Bremer about his apparent good humor, responded:

We endeavor to keep ourselves up as well as we can. What can we do unless we keep a good heart? If we were to let it weaken, we should die.

More observant listeners heard the plaintive melancholy overtones in the singing and were occasionally startled by "wild and unaccountable" melodies.

Frederick Douglass and Solomon Northup were the most articulate of the ex-slaves who tried to explain the meaning of slave songs. Douglass observed in his 1845 autobiography that slaves sang most when they were unhappy. He remembered in particular the singing of two slaves on his Maryland plantation when they made their monthly trips to the Great House Farm for supplies.

While on their way, they would make the dense old woods, for miles around, reverberate with their wild songs, revealing at once the highest joy and the deepest sadness. They would compose and sing as they went along, consulting neither time nor tune. . . . "I did not, when a slave, understand the deep meanings of those rude, and apparently incoherent songs. I was myself within the circle, so that I neither saw nor heard as those without [the circle] might see and hear. They told a tale which was then altogether beyond my feeble comprehension; they were tones loud, long and deep, breathing the prayer and complaint of souls boiling over with the bitterest anguish. Every tone was testimony against slavery, and a prayer to God for deliverance from chains."

HOLIDAYS AND FROLICS

While it was generally true, as Lewis Paine observed, that slaves followed the "same monotonous course" day in and day out, year in and year out, until old age brought them to the grave, it was also true that there were times of the year when welcome breaks interrupted the routine. All over the rural South the population—whites as well as blacks, and particularly the white small planters and common laborers—looked forward to such work festivals as logrolling, hog killing, corn shucking [cornhusking], and rice threshing to give some respite from the heavy labor of everyday life and to bring some brightness into the monotony of existence. On such occasions it was the custom of the people in a community to gather at one plantation, the planters coming in from miles around and bringing with them their slaves. The work to be done was then tackled by the entire group and followed by feasting and dancing.

Paine provides vivid descriptions of the corn-shucking jubilees that involved small planters and their slaves in Georgia:

A farmer will haul up from his field a pile of corn from ten to twenty rods long, from ten to twenty feet wide, and ten feet high. . . . It is so arranged that this can be on a moonlight evening. The farmer then gives a general "invite" to all the young ladies and gentlemen in the neighborhood, to come and bring their slaves; for it takes no small number to shuck such a pile of corn. . . .

The guests begin to arrive about dark, and in a short time, they can be heard in all directions, singing the plantation songs, as they come to the scene of action. When they have all arrived, the Host makes the following propositions to his company, "You can shuck the pile, or work till eleven o'clock, or divide the pile and the hands, and try a race."

The last offer is generally accepted. Each party selects two of
the shrewdest and best singers among the slaves, to mount the
pile and sing, while all join in the chorus. The singers also act
the part of sentinels, to watch the opposite party—for it is part
of the game for each party to try to throw corn on the other's pile.

Singing was essential to the success of the evening. No huge
work project was successfully tackled at a jubilee without singing, whether shucking corn, rolling logs, or threshing rice. Mallard, in recalling the rice frolics on his plantation, thought first
of the singing of the workers:

> The dirt floor is beaten hard and swept clean and the sheaves of
> golden rice arranged upon it side by side. And now the stalwart
> laborers, with their hickory flails, beat off the heads of grain from
> the yellow straw. . . . The rhythmical beat of the numerous flails
> is accompanied by a recitative and improvised song of endless pro-
> portions, led by one musical voice, all [the others] joining in the
> chorus, and can be heard a mile.

There are numerous references in the sources to the singing
of the slaves as they marched along the roads leading to the
site of the work jubilee. The slaves assembled from plantations
as far as six to eight miles away and merged into large gangs
as they met on the road. Their "rich deep voices," which could
be heard for miles around, would swell out in a huge roar as
the singers came in on the refrains of the song.

No celebration was complete without a dance. Events of the
evening always occurred in the same order: working, feasting,
dancing. If the dance was to be held indoors, the long tables
on which the meal had been served would be cleared and the
room quickly stripped of all its furniture; for outdoor dancing,
the yard was swept and torchlights placed about. Then the fiddler
struck up a reel and the dancing began. Those who did not
dance sang along with the fiddler and tapped their feet.

All contemporary accounts of slave dancing emphasize its
vigor and vitality. The visitor to Virginia in 1787 (mentioned
above) observed with amazement that after a day of hard labor
the slave, instead of retiring to well-earned rest, walked six or
seven miles in the night to the site of a dance, where:

he performs with astonishing ability, and the most vigorous exertions, keeping time and cadence, most exactly, with the music . . . until he exhausts himself, and scarcely has time, or strength, to return home before the hour he is called forth to toil the next morning.

Paine reports an amusing episode in Georgia when, after a logrolling, masters and slaves had begun dancing at the same time. As the slave musicians became more and more intoxicated with the spirit of the dancing, they played faster and "wilder," until finally the whites could keep up no longer and withdrew from the dancing. This was exactly what the slave dancers desired! They sang out, "Now show de white man what we can do!" and threw themselves with wild abandon into their "frolic."

Slaves were very proud of their dancing prowess, and generally considered the "measured, listless and snail-like steps" of the society cotillions much inferior to their lively reels and jigs. As we have observed, however, the whites themselves, and especially the younger ones, were apt to move into reels and jigs at their own dances after a few perfunctory bows in the direction of "society sets" such as minuets and cotillions. The slave fiddlers had their own methods for producing "hot" music as the dancing became wilder and more abandoned.

A boy would stand behind the fiddler with a pair of knitting needles in his hands. From this position the youngster would reach around the fiddler's left shoulder and beat on the strings in the manner of a snare drummer.[1]

The fiddler sang and stomped his feet as he played, the boy handling the needles all the while. An expert fiddler "could stomp the left heel and the right forefoot and alternate this with the right heel and the left forefoot, making four beats to the bar."

Holiday dances were generally all-night affairs. When the fiddler grew tired, the slaves provided a different kind of dance music by "pattin' juba." Basically, this procedure involved foot tapping, hand clapping, and thigh slapping, all in precise rhythm. There seem to have existed, however, a number of ways to

[1] William C. Handy, *Father of the Blues* (New York, 1941; paperback reprint, 1970), p. 5.

accomplish this feat. According to Paine, in Georgia the patter tapped his foot in regular time while he alternately clapped his hands lightly and slapped his thighs. This made a "most curious noise, yet in such perfect order that the slaves had no difficulty in dancing to it." On the plantation in Louisiana where Northup was enslaved, the patting was performed by

> striking the hands on the knees, then striking the hands together, then striking the right shoulder with one hand, the left with the other—all the while keeping time with the feet, and singing, per-haps, this song:

> > "Harper's creek and roarin' ribber,
> > Thar, my dear, we'll live forebber;
> > Den we'll go to the Ingin Nation,
> > All I want in dis creation,
> > Is pretty little wife and big plantation."

In Virginia, Hungerford reports that a boy also sang as he patted juba; or rather, "he recited the words of a jig in a monotonous tone of voice." As we have seen, slaves in northern urban areas also utilized "patting" as a way of providing dance music.

ENTERTAINMENT FOR THE PLANTERS

Slaves were frequently called upon to entertain their masters, particularly when visitors were about, as we learn from nu-merous anecdotes in nineteenth-century sources. Paine declared that there was no match for the "comic actions, ludicrous sights, and laughable jokes and truly comic songs" of talented slaves. As for dancing, he wrote:

> One would think they had steam engines inside of them, to jerk them about with so much power; for they go through with more motions in a minute, than you could shake two sticks at in a month.

He dismissed the Fellow's Minstrels (a popular white minstrel group of the 1850s) as not "bearing comparison" with the plan-tation slaves, chiefly because of the former's artificiality. More often than calling slaves up to the big house, the slaveowner would take his guests down to the slave quarters to watch a frolic or a shout. It is from these curious guest-observers that many detailed descriptions of slave musical practices have come down to us.

But the slaves, too, were aware of their usefulness. The ex-slave Isaac Williams wrote:

> When our masters had company staying with them, they would often collect all the slaves for a general jubilee frolic.

A more pointed anecdote is found in the Slave Narrative Collection:

> Charlie could make up songs about de funniest things. . . . Marsa say, "Come here, Charlie, and sing some rhymes for Mr. H." "Don't know no new ones, Marsa," Charlie answered. "Come on, you black rascal, give me a rhyme for my company, one he ain't heard." [2]

Fiddlers were always in great demand. Rare was the plantation that did not have someone around like Old John Drayton, who played for all the dances on his plantation. His fellow slaves were very proud of Drayton's fiddling:

> He fair make the fiddle talk. When Master give a dance he always call upon John. Yes sir, that man sure could play. When he saw down on the fiddle and pull out that tune, "Oh, the Monkey Marry to the Baboon Sister," he make a parson dance.

An old ex-slave from another plantation boasted:

> I was a good fiddler; used to be a fiddler for the white girls to dance. Just picked it up, it was a natural gift. I could still play if I had a fiddle. . . . Played all those old-time songs . . . *Soldier's Joy, Jimmy Long Josey, Arkansas Traveler*, and *Black-eyed Susie*.

A good violinist found that his fiddle gained him entry into places otherwise closed to slaves and exempted him of many a day of hard work in the fields. Nothing could better illustrate

[2] Cited in Milton Meltzer, ed., *In Their Own Words: A History of the American Negro*, I (New York, 1964), p. 47.

this than the experience of Solomon Northup in Louisiana. His master's wife induced her husband Edwin, a crude, vicious man, to buy a violin for Northup because she was "passionately fond of music." As a consequence, Northup was frequently called upon to play for the Epps family in the evenings. When Northup finally obtained his freedom "Mistress Epps was actually affected to tears," primarily because she no longer would have someone to play for her on the violin.

As the owner of Northup, Epps received numerous requests for his slave's services from townsmen and planters on neighboring plantations. The white people in the nearby villages got to know him well:

> [They] always knew there was to be a jollification somewhere, whenever Platt Epps [Northup's slave name] was seen passing through the town with his fiddle in his hand. "Where are you going now Platt?" and "What is coming off tonight, Platt?" would be interrogatories issuing from every door and window, and many a time when there was no special hurry, yielding to pressing importunities, Platt would draw his bow, and sitting astride his mule, perhaps, discourse musically to a crowd of delighted children, gathered around him in the street.

To the slaveowner went all payments, of course, for his slave's fiddling, but Northup sometimes received a little money for his musical exertions. On one occasion he collected seventeen dollars in tips—a large sum for a slave to receive at one time. To play for dances of the planters the slave musician could not get by with only reels and jigs; he was expected to be able to play minuets and cotillions as well. The demands upon his violin technique, consequently, were almost as great as if he had been a city-slave musician.

CHAPTER VII

The Ante-Bellum Period:
General Character of the Folk Music

By the time of the Civil War the music of black folk in the
United States had developed its own characteristic style. As we
have pointed out, white observers had begun to notice differences between African-style music and European music as early
as 1637. They revealed this awareness by the kinds of observations they made—by the things that caught their attention and
by the things they left unsaid. The early writers spoke largely
about performance practices—about concepts of sound, instruments, and the black man's attitude toward music making. While
the writers were vaguely aware that the music itself was different, they were unable to explain its divergencies and, unfortunately, did not record any of the music. Later observers paid
closer attention to what they saw and heard. They jotted down
the words of songs, observed how the songs were sung, described
in detail the body movements of dancers and workers, commented upon the instruments used, how the instruments were
constructed and how played. Finally came the song collectors,
who patiently listened to the "weird and barbaric madrigals" or
"sweet, impressive melodies" and attempted to record them in
European musical notation.

Few of these persons were professional musicians, however,
and errors were inevitably made in the process of transcribing.

It must be remembered, too, that their work was accomplished without the aid of the phonograph, an indispensable item of equipment for the modern-day folksong collector. Moreover, they rarely had the opportunity of hearing a song performed several times in succession; they were required to "catch the tune" the first time, for the same song, if sung a day later or by a different person, would have been altered—sometimes beyond recognition.

THE MUSICAL SOURCES

As we have seen, it was not until 1867 that the first song collection was published in book form. Before that year, isolated examples of slave songs had appeared in various books and periodicals: two songs were written down in 1832 by James Hungerford and published in his book *The Old Plantation;* two songs appeared in a letter written by Lucy McKim Garrison to *Dwight's Journal of Music* (1862); five songs, in an article by H. G. Spaulding, "Under the Palmetto" in the *Continental Monthly* (1863); one song, in an article by the Reverend L. C. Lockwood, *The Song of the Contraband* (1861); and a large number of song texts in an article by Colonel Thomas W. Higginson in the *Atlantic Monthly* (1867). The songs of Garrison and Higginson were included in the 1867 publication *Slave Songs of the United States.* The editors of that source also drew upon a number of private collections. According to their statements, they failed to use many songs from those sources. Consequently, there is an unknown quantity of slave songs collected during the period that remains unpublished.

It is possible to discuss the texts and musical features of slave songs with some degree of authority on the basis of the songs listed above and other songs published soon after the Civil War, representing (with a few exceptions) an ante-bellum repertory. The songs referred to above make a total of 144 songs. To that number should be added six slave songs included in an article by John Mason Brown, "Songs of the Slave," published in *Lippincott's Magazine* (1868). A collection with 128 slave songs, *Jubilee Songs as Sung by the Fisk Jubilee Singers,* was published in the year 1872, and was followed in 1874 by a similar publication containing fifty songs, *Hampton and Its Students . . . with Fifty Cabin and Plantation Songs Arranged by Thomas P. Fenner*, edited by Mary Frances Armstrong and Helen Ludlow. And finally, the collection of William E. Barton, *Old Plantation Hymns* (first published as three magazine articles in 1898), includes a group of fifty-four songs—some "of unquestioned antiquity" and others "which show the influence of the war." All in all, the slave-song repertory recorded in music notation comprises no fewer than 382 songs.

Whether or not they were aware of it, the first folksong collectors in the United States were acting in the tradition of the nationalistic movement in nineteenth-century Europe. Political nationalism had its musical counterpart; composers were expected to contribute by drawing upon the folk music and dance of their countries as inspiration for their composed music and by using subjects from national history and legend. But before this could be done, there had to be a collection and codification of the national folk-music heritage. A second step involved the arrangement of these songs for the use of city folk and professional musicians.

Probably the oldest folksong repository of modern times is *The Beggar's Opera* (1728), which was not intended at all to be a collection of folksongs, but was written as a ballad opera—that is, a play with interspersed songs. Nevertheless, the work does contain sixty-nine folk tunes arranged by John Pepusch. Fourteen years later there appeared the first volume of a genuine collection of folk music, *Ancient British Music* (1742–81), edited by John Parry and Ivan Williams. In 1806, the Germans began to publish folksongs, beginning with *Das Knaben Wunderhorn* (The Boy's Magic Horn), edited by Ludwig Arnim and Clemens Brentano. The poet Sir Walter Scott published in 1802–03 a collection of ancient Scottish ballad texts in three volumes, *Minstrelsy of the Scottish Border*. By the 1860s the folksong-collecting movement was well on its way. During the same time that some Americans were recording slave melodies, other collectors were tracking down the folk music of the British peoples and their descendants in the United States—notably, Harvard University professor Francis Child and an English musician, Cecil Sharp. On the continent, Jaromir Erben of Bohemia

(Czechoslovakia) began collecting examples of his national songs as early as 1820, and Ludwig Erk and Franz Boehme of Germany undoubtedly began their work not too much later, for their monumental collection of German folksongs appeared in 1893–94. Nationalistic composers consciously employed folksongs in their composed music, either by literally quoting the tunes or by inventing melodies in the spirit of, and using the characteristic idioms of, folk music.

SONG TYPES

The slaves distinguished many different types among their songs according to the ways in which the songs were used, and they employed special terms to apply to the different categories. In this regard they followed in the tradition of their African forbears. Obviously, the complex social and political organization of African society cannot be compared to the simple slave society of ante-bellum times. Nevertheless, the African tradition of using music on all occasions and of classifying the music according to its function is reflected in the slaves' plantation songs. For the few rites the slaves were permitted to observe—chiefly those involved with death and, in some places, religion—and for the few activities in which they engaged, there was always relevant music.

The larger part of the songs in the extant ante-bellum repertory is of a religious nature. It is probable, however, that religious songs accounted for a much smaller part of the actual repertory in use than the preserved sources seem to indicate. The song collectors were aware that the songs they were able to record did not represent the "purest specimens" of the folk music nor the most numerous types. They gathered songs, for the most part, in places where they "never heard a secular song" or "saw a musical instrument." The black folk in those areas had been converted to Christianity and, consequently, sang only religious songs.

But there is no evidence to support an assumption that such a condition was typical. In fact, it seems that on most plantations the opposite was true. The song types referred to most frequently in ante-bellum literature were rarely religious, and there were many more references to working and dancing than to praying. A "gentleman of Delaware" emphasized this point in 1867 (quoted in the 1867 collection):

> We must look among their non-religious songs for the purest specimens of negro minstrelsy. . . . Some of the best *pure negro* songs I have ever heard were those that used to be sung by the black stevedores, or perhaps the crews themselves, of the West India vessels, loading and unloading at the wharves in Philadelphia and Baltimore. I have stood for more than an hour, often, listening to them, as they hoisted and lowered the hogsheads and boxes of their cargoes; one man taking the burden of the song (and the slack of the rope) and the others striking in with the chorus. They would sing in this way more than a dozen different songs in an hour . . . generally rather innocent and proper in their language, and strangely attractive in their music; and with a volume of voice that reached a square or two away. . . .

Ex. VII.1   *Sold Off to Georgy*, from Hungerford

1. Fare-well, fel-low sar-vants! O — ho! O — ho! I'm gwine way to leabe you; O — ho! O-ho! I'm gwine to leabe de ole coun-ty; O — [leave] ho! O — ho! I'm sold off to Geor-gy! O — ho! O — ho!

2. Farewell, ole plantation, (Oho! Oho!)
   Farewell, de ole quarter, (Oho! Oho!)
   Un daddy, un mammy, (Oho! Oho!)
   Un marster, un missus! (Oho! Oho!)

3. My dear wife un one chile, (Oho! Oho!)
   My poor heart is breaking; (Oho! Oho!)
   No more shall I see you, (Oho! Oho!)
   Oh! no more foreber! (Oho! Oho!)

The nonreligious songs fall into several major categories: work-songs of many kinds, dance songs, play songs, story songs or ballets, songs of social comment, gossip songs, satirical songs, field hollers and street cries, and sorrow songs. The religious songs include those associated with worship, worship-related activities, and death. Generally these songs are called spirituals.

THE WORKSONGS

As has been observed, the style of a worksong was related to the work activity it was intended to accompany. Rowing songs, like rowing songs the world over, have smooth flowing rhythms. The earliest recorded music example of a slave boat song is the melody Hungerford transcribed in 1832, reproduced in Ex. VII.1. To Hungerford the song was an "inexpressibly plaintive, . . . melancholy tune." Charley, the boatman, sang the verses and the other oarsmen came in on the refrains, "all timing the strokes of their oars to the measure." Afterward, when Hungerford reproached the slaves for singing so depressing a song, Charley answered, "De boat-songs is always dat way . . . dat is, mo' er less."

This song, or variants of it, was widely dispersed through the South. An early text was written down in 1808 by a British traveler, John Lambert, who observed that the tune was "rather monotonous, but had a pleasing effect. The boatman kept time with it at every stroke of their oars":

> We are going down to Georgia, boys, Aye, aye,
> To see the pretty girls, boys, Aye, aye,
> We'll give them a pint of brandy, boys, Aye, aye,
> And a hearty kiss besides, boys, Aye, aye.

A song heard by Frances Kemble in 1838 seems to represent still another variant. She commented that the song had "an extremely pretty, plaintive, and original air."

Fare you well and good bye, oh, oh,
I'm going away to leave you, oh, oh.
Oh, my massa's told me, [oh, oh],
There's no grass in Georgia, [oh, oh].

We have no way of knowing, of course, whether the same tune
or variants of the tune were used for the different text versions,
but it is possible that such may have been the case.

Stevedore and roustabout songs reflected the tremendous out-
pouring of energy involved in waterfront jobs, and their texts
were often unprintable. One of the oldest roustabout song texts
on record is the following, heard in the Philadelphia area about
1800:

Nancy Bohannan, she married a barber,
Shave her away, shave her away;
He shaved all he could, he couldn't shave harder,
Shave her away, shave her away.

When Lafcadio Hearn, a white journalist, went to Cincinnati in
1869 (i.e. after Emancipation) he found that more than two-
thirds of the stevedores and longshoremen there were black.
He was fascinated by their roustabout songs, which obviously
had a long history, and wrote down the texts of several. One
of the "most melancoly of these plaintive airs" was *O Let Her
Go By.*

I'm going away to New Orleans,
Good-bye, my love, good-bye;
I'm going away to New Orleans,
Good-bye, my love, good-bye;
O let her go by.

She's on her way to New Orleans,
Good-bye, my love, good-bye;
She's bound to pass the Robert E. Lee,
Good-bye, my love, good-bye;
O let her go by.

I'll make this trip and I'll make no more,
Good-bye, my love, good-bye;
I'll roll these barrels and I'll roll no more,

> Good-bye, my love, good-bye;
> O let her go by.
>
> An' if you are not true to me,
> Farewell, my lover, forever;
> An' if you are not true to me,
> Farewell, my lover, forever;
> O let her go by.

One of the most popular songs among the men was:

> Molly was a good gal and a bad gal, too,
> Oh, Molly, row, gal;
> Molly was a good gal and a bad gal, too,
> Oh, Molly, row, gal.
>
> I'll row this boat and I'll row no more,
> Row, Molly, row, gal;
> I'll row this boat and I'll row no more,
> Row, Molly, row, gal.

Each plantation had its own repertory of worksongs, which grew out of the work activities of the plantation. According to an ex-slave, the following example of a woodcutter's song was sung in a woods, where hundreds of slaves, paired off in twos in front of the trees, "marked the blows by the song."

> A cold frosty morning,
> The niggers feeling good,
> Take your ax upon your shoulder,
> Nigger, talk to the wood.[1]

The term "corn song" was used throughout the South to refer to the songs sung at corn-shucking frolics. On many plantations there was a slave, or perhaps two, whose special job it was to supply songs for the annual jubilees. On Hungerford's plantation the young girl Clotilda could be depended upon to furnish "jingling rhymes" for the cornhusking season. She could also "make melodies as well as rhymes." The texts of corn songs invariably include phrases referring to the work action, such as "round the corn" and "shuck the corn." Two songs have come

[1] Cited in Meltzer, *In Their Own Words,* p. 43.

down to us with the title *Roun' de Corn, Sally*, but their texts and music are unrelated. This example from Virginia was recorded in 1832.

Ex. VII.2   *Roun' de Corn, Sally*, from Hungerford

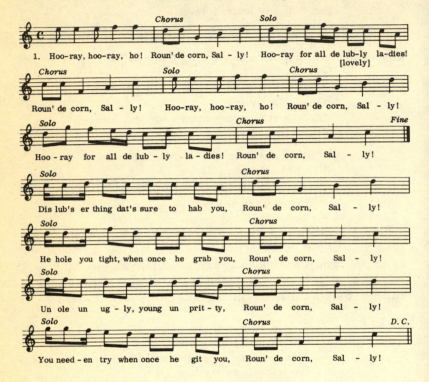

2. Dere's Mr. Travers lub Miss Jinny;
   He thinks she is us good us any.
   He comes from church wid her er Sunday,
   Un don't go back ter town till Monday.
                    Hooray, hooray, ho! etc.

Corn songs used to aid in the coordination of movements during the husking activity fall into a different category from songs describing the work, which were intended for singing in social context. The texts of the former are not as important as the rhythm. In *Shock Along, John*, for example, the only

words intelligible to the recorder of the song were the words
of the refrain:

Ex. VII.3 *Shock Along, John,* from *Slave Songs of
the United States*

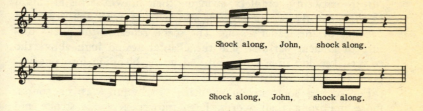

Shock along, John, shock along.

Shock along, John, shock along.

In another corn song, the slaves obviously borrowed some
verses from nursery rhymes:

> Massa in the great house counting out his money,
> Oh, shuck that corn and throw it in the barn;
> Mistis in the parlor eating bread and honey,
> Oh, shuck that corn and throw it in the barn.
> Sheep shell corn by the rattle of his horn,
> Oh, shuck that corn and throw it in the barn;
> Sent it to the mill by the whippoorwill,
> Oh, shuck that corn and throw it in the barn.

In contrast, the texts of the social corn-songs were quite important. William Wells Brown recorded the texts of several
"marching" corn songs as sung in 1820 by the slaves on the
plantation from which he escaped, Poplar Farms near St. Louis,
Missouri. One example follows:

> All them pretty gals will be there,
> Shuck that corn before you eat;
> They will fix it for us rare,
> Shuck that corn before you eat.
> I know that supper will be big,
> Shuck that corn before you eat;
> I think I smell a fine roast pig,
> Shuck that corn before you eat. . . .

James Mason Brown includes a slave harvesting-song in his

magazine article and tells of the condition under which it was sung:

> Long ago, when the mowing-machine and reaper were as yet un-thought of, it was uncommon to see, in a Kentucky harvestfield, fifteen or twenty "cradlers" swinging their brawny arms in unison as they cut the ripened grain, and moving with the regulated cadence of the leader's song. The scene repeated the poet's picture of ancient oarsmen and the chanter seated high above the rowers, keeping time with staff and voice, blending into one impulse the banks of the trireme.

For such a song strong emphasis of rhythm was, of course, more important than words. Each mower kept his stroke and measured his stride by musical intervals. A very favorite song for these harvesting occasions commenced thus:

Ex. VII.4   *Rise Up in Due Time*, from Brown

DANCE SONGS AND PLAY SONGS

The slaves referred to their dance songs as "fiddle songs," "jig tunes," and "devil songs." "Patting songs," those used for dancing when no musical instrument was available, rarely expressed any distinct ideas in the lyrics, but were valued for the rhythm of the words. Indeed, most often the texts were nonsensical, as in the following one remembered by Northup. The singer "patted" as he sang:

> Who's been here since I've been gone?
> Pretty little gal wid a josey on.
>   Hog eye!
>   Old Hog eye!
>   And Hosey too!
> Never see de like since I was born,

Here comes a little gal wid a josey on.
   Hog eye!
   Old Hog eye!
   And Hosey too!

There are several genuine dance songs in the preserved slave-music repertory, all of them "obtained from a lady who heard them sung before the war on the Good Hope Plantation, St. Charles Parish, Louisiana," according to the editors of the 1867 collection. As we have observed, the majority of the slave songs in the extant repertory were gathered from slaves who, having been converted, consequently no longer danced. In Catholic Louisiana, however, the slaves' religion did not prohibit their dancing. The *calinda* was a kind of contradance in which the two lines of dancers faced each other, advancing and retreating in time to the music. The title of the song and the name of the dance were identical. The *bamboula* was a lively couple-dance; its name probably points to the African bamboo-drum music originally associated with the dance. At least two bamboula songs have survived from ante-bellum times: *Musieu Bainjo* (Mister Banjo) and *Quand patate la cuite* (When the [Sweet] Potato Is Cooked). Four songs in the 1867 collection served as accompaniment songs for the group dance *coonjai* (counjaille): *Belle Layotte* (Pretty Layotte), *Remon, Aurore Bradaire*, and *Caroline*. The 1867 collection includes a description of the music for the dancing:

When the *Coonjai* is danced, the music is furnished by an orchestra of singers, the leader of whom—a man selected both for the quality of his voice and for his skill in improvising—sustains the solo part, while the others afford him an opportunity, as they shout in chorus, for inventing some neat verse to compliment some lovely *danseuse*, or celebrate the deeds of some plantation hero. The dancers themselves never sing, as in the case of the religious "shout" of the Port Royal negroes; and the usual musical accompaniment, besides that of the singers, is that furnished by a skilful performer on the barrel-head-drum, the jaw-bone and key, or some other rude instrument.

The slave dance known throughout the South was the juba, for which the customary accompaniment seems to have been "patting," with or without the singing of a duple-meter song. ("Jig" and "juba" seem to have been used synonymously in nineteenth-century references to slave dancing.)

Children often sang religious songs when at play. C. G. Parsons, who visited a plantation in 1855, noticed that the children played a game in which they joined hands and circled around a tree, singing as they moved such songs as *I'm Going Way Up Yonder, See God Feeding the Lambs*, and *When I Get Over Jordan.*

STORY SONGS OR BALLETS

The narrative song seems not to have had the important place in the slave-song repertory that it occupied in other comparable repertories of the time—for example, Anglo-American folksongs. It may well be that the simple, unvarying routines of slave life precluded the development of a song type dependent upon the adventures of a hero or heroine. Without control of his own body, the slave had few adventures. He knew in advance the consequences of any action he might take, and he knew that there was nothing he could do to avert the consequences. Only three or four songs in the repertory can be remotely classified as story songs and one of these is an animal song. There must have been hundreds of these animal songs in circulation, just as there were hundreds of folktales about Brer Rabbit and his friends, but only one, *Charleston Gals*, has come down to us from this period in a musical source.

SATIRICAL SONGS

The traditional African penchant for musical satire is also poorly reflected in the surviving slave songs, the 1867 collection containing only two or three genuine satirical songs. A song of Creole origin pokes fun of the city dandy:

Ex. VII.5 *Musieu Bainjo,* from *Slave Songs of the United States*

[Look at that puffed-up Mr. Banjo over there,
See how he puts on airs.
    Hat perched on the side of his head, Mr. Banjo,
    Fancy cane in his hand, Mr. Banjo,
    New boots that go squeak, squeak, Mr. Banjo,]

A song called *Away Down in Sunbury* is provided with just one stanza in the 1867 collection, but one can easily imagine that succeeding stanzas, continuing in the same satirical vein, related other instances where the slave deceived the unsuspecting master:

> O massa take that bran' new coat and hang it on the wall,
> That darky take the same ole coat and wear it to the ball.

Chorus: O don't you hear my true love sing,
      O don't you hear him sigh,
      Away down in Sunbury
      I'm bound to live or die.

According to the sources, satirical songs were common, notwithstanding their absence in the extant slave-repertory. As we have seen, Cresswell's account—one of the earliest comments upon slave singing—refers to this kind of song: "In their songs they generally relate the usage they have received from their Masters or Mistresses in a very satirical manner" (see p. 66). Numerous other sources refer to similar practices. It is understandable, however, that slaves would not have allowed whites to

hear them singing such songs—at least not clearly enough to
write them down. The white man heard only what the slave
wanted him to hear.

The slaves were not averse, however, to letting whites hear
them shoot a few barbs at their fellows in religious songs. The
first verses of a song entitled *O Daniel* aim at deflating the ego
of a self-righteous member of the church:

> You call yourself church-member,
> You hold your head so high,
> You praise God with your glittering tongue,
> But you leave all your heart behind.

In another example, *On to Glory*, the final stanza includes a
little chastisement for a wayward sister:

> There's Chloe Williams, she makes me mad,
> For you see, I know she's going on bad;
> She told me a lie this afternoon,
> And the devil will get her very soon.

Then there is a song that begins:

> Hypocrite and the concubine,
> Living among the swine;
> They run to God with the lips and tongue,
> And leave all the heart behind.

FIELD AND STREET CRIES

Among the various labels given to the cries of the field are
"cornfield hollers," "cotton field hollers," "whoops," "water
calls," and "field calls." A slave's call or cry could mean any
one of a number of things: a call for water, food, or help, a
call to let others know where he was working, or simply a cry
of loneliness, sorrow, or happiness. As in the African tradition,
one cry might be answered by another from a place far distant.

In 1853 a traveler in South Carolina described the sound of a cry:

> Suddenly one [a slave] raised such a sound as I had never heard before, a long, loud musical shout, rising and falling, and breaking into falsetto, his voice ringing through the woods in the clear frosty night air, like a bugle call. As he finished, the melody was caught up by another, and then another, then by several in chorus.[2]

The call of the street vendor was intended to carry a distinct message and rarely, therefore, left the listener in doubt of its meaning. Sometimes the calls were just a phrase or two sung in a "novel manner." Often they were parody versions of folksongs, such as the following parody of the spiritual *I Am Going to Glory*. William Wells Brown heard the song and commented: "A woman with some really fine strawberries put forth her claims in a very interesting song; the interest centered more upon the manner than the matter":

> I live four miles out of town,
> I am going to glory;
> My strawberries are sweet and sound,
> I am going to glory.
> I fotch them four miles on my head,
> I am going to glory;
> My child is sick, my husband dead,
> I am going to glory.
> Now's the time to get them cheap,
> I am going to glory;
> Eat them with your bread and meat,
> I am going to glory.
> Come sinner get down on your knees,
> I am going to glory;
> Eat these strawberries when you please,
> I am going to glory. . . .

SPIRITUALS

The spirituals represent the religious musical expression of the slaves. Some spirituals were classified by the slaves as songs to

[2] Frederick Olmstead, *Journey in the Seaboard Slave States, with Remarks on Their Economy* (1856; paperback reprint, New York, 1969), p. 114.

be sung during services or while "just sitting around"; other spirituals were intended for use during the shout. To the latter were given such labels as "ring spirituals," "shout spirituals," or "running spirituals." Among the spirituals most closely associated with the shout throughout the South were *Oh, We'll Walk Around the Fountain; I Know, Member, Know Lord; The Bells Done Ring; Pray All the Members; Go Ring That Bell;* and *I Can't Stay Behind.*

Ex. VII.6   *I Can't Stay Behind,* from *Slave Songs of the United States*

2. I been all around, I been all around,
    Been all around de Heaven, my Lord.

3. I've searched every room—in de Heaven, my Lord.

4. De angels singin'—all round de trone.

5. My Fader call—and I must go.

6. Sto-back, member; sto-back, member.

A few spirituals fall into the sorrow-song category, songs with texts that express only despair and hopelessness. Perhaps the best known of these was *Lay Dis Body Down,* called by Colonel Higginson "a flower of poetry in the dark soil."

Ex. VII.7 *Lay Dis Body Down*, from *Slave Songs of the United States*

O   grave-yard,___   O   grave-yard,___   I'm

walk-in' troo de grave-yard;___   Lay dis bod-y   down.

2. I know moonlight, I know starlight,
I'm walkin' troo de starlight;
Lay dis body down.

Alternate version with Higginson's text, from *Slave Songs of the United States*

I   know moon-light, I   know star-light;   I   lay dis bod-y   down.

2. I walk in de moonlight, I walk in de starlight;
I lay dis body down.
3. I know de graveyard, I know de graveyard,
When I lay dis body down.

POETIC FORMS

The most common poetic structure is the call-and-response form, in which solo verses alternate with refrain lines. There seems to be no typical pattern with regard to length of lines or to relationship between solo and refrain lines. In some texts all of the lines have four metric feet (that is, four accents in each line), while in other texts four-foot lines alternate with three-foot lines (the so-called "ballad meter"). Moreover, some texts have refrain lines of two metric feet. The following two texts are examples of the most typical arrangements:

I meét little Rósa eárly in the mórning, (4)
Ó Jerúsalem! eárly in the mórning. (4)

And I aśked her, Hów [do] you dó, my daúghter, (4)
Ó Jerúsalem! eárly in the mórning. (4)
I meét my móther eárly in the mórning, (4)
Ó Jerúsalem! eárly in the mórning. (4)

I wánt to gó where Móses tród, (4)
Ó the dýing Laṁb. (3)
For Móses goṅe to the prómised laṅd, (4)
Ó the dýing Laṁb. (3)
To dŕink from spŕings that néver run dŕy, (4)
Ó the dýing Laṁb. (3)

The call-and-response structure points, of course, directly to
Africa.

Another common form is strophic, in which a four-line stanza
alternates with a four-line chorus, the chorus typically consisting
of three repeated lines and refrain (as a-a-a-Refrain), and the
stanza of varying form (as a-R-a-R, a-b-c-R, or a-b-a-c):

We'll run and never tire, (a)
We'll run and never tire, (a)
We'll run and never tire, (a)
Jesus sets poor sinners free. (R)

Way down in the valley, (a)
Who will rise and go with me? (b)
You've heard talk of Jesus, (c)
Who set poor sinners free. (R)

The lightning and the flashing, (a)
The lightning and the flashing, (a)
The lightning and the flashing, (a)
Jesus sets poor sinners free. (R)

In a publication of William C. Nell, *The Colored Patriots of
the American Revolution* (1855), there appears what is possibly
the earliest record of a slave song text with three-line stanzas
instead of the conventional four-line stanzas:

You may beat upon my body,
But you cannot harm my soul;
I shall join the forty thousand by and by.

You may sell my children to Georgy [Georgia],
But you cannot harm their souls;
They will join the forty thousand by and by.

Come, slave trader, come in too;
The Lord's got a pardon here for you;
You shall join the forty thousand by and by.

According to Nell, this song was sung at a slave religious meeting held in a deep forest, "in the lone sanctuary of Nature's primeval majesty," where hundreds of slaves joined in on the refrain lines.

It is noteworthy that all the songs with three-line stanzas in the 1867 collection are sorrow songs. One of the songs is discussed above, *Lay This Body Down*. Another, *I Want to Go Home* (No. 61 in the collection), seems more like a chant than a genuine song.

Ex. VII.8   *I Want to Go Home*, from *Slave Songs of the United States*

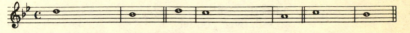

Dere's no rain to wet you. O yes, I want to go home, Want to go home.

2. Dere's no sun to burn you.—O yes, etc.

3. Dere's no hard trials.

4. Dere's no whips a-crackin'.

5. Dere's no stormy weather.

6. Dere's no tribulation.

7. No more slavery in de kingdom.

8. No evil-doers in de kingdom.

9. All is gladness in de kingdom.

The three-line stanza apparently points to the African tradition. There is an example of such an old African song in W. E. B. DuBois's book, *Souls of the Black Folk*. The song was sung by the great-great-grandmother of DuBois and passed down from parents to children for over two hundred years.

Ex. VII.9 *Do Bana Coba,* from DuBois *

* The rhythms of measures 1 and 3 are reproduced exactly as notated in the source.

The three-line sorrow song was probably the prototype for the blues of a later time.

Of course, not all of the slave songs employ the typical forms as outlined above. Sometimes a text, while utilizing the predictable repetition, reflects an unusual arrangement of words into patterns:

> Bow low, Mary, bow low, Martha,
> For Jesus come and lock the door,
> And carry the keys away.
> Sail, sail, over yonder
> And view the promised land.
> For Jesus come and lock the door,
> And carry the keys away.
> Weep, O Mary, bow low, Martha,
> For Jesus come and lock the door,
> And carry the keys away.
> Sail, sail, my true believer,
> Sail, sail, over yonder;
> Mary, bow low, Martha, bow low,
> For Jesus come and lock the door,
> And carry the keys away.

POETIC LANGUAGE AND THEMES

The song texts are marked by vivid imagery, with emphasis on metaphoric figures of speech. A slave sings "my brother's sitting on the tree of life"; he exults "I cast my sins in the middle of the sea." Sometimes he thinks of his sins as a heavy load on his back: "my sins so heavy I can't get along." To be sure, there is always the possibility of forgiveness: "Jesus give me a little broom for to sweep my heart clean." Often his wretched existence makes him long for the security of his infancy: "Rock o' my soul in the bosom of Abraham."

Occasionally, the technique of personification is used. The slave reminds himself: "Death's gonna lay his cold icy hand on me." He sings, "Death go from door to door" in his search for men; "he knock down some, and he cripple up some." In some songs the "mournful" thunder or the "lumbering" thunder "rolls from door to door," "calling home God's children," or the "forked" lightning calls God's children home.

Above all, the language is forceful and direct. The slave longs to "go home" where there is "no rain to wet," "no sun to burn," and "no whips a-cracking." He holds onto his brother or sister "with a trembling hand." If he remains in the wilderness too long, his "head will get wet with the midnight dew." He says to his wayward brother "O Sinner, ain't you tired of sinning?" Trouble becomes a "gloomy cloud," but it can be dispelled because "the sun give a light in the heaven all round."

The use of rhyme was apparently not essential to the slave singer, probably because the songs originated as improvisations. The lead singer extemporized the words of a song as he went along, and had no time to think about rhyme, so great was his concern for the idea he wanted to express. Perhaps during the choral response he could think ahead a bit, but not always to the extent of perfecting the rhyme. The next time the song was sung, the leader might improvise different words in response to a different set of circumstances, or a different person might lead the singing. The choral refrain was the most permanent feature of the song. Bremer, as well as many others, observed this characteristic and wrote:

> All these songs are peculiarly improvisations. . . . This improvisation goes forward every day. . . . The rhyme comes as it may, sometimes clumsily, sometimes no rhyme at all, sometimes most wonderfully fresh and perfect.

There are some words, some phrases, some lines that reappear so consistently from song to song that they can be regarded as "wandering" phrases and verses. Obviously at one time these wandering bits of text were associated with specific songs, but it is now impossible to trace them back to the original settings. There are, for example, the places to which the slaves refer in their songs—the wilderness, the valley, Jerusalem, Jericho, and the promised land. Any of these may be accompanied by adjectives—for example, "the lonesome valley" or "new Jerusalem." To get to one's destination, one travels up or down the road, which is "rocky" or "stormy" or "rough" or "heavenly," depending upon the circumstances. Occasionally there are references to chariots, but the slave knew from experience that the chief mode of travel was necessarily by foot. Then there are the ubiquitous allusions to water—particularly to the Jordan river or stream or banks—and to the boats that sail on the water, or to ships—particularly the Ship of Zion.

The slaves had their own scriptural heroes, their favorite—judging by the number of times they sang about him—being Jacob. The favorite antihero was Satan, needless to say. Among other favorites mentioned in songs were Daniel, Moses, and Gabriel, the trumpet blower. But the blowing of trumpets occurs as well without Gabriel, as does the ringing of bells again and again—sometimes "heavenly" bells. Another musical reference is to "the band," which listeners and singers were admonished to join. Among the whole stanzas that are carried from one song to another is this one:

> One morning as I was walking along,
> I saw the berries hanging down;
> I pick the berries and I suck the juice—
> It's sweeter than the honey comb [or Jes' as sweet as the
>   honey in the comb].

The stanza occurs in spirituals as well as social texts. Common refrain lines include: "Roll, Jordan, roll"; "Glory, Hallelujah"; "I look to the East and look to the West" (or "bury me in the East and bury me in the West," or "there's a fire in the East and fire in the West"); and "Ashes to ashes and dust to dust."

Thus in their songs the slaves reflected their way of life. While the original inspiration for a spiritual may have been a

Biblical story or a Protestant hymn (we shall return to this point), the poetic material was reshaped to the slaves' own immediate concerns. The religious songs are as down-to-earth and practical as the social songs. As we have seen, religious concepts are interpreted in the light of the slave's everyday experiences. Numerous examples could be cited but one will suffice to illustrate this point.

In the *Slave Songs* there is a spiritual, *Pray All de Members*, with a text about prayer and symbolic journeys to Jericho and Jerusalem. Suddenly, the sixth and seventh stanzas jerk the listener back to the concrete everyday world: "Patrol around me, Thank God he no catch me." Now there are no patrols in the spiritual world waiting to catch unwary pilgrims, and one cannot help thinking that the singer is concerned not so much with a journey to Jerusalem as with a trip to the next plantation for a secret religious meeting, perhaps, or to freedom in the North. Jerusalem and Jericho are being used as code names for actual places, and the maker of the song simply has neglected to invest the patrols with similar symbolic garb. We know, of course, from the testimony of ex-slaves that the religious songs, more than any others, often had double meanings and were used as code songs.

Again and again the same themes are represented in the folksongs, both religious and nonreligious. Some of these themes can be anticipated, for they are the themes of any oppressed people who are determined "to overcome." First, there is *faith*—faith that someday slavery will be no more. The slave knows that Jesus will come to his rescue, whether he is wrestling with Jacob, fighting Satan, or searching for a way out of the wilderness. Closely associated with faith is *optimism*. A song proclaims that the winter will soon be over; other songs remind the slaves that the sun is shining and the bells are ringing. *Patience* is necessary. If one cannot depend upon his own inner resources, then one must pray to the Lord for help, ask Jesus to give more patience. At the same time, the song maker cries out, "how much longer?" He is discouraged, weary, and ill; his body is wracked with pain and fever. He even welcomes death as a reliever of his misery. The *weariness* theme sounds in almost all the songs, sometimes in the opening verses but more frequently in the later ones. Surprisingly, for a so-called meek people, there is a great deal of emphasis on the theme of *fighting*. True, the fight is frequently symbolic—a fight with Satan or Jacob or sin. But in numerous instances all pretense is dropped; the slave plans to fight until he dies.

Despite their isolation on the plantations, the slaves were aware of the bitter conflict shaping in the United States during the middle decades of the nineteenth century that was to result in the Civil War. There was constant movement from plantation to plantation and from state to state—particularly from Virginia to the states in the deep South—as slaves were sold, exchanged, or sent out "for hire." The news was spread of aborted slave revolts, of the militance of the abolitionists and their Underground Railroad to freedom. Eventually, a body of plantation war songs developed in the South, in response to the unsettled condition of the nation.

RELATIONSHIP BETWEEN TEXT AND MUSIC

Generally, but not always, the opening verses of Negro folksongs tend to be syllabic—that is, there is one note for each syllable. Succeeding verses are another matter! Once a pattern has been set, any number of syllables may be sung on a single pitch. One of the editors of the *Slave Songs* explained it thus:

> Neither should any one be repelled by any difficulty in adapting the words to the tunes. The negroes keep exquisite time in singing, and do not suffer themselves to be daunted by any obstacle in the words. The most obstinate Scripture phrases or snatches from hymns they will force to do duty with any tune they please, and will dash heroically through a trochaic tune at the head of a column of iambs with wonderful skill.

The melisma, a passage of several notes sung to a single syllable, is not characteristic of Negro folksong style, but can be found occasionally, as in the following example:

Ex. VII.10 *I'm Gwine to Alabamy*, from *Slave Songs of the United States*

2. She went from Ole Virginny,—Oh,
   And I'm her pickaninny,—Ah.
3. She lives on the Tombigbee,—Oh,
   I wish I had her wid me,—Ah.
4. Now I'm a good big nigger,—Oh,
   I reckon I won't git bigger,—Ah.
5. But I'd like to see my mammy,—Oh,
   Who lives in Alabamy,—Ah.

One might expect that text repetition should be matched by musical repetition, and this does happen in the simpler songs:

Ex. VII.11 *Tell My Jesus "Morning,"* from *Slave Songs of the United States*

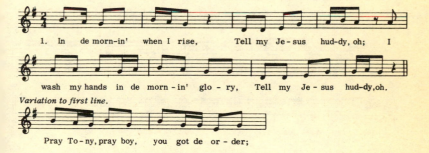

2. Mornin', Hester, mornin', gal,
   Tell my Jesus, &c.

(To the Variation.)

2. Say, brudder Sammy, you got de order,
   Tell my Jesus, &c.
3. You got de order, and I got de order.

More often, however, exact repetition of poetic lines is not matched by repeating musical phrases. In the first place, the music of a song is typically organized into four-phrase units, regardless of the text form. Within each unit the first and third phrases correspond (see Examples VII.12 and 13). If the song consists of two units, the units are pulled together into an eight-phrase form because of the correspondence between phrases 4 and 8 which carry the refrains. There may, or may not, also be a correspondence between phrases 2 and 6. In the first of the two examples given below, the text form is call-and-response, while in the second the text has an a-a-a-Refrain structure. Observe, however, that the musical patterns for both songs are similar.

Ex. VII.12 *I Heard from Heaven To-Day*, from *Slave Songs of the United States*

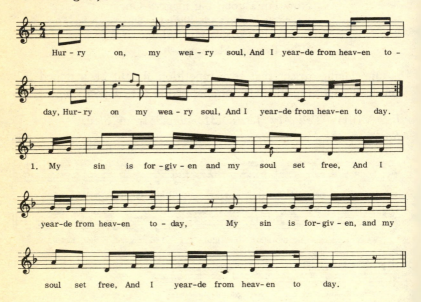

2. A baby born in Bethlehem,
      And I yearde, &c.
3. De trumpet sound in de oder bright land.
4. My name is called and I must go.
5. De bell is a-ringin' in de oder bright world.

Ex. VII.13 *Hail, Mary,* from *Slave Songs of the United States*

A third music pattern consists of four different phrases, a-b-c-d, associated with the text pattern a-a-a-b.

Ex. VII.14 *Huntin' for a City,* from *Slave Songs of the United States*

MUSICAL FEATURES OF THE SONGS

It is impossible in light of the available evidence to gain an accurate insight into the true musical nature of slave music. As we have pointed out, in the collecting process the large body of social music was neglected in favor of the smaller, less typical religious repertory. Moreover, the early transcribers of the songs, by their own admission, were unable to record the more exotic songs they heard—that is, the songs most African in expression and, consequently, most characteristic. And the transcribers admitted to uncertainty about the accuracy of the songs they did record. In this regard Lucy McKim Garrison wrote in 1862:

> It is difficult to express the entire character of these negro ballads by mere musical notes and signs. The odd turns made in the throat, and the curious rhythmic effect produced by single voices chiming in at different irregular intervals, seem almost as impossible to place on the score as the singing of birds or the tones of an Aeolian Harp.

A year later Spaulding admitted to the same difficulty in his recording of melodies:

> The tunes to which these songs are sung, are some of them weird and wild—barbaric madrigals—while others are sweet and impressive melodies. The most striking of their barbaric airs it would be impossible to write out.

And the compiler of the Hampton spirituals reports in a similar vein on his problems:

> Tones are frequently employed which we have no musical characters to represent. Such, for example, is that which I have indicated as nearly as possible by the flat seventh. . . . The tones are variable in pitch, ranging through an entire octave on different occasions, according to the inspiration of the singer.

Obviously then, the songs as written down in extant collections must represent only an approximation of slave music as it actually sounded. The twentieth-century ethnomusicologist Bruno Nettl has explained carefully the problems confronting a transcriber whose ears are accustomed to the sound of western music. He cautions:

> . . . make no mistake about this: What you hear is conditioned not only by what sound is actually produced, but also by what sound your mind is attuned to and expects. Consequently, transcribing is a process that requires hearing and rehearing a piece; a minute of music may take two hours to transcribe.

MELODY AND SCALES

As written down in the documents, most melodies use the tones of either the major scale or the pentatonic scale. These scales tend to produce bright, cheerful melodies. But according to contemporary reports, the slaves' singing rarely was bright and cheerful; it was generally described as being in a minor key or as being plaintive, mournful, or wild. Bremer wrote about a song, for example: "I wish I could give you an idea of [it], so fresh was the melody, and so peculiar the key." Even in their gayest songs there were "overtones of melancholy." It seems unlikely, therefore, that the original versions of slave songs were actually in the major mode. More probably, these songs, like many Negro folksongs of the twentieth century, did indeed use the major and pentatonic scales but with some tones of these scales altered—most often, to a lower pitch.

There are just enough hints in the 1867 collection to suggest how this alteration may have operated. In many songs, the editors have used accidentals to indicate such alterations. Most frequently in a major melody, it is the seventh tone of the scale that is flatted, indicating that the tone was sung lower than normally (as C D E F G A B♭ C). Frequently, such a song includes both flatted and normal seventh tones.

Ex. VII.15   *Roll, Jordan, Roll,* Traditional

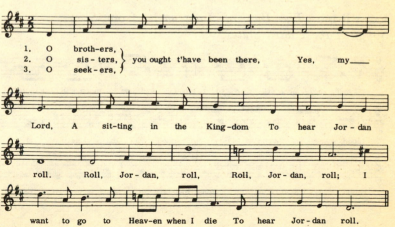

Some songs include more than one altered tone, as in the following examples:

Ex. VII.16a *Sabbath Has No End*, from *Slave Songs of the United States*

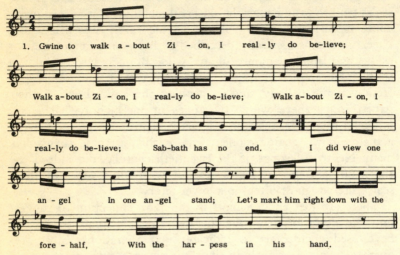

1. Gwine to walk a-bout Zi - on, I real-ly do be-lieve; Walk a-bout Zi - on, I real-ly do be-lieve; Walk a-bout Zi - on, I real-ly do be-lieve; Sab-bath has no end. I did view one an - gel In one an-gel stand; Let's mark him right down with the fore - half, With the har - pess in his hand.

2. Gwine to follow King Jesus, I really do believe.
3. I love God certain.
4. My sister's got religion.
5. Set down in the kingdom.
6. Religion is a fortune.

Ex. VII.16b *The Day of Judgement*, from *Slave Songs of the United States*

And de moon will turn to blood, And de moon will turn to blood, And de moon will turn to blood in dat day. O joy, my soul! And de moon will turn to blood in dat day.

2. And you'll see de stars a-fallin'.
3. And de world will be on fire.
4. And you'll hear de saints a-singin'

To be sure, the observations of contemporary reporters were not altogether incorrect; a small number of the songs actually are based on the minor scale. And there are a few songs that use tones of the so-called medieval church modes (Dorian, Phrygian, Lydian, Mixolydian, Aeolian). For example, the following song suggests the minor but actually uses tones of the Dorian mode (as D E F G A B C D).

Ex. VII.17   *Dis Is de Trouble of de World*, from
Slave Songs of the United States

Finally, there are some songs with implications so vague that it is difficult to decide which scale serves as a basis for the melodies.

According to the testimony of nineteenth-century writers, the slaves also sang melodies using only one, two, or three tones. None of these are preserved, however, in the musical records. Significantly, these melodies were labeled as African and were associated with rituals of various types. It will be recalled that Latrobe, watching the dancers in the Place Congo of New

Orleans, described the singing that accompanied one group as follows:

> The women squalled out a burden [that is, refrain] . . . consisting of two notes.

For another group:

> A man sung an uncouth song . . . which I suppose was in some African language . . . and the women screamed a detestable burden on one single note.

With regard to three-tone melodies, Fredrika Bremer relates that she persuaded an elderly slave in Charleston, South Carolina, to sing for her "an Ethiopian death-song, which seemed to consist of a monotone vibration upon three semi-tones." Although no written examples of two- or three-tone melodies are preserved in American sources, we can obtain some understanding of the nature of these songs by referring to African music—for in some parts of Africa such songs are common.

The slave songs exhibit varying types of melodic contours and lines. Some melodies rise gently in an undulating line to high pitches, then fall slowly to the final tones, thus taking on the contour of symmetrical curves.

Ex. VII.18   *I Am a-Trouble in de Mind*, from *Slave Songs of the United States*

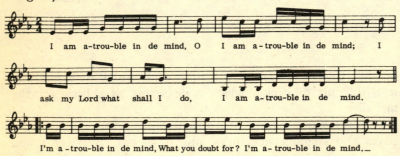

Other melodies show a succession of such curves, each phrase having its own rise and fall. In contrast, there are melodies composed of successive concave curves.

Ex. VII.19   *Satan's Camp a-Fire*, from *Slave Songs of the United States*

The songs vary in regard to compass—that is, in regard to the difference in pitch between the lowest and the highest notes of a melody. With the exception of the sorrow songs, few songs have compasses smaller than an octave, and many extend over a range of a tenth or a twelfth. Within the confines of the melodic range there is an emphasis on pentatonic patterns, even when the melodies derive from six- or seven-tone scales. One example will illustrate this point. The following melody uses the tones of the E♭-major scale, but because of the persistent emphasis on the tones E♭-F-G-B♭-C it suggests the pentatonic instead of the major:

Ex. VII.20   *Jesus on de Water-Side*, from *Slave Songs of the United States*

The sorrow songs as a group tend to have a small compass—sometimes as small as a third or fourth from lowest to highest tones.

RHYTHMIC FEATURES

Rhythm is the most striking feature of the slave music. This is obvious even though the transcribers made errors in some of the rhythmic notation as they did in their notation of pitch. The rhythms were much more complex in actual performance than the music scores indicate. Allen freely admits this:

> What makes it all the harder to unravel a thread of melody out of this strange network is that, like birds, they [that is, the black singers] seem not infrequently to strike sounds that cannot be precisely represented by the gamut, and abound in "slides from one note to another and turns and cadences not in articulated notes." . . . There are also apparent irregularities in the time [that is, rhythm], which it is no less difficult to express accurately.

Nevertheless, certain general observations can be made. Except for the field hollers, which have their own free rhythmic patterns, the slave songs show a decided preference for simple duple meters, as distinguished from triple meters. In performance, the steady beats of a song's meter were maintained by hand clapping and foot tapping.

The modern scholar Richard Waterman has used the term *metronome sense* to refer to the African tradition for

> conceiving music as structured along a theoretical framework of beats regularly spaced in time . . . whether or not the beats are expressed in actual melodic or percussion tones. . . . Since this metronone sense is of such basic importance . . . it is assumed without question or consideration to be part of the perceptual equipment of both musicians and listeners and is, in the most complete way, taken for granted.

Typically the slave melodies are marked by syncopation. As a consequence the melodic accents are shifted from the strong beats of the music to the weaker beats, and there is a conflict set up between accents in the melody and the foot tapping or hand clapping, which represents metrical accents. Example

Ex. VII.21 *Nobody Knows de Trouble I've Had,*
from *Slave Songs of the United States*

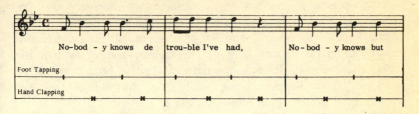

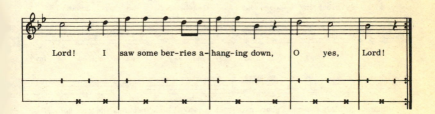

2. I pick de berry and I suck de juice, O yes, Lord!
   Just as sweet as the honey in de comb, O yes, Lord!
3. Sometimes I'm up, sometimes I'm down,
   Sometimes I'm almost on de groun'.
4. What make ole Satan hate me so?
   Because he got me once and he let me go.

VII.21 illustrates this point; the top line indicates the melody of a song, the second line the strong-beat accents, and the bottom line the syncopated patterns.

Syncopation, if constant and continuous, is extremely exciting, particularly when it not only shifts accents from the regular beats 1 and 3 to beats 2 and 4 but also emphasizes subdivisions of the beats (as in mm. 1–7 of the melody above). When the song also includes dotted-note patterns (as happens frequently) and triplets (as happens occasionally) the rhythmic interest becomes even greater (see Example VII.20).

The tempos of the slave songs varied according to the social context in which the songs were performed. The observations of Lucy McKim Garrison illustrate how the tempo of a song was changed according to its function:

> As the same songs . . . are sung at every sort of work, of course the *tempo* is not always alike. On the water, the oars dip "Poor Rosy" to an even *andante;* a stout boy and girl at the hominy mill will make the same "Poor Rosy" fly, to keep up with the whirl-

Ex. VII.22 *Poor Rosy,* from *Slave Songs of the United States*

1. Poor Ro-sy, poor__ gal; Poor Ro-sy, poor__ gal;
Ro-sy break my poor heart, Heav'n shall-a be my home.
I__ can-not stay_ in_ hell one day, Heav'n shall-a be my
home; I'll_ sing and pray_my_ soul a-way, Heav'n shall-a be my home.

2. Got hard trial in my way,
    Heav'n shall-a be my home.
  O when I talk, I talk wid God,
    Heav'n shall-a be my home.
3. I dunno what de people want of me,
    Heav'n shall-a be my home.

ing stone; and in the evening, after the day's work is done, "Heab'n shall-a be my home" [the refrain of *Poor Rosy*] peals up slowly and mournfully from the distant quarters.

One old slave, who had seen more than her share of tragedy, said, "I likes 'Poor Rosy' better than all the songs, but it can't be sung without a *full heart and a troubled spirit*."

A spiritual sung during a prayer service was performed at a slower tempo than when used to accompany a shout. The tempo of a song might also vary during the course of the singing—as, for example, during the shout, when the shouters begin shuffling slowly around in a circle, then gradually move more rapidly,

the song getting faster and faster, till at last only the most marked part of the refrain is sung, and the shuffling, stamping, and clapping get furious.

MUSICAL TEXTURE

Normally we classify music as (1) *monophonic*, when there is just the melody, one note at a time; (2) *polyphonic*, when there are two or more melodies going on simultaneously; or (3) *homophonic*, when the melody has subsidiary accompanying parts. The scores of the slave songs indicate that the music was monophonic. And more than one nineteenth-century writer states that the singing was in unison. But some evidence contradicts this testimony. Again and again the choral singing of the slaves is described in terms of homophony; for example, as "a torrent of sacred harmony." Moreover, several writers refer to the songs of the slaves as "barbaric madrigals." Since the madrigal is a polyphonic form, presumably the term madrigal was used with reference to the polyphonic character of the songs.

The song collectors frankly admitted the difficulties involved in trying to put into musical notation the sounds of the slave songs when sung by groups. Allen, chief editor of the *Slave Songs*, writes:

The voices of the colored people have a peculiar quality that nothing can imitate; and the intonations and delicate variations of even one singer cannot be reproduced on paper. And I despair of conveying any notion of the effect of a number singing together, especially in a complicated shout. . . . There is no singing in *parts*, as we understand it, and yet no two [singers] appear to be singing the same thing.

He continues to describe in detail what happens during the course of the singing. The lead singer always began the song. The others joined the singing on the refrains, or even in the verses if they knew the words. Most often, however, the lead singer improvised new words for the verses as he sang. Those who constituted the chorus called themselves "basers"; when they came in on the refrains, they were "basing" the leader.

. . . the "basers" themselves seem to follow their own whims, beginning when they please and leaving off when they please, striking an octave above or below (in case they have pitched the tune too low or too high), or hitting some other note that chords, so as to produce the effect of a marvellous complication and variety, and yet with the most perfect time, and rarely with any discord.

It is important to emphasize that individuals might begin to sing the refrain before the leader concluded his solo, and that the leader might begin his next solo before the chorus had finished. Scholars refer to this phenomenon as *overlapping call-and-response* patterns. Obviously, these procedures produced unorthodox harmonic sounds, as Allen observed, but the diverse elements were tied together because of the governance of the strong rhythms.

William Barton makes an effort to write down in a few songs some of the "extra tones" that he heard accompanying melodies. He introduces *In Dat Great Day* with these sentences:

In theory the song is sung in unison, and there is no harmony proper. But in practice the more independent singers introduce grace notes and slurs, and the higher and lower voices range above and below in fifths and thirds in the more descriptive portions [of the text], especially in the latter verses. In this song the melody of "O Israel, O Israel" is given in the first line [that is, the soprano part] where those words are used, and in the notes which run nearest the tonic; but as the song proceeds this simple theme is worked out quite elaborately and with much greater variety than the notes here indicate.

Ex. VII.23   *In Dat Great Day*, from Barton

2. Don' you see de dead arisin'? etc.
3. Don' you heah de trumpet soundin'?
4. Don' you see dem tombs a-bustin'?
5. Yes, we'll see our chillen risin'.
6. Don' you see de chariot comin'?
7. Don' you see de sinnah tremblin'?
8. Don' you heah de saints a-shoutin'?

To summarize, the slave songs were not typically sung in unison, despite evidence to the contrary in the music sources, where most of the songs are written down as melodies. And yet the term polyphonic, in its true meaning, hardly applies to the singing, for the slaves did not believe themselves to be singing different melodies at the same time. Perhaps the best descriptive word is *heterophony*, in that the singers followed the lead melody for the most part but allowed themselves to wander away from it when its tones were too high, or when the text called for special emphasis, or simply when their whims indicated the need for more variety. Since, in an important aspect, the musical texture of the songs is closely related to performance practices, we shall touch upon this matter again.

PERFORMANCE PRACTICES

By all accounts the music of the slaves was inseparable from some form of body movement—if not dancing or working, then hand clapping, foot tapping, or swaying of the body. A reporter writing for the *Knickerbocker Magazine* in 1845 identified this quality in the following statement:

> Without any teaching, the Negroes have contrived a rude kind of opera, combining the poetry of motion, of music, and of language . . . all the Negro songs were intended to be performed as well as sung and played.

In the eighteenth and early part of the nineteenth centuries the performances of the slaves were, of course, more spectacular than in later years, involving as they did hundreds and sometimes thousands of slaves performing the traditional ring dances.

We have discussed already the various examples of this spectacle: the Pinkster dances in New York, the jubilees in Philadelphia, and the Place Congo dances in New Orleans. The musical forces were elaborate in all of these performances. Almost always there were several sizes of drums, string instruments, sometimes woodwinds and horns, and various types of small percussion instruments. To the sound of instruments was added that of human voices and hand clapping. All these elements blended to make the whole. The human voice, given a song of chantlike character with little emphasis on its text, was employed essentially as a melody instrument, while hand clapping functioned as a percussive element.

The demise in the nineteenth century of the huge spectacle effected no basic changes in the character of the slave performance, merely a reduction of forces. In the ring shout, for example, melodic elements were represented by human voices and percussive elements by hand clapping and foot tapping. As in the earlier spectacles, poetic elements were almost entirely absent, for the song fragments that composed the shout spirituals were hardly meant to convey verbal messages. Black folk used other types of songs for this purpose.

The work songs of the slaves generally followed in the same tradition, although on a smaller scale. Stevedore songs, rowing songs, rice-threshing or corn-shucking songs—in all of these, percussive effects were employed to support the melodies, which were sung in coordination with the body movements of the work activity. The percussive sounds may have derived from actions as obvious as pounding, chopping, and flailing, or as subtle as the dipping of oars into water, but to the singers such sounds were an important part of the performance. The relative unimportance of the text is indicated by the fact that frequently it consisted of nonsense phrases or syllables, with only the refrain alluding to the work activity itself. Even when performing alone the black musician tended to add percussive effects to the melody produced by his voice or a string instrument. A slave singer drummed an accompaniment on a board as he sang; the banjo player tapped his foot as he played and sang; a boy "patted juba" at the same time as he recited the words of a jig so that his companions could dance without music of the fiddle.

It may be that the *performance* of vocal music should be regarded as the single most important factor in slave music. It was the performance that shaped the song, that determined its rhythm, melody, texture, tempo, text, and, finally, its effect upon listeners. This was largely because of the importance of improvisation in the African tradition. The song as written down represented but one performance, in which the chief stable elements were the meter, the refrain texts, and the basic outlines of the melody. All else changed from performance to performance: syncopations and dotted rhythms were introduced at different places; embellishments and pitch alterations were added to or eliminated from the melody; the "basers" joined the singing or dropped out of it at varying time intervals and provided different harmonizing tones for the melody. Even the general form of the piece might have been changed by the repetition of refrain lines or choruses.

In regard to all these matters, Allen directs a note of encouragement to the users of his collection:

> We have aimed to give all the characteristic variations [for the songs] which have come into our hands, whether as single notes or whole lines, or even longer passages; and of words as well as

tunes. . . . It may sometimes be a little difficult . . . to determine precisely [the relationship between all these things]. . . . However much latitude the reader may take in all such matters, he will hardly take more than the negroes themselves do. . . . The rests [in the notated songs], by the way, do not indicate a cessation in the music, but only in part of the singers. They overlap in singing, as already described, in such a degree that at no time is there any complete pause.

Adding to all this complexity was the practice of audience participation—indeed, in the strict sense of the term there was no audience; there were only singers and nonsingers. The white listeners might sit quietly, showing their appreciation of a performance by facial expression and applause at appropriate times, but the slaves actively participated in the performance, not only by clapping and tapping, but also by constantly interjecting spoken or chanted words to reinforce the meaning of the text, such as "Yes, Lord," "O Lord," "I say now," and similar short phrases. The nature of these interjections depended upon the occasion. Colonel Higginson observed that on one occasion the men watching a shout gave encouragement by yelling, "Wake 'em, brudder!" and "Stan' up to 'em, brudder!"

The voice quality cultivated by the slaves was high-pitched and of great intensity. Without exception, contemporary accounts refer to the "far-sounding harmony," "vigorous chorus," or the "great billows of sound" produced by the slaves' singing. When the slaves gathered for corn-shucking jubilees, in some places as many as three hundred or more would participate in the singing as they marched along the roads, their "rich, deep voices swelling out" on the refrains. Even the singing of two slaves as they walked through a forest "would make the dense old woods, for miles around, reverberate with their wild songs." When the slaves sang psalms and hymns during their religious services, they sang "loud and slow." Many a white slaveholder and his guests dropped off to sleep at night with the loud songs of the slaves ringing in his ears and awoke to the same sound the next morning. With regard to the individual voice, there are few contemporary references except those noting some slave's unusually wide range. Kemble does remark, however, that the voices of the slaves on her plantation seemed "oftener tenor than any other quality." And a number of reporters comment upon the free use of falsetto among the slaves, particularly in the field hollers.

ORIGIN OF THE FOLKSONGS

Rarely is it possible to identify the author of a folksong and to pinpoint its original form. Typically, folksongs are created by nonprofessional musicians, are performed by the common people, and are passed along from one generation to the next by oral transmission. In the process, the music is adapted to the taste of both those who sing and those who listen. The changes that take place become a part of the music, and inevitably the music takes on a different form than it originally had. Over the span of years the authors' names are forgotten.

There are three choices available to the folk composer who wishes to create a new song. Consciously or unconsciously, he may (1) improvise upon a song already in existence; (2) combine material from several old songs to make the new one; or (3) compose the song entirely of new materials. The African tradition favors the first process. Indeed, improvisation is so strong a factor in this tradition that changes are introduced into songs with each new performance. Above all, music in the African tradition is functional. Consequently, the melody of a song often serves chiefly as a vehicle for the text, and is constantly adjusted to fit, even as the singer extemporizes from one verse to the next.

As we have seen, slave music was squarely in the African tradition with respect to improvisation. All the evidence indicates that a large number of the slave songs represent "variations upon a theme"—that is, the songs seem to be altered versions of very old songs. No doubt many of these songs—the social songs, in particular—were brought over from Africa and passed down from parents to children. Almost every contemporary source contains references to slaves born in Africa who helped to keep African traditions alive in their communities during the eighteenth and nineteenth centuries. And the continuous influx of new slaves helped to revive traditions that were in danger of dying out, whether the newcomers came from Africa, the West Indies, or another state. Thus, it has been possible for researchers to find a number of direct parallels between African melodies and slave tunes, and future research will undoubtedly reveal many more.

Contemporary reporters were very much aware of the African originals and used such words as "wild," "barbaric," "uncivilized," and "strangely attractive" in referring to these songs. The song collectors, too, identified these songs and, as we have noted, for the most part did not even try to notate them because of the difficulties involved. Editor Allen regarded several songs of the 1867 collection as being either partly or wholly of African origin. He points out that, although the majority of the songs in his collection are "civilized,"

> It is very likely that if we had found it possible to get at more of their secular music, we should have come to another conclusion as to the proportion of the barbaric element.

To return to our list of the choices available to folksong composers, it would appear that the second accounts for a considerable number of the spiritual texts (as distinguished from the social songs), except that the songs used lines from the Scriptures and Protestant hymns, rather than older existing songs, as raw material. To the sacred verses the slaves added their own verses, refrains, and choruses to make up complete songs. As we saw in Chapter IV, black folk in the United States had developed their own Protestant-hymn tradition by the end of the eighteenth century, the core of which was a body of Dr. Watts' hymns, supplemented by the hymns of black preachers and the folk hymns in oral circulation among the Baptists and Methodists of the time. Richard Allen's hymnal of 1801, being a "folk-selected anthology," indicates clearly which hymns were favored among the blacks. The literary sources of the nineteenth century refer again and again to certain of these hymns, and the music sources include spirituals obviously derived from them. One or two examples will suffice here to illustrate this point.

By all accounts, one of the most popular of all hymns among Negroes during the ante-bellum period was written by Dr. Watts, *When I Can Read My Title Clear*, which is No. 26 in Allen's collection:

When I can read my title clear
    To mansions in the skies,
I'll bid farewell to ev'ry fear,
    And wipe my weeping eyes.

Should earth against my soul engage,
    And hellish darts be hurl'd,
Then I can smile at Satan's rage
    And face a frowning world.

Let care, like a wild deluge come,
    And storms of sorrows fall;
May I but safely reach my home,
    My God, my heav'n, my all:

There shall I bathe my weary soul,
    In seas of heav'nly rest,
And not a wave of trouble roll
    Across my peaceful breast.

The hymn gave rise to several spirituals, one of which is the following:

Good Lord, in the mansions above,
Good Lord, in the mansions above,
My Lord, I hope to meet my Jesus
In the mansions above.

My Lord, I've had many crosses,
And trials here below;
My Lord, I hope to meet you,
In the mansions above.

Fight on, my brother,
For the mansions above;
For I hope to meet my Jesus there,
In the mansions above.

In this spiritual, the folk composer has taken the basic concept of the Watts hymn—which was written for white Protestants—and has restated it in the language of his own people. The second line of the hymn, with a slight change, becomes the refrain of the spiritual. The essence of the hymn is caught in the second stanza of the spiritual—that the singer wishes to exchange the conflicts of earthly life for the peace of a heavenly one. The rest of the hymn is unimportant to the slave composer.

Another hymn, No. 10 in Allen's hymnal, served as an inspiration for an even larger number of spirituals:

> Behold the awful trumpet sounds,
>   The sleeping dead to raise,
> And calls the nations underground:
>   O how the saints will praise!
>
> Behold the Saviour how he comes
>   Descending from his throne
> To burst asunder all our tombs
>   And lead his children home.
>
> But who can bear that dreadful day,
>   To see the world in flames:
> The burning mountains melt away,
>   While rocks run down in streams.
>
> The falling stars their orbits leave,
>   The sun in darkness hide:
> The elements asunder cleave,
>   The moon turn'd into blood!
>
> Behold the universal world
>   In consternation stand,
> The wicked unto Hell are turn'd
>   The Saints at God's right hand.
>
> O then the music will begin
>   Their Saviour God to praise,
> They all are freed from every sin
>   And thus they'll spend their days!

One of the best known of the derivative spirituals is the following, found in both the Fisk and Hampton collections:

> My Lord, what a morning,
> My Lord, what a morning,

> My Lord, what a morning,
> When the stars begin to fall.
>
> You'll hear the trumpet sound,
> To wake the nations underground,
> Looking to my God's right hand,
> When the stars begin to fall.

Here the vivid imagination of the folk composer seizes upon the significance of the awesome events that will take place on Judgement Day according to the hymn, and gives first his personal reaction: "My Lord, what a morning." Then he proceeds to enumerate the events, using for the most part the same phrases as in the hymn. The result is, however, an entirely new song with new music and a new form. (Obviously the old hymn tune, whatever it was, no longer fits.)

There are several more elaborate variations on the theme of this original hymn. In one song, Judgement Day has become "that great getting-up morning." The structure of the song is the call-and-response form, with the refrain "fare you well, fare you well" occurring after each single line. The chorus of the song establishes the basic mood:

Ex. VII.24   *In That Great Getting-Up Morning*, Traditional

After a twenty-line introduction consisting of original material, the slave composer takes the first stanza of the hymn and expands it into a little story. He gives the trumpet to Gabriel, who holds a lengthy conversation with the Lord about how he is to blow:

> The Lord spoke to Gabriel
>
> [*Throughout the song the refrain follows each line of the text, as in the first stanza.*]
>
> Go look behind the altar
> Take down the silver trumpet
> Blow your trumpet, Gabriel

> Lord, how loud shall I blow it
> Blow it right calm and easy
> Do not alarm my people
> Tell 'em to come to judgement
>
> Gabriel blow your trumpet
> Lord, how loud shall I blow it
> Loud as seven peals of thunder
> Wake the living nations

Further instructions are given to Gabriel and he is forewarned of what will happen upon the sounding of the trumpet—all this in accordance with the text of the original hymn, but in the idiomatic language of the slaves.

> Place one foot upon the dry land
> Place the other on the sea
> Then you'll see the coffins bursting
> See the dry bones come a-creeping
>
> Hell shall be uncapped and burning
> Then the dragons shall be loosened
> Where you running poor sinner?
> Where you running poor sinner?
>
> Then you'll see poor sinners rising
> Then you'll see the world on fire
> See the moon a-bleeding
> See the stars a-falling
>
> See the elements a-melting
> See the forked lightning
> Then you'll cry out for cold water
> When the Christians shout in glory
>
> Hear the rumbling of the thunder
> Earth shall reel and totter
> Then you'll see the Christians rising
> Then you'll see the righteous marching

The song concludes with the arrival of the Christians in heaven:

> See them marching home to heaven
> Take the righteous home to glory
> There they'll live with God forever
> On the right handside of my Saviour

Thus a spiritual of almost heroic proportions has been fashioned from the material of a single hymn (less than half of the spiritual text is quoted above; the interpolation of the refrain line after each line of text and the choruses after the stanzas draw out the song to considerable length). The original hymn did not satisfy the needs of the slaves so they improvised upon it to such an extent that a new song was created.

Not always does a spiritual point back to a single hymn or scriptural passage. In the following example ideas are drawn from both the hymns cited above (observe the italicized lines):

> *When every star refuses to shine,*
> Rocks and mountains don't fall on me;
> I know that King Jesus will-a be mine,
> Rocks and mountains don't fall on me.
> *The trumpet shall sound and the dead shall rise,*
> Rocks and mountains don't fall on me;
> *And go to the mansions in-a the skies,*
> Rocks and mountains don't fall on me.

Of the songs created from new materials, those songs that relate to current events or specific activities or specific persons are most numerous. Into this category fall also the sorrow songs and many of the songs associated with recreational activities—for example, the patting songs. Some spirituals were composed as homiletic songs and taught to the congregation by the preacher or the deacon. Black ministers took seriously the admonition of Dr. Isaac Watts:

> Ministers are to cultivate gifts of preaching and prayer through study and diligence; they ought also to cultivate the capacity of composing spiritual songs and exercise it along with the other parts of worship, preaching and prayer.

The congregations contributed their share to the composition of these songs, their interjected expressions developing into song refrains.

Sometimes an excited preacher would be carried away by his emotion and compose a song on the spot—that is, during the sermon itself. More than one contemporary writer witnessed such occurrences. William Wells Brown writes, for example, of visiting a church in Nashville, Tennessee, where the sermon was preached by "an educated minister from Cincinnati" whose aim was "to set the congregation to shouting." Although Brown disapproved of the procedures, he remained for the service and later described what had happened. At a certain point in the sermon, the minister took from his pocket a letter and said, "When you reach the other world you'll be hunting for your mother, and the angel will read from this paper." This statement was repeated again and again as the minister walked back and forth on the pulpit platform. His voice grew higher and higher in pitch as he repeated the words, until he was almost singing. The congregation became excited; soon various members began to cry out: "Let that angel come right down now and read that letter," "Yes, yes, I want to hear the letter," "Come, Jesus, come or send an angel to read the letter," "Lord, send us the power," in addition to the more usual cries, "Amen," "Glory, Hallelujah," "Yes, Lord." It does not take too much imagination to recreate the scene, for parallel occurrences can be found today among black churches in rural areas and in ghetto areas of the cities. The spirituals that originated in the emotionally charged atmosphere of the religious service have been called "preaching spirituals" by some modern writers.

The melodies of the slave songs typically represent original composition rather than a borrowing of older tunes. In the preface to the *Slave Songs*, Allen pointed out that although he had searched diligently in white hymnals, he was able "to find hardly a trace of the tunes" of the spirituals. Other writers as well refer to the wild, original tunes of the slaves. Not that the slaves were averse to borrowing tunes for their improvised verses from popular songs, Anglo-American folksongs, minstrel songs, and even hymns. The fact was, as Higginson noted,

> As they learned all their songs by ear, they often strayed into wholly new versions, which sometimes became popular, and entirely banished the others.

In effect, slave-song melodies were reshaped by the process of "communal re-recreation"—regardless of their origin—into characteristic Afro-American music. A stylistic unity among these melodies results from the traditional preference for pentatonic-scale patterns (or major and minor patterns with altered tones) and rhythmic complexities, particularly syncopation.

DISPERSION OF THE FOLK MUSIC

While any positive pronouncements on the origin and dispersion of the slave songs would necessarily be speculative, one can venture a few assumptions based on clues provided by nineteenth- and twentieth-century writers. It would seem that Philadelphia was a major focal point of creative activity. That city saw the birth of the independent black church, whose minister published the first hymnal for black congregations and thereby helped to shape the development of a Protestant-hymn tradition among Negroes. As the A. M. E. and the later A. M. E. Zion Churches grew and established branches throughout the East and the South, they exported their favorite hymns, accompanied by the related spirituals, to other communities. As we have seen, Negroes were heard singing their own composed spirituals and stevedore songs in the Philadelphia area early in the nineteenth century. And as late as 1867, song collectors were still acknowledging their indebtedness to black folk of Philadelphia for original versions of some of the slave songs; for example, in the introduction to the *Slave Songs*.

In his study, *The Philadelphia Negro* (1899), W. E. B. DuBois points out the primacy of Philadelphia with regard to Negro life in the nineteenth century:

> Philadelphia was the natural gateway between North and South; through it passed a stream of free blacks and fugitive slaves toward the North, and of recaptured Negroes and kidnapped blacks toward the South.

Not only would black preachers have served as song carriers when they went South to organize congregations, but slaves and ex-slaves also would have helped to disperse Negro songs. Not to be forgotten are the black watermen who loaded and unloaded their cargoes on the wharves of Philadelphia and Baltimore and carried their songs from one port of the nation to another as well as down into the West Indies.

Our first assumption, then, is that the Negroes of Philadelphia, and the independent black church especially, were catalytic forces in the dispersion of the slave songs. A second assumption is that the camp meeting was a place where the spiritual songs, in particular, originated and were dispersed. We discussed in Chapter IV how blacks would gather in their quarters after the services and improvise songs for "hours together." There can be no doubt that when these campers went back to their local communities they took the camp-meeting songs with them to be sung in their religious services. Few of these songs found their way into official hymnals, although an 1837 edition of the A. M. E. hymnal does include a single song entitled *A Camp-Meeting Hymn* (No. 502):

> Ye weary, heavy laden'd souls,
> Who are oppressed sore;
> Ye travelers through the wilderness
> To Canaan's peaceful shore;
> Through chilling winds and beating rains,
> The waters deep and cold,
> And enemies surrounding you—
> Take courage and be bold.

To the "Second Awakening" and its attendant camp meetings is given credit for having produced two other kinds of spirituals —the so-called white spiritual and the Pennsylvania Dutch spiritual. Just what the precise relationship was among the three strands of spiritual songs is not clear, except that all three point back to Protestant hymnody. This is not the place to examine the involved argument over whether blacks borrowed from whites or vice versa. Undoubtedly there was a great amount of interchange among all three groups, particularly in the Philadelphia area, which seems to be as important in the history of the white and the Pennsylvania Dutch spiritual as in that of the Negro spiritual. It should be noted, however, that long before Negroes began to attend camp meetings in large numbers, they were singing many of the songs regarded by some scholars as camp-meeting hymns. The evidence for this is provided by Richard Allen's hymnal of 1801, in which these hymn texts are printed.

CHAPTER VIII

The War Years and Emancipation

The 1860s were ushered in by a bitter intersectional war between white pro-slavery and anti-slavery forces, bringing drastic changes in the existing relationship between black men and white men in the United States. In the years just before the war, several events forewarned of the trouble to come. One of the first was the Compromise of 1850, which was intended to settle both the problem of the fugitive slave and the question of whether slavery should be permitted in the territories being annexed to the United States—California, Utah, and New Mexico (including what is now Arizona). The compromise was unsuccessful; abolitionists only increased their efforts in helping slaves to escape, and slaveholders stepped up their activities in recovering the fugitives, often kidnapping free blacks as well as runaways. The publication of Harriet Beecher Stowe's anti-slavery novel, *Uncle Tom's Cabin*, in 1852 served to further widen the growing gulf between North and South. When the Supreme Court decided in 1857 that a Negro could not be regarded as a citizen of the United States and, consequently, had no civil rights (in the so-called Dred Scott case), many of the abolitionists were convinced that war was inevitable if the slaves were ever to be freed.

Then came John Brown's raid on the federal arsenal at Harpers Ferry, Virginia, in 1859. He had planned—with the help of ardent abolitionists like himself, including several black men—to obtain enough ammunition in his raid to open fire on the slaveholders of Virginia. These plans were thwarted and Brown was hanged, but in the process he became a martyr to the cause of freedom. In 1860 an aroused people voted into the presidency of the

United States a man who was determined to prevent the country from falling apart and who had pronounced anti-slavery sentiments, although he was not an abolitionist.

When President Abraham Lincoln was called upon to defend Fort Sumpter on April 12, 1861, against an attack by secessionists, he called out federal troops, and the War Between the States began. As in previous wars, black men were among the first to offer their services to the Union—and, as in previous wars, their offers were at first rejected. It was not until the Fall of 1862 that blacks were permitted to enlist for service. Among the first troops to be organized were the First South Carolina Volunteer Regiment, the Fifty-fourth Massachusetts Regiment, a New Orleans regiment called the *Corps d'Afrique*, and the First Regiment of Kansas Colored Volunteers.

By the end of the Civil War in 1865, more than 186,000 black men had been inducted into the army as the "United States Colored Troops." They had been organized into the various existing kinds of regiments—166 in all, including 137 regular infantry, 13 heavy artillery, 10 light artillery, and 6 cavalry. Most troops were led by white commanding officers, but some regiments were staffed by black officers. Relatively large numbers of black musicians performed in army bands and afterward put to good use the skills they had developed during the war. In the Confederate army, slaves were employed in essential noncombatant services and in important war industries. Many southerners took their slaves with them to the front, mostly to serve as body servants, but also to perform other duties. The slave Josephus Blake and two fellows, for example, played fifes and drums for the regiment of their master, General John B. Gordon.

In addition to the black serviceman and the southern slave laborer, there was yet a third role played by the black man during the war years—that of "contraband of war." The term was applied to the fugitive slaves who fled by the thousands to the Union army lines, were settled in contraband camps, and placed under the supervision of federal forces. So much confusion resulted from the government's handling of the contrabands that various private elements among the whites organized themselves to assist the refugees. Chief among the newly established groups were educational missions and freedmen's relief associations.

The whites who came into contact with blacks as commanding officers, supervisors in contraband camps, and agents of educational missions were usually northerners, and most frequently these contacts represented their first close association with blacks. They brought to the experience a sincere desire to help and, at the same time, considerable curiosity about the recipients of their aid. They recorded their impressions and the events of everyday life among the blacks in a steady stream of published letters, journals, diaries, and narratives that ebbed only in the closing years of the nineteenth century. For the most part, the persons responsible for disseminating information about the musical practices of the black man and for collecting examples of Negro song during the 1860s were members of this group of concerned northerners.

Best known was Colonel Higginson of the South Carolina Volunteer Regiment—Harvard graduate, minister, and abolitionist. Higginson first published an article in the *Atlantic Monthly* (June, 1867) about the black man's songs and later wrote a book, *Army Life in a Black Regiment*, that contained additional information. The compilers of the historic 1867 collection of slave songs were all members of an educational mission that had been sent in 1861 to Port Royal on the coast of South Carolina, and most of the contributors to the collection were members of later missions sent to one or another of the islands off the coast of South Carolina and Georgia. The contributor Laura Towne, who spent thirty-eight years among the ex-slaves on St. Helena Island, made a number of sharp observations about musical practices there and also collected song texts. Among the most useful sources on music in the contraband camps is Elizabeth Botume's *First Days Amongst the Contrabands*.

MUSIC IN THE UNION ARMY

One of the first acts of the white commanding officers of Negro regiments was to procure instruments and music instructors for the formation of bands. In Massachusetts, for example, a special fund of $500 was contributed early during the recruiting stage to Colonel Robert Gould Shaw's Fifty-fourth Regiment for the purchase of musical instruments and uniforms, and a musician of the Fifty-eighth Regiment of New York was obtained to instruct the band. During the first months of organization a great deal of attention was given to drilling and evening parades. Recruits for the First Regiment of Kansas Colored Volunteers spent as many as five hours daily in drills and ended each day with a dress parade. The Fifty-fifth of Massachusetts had its first evening parade even before uniforms and arms had arrived from the government. White army bands and special drum corps composed of young black boys were used to provide music for drills during the period when black servicemen were being taught how to play band instruments.

A list of all the names of black army musicians is too long to be included here. We may cite, however, the names of several who early achieved a degree of fame for their musical skills as bandleaders or performers. Most of these men held the rank of principal musician or chief bugler in their regiments. Associated with regiments of Massachusetts were William DuPree, Eli Lett, Thomas Edward Platner, William Porter, John H. Moore, and Alfred C. Peleter. Since men were recruited from all over the nation for the first black regiments, it does not follow that all these men were natives of Massachusetts or even of New England. William Porter, for example, came from New York. Black music-biographer James M. Trotter singled out John Moore for special praise:

> He was a born musician, so to speak, and was ever "full of music." I remember him as the leader of the band of the Fifty-fifth Massachusetts Regiment. . . . Although in this position he generally played upon the E♭-cornet, he could also play most of the other instruments used in the band; and was, besides, a good performer on the flute. . . . [in the band he] enjoyed the reputation of being the best in the Department of the South.

Musicians associated with Kansas units were Thomas Brightwell, John Colwell, John Corowell, John Crump, Madison Craton, Absalom Dimmery, Samuel Davis, Nelson Hoas, Rolla Isence, William Madden, and William Nelson.

Black servicemen brought to army life their love of music. More than one officer was entranced by the continous singing that went on day and night in army camps and later wrote about it in a regimental history, a camp diary, or a personal memoir. Black ex-soldiers, too, have left written records of army life that included references to group singing. Since the report of Colonel Higginson agrees with the published records of other army men, we quote from it as representative of life in a black army camp. The white officer strolling among his men as they sat around evening campfires rarely failed to be amazed by the wide variety of activities in which they were engaged. While some men were cleaning their guns or rehearsing their drills, others were swapping stories and jokes, especially at the expense of their white officers. To be sure, these were typical scenes in the white camps as well, but the religious activities of the blacks probably were unmatched by parallel scenes among the whites. Higginson wrote:

> The everlasting "shout" is always within hearing, with its mixture of piety and polka, and its castenet-like clapping of the hands. Then there are quieter prayer-meetings, with pious invocations and slow psalms, "deaconed out" from memory by the leader, two lines at a time, in a sort of wailing chant. . . . Elsewhere, it is some solitary old cook, some aged Uncle Tiff, with enormous spectacles, who is perusing a hymn-book by the light of a pine splinter, in his deserted cooking booth of palmetto leaves.

Of course, not all activity was of a serious nature:

> By another fire there is an actual dance, red-legged soldiers doing right-and-left, and "now-lead-de-lady-ober," to the music of a violin which is rather artistically played, and which may have guided the steps, in other days, of Barnwells and Hugers.

On rainy evenings, "mingled sounds of stir and glee" would come from the tents to the ears of the commanding officers:

> . . . a feeble flute stirs somewhere in some tent, not an officer's,—a drum throbs far away in another . . . and from a neighboring cook-fire comes the monotonous sound of that strange festival, half pow-wow, half prayer-meeting, which they know only as a "shout."

For the shout the men would have crowded into one tent or hut, singing at the "top of their voices . . . quaint, monotonous, endless, negro-Methodist chants." Invariably the excitement would spread to other parts of the camp, and soldiers from all over would join in the performance—inside and outside the enclosure—all "steadily circling like dervishes." Higginson and others marveled that the shout should take place "not rarely and occasionally, but night after night."

In some places black servicemen formed glee clubs that occasionally gave concerts for the community, gaining thereby not only good will but also money for the company fund. Service units came into contact with members of the community on many occasions, the most common of which were the periodic drills and parades and the celebration of holidays to which spectators were invited. The historian of the Fifty-fifth Massachusetts describes one such occasion:

On the 4th of July, 1863, a festival was prepared for the regiment by the ladies in the vicinity. Music and dancing, with games and prizes were the order of the day, and in the evening a display of fireworks from the high embankment of the railroad overlooking the camp. The leader of the regimental band was presented with a silver cornet. . . .

But it was the black servicemen's singing of folksongs that most frequently drew the attention of commanding officers and friends of the regiments. Higginson was moved thereby to record the texts of the songs sung by his men. He explained his action:

The war brought to some of us, besides its direct experiences, many a strange fulfilment of dreams of other days. For instance, the present writer had been a faithful student of the Scottish ballads, and had always envied Sir Walter [Scott] the delight of tracing them out amid their own heather, and of writing them down piecemeal from the lips of aged crones. It was a strange enjoyment, therefore, to be suddenly brought into the midst of a kindred world of unwritten songs, as simple and indigenous as the Border Minstrelsy, more uniformly plaintive, almost always more quaint, and often as essentially poetic.

This interest was rather increased by the fact that I had for many years heard of this class of songs under the name of "Negro

Spirituals," and had even heard some of them sung by friends from South Carolina. I could now gather on their own soil these strange plants, which I had before seen as in museums alone.

Singing was for black servicemen not only a recreational activity, but a release from the predictable tensions involved in fighting a war, particularly one in which the problem of the freedom of the race was to be settled. Black soldiers sang, along with their own folksongs, the war songs of white composers that were popular with all servicemen, such as George Root's *Tramp, Tramp, Tramp, Battle Cry of Freedom,* and *Just Before the Battle, Mother;* Henry Clay Work's *Marching Through Georgia;* Patrick S. Gilmore's *When Johnny Comes Marching Home;* and Walter Kittredge's *Tenting on the Old Camp Ground.* But their all-time favorite was *John Brown's Body.* The four-phrase melody for this song belonged originally to a camp-meeting song composed in 1852 by a white song-leader, William Steffe. To the original chorus, "Glory, Glory, Hallelujah," an anonymous soldier added some stanzas about John Brown.

Ex. VIII.1   *John Brown's Body*, William Steffe

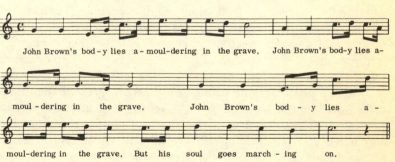

In 1862 Julia Ward Howe wrote a stirring poem, *The Battle Hymn of the Republic,* to be sung to the popular tune, which was used for both stanzas and chorus. Black soldiers seemed to prefer their own texts, however, and used the tune for marching songs, camp songs, social songs, and even religious songs. Among

the different versions that were in circulation during the war
years was this one:

> We are done with hoeing cotton, we are done with hoeing corn,
> We are colored Yankee soldiers, as sure as you are born;
> When Massa hears us shouting, he will think 'tis Gabriel's horn,
> As we go marching on.

John Brown's Body came to be the unofficial theme song of
black soldiers. Early in the war it was invested with a special
sentiment for them. Historians report, for example, that when
the band of the Fifty-fourth of Massachusetts, one of the first
black regiments to go South, played the melody as the soldiers
marched down State Street in Boston en route to Battery Wharf,
tears came to the eyes of the proud black women watching the
parade and the mother of the white commanding officer, Mrs.
Shaw. Another popular song was the so-called *Negro Battle
Hymn*, also known as *They Look Like Men of War*.

Under informal circumstances, servicemen on the march used
the "route step"—that is, they were allowed to talk and sing and
were not required to keep in step but could simply remain four
abreast as long as they did not lag behind. Nevertheless, the black
soldiers would instinctively keep in step, singing enthusiastically
and loudly as they walked along. To everybody, known or
unknown, who gathered along the roads to watch them pass,
they would sing out greetings: "Howd' you, brother?" Higginson provides a description of route stepping on an occasion
when his men were "at the top of exhilaration." His "laughing
and utterly unmanageable drummers" heartily greeted the grave
little boys on the roadside with, "Dem's de drummers for de
nex' war!" They flirted with the girls and saluted the venerable
kerchiefed matrons, singing briskly all the while. When Higginson reined up to watch them pass, the strains of one company's songs blended with those of the preceding and following
companies.

> Such an odd mixture of things, military and missionary, as the
> successive waves of song drifted by! First, "John Brown", of course;
> then, "What make old Satan for [to] follow me so?" then, "March-
> ing Along"; then, "Hold your light on Canaan's shore"; then, "When
> this cruel war is over" (a new favorite, sung by a few); yielding pres-

ently to a grand burst of the favorite marching song among them all, and one at which every step instinctively quickened, so light and jubilant its rhythm,—

> "All true children gwine [going] in de wilderness,
> Gwine in de wilderness, gwine in de wilderness,
> True believers gwine in de wilderness,
> To take away de sins ob de world,"—

ending in a "Hoigh!" after each verse,—a sort of Irish yell. For all the songs, but especially for their own wild hymns, they constantly improvised simple verses, with the same odd mingling,— the little facts of to-day's march being interwoven with the depths of theological gloom, and the same jubilant chorus annexed to all. . . .

William Barton recorded several "war songs" in his collection, *Hymns of the Slave and Freeman*. His comments about the improvisatory nature of the verses in these songs support Higginson's statement. Sometimes only a single line represents the stable element, the rest of the song being "built up as occasion demands." In the following song, however, the entire chorus was typically sung without alteration.

Ex. VIII.2   *Stay in the Field*, from Barton

1. { I've   got my breast-plate, sword and shield,   Till the war is   end-ed.
     And   I'll go march-ing   thro' the field,

2. Satan thought he had me fast,
       Till the war is ended;
   But thank the Lord I'm free at last,
       Till the war is ended.

MUSIC IN THE CONFEDERATE ARMY

Little is known about the activities of Negro musicians in the Confederate army except that slaves were pressed into service as fifers and drummers. But there is evidence in the official records of the army that suggests that some blacks may have been given the rank of musician or bugler. An act entitled "An Act for the payment of musicians in the Army not regularly enlisted" reads as follows:

> The Congress of the Confederate States of America do enact, That whenever colored persons are employed as musicians in any regiment or company, they shall be entitled to the same pay now allowed by law to musicians regularly enlisted: Provided, That no such persons shall be employed except by consent of the commanding officer of the brigade to which said regiments or companies may belong. Approved April 15, 1862.

MUSIC IN THE CONTRABAND CAMP

Life in the contraband camp was in many ways similar to life on the plantation. Black people lived in special quarters under supervision of the whites and worked at jobs that would aid in the war effort. The ex-slaves adjusted to the incredible inconveniences of camp life, to the lack of sufficient clothing and, occasionally, of adequate food. It was enough for them that freedom was in the air! Botume, like other writers of her time, noticed that songs, too, were in the air, night and day. Her campers had been forced to resort to very primitive means in order to obtain the basic food staple of the camp:

> This hominy was ground between two flat stones, one of which was stationary and the other was moved by hand by means of an upright stick inserted in a groove in the stone. It was a slow and tedious process, but always enlivened by songs . . . and jokes of the colored people when grinding. At night the older people came and ground by the light of a pine torch fastened to a post. All

night long I could hear the whizzing of the wheel and the shouts of the people. I have dropped to sleep hearing,—

> "O believer, go ring that bell, ring that bell,
>   ring that bell,
> O believer, go ring that bell, ring that charming bell."

the words and the tunes mingling with my dreams. When I awoke in the morning they were still singing, but it was now—

> "Roll Jordan, roll Jordan, roll Jordan, roll."

When the camp held its periodic festivals, there was always the ubiquitous shout. The favorite shout spirituals among all the contrabands apparently were *I Can't Stay Behind* and *Nobody Knows the Trouble I've Had.*

The whites who lived in contraband camps were sometimes asked to fulfill unusual requests. Botume, for example, was once asked to "funeralize"—that is, to read the burial service for a funeral and lead the singing. She wrote later in her diary, "I lined the hymns as distinctly as possible, which the entire crowd sang loud and slow in a minor tune." Funerals were invariably held at night. The ex-slaves believed that the spirit remained with the body until daylight, then went home to God as the morning stars disappeared. All night long the friends of the deceased would sit together in a watch meeting, called a "setting up," chanting and clapping their hands. At dawn would begin the long procession from the burial site, the marchers beating muffled drums and singing spirituals. To more than one white observer, "it was a somber sight as this sable procession wound around through the grove." On one occasion Botume was reminded of the *Pilgrim's March* in Wagner's opera, *Tannhäuser,* as the tones of the spirituals "reverberated through the arches of 'God's first temple.' "

EMANCIPATION

Over the years the slaves had developed a sizable repertory of songs about the day when freedom should come. While few song texts of this kind were recorded in contemporary sources, and understandably so, there are numerous references to such songs. As the war tensions mounted throughout the nation, blacks were restricted more and more. In Georgetown, South Carolina, for example, slaves were whipped for singing the following spiritual on the occasion of Lincoln's election:

> We'll fight for liberty,
> We'll fight for liberty,
> We'll fight for liberty,
> Till the Lord shall call us home;
> We'll soon be free,
> Till the Lord shall call us home.

In the Fall of 1862, President Lincoln issued a preliminary proclamation stating that on January 1, 1863, "all persons held as slaves within any State, or designated part of the State, the people whereof shall be in rebellion against the United States, shall be then, thenceforward and forever free." Black men assembled in "rejoicing meetings" all over the land on the last night of December in 1862, waiting for the stroke of midnight to bring freedom to those slaves in the secessionist states. At the contraband camp in Washington, D. C., the assembled blacks sang over and over again:

> Go down, Moses,
> Way down in Egypt land;
> Tell old Pharaoh,
> Let my people go.

Then, according to William Wells Brown, "a sister broke out in the following strain, which was heartily joined in by the vast assembly":

> Go down, Abraham,
> Away down in Dixie's land;
> Tell Jeff Davis
> To let my people go.

In a lowly cabin in South Carolina a slave said to those gathered there, "By the time I counts ten, it will be midnight and the land will be free. . . ." A man began to sing:

Oh, brethren, my way, my way's cloudy
Go send dem angels down

[*Throughout the song the refrain follows each line of
text, as in the first stanza.*]

There's fire in the east an' fire in the west
An' fire among the Methodists
Ole Satan's mad and I'm glad
He missed the soul he thought he had
I'll tell you now as I told before
To the promised land I'm bound to go
This is the year of Jubilee
The Lord has come to set us free

In some places the first songs that came to the lips of the
huge assemblies of Negroes gathered in great halls or in open
fields were not spirituals but beloved hymns that had been consolation for decades. At Tremont Hall in Boston, for example, it
was *Blow Ye the Trumpet, Blow.* At a celebration at Camp
Saxton in South Carolina, where white and black had assembled,
it was a patriotic hymn that the freed slaves began to sing after
the speeches and the band music—*My Country 'Tis of Thee.*
A handful of blacks began the singing, and others joined in.
When some whites also attempted to join the singing, Colonel
Higginson waved them to silence; the new citizens of the Union
alone sang all the verses of their new national hymn.

New Year's Day took on a special significance for black
people of the nation. Formerly known as "Heartbreak Day"
because of the custom of holding big slave auctions on that day,
the first day of the year now became associated with freedom
and hope for the future. For many years after 1863, celebrations
were held in Negro communities in honor of the Emancipation
Proclamation. In 1866 celebrations were especially important,
for in 1865 Congress added the Thirteenth Amendment to the
Constitution, abolishing slavery in *all* the states; the 1863 Act
had eliminated slavery only from those states that had seceded
from the Union.

The slaves had wisely refrained from singing their freedom
songs in the presence of whites before Emancipation; now they
came out into the open. From this period dates such songs as

No More Auction Block for Me, I Want Some Valiant Soldier, Babylon Is Fallen, Bobolishion's [Abolition's] *Coming, Before I'd Be a Slave; The Massa Run,* and *Done wid Driber's Dribin'* (i.e. the slave driver's or overseer's driving).

Ex. VIII.3   *Done wid Driber's Dribin'*, Traditional

2. Done wid massa's hollerin',
3. Done wid missus' scoldin'.

Of these songs, *Before I'd Be a Slave* was destined to be long-lived. Barton heard the song many times during the 1880s. He associated it especially with an old ex-slave, Uncle Joe Williams, to whom slavery had not been unkind, but who nevertheless had looked forward to freedom as eagerly as the most persecuted of slaves. This was the song Williams "loved to sing, sitting before his door in the twilight":

Ex. VIII.4   *Before I'd Be a Slave (Oh, Freedom)*, from Barton

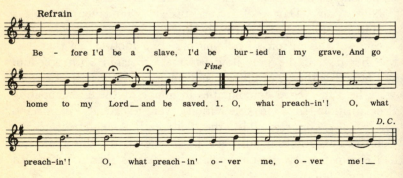

2. O, what mourning, *etc.*
3. O, what singing, *etc.*
4. O, what shouting, *etc.*
5. O, weeping Mary, *etc.*

6. Doubting Thomas, *etc.*
7. O, what sighing, *etc.*
8. O, Freedom, *etc.*

In 1909 the same song appeared in a collection of Hampton Institute songs. Half a century later, during the early 1960s, the song was adopted by workers in the civil rights movement in the United States and in a few short years had spread throughout the world, a musical standard-bearer for those—regardless of race, color, or religion—in search of equal opportunity to achieve the good things in life.

III

Blow Ye the Trumpet

1867-1919

Important Events

1867   First publication of a collection of Negro spirituals, *Slave Songs of the United States*, by William Allen, Charles Ware, and Lucy McKim Garrison: New York, N. Y.

Founding of New England Conservatory of Music: Boston, Mass.

Establishment of the first of the philanthropists' funds that worked to advance Negro education, the Peabody Education Fund. In later years came the John F. Slater Fund (1892), the General Education Board (John D. Rockefeller, 1902), and the Julius Rosenwald Fund (1912).

1869   Completion of the first transcontinental railroad, the Union Pacific.

1871   First tour of the Fisk Jubilee Singers.

1872   World Peace Jubilee, produced by Patrick S. Gilmore: Boston, Mass.

1876   Celebration of the Centennial of American Independence. Black Americans presented a show: Philadelphia, Pa.

241

1881 Founding of the Boston Symphony Orchestra.

1882 Organization of the largest black minstrel group ever assembled, Callendar's Spectacular Colored Minstrels.

1883 Founding of the Metropolitan Opera Company: New York, N. Y.

1886 Organization of the National Baptist Convention (Negro).

1887 Invention of disc recording method by Emile Berliner, whose organization was the beginning of the Victor Recording Company.

1890 First all-black musical show to employ Negro women on the professional stage, *The Creole Show*, produced by white management: Haverhill, Mass.

Beginning of the enactment of Jim Crow legislation in the South which provided for segregation of blacks in education, housing, travel, and recreation.

1893 World's Columbian Exhibition; included African and black American exhibitions: Chicago, Ill.

1894 *Black America* extravaganza: Brooklyn, N. Y.

1896 First black musical show to play Broadway, *Oriental America:* New York, N. Y.

1897 First ragtime piece published by a black man, *Harlem Rag,* by Tom Turpin.

1898 Production of first musical-comedy sketch written and performed by Negroes, *Clorindy, the Origin of the Cakewalk* by Will Marion Cook: New York, N. Y.

Production of the first full-length musical comedy written, produced, and performed by Negroes, *A Trip to Coontown,* by Robert Cole: New York, N. Y.

Spanish-American War

1899 Publication of the *Maple Leaf Rag* by the "King of Ragtime," Scott Joplin.

1900 Flourishing of "Black Bohemia" neighborhood in New York where black musicians and artists congregated at the Marshall Hotel.

Founding of the Philadelphia Symphony Orchestra.

1903 Flourishing of Bob Mott's Pekin Theatre (Negro): Chicago, Ill.

1905 Organization of the Niagara Movement under leadership of W. E. B. DuBois in protest against racial discrimination and lynching: Niagara Falls, Canada.

First public performance of a black "syncopated orchestra," the Nashville Students: New York, N. Y.

1909 Organization of the National Association for the Advancement of Colored People (incorporating members of the Niagara Movement): New York, N. Y.

1910   Organization of the Clef Club (a black musician's union): New York, N. Y.

1911   Incorporation of the National League on Urban Conditions among Negroes (known as the National Urban League).

Performance (concert version) of the Negro folk opera *Treemonisha*, written by Scott Joplin: New York, N. Y.

1912   Publication of the *Memphis Blues* by W. C. Handy.

1914–18   World War I

1914   Presentation of James Reese Europe's all-black orchestra of 125 performers at Carnegie Hall: New York, N. Y.

Publication of the *St. Louis Blues* by W. C. Handy.

Institution of the Springarn Medal awards by the NAACP for achievement by an individual Negro.

Founding of the American Society of Composers, Authors, and Publishers.

1915   First publication in history of a jazz arrangement: *Jelly Roll Blues* by Ferdinand Morton.

1916   Publication of first solo arrangement of Negro spirituals by Harry Burleigh.

1917   Entrance of the United States into World War I.

Closing of Storyville: New Orleans, La.

1918   Jazz Concert of Jim Europe's 369th Infantry Band at the Théâtre des Champs-Elysées "conquers Paris."

1919   Founding of the National Association of Negro Musicians.

Southern Syncopated Orchestra, under direction of Will Marion Cook, tours Europe.

CHAPTER IX

After the War

The year 1865 brought to an end the enslavement of four million blacks. By the thousands the ex-slaves fled the hated plantations to urban areas of the South, to the North, and out into the great plains of the West. Inevitably there was a tremendous amount of suffering, for the freedmen were suddenly thrust without preparation into a new way of life. The federal government set up the Bureau of Refugees, Freedmen, and Abandoned Lands (called Freedmen's Bureau) to provide basic food and health services, to arrange for employment, and to establish schools. The American Missionary Association and various other religious groups also assisted in the establishment of schools, and hundreds of teachers came down from the North to work in them. Among the Negro institutes and colleges founded just after the war were Atlanta, Biddle Memorial (now Johnson C. Smith), Fisk, Hampton, Howard, and St. Augustine.

It had been rumored that each ex-slave family was to receive "forty acres and a mule" from the government as a start toward building a new life, but this proved to be unfounded. Some amount of land was distributed to ex-slaves, however, particularly under the Southern Homestead Act. Freedmen also received help from another quarter—the Negro Church. With the demise of slavery, blacks were no longer forced to attend the churches of the whites, and they began to organize their own. Those independent Negro sects already in existence, the A. M. E. and A. M. E. Zion denominations, greatly expanded their membership, and a new denomination, the Colored Methodist Episcopal Church (now Christian Methodist Episcopal Church) appeared on the scene.

Despite the migration of thousands out of the South, within a few years most of the newly freed slaves were resettled there and engaged in agricultural occupations as before. They worked under a system called "sharecropping," wherein the landowner provided land and tools for the worker, whose responsibility it was to raise crops. At harvest time the worker was given a share of the crops as pay for his labor. The built-in evils of the system militated against the ex-slaves' prospects of improving their lot. In some ways they were worse off than under slavery. The southern states began to pass the so-called Jim Crow laws that infringed upon the freedmen's rights in every area of daily life. Their precarious situation was not helped by the emergence of white secret societies such as the Ku Klux Klan, whose avowed purpose was to establish control over the black population and maintain "white supremacy." Under cover of darkness, hooded white riders tore black men from their homes—beat them, tarred and feathered them, and lynched them.

SONGS OF THE PEOPLE

In keeping with his traditions, the ex-slave sang about his experiences—his new freedom, his new occupations, the strange ways of the city, current events, and his feelings of rootlessness and loneliness. Above all he sought a self-identity. Slavery had deprived him of a name, a homeland, and a family. The original African names of his forbears had long ago been forgotten, the land of Africa no longer beckoned after almost two hundred and fifty years of exile, and his relatives had been dispersed, for the slave auction block had separated husband from wife, mother from child, brother from sister, and lover from lover. Now that freedom had come, some freedmen set out in search of long-lost loved ones. The black singer recounted their adventures, too. In an uneasy society that used the slightest pretext for putting black men in prison, large numbers of them found themselves behind bars. Consequently, a new type of song was born, the prison song.

Many erstwhile black farmers sought work in lumber camps, on steamboats, in coal and iron mines, on the cattle range, in factories, and on railroads. Even before the completion in 1869 of the first transcontinental railroad, the Union Pacific, hundreds of ex-slaves were following the railroad tracks in search of jobs. As they worked they sang such songs as:

> Captain, go side-track yo' train,
> Captain, go side-track yo' train,
> Number three in line, a-coming in on time,
> Captain, go side-track yo' train.

The most popular railroad song of all was a ballad about John Henry, the black, 220-pound, "steel driving" railhand who became a folk hero to his people. No one could work as long as

Ex. IX.1 *John Henry*

* The rhythm of measure 9 is reproduced exactly as notated in the source.

> John Henry says to his Cap'n,
> "Send me a twelve-poun' hammer aroun',
> A twelve-poun' wid a four-foot handle,
> An' I beat yo' steam-drill down,
> An' I beat yo' steam-drill down."
> John Henry went down on de railroad.
> Wid a twelve-poun' hammer by his side,
> He walked down de track, but he never come back,
> 'Cause he laid down his hammer an' he died,
> Yes, he laid down his hammer an' he died.

John Henry could; the women would all come out just to watch him work and to hear him make the cold steel ring. Many versions of his story came into being, the tale of a proud, hard-working "hammer man" who refused to let a "new-fangled steel drill beat him down," but who "hammered himself to death" in the struggle of man against the machine.

Railroad songs of the nineteenth century were not usually ballads, however, but long, drawn-out, monotonous chants. William Barton describes the singing of some of these songs in his book. Only the leader sang the words of the verses; the workers sang out the refrains, which came at irregular intervals, "just often enough to quicken the lagging interest of any who may have dropped out." The melody was apt to be quite dull, using chiefly the sixth and eighth tones of the scale, but its rhythm was sharp, setting the pace for the work activity—the spades sinking into the clay and the picks stabbing the ground in time to the music. Barton writes:

> To hear these [railroad] songs . . . at their best, one needs to hear them in a rock tunnel. The men are hurried in after an explosion to drill with speed for another double row of blasts. They work two and two, one holding and turning the drill, the other striking it with a sledge. The sledges descend in unison as the long low chant gives the time [i.e. the rhythm]. . . . Imagine the effect of it all, the powder smoke filling the place, the darkness made barely visible by the little lights on the hats of the men, the echoing sounds of men and mules toward the outlet loading and carting away the rock thrown out by the last blast, and the men at the heading droning their low chant to the *chink! chink!* of the steel. A single musical phrase or a succession of a half dozen notes caught on a visit to such a place sticks in one's mind forever.

The men who worked on steamboats and on the levees of the river towns continued to contribute material to the store of "water" songs built up during ante-bellum days. Ex-slaves who came into possession of land for the first time found themselves concerned about things that formerly had interested only their masters—such as, for example, the price of cotton, the weather, or the boll weevil. Often their songs about the vagaries of land ownership were parodies of spirituals, such as the following one heard by William Wells Brown:

Sing your praise, bless the Lamb,
Getting plenty money;
Cotton's going up, 'deed it am,
People, ain't it funny.

Rise, shine, give God the glory, glory,
Rise, shine, give God the glory, glory,
Rise, shine, give God the glory, glory,
Soldiers of the cross.

Don't you think it's going to rain?
Maybe 'tis, a little;
Maybe one old hurricane
Is boiling in the kettle.

Out on the western plains Negro cowboys joined the crews that drove millions of longhorns over the Chisholm and the Western Trails, from the Rio Grande to such cattle towns as Dodge City, Kansas. Between the years 1868 and 1895 more than 5,000 black cowboys went up the trails, delivering the Texas cattle to railroad centers for shipment to northern and eastern markets. On the lonesome journeys they sang the sad, lonely songs that all cowboys sang as well as their own plaintive songs. At night around the campfires the black cowboys entertained their trail mates with songs and sometimes fiddle music. A typical trail crew of eight cowboys invariably included two or three black men.

Best known of the black cowboys was Nat Love, or Deadwood Dick as he called himself. Unfortunately, for our purposes, Love cared little about music and did not discuss it in his autobiography. Some names of black cowboy minstrels have been preserved, however, in other sources of the period. Big Jim Simpson, for example, was a cowboy-fiddler who came up the Chisholm Trail from Texas and finally settled down on the Flying-E Ranch in Wyoming. Among the cowboys who rode with Billy the Kid in the Lincoln County bloody feud were George Washington and Sabrien Bates, both black fiddlers. Blind Sam and his brothers settled down as entertainers in Deadwood City during 1870s after spending many years fighting Indians. And old Jim Perry, respected in the West as an all-around cowboy, also built up a reputation as a fiddler.

THE SPIRITUALS

The post-war spirituals, like the social songs, employed the old forms and musical idioms of the slave songs, but the content of these songs reflected the new status of the singers and the different circumstances under which they lived. The growing importance of the railroad in the lives of black men, for example, revealed itself in the number of songs that included phrases about "getting on board the Gospel train" and about the railroad-car wheels "rumbling through the land." Although the folksongs of the Negro began to appear in print early in the 1860s, the songs were unknown to most whites of the country. It remained for a group of young black singers to bring the songs to the attention of the American public and eventually to the people of Europe. This was as it should have been, for as we have seen, the beauty and "quaint charm" of the spirituals derived as much from the way in which they were sung as from the music itself.

The singers were students at the newly established Fisk University in Nashville, Tennessee, which opened its doors in 1866. Fisk's administrator John Odgen asked George L. White, one of the school's young white teachers, to devote his leisure hours to music instruction. In addition, White gave a thorough training in musicianship to selected students that showed great promise. Wisely, he let them sing "their own music" as well as standard classical music. In 1867 the students under White's direction presented a concert to the Nashville public and were well received. Encouraged, White began to take his singers on short trips to nearby towns. In 1871 he conceived the idea of taking the singers on a tour in order to raise money to help with the building program at Fisk, which remained continuously in financial straits during those early years.

This was not a decision lightly made. The students were not minstrel singers; their program included no jokes, no dances, no catchy tunes. The American public had not yet heard the religious music of the slaves and had given no indication that it was ready to hear it. With great misgivings but determined, White set out on October 6, 1871, with eleven singers, a "skillful young Negro pianist" (Ella Shepherd), and a teacher-chaperon (Miss

Wells)—on borrowed funds! The experiment was not an immediate success. In Cincinnati a newspaper critic wrote:

> This is probably the first concert given by a colored troupe in this temple, which has resounded with the notes of the best vocalists in the land.

When Henry Ward Beecher, the noted abolitionist, sponsored a presentation in New England, the newspapers referred to the singers as Beecher's Negro Minstrels.

Despite several depressing occurrences, White determined to continue with the tour. It was in Columbus, Ohio, after a sleepless night, that he conceived the idea of giving his singers a name. For many years the slaves had talked about their "year of jubilee" when slavery should be ended; why not call the singers the "Fisk Jubilee Singers"? The name had a euphonious sound and it caught on with the public. In Boston a newspaper reporter wrote that when the Jubilee Singers sang *Home, Sweet Home* to an audience that had heard the renowned Jenny Lind sing it, the song as presented by the black students was "rendered with a power and pathos never surpassed." The format of the Fisk Jubilee Singers' concerts was similar to that of concerts presented by white artists of the time, except that a large number of spirituals were included. Among audience favorites were the slave songs *Keep Me from Sinking Down; O Brothers, Don't Stay Away; Go Down, Moses;* and such popular songs as *Old Folks at Home, A Temperance Medley,* and *Home, Sweet Home.*

The event that catapulted the singers to fame took place in Boston on the occasion of the mammoth World Peace Jubilee in 1872. The huge festival chorus, which included the Fisk Jubilee Singers, was scheduled to sing the refrain of the popular *Battle Hymn of the Republic,* the verses to be performed by a local Negro singing group. The orchestra began the song on too high a pitch level, however, and the opening verses were a "painful failure." The Jubilee Singers then sang out strongly and, with their well-trained voices, easily reached the high notes. Marsh gives an account in his book, *The Story of the Jubilee Singers* (1880), of the historic occasion:

> Every word . . . rang through the great Coliseum as if sounded out of a trumpet. The great audience was carried away with a

whirlwind of delight. . . . Men threw their hats in the air and the Coliseum rang with cheers and shouts of, "The Jubilees! The Jubilees forever!" Mr. [Patrick Sarsfield] Gilmore brought the Singers from their place below and massed them upon his own platform, where they sang the remaining verses.

The reputation of the Fisk Jubilee Singers was made! They went on to sing at places in the United States that had never before heard the black man's folk music—before crowned heads of Europe, and before the common people in Germany, Switzerland, and Great Britain. Everywhere the Singers "carried their audiences by storm" and won acclaim from the critics. Within seven years they raised $150,000, a tremendous sum for those days, and turned it over to the university to help with the erection of a new building, called Jubilee Hall, on the campus.

In the Winter of 1872–73, student singers at another college, Hampton Institute in Virginia, were organized into a singing group and taken on tours to raise money for the school. Like the Fisk Jubilee Singers, this group sang spirituals and other "plantation songs"; and like the Jubilees, it, too, met with success. Other struggling Negro colleges were inspired to send out spiritual-singing fund-raisers, and a tradition was established that lasted through the twentieth century. The Fisk Jubilee Singers became a permanent institution at their college, the work being carried on by two generations of Negro music instructors at Fisk—John Wesley Work, Sr. (1873–1925) and John Wesley Work, Jr. (1901–67).

To be sure, the spirituals as performed on the concert stage represented adaptations of the folksongs rather than the genuine product. When the spirituals were removed from the original setting of the plantation or the Negro Church and sung by persons who had not directly experienced slavery, these songs no longer served their primary function. Concert singers could present to the public only an approximation of how the spirituals had been sung by the slaves.

CONCERT ARTISTS

After the war, black artists began to attain national and international reputations in the field of concert music. Most widely traveled of these pioneer artists was an ex-slave. Thomas Greene Bethune (1849–1908) was born in Columbus, Georgia, a slave of the Oliver family, and later sold along with his mother, Charity Wiggins, to a Colonel Bethune. Blind from birth, Thomas gave no indication of possessing musical talent until the age of seven, at which time he amazed his owners by his ability to play on the piano some difficult exercises he had heard others perform. Although Blind Tom was not given musical instruction, he was allowed free access to the piano and soon developed a large repertory of classical and popular music and, as well, of his own compositions. His musical memory was so highly developed that he could play any piece to which he had listened. The young prodigy was continually subjected to rigorous tests of his unusual gift, all of which he passed with ease. On one occasion, at the White House, Blind Tom played correctly a piece twenty pages in length a short time after hearing it.

Bethune's owner-guardian first presented him in a recital at Savannah, Georgia, in 1858. On his extensive tours throughout the United States and Europe he impressed critics and audiences with his "clearness of conception," his technical skill, and, above all, his prodigious memory. Ironically, Blind Tom was forced by circumstances to aid the cause of the South during the Civil War. During the Summer of 1861 he gave concerts for the benefit of the sick and wounded of the Confederate army. Bethune's recitals typically consisted of eight parts, each with a title, e.g. *Classical Selections, Piano-Forte Solos, Fantasias and Caprices, Marches, Imitations, Descriptive Music, Songs,* and *Parlor Selections.* Audiences were given a list of the pieces in his repertory and allowed to select the ones they wished to hear. One program, for example, listed eighty-two pieces, each category including from eight to twelve pieces.

The classical selections consisted of the music of Bach, Beethoven, Chopin, Mendelssohn, and Rossini; the fantasias and parlor selections, of the music of Heller, Hoffmann, Thalberg, Gottschalk, Liszt, and obscure men no longer remembered today. Approximately one fourth of the program was devoted to variations on popular ballads, operatic airs of Verdi, Bellini, and Gounod—this part of the performance allowing Tom to demonstrate his improvisational skills. His compositional abilities were displayed in the "imitations" and "descriptive music"; for ex-

ANECDOTES, SONGS,

SKETCH OF THE LIFE,

Testimonials from the most Eminent Composers,

AND

OPINIONS OF THE AMERICAN AND ENGLISH PRESS,

OF

BLIND TOM,

THE MARVELLOUS MUSICAL PRODIGY,

THE NEGRO BOY PIANIST

(FROM AMERICA.)

Whose recent Performances at the Great St. James's and Egyptian Halls,
London, have created such a profound sensation.

MUSICAL GUARDIAN OF "BLIND TOM," · · · · W. P. HOWARD, ESQ.

Title page of *Sketch of the Life of Blind Tom*, ca. 1866. (*Courtesy
M. A. Harris.*)

ample, *Imitation of the Music-Box, of the Church Organ, of the Dutch Woman and Hand-Organ, of Douglass's Speech* (i.e. Frederick Douglass), and *of Uncle Charlie; or The Rain Storm* and *The Battle of Manassas.*

Over the years Colonel Bethune and members of his family made fortunes on the exploitation of Tom's phenomenal ability. The blind baby had been "thrown in" upon Bethune's purchasing of the mother at no extra cost to the slaveholder. Tom's long career began when he was only eight years old and lasted until a few years before his death in 1908, for as late as 1904 he was sent out on a tour for the benefit of his guardians. His management increased his repertory by hiring professionals to play for him. According to their advertisements, Tom could play as many as seven hundred pieces upon demand. Once he had learned a piece, he never forgot it. A visitor to his home in 1898 requested a piece, *The Maiden's Prayer* that he had not played for many years. "Without a moment's hesitation, he played it." After Bethune's death in 1883, his son John took over Tom's guardianship, and after John's death his widow and her husband, Albert Lerché, assumed Tom's management.

In 1867 at Sacramento, California, two sisters, Anna Madah Hyers (1854–?) and Emma Louise Hyers (1853–?), won press acclaim for their striking soprano and contralto voices upon the occasion of their debut recital at the Metropolitan Theatre in Sacramento, California, April 22, 1867. Subsequent concert tours by the sisters in the northern and western sections of the United States, beginning in 1871, brought more praise from the critics. Later the Hyer sisters added to their entourage the tenor Wallace King (of minstrelsy fame) and the bass-baritone John Luca (of the Luca Family Singers). In 1869 a Boston critic wrote:

We were invited with some fifty other persons this forenoon to hear the singing of two colored young ladies, named Anna and Emma Hyers, of San Francisco, at the Meionaon. They are aged respectively sixteen and fourteen years, and, after a casual inspection, may be called musical prodigies. They are, without doubt, destined to occupy a high position in the musical world.

Anna sings not only alto, but tenor, and both with great excellence. They sang "Ah fors'è lui" from *Traviata,* "M'appari" from *Martha,* and the "Miserere" from *Trovatore,* each with remarkable clearness and accuracy, and surprised all with the general skill they displayed. Anna has also the faculty of reaching E-flat above the staff. Judging from present data, they are on a par vocally with our better concert-singers; and a further hearing may place them in rank with more pretentious vocalists.

In 1877 the Hyers organized a company that produced three musical shows: *Out of Bondage, The Underground Railway,* and *Princess Orelia of Madagascar.* The starring roles were shared by the two sisters, the noted minstrel star Sam Lucas, and singer Tom Fletcher.

Probably the most talented of the black concert artists during this era was Marie Selika (1849–?). Madame Selika (in private life Mrs. Sampson Williams) toured the United States and abroad during the 1880s, winning the praise of the critics for the "surprising sweetness and extraordinary compass" of her coloratura soprano voice. When Madame Selika sang in Paris, the critic of *Le Figaro* wrote:

> Madame Selika sang in great style. She has a very strong voice, of depth and compass, rising with perfect ease from C to C, and she trills like a feathered songster. Her range is marvelous and her execution and style of rendition show perfect cultivation. Her *Echo Song* cannot be surpassed. It was beyond any criticism. It was an artistic triumph.

Several other performers not as well known and perhaps with smaller talents were active on the regional level during the 1860s and 70s. In New England, pianist-organist Rachel Washington, the first Negro to receive a diploma from the New England Conservatory in Boston, was active as a music teacher and choir director as well as occasional recitalist. Soprano Nellie Brown of Dover, New Hampshire, began to sing professionally in 1865. Her concert career carried her to the major cities of New England and as far south as New York, Baltimore, and Washington, D. C. Samuel Jamieson, born in Washington, D. C., moved to Boston in his youth and won a diploma in piano from the Boston Conservatory in 1876. As a concert pianist Jamieson won a number of favorable notices from the press. James Gloucester Demarest achieved recognition as a guitarist in the Boston area, and a contemporary, Frederick Elliot Lewis, gained repute as a proficient player on many instruments, string and wind. In the New York area John T. Douglass rated attention for his artistry on the guitar and the violin and also for his compositions. Walter Craig attracted the attention of the critics for his violin playing at his debut recital in 1870. His skill developed to the degree that in 1886 the *New York Freeman* labeled him the "Prince of Negro violinists," and in 1887 the *New York Herald* reported him to be a "perfect master of his instrument."

Black instrumentalists in the United States were greatly inspired by the accomplishments of two violinists of African parentage who were active in the European musical world. George Polgreen Bridgetower (1779–1860), son of an African father and a Polish mother, was recognized as a violin prodigy at the age of ten and later became known as "the Abyssinian Prince." A student of Haydn and friend of Beethoven, the violinist enjoyed a short but highly successful concert career in Europe and left a sizable quantity of composed music. Beethoven's Violin Sonata, Op. 47, the "Kreutzer Sonata," was originally written for Bridgetower, who gave its first performance at Vienna in 1803. The other artist, José (Joseph) White (1833–1920), was a native of Cuba. At an early age he entered the Conservatory at Paris where he repeatedly won prizes for his skill in violin playing. In Europe, White was reported to be "one of the most distinguished violinists of the French school" and also "a composer of note." In 1876 White visited the United States where he impressed critics and audiences with his mastery of the violin. In New York he appeared with the Philharmonic and also the orchestra of Theodore Thomas, playing the Mendelssohn Concerto in E minor, among other works.

VOCAL ENSEMBLES

Small ensembles became increasingly popular among black musicians after the war, undoubtedly because it was easier for four or five singers to develop an audience following than for a single singer. It was difficult enough for a white American to earn a livelihood as a concert artist in the nineteenth century; with the exception of Louis Gottschalk, the brilliant pianist-composer of New Orleans, the concert field was dominated entirely by European artists—for example, Ole Bull, the Nor-wegian violinist; Jenny Lind, the "Swedish Nightingale"; Maria Malibran and Adelina Patti, operatic prima donnas; the sensa-tional soprano Henriette Sontag; and Sigismund Thalberg, vir-tuoso pianist. During this period, America generally ignored its own musicians, white as well as black, preferring to import its musical culture from Europe. Black performers were further handicapped by racial predjudice, especially when they at-tempted to sing anything other than spirituals or minstrel songs. Even the most gifted black artists of this period were forced to turn to ensemble singing in order to continue their musical activities. Thus the Hyer sisters formed a mixed quartet with Wallace and Luca.

Male quarters, however, were more common. In New England the Lew Male Quartet, managed during the 1880s by the Redpath Lyceum Bureau, toured with considerable success, including ap-pearances before Chautauqua assemblies at Chautauqua, New York, in 1887. Second tenor William Lew was a direct descendent of the colonial musician Barzillai Lew (see Chapter IV). During the next decade, male quartets came into even greater prominence. One of the best and most popular was the Golden Gate Quartet, organized in Baltimore in 1892.

The success of the Fisk and Hampton student singers inspired the organization of professional mixed ensembles that specialized in singing spirituals. Best known of the groups were the Mc-Millen and Sourbeck Jubilee Singers (later, called the Stinson Singers), the Stewart Concert Company, and the McAdoo Jubi-lee Singers. Minstrel shows and other kinds of road shows gen-erally featured quartet singing.

MUSICAL ORGANIZATIONS

During the 1870s Negro musical societies were organized in several of the nation's cities: the Colored American Opera Com-pany in Washington, D. C., in 1872; the Mozart Circle in Cincin-nati and the Progressive Musical Union in Boston, both in 1875; a Philharmonic Society in New York in 1876; a Musical Soci-ety in Louisville, Kentucky, in 1877; and in San Francisco, the Pacific Musical Association in the same year. In Philadelphia and Washington in 1873 the opera company presented several performances of an opera, *Doctor of Alcantara*, composed by Julius Eichberg, a German composer who came to the United States in 1859. One of the Philadelphia performances drew these comments from the press:

> . . . It must be remembered that this troupe is composed entirely of amateurs, and is the first colored opera-troupe in existence. We have had the "Colored Mario" [Thomas J. Bowers], the "Black Swan" [Miss Greenfield], & c.; but never until now have we had a complete organization trained for ensembles.
>
> [*All-Day City Item*, Philadelphia, February 22, 1873]

A number of Negro brass bands came into being after the war. Thanks to the army bands, black men were trained as bandmasters as well as instrumentalists. Quite a few of these men elected to remain in the service after the war was over; other men joined army bands for the first time during the 1870s and 80s. Among those who established reputations for themselves as fine bandsmen during the last decades of the nineteenth century were Walter Loving of the United States Philipine Constabulary Band; Joseph Anderson of Philadelphia, a band instructor; J. Paul Wyer of Pensacola, Florida; N. Clark Smith, who later became the bandmaster of Tuskegee Institute in Alabama; and George A. Swan and Wade Hammond of the Ninth Cavalry. Many Civil War ex-bandsmen attached themselves to independent town bands or toured with the bands of minstrel troupes, circuses and carnivals, medicine shows, or drama companies.

New Orleans maintained its position as the leading producer of good brass bands, both white and Negro, a position it had held from the beginning of the nineteenth century. Kelly's Band and the St. Bernard Brass Band led by E. Lambert were especially noted for the fine musicianship of the bandsmen. In Baltimore, Maryland, the Monumental Cornet Band was active under the leadership of C. A. Johnson, and in New York Walter Craig organized a band in 1872. In Philadelphia, the successor to Frank Johnson's band was called the Excelsior. The leading band in Boston during this period was the Boston Brass Band under the direction of George Sharper.

BLACK MINSTRELSY

After the war, genuine Negro minstrel companies were organized. To be sure, there had been isolated performances by Negro troupes earlier. A troupe billed as the Extraordinary Seven Slaves put on a show in Massachusetts in the 1850s under the sponsorship of "northern friends." And in 1863 a group of slave refugees from Charleston, South Carolina, calling itself the Charleston Minstrels, presented a show for the benefit of the sick and wounded of Colonel Higginson's First South Carolina Volunteers. Of the professional troupes organized during the 1860s the most successful were Lew Johnson's Plantation Minstrel Company and the Georgia Minstrels, the latter founded by a black man, George Hicks. Some of the troupe's members had been slaves, few had had musical training, but all possessed much natural talent. Hicks ran into racial discrimination in trying to book his show into theaters and opera houses, which were owned by whites, so eventually he sold the company to a white manager, George B. Callendar. The troupe's name was changed first to Callendar's Original Georgia Minstrels; after reorganization it became Haverly's International Minstrels; and finally Callendar's Consolidated Spectacular Colored Minstrels.

The minstrel show had come to represent America's unique contribution to the entertainment stage, and during the last quarter of the nineteenth century and the first decade of the twentieth, both white and black troupes enjoyed an international vogue. At the peak period there were three large Negro-owned and -managed troupes: the Hicks and Sawyer Minstrels, Richard and Pringles Famous Georgia Minstrels, and the McCabe and Young Minstrels. Among the giants of the white-managed Negro companies were Sprague's, F. L. Mahara and W. A. Mahara (shows owned by two brothers), and Callendar's. The Primrose and West Minstrel Company developed a new approach; it sent on road tours a mixed troupe consisting of "forty whites and thirty blacks." The stage manager was a Negro, Jesse Shipp, who later contributed much to the development of Negro musical comedy. Another troupe that employed both white and black minstrels was Lew Dockstader's. Neither company had integrated performances, however, except perhaps in the finales.

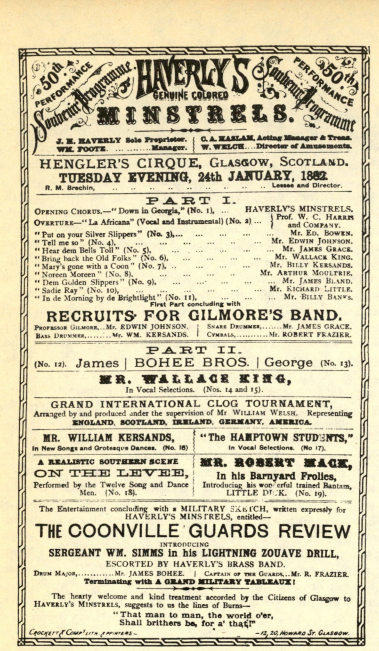

Playbill for a Glasgow performance by Haverly's Genuine Colored
Minstrels, 1882.

Typically the first half of a show was presented by whites and the second half by Negroes.

Many talented black musicians of the turn of the century began their careers in minstrel troupes. Indeed, the minstrel show generally offered the only profitable vocation for black creative talent. As a consequence, song writers, singers, dancers, instrumentalists, and comedians all "joined the band." Minstrel-troupe life has been described by several of the old-timers in their memoirs; best known of the writings by black authors are *Father of the Blues* by William Christopher Handy and *100 Years of the Negro in Show Business* by Tom Fletcher. Both Handy and Fletcher played with small minstrel groups when in their early teens; both later became attached to one of the big companies. One of the most informative of the books written by white authors is *They All Sang* by Edward B. Marks.

Life in a small company was pretty rough! There might not even be a band, just two or three musicians playing on banjos and guitars. On the day of a show, the manager would take his musicians to the site of the town's factories or mines to play during the workers' lunch hour in order to advertise the evening's show. In small towns the troupe frequently had to clean the rented hall or schoolhouse or "opera house" where the show was to be presented and to make its own scenery and footlights. After the show, the troupe might have difficulty in finding a place which would accommodate them overnight, particularly in small towns where there were few Negroes. Often there were signs in southern towns that warned, "Nigger Don't Let the Sun Go Down on You!" or "Nigger, Read and Run!" Old showmen avowed that frequently the latter had an additional message, "If you can't read, run anyway!" Even in places where there were Negro residents, it was not easy to obtain lodging, for the local Negroes were often too poor to provide it. Consequently, the minstrels sometimes found themselves sleeping in the unheated hall where the show had been presented, or in a railroad station.

With one of the well-established giant companies, life was quite different. The management provided private Pullman cars for traveling, which were used as a hotel when the troupe stopped overnight in a town to put on a show. The day of a minstrel company typically began at 11:45 A.M. with the traditional parade through the principal streets of the town or city. Sometimes the parade began at the railroad tracks, where the Pullman cars were put on a siding off the regular tracks. The procession started off with the managers in their carriages. Then, also in carriages, followed the stars of the show, in their tall silk hats and scarlet or plum-colored long-tailed coats. Next in line was the "walking company" dressed in brilliant coats with brass buttons—the singers, comedians, acrobats and dancers, and instrumentalists—accompanied by local boys who had begged for the opportunity to carry the banners that advertised special features of the show. The bandsmen marched in pairs, maintaining a distance of from ten to twelve feet between pairs so that the parade might stretch out as long as possible.

According to old-timers, bandsmen rarely made concessions to "low-brow taste" in their choice of music for the parades. Only when their lips grew weary would they "ease off" into the light marches of John Philip Sousa or R. B. Hall. Typically a band was composed of twelve or fourteen men, who played clarinets, cornets, trombones, the tuba, percussion, and occasionally flutes or piccolos. (For the show concert at night, some players had to "double," exchanging their wind instruments for fiddles, guitars, banjos, mandolins, and percussion.) The parade would come to a halt on the public square, and there the band would present a concert consisting of classical overtures and of popular-tune medleys, with a few clarinet, cornet, or trombone solos. At the close of the concert there was another parade to the hall or opera house, after which the company was free until show time. Before the evening performance, the band played once more in front of the hall in order to draw a crowd. This accomplished, the ticket seller would go to work on the people in much the same manner as a circus or carnival barker. The combination of the band's "sizzling" music and the barker's hokus-pokus rarely failed to round up a full house for the evening show.

A minstrel show lasted for an hour and forty-five minutes. The bandsmen sat on an elevated platform on the stage. Before them sat the performers in the traditional semicircle formations, soloists in front and supporting company behind. Immediately after the curtain rose, the company burst into song. Then the interlocutor, dressed in silk and lace, would come out front to introduce the stars:

> Ladies and gentlemen! We have come out tonight to give you a pleasing entertainment. With bones on the right and tambourines on the left, we shall now proceed with the overture. Gentlemen, be seated!

The first part of the show generally was followed by an *olio*, a kind of variety show which featured one or more specialty acts. At the end of the second part, the entire company came on for the *afterpiece* or finale.

Black minstrelsy had its own established traditions. It was traditional, for example, that a would-be minstrel should join a company as a young boy and serve a period of apprenticeship, learning the tricks of the trade from the older men. Typically, the troupes of the nineteenth century were composed only of males; in addition to the tenors with extraordinary ranges, there were male sopranos and altos who could soar to high C as easily as any woman. Moreover, male singers freely used falsetto to obtain desired effects. In later years the bar against women was lowered and women took their places on the stage alongside men. Indeed, Handy notes that a "lady trombonist" played in the Mahara minstrel band as early as the 1890s.

Minstrel songs generally fell into three categories: ballads, comic songs, and specialties. The songs of three Negro song-writers, James Bland, Gussie Davis, and Samuel Lucas, and of the white writer, Stephen Foster, were most popular among black minstrels. In addition, spirituals and other religious songs as well as operatic airs were used. The roles of the singers were fixed by tradition. It was the task of the tenor, for example, to sing ballads that "jerked the tears"; to the comedians were given comic songs; to the rich, deep bassos, specialty numbers.

While minstrel bands generally were small and composed of versatile musicians who were expected to play more than one instrument, some companies did have big bands. At one time the W. A. Mahara Minstrels had a thirty-piece band for day parades and a forty-two-piece band for night shows. The band-leader was an important member of the company; his attire reflected his status, consisting of a brightly colored uniform with golden epaulettes and a high silk hat. He was expected to rehearse the band, train those men who needed it, train the vocal ensembles, coach soloists, and make orchestrations if necessary. If he were a composer, he seized the opportunity to write music and hear it performed by a professional company. Ideally, bandsmen were supposed to be music readers. But since many black instrumentalists could play the traditional repertory as proficiently "by ear" as did music readers, it was frequently difficult for the bandmaster to distinguish the musically literate from the illiterate. Sometimes leaders resorted to ingenious methods to discover the fakers. Fletcher tells us, for example, that in his company:

> There was never any band rehearsal. The band leader . . . would pass out the books that had all of the tunes, but with the names of the tunes cut off. . . . [Then] the leader would give the signal to start playing the march.

Naturally, those musicians who could not read music would be unable to play.

The minstrel repertory included a wide variety of works currently in vogue. For the parades the band played marches by such composers as W. P. Chambers, C. W. Dalbey, and C. L. Barnhouse—all of them forgotten today but well known in their time. One of the most popular medleys for featuring at the outdoor concerts was *Brudder Gardner's Picnic*, a selection of Stephen Foster tunes. Since black minstrel troupes played most of their engagements in the South, the bands always played *Dixie*, the favorite tune of all southern audiences. For the evening show, the minstrels preferred to use "new" music or unusual arrangements of familiar pieces. Many singers wrote their own songs or paid a song writer to compose special songs for them, just as minstrels had done in Europe during the Middle Ages. The songs then "belonged" to the minstrel who had introduced them to the public. In a similar way, specialty dances became associated with individual minstrels. A composer-bandmaster such as Handy was always on the alert for a novel way to present familiar material. On one occasion, for example, he planned to use *The Holy City* as a "religioso," featuring a cornet solo against a saxophone-quartet accompaniment.

AMERICA'S BLACK TROUBADOUR

When the renowned white minstrel-songwriter Stephen Foster died in 1864, at first it seemed that there was no one of sufficient stature to take his place. There soon appeared, however, a young Negro composer, James Bland (1854–1911), who proved to be a worthy heir to Foster's laurels. At the height of his fame, Bland was the brightest star of minstrelsy in the United States, London, and Paris. He was advertised as "The World's Greatest Minstrel Man" and "The Idol of the Music Halls." His songs were sung by all the minstrels—black and white—by college students, and by the American people in their homes and on the streets. Most of the singers did not even know that they were singing songs written by a black man. The big white stars of minstrelsy for whom he wrote songs often published the songs under their own names. To be sure, this was rather a common practice; some of Stephen Foster's songs were expropriated in the same way. Before the days of copyrights and royalties song writers generally sold their songs outright for ten or fifteen dollars per song. This practice continued into the twentieth century.

Bland was born in Flushing, Long Island, but the family moved to Washington, D. C., upon the father's appointment as the first Negro Examiner in the United States Patent Office. James finished high school in Washington and upon graduation enrolled at Howard University. It was there that he came to know and appreciate the spirituals and other folksongs of this people. The manual labor on Howard's campus was performed by ex-slaves, and young Bland listened avidly to their songs and stories of slavery time. Meanwhile, he taught himself to play the banjo and soon began to earn money by singing and playing for private gatherings. His talent and skill, and especially his ability to compose his own songs, contributed to a demand for his services and led to his employment as an entertainer at a hotel in Washington. Bland's reputation grew. He soon found himself in constant demand for private parties and dinners, for weddings, and other social gatherings of both black and white groups. At his recital for the annual dinner meeting of the exclusive Canvasback Club (of which President Grover Cleveland was a member), Bland introduced some of the songs that later were to make him famous. He returned many times to the Club's annual dinners, even after he was an international figure in the entertainment world.

Eventually Bland left college, "banjo under his arm," to join Haverly's Colored Minstrels (i.e. the Original Georgia Minstrels), much to the distress of his family. James's father, Allen Bland, who had attended Wilberforce and Oberlin and had received a law degree from Howard University, had hoped that his son would become a lawyer rather than an entertainer, a career with little status among middle-class Negroes. Bland was an immediate success in the minstrel troupe, which toured the United States soon after he joined them and traveled to England in 1881. Many of his best songs were introduced in the music halls of London, Liverpool, and Manchester. When the troupe returned to the United States the next year, Bland remained in London. He dispensed with the blackface make-up he had worn as a minstrel and toured the music halls and theaters of England and the Continent as an elegantly dressed singer-banjoist. Germany was especially sympathetic to Bland's music. Germans rated him as one of the three Americans of the time who had "made an appreciable dent in the German consciousness," along with Stephen Foster and John Philip Sousa.

In 1890 Bland was at the peak of his career. He was thirty-six years old; he was truly the music-hall idol of Europe, and he was launching his songs at the rate of almost one a week. He traveled incessantly, helping others to get careers started, performing for charitable affairs, inspiring young black entertainers, and always living the "high life" of a showman. By the early 1900s, however, life had changed for Bland. The world was no longer interested in his kind of entertainment, for vaudeville had replaced minstrelsy. Bland left England permanently, returning to Washington where he tried to begin a new career. But his efforts were useless. His last work was for a musical show, *The Sporting Girl*, a two-act production with eighteen songs which met with little success. Bland moved to Philadelphia, where he died penniless and alone.

Of the approximately seven hundred songs written by James Bland, the best remembered are *In the Evening by the Moonlight; In the Morning by the Bright Light; Oh, Dem Golden Slippers;* and *Carry Me Back to Old Virginny*. The last-named song was published by Bland in 1878, when he was twenty-four years old.

Sixty-two years later (in 1940) the state of Virginia adopted the song as its official state song. Few realized that it was the composition of a Negro minstrel who sang his way into the hearts of the public during the turn of the century. *Oh, Dem Golden Slippers* was used as the theme song for the Mummers' Annual New Year's Day parade in Philadelphia for over fifty years. The opening bars of *In the Evening by the Moonlight* seems to have been the direct inspiration for the popular World War I song *There's a Long, Long Trail a-Winding*, for the beginning of the chorus in the later song is identical, note for note, to the beginning of Bland's melody. Other melodies have been used over the years as campaign songs (*The Missouri Hound Dog*), marching songs (*Dandy Black Brigade*), and in background music for movies, for radio, and television shows. A number of Bland's songs are on file at the Library of Congress, among them sentimental ballads as well as minstrel types. A good minstrel was expected to bring tears to the eyes as well as laughter to the lips, and James Bland was one of the best.

BLACK MINSTREL STARS

The Georgia Minstrels had more than its share of musical talent over the years; Bland was simply the best of a number of superior men. Billy Kersands (d. 1915) joined the original company in 1865 and spent the remainder of his life in one or another of the big troupes. At one time, he even owned his own company. It was said in the South that a minstrel show without Bill Kersands was like a circus without an elephant. While Kersands seems not to have been a song writer, his top billing as a minstrel endman and comedian enabled him to successfully launch the songs of others. The special dances associated with Kersands were the buck-and-wing and the soft shoe, sometimes called the "Virginia essence." He usually danced the latter to the music of Stephen Foster's *Old Folks at Home*.

A contemporary of Kersands, and like him a lifetime showman, was Samuel Lucas (1840–1916), the "Grand Old Man of the Stage." Lucas was born of free parents in Washington, Ohio. Before he joined the Union army, he had been a barber in his own town. After the war he went into show business—first playing with minstrel troupes, then later playing with vaudeville

Ex. IX.2   *Carve Dat Possum*, Sam Lucas

2. I reached up for to pull him in,
    Carve him to de heart;
    De possum he began to grin,
    Carve him to de heart;
    I carried him home and dressed him off,
    Carve him to de heart;
    I hung him dat night in de frost,
    Carve him to de heart.

    Carve dat possum,
       Carve dat possum, children,
    Carve dat possum,
       Carve him to de heart;
    Oh, carve dat possum, . . .

and musical comedy after minstrelsy had died out. Lucas always looked the part of the star, whether on or off the stage. During a tour of England he had been given a "big diamond cluster" by Queen Victoria, which he always wore, and a gold-headed cane by a member of the English nobility. He dressed very well, wearing in addition to the ring a big gold watch with a gold chain, so that sometimes he was mistaken for the owner of the company instead of its star. The diamond ring and gold watch were pawned more than once to rescue some minstrel troupe that had gotten stranded in a small town for lack of funds.

Lucas liked to write his own songs in order to be sure, as he used to say, that he would "never have to worry about running into anyone doing [his] stuff." Among the songs he made famous were *Grandfather's Clock, Turnip Greens,* and *Carve Dat Possum* (see Ex. IX.2).

Among the other stars attached to the minstrel troupes at one time or another in their careers were the celebrated banjoists the Bohee brothers, who introduced the specialty of dancing and playing banjos at the same time; the banjoist-composer Horace Weston (see p. 123); Billy Windom and Wallace King, both "heart-breaking" tenors; Robert Leach and Lorenzo Tio, Sr., first of the great Negro clarinetists; song writers Ernest Hogan (Reuben Crowder, 1865–1900) and Irving Jones; and, of course, bandleader-composer W. C. Handy. In addition to those who gained international fame and star billing there were hundreds of good instrumentalists, singers, dancers, and comedians who contributed to the development of this first Negro entertainment industry, the minstrel show.

The black minstrel has been much maligned by many, including members of his own race, for perpetuating the Jim Crow and Zip Coon stereotypes and other caricatures of Negroes that were established by white minstrels. It is true that black minstrels blackened their faces with burnt cork (no matter how dark their skins), made up enormous red lips, and used traditional slapstick jokes and gestures, comic patter-songs, and stylized dances. But they also brought to the stage much genuine humor, original dancing, the poignant songs of their people, and superb solo and ensemble performance, both vocal and instrumental. After the war, minstrelsy offered to the creative black man an opportunity to acquire experience in the theatrical arts that could scarcely have been obtained any other way during the period. Because so many gifted men were able to acquire this experience, they were able to contribute, directly or indirectly, to the development of musical comedy and the new music called "jazz" in a later era. Moreover, the black minstrel stars served as models for black youngsters to emulate. Many a budding singer or composer surmounted the hurdles and obstacles that might have prevented his obtaining music training because he wanted to become another James Bland or Sam Lucas or Billy Kersands.

A WRITER OF BALLADS

Gussie Davis (1863–99), who commanded the attention of the entertainment world for his talent in writing sentimental ballads, was the first black song writer to succeed in Tin Pan Alley. Born in Dayton, Ohio, Davis first worked as a Pullman porter on the railroad, but later took a job as a janitor at the Cincinnati Conservatory of Music because of the opportunity it afforded him to come into contact with music. While attending to his custodial duties, he paid close attention to the music lectures and learned to read and to write music. His enormous talent did the rest. During his brief lifetime, he wrote over three hundred songs and earned a place in the "star-studded galaxy of brilliant American song writers" during the "gay nineties."

Davis's first songs were published in Cincinnati, among them, *'Neath the Maples Long Ago* (1886); *In a Lighthouse by the Sea* (1886); and *The Hermit* (1888). He moved to New York in 1890, becoming one of the "mainstays" of the young firm of Edward B. Marks, according to the owner. Davis wrote one hit after the other, including *The Fatal Wedding* (1893); *Down in Poverty Row* (1895); and *The Baggage Coach Ahead* (1896). The latter sold more than one million copies of sheet music soon after it was published. The song was popularized by the noted white "female baritone," Imogene Comer, the "Queen Regent of Song." Its lyrics derived from an incident that had occurred during Davis's period of working on the railroad. It was this kind of song that led observers to state that Davis "did more than his share to open up the tear ducts of America."

Ex. IX.3 Chorus of *In the Baggage Coach Ahead*, Gussie L. Davis

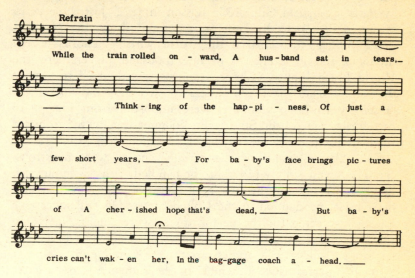

Two of the most popular songs in the 90s that were of Negro origin were written down and popularized by whites. The songs *Ta-ra-ra-boom-der-e* and *The Bully* originated in the notorious "Babe Conner's place" in St. Louis, where a black woman called Mama Lou with a powerful voice sang a large variety of Negro songs to the accompaniment of a blind pianist. White publishers retained the melodies, titles, and refrains, but "cleaned up" the lyrics for the public's benefit. *Ta-ra-ra-boom-der-e* was first introduced into the music halls of London by the white singer Lottie Collins and brought to New York as the sensational song of the year. *The Bully* was featured by white singer May Irwin on Broadway.

FESTIVALS, ROAD SHOWS, AND EXTRAVAGANZAS

The last three decades of the nineteenth century witnessed one big spectacular event after another, all of them providing

Negro entertainers with the opportunity to appear before the American public either in white shows or in all-black extravaganzas. The first of these was the World Peace Jubilee produced by Patrick Sarsfield Gilmore in Boston in 1872. Just three years earlier in Boston he had put on a colossal show, the National Peace Jubilee, that amazed the world with its chorus of ten thousand and its orchestra of one thousand players. For the World Peace Jubilee, Gilmore's chorus was doubled to twenty thousand singers and the orchestra to two thousand instrumentalists. World-famous soloists were imported from Europe to participate, and Johann Strauss the Younger was invited to direct the huge orchestra in the playing of *The Blue Danube Waltz*.

The musical results of the daring venture were disastrous; the forces were simply too big to be handled. What is significant, however, is that for the first time Negroes were included in a big musical production in the United States. On the huge stage especially erected for the performances were soloists, including the Hyer sisters, and singing ensembles, including the Fisk Jubilee Singers, and in the orchestra pit were two Negro violinists. After one performance a member of the audience wrote a letter to the *Progressive American:*

> Having occasion to visit Boston, I attended one of the unrivalled concerts at the Coliseum, where to my great astonishment, I saw undoubtedly the greatest assemblage of human beings ever congregated under one roof, and heard a chorus of nearly or quite twenty thousand voices, accompanied by the powerful organ and an orchestra of two thousand musicians. I was highly delighted. But what gave me the most pleasure was to see among some of the most eminent artists of the world two colored artists performing their parts in common with the others; viz, Henry F. Williams and F. E. Lewis. Each of these was competent to play his part, or he could not have occupied a place in the orchestra. I was informed by the superintendent of the orchestra that both these men were subjected to a very rigid examination prior to the commencement of the concerts.

> [July 17, 1872]

In 1876 the celebration of the Centennial of American Independence at Philadelphia was attended by crowned heads of Europe, presidents, and common people of three continents.

Among the exhibits was a plantation scene featuring the singing of Negro folksongs by ex-slaves and free-born blacks. A special attraction was the performance of an old folk dance dating back to ante-bellum times, called "chalk-line walk" or "cakewalk." Originally, the dance had been performed on the plantation by slave couples who competed for a prize, generally a cake, awarded to the pair that pranced around with the proudest, high-kicking steps. On some plantations the dancers moved with pails of water on their heads. Those who spilled the least water and yet maintained erect posture were declared the winners.

In Chicago, in 1893, a celebration was held in honor of the four-hundredth anniversary of the discovery of America (a year late, to be sure). Called the World's Columbian Exposition, it attracted more than 27,500,000 visitors. One of the exhibits consisted of the reproduction of a tiny African village, as we noted in Chapter I, where Dahomans performed dances several times a day to the music of drums, bells, and singing. On the day designated as "Colored American Day," the musical performances included singing by Harry Burleigh, a rising young baritone; the reading of poems by young Paul Laurence Dunbar; and violin playing by Joseph Douglass, a grandson of the fiery old abolitionist Frederick Douglass (see Plate IX). The amusements of the exposition were centered along a road called the Midway Plaisance. Entertainers from all over the land, black and white, flocked to the Midway seeking employment in the night spots and dance halls. Black musical talent was also employed in less spectacular events during this period; for example, the inauguration of President James A. Garfield on March 4, 1881, when a Negro band played march arrangements of Bland's melodies in the inauguration parade.

After the war a number of traveling road shows that included plantation or levee scenes employed Negroes in singing and dancing roles and in walk-on parts "to provide atmosphere." The perennial favorite was *Uncle Tom's Cabin*, which used whites with blackened faces for the leading roles but Negroes for the minor parts. History was made in the 1880s when for the first time a black man, Sam Lucas of minstrel fame, was hired to play Uncle Tom. A second long-lived show was *In Old Kentucky*, which was based on a plot about thoroughbred race horses and plantation life in Kentucky and which used black singers and dancers in the stable scene. An added feature in the scene was a so-called "pickaninny band" composed of small boys playing brass instruments. The show opened each year in New York at the old Academy of Music, then went out on the road to play cities, towns, villages, and hamlets all over the country. Among the other traveling shows that provided employment for black entertainers were *Down in Dixie, On the Mississippi,* and *South Before the War.*

Negro brass "boy bands" became very popular, especially because of the novelty they added to almost any plantation scene. The first of these bands was organized in Cincinnati by John Brister, who was also the leader of an adult brass band, for one of the *In Old Kentucky* companies. According to Tom Fletcher, Brister's Boy Band was the first black touring boy band in the country. One year, the boys were given silver instruments with gold bells by the C. G. Conn Company of Elkhart, Indiana, a leading instrument-manufacturing company. During the 1880s many road shows were accompanied by these bands, most of which originated in Cincinnati.

It was inevitable that eventually an all-black extravaganza should be produced. The idea was conceived by Billy McClain, an old-time minstrel man, who already had helped launch the *South Before the War* company. About 1893 he found a promoter for his show in Nate Salsbury, an ex-impresario of Buffalo Bill's. The plans called for a big outdoor pageant with a cast of five hundred. Ambrose Park in Brooklyn, New York, and the Huntington Avenue grounds in Boston were selected as sites, and the show, *Black America,* was produced in the Summer of 1894. The park grounds were transformed into plantation scenes with real cabins, livestock, cotton fields, and cotton gins, about which people could wander until the show began. The performance itself took place in a huge amphitheater. The first part of the show was devoted to a re-creating of African episodes in dance and song; the second part consisted of American songs and dances (i.e. in the European and Afro-American traditions); and for the finale there was a grand cakewalk contest. McClain assembled his cast from all over the nation. Because show people were generally free in the Summer, he was able to obtain the best talent of the period. Sixty-three male quartets added their rich voices to the singing of the "field hands" in the plantation scenes and to the operatic choral numbers. One of the quartets was the well-known Golden Gate Quartet. A small company from the United States Ninth Cavalry put on a spectacular drill act, accompanied by costumed girls riding horses. The extravaganza was a success musically and financially. More important, it impressed white managers that a huge reservoir of Negro talent was available for employment in the entertainment world.

ITINERANT AND COMMUNITY MUSICIANS

The post-war years saw the emergence of a class of black musicians who, though humble and without public recognition, nevertheless contributed their share to the musical traditions of black folk in the United States. They provided essential music services for the newly established Negro communities, playing organ or piano in the churches, playing in the opera houses for musical events staged by local groups, playing in the dance halls, beer parlors, and saloons. Sometimes these men were professionals who had been traveling with a minstrel troupe or a circus or medicine show that was left stranded in a town. Frequently the musicians were self-taught drifters who were never to settle down permanently. Then there were those who were natives of the towns where they assumed the roles of community musicians. Perhaps they had studied music with a local white musician or, like the drifters, had taught themselves and developed some degree of skill by virtue of continuous practicing.

In addition to providing service music, these men often organized bands and orchestras or vocal and choral ensembles, infusing new spirit into community life during their temporary or permanent sojourns. Such a man was Jim Turner, who visited Florence, Alabama, when W. C. Handy was a schoolboy. Originally from Memphis, Turner had suffered through a tragic love affair and landed in Florence after asking the railroad ticket agent to sell him a ticket to "anywheres, just anywheres." Handy observed that "the proud little town entertained a genius unawares." Turner was a good violinist. He organized an orchestra, taught dancing, and brought a glimpse of another world to the provincial little town. Moreover, he planted the "seed of discontent" in Handy's mind and caused the boy to "yearn" for the gayer world of Memphis.

In the larger towns and cities, wandering musicians staged impromptu song recitals on street corners or in eating places and saloons, passing around a hat afterward to collect coins from listeners. Sometimes they boarded the riverboats and played for passengers in the staterooms, or they sang and played on trains and in railroad stations. Youngsters formed quartets that serenaded the neighbors, sang on street corners in cheap restaurants, and performed for community dances and picnics.

The part-time musician was as common in black communities as in white communities of the period. When Handy went to Bessemer, Alabama, in the 1890s, for example, he worked at the Howard and Harrison Pipe Works during days and engaged in musical activities during his free time. He organized a brass band, led a string orchestra and taught its members to read music, played trumpet with the choir in one of the churches, and sang to his own guitar accompaniment on social occasions. Waiter-musicians frequently provided entertainment for patrons in the places where they worked, particularly on the packet boats that ran the Ohio, Missouri, and Mississippi Rivers. Fletcher tells of boarding one of the riverboats on the Ohio to join with the boat's barber and a waiter in forming a vocal trio, accompanied by guitar and jew's-harp, to serenade the passengers.

According to a note in the diary of Cornelia Adair, a woman traveling in 1874 by steamboat down the Mississippi from St. Paul to St. Louis, the entertainment provided by waiters could be quite extensive. After dinner the tables in the saloon were cleared away and a band came out, composed of some of the waiters, "all black," who had just finished serving the meal. First the men played "uncommonly well" an overture from some opera. Then a tenor sang some arias and other "heart-breaking" melodies. About nine o'clock the band began to play dance music, beginning with a quadrille. The dance figures were called out by the big double-bass player, whose voice could be heard roaring over the sound of the music, the din of the boat engines, and occasional steam whistles: "Ladies' chain—Gents to the right —Dos à dos—Allemand all—Ladies in the center—Promenade!"

The barber and his shop played an important part in the musical life of early Negro rural and small-town communities.

Owned and operated by black men, open from early morn until late at night, barbershops provided congenial meeting places where the musically inclined could discourse on music or practice in a back room without interruption. It was no accident that many of the early musicians were barbers, some of whom became famous—such as Richard Milburn, the guitarist-whistler; Sam Lucas, the minstrel king; and Buddy Bolden, the famous trumpeter of New Orleans. Barbers could not leave their shops during the day, yet there were periods when no patrons came in and time hung heavy on their hands. If they had musical skills, there was unlimited time to practice and develop those skills. Musicians frequently received their first lessons in the community barbershop. It was there, for example, that W. C. Handy first learned to play the cornet. A white bandmaster who had been traveling with a circus that became stranded trained the Negro band of Florence, Alabama, in the neighborhood barbershop. Handy could see the bandleader's fingering charts through the windows of the shop as he passed by on the way to school. It was only a matter of time before he had joined the bandsmen inside the shop.

CHAPTER X

The Turn of the Century

The last decade of the nineteenth century brought a period of unprecedented opportunity for black men to develop and exercise their talents, despite the fact that for every new avenue open to them twice as many barriers were thrown up to prevent their advance. This was the era that saw the ascendency of such race leaders as educators Booker T. Washington (1856–1915), John Hope (1864–1936), William E. B. DuBois (1868–1963), Carter G. Woodson (1875–1950), and Mary McLeod Bethune (1875–1955); the surgeon Daniel Hale Williams (1856–1931) and the scientist George Washington Carver (1864–1943); the business tycoons Madame C. J. Walker (1869–1919) and Charles Clinton Spaulding (1874–1952); the sculptress Edmonia Lewis (1845–1890); the historian George Washington Williams (1849–1891); the novelist Charles Waddell Chesnutt (1858–1932); the artist Henry Ossawa Tanner (1859–1937); and the poet Paul Laurence Dunbar (1872–1906). Other names could be added to the list, names of black pioneers in the fields of politics, religion, business, and the professions, who were recognized by America for achievement. In the field of music, perhaps more than in any other field, the black man's pre-eminence was acknowledged by the nation. As we shall see, his contributions not only made a decisive impact on the existing style of music in the western tradition, but also gave birth to a new style of music.

THE GENERAL STATE OF MUSIC

During the last decades of the nineteenth century the United States entered upon a new era in her musical history. Symphony orchestras and major opera companies were established, a native American school of composers emerged, and promising developments took place in the area of music education. The Philharmonic Society of New York, oldest professional orchestra in the country (1842), was reorganized in 1901 and renamed the New York Philharmonic Society. Guided by a succession of distinguished directors, the orchestra won for itself a reputation as one of the world's leading symphonies. Other permanent major orchestras founded during these years include the Boston Symphony (1881), the Philadelphia Symphony (1900), the Minneapolis Symphony (1903), the Chicago Symphony (1904), and the Cincinnati Symphony (1909).

With regard to opera, New Orleans continued its dominance until the end of the nineteenth century, importing famous opera stars to sing with its highly trained opera companies. New York had had impressive opera performances since 1825, but it was not until 1883 that the permanent Metropolitan Opera Company gave its opening performance in a new Opera House. In Chicago, a new auditorium was provided for the Chicago Opera in 1889, and soon afterward the company was established on a firm basis.

One of the main purposes of the Boston Academy of Music, founded in 1832 by Lowell Mason (1792–1872) and others, was to serve as a center where children could receive music education. Primarily because of Mason's pioneering activity in music education, Boston became in 1838 the first city in the United States to introduce music into the public-school curriculum. Mason then organized "musical conventions" where teachers could be trained, first in Boston, later in New York. The movement continued to grow; by the beginning of the twentieth century most public schools were including music instruction as part of the course of study. Meanwhile, schools devoted to the training of professional musicians were being established: in 1857, the Peabody Conservatory in Baltimore; in 1865, Oberlin School of Music; in 1867, the New England Conservatory of Music, the Cincinnati Conservatory, and Chicago Musical College; and in 1870, the Philadelphia Musical Academy. The next two decades saw the founding of the New York College of Music in 1878, the National Conservatory of Music at New York in 1885, and the American Conservatory at Chicago in 1886. The last major music school to be established before World War I was the Institute of Musical Art, founded in New York in 1904.

While black musicians were generally barred from participation in the activities of the symphony orchestras and opera companies, they were freely admitted to some of the music schools and conservatories. Moreover, a few Negro students enjoyed the patronage of such eminent musicians as the Bohemian composer Antonín Dvořák (1841–1904), director of the National Conservatory of Music during the years 1892–95, and the violinist-composer Julius Eichberg, director of the Boston Conservatory. A number of Negroes took advantage of the opportunity to obtain an excellent music education, and some completed their studies by going to Europe to work with musicians there. It was no accident that the most active and most creative colonies of black musicians should develop in those places where musical training—formal or informal—was available to them and where, after they were trained, they found opportunities to employ their talents.

The first "school" of white American composers appeared in New England and was active from about 1875 to the time of World War I. Among the most important of the pioneering composers were John Knowles Paine (1839–1906), who became the first professor of music at Harvard University in 1875 (he had begun teaching there in 1862 as an instructor); Arthur William Foote (1853–1937), who helped to found the American Guild of Organists in 1896; George Whitefield Chadwick (1854–1931), who taught at the New England Conservatory and later became its director; and Horatio William Parker (1863–1919), who taught first at the National Conservatory in New York, then later at Yale University. These men and others of their circle have been called the "Boston Classicists" or the "New England Academicians." Trained for the most part in Germany, they composed under the spell of German romanticism and produced works that have been labeled "academic." Of the group, only Chadwick has been credited with having a "spark of genuine inspiration, flavored with a sense of humor" in his music. But they did succeed in giving to the native American composer, both in the United States and in Europe, a social and professional prestige that he had not had in the past. Their works were performed at home and abroad; their musical ideas influenced the later generations of native American composers who studied under their tutelage. More than one of these men had Negro students, if not in their immediate classes then in the conservatories or university music departments that they headed. Chadwick gave lessons in composition to a man who would be acclaimed the "Dean of Afro-American Composers"—William Grant Still.

There are at least two other white composers of this period who influenced, directly or indirectly, the development of the first school of black composers in the United States. Edward Alexander MacDowell (1861–1908), a native of New York, was the foremost composer of the period, but like the "Boston Group," he represented the past and contributed little that younger composers found of value. Daniel Gregory Mason (1873–1953) was a New Englander and followed in the tradition of the New England composers, although he spent his later years in New York as a music professor at Columbia University.

THE NATIONALISTIC MOVEMENT IN THE UNITED STATES

In the first part of the nineteenth century at least two white composers had shown interest in developing a truly "American" music, inspired by the nation's history and by the native Indian and Negro folk music. Anton Philipp Heinrich (1781–1861), a native of Bohemia who came to the United States about 1818, was so impressed by the country's natural scenery, its exciting history, and the music of the Indians, that he was inspired to write a large quantity of music about these things. His publications, which now have little more than historic value, include works with such titles as *The Dawning of Music in Kentucky*, *Yankee Doodliad*, *Indian Carnival*, and *Indian Fanfares*. Louis Moreau Gottschalk (1829–69), the first American concert artist and composer to achieve international renown, was born in New Orleans and consequently fell heir to the rich music traditions of that colorful city. Three of his most popular compositions, *Bamboula*, *La Savane* (or *Ballade Créole*), and *Le Bananier* (or *Chanson Nègre*) used Negro folk tunes of New Orleans. He also wrote pieces inspired by Afro-Cuban folk music.

It was not until the decade of the 1890s, however, that a nationalistic school of music actually got under way in the United States. Dvořák started it all. Soon after he came to America as director of the National Conservatory in New York in 1892, he revealed his enthusiasm for the native folk music of the land and called for the formation of an American school of composition. Dvořák became particularly fond of one of his Negro students at the conservatory, Harry Burleigh, and spent many hours listening to him sing the folksongs of his people and discussing with him the possibilities for utilizing the folk music as the basis for composition. Within three months of his arrival, Dvořák had begun work on a symphony, *From the New World* (No. 5 in E minor), that employed themes invented in the spirit of Negro and Indian folk melodies. Just before its New York première in 1893, Dvořák stated:

> These beautiful and varied themes are the product of the soil. They are American. They are the folksongs of America, and your composers must turn to them. In the Negro melodies of America I discover all that is needed for a great and noble school of music.

Dvořák wrote two other works in which he used themes employing the idioms of Negro spirituals, the so-called "American" Quartet (Op. 96) and a quintet (Op. 97). He returned to Bohemia in 1895, leaving behind an awakened interest in America's folk music among the composers of the time, which led to the rise of a genuine musical nationalism for the first time.

Two of Dvořák's white students at the conservatory accepted his challenge. William Arms Fisher (1861–1948) made settings of Negro spirituals, publishing one collection as *Seventy Negro Spirituals* (1926). Fisher's arrangement of the second-movement theme of Dvořák's *From the New World* Symphony as a pseudo-spiritual with the text *Goin' Home* was popular at one time. Rubin Goldmark (1872–1936), who became a teacher at the conservatory and, later, at the Institute of Musical Art, wrote *A Negro Rhapsody*. Among other white Americans who were inspired to use Negro folk materials during this period were Henry F. B. Gilbert (1868–1928) and John Powell (1882–1963), both of them writing Negro rhapsodies and other symphonic

Traditional African instruments: trumpets, drums, and other percussion. *(Courtesy New York Public Library, Schomburg Collection.)*

II

MOORS

BERBERS

A

F

Senegal River

St. Louis
de Senegal

FULANI

Timbuktu

Cape
Verde

JOLOF

Gambia River

James
Fort

MANDINGOS

Niger River

Segu

SUSU

Sierra Leone

VAI

Sherbro
Island

KRUMEN

AWIKAM

Grain Coast

Ivory Coast

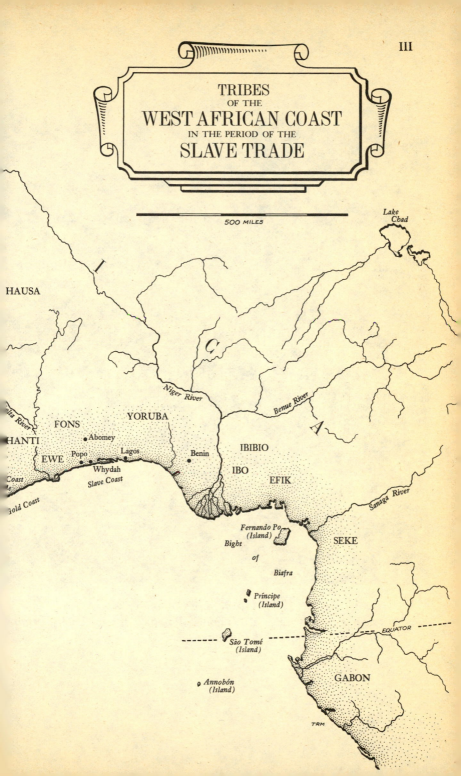

III

TRIBES
OF THE
WEST AFRICAN COAST
IN THE PERIOD OF THE
SLAVE TRADE

500 MILES

Lake
Chad

HAUSA

Niger River

Benue River

Volta River

FONS   YORUBA

HANTI   IBIBIO

EWE   Popo   Lagos   Benin

ABOMEY

Whydah   IBO

Coast   Slave Coast   EFIK

Gold Coast   Sanaga River

Fernando Po
(Island)   SEKE

Bight

of

Biafra

Príncipe
(Island)

EQUATOR

São Tomé
(Island)

Annobón
(Island)   GABON

TRM

The First Day of the Yam Custom in Dahomey, 1818. After a colored engraving made by Edward Thomas Bowdich for his book *Mission from Cape Coast Castle to Ashantee.*

The Bamboula. Reproduction of a drawing by E. W. Kemble, included in an article by George Cable, "The Dance in Place Congo," *Century Magazine* 31 (1885-86). African-type instruments were generally used in the slaves' own jubilees.

Merrymaking at a Wayside Inn. White Americans danced to the music of black fiddlers in the early years of the nation. The Russian traveler Paul Petrovich Svinin included the above scene in his collection, "A Portfolio of Water Color Sketches of the United States: 1811-1813."

The Coffle Gang. "There is not a village or road that does not behold the sad procession of manacled outcasts, whose chains and mournful countenances tell that they are exiled by force from all that their hearts hold dear." Picture and quotation from George Carleton, *The Suppressed Book About Slavery* (New York, 1864), p. 164.

De Jubilee Am Come! Contemporary cartoon depicting the slaves' celebration of Emancipation. *(Courtesy New York Public Library, Schomburg Collection.)*

The Original Fisk Jubilee Singers. Copy of a painting made in London for Queen Victoria. (*Courtesy New York Public Library, Schomburg Collection.*)

Sissieretta Jones, the "Black Patti."

James A. Bland.

lale quartet of the post Civil-
Var period (possibly the Lew
Juartet).

Joseph Douglass and his grandfather, Frederick Douglass.

Civil War army band, 107th U. S. Colored Infantry. *(Courtesy Library of Congress.)*

X

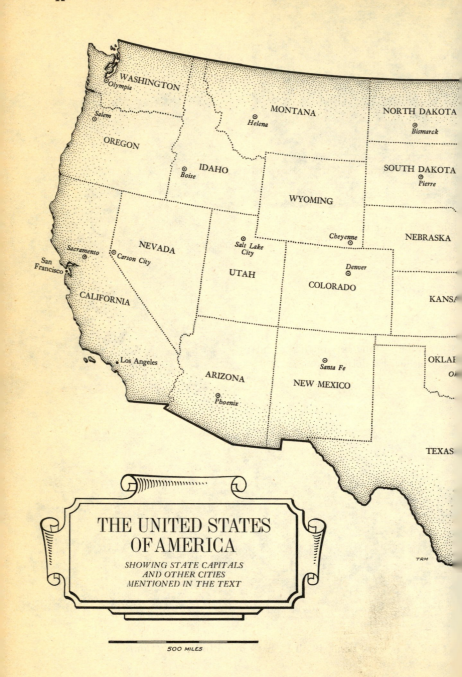

THE UNITED STATES
OF AMERICA

SHOWING STATE CAPITALS
AND OTHER CITIES
MENTIONED IN THE TEXT

500 MILES

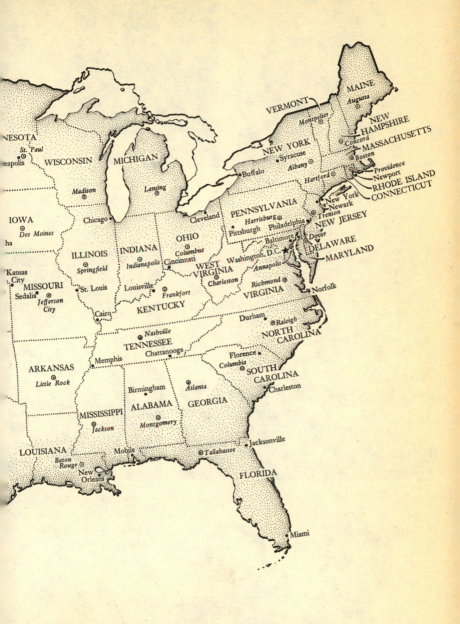

XII

Scott Joplin.

Jelly Roll Morton. *(Courtesy New York Public Library, Americana Collection of the Music Division.)*

Eubie Blake.

James P. Johnson. *(Co New York Public Li Americana Collection Music Division.)*

Robert Cole and J. Rosamond Johnson.

A Clef Club orchestra, 1910; James Reese Europe, director.

Will Marion Cook. *(Courtesy New York Public Library, Theatre Division.)*

World War I parade of an unidentified army band. *(Courtesy New York Public Library, Schomburg Collection.)*

Small dance orchestra of the 1920s. At the piano is A. Jones, the orchestra director; Ferman Tapp is playing the banjo; others unidentified.

Original orchestra of *Shuffle Along*, 1921. Among those than can be identified are cellist Leonard Jeter (center), oboist William Grant Still (fourth from right), violist Hall Johnson (third from right), and Eubie Blake (piano).

Harry T. Burleigh.

Clarence Cameron White.

R. Nathaniel Dett.

The Negro String Quartet; active in New York during the 1920s: Arthur Boyd, violin; Felix Weir, violin; Hall Johnson, viola; Marion Cumbo, cello.

Eva Jessye.

Roland Hayes.

Marian Anderson. (
tesy *Hurok Concerts*

A Hall Johnson Choir during the mid-century years.

W. C. Handy and Duke Ellington. *(Courtesy New York Public
Library, Americana Collection
of the Music Division.)*

World War II jam session (unidentified
musicians). *(Courtesy New York Public
Library, Schomburg Collection.)*

eontyne Price, as Leonora in
*erdi's Il Trovatore. (Courtesy
ouis Melançon, Metropolitan
pera House.)*

George Shirley. *(Courtesy
Metropolitan Opera Archives.)*

Arthur Cunningham.

Hale Smith.

William Grant Still.

works with Negro themes. Daniel Gregory Mason (1873–1953) wrote a string quartet on Negro themes. Arthur Farwell (1872–1952) not only wrote nationalistic music and collected folksongs, but also founded the Wa-Wan Press in 1901 for the express purpose of publishing compositions of American composers and collections of Indian and Negro folksongs. However, no black composers were represented in the Wa-Wan Press catalogue.

BLACK NATIONALISTIC COMPOSERS

Almost the entire first group of post-slavery black composers —i.e. those born before 1900—may be regarded as nationalists in the sense that they consciously turned to the folk music of their people as a source of inspiration for their composed music, whether in the fields of concert music, show music, or dance and entertainment music. Most of those who achieved distinction, and some of lesser stature as well, were excellently trained; they had studied at Oberlin, the New England Conservatory, and the National Conservatory in New York, or privately with competent, European-trained white musicians. Consequently, they knew how to write music in traditional European style and, indeed, often did so, particularly when they wanted the music to sell. But they reserved much of their creative energy for Negro-inspired composition. The song writers set the poems of black poets and made vocal and choral arrangements of spirituals and other folksong types. The instrumental composers wrote program music, drawing heavily upon characteristic Negro melodic idioms and dance rhythms. All the composers placed special emphasis upon traditional Negro performance practices, and made efforts to reflect the individualities of these practices in their composed music.

The composers who won recognition in the field of concert music generally began to publish late, first pursuing careers as performers or teachers. The composers of show music and entertainment music wrote prolifically from the beginning, and although much of their music remained unpublished, it was performed and consequently was known to the appropriate segment of the public for which it was written.

HARRY BURLEIGH

Harry Thacker Burleigh (1866–1949) was the earliest of the black nationalistic composers. He also was the first Negro to achieve national distinction as a composer, arranger, and concert singer. A native of Erie, Pennsylvania, Burleigh revealed an interest in music as a child, although he was not provided with an opportunity to study then. His mother, who was educated, was forced to do household work after her husband's death left her with five children to support. On one occasion he stood for hours in the snow outside the Russell home where his mother was employed, waiting to hear the piano artistry of Rafael Joseffy through the drawing-room windows. When Mrs. Russell heard of it, she arranged for the boy to serve as a doorman whenever she had musical evenings in her home so that he could come into direct contact with her guest artists.

Until he was twenty-six, Burleigh had little formal training in music, but he sang in churches and synagogues of Erie whenever the opportunity arose. In 1892 he went to New York, after obtaining a scholarship to the National Conservatory of Music with the assistance of friends, one of whom was the mother of MacDowell. During his second year there he began to study with Dvořák. As we have observed, Dvořák took an interest in Burleigh, and the singer became a constant visitor to the composer's apartment on East Seventeenth Street. While at the conservatory Burleigh acquired practical experience with orchestral music as well as vocal music—he played double bass and, later, timpani in the orchestra. As a senior he was given the opportunity to teach voice at the conservatory and continued to do so for two years after graduation.

By 1894 Burleigh found himself launched on a career as a singer. He had applied for the position of baritone soloist at St. George's Episcopal Church and was selected over fifty other applicants, though not without opposition from some of the parishioners because of his race. In 1900 he was appointed to a similar position at Temple Emanu-El. During these years Burleigh concertized extensively in the United States and in Europe, his appearances in England including a command performance before King Edward VII. About 1898 he began to compose songs—at first, sentimental ballads in the conventional style of the time, then later, as his skills developed, sensitive settings of fine poems. Eventually Burleigh shifted his attention from singing to composing, although he continued to give occasional recitals and retained his posts at St. George's and Temple Emanu-El. The position he took as a music editor with G. Ricordi and Company in 1900 permitted him to concentrate on composing and provided him with a publishing contact. In 1917 Burleigh was awarded the Spingarn Achievement Medal for excellence in the field of creative music. Later he received an honorary master's degree from Atlanta University and an honorary Doctor of Music from Howard University, Washington, D. C. In Indiana, an organization devoted to the performance of Negro music named itself the Harry T. Burleigh Association.

Burleigh left more than ninety songs, fifty or more choral pieces, approximately fifty arrangements of spirituals for solo voice, and some miscellaneous works, including the early *Six Plantation Melodies for Violin and Piano* (1901). Other nonvocal works include *From the Southland* for piano (1914) and *Southland Sketches* for violin and piano (1916). Among the best of his art songs are *I Love My Jean* (Robert Burns poem, 1914), *Saracen Songs* (1914), *The Prayer* (1915), *Five Songs* (poems of Lawrence Hope, 1919), and *Lovely Dark and Lonely One* (poem of the black poet Langston Hughes, 1935). The *Saracen Songs* cycle was acclaimed at the time of its publication as Burleigh's "most ambitious and successful achievement." W. J. Henderson, music editor of the *New York Sun* wrote:

> The rich Orientalism of the text has warmed the composer's imagination so that it has found eloquent and captivating musical setting for the thoughts. . . . [The composer's] poetic conceptions are paired with his masterly musicianship.

His ballads and art songs were popularized by such well-known white concert singers of the period as Lucrezia Bori, Ernestine Schumann-Heink, and John McCormack. McCormack, in particular, was responsible for acquainting the public with Burleigh's *Little Mother of Mine* (1917), *Dear Old Pal of Mine* (1918), *Under a Blazing Star* (1918), and *In the Great Somewhere* (1919). One of the several war songs that Burleigh wrote,

The Young Warrior (poem by the black poet James Weldon Johnson, 1916), was translated into Italian and used as a marching song by regiments of the Italian army during World War I. Another song, *Ethiopia Saluting the Colors* (1916), preserves the vitality of the Walt Whitman poem that it sets.

Burleigh's determination to capture the spirit of Negro folksong in composed music marks him a true disciple of his teacher, Dvořák. It was as an arranger of spirituals for the solo voice that Burleigh made a unique contribution to the history of American music. Before he published his arrangement of *Deep River* in 1916, the nation had heard only ensemble and choral performances of spirituals. Burleigh gave to the 1916 collection the title *Jubilee Songs of the United States of America*. His achievement made available to concert singers for the first time Negro spirituals set in the manner of fine art songs. The piano accompaniment in his arrangements never overpowers the simple

Ex. X.1   *Deep River*, arr. Burleigh

melody, but rather sets and sustains a dominant emotional mood throughout the song. Chromatic harmonies are used within the basically diatonic coloring, but discreetly, so as not to destroy the balance between piano and vocal line (see Ex. X.1).

After Burleigh, many concert singers developed the tradition of closing their recitals with a group of Negro spirituals, sometimes intermixed with other arranged folksongs. One critic wrote about the Burleigh arrangements:

> They are one and all little masterpieces, settings by one of our time's most gifted song-composers of melodies, which he penetrates as probably no other living composer.
>
> [*Musical America*, October 17, 1917]

Burleigh himself wrote about his aim:

> My desire was to preserve them [the spirituals] in harmonies that belong to modern methods of tonal progression without robbing the melodies of their racial flavor.
>
> [*New York World*, October 25, 1924]

In 1929 Burleigh published the *Old Songs Hymnal*, a collection of very simple arrangements of Negro songs for nonprofessionals "to be used in church and home and school, preserving to us this precious heritage."

CLARENCE CAMERON WHITE

Clarence Cameron White (1880–1960), composer and violinist, was born in Clarksville, Tennessee, but spent his early childhood in Oberlin, Ohio, where his father practiced medicine. Upon the death of his father, his mother remarried and the family went to live in Washington, D. C. There White attended public schools and Howard University, and upon graduation, entered the Oberlin Conservatory of Music with the goal of becoming a concert violinist. Even before he completed his studies there he had embarked upon a career as a recitalist. After graduation from Oberlin in 1901, White returned to Washington, D. C., taking a position as a violin teacher in the newly founded (Negro) Washington Conservatory of Music and teaching also in the

THE H. T. BURLEIGH MUSIC ASSOCIATION

presents

THE WORLD PREMIERE
OF

"OUANGA"

AN OPERA IN THREE ACTS

Music by
Clarence Cameron White

Libretto by
John Frederick Matheus

Conducted by
The Composer and Zigmont G. Gaska

Stage Director
James Lewis Casaday

Choreography
by
Katherine Flowers, Vernon Duncan,
Madge Rose Brockevelt

▼

Friday and Saturday, June 10th & 11th, 1949

8:15 P. M.

Central High School Auditorium

SOUVENIR PROGRAM, 50c

Title page of the program for the stage première of Clarence White's
Ouanga, 1949. (*Courtesy John F. Matheus.*)

public schools. In the Summer of 1906 and again during the years 1908–11 White lived in London, where he studied violin with the Russian violinist Zakarevich and composition with the African-English composer Samuel Coleridge-Taylor.

Returning to the United States in 1910, White settled in Boston, opened a music studio, and took up again his periodic concert tours, his wife (the former Beatrice Warrick) serving as accompanist. It was during this period (1912–23) that he began to publish some of the pieces he had been composing over the years. His first publications were salon pieces and teaching materials written in the conventional style of the time. Then he turned to the folk music of his people as a source of inspiration for his work, making arrangements of spirituals and writing violin compositions that utilized spirituals as thematic material. In 1924 White was appointed director of music at a Negro institution, West Virginia State College; his teaching responsibilities there, however, did not prevent him from composing and occasionally concertizing. During the Summer of 1928 White and John F. Matheus, a professor of romance languages at the college, visited the black republic of Haiti for the purpose of studying the folk music and lore of that country. After returning to the United States, Matheus wrote a play, *Tambour*, for which White composed incidental music, including the ballet number *Meringue*.

But the most important outgrowth of the Haitian visit was the decision of the two men to write an opera based on the life of Dessalines, Haiti's liberator and first ruler. Matheus wrote the libretto for the opera, which was given the title *Ouanga* (meaning "charm" or "talisman" in Haitian Creole), and White began work on the music. In two successive years (1930, 1931) White received grants from the Julius Rosenwald Fund that enabled him to study abroad and work on the opera he had begun. While in Paris he studied with Raoul Laparra, completing the opera; a string quartet using Negro themes, entitled *Prelude*, *Dawn*, and *Jubilee Hallelujah;* and also several small violin pieces. The string quartet was performed at the École Normale de Musique by a faculty ensemble.

In November, 1932, the White-Matheus opera was presented in concert form by the American Opera Society in Chicago. Seventeen years later, in June, 1949, the Burleigh Musical Association gave the world stage première of *Ouanga* in South Bend, Indiana. The critic of the *South Bend Tribune* wrote:

> This is a rich score. The themes are on a rhythmic pattern that jolts and sways with a jungle beat and often sweeps to majestic, terrifying heights. The production was colorful and tumultuous. The settings were eye-filling and handsome.
>
> [June 11, 1949]

In 1950, a Negro opera company of Philadelphia, the Dra-Mu, produced *Ouanga* at the Academy of Music. The National Negro Opera Company gave a concert version of the opera with ballet in May, 1956, at the Metropolitan Opera House and repeated the performance at Carnegie Hall in September of the same year.

During the years 1931–35 White served as the director of Music at Hampton Institute; from 1937 to 1941 he was an organizer of community music programs for the National Recreational Association. White won several awards and prizes in addition to the Rosenwald grants: the Harmon Foundation Award (1927), the David Bispham Medal for his opera (1932), an honorary M.A. from Atlanta University (1928), an honorary Doctor of Music from Wilberforce University (1933), and the Benjamin Award for "tranquil music" for his *Elegy* (1954). His activity as a concert violinist earned him a place in *Who's Who in America* for several years.

White composed works for violin, piano, solo voice, chorus, orchestra, band, chamber ensemble, and organ. Best known of his works were the violin *Bandana Sketches* (1920); *Cabin Memories* (1921); *From the Cotton Fields* (1921); two collections of spirituals, *Forty Negro Spirituals* (1927) and *Traditional Negro Spirituals* (1940), arranged for voice and piano accompaniment; three orchestral works, *Piece for Strings and Timpani, Kutamba Rhapsody*, and Symphony in D minor; a ballet, *A Night in Sans Souci;* and the Violin Concerto No. 2 in E minor. His arrangements of spirituals for violin and piano were regarded as effective concert pieces by violinists during the 1920s and 30s and were played by such noted violinists as Fritz Kreisler, Albert Spalding, and Irma Seydel.

R. NATHANIEL DETT

Robert Nathaniel Dett (1882–1943) achieved recognition as a composer, arranger, pianist, and choral conductor. Born in Drummondsville, Ontario, where fugitive slaves had established a thriving Negro community, Dett heard his people singing their spirituals and other songs from earliest childhood on. He obtained his early musical training at the Oliver Willis Halstead Conservatory in Lockport, New York, and afterward attended Oberlin Conservatory, where he received the Bachelor of Music degree in 1908. In later years Dett continued his musical studies at the American Conservatory of Music in Chicago, Columbia University, the University of Pennsylvania, and Harvard.

Dett toured briefly as a concert pianist and taught at Lane College (1908–11) and Lincoln Institute in Missouri (1911–13) before he accepted in 1913 the position of director of music at Hampton Institute, where he remained for eighteen years. Dett took a leave of absence from his teaching duties in 1920, going to Boston where he studied piano with Arthur Foote and composition at Harvard. Again in 1929 Dett took time off to study, this time in France with the noted teacher Nadia Boulanger at the American Conservatory at Fontainebleau. In 1932 he went to Rochester, New York, where he maintained a music studio, although returning twice to college teaching, in 1935 at Sam Houston College (then in Austin, Texas), and in 1937 at Bennett College in North Carolina. Over the years Dett composed continuously, arranged spirituals and other Negro folksongs for voice and chorus, and developed fine choral groups at the colleges where he taught and in various communities. Under his leadership the forty-voice Hampton Institute Choir won special recognition for its high level of musicianship, being called to appear at such places as the Library of Congress for a music festival (1918), Carnegie Hall in New York, and Symphony Hall in Boston. In 1930 the Hampton Choir made a tour of seven European countries and won the critical acclaim of the press. In 1931 the choir repeated its successes in a tour of the United States.

Among Dett's best-known works were five piano suites, *Mag-*

nolia (1912), *In the Bottoms* (1913), *Enchantment* (1922), *The Cinnamon Grove* (1928), and *Tropic Winter* (1938); three motets, *Listen to the Lambs, I'll Never Turn Back No More*, and *Don't Be Weary, Traveler;* two songs, *Magic Moon of Molten Gold* and *A Thousand Years or More;* and three choral works in large form, *Music in the Mine* (1916), and the oratorios *The Chariot Jubilee* (1921) and *The Ordering of Moses* (1937). The last of these has had an impressive performance history, including presentations at the Cincinnati Festival of 1927 and at the Worcester (Massachusetts) Festival of 1938; by the Oratorio Society in New York in 1939 and the National Negro Opera Company Concert in 1940; and at Carnegie Hall in New York in 1941. Later, the oratorio was recorded by the Voice of America for distribution overseas. In 1969 Dett's oratorio was chosen for performance at the Golden Jubilee Convention of the National Association of Negro Musicians held at St. Louis, Missouri.

Percy Grainger, the Australian pianist, helped to bring Dett's piano compositions to the attention of the American public; he often included in his recitals such pieces as the *Dance: Juba* from *In the Bottoms Suite.*

Ex. X.2 Beginning of *Dance: Juba*, R. Nathaniel Dett

In October, 1933, *Etude* music magazine published Dett's *Adagio Cantabile* from *The Cinnamon Grove Suite* in its section devoted to "fascinating pieces for the musical home." Dett, like his contemporary, Clarence White, published two collections of the spirituals he had arranged during his career, *Religious Folksongs of the Negro* (1926) and *The Dett Collection of Negro Spirituals*

(1936; in four volumes). As a youth Dett also tried his hand at ragtime music, publishing in 1900 a piano rag entitled, *After the Cakewalk—March—Cakewalk*. (See p. 313 for a description of ragtime style.)

Dett was the recipient of a number of awards and prizes. In 1920 he won the Bowdoin Prize at Harvard for an essay, "The Emancipation of Negro Music," and the Francis Boot prize for composition. In 1927 he won the Harmon Foundation Award for composition. Eastman School of Music awarded him an honorary Master of Music degree; Oberlin and Harvard gave him honorary doctorates in music. From the Royal Belgian Band in Europe he received the Palm and Ribbon Award. In 1938 Dett received a commission from the Columbia Broadcasting Company to write a work for radio.

JOHN WESLEY WORK, SR.

John Wesley Work, Sr. (1873–1925) was better known as a folksong collector and arranger than as a composer, although he did leave a small quantity of vocal music. A graduate of Fisk University, he studied Latin at Harvard for one year, then returned to Fisk to teach Latin. But his first love was music. He turned to the serious study of voice, and thereby came into close contact with Negro folksongs. His enthusiasm for folk music led him to revive the idea of the college's sponsoring a Fisk Jubilee Singers ensemble. Work went into the field to collect folksongs for his singers and made special arrangements of the songs. From about 1900 to 1916 he took successive college generations of Jubilee Singers (i.e. vocal quartets) on concert tours, raising money for the college.

After he gave up the tours, he directed the Fisk Mozart Society and a three-hundred-voice chorus that gave annual concerts devoted solely to Negro spirituals. In 1901 Work published, with his brother Frederick, a collection of songs entitled *New Jubilee Songs* and in 1907 another collection, *Folk Songs of the American Negro*. In 1915 there followed a treatise, *The Folk Song of the American Negro*. Work's composed songs include *Negro Lullaby*, *Negro Love Song*, *If You Were Only Here*, and *Song of the Warrior*.

BLACK NATIONALISTS ON BROADWAY

Some black composers active at the turn of the century elected to employ their talents in the field of musical comedy and popular music. When Negro composers began gravitating toward New York in the 1890s, minstrelsy was still an important form of entertainment, and song writers who wanted their songs to be successful tried to get minstrel stars to introduce the songs. Within a few years the picture had changed. Musical comedy and vaudeville began to replace the extravaganza and the minstrel or variety show. Actually, the change had been in the making for some time. *The Black Crook*, which was produced (with all-white personnel) in New York in 1866, is credited with being the world's "first musical comedy." It was little more than an elaborate spectacle, but it was distinctly American and therefore different from the European operettas and comic operas that were being performed in the United States. And the show appealed to sophisticated taste with its beautiful girls, elaborate scenery, and careful staging.

The first show to put beautiful Negro women on the stage opened for a trial run in Haverhill, Massachusetts, on August 4, 1890. Sam T. Jack, the white producer, had gathered together sixteen of the prettiest girls he could find and some good minstrels, including Sam Lucas, and cast them in a show with minstrel format called *The Creole Show*. The idea was novel for the times, and it worked. The girls were given the spotlight —there was even a female interlocutor—the costumes were smart, and the songs and jokes were up to date. The show had a long run in Boston after its official opening at the Howard Theater. Jack carried his show to Chicago in 1891, where it was as successful as it was in Boston, and again to Chicago in 1893 for the Columbian Exposition. In 1894, *The Creole Show* opened at the Standard Theater in New York's Greeley Square and enjoyed four or five successful seasons.

The second show to use Negro girls was *The Octoroons*, which opened in 1895 under white management. It departed more from the minstrel formula than had its predecessor, having a thread of a plot and using girls in starring roles as well as in chorus numbers. In 1896 the same manager, John Isham, opened a more ambitious show, *Oriental America*, which concluded with an afterpiece consisting of a medley of operatic airs. Consequently, the production demanded the use of good singers as well as clever comedians and pretty girls. *Oriental America* was the first show with an all-Negro cast to play Broadway and the first all-Negro show to make a definite break with minstrel traditions and the burlesque theaters where minstrel shows were customarily presented. The time was ripe for genuine Negro musical comedy written and produced by black men!

WILL MARION COOK

In 1898 Will Marion Cook (1869–1944) directed a musical-comedy sketch, *Clorindy, the Origin of the Cakewalk,* that created a sensation on Broadway. He had composed the music to lyrics written by Paul Laurence Dunbar, rehearsed for weeks a hastily gathered group of twenty-six black performers, then finally wrangled the opportunity of having it produced at the Casino Roof Garden, after much travail. One publisher, for example, had informed Cook flatly that Broadway audiences would not listen to Negroes singing Negro opera. Cook later wrote about the performance:

> My chorus sang like Russians, dancing meanwhile like Negroes, and cakewalking like angels, black angels! When the last note was sounded, the audience stood and cheered for at least ten minutes. . . . It was pandemonium, but never was pandemonium dearer to my heart. . . . Negroes were at last on Broadway, and there to stay. . . . Nothing could stop us, and nothing did for a decade.

Cook was well equipped to present New York with its first Negro musical-comedy sketch. Born in Washington, D. C., he achieved distinction as a composer, conductor, and violinist. His father and mother were both graduates of Oberlin College; his father later became a law professor at Howard University. The boy early revealed musical talent and at the age of thirteen was sent to Oberlin Conservatory to study violin. Three years

Produced at The Shaftesbury Theatre
May 16th 1903.

IN DAHOMEY.

A NEGRO MUSICAL COMEDY

BOOK BY

JESSE A. SHIPP

LYRICS BY

PAUL LAWRENCE DUNBAR & OTHERS.

Music by

WILL MARION COOK.

LONDON,
KEITH, PROWSE & CO. LTD. 48, CHEAPSIDE, E.C.
Publishing Depôt, 42, Poland St, W.

Title page of the British edition of *In Dahomey*, 1902. (*Courtesy New York Public Library, Schomburg Collection.*)

later Cook left for Berlin, where he attended the Hochschule and took lessons from the renowned violinist Joseph Joachim. After several years of study he returned to New York and matriculated at the National Conservatory of Music, studying harmony and counterpoint with John White and composition with Dvořák.

In New York, Cook became a member of a circle that included some of the most talented black artists in the entire nation. There were Harry Burleigh, the singer-composer; Theodore Drury, a young impressario; Paul Dunbar, the poet; Bob Cole, a writer, composer, and performer; J. Rosamond Johnson, a pianist-composer; and James Weldon Johnson, teacher, poet, writer, and later U. S. Consul and race leader. Cook was regarded by his fellows as the "most original genius among all the Negro musicians"—a sentiment that later was to be echoed by white critics.

After *Clorindy*, Cook was the "composer in chief" for a steady succession of musical comedies, most of which featured the celebrated vaudeville team of George Walker and Bert Williams and their theatrical company. Among the collaborators with Cook over the years were librettists and lyricists Paul Dunbar, James Weldon Johnson, Alex Rogers, Jesse Shipp, and Harry Smith; song writers J. Leubrie Hill and James Vaughn. Cook's first three shows failed to duplicate the success of *Clorindy: Jes Lak White Folks* (1899), for which Cook wrote his own libretto; *The Casino Girl* (1900); and *The Policy Players* (1900). Then came three hits: *In Dahomey* (1902), a satire on the American Colonization Society's "back to Africa" movement; *In Abyssinia* (1906), an extravaganza with an African locale and a huge cast, including live camels; and *In Bandana Land* (1907), a gentle spoof of Negro life in the South. *In Dahomey* made Negro theatrical history by opening in Times Square on Broadway.

The illness of Walker and his eventual death in 1911 brought an end to the winning combination of Williams and Walker. These two men had been responsible for the production of over a dozen musical comedies written and performed by blacks during the first years of the twentieth century. Williams left the Negro stage to star for ten seasons (1912–19) in Broadway's famous *Ziegfeld Follies*. Cook wrote the music for two more comedies, *In Darkeydom* (1914) and *The Cannibal King* (which was never produced). Cook's shows gave audiences tunes to whistle as they left theaters and songs to try out on their pianos at home. The early shows helped to make the cakewalk the dance craze of the nation and Europe for several years—particularly *In Dahomey*, which toured Europe. Most popular of

Ex. X.3   Beginning of *Rain Song*, Will Marion Cook

Copyright 1912 by G. Schirmer, Inc. Used by permission.

the songs were *Who Dat Say Chicken in Dis Crowd?*, *That's How the Cakewalk's Done*, *Emancipation Day*, *Darktown's Out Tonight*, and *Swing Along*.

The last-named song belongs to *A Collection of Negro Songs*, published by Cook in 1912, which represents an original, distinctive approach to the composition of songs inspired by Negro folk music. Among other songs of the series are *Rain Song, Exhortation—A Negro Sermon*, *My Lady*, and *Wid de Moon, Moon, Moon*. Over the years, recitalists have drawn upon these songs as concert numbers and choral ensembles have used them in choral arrangements. In later years Cook composed a Negro folk opera, *St. Louis Woman* (1929), based on a libretto by his son Mercer Cook, about Negro life along the Mississippi in the 1890s. A discussion of Cook's activities as an orchestra leader will be taken up later.

ROBERT COLE AND J. ROSAMOND JOHNSON

E. B. Marks avowed in his book *They All Sang* that "no pair or trio, black or white, Viennese or Alabaman" wrote so many hit tunes as Robert Cole and the two Johnson brothers, J. Rosamond the musician and James Weldon the lyricist. These three men were also responsible for two Negro musical comedies that were produced during the first decade of the twentieth century and for a large number of specialty songs featured by white entertainers in New York and London musicals. Robert Cole (1863–1911), who was born in Athens, Georgia, went to New York after graduation from Atlanta University. A versatile man and a serious drama student, though not a trained musician, he found employment as an entertainer—he could sing, dance, and play several musical instruments—writer, actor, and stage manager. At Worth's Museum in New York, Cole was the playwright and manager of the All-Star Company, the first Negro stock company. In 1893 he was engaged to write the show for "Black Patti's Troubadours" but left after the first season because of a disagreement with the white management. Thereafter he worked on plans for a show of his own.

In the Fall of 1898 Cole presented New York—and the nation —with its first all-black *full-length* musical comedy, *A Trip to Coontown*. This was also the first show to be written, organized, produced, and managed by Negroes. The musical broke away from the minstrel tradition, previously favored by all-Negro shows, in having a genuine plot and some character development as well as songs, dances, and pretty girls. Some of the veteran entertainers in New York joined with Cole to make the musical a success; among them, Jesse Shipp, Sam Lucas, and Billy Johnson, who became Cole's partner in future productions. In 1901 Cole teamed up with the Johnson brothers (not related to Billy Johnson) to write show tunes and popular songs. Among their most impressive products were *The Shoo-Fly Regiment* (1906) and *The Red Moon* (1908), two Negro musicals written in typical Broadway tradition with good melodies, well-orchestrated scores, and plot continuity, but, unlike the Walker and Williams shows, without inclusion of minstrel comedy scenes.

An earlier work of Cole and the Johnsons, *The Evolution of Ragtime* (1903), is subtitled "a musical suite of six songs tracing and illustrating Negro music" and includes the following numbers: *Voice of the Savage (With Zulu Dance); Echoes of the Day: Daylight Is Fading; Echoes of the Jug: Lay Away Your Troubles; Darkies' Delight; The Spirit of the Banjo;* and *The Spirit of the Times*.

J. Rosamond Johnson (1873–1954) was the trained musician of the trio. Born in Jacksonville, Florida, Johnson received his musical training at the New England Conservatory of Music in Boston. By 1901, the year he settled permanently in New York, Johnson had traveled the vaudeville circuit with *Oriental America*, had taught music in Jacksonville, and had written a number of songs in collaboration with his brother James. Two of the songs, *Li'l Gal* and *Since You Went Away*, became staple items in the concert repertory of American singers of the time, white and black. A third song, *Lift Every Voice and Sing*, became so popular with blacks that it picked up the subtitle "The Negro National Anthem."

Ex. X.4 *Lift Every Voice and Sing,* James Weldon
Johnson and J. Rosamond Johnson

Lift ev'-ry voice and sing, till earth and heav-en ring, ring with the
har-mo-nies of lib-er-ty; Let our re-joic-ing
rise, high as the list-'ning____ skies, let it re-sound loud as the
roll-ing sea. Sing a song full of the faith that the dark past has
taught us; Sing a song full of the hope that the pres-ent has
brought us. Fac-ing the ris-ing sun of our new day begun, let us march on till vic-to-ry____ is won.

Stony the road we trod, bitter the chastening rod
Felt in the days when hope unborn had died;
Yet with a steady beat, have not our weary feet
Come to the place for which our fathers sighed?
We have come over a way that with tears has been watered;
We have come, treading our path through the blood of
    the slaughtered;
Out from the gloomy past, 'til now we stand at last
Where the white gleam of our bright star is cast.

God of our weary years, God of our silent tears,
Thou who hast brought us thus far on the way;
Thou who hast by Thy might led us into the light,
Keep us forever in the path, we pray.
Lest our feet stray from the places, our God, where we
    met Thee,
Lest our hearts, drunk with the wine of the world, we
    forget Thee;
Shadowed beneath Thy hand, may we forever stand,
True to our God, true to our native land.

In 1901 Cole and the Johnson brothers signed with Joseph W. Stern and Company a three-year contract that included guaranteed monthly payments (to be deducted from their royalties). This, apparently, was the first contract ever made between black song writers and a Tin Pan Alley publisher. Such white Broadway stars as May Irwin, Anna Held, Marie Cahill, and Lillian Russell used Cole and Johnson songs in their musicals and popularized a succession of hits including *The Maiden with the Dreamy Eyes, The Old Flag Never Touched the Ground, My Castle on the Nile, Under the Bamboo Tree,* and *Didn't He Ramble.* The last one became a special favorite of brass bands in New Orleans. The Cole-Johnson trio wrote music for exclusive Klaw and Erlanger productions—*The Sleeping Beauty* and *Humpty Dumpty*—and saw their songs published in the *Ladies' Home Journal.* (During this period both the *Journal* and the *Etude* published songs and piano pieces in the regular editions.)

The Cole-Johnson combination was dissolved in 1906 when James Weldon was appointed a United States consul to Venezuela. J. Rosamond wrote only one more musical show, the score for *Mr. Lode of Kole* (1909), which starred Bert Williams, but continued to work with Cole as a top vaudeville attraction until the latter's death.

During the years 1912 and 1913 Johnson was the music director at Hammerstein's Opera House in London. After his return to the United States, he worked for a number of years at the Music School Settlement in New York, then returned to the stage again with a Rosamond Johnson Quintet. Johnson published two song collections, *Shout Songs* (1936) and *Rolling Along in Song* (1937), and collaborated with his brother on two other collections, providing song arrangements for *The Book of American Negro Spirituals* (1925) and *The Second Book of Negro Spirituals* (1926). Best known of his choral works was *Walk Together Children,* for chorus and orchestra (1915).

Whatever opinion critics of the future may have regarding the intrinsic value of the music of the black pioneers just discussed, these men remain historically important as the first composers to truly assimilate the characteristic idioms of Negro folksong into a body of composed music. Unlike the white composers of so-called Negro music who preceded and followed them, these men did not have to first understand the "exotic" music before employing it in their composition; to them this music was not exotic but natural. Surrounded by the sound of Negro singing from birth, they absorbed the music with each breath they took. The challenge, rather, was to pour their music into traditional European forms—the art song, the motet and chorus, the instrumental suite, the music drama, and the operetta or musical comedy—and their training enabled them to do this. They naturally wrote in the Negro style and scored for ensembles in the Negro way without even being conscious of doing so.

To be sure, there were times when they "quoted" rather than invented melodies in the spirit of Negro folksong—whether consciously or not, we cannot say. Negro composer Margaret Bonds points out, for example, that Burleigh used the spiritual melody *Somebody's Knocking at Yo' Door* in one of his *Saracen Songs—Ahmed's Farewell*.

Ex. X.5   *Somebody's Knocking at Yo' Door*

Some-bod-y's knock-ing at yo' door, Some-bod-y's knock-ing at yo' door.

Ahmed's Farewell, Harry T. Burleigh

Nev-er so state-ly a   star   Rode the fair man-sions of

Heav'n;   Gods   gather'd beau-ties a-far,

An amusing anecdote related by old-timers indicates that two composers, at least, knew what they were doing when they employed a spiritual melody in a popular tune. It seems that on one occasion when Bob Cole and J. Rosamond Johnson were urgently in need of a good tune, Cole suggested using the old familiar spiritual *Nobody Knows the Trouble I've Seen*. Upon his companion's protest that to use a spiritual would be sacriligious, Cole is reputed to have said, "What kind of a musician are you, anyway? Been to the Boston Conservatory and can't change a little old tune around." That did it! Johnson and Cole used the melody in an altered form for one of their biggest hits, *Under the Bamboo Tree*. The song was featured by Marie Cahill in the show *Sally in Our Alley*. During the 1940s film star Judy Garland sang the song in the movie *Meet Me in St. Louis.*

Ex. X.6 *Nobody Knows the Trouble I've Seen*

No-bod-y knows the trou-ble I've seen,   No-bod-y knows my   sor-row;

Chorus of *Under the Bamboo Tree*, Bob Cole and J. Rosamond Johnson

If you lak-a-me, lak I lak-a-you, And we lak-a both the   same,

Other composers active in show music at the beginning of the twentieth century include Tim Brymn, Henry S. Creamer, Ford Dabney, J. Leubrie Hill, J. Turner Layton, Alex C. Rogers, and James Vaughn. In addition to the composers of concert music and show music, there was yet a third group of composers during this period which turned to folk music of the race for use in composed entertainment music, particularly for dancing. The folk music they employed was not "respectable" as were the spirituals and worksongs, but was to have farther-reaching influences on the music of the world in the course of time. We shall discuss this music—ragtime and the blues—and its composers in a later chapter.

IN THE CONCERT WORLD

Sissieretta Jones (1868–1933), soprano, was born in Virginia, but spent her childhood in Providence, Rhode Island. After completing her studies at the New England Conservatory, she sang professionally for several years. It was not until 1892, however, when she appeared at a Jubilee Spectacle and Cakewalk held in Madison Square Garden in New York that she attracted the notice of the critics. Her press notices were enthusiastic, one critic calling her the "Black Patti," after the Italian prima donna Adelina Patti. After the close of the jubilee she gave two successful recitals at the Academy of Music. Her performance on these occasions brought her to the attention of the managers of the Metropolitan Opera Company, Abbey, Schoffel, and Grau, who are reputed to have approached her with regard to singing the African roles in Verdi's *Aïda* and Meyerbeer's *L'Africaine*. But the musical world was not ready to accept black prima donnas, and the project fell through. Sissieretta's management sent her out on a concert tour, which included an appearance at the White House by invitation of President Harrison and appearances at the Pittsburgh Exposition in 1892 and 1893. After a tour of Europe in 1893, Sissieretta's managers organized a Negro company, called "Black Patti's Troubadours," whose shows featured the soprano in the singing of operatic arias. "Black Patti" and her troupe remained active for seventeen years.

One of the performers of this period was a grandson of the abolitionist Frederick Douglass. Joseph Douglass (1869–1935), the first Negro violinist to tour the United States, began the study of music in Washington, D. C., as a child and continued his studies at the New England Conservatory; later he studied in Europe. Douglass married a pianist, Fannie Howard (b. 1885), who attended Oberlin Conservatory after graduating from Atlanta University and who occasionally accompanied her husband on tours. Douglass's tours took him throughout the country and included appearances before both President William McKinley and President William Taft. As was pointed out, he was one

of the featured attractions in 1893 at the Chicago World's Fair
on "Colored American Day." Douglass's recitals, the first of
their kind in Negro communities, helped to inspire young black
boys to study seriously the violin. To Douglass also goes
credit for another "first"—he was the first Negro violinist to
make recordings for the Victor Talking Machine Company (now
a part of RCA). The press accorded to his playing "a broad
sympathetic tone" and named him "a thorough master of the
instrument." After leaving the concert stage, Douglass taught
at Howard University and at the Music School Settlement in
New York.

Two talented singers of lesser fame than Sissieretta Jones
were Flora Batson (1870–1906) and Sidney Woodward (1860–
1924). Batson, a native of Providence, Rhode Island, achieved
recognition as a singer of ballads. Her concert tours carried her
throughout the United States and to Europe, Australia, New
Zealand, and Africa. Woodward was born a slave on a Georgia
plantation, but his ambition to become a singer helped him to
overcome the obstacles of poverty and orphanhood. He made
his way to Boston, where he studied privately. Woodward began
touring in 1890. In 1896 he joined Isham's *Oriental America*
company, which went on a tour of England the following year.
Woodward did not return to the United States with the company,
remaining instead to tour England and the Continent as a singer
from 1897 through 1900. In later life Woodward taught at the
Music School Settlement in New York.

Hazel Harrison (1881–1969) and Carl Diton (1886–1969)
achieved distinction as pianists. Harrison studied first with a
local white musician in her native town, Laporte, Indiana, then
continued her study of piano with Victor Heinze (at that time
in Chicago) and later with Ferruccio Busoni and Egon Petri in
Germany. While in Berlin during the years 1903–06, she played
with the Berlin Philharmonic Orchestra. She returned to Germany again in 1928 to study with Heinze (now in Munich) and
Petri. Her concert tours, beginning in the 1920s, carried her
throughout the United States and included appearances with the
Chicago Symphony, Minneapolis Symphony, and Los Angeles
Symphony. Press notices referred to her "sweeping bravura passages," "brilliantly crisp tone, with sonority when that quality
is to be brought forward," and "wholly matured art conception

and universally smooth flowing technic." In later life Harrison combined concertizing with teaching at Howard University.

Diton, the first Negro pianist to tour the nation, was graduated from the University of Pennsylvania in 1909 and studied further in Germany. After a brief career as a full-time concert artist, Diton combined his playing with teaching. During the years 1911–18 he was director of music at Paine College in Georgia, Wiley College in Texas, and Talladega College in Alabama. Thereafter he settled in Philadelphia, his native town, where he continued to concertize and teach and, in addition, to publish some of his compositions. His works include *Four Spirituals* (1914) and the oratorio, *The Hymn of Nebraska* (1921).

Several new Negro music organizations came into being during the turn of the century; among them, the Lyre Club Symphony Orchestra in New Orleans in 1897, the Drury Opera Company in New York, which presented annual evenings of grand opera at the Lexington Opera House (1900–05); the Samuel Coleridge-Taylor Choral Society, founded in Washington, D. C., in 1901; the Camden Negro Symphony, organized in Camden, New Jersey, in 1912; and the Anderson Orchestra of Philadelphia, a symphony orchestra also founded in 1912. The Choral Society was responsible for bringing the African-English composer Samuel Coleridge-Taylor (1875–1912) to the United States in 1904. In November of that year, the society produced a Coleridge-Taylor Festival, its two-hundred-voice choir singing the composer's choral works on two evenings in Washington and on a third in Baltimore; the composer himself conducted the United States Marine Band.

Coleridge-Taylor subsequently toured the United States, performing his works and conducting orchestras and choruses in the performance of the works. Regarded as one of England's rising young composers, Coleridge-Taylor made a marked impression upon the American public and particularly upon Negroes. Best known for his trilogy of oratorios, *Hiawatha's Wedding Feast*, *The Death of Minnehaha*, and *Hiawatha's Departure*, he had also composed other choral works, an opera, a symphony, a number of instrumental works, and art songs. In addition to his teaching at the Trinity College of Music, Coleridge-Taylor conducted choral societies in England and organized the Croydon String Orchestra. In 1899, after attending a concert of the Fisk

Jubilee Singers in England and becoming interested in Negro folksong, Coleridge-Taylor made a collection of piano arrangements of African and Afro-American melodies, *Twenty-Four Melodies Transcribed for the Piano* (published in 1905). The *Bamboula* from this collection became very popular with pianists. Again in 1906 the composer returned to the United States for a tour, stopping in Chicago for two recitals at the Pekin Theatre. Included among the performers on that occasion was Harry Burleigh.

MUSIC MANUALS AND A BOOK ABOUT NEGROES

Wendell P. Dabney (1865–1952), born in Richmond, Virginia, and active in Cincinnati, was a graduate of Oberlin Conservatory. Among his publications were *Dabney's Complete Method of Guitar* and *Dabney's Complete Method of Mandolin and Guitar*. In 1878 the first historical survey of Negro music was written by James Monroe Trotter, an office holder in the federal post office in Boston. The book is invaluable today for the unique information it provides about black musicians of the nineteenth century. Trotter's qualifications for writing on the subject of music are unknown, but his approach to the subject and the thoroughness with which he handled the material demand respect. He quoted extensively from press notices about the artists discussed and provided reproductions of recital programs and advertisements. The book, *Music and Some Highly Musical People*, was a landmark in the field of writings about Negro music and was not to be matched by a similar study for more than fifty years.

THE SPANISH–AMERICAN WAR

When the Spanish-American War broke out in 1898, black men immediately volunteered for service as they had done in previous wartimes. As before, they met with rebuffs from the War Department. To be sure, there were already in the regular army four groups of Negro servicemen: the Ninth Cavalry, the

Tenth Cavalry, the Twenty-fourth Infantry, and the Twenty-fifth Infantry, all stationed in the West. (It was the Tenth Cavalry, as we pointed out earlier, that sent a delegation to the Black America extravanganza at Brooklyn, New York in 1894.) After considerable red tape, four new all-black regiments were organized under a special recruitment act of Congress. In addition, a number of Negro outfits organized on the state level were permitted to enter the war. One of these groups, Company L of the Sixth Massachusetts Infantry, traced its military lineage back to the all-Negro company, "Bucks of America," that had fought in the Revolutionary War.

The white commanding officer of the Tenth Cavalry, Colonel Grierson, himself an ex-music teacher, saw to it that his outfit was given an opportunity to develop a first-rate band. The Tenth Cavalry Band was composed of twenty-six men, including Chief Musician Washington Darrow, Chief Trumpeter John Campbell, and George Tyrell, chief musician after Darrow's death. Two well-known musicians in the Ninth Cavalry Band were bandleader Wade Hammond and bugler George Swan. Out of the war came the inevitable anecdote about black soldiers and a song. It is said that when the soldiers "mowed down the enemy" in the storming of San Juan Hill in Puerto Rico, they sang loudly *There'll Be a Hot Time in the Old Town Tonight.*

CHAPTER XI

Precursors of Jazz: Ragtime and Blues

THE GENERAL STATE OF MUSIC

The beginning of the twentieth century brought the promise of new musical developments both in Europe and in the United States—here, in areas affecting both black men and white. The century opened auspiciously with the Exposition Universelle in Paris. Those attending heard for the first time a strangely exciting music from America called "ragtime." During the first decade of the century, European composers began to produce works that started a revolution in the art of music. Startled and bewildered audiences reacted violently to the "New Music"— i.e. the music of Igor Stravinsky(1882–1971), Arnold Schoenberg (1874–1951), and their contemporaries, which broke away from traditional concepts of melody, rhythm, texture, form, and instrumentation.

Stravinsky was in the forefront of the movement. He came to Paris in 1910 to write ballets for the choreographer Sergei Diaghilev and his Ballet Russe, which had opened its first season in Paris in 1909. Stravinsky's music for a ballet produced in the Spring of 1913, *Le Sacre du printemps* (The Rite of Spring), touched off a near-riot on opening night. The label "primitivism" was applied to this work and to similar ones—such as, for example, the *Allegro barbaro* (1911) of the Hungarian composer Béla Bartók (1881–1945). In Vienna during the same period, Schoenberg was writing music that was described as "expressionistic." It was an abstract kind of music with highly chromatic melodies and dissonant harmonies. Eventually Schoenberg and his disciples entirely rejected tonality—i.e. the system of tonal relationships underlying music of the eighteenth and nineteenth centuries— and arrived at a music in which a single note no longer functioned as a tonal center; all twelve tones of the octave were of equal importance. The new system of tonal relationships, called the "twelve-tone method" (later, "serial technique"), was developed to take the place of the old system based on major and minor scales.

In the United States most white and black composers continued for many years to write in the tradition of nineteenth-century music. The composer whose music was closest in style to the "New Music" of Europe was Charles Ives (1874–1954) of Danbury, Connecticut, an organist who followed a career in insurance business. In fact, Ives anticipated many of the European developments, but he did not begin to publish his music until the 1920s. If any twentieth-century European composer was emulated by Americans during this period, it was the French composer Claude Debussy (1862–1918), a figure of the late nineteenth century as well as the twentieth. His best-known work, *Prélude à "L'Après-midi d'un faune"* (Prelude to "The Afternoon of a Faun"), was published in 1894. Debussy's music was innovative in its use of scales other than major and minor—the church modes, for example, oriental scales, and a new whole-tone scale; in its use of parallel chords (which gave the effect of blocks of tones sliding up and down); of vague, restless rhythms; of wispy, indefinite melodies; and of veiled, shimmering orchestra sounds. The critics called Debussy's music "impressionistic," although Debussy himself disliked the term.

THE EMERGENCE OF RAG MUSIC

Not all composers in the United States were writing music in the orthodox European style. Large numbers of musically illiterate black music makers were not aware of its existence, and many blacks who could read music were unconcerned about it. The effect of slavery had been to create distinct and separate communities of blacks within the larger white communities of the nation, and the emancipation of the slaves did nothing to change this situation. Blacks lived, for the most part, in their own world and developed their own institutions and culture. Of particular relevance here is the fact that the black music maker developed a distinctive style of entertainment music, fitted to his own personal needs and expressive of his own individuality. It was not intended to be heard or understood by whites. Rag music was one of the earliest manifestations of this distinctive music. The other was the blues.

It is noteworthy that from the time of its origin rag music seems to have been associated primarily with the piano. As slaves, black musicians had little access to the piano, of course, but after freedom they displayed a marked predilection for keyboard instruments. Families purchased small organs (i.e. Estey organs or harmoniums) for use in the home (pianos were too expensive), often paying fifty cents down and fifty cents per week for a lifetime. In this regard Booker T. Washington recounts an illuminating experience in his autobiography, *Up from Slavery* (published 1901):

> I remember that on one occasion when I went into one of these cabins [in the plantation districts of Alabama] for dinner, when I sat down to the table for a meal with the four members of the family, I noticed that, while there were five of us at the table, there was but one fork for the five of us to use. Naturally there was an awkward pause on my part. In the opposite corner of that same cabin was an organ for which the people told me they were paying sixty dollars in monthly installments. One fork, and a sixty-dollar organ!

Washington was outraged, naturally, that the ex-slaves should be so impractical as to buy an organ when such a necessity as tableware was overlooked. Undoubtedly he was right in one respect; he was wrong, however, in assuming that music was not a necessity to the ex-slaves. One of the first ways they showed their independence was to purchase the musical instruments for which they had longed as slaves. If they could not play these instruments, then their children would learn to do so. And many of the black pioneering musicians actually did begin their childhood musical training with lessons on the home organ; among others, W. C. Handy and the ragtime pianist Eubie Blake.

The earliest rag-music players were anonymous drifters in the Mississippi River country and on the eastern seaboard who played piano music in cheap eating-places, honky-tonk spots, saloons, and riverside dives—often for meager wages, sometimes only for tips. It was the job of the lone musician to substitute for an orchestra in providing music for listening or dancing. With his left hand he maintained the steady regular beat of the dance-orchestra bass; with his right hand he carried a sharply syncopated melody, altering and embellishing it as he played. W. C. Handy remembered having heard one of these "piano thumpers" during a visit to Memphis in the late 1880s:

> As I was walking down Beale Street one night, my attention was caught by the sound of a piano. The insistent Negro rhythms were broken first by a tinkle in the treble, then by a rumble in the bass; then they came together again. I entered the cheap café and found a colored man at the piano, dog tired. He told me he had to play from seven at night until seven in the morning, and [so he] rested himself by playing with alternate hands.

The fact that few of the early ragtime piano players could read music seemed to stimulate rather than to deter them in the production of a novel style of piano music.

The style of piano-rag music—called "jig piano" by some—was a natural outgrowth of dance-music practices among black folk. As we have seen, the slaves danced in ante-bellum times to the music of fiddles and banjos, the percussive element being provided by the foot stomping of the musicians and the "juba patting" of the bystanders. In piano-rag music, the left hand took over the task of stomping and patting while the right hand performed syncopated melodies, using motives reminiscent of fiddle and banjo tunes. White America first became aware of the new style through the syncopated rhythms employed in dance music and minstrel songs. For years rag music was the exclusive possession of black communities; suddenly it was snatched from its original habitat, catapulted into the national spotlight, and adopted by white society. New York was made conscious of the infectious new rhythms in 1896 when a popular pianist, Ben Harney of Kentucky, played for the buck-and-wing dancing of a diminutive black dancer known as Strap Heel on the stage of Tony Pastor's Fourteenth Street Variety House.

But it was in partnership with the dance called the cakewalk that syncopated music made its most impressive showing. That dance of plantation origin had been taken up by minstrels and given a special place in their shows, sometimes as a feature entitled "walking for that cake" or "peregrination for the pastry." The dance took over everywhere—in hamlets, towns, and cities —and with everyone. Throughout the nation contests and jubilees were held in which, for substantial prizes, cakewalking couples improvised steps, prances, and kicks to the accompaniment of syncopated music. The music used for cakewalking shared in its popularity, although the term *ragtime* was not used to apply to this music until later. By the end of the century, contests were offering two sets of prizes, one set for cakewalkers and the other for ragtime pianists, who were given an allotted time in which to demonstrate their ability to improvise upon given songs in ragtime style.

RAGTIME SONGS

Beginning in the 1890s song writers began more and more to use syncopation, particularly in the new so-called "coon songs." To be sure, the coon song had been a basic stock in trade of the early minstrel stage, but its importance had diminished considerably by the end of the Civil War. A list of the 130 most successful popular songs of the 80s, as compiled by Edward B. Marks, included only seven coon songs, all written by whites, and of the seven, only one, J. S. Putnam's *New Coon in Town* (1883), employed enough syncopation as "to foreshadow the true, shouting, ragtime school." The others, according to Marks, were "mere blackface numbers . . . no more essentially Negroid than the minstrel men who sang them in their curiously conventional style."

Matters changed in the next decade. The black actor and song writer Ernest Hogan wrote a song, *All Coons Look Alike to Me*, that contributed to a tremendous vogue for syncopated coon songs, from which both black and white song writers profited. Published in 1896, the song was an immediate hit and "sold like wildfire all over the United States and abroad." When ragtime pianists from all over the country gathered for the Ragtime

Ex. XI.1 Excerpts from *All Coons Look Alike to Me*, Ernest Hogan

Championship of the World Competition held at Tammany Hall in New York City on January 23, 1900, it was Ernest Hogan's song that was recommended for the final test. The three pianists who had reached the semifinals were asked to demonstrate their skill in ragging a song by playing *All Coons Look Alike to Me* for two minutes.

Despite its success, the song brought unhappiness to its originator. Although the lyrics of the song were innocuous, Negroes did not like the title, which was derisive when separated from the lyrics.

The ragtime song, as distinguished from the piano rag, was characterized by a regular, straightforward bass and a lightly syncopated melody. Frequently the syncopation was confined to the vocal line, the piano providing an "um-pah um-pah" accompaniment based chiefly on simple harmonic progressions (see Example XI.1, on p. 315).

EARLY RAGTIME SONG WRITERS

Like many of the pioneer ragtime pianists, some of the early black song writers were musical illiterates. They played their songs on the piano for professional arrangers in Tin Pan Alley, who wrote down the notes as fast as the ragtimers played. Inevitably more songs were "lost" by this method than were turned over to publishers. Nevertheless, such writers as Cris Smith of South Carolina and Irving Jones of New York were responsible for a large number of the hit songs written in ragtime style that were on the lips of everyone around the turn of the century. Other ragtime song writers of the early twentieth century were James T. Brymn, Bob Cole, Will Cook, James Europe, Harry P. Guy, Ernest Hogan, J. Rosamond Johnson, Joe Jordan, Cecil Mack, Fred Stone, Charlie Warfield, Bert Williams, and Clarence Williams. One of the most popular ragtime songs on record, *My Ragtime Baby* (1898), was written by a member of this group, Fred Stone. According to Tom Fletcher, this piece won a prize for the band of the famous white bandleader John Philip Sousa at the Paris Exposition in 1900 and, at the same time, gave Europe its first sound of ragtime music.

A list of the successful syncopated songs of black writers during this period should also include such favorites as *Cuban Cake Walk* (Brymn); *Bon Bon Buddy* (Will Marion Cook); *Under the Bamboo Tree* (Cole and Johnson); *When the Band Plays Ragtime* (Cole and Johnson); *Didn't He Ramble* (Cole and Johnson, under the nom de plume of Will Handy); *Darktown Is Out Tonight* (Cook); *My Home Ain't Nothing Like This* (Jones); *Possumala* (Jones); *Wouldn't That Be a Dream* (Jordan); *Miss Dora Dean* (Bert Williams); and *Good Morning, Carrie* (Smith).

INSTRUMENTAL RAGS

The instrumental pieces of the ragtime composers generated an excitement and emotional power not previously associated with entertainment music in America. Much of the power derived from the rhythm, which had numerous cross-accents resulting from a conflict of metrical patterns between the duple-meter bass and the syncopated treble that tended toward the use of 6/8 rhythmic motives. The influence of Negro folksong was particularly evident in the chromatic turns of melody and harmony, which often derived from the occurrence of flatted thirds and sevenths in the major scale. Many piano rags were written in march and quadrille (or altered-quadrille) forms—the former, a multisectional form that includes the return of the first section after one or two trios (m-t-m-t-m); the latter, a French dance form, consisting of five sections (a-b-c-d-e or a-b-a-c-d) alternately employing 6/8 and 2/4 meters.

A white bandleader, William Krell of Chicago, was the first to publish the kind of music that black pianists had been playing for years in cabarets and cheap cafés. Krell had toured widely in the South, coming into contact with folk ragtime and other forms of Negro music and dance. He tacitly acknowledged his debt to the black creators of ragtime style in his piece, stringing together four sections (called *Cakewalk*, *Plantation Song*, *Trio*, and *Buck-and-Wing Dance*), adding introduction, coda, and interludes, and naming the work *Mississippi Rag* (1897). The cover of the sheet music depicts dancing, singing, and banjo-playing black folk in the typical minstrel tradition of stereotyped "happy blacks." Within the same year, black pianist-composers began finding publishers for their music and together with a few whites were able to produce a considerable number of superior works before the music-publishing industry in New York glutted the market with a vast quantity of mediocre music.

A distinctive group of black pianist-composers was active in or near St. Louis, Missouri, during the years ca. 1890–1910. Rag-music pioneers Scott Joplin and Thomas Million Turpin were followed by James Scott; two of Joplin's protégés, Arthur Marshall and Scott Hayden; and three men who developed under the guidance of Turpin, Louis Chauvin, Sam Patterson, and Joe Jordan. To this list should be added the names of four pioneering white rag composers: Charles L. Johnson, Charles Hunter, George Botsford, and Percy Weinrich. Along the Atlantic seaboard there was developing at the same time a different kind of rag music, some of it played by phenomenal pianists. Only two of these men, however, found publishers for their rag music: James Hubert "Eubie" Blake and the white composer Joseph Lamb.

SCOTT JOPLIN, KING OF RAGTIME

Scott Joplin (1868–1917), generally acknowledged as the "King of Ragtime," was born into a musical family in Texarkana, Texas—his father played the violin, his mother played the banjo, one brother played both violin and banjo, and another possessed a fine voice. Scott showed musical promise at the piano before the age of seven. His father, despite meager earnings as a railroad laborer, managed to scrape together enough money to buy an old square grand piano, and the boy soon taught himself to play. His skill at the piano became a source of local pride, eventually winning for him the opportunity to study with an old German musician in the area, who not only gave him free instruction in piano and theory, but also helped him to develop an appreciation for the music of the great European masters. While still in his early teens, Scott joined the ranks of itinerant musicians, earning his way by playing piano in the honky-tonks of villages and towns in the Mississippi Valley country and absorbing all the while the folk music of his people and the "jig piano" style of the self-taught pianists with whom he worked.

In 1885 Joplin arrived at St. Louis, at that time a frontier town with a thriving black population and a prosperous sporting-life district. Chestnut and Market Streets were especially notorious for their bawdy houses and saloons, from which came forth the sound of piano thumping day and night. Joplin got a job playing piano in the Silver Dollar, a saloon owned by "Honest" John Turpin, one of the important men of the district. The Turpins —first the father and later the sons—were true patrons of ragtime music; their saloons and clubs provided hospitable centers for local and visiting pianists, places where they could exchange ideas and engage in friendly competition.

During the next decade Joplin played in St. Louis and other Missouri towns, organized vocal and instrumental groups, and began to write down some of his musical ideas. In 1893 he spent a brief period at the World's Columbian Exposition in Chicago, where he came into contact with some of the hundreds of black musicians who had converged on the exposition's Midway seeking employment. In 1895 Joplin toured widely with a vocal group he had organized, the Texas Medley Quartette (actually a double quartet), and was thereby able to plug his music as well as contact interested publishers. During the next two years Joplin published five pieces, two songs and three piano pieces, all written in typically Victorian style: the songs were mediocre, with attractive melodies but conventional harmonies and sentimental lyrics; the piano pieces, two marches and a waltz, equally undistinguished. None of them contained more than a few bars of syncopation. The evidence indicates, however, that Joplin played his music in syncopated style despite his use of traditional notation in the published versions. He would hardly have been able to find a publisher at that time for his music had he written it as he played it.

In 1896 Joplin settled in Sedalia, Missouri, where he had previously lived during 1894. There he played piano at the Maple Leaf Club, took courses in advanced harmony and composition at the George Smith College for Negroes, played with a local brass band, worked seriously at his composition, and generally kept in the center of the town's musical activities. By 1898 the ragtime craze was sweeping the country and Joplin was able to find, for the first time, a publisher for one of his syncopated pieces. His *Original Rags* was published in March, 1899. Later

Ex. XI.2 Excerpts from *Maple Leaf Rag*, Scott Joplin

that same year a white music publisher, John Stillwell Stark, heard Joplin play a piano rag at the Maple Leaf Club, liked what he heard, and bought the piece for fifty dollars and royalties to the composer. The *Maple Leaf Rag* was a financial success, and it became a landmark in the history of American music. The Joplin-Stark partnership, which was responsible for a number of ragtime masterpieces, made Joplin's name a household word and made Stark the leading ragtime publisher in the country. Their first publication set high standards for the "classic" rags that were to be published later. The *Maple Leaf Rag* became a test piece for every ragtime pianist; its technical brilliance ushered in "a new order" for showy, virtuoso instrumental exercises in syncopated style (see Ex. XI.2).

The *Maple Leaf Rag* sold hundreds of thousands of copies in the first decade of its publication. Scott Joplin gave up his piano playing, moved back to St. Louis, and devoted himself wholly to teaching music and composing. In addition to publishing piano rags, he experimented with larger musical forms. In 1903 he produced a concert version of *A Guest of Honor, a Ragtime Opera* at St. Louis. The manuscript of this ill-fated work has disappeared, but contemporaries remarked on its "beautiful raggy music." In 1903 Joplin also produced *The Rag-Time Dance*, a folk ballet with narrative soloist, in Sedalia's Opera House. The work, which lasted about twenty minutes in performance, featured the popular dances of the period, particularly the cakewalk and the "slow drag," with the narrator singing such verses as:

> Let me see you do the rag-time dance,
> Turn left and do the cakewalk prance,
> Turn the other way and do the slow drag—
> Now take your lady to the World's Fair [i.e. at St. Louis]
> And do the rag-time dance.

The years 1906–09 were restless ones for Joplin. After moving from one place to another, he set out on a series of vaudeville tours. During these years he also made a number of piano-roll recordings, intended for performance on the then popular Pianola player piano. Finally he settled permanently in New York City.

Despite the publication of several piano rags during the first years of his stay in New York, Joplin concentrated most of his creative energy on his second opera, *Treemonisha*. In 1911 he published the 230-page piano score at his own expense, for he could find no publisher willing to accept a work with little likelihood of financial success.

Joplin became obsessed with the necessity for producing his opera. He determined to produce it in a concert version at least, hoping thereby to attract a backer. After months of orchestrating the score (Sam Patterson helped with the herculean job), writing out the instrumental parts, and training a cast, he succeeded in putting the opera on the stage for one night. The performance took place without costumes, scenery, lighting, or orchestra in a Harlem hall in 1915. Joplin himself played the orchestral parts at the piano. From the standpoint of its public reception, the performance was a failure. Joplin was crushed; his mind, which had begun to show some evidences of strain even before 1915, gave way completely and in 1917 he died a broken man.

OTHER BLACK COMPOSERS OF RAGS

Thomas Million Turpin (1873–1922) was the first Negro to publish a piano rag, the *Harlem Rag* (1897). Owner of the Rosebud Café and other places in St. Louis's tenderloin, Turpin wrote and featured most of his piano rags at the café. Like his father's saloon in earlier days, his café became a rendezvous for ragtime pianists; to Turpin, the ragtime patriarch, his contemporaries gave the title "Father of St. Louis Ragtime." Despite Turpin's many business ventures, he found time to publish a number of his piano rags and to encourage the development of a younger generation of ragtime pianists, some of whom became important figures in the diffusion of ragtime. Best known of Turpin's compositions, in addition to the *Harlem Rag*, were the *Bowery Buck* (1899), *A Ragtime Nightmare* (1900), *St. Louis Rag* (1903), and *The Buffalo Rag* (1904).

James Sylvester Scott (1886–1938) is regarded by some as ragtime's second-ranking composer after Joplin. He was born in Neosho, Missouri, and received his early musical training there from a black pianist, John Coleman. Later the family moved to

Carthage, Missouri, where Scott's father managed to buy a piano for his talented son. At the age of sixteen Scott went to work at a local music store, starting out as a handyman. After the owner heard his piano playing, however, he was given the job of a music clerk, playing for customers to promote the sale of sheet music. Scott published his first piano rags at the age of seventeen. Although these early pieces revealed the influence of Joplin's *Maple Leaf Rag* (as did, indeed, most rags of the time), the pieces nevertheless reflected the young composer's originality and creativity. Scott's later works were entirely his own and represent the highest level of classic ragtime composition.

In 1914 Scott moved to Kansas City, Missouri, where he established himself as a music teacher and theater musician, playing the organ and working as a music arranger for various theaters in the city. Later he organized an orchestra that played in Kansas City theater pits until about 1930, when the advance of sound films made theater orchestras all over the country obsolete. Although Scott was a prolific composer, fewer than forty of his compositions were published. These include thirty piano rags, four songs, and miscellaneous pieces. Best remembered of his works are the *Frog Legs Rag* (1906), *Kansas City Rag* (1907), *Quality—A High-Class Rag* (1911), *Climax Rag* (1914), and *Pegasus—A Classic Rag* (1920). Scott's last rag was the *Broadway Rag—A Classic*, published in 1922.

Two composers of the St. Louis group, Scott Hayden (1882–1915) and Louis Chauvin (1883–1908), wrote piano rags only in collaboration with others. Arthur Marshall (1881–1956) left several compositions, two written in collaboration with Joplin, four published by Stark, and three of them unpublished but copyrighted and recorded on Circle Records. Sam Patterson (1881–?) published a piano rag and several songs in collaboration with Chauvin, and also a musical show, *Dandy Coon*. In 1906 he left St. Louis to travel with a variety act, the Musical Spillers. Some composers who played important roles in the development of instrumental rag style later became involved with other kinds of music—for example, Joe Jordan and Eubie Blake. Others made "experiments" in the style at the same time as they were writing show music, dance music, or concert music; among them, Blind Boone, Will Cook, R. Nathaniel Dett, Ford Dabney, James Reese Europe, J. Leubrie Hill, Wilbur Sweatman, and Will H. Tyers.

JOE JORDAN

Joe Jordan (b. 1882) was born in Cincinnati, Ohio, but later moved to St. Louis and attended the nearby Lincoln Institute (now Lincoln University). Back in St. Louis he studied music privately, played piano-rag music in cafés, played and sang with small ensembles (such as a piano quartet including Turpin, Chauvin, Patterson, and himself), and played violin and drums in brass bands (such as the Taborin Band). In 1903 Jordan went to Chicago, played for a brief period at the Pekin Beer Garden on State Street, then left for New York the following year, where he became involved with show music and syncopated dance orchestras. He was back in Chicago in 1906 as the director of music at the Pekin Theatre.

The Pekin had had a short but eventful history. Originally a saloon and gambling joint, in 1903 its black owner, Robert Motts, converted it into a beer garden frequented by both black and white patrons. In 1905, Motts changed the place into a "Temple of Music," where variety shows were presented; in 1906 he razed the old building and built a new Pekin Theatre. It was at this place that Coleridge-Taylor gave his recitals in 1906; Jordan was music director and conductor of the theater orchestra at the time. Jordan went back to New York in 1909 to collaborate with Cole and Johnson in the writing of *The Red Moon*, then returned in 1911 to resume his position at the Pekin.

All during this period Jordan was writing music: piano rags, ragtime songs, show music, dance music, and concert music. Much of this music was not published, of course, but enough was published to reveal his great talent. Included among the piano rags were *Nappy Lee—A Slow Drag* (1903), *Pekin Rag* (1904), and *J. J. J. Rag* (1905). The list of published ragtime songs is long and includes two of the period's favorites, *Oh, Say, Wouldn't That Be a Dream* and *That Teasing Rag*.

EUBIE BLAKE

Eubie Blake (b. 1883), the leading exponent of the eastern school of rag music, was born in Baltimore. His music lessons began when he was six years old; an enterprising merchant placed an Estey organ in his home, over his mother's hesitations, when the boy demonstrated a talent for playing on the instrument in a department store. Soon little Eubie was "raggin'" the hymns assigned to him for study by his music teacher, Margaret Mitchell, organist at the Negro Methodist Church. When his mother, a deeply religious person, heard this, she was upset and ordered him to "take that ragtime out of [her] house." But Eubie was to sink even lower in *her* view. He began to frequent the bawdy houses of the tenderloin, fascinated by the exciting music he heard coming from the pianos. He soon learned from the piano players how to produce similar music and took his first job as a pianist in a sporting house when he was about sixteen years old. It was in 1899 that he composed his first rag, *The Charleston Rag*, although it was not published until many years later. Many of Blake's best rags were never published. His published rags include *Chevy Chase* (1914), *Fizz Water* (1914), and *Bugle Call Rag* (1926). Among rag fanciers, the most popular unpublished rags (which have been recorded) include *Eubie's Boogie*, *Troublesome Ivories*, and *Brittwood Rag*. In later years Blake studied theory and composition with Llewellyn Wilson, conductor of the Baltimore Negro Symphony. As late as 1969 he was still composing rags, after having spent many years in other fields of music composition. His latest work was *Blue Rags in Twelve Keys*.

Blake played rag piano in various "houses" of Baltimore, Atlantic City, and New York until 1915. In that year he met a young singer from Indianapolis, Indiana, Noble Sissle (b. 1889), who had written lyrics for songs, toured with the Thomas Jubilee Singers, and organized his own dance orchestra. The two men went into partnership, Sissle writing the lyrics and Blake writing the music for songs and musicals, and six years later they wrote a show that made music history—*Shuffle Along*.

RAGTIME PERFORMERS

By the end of the nineteenth century there were several important ragtime areas in the United States, each with its own coterie of black players, favorite rendezvous spots, and distinctive style of performance. Generally the gathering places were located in the heart of a sporting-life district, for it was there that black performers of rag music found ready employment and warm acceptance. Among the pianists—many of now legendary fame—who congregated in the back rooms of bars to play for one another and for other connoisseurs of good ragtime were "habitual winners" of contests. Composers as well as performers, few bothered to publish their music—either they were too busy, or they felt that at the going rate of ten or fifteen dollars per piece it was hardly worth the trouble.

The Missouri area, with St. Louis at the core, may not have produced the earliest school of ragtime players, but its composers were the first to be published and to win national recognition. In addition to the men already discussed, other black pianists belonging to the group included Otis Saunders, Bob and John Moore, Charlie Warfield, and a man known as Klondike.

A big ragtime contest, sponsored by the Turpins, was held in St. Louis during the time of the Louisiana Purchase Exposition (the "St. Louis Fair") in 1904. Black pianists came from all over the nation to enter the competition—as much for the thrill of competing with the country's best rag pianists as for the prizes. Top honors were won by a pianist from New Orleans, Alfred Wilson, and second place went to Charlie Warfield. Beginning about 1906 the St. Louis men began to drift away—to Chicago, Kansas City, and New York.

In New Orleans at the turn of the century, the city's best rag pianists were accustomed to gathering in the back room of Frenchman's Saloon after leaving their regular places of employment; among them were Albert Carroll, Anthony Jackson, Alfred Wilson, and the somewhat younger Buddy Carter, Sammy Davis, and Ferdinand "Jelly Roll" Morton. All knew about the legendary rag pianist called John the Baptist who had been active in the 70s and 80s, but none had actually heard him play. Of the group, Tony Jackson was most famous; singer as well as pianist, he became known as the "World's Greatest Single-Handed Entertainer." The rag music played by the New Orleans group was faster, the rhythms more strongly marked, the texture contrapuntal, and the harmonies more chromatic than that of the St. Louis ragtimers. While each player had his own distinctive style, they all favored the use of "walking" or "rolling" basses in the left hand (see Example XI.3).

Ex. XI.3   A walking bass

[walking]

etc.

First-rate rag pianists were to be found in smaller cities of the
South as well as in old, sprawling New Orleans. At one period
during 1905, for example, there were four well-known raggers in
Mobile, Alabama, at the same time: Porter King, Baby Gryce,
Frazier Davis of Florida, and Frank Rachel of Georgia. Louisville,
Kentucky, was known for its rag pianists Glover Compton and
Piano Price Davis. In Memphis, Tennessee, Pee Wee's saloon on
Beale Street was the chief headquarters for musicians, but piano
thumpers were to be heard all up and down the street. In the
northern city of Pittsburgh, Pennsylvania, the best pianist was a
woman known as "Ragtime Mame." Indianapolis, Indiana, was the
home of Russell Smith, whose rags were published by a local
company.

When the southern pianists began drifting into Chicago during
the first decade of the twentieth century, they found there an
established tradition for rag music dating back at least to the time
of the World's Fair in 1893. The patriarch of the group in Chicago, Plunk Henry (ca. 1850–1906), had been one of ragtime's
earliest pioneers. One of the younger men, Johnny Seymour, had
made a name for himself with his sensational playing at the Chicago Fair. Other outstanding players were Eddie James, Harry
"Squirrel" Crosby, Needham Wright, Fred Burke, George
"Sparrow" Kimbrough, James "Slap Rags" White, and Ed Hardin,
"chief of the ragtime roost." When the newcomers to Chicago—
including such men as Charlie Warfield, Tony Jackson, Joe
Jordan, and Jelly Roll Morton—added their talents to the existing
store, the results were impressive. Chicago became the center of
ragtime playing that St. Louis had been a decade earlier.

Ragtime on the eastern seaboard also had its legendary figures.
The pioneers included Old Man Sam Moore of Philadelphia,
Bud Minor of Washington, D. C., and Old Man Metronome
French of Baltimore (a rag-playing banjoist). Among the mem-
bers of a later generation born in the 1860s and 70s were Sam

Gordon of Trenton, Walter "One-Leg Shadow" Gould of Philadelphia, and John "Jack the Bear" Wilson, originally from Pennsylvania or Ohio. In 1969 Eubie Blake, reminiscing about the
Baltimore of his youth (i.e. in the 90s), discussed the eastern style
of ragtime music and named several "piano sharks" who played
this music: Jesse Pickett, Big-Head Wilbur, Big Jimmy Green,
Shout Blake (not related to Eubie), William Turk, Sammy Ewell,
"Slew-Foot" Nelson, and Willie "Egg Head" Sewell. Shout Blake
was the only one of the group who could read music, but "all of
the men could play in any key." It was Jesse Pickett ("some say
he was from Philadelphia") who taught Eubie Blake how to play
ragtime, using the famous Pickett rag *The Dream* as the demon-
stration piece. Other members of Blake's generation who were
widely known for their ragtime skill were Richard "Abba Labba"
McLean of New York, "One-Leg" Willie Joseph of Baltimore
(originally from New England and a graduate of the Boston Conservatory of Music), and Sticky Mack and Louis Brown of
Washington, D. C. Many of these pianists eventually settled in
New York, going there during the opening decade of the
twentieth century. There was also a continuous influx into New
York of rag pianists from other centers—particularly from Baltimore, Chicago, St. Louis, Memphis, and New Orleans—who
stayed there briefly, then moved on to other places.

Since none of the music of the eastern pioneers, except for
Eubie Blake's, was published or recorded, it is impossible to know
how this music actually sounded. Some insight into the early
eastern style is afforded, however, by the playing of Blake, although his personal style undoubtedly underwent many changes
over the long span of years from the time of his first job in the
Baltimore tenderloin district in 1899 and the release of his album
The Eighty-Six Years of Eubie Blake in 1969. The most striking
features of Blake's rags are the fast tempos and the powerful
pulsating basses. The latter, consisting chiefly of "um-pah"
skips from low octaves to mid-keyboard chords and octave
passages are generally referred to as "stride basses." But Blake occasionally interrupts the straightforward patterns in his left hand
to inject a few measures of stentorian broken octaves, his right
hand continuing all the while in its flowing embellishing of the
syncopated melody (he calls the embellishments "tricks").

Blake's strongest complaint about modern piano playing, which he generally admires, concerns the neglect of the bass—"they don't play a bass!" The old-timers realized that their piano playing served in lieu of an orchestra and compensated for the absence of percussion instruments by emphasizing the left-hand bass. Blake's simple statement, "We had to do it because we had no drums to help us," reflects, perhaps unconsciously so, a basic premise of Afro-American music—there is no music without the drum.

Just when rag music—this music developed by black musicians for the entertainment of their own people—first emerged on the wider stage of American music is not known. In the South, piano playing among the common folk developed only after freedom came, except for one or two professionals such as Blind Tom, of course. It is probable, however, that on the East coast, particularly in the New York-Philadelphia-Baltimore area, "jig piano" may have been played much earlier than in the South. As we have seen, middle-class Negroes began purchasing pianos for use in the home in the early part of the nineteenth century. There is some evidence suggesting that not only daughters of the middle classes were given piano lessons, but occasionally men also. In Baltimore in 1856, for example, a black pianist billed as Tom Thumb appeared at the New Assembly Rooms, where "his intuitive playing filled everyone with wonder." On May 21, 1881, a concert given in New York by black artists of Baltimore featured, along with "Baltimore's Black Swan" (Madame Mahoney) and "Baltimore's favorite tenor" (J. T. Meredith), a man acclaimed as "Baltimore's grand pianist" (Professor J. Dunger).

In 1850 the writer G. G. Foster could observe in his book, *New York by Gas Light*, that every dance hall in the notorious "Five Points" area was "provided with its fiddler, ready to tune up his villainous squeaking for sixpence a [dance] piece." On gala nights, as we have seen, trumpets and drums were added to fiddles to make up the dance "orchestras." The white reporter Lafcadio Hearn, writing in the 1870s about the dance music he heard in Negro dance houses of Cincinnati, reported that the instruments used were violin, banjo, and bass fiddle. Similarly constituted groups provided dance music for Negroes in other places, wherever the ubiquitous fiddler was joined by others. It seems clear then that at midcentury, the black fiddler still held sway over Negro dancing spots. This state of affairs could not have existed, however, too long in the East. According to the evidence, the rag-playing pioneer Old Man Sam Moore was "ragging the quadrilles and schottisches" in Philadelphia before 1875. Moore played in dance ensembles of the time, doubling on the bass fiddle and the piano.

Sometime during the 1860s or 70s an historic event took place —the piano was brought for the first time into a dance combo. And it happened in some night spot of a black tenderloin district—probably in the East. It did not take long for canny nightclub owners to discover that piano music could be used as a substitute for the traditional combination of fiddle, wind instrument, and bass fiddle and, more important, that it was less expensive.

Rag players were called "professors," titles given also to bandmasters and music teachers. By 1910 the rag professors were either writing fewer and fewer rags or were moving over into other areas of music activity. The publication of 1911 of white song writer Irving Berlin's *Alexander's Ragtime Band* was in reality the swan song of the ragtime-song period, although it brought about a brief revival of interest in the music. The vogue for instrumental rags in the classic style may be regarded as symbolically ending with the death of Scott Joplin in 1917. Upon hearing of Joplin's death, publisher John Stark eulogized: "Scott Joplin is dead. A homeless itinerant, he left his mark on American music." In memory of the Ragtime King, Stark published *Reflection Rag—Syncopated Musings*. He continued to publish instrumental rags for several years more, notably by the black composer James Scott and three younger black rag men active in St. Louis: Artie Matthews, Robert Hampton, and Charles Thompson. But the kind of piano playing that was developing in the former ragtime centers of the nation was no longer in the classic rag tradition; it was more a jazz-piano style that derived its distinction from improvisation. Its principal exponents on the East coast were James Price Johnson, Charles Luckeyeth "Luckey" Roberts, Willie-the-Lion Smith, and Thomas "Fats" Waller. In the Midwest there were the St. Louisians mentioned above, and some of the old-timers in Chicago, who were gradually changing their style of playing.

RAGTIME STYLE IN THE MUSIC OF
WHITE SONG WRITERS AND COMPOSERS

Ragtime writer Benjamin Harney (1871–1938) is of historic importance because, as ragtime historian Rudi Blesh points out, he "publicly pioneered it [i.e. rag music] in an early day when Negro ragtimers were cautious about presenting it full-strength to any but their own race." As we have seen, Harney was the first to introduce ragtime to sophisticated New York audiences; he also wrote two of the period's most popular songs, *You've Been a Good Old Wagon but You Done Broke Down* and *Mister Johnson Turn Me Loose*. A white writer of Tin Pan Alley, Kerry Mills, was responsible for another favorite of the time, *At a Georgia Camp Meeting*. A discussion of the development of a white school of ragtime composers is beyond the scope of this book. (The subject is ably handled in several sources, particularly in Rudi Blesh's *They All Played Ragtime*.) The 1950s saw a revival of interest in the classic rag music of Joplin and his contemporaries. During the following decade, groups concerned with the preservation of rag music began to spring up over the country, one of the most active of which was the Maple Leaf Club in Los Angeles, California. This group published a newspaper, *Rag Times*, and contributed to the growth of the movement by sponsoring concerts, rag festivals, and lecture-concerts. In 1969, the club saluted Eubie Blake as the greatest living ragtimer and presented him in a lecture-concert.

Of the great European art-music composers who were writing during this period, Debussy was the first to take notice of the new music of Negro folk origin; his *Golliwog's Cakewalk*, a movement of the piano suite *Children's Corner* (1905), bounces along in typical ragtime song style with a syncopated melody in the right hand and "um-pah" accompaniment in the left. Stravinsky wrote *Piano Rag-Music* (1920), *Ragtime* for eleven instruments (1918), and included a ragtime movement in the popular *L'Histoire du soldat* (The Soldier's Tale, 1918). The French composer Erik Satie (1866–1925) wrote a ballet, *Parade* (1917), in which *The American Girl's Dance* is in ragtime style. The German composer Paul Hindemith (1895–1963) inserted a

Ragtime finale in his piano suite of 1922. In the United States, John Alden Carpenter (1876–1951) seems to have been the first white composer to use ragtime style in art music, in his concertino for piano and orchestra (1916). All of this music reflects the captivating but rather vapid style of the ragtime song rather than the essence of serious rag music. But then, few persons outside the Negro world had the opportunity to hear rag music as played by the legendary figures. The music composed by Joplin, Scott, Turpin, Blake, and others was too difficult to be taken home "and tried out on the piano." The public came to know instead a pseudo-ragtime style popularized by Tin Pan Alley and exemplified in the playing of the white pianist Mike Bernard and his followers.

THE BLUES

We know even less about the origin of the blues than we know about the beginning of ragtime. W. C. Handy, the first man to popularize the blues, was struck with the possibilities of utilizing it in musical composition in 1903 when he heard a man singing a song in a Mississippi train station. The singer was a "lean, loose-jointed Negro" clothed in mere rags, whose face reflected the "sadness of the ages." As he sang, he plunked on a guitar, producing some of the "weirdest music" Handy had ever heard. Handy recognized the song type, an earthy kind of music that he had known as a boy in Alabama.

The earliest professional blues singer, Ma Rainey (Gertrude Malissa Nix Pridgett Rainey), remembered first hearing the blues in 1902. She was touring in Missouri with the Rabbit Foot Minstrels when she heard a local girl sing a song about the man who had deserted her. Its plaintive poignancy haunted Ma, who learned the song and used it in her act, where it became so popular with audiences that Ma began to specialize in the singing of such songs. She claimed that it was she who gave to the songs the name "blues" after being asked time and time again about the kind of song she was singing and having finally answered in an inspired moment, "It's the blues." But old-timers who sang and played the blues in tenderloin districts across the country scoffed when asked about the origin of the blues. In New Orleans an old fiddler said, "The blues? Ain't no first blues! The blues always been." Eubie Blake answered, "Blues in Baltimore? Why, Baltimore is the blues!" Bunk Johnson, a pioneer bluesman, told an interviewer, "When I was a kid [i.e. in the 1880s] we used to play nothing but the blues." In New Orleans, even the street vendors used the blues, advertising their wares by playing blues on toy horns bought from Kress's dime stores.

CHARACTERISTICS OF THE BLUES

The blues has few absolute features. It is an aural music, intended to take on its shape and style during the performance. The notation of a blues gives only an approximation of how it may sound during performance. Generally, but not always, the blues reflects the personal response of its inventor to a specific occurrence or situation. By singing about his misery, the blues singer achieves a kind of catharsis and life becomes bearable again. A stevedore has lost his job, for example, and he wails:

> Ain't got no place to lay my head,
> Ain't got no place to lay my head, Baby,
> Ain't got no place to lay my head.
>
> Steamboat done put me out of doors,
> Steamboat done put me out of doors, Baby,
> Steamboat done put me out of doors.
>
> Don't know what in this world I'm goin' to do,
> Don't know what in this world I'm goin' to do, Baby,
> Don't know what in this world I'm goin' to do.

Most often the blues singer bemoans the fickleness or departure of a loved one. He doesn't need an audience for his singing, although others may listen to him if they wish. When others do listen to the blues singer, they frequently find that they have shared his experiences in one way or another.

The antecedents of the blues were the mournful songs of the stevedores and roustabouts, the field hollers of the slaves, and the sorrow songs among the spirituals. Such spirituals as *Lay This Body Down*, for example, would probably have been called blues had the term been in use at the time. Most frequently the blues has a three-line stanza, of which the second line is a restatement of the first and the third line is a contrasting statement. The latter may supply an explanation for the question raised by the first two lines, or it may simply provide a philosophical comment upon the situation:

> Woke up this morning, feeling sad and blue,
> Woke up this morning, feeling sad and blue,
> Didn't have nobody to tell my troubles to.

or

> I've got the blues, but I'm too darn mean to cry,
> I've got the blues, but I'm too darn mean to cry,
> Before I'd cry I'd rather lay down and die.

or

> When a woman gets the blues she hangs her head and cries,
> When a woman gets the blues she hangs her head and cries,
> But when a man gets the blues, he grabs a train and flies.

Like most Negro folk music, the blues tends to move in duple rhythms and have syncopated melody. Its musical form parallels the poetic form, generally with an a-a'-b arrangement for the three-line text, each phrase consisting of four measures and the entire song of twelve measures. To be sure, a blues form may be contracted to eight measures or expanded to sixteen. The melody for each line is typically condensed into a little more than two measures of the four-measure phrase (see Example XI.4); this allows for a "break" at the end of each line, for improvisation on the accompanying instrument (guitar, piano, or instrumental ensemble), during which the singer interjects spoken asides such as "Oh, Lordy," "Yes, man," "Oh, play it," etc. The resulting effect is a call-and-response structure, the instrumental improvisation representing the "response" to the voice's "call."

The blues melody derives from an altered scale in which the third, fifth, seventh, and occasionally the sixth degrees are treated very casually, sometimes being lowered and at other times being used at the natural pitch levels of the major scale. At these points in the scale the singer is apt to "scoop," "swoop," or "slur." The altered tones are commonly called "blue notes."

Ex. XI.4   Traditional blues melody with chords,
Joe Turner Blues

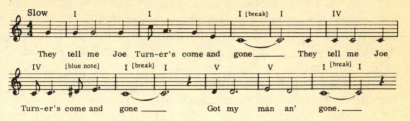

The blues singer invariably employs a relaxed singing style, freely using such special vocal devices as falsetto, shouting, whining, moaning, and growling.

Most of the features discussed so far are in the African tradition; as demonstrated in Chapter VII, we could describe many other kinds of Negro folksong in a similar way. One of the unique features of the blues is its harmonic character, which points to the influence of the European tradition. The accompaniment for the blues uses three chords in a prescribed way. The first line of the blues is supported by the tonic chord of the key (i.e. a chord built on the first degree of the scale, as C-E-G in the key of C). The second line is accompanied by the subdominant chord (i.e. a chord built on the fourth degree), which moves to the tonic chord by the end of the line. The third line employs the dominant chord (i.e. a chord built on the fifth degree) resolving to the tonic at the end of the song. The chord progressions (i.e. the movements from one chord to the other) can be expressed in the formula I–IV–I–V–I. To be sure, this harmonic framework may be altered in actual performance or in a particular song, but it may be generally regarded as typical of blues harmony. In performance, the twelve-measure blues melody is repeated with each new stanza of the text, but very freely in an improvisatory manner, so that the repetitions become variations on the first statement rather than strict restatements.

Blues analysts of the present day tend to classify blues into three categories: country or rural blues, city or "classic" blues, and urban blues. The *country blues* represents the earliest type, the singing of one man to the accompaniment of his guitar. Later these men were accompanied by "string bands" and "jug bands" —the string bands consisting of fiddles, guitars, banjos, mandolins, and basses; the jug bands using ordinary crockery jugs, banjos, harmonicas, mandolins, washboards, and kazoos (toy instruments). The *city blues* was sung by women in the 1920s and 30s to the accompaniment of a piano or orchestra, and was apt to be more sophisticated in tone than the country blues. The term *urban blues* is used to apply to blues of the 40s and later, with accompaniment that includes electric guitars and/or basses, drums, and brass instruments, but no harmonicas or similar "country" instruments. Each of the three types includes, of course, a wide diversity of styles and structures, although the city blues generally retains the "classic" three-line a-a-b form.

The early anonymous singers of the blues were often wanderers, sometimes blind, who carried their sorrowful songs from one black community to another, some of them sauntering down the railroad tracks or dropping from freight cars, others coming in with the packet boats, and yet others coming via the dirt road, having caught a ride on a wagon or in a later time, on a truck. They sang their songs in the railroad stations, on the street corners, in eating places, in honky-tonk night spots, and even on the trains. They also sang for community social affairs, dances, and picnics. From the time of its origin, however, the blues was generally associated with the lowly—received with warmth in the brothels and saloons of the sporting world, but rejected by respectable people.

BLUES AND SPIRITUALS

The dividing line between the blues and some kinds of spirituals cannot always be sharply drawn. Many spirituals convey to listeners the same feeling of hopelessness and despair as do the blues. The spiritual is religious, however, rather than worldly and tends to be more generalized in its expression than specific, more figurative in its language than direct, and more expressive of group feelings than individual ones. Despite these differences it is nevertheless often difficult to distinguish between the two kinds of songs. Some songs have such vague implications that they are classified as "blues-spirituals."

Singers of spirituals wandered from place to place, as did blues singers. Handy describes in his book a scene of Clarksdale, Mississippi, that depicts the "blind singers and the footloose bards" in their natural habitat:

> A favorite hangout with them was the railroad station. There, surrounded by crowds of country folks, they would pour out their hearts in song while the audience ate fish and bread, chewed sugar cane, [and] dipped snuff while waiting for trains to carry them down the line.
>
> They earned their living by selling their own songs—"ballets," as they called them. . . . Some of these country boys hustled on trains. Others visited churches. I remember buying such a ballet entitled *I've Heard of a City Called Heaven*. It was printed on a slip of paper about the size of a postcard. Fifty years later . . . I heard the number sung with great success by the Hall Johnson singers in *The Green Pastures* [a Broadway show first produced in the 1930s].

Not all blues are sorrowful. Almost always there is a note of humor, and sometimes the blues singer audaciously challenges fate to mete out further blows. Sure, he has lost his job, and his woman has left him, and he has the blues, but he will go out the next morning to look for another job, and perhaps another woman will come along. Such a blues may have all of the jubilance of a shouting, foot-stomping spiritual.

W. C. HANDY, FATHER OF THE BLUES

When William Christopher Handy (1873–1958) published his first blues composition, the *Memphis Blues*, in 1912 he created an unprecedented vogue for that kind of music. Originally written in 1909 as a campaign song for one of the mayoral candidates in a Memphis election, Edward H. Crump, it was an immediate success upon its first performance. Handy's bandsmen became "intoxicated" with the melody and rhythm of the piece even during the rehearsal. Once the playing began, both the crowd and the band went wild! People danced on the streets; in the office buildings the "white folks pricked up their ears" and "stenographers danced with their bosses." As a result of this performance Handy's band jumped to the top spot among Memphis bands. Two years later Handy published the world-famous

St. Louis Blues, a composition that has carried the blues all over the world.

Handy was well equipped for his role as a musical pioneer. Although his father, minister of a church in Florence, Alabama, was not musical, his mother "admitted [to] a fondness for the guitar" and at least two maternal relatives were skilled ex-slave fiddlers. At the Florence District School for Negroes, the boy studied solfeggio under the guidance of Y. A. Wallace, a member of the first graduating class of Fisk University. So thoroughly did the teacher train his students that Handy at the age of ten could "catalogue" any sound he heard, using the sol-fa syllables. As we have seen, Handy was given organ lessons as a boy, and surreptitiously he learned to play the cornet from the white bandmaster who worked with the town's Negro band in the community barbershop. Handy's parents thoroughly disapproved of his learning to play anything but hymns on the organ. When he brought home a guitar, which he had purchased with his own money after several months of hard work, his parents were aghast and ordered him to exchange it, "a sinful thing brought into a Christian home," for something "useful,"–a *Webster's Unabridged Dictionary!* Despite his family's stand against worldly music, Handy began to play with the local Negro brass band, to sing with local quartets, and eventually to play with the Negro dance orchestra.

Handy began the life of a "trouper" soon after graduation from high school. His varied career included a year or so on the road as an itinerant musician, several stints with minstrel troupes as a bandsman and bandleader, a brief period of teaching at the Teacher's Agricultural and Mechanical College for Negroes in Huntsville, Alabama, several years as a brass-band and dance-orchestra leader in Mississippi and Tennessee (particularly in Memphis), and led to his establishing a music publishing company in Memphis in 1907 with a young lyricist and singer, Harry Pace. In 1918 Handy and Pace moved to New York with their company.

All those years Handy had been making arrangements of melodies and pieces for the choral and instrumental groups under his direction in order to obtain the special effects he wanted in performance. It was not until the tremendous popularity of the *Memphis Blues,* however, that he thought about publishing any of his works. After it appeared in print, Handy published a steady stream of blues, spiritual arrangements, marches, hymns, and miscellaneous songs. His collections include *Blues: An Anthology* (1926) and *Book of Negro Spirituals* (1938); his books include *Negro Authors and Composers of the United States* (1936), *Father of the Blues* (1941), and *Unsung Americans Sung* (1944).

Although Handy was the first man to write a blues composition and the first to popularize the blues, two blues pieces actually appeared in print prior to his *Memphis Blues*. The *Baby Seals Blues*, written by the black rag-pianist Artie Matthews, was published in August, 1912; the *Dallas Blues*, written by the white song writer Hart A. Wand, appeared the following month. Handy's blues piece came out three weeks later, followed by his *Jogo Blues* in 1913, *St. Louis Blues* in 1914, and *Joe Turner Blues* in 1915. Matthews wrote another blues in 1915, the *Weary Blues*, that became very popular. In the same year, Morton published his *Original Jelly Roll Blues*. These early pieces, along with some traditional folk-blues melodies, provide a basic repertory of stock melodies that have been drawn upon innumerable times by jazz composers. As we shall see, the essence of jazz is improvisation upon a given melody.

The foregoing discussion serves as an introduction to the blues. Its history cannot properly begin until 1920, the year of the first recorded blues, for phonograph records are the chief sources of blues history. We can surmise how the blues sounded before that date, but critical discussion must be concerned with the music itself. The blues performer is at the same time its composer.

CHAPTER XII

Precursors of Jazz: Syncopated
Dance Orchestras and Brass Bands

At the end of the nineteenth-century Negro brass bands and dance orchestras were flourishing all over the country, particularly in the large cities of the nation. The black dance-orchestra tradition on the eastern seaboard reached back to the beginning of the century, as we have seen, with the orchestras of Frank Johnson of Philadelphia, Peter O'Fake of Newark, New Jersey, and Sy Gilliat and George Walker of Richmond, Virginia. During the 1880s New York began to establish itself as a center of Negro dance-orchestra activity. Even before the 80s, there were two good brass bands, Johnson's Brass Band and Becker's Brass Band. During the decade the violinist Walter Craig organized a society dance orchestra that developed a fine reputation for itself and was soon in constant demand by white society groups and musical-show producers. It was Craig's Celebrated Orchestra, for example, that provided the music for the big cakewalk competition held at Madison Square Garden in February, 1892. Craig was also heavily patronized by Negroes; the biggest social event of the year was his annual Christmas Dance and Reception for his own people, which was begun in 1880 and continued for over forty years.

In Detroit, Michigan, "Old Man" Finney established a musical dynasty during the 1860s that flourished up until the 1920s. Originally from Canada, Finney formed with his wife and son an ensemble called Finney's Quadrille Orchestra. As the demand for his services grew, he added players to the family ensemble. Eventually there resulted the Detroit City Brass Band and a society dance orchestra of over forty men. Finney often found it necessary to divide his men into smaller groups to cover all of the engagements for which he had been contracted. A second generation in the Finney entourage included some of his protégés: John Johnson, Ben Shook, Harry Guy, and the Stone brothers. All of these men were known for their band compositions or popular songs as well as their skill as instrumentalists. It was Fred Stone of this group who wrote the popular *My Ragtime Baby*. In San Francisco, an ensemble called La Estrella Mandolin Club under D. W. McDonald played for the social affairs of the Nob Hill society set.

Even in sparsely populated areas of the country there were opportunities for Negro dance ensembles, often referred to as "string bands," to find employment. George Morrison, a bandleader from Denver, Colorado, recalled that as a boy in Boulder, during the early 1900s, he organized a boys' string band that played for all the dances held in the mining camps and in the mountain towns. There was simply no other music group available to the mountain people. Morrison and other old-timers give the reason for this state of affairs: throughout the nineteenth century and on into the twentieth, white youths were discouraged from preparing for careers as dance musicians. We know that since colonial times black men had traditionally provided music for the dancing of whites. In many places the profession of dance musician was reserved by custom for Negroes, just as was, for example, the occupation of barber. Consequently, black dance orchestras held widespread monopolies on jobs for a long period in the nation's history—even after World War I.

A number of the Negro bands that were active at the end of the nineteenth century won national reputations, some of them touring on the road, as did vocal groups and music shows. When W. C. Handy arrived in Evansville, Indiana, in the 1890s, he found there three good bands: Warren's, Schreiber's, and the Hampton Cornet Band. In nearby Henderson, Kentucky, the noted David Crutcher had a band. During the same decade, Sedalia, Missouri, a town of only moderate size, had several bands, including the twelve-piece Queen City Concert Band, which was a competition winner. When Handy went to Memphis in 1903 to take over Thornton's Knights of Pythias Band, the city had already three well-established bands. In Baltimore, Eubie Blake, as a twelve year old, played cornet in the Monumental City Guards Band led by Charles Harris. In Cleveland, Ohio, the Excelsior Reed Band under H. C. Smith was regarded as first-rate. The list of bands is far more extensive than can be given at this point, but the names cited above suggest the extent to which brass-band music was being played by black men at the end of the nineteenth century.

The town brass band was a traditional American institution, and every little village aspired to have its own band to provide Sunday afternoon concerts in the village square and to play for parades on civic occasions and holidays. Although some towns hired their own bandmasters to organize town bands and to train the bandsmen, generally the Negro bands were independently sponsored by fraternal and benevolent societies, or social clubs, or by the bandsmen themselves. In the latter instance the black bandsmen could often depend upon the patronage of wealthy white townspeople in helping with the purchase of uniforms and instruments. A good Negro band found itself in great demand by both whites and blacks for all kinds of occasions. The opening of a country store, for example, called for brass-band music after the ceremonies. Band music was demanded for political rallies and Election Day ceremonies. Large cities in the South maintained amusement parks for blacks, where dances were among the chief attractions and brass bands provided the dance music in open-air pavillions. The dance floor in Memphis's Dixie Park could, and often did, accommodate a thousand dancers at a time; at Lincoln Park in New Orleans there were two dance places—an open-air pavillion and a dance hall. The bands in towns and cities located along the Mississippi or its main tributaries, the Ohio and the Missouri, found opportunities to play on excursion boats and packet boats that plied up and down the rivers.

Typically, a brass band was composed of twelve to fourteen men and used the following instruments: trumpets or cornets, trombones, horns, clarinets, and drums. To this basic ensemble might be added melophones, tubas, flutes, piccolos, and other instruments, depending upon the place and the availability of players. In Maryland, Virginia, and the Carolinas, for example, the euphonium was a popular band instrument. Generally, brass bands had their own little satellite dance orchestras, composed of seven or eight bandsmen who could double on other instruments. For dances, the bandsmen added violins, guitars, banjos, mandolins, and basses to a few winds and the drums.

Except for some of the bands in New Orleans, bandsmen were expected to read music and to play the music as written. (We shall take up the discussion of New Orleans bandsmen later.) Undoubtedly there was some "ragging" of the music, but there seems to have been very little improvisation or embellishing of melodies. Brass-band repertories included marches of all kinds, hymns, overtures, medleys of popular songs or operatic arias, and "light classics." Bands were frequently called upon to play for funerals, particularly in southern cities. On the way to the cemetery it was customary for the band to play very slowly and mournfully a dirge, or a Protestant hymn such as *Nearer My God to Thee*, but on the way back the band would strike up a lively spiritual such as *When the Saints Go Marching In*, or a ragtime song such as *Didn't He Ramble*, or a syncopated march. For dances, bands were expected to provide music for the popular dances of the period: waltzes, schottisches, polkas, quadrilles, and two-steps. By the turn of the century, one-steps and "slow drags," as well as the cakewalk, were becoming popular.

An integral part of life for brassmen was the band competition. Just as ragtime pianists and cakewalkers competed in regional and national contests, so did brass bands. A town or city expected its brass band to bring back honors from a competition, just like its baseball team. In some places, particularly in New Orleans, brass bands engaged in local battles. One band would literally play another off the streets by playing louder or more brilliantly or with sweeter tones, much to the delight of the hundreds of band watchers on the streets who would assemble at the first sounds of a *ta-ta-ta-ta ta-ta* from the trumpets calling the bandsmen together. In New Orleans the contests were called "cutting" or "bucking" contests. When on parade, bands were generally accompanied by a grand marshal, his aides, and a host of non-musicians, chiefly children who danced along in time to the music, called the "second line." For an important occasion the fraternal organization or benevolent society sponsoring the parade might hire three or four bands to participate, the members themselves also parading in fancy uniforms.

SYNCOPATED DANCE MUSIC IN
NEW YORK

In 1900 the center of Negro fashionable life at New York was an area on the West Side of Manhattan known as Black Bohemia; the headquarters of black artistic talent in the area was the Marshall Hotel on West Fifty-third Street. Here were to be found the actors, musicians, artists, composers, writers, and poets who were the celebrities of the time. Here also came white actors, musicians, and composers from the nearby Broadway theater district, to see and be seen. Robert Cole and the Johnson brothers lived in the hotel, and their rooms were gathering places for the elite of the group. Entertainers would gather in the bar, waiting for calls to go out on private engagements, for it was known all over the city that one could always find dance musicians and singers at the Marshall. In the first decade of the twentieth century there came to the West Fifty-third Street area several young musicians who would make a decisive impact on the social life of the city, among them: Tim Brymn (1881–1946), Ford Dabney (1883–1958), James Reese Europe (1881–1919), J. Leubrie Hill (1873–1916), William H. Tyers (1876–1924), and Will Vodery (1885–1951). They were caught up immediately in the exciting life of Black Bohemia and began to organize and train dance-music ensembles to go out on engagements.

JAMES REESE EUROPE

James Europe was born in Mobile, Alabama, but moved with his family to Washington, D. C., during childhood. As youngsters, James and his sister Mary gained a reputation in Washington for their pianistic skills. Europe also studied violin with Enrico Hurlei, the assistant director of the United States Marine Band. In 1904, Europe went to New York, attracted by the possibilities for obtaining employment with one of the musical-show companies. In 1906 he signed on as musical director for the Cole-Johnson production of *The Shoo-Fly Regiment*, remained with the show for three seasons, then signed up with *Mr. Lode of Kole* for another season. But before that he had participated in a

unique experience. A group of about twenty experienced enter-
tainer-instrumentalists organized themselves into an orchestra at
the Marshall Hotel and decided to give a concert. The music to
be used was original—written and orchestrated by Joe Jordan.
Will Marion Cook took a hand in rehearsing the group and
developing its ensemble sound.

In the Spring of 1905, the orchestra made its debut at the
Proctor Twenty-third Street Theater. This was the first public
concert of syncopated music in America. Heretofore dance music
had been reserved for dance halls or the orchestra pits of
theaters. The group called itself the Nashville Students, although
none was from Nashville and none was a student. The instrumentation consisted primarily of banjos, mandolins, guitars, saxophones, and drums, to which were added a violin, one or two
brasses, and a double bass. Among the featured soloists were the
minstrel star Ernest Hogan, the soprano Abbie Mitchell, and the
dancer Ida Forsyne. The success of the show brought it a booking at Hammerstein's Victoria Theater on Broadway, on the
vaudeville schedule daily, and in the Roof Garden at nights.
Later, the orchestra toured Europe as the Tennessee Students,
playing at the Olympia in Paris, the Palace Theatre in London,
and the Schumann Circus in Berlin.[1]

The performances of the Nashville Students were innovative in
several ways. First and most impressive was the syncopated
music. Second, and closely related to the first, was the "dancing
conductor," Will Dixon. James Weldon Johnson describes
Dixon's style in the book *Black Manhattan:*

> All through a number he would keep his men together by dancing
> out the rhythm, generally in graceful, sometimes in grotesque,
> steps. Often an easy shuffle would take him across the whole front
> of the band. This style of directing not only got the fullest possi-
> ble response from the men, but kept them in just the right humour
> for the sort of music they were playing.

[1] In several books there exists some confusion about whether the name
of the first Students group was the Nashville Students or the Memphis
Students. Tom Fletcher, who performed with the Students, makes it very
clear in his book, *100 Years of the Negro in Show Business* (New York,
1954), that the 1905 group, which starred Ernest Hogan, was named the
Nashville Students. In 1908 a second Student group was formed and called
the Memphis Students. Fletcher took over the former role of Hogan, who
was ill. See further in Fletcher, pp. 129–34.

Title page of a Clef Club program, 1910. (*Courtesy New York Public Library, Schomburg Collection.*)

The drummer, Buddy Gilmore, contributed his share to the excitement by performing juggling and acrobatic stunts while drumming. His use of other noisemaking devices in addition to the drums—unusual at that time—drew added attention to the rhythms of the music. The unorthodox combination of instruments attracted attention to the novel sound of the group's music. The traditional dance orchestra's violin-dominated combination of strings and woodwinds was almost entirely replaced by instruments formerly associated with folk music—mandolins, guitars, and banjos—or with symphonic music, such as the saxophone. (Up to this time, the saxophone had been used only by Europeans, first French and later German composers, for special effects in their symphonic music and operas.) A final novelty was that the instrumentalists, except for those playing wind instruments, sang as they played. First to introduce the concept of the "singing band" to the entertainment world, the Students added four-part harmony (now known as "barbershop harmony") to several of the musical numbers.

The success of the Nashville Students made a considerable impression upon Jim Europe. In 1910 he gave up his duties with musical shows and organized a black musician's union, the Clef Club. All the best performing musicians in the city were drawn together into the chartered organization, and a house was purchased to serve as a club and booking office. The Clef Club boasted that it could furnish a dance orchestra of from three to thirty men upon request at any time, day or night. In honor of its founding, the Clef Club gave a big concert at the Manhattan Casino on 155th Street and Eighth Avenue (now the Rockland Palace) on October 20, 1910. It was a warm, friendly concert, intended to entertain the patrons, not to impress. Afterward everyone was invited to dance to the music of Craig's Celebrated Orchestra and Hallie Anderson's Orchestra. The instrumentation of the Clef Club Orchestra was unconventional; mandolins were used in place of first and second violins, but there were also a few violins along with the banjos, harp-guitars, cellos, trap drums, and timpani. Finally, there were eleven pianos. This largely string orchestra played marches, dances, operatic medleys, and popular songs of the day.

In May of 1912 Jim Europe took his Clef Club orchestra of 125 players to Carnegie Hall. Again the instrumentation was unorthodox, with forty-seven mandolins and bandores, twenty-seven harp-guitars, eleven banjos, eight violins, one saxophone, one tuba, thirteen cellos, two clarinets, two baritones, eight trombones, seven cornets, one timpani, five trap drums, two double basses, and ten pianos. The program for the evening was equally unorthodox. James Weldon Johnson later wrote about the effect of the opening number, Europe's *Clef Club March*, upon the audience, which was composed of the regular patrons of Carnegie Hall in addition to friends of the orchestra and many serious musicians and music critics as well, who had come out of curiosity.

> New York had not yet become accustomed to jazz; so when the Clef Club opened its concert with a syncopated march, playing it with a biting attack and an infectious rhythm, and on the finale bursting into singing, the effect can be imagined. The applause became a tumult!

The orchestra also performed and sang three of Will Marion Cook's songs: *Swing Along, Exhortation*, and *Rain Song*. According to Fletcher, who was attending the concert, the audience's reception of Cook's music was "thunderous." Europe had insisted that Cook play with the orchestra. Cook had given in on one condition—that he not be introduced on the stage—and Europe promised to observe the condition. But the persistent applause of the audience in response to Cook's music forced Europe to break his promise. When the audience yelled, "Speech, speech!" Cook was so overcome that tears came to his eyes and he could say nothing.

Not all reaction to the concert was as favorable as that of the audience. A white critic wrote in *Musical America*:

> If the Negro Symphony Orchestra will give its attention during the coming year to a movement or two of a Haydn symphony and play it at its next concert, and if the composers, who this year took such obvious pleasure in conducting their marches, tangos, and waltzes, will write short movements for orchestra, basing them on classic models, next year's concert will inaugurate a new era for the Negro musician in New York and will aid him in being appraised at his full value and in being taken seriously.

And a black musician of Philadelphia wrote in an open letter:

> All the renditions of the Club were good, spicy and catchy. . . .
> All races have their folksongs and dances, but all races try to de-
> velop their art from examples set by masters of other periods; and
> if we expect to do anything that is lasting from an artistic stand-
> point, we, too, must study the classics as a foundation for our work.

But Europe defended his position. He told an interviewer:

> You see, we colored people have our own music that is part of us.
> It's the product of our souls; it's been created by the sufferings and
> miseries of our race. Some of the melodies we played Wednesday
> were made up by slaves of the old days, and others were handed
> down from the days before we left Africa. . . . [Some] would
> doubtless laugh heartily at the way our Negro Symphony is
> organized, the distribution of the pieces, and our methods of
> organization.

Europe pointed out that mandolins and banjos were used in place
of second violins, two clarinets instead of an oboe, baritone
horns and trombone instead of French horn and bassoon. He felt,
however, that it was the "peculiar steady strumming accompaniment" of the mandolins and banjos that made the music distinctive, and that the use of ten pianos in the ensemble gave the
background of chords "essentially typical of Negro harmony."
He concluded:

> We have developed a kind of symphony music that, no matter
> what else you think, is different and distinctive, and that lends itself
> to the playing of the peculiar compositions of our race.

Europe was never to retreat from that stand. Seven years later,
after extensive touring and service in the United States Army,
he stated emphatically:

> I have come back from France more firmly convinced than ever
> that negroes should write negro music. We have our own racial
> feeling and if we try to copy whites we will make bad copies. . . .
> We won France by playing music which was ours and not a pale
> imitation of others, and if we are to develop in America we must
> develop along our own lines. . . . Will Marion Cook, William Tires

[Tyers], even Harry Burleigh and Coleridge-Taylor are [only] truly themselves in the music which expresses their race. . . . The music of our race springs from the soil, and this is true to-day with no other race, except possibly the Russians. . . .

[*Literary Digest*, April 26, 1919]

A dance craze swept over the United States beginning in the second decade of the century. Nowhere was it more obvious than in New York. In the 1890s the public had wanted songs to sing and to try out on the piano at home; after 1910 the public wanted only dance music. The Clef Club men profited from the new fad. Their orchestras played in the big hotels, restaurants, clubs, and in private homes, on yachts, and at resorts. Jim Europe left the Clef Club and organized his own Tempo Club, an organization similar to the Clef Club, that sent out small dance orchestras to play upon call. In 1914 Europe began an association with Vernon and Irene Castle, a white dance team, that brought fame to all three. The Castles made popular several ballroom dances; notably the turkey trot, the fox-trot, the one-step, and the Castle walk. Europe produced the kind of music for the Castles that helped them to become an institution in New York. He composed special music for their dances and directed the resident orchestra at their dance salon, the Castle House or "Castles-in-the-Air" as it was called. Europe even invented several of the dances featured by the Castles; for example, the fox-trot and the turkey trot. His eleven-piece orchestra consisted of violins, cornets, clarinets, mandolins, drum, and piano. In 1914 Europe was signed to a recording contract by the Victor Record Company.

OTHER BAND LEADERS

A tiny item appeared in *Variety* magazine during these years: "Since the turkey-trot craze, the colored musicians in New York have been busy dispensing syncopated music for the 400" (i.e. the cream of white society). In 1915 society orchestras of the Tempo Club (with over two hundred members) and the Clef Club were kept busier than ever playing for dance-crazed New Yorkers. Tim Brymn led a twenty-piece band at the New York

Roof Garden, Will Tyers played at the Strand Roof, Will Vodery conducted for the Coconut Grove on the Century Roof, and Ford Dabney directed for the *Ziegfeld Follies* at the New Amsterdam Roof Garden. Like Jim Europe, these men wrote much of the music that they played. According to music publisher Edward B. Marks, Jim Europe and Ford Dabney wrote so many dance hits that their names were spelled backward on some pieces of sheet music in order to "lend an appearance of variety." It was not true ragtime, but a lusty, joyful music, full of zest. Its distinction derived not so much from the kind of syncopation found in rag music as from the instrumentation, the way the men handled their instruments, and the noisy way that they shouted back and forth to each other as they played. But it was indoor music, for all that. The ensembles were small, and the violin, clarinet, or flute generally played the lead.

The bandleaders who directed the "dispensing" of syncopated music for New York society were well trained, experienced, and ambitious. Ford Dabney, a native of Washington, D. C., had studied music with his father and local white musicians. From 1904 to 1907 he served as the official court musician to the president of Haiti. After returning to the United States, Dabney organized a quartet and later operated a theater where vaudeville shows were produced. By 1913 he was in New York, working with Jim Europe and the Tempo Club. Dabney also worked with the Castles and wrote music for some of their dance numbers. It was during this period that he conducted the *Ziegfeld Follies* orchestra. James Tim Brymn was born in Kingston, North Carolina, and was graduated from Shaw University in that state. Coming to New York at the beginning of the twentieth century, he studied further at the National Conservatory of Music. Among other places, Brymn's orchestra played at the sophisticated Reisenweber Café off Columbus Circle.

William H. Tyers was born in Richmond, Virginia, but moved with his family to New York at an early age. Educated in the public schools, he studied music privately. In addition to conducting dance orchestras, Tyers worked as a staff arranger for music publishing companies in the city; among them, the Joseph Stern Company. His instrumental dance compositions were widely known during the time, particularly *Maori*, *Trocha*, *The Call of the Woods* (a waltz), and *Panama*. Will Vodery, originally from Philadelphia and a graduate of the University of Pennsylvania, was also a professional arranger as well as bandleader. He first commanded attention with his music for an all-white production, Joe Howard's *The Time, the Place, and the Girl*. From 1911 until 1932 Vodery was music supervisor for the Florenz Ziegfeld productions. One of the Negro plays for which he wrote songs, *The Oyster Man* (1910), starred the celebrated minstrel Ernest Hogan. One other musician who belongs to this group was John Leubrie Hill, arranger and writer of popular songs, instrumental rags, and musical comedies.

Willie-the-Lion Smith, who was playing rag music in tenderloin clubs during this period, said that Clef Club musicians were "not allowed to rag it [their music] or beautify the melody [by] using their own ideas—they had to read those fly-spots [the music notes] closely and truly." This was not the case in the dance halls and night clubs of the "district." There, dance music was furnished by a three-man combination, consisting of piano, drummer, and banjoist or harmonica player. Salaries were low but the tips were good. The pianists tried to get an orchestral effect in their playing, chiefly by using a loud, heavy left hand; they also used a great deal of syncopation and improvisation. During this period Chicago was reputed to have the best Negro bands, but it was acknowledged that New York had the best pianists and drummers; after all, there was a long-standing tradition in the East for drumming, dating back to the Pinkster festivals and Philadelphia jubilees. And New York pianists played the piano not only as a melody instrument but also as a percussive one.

During the crowded years before World War I, many things happened in the Negro world of New York. Before 1910 black folk began to move north into Harlem. During the same period the last black musical comedy left Broadway, and none was to return there for eleven years. For a while black New Yorkers were dismayed at the loss of all-Negro shows; then theaters began to spring up in Harlem, two of which—the Lafayette and the Lincoln—became the homes of Negro stock companies. In 1913 the Lafayette presented a musical show, J. Leubrie Hill's *Darktown Follies*, that brought Broadway audiences up to Harlem to see it. One of the chief representatives of Broadway, Florenz Ziegfeld, liked what he saw and bought the rights to use several numbers in his own *Follies* on Broadway. Especially striking was *At the Ball,* the finale to the first act of *Darktown Follies,* based on a Negro dance that had become a fad across the nation, called "balling the jack." In 1914 Cris Smith wrote a song, *Balling the Jack,* to match the dance step. Once white New Yorkers had come to Harlem in search of entertainment, they continued "the nightly migration" for almost twenty years.

W. C. Handy's *Memphis Blues* made a big impact on New York in 1912, but the *St. Louis Blues* in 1914 made an even greater impression, especially on Harlem. Everyone began to sing blues, and all the song writers began to write blues. In response to the public's interest in dancing, composers such as James P. Johnson and Luckey Roberts published dance rags and other kinds of dance music. Marks wrote that his publishing company fell back on its "corps of colored writers":

> The new dancing rhythm, almost bare of melody, and Luckey Roberts, one of the hardest-pounding colored piano players of any weight, gave us *Pork and Beans* [1913], a perfect example of the genre. An Englishman once asked the Castle House orchestra for "that song without any tune," and they immediately responded with Luckey's composition.

The year 1914 was notable in yet another regard. It was during this year that a group of New York composers, lyricists, and music publishers met at a restaurant on Fourteenth Street, Lüchow's, and formed an organization to protect the performing rights of copyright owners of musical compositions. The resulting American Society of Composers, Authors, and Publishers (commonly known as ASCAP), counted 170 composers and lyricists among its charter members, including six Negroes: Harry Burleigh, Will Marion Cook, J. Rosamond and James Weldon Johnson, Cecil Mack (Richard McPherson), and Will Tyers. The society determined that anytime a musical composition was performed for profit the originators of the composition should be recompensed. Over the years the society was to prove of great benefit to song writers (who previously had had little protection from music pirates), and particularly to black composers. This meant that such writers as James Bland or Gussie Davis would no longer be forced to retire to poverty while others made thousands of dollars on the sale or performance of their music. Most of the successful black song writers and composers would join ASCAP over the years—that is, until 1940, when a rival organization, Broadcast Music, Incorporated (BMI) was founded.

Harlem was unmoved by the performance of Joplin's rag opera *Treemonisha* in 1915, but stopped to pay a last tribute to the King of Ragtime upon his death in 1917. In 1918 the music publishing firm of Pace and Handy opened an office on Broadway. The firm had had previous association with New York publishers, to be sure, because of its activity in Memphis, and Handy himself had visited New York on several occasions before his final move there. At one time during 1917 he had talked with Jim Europe, Will Vodery, and Tim Brymn about the prospects of the United States entering World War I, and the men had discussed the idea of organizing Negro bands for overseas service. On Broadway, the Pace-Handy firm could advertise itself as the publisher of a new hit, *A Good Man Is Hard to Find*. Sophie Tucker, noted white singer of show music, helped to make the song a success by singing it on Broadway. She also featured other songs by black writers—for example, Charlie Warfield's *I Ain't Got Nobody* and Shelton Brooks' *Some of These Days*.

ENTERTAINMENT MUSIC IN CHICAGO

In Chicago, the new Pekin Theatre on State Street became the center of Negro musical activity early in the century. Joe Jordan was the music director there on and off until 1913; the rag pianist Tony Jackson was the chief entertainer. Jackson had composed many songs since arriving from New Orleans in 1905, but chose not to publish until about 1915. His first two songs, *Pretty Baby* and *You're Such a Pretty Thing*, were immediate hits. Later songs—among them, *Some Sweet Day*—were equally popular. Motts' Pekin was the first theater in the country to be staffed entirely by black men. First-rate vaudeville shows—black and white, American and European—were brought to the Pekin. Several of the celebrated black entertainers of New York performed there at one time or another, including orchestra directors Tim Brymn and Will Vodery. Motts, as the owner, gave many newcomers to the field of theatrical entertainment the opportunity to exercise their talents and gain experience. As we have seen, he did not confine himself to the presentation of show music, but made his theater a place where the music of such composers as Harry Burleigh and Coleridge-Taylor could also be heard.

In 1907 Motts hired two young graduates of Fisk University, Flournoy Miller and Aubrey Lyles, to write plays for his Pekin Theatre Company. Their very first play, *The Mayor of Dixie* (which included songs), was a success; years later, it was re-written and used as the book for the Broadway musical *Shuffle Along*. During the same year, 1907, a wanderer from New Orleans who was known as a good bluesman came into Chicago but did not remain. The wanderer, Jelly Roll Morton, returned in the 20s to stay for awhile and to make a national reputation in the entertainment world for himself and his band.

Beginning in the second decade, other places in Chicago began to compete with the Pekin in offering syncopated dance music —for example, the Lincoln Gardens (Royal Gardens) at Thirty-first Street and Cottage Grove Avenue; the De Luxe Café at Thirty-fifth and State Streets; and the Dreamland Café in the same area. Among the Negro orchestras on Chicago's South Side during this period were Wilbur C. Sweatman's Orchestra at the Monogram Theater, Erskine Tate's Orchestra at the Vendome Theatre, and Dave Peyton's Symphonic Syncopators at the Grand Theatre. All three men were active later during the jazz era; some of the members of their orchestras went on to achieve world renown.

Wilbur Sweatman (1882–1961) was better known as a clari-netist and a vaudeville performer than as an orchestra leader. Having been taught the piano as a child by his sister, Sweatman learned to play clarinet and violin by himself. Before going to Chicago about 1910, he had traveled with circus bands, played in W. C. Handy's minstrel band of the Mahara's Minstrels, and directed music in various theaters of the Midwest. He is credited with having introduced syncopated clarinet-solo playing to the entertainment world during his engagement at Hammerstein's Victoria Theater on Times Square in the early 1900s. His sweet tone, coupled with his syncopation and high-register playing (an octave higher than New Yorkers were accustomed to hearing) won him the plaudits of the press as well as the crowd. On the vaudeville circuit Sweatman's specialty was playing three clarinets at the same time, each instrument producing a different note to create three-part harmony. Audiences particularly liked his three-clarinet performance of *The Rosary*, a popular sentimental song by the white composer Ethelbert Nevin.

BANDS AND ORCHESTRAS IN NEW ORLEANS

In New Orleans at the end of the nineteenth century, there were dozens of marching brass bands, dance orchestras, and strolling groups of players. The most outstanding of these bands were the Excelsior Brass Band and the Onward Brass Band, both organized in the 1880s. As in the early part of the century, some bandsmen had taken music lessons from members of the French Opera House orchestra, and two bandsmen, the Tio brothers, had graduated from the Mexican Conservatory before coming to New Orleans about 1885. A marching band typically included from ten to twelve men; its usual instrumentation was two or three cornets, two trombones, an alto horn, a baritone horn, a tuba, one or two clarinets, a snare drum, and a bass drum. When the relatively small bands played for parades and funerals on the streets of New Orleans, they produced a sound that was "beautifully light" and sweet and yet at the same time full-bodied, reflecting the excellent training of the musicians and their concern for good ensemble playing.

The standard repertory of brass bands included light concert music as well as marches, for as in other places the bands of New Orleans were often called upon to present concerts. The Excelsior Band played a program, for example, at the New Orleans Exposition in February, 1885. Moreover, since brass bands were frequently hired to play for dances held in the larger halls, a band's repertory also included the required quadrilles, polkas, schottisches, two-steps, and waltzes.

Generally, however, smaller ensembles were used for dances —orchestras composed of seven or eight men with a typical instrumentation of violin (or mandolin), guitar, cornet (or trumpet), clarinet, trombone, bass, and drum. Best known of the dance ensembles were the Excelsior String Band, an affiliate of the Excelsior Brass Band, led by the violinist Henry Nickerson, and the society orchestra of John Robichaux, a versatile instrumentalist who played drums in the Excelsior Brass Band from 1891 to 1903. The "string bands" that played for neighborhood affairs were quite small, of course, often consisting only of guitar, trumpet, clarinet, and bass.

At first, the Excelsior and Onward Brass Bands were composed primarily of creoles of color, who lived in the French-speaking downtown district of New Orleans. Uptown, the musicians were blacks, who preferred a more exciting kind of music than the genteel quadrilles and marches of the creoles. The star attractions of the uptown district in the 1890s were the barber-trumpeter Charles "Buddy" Bolden (1868–1931) and a young cornetist, William Geary "Bunk" Johnson (1879–1949), who joined Bolden about 1895. When Bolden and his men played at the uptown Lincoln Park, Bolden's powerful trumpet "could be heard for miles around, especially on a clear night." Lincoln Park catered to middle-class patrons as well as the working class; Bolden's ability to play "sweet music" at five o'clock matinees on Sundays endeared him to the former, and his "ragged" versions of street songs and blues made him the idol of the latter. In the tenderloin district, Bolden was the "King"; for the district folk he brought out some of his specialties such as *Make Me a Pallet on the Floor, Buddy Bolden's Blues,* and *Bucket's Got a Hole in It.*

It was during the Summer of 1894 that Bolden and his band improvised a "hot blues" at a dance hall and Bolden thereby became known as the man "who invented the hot blues" and "the first man that began playing jazz." There is no evidence, however, that the music generally played by Bolden's band was genuine jazz, as defined by modern scholars. Rather, they played a music characterized by embellishment of the melody, strong rhythms, and fiery, powerful instrumental tones.

The downtown musicians were proud of their ability to read music and to play "legitimately"; the uptown musicians were equally proud of their inability to read music. They feared that learning to read might dull their ability to improvise and to play "with the heart." Bolden was a music reader, as were one or two of his men, but all preferred to play by ear. At dances the violinist generally played the "lead" or the melody, while the other instrumentalists played variations on the melody. In parades the trumpet or cornet played the lead. The performer playing the lead instrument (violinist or cornetist) was in effect the bandleader. He decided which pieces were to be played, set the tempo, kept the band together, and determined when solo passages would be introduced.

Two events occurred during the 90s that greatly affected the development of entertainment music in New Orleans. In 1894, the city enacted a segregation code that sent colored creoles to live in the uptown district and consequently brought them into closer cultural contact with the blacks. In 1897, the city passed a resolution that instituted vice segregation, setting up a tenderloin district, later called Storyville after the resolution's sponsor, Alderman Sidney Story. Eventually the best musicians, colored creole and black, found their way to Storyville, where the wages were good and the work was regular. They played together in bands, exchanging musical ideas and teaching each other the things they knew best—the creole professors giving music lessons, the uptowners teaching the creoles to understand and to enjoy ragtime and the blues. Basin Street was the important street of the district; the Tuxedo, one of the large dance halls in the area. The street was later immortalized in the *Basin Street Blues*. About 1910 a band was organized under the leadership of Oscar Celestin that soon rivaled the Excelsior and the Onward in popularity—the Tuxedo Brass Band. Among the other bands that became widely known for their hot music during this period were the Olympia, Bunk Johnson's Superior Band, the Eagle (the successor to Bolden's band), and the Imperial. All of the cabarets had orchestras, too numerous to list here. Probably the best music was to be heard at Café "25" and at Pete Lala's Café.

When the brass bands and dance orchestras began to incorporate into their music the styles of the ragtime pianists and blues singers, the music that was produced was new—and exotic. The bandsmen used the written music for a piece only once—to learn the melody. Then the music was discarded, and everyone played variations on the melody. Trumpeters and clarinetists forced their instruments to sing the blues. They stretched the ranges of the instruments, ascending to dizzy heights and descending to incredible depths. In order to get the "dirty" tones they wanted, they used an endless variety of mutes—plungers, cups, drinking glasses, and pop bottles. These pioneers passed on the traditions of their music to the youngsters who idolized them, who followed after them in the street parades, who took music lessons from them, who watched them perform from the swinging doors of the saloons, and who finally took places beside them in the endless parades and in the dance halls, "parlors," and saloons of Storyville.

The legendary figures of the pioneer group included clarinetists Frank Lewis (d. 1924), Alphonse Picou (1878–1961), Lorenzo Tio, Sr. (ca. 1865–1920) and his brother Louis (1863–1927); cornetists or trumpeters (in addition to Bolden and Johnson) Theogène Baquet (ca. 1860–1920), Jim Humphrey (ca. 1870–?), Manuel Perez (1879–1946); trombonist Buddy Johnson (1875–1927), bassist Henry Kimball, Sr. (1870–?), guitarist Charles "Happy" Galloway (ca. 1865–1914); and drummers Black Benny Williams (d. 1922) and Dee Dee Chandler (ca. 1870–1925). Despite the wide variation in ages among these men, they may be regarded as contemporaries, for they played alongside each other in the musical organizations of the 1890s. To be sure, the same statement can be made regarding the members of the next generation, two of whom were sons of the older men and several of whom were students. Among the outstanding figures were clarinetists George Baquet (1883–1949), Louis "Big Eye" Nelson (1885–1949), and Lorenzo Tio, Jr. (1885?–1933); trumpeters Freddie Keppard (1889–1933) and Joseph "King" Oliver (1885–1938); trombonist Frank Dusen (ca. 1880–1940), and drummer Henry Zeno (ca. 1884–1917).

About 1908, a band organized by Keppard went out on a tour, the first of the New Orleans bands to do so. Starting out with a seven-piece band (composed of violin, guitar, clarinet, trombone, trumpet, drums, and bass), Keppard later dropped the violin, bass, and guitar for economic reasons and added a piano. In 1913 the band came under the management of the powerful Pantages vaudeville-circuit agency; its name was changed to the Original Creole Band, and it was sent on a transcontinental tour beginning in New York and ending in Los Angeles. The music played by the band was novel for the time and impressive to those who heard it. It was in the blues tradition established by King Bolden, with a style distinctive for its variation procedures. After the first playing of the basic blues theme, each succeeding chorus consisted of a variation on the theme. All of the big-name bands in the Storyville district of New Orleans played in much the same way. Trumpeter King Oliver was one of those who would, along with Keppard, help to establish the New Orleans style in Chicago. Until 1918, however, he played in New Orleans, first with the Olympia, then with a band led by Edward "Kid" Ory.

JELLY ROLL MORTON

The towering figure of this generation was Ferdinand "Jelly Roll" Morton (1885–1942)—composer, performer, and jazz historian. Morton began to perform early in life. As a child, he played guitar in a three-piece string band (guitar, mandolin, and bass) and sang with a strolling quartet that specialized in spirituals, particularly at funeral wakes and burials. Like other music-struck youngsters in New Orleans, he followed the great brass bands as a second-liner, sometimes carrying the instrument cases of the great ones and on one occasion riding a horse in a parade as a club's mascot. By the time he was fifteen, Morton had obtained his first job, playing piano in one of the tenderloin district's brothels. Contemporaries remembered him as a blues player and singer: "Jelly would sit there and play that barrelhouse music all night . . . he'd play and sing the blues until way up in the day." When Morton was seventeen he composed his first blues, the *New Orleans Blues*, which became one of the favorites of the city's bands. In Morton two traditions merged, those of the French colored-creoles and of the African uptown blacks; and in him three styles merged, those of ragtime, blues, and brass-band music.

WORLD WAR I

The First World War began on July 28, 1914; nearly three years later, on April 6, 1917, the United States joined the struggle by declaring war on Germany. At this time there were about 20,000 blacks in the United States Army—10,000 in the four units of the regular army and 10,000 in various units of the National Guard. Upon the declaration of war, black men immediately began volunteering, to such an extent that the quota for Negro volunteers was filled within a week. Other blacks entered the service as draftees. By the end of the war, more than 200,000 blacks had served with the United States Army, in ranks from lowly private to captain and in all kinds of units except pilot sections of the aviation corps. Blacks were not accepted into the Marines or Coast Guard, however, and were generally confined to menial duties in the Navy. Most of the Negro units maintained their own bands, with black bandmasters, and some of the bands won distinction overseas for their exciting music and for their efforts to raise the morale of soldiers on the front and in hospitals.

Among such bands were the 349th Infantry under Norman Scott; the 351st under Dorsey Rhodes; the 367th, the so-called "Buffaloes," under Egbert Thompson; the 368th under Jack Thomas; and the 370th under George Duff. Rhodes was a clarinetist and a graduate of the Institute of Musical Art in New York. One of his saxophonists, Ernest Hayes, was a graduate of the New England Conservatory and a professional organist. The assistant bandmaster of the 809th Infantry Band, Wesley Howard, had also graduated from the New England Conservatory with a major in violin. The first Negro bandmaster of the U. S. Navy was Alton Augustus Adams (1889–?), who was detailed by the government to organize a band in the Virgin Islands in 1917. Adams had studied privately in St. Thomas (one of the Virgin Islands) and had also taken correspondence courses in composition at the University of Pennsylvania. In 1924 Adams visited New York and conducted the famous Goldman Band in the playing of one of his compositions at a concert on the Mall of Central Park. His works include the *Virgin Islands March* and *Spirit of the United States Navy*.

The most widely known bands were those under the direction of Clef Club musicians: the 350th Infantry (formerly the Eighth Illinois) under Tim Brymn, the 807th under Will Vodery, and the 369th (formerly the Fifteenth New York) under Jim Europe. Brymn's band was known as the Seventy Black Devils of the U. S. 350th; rag pianist Willie-the-Lion Smith, was a drum major in the band. The band was as well known for its "jam sessions" (i.e. impromptu, informal gatherings of musicians to play dance music) as for its formal military concerts. Vodery was among the bandmasters sent to Fort Betev, France, after the war to receive an award for excellence from the French musician Robert Casadesus. From all evidence, he was the only black man in the group so honored. Among the musicians in Vodery's band was a young violinist, Louis Vaughn Jones, who played saxophone and later made a name for himself as a professional violinist.

But it was the 369th Band, under the direction of Jim Europe, that won the most honors abroad for the United States. From the beginning of its organization, the band was marked for distinction. Europe, who had enlisted in the Fifteenth New York, was asked by the colonel in charge, William Hayward, to organize an army band that would measure up to his Clef Club and Tempo Club groups. Europe accepted the charge, but found that it was impossible to gather together enough men from the New York area. He explained later that the New York black musicians "were paid too well to have to give up their jobs to go to war." Hayward was not daunted, however; he was determined to have a good Negro band. Apparently he contacted the wealthy Daniel Gray Reid (a director of the United States Steel Corporation), for soon afterward Mr. Reid publicly announced that he would provide $10,000 for a national canvas to recruit black musicians who could measure up to Jim Europe's standards for bandsmen. Within a few months a large number of men from all over the country had been recruited, many of them coming from the Hampton Institute in Virginia and some from as far away as Puerto Rico. Egbert Thompson worked with Europe in training the band; Noble Sissle was a drum major.

An account of the war experiences of Europe's band is contained in the book *From Harlem to the Rhine* by Arthur Little, one of the officers of the regiment. Some of the band's experiences may be cited as generally illustrative of the activity of black bands in the armed services. When the band played for its first parade up Fifth Avenue in New York, the newly recruited soldiers of the regiment had had no official drill practice. But, as Little points out, the men were

. . . natural born marchers and cadence observers. With a band playing, or with spectators cheering, they just couldn't be held from keeping step. That bright, sunny, Sunday morning we had both—the playing band and the cheering spectators. The churches had just concluded their services; and the crowds . . . were strolling along New York's wonderful promenade avenue as our picturesque organization swung up the line, to the brass toned expression of *Onward Christian Soldiers.*

On the camp site the band was expected to play for evening parades and to give concerts at various times. When stationed in Spartanburg, South Carolina, Europe's band developed the practice of giving a short concert every afternoon at retreat, immediately after playing the national anthem. These concerts were generally attended by visitors from the town as well as soldiers. Bands also played for the occasional dances held for the men at the camp site. On board ship, bands added to their duties the playing of hymns for religious services. A band was expected to be familiar with the old basic Protestant hymns, such as *Onward Christian Soldiers, Nearer My God to Thee, Rock of Ages, Holy, Holy, Holy,* and *Come All Ye Disconsolate.* These hymns were staple items in black-church repertories, of course, and the bandsmen heartily joined in the singing with their fellow soldiers.

Once in France, Jim Europe's band became unique. Although several of the Negro bands overseas spent some time in entertaining soldiers in hospitals and rest camps as well as those of their own units, Europe's band was the only one sent on a special mission to Aix-les-Bains (during the period February 12 to March 20, 1918) to play for the soldiers there on "rest and recreation" leave. En route, the band gave concerts in the public squares of the towns and villages through which the army train passed. Its concerts were attended by thousands who crowded into the squares, maintaining perfect silence during the playing but after each number applauding wildly and giving out shrill whistles or catcalls. A French officer explained to the surprised American band that among the French such sounds were "the supreme effort of applause." At Aix-les-Bains the band rehearsed every morning, played a concert every afternoon (in the park on Tuesdays and Thursdays), and played an evening concert every night as part of the vaudeville shows held at the Casino Theatre.

The townspeople were as thrilled as the soldiers by the playing of Europe's men. Frequently, someone would give Europe an original composition, requesting that the band play it at the next concert.

> It might be a song written by a daughter who had died. It might be a valse composed by the firstborn son of the family now serving at the front. Europe's sympathy and courtesy went out to all alike. No such request was ever refused.

On one occasion Captain Little noticed that Europe seemed particularly tired. When he asked for an explanation he was told that Europe had spent most of the previous night in orchestrating one of those "amateur compositions." Europe jokingly maintained that he wrote more than "three million notes" in the twenty different instrumentations he had made during the six-week period. To listeners, the band arrangements were "marvels of effective harmony." Captain Little firmly believed that no more than two men in the band played the same part. This could not have been possible, of course, because the band included fifty or sixty men, and Europe would hardly have written out twenty-five or more different parts for each band number. What is more likely is that his arrangements called for ten or twelve different parts, as in the style of modern symphonic music, and consequently sounded very full, rich, and complex to listeners accustomed to hearing traditional soprano-alto-tenor-bass arrangements.

In August, 1918, Jim Europe was sent by Colonel Hayward to Paris to give only a "single concert." The band played in the Théâtre des Champs-Elysées. Europe later recalled the occasion for a reporter:

> Before we had played two numbers the audience went wild. We had conquered Paris. General Bliss and French high officers who had heard us insisted that we should stay in Paris, and there we stayed for eight weeks. Everywhere we gave a concert it was a riot, but the supreme moment came in the Tuileries Gardens when we gave a concert in conjunction with the greatest bands in the world—the British Grenadiers' Band, the band of the Garde Républicain [sic], and the Royal Italian Band. My band, of course, could not compare with any of these, yet the crowd, and it was such a crowd as I never saw anywhere else in the world, deserted them for us. We played to 50,000 people at least, and, had we wished it, we might be playing yet.

Later the music of Jim Europe's band would be called jazz. But it was not actually jazz for, as Europe stated, his men played the music strictly as it was written—that is, with regard for accuracy of pitch and note values. But Europe admitted to introducing certain innovations:

> With the brass instruments we put in mutes and make a whirling motion with the tongue, at the same time blowing full pressure. With wind instruments we pinch the mouthpiece and blow hard. This produces the peculiar sound which you all know. To us it is not discordant . . . we accent strongly in this manner the notes which originally would be without accent. It is natural for us to do this; it is, indeed, a racial musical characteristic. I have to call a daily rehearsal of my band to prevent the musicians from adding to their music more than I wish them to. Whenever possible they all embroider their parts in order to produce new, peculiar sounds.

The bandsmen of the French Garde Républicaine were so impressed by the sound of Europe's band that they borrowed his orchestrations in order to try to duplicate the sound. When their efforts were unsuccessful, they insisted upon examining the musical instruments of the black bandsmen, thinking perhaps that the instruments were different. So Paris came to know the sound of the music of black men that would later develop into jazz. The United States was immensely proud of Europe's band. A newspaper reporter for the *New York Times* wrote that Jim Europe produced an organization that "all Americans swore, and some Frenchmen admitted, was the best military band in the world."

SONGS OF THE WAR

Inevitably the war produced special war songs and a large amount of impromptu singing around campfires. Black and white soldiers sang such songs as *Over There, Keep the Home Fires Burning, There's a Long, Long Trail a-Winding, My Buddy*, and *Tipperary*. The Cole-Johnson trio made a contribution to war-song literature with *The Old Flag Never Touched the Ground*. And, as we have seen, Harry Burleigh wrote several war songs.

Overseas, Negro units were generally bypassed by white entertainment groups, and there were no black entertainers as there
would be in later wars. But a small enterprising group, including
a speaker, the Reverend H. H. Proctor, a song leader, J. E. Blanton and the pianist Helen Hagan traveled through France under
the sponsorship of the War Camp Community Service and staged
entertainment for Negro troops. One of Blanton's aims was to
lead the soldiers in singing spirituals and to teach them new Negro
folksongs. The Negro baritone William H. Richardson was also
active in the "community sing" movement in the States during
the war years.

Overseas a white pilot, John Jacob Niles, made a collection of
the songs he heard sung by Negro soldiers and later published it
in a book, *Singing Soldiers*. He avoided the music-hall ditties and
Tin Pan Alley ballads, preferring to write down the songs of

> . . . the natural-born singers, usually from rural districts, who,
> prompted by hunger, wounds, homesickness, and the reaction to
> so many generations of suppression, sang the legend of the black
> man to tunes and harmonies they *made up* as they went along.

Of the total number of twenty-nine melodies and many more
song texts in the Niles collection, a considerable number are
worksongs and blues. The soldiers sang parodies of ancient
spirituals such as *Roll, Jordan, Roll* or *The Old Ark's a-Movering*.
They contracted all kinds of blues: "the awful, deep-sea blues,"
"the holy hell, soldier-man blues," and "the jail-house blues."
They sang about their labors, "diggin' in France," and how the

> Black man fights with the shovel and the pick . . .
> Never gets no rest 'cause he never gets sick . . .

and complained about their mode of life, "it's a hell of a life
aboard of a destroyer." And there were the inevitable "lonesome
songs":

> Oh, we're long gone from Alabama . . . from Georgia . . .
> And we may never see home again.

> I don't want anymore France,
> Jesus I want to go home.

Oh, my, I'm too young to die—
I want to go home.

At one performance of a traveling army show, Niles heard ten black soldiers sing a song in the ubiquitous call-and-response form, one man singing the innumerable verses and the others coming in on the refrain:

My mama told me not to come over here
But I did, did, did.

Niles was apparently unaware that in collecting songs of Negro soldiers he was following in the tradition established by the Civil War collectors Higginson, Ware, and Allen; at any rate, he does not mention the earlier collectors in his book.

AFTER THE WAR

The various Negro army bands that had "filled France with jazz" returned in triumph to proud, welcoming crowds in the United States. Jim Europe soon embarked on a world-wide tour with his sixty-five musicians, the "best band the war produced." A critic reported on one of the concerts staged at the Manhattan Opera House in New York on March 16, 1919:

There was a flood of good music, a gorgeous racket of syncopation and jazzing, extraordinarily-pleasing violin and cornet solos, and many other features that bands seldom offer.

The band's repertory included all kinds of music, from medleys of operatic arias and overtures to blues. The former kind was frequently identified on the printed program as "highbrow" selections. In one of the band's favorite featured numbers, the *St. Louis Blues,* one player after another would play a solo (consisting of a variation on the blues melody), then the entire band would join in a rousing finale. According to contemporary reports, this performance never failed to bring audiences to their feet, "applauding and cheering." Invariably programs listed syncopated versions of standard works—such as Grieg's *Peer Gynt* Suite, for example, to which would be added the phrase "with respectful apologies to Mr. Grieg." The world was shocked to learn of Jim Europe's death on May 10, 1919, after a band concert held at Symphony Hall in Boston. A *New York Times* editorial stated the sentiments felt by Americans in mourning the "untimely death of a man who ranked as one of the greatest ragtime conductors, perhaps the greatest, we ever had" and one who had enhanced American prestige overseas.

Toward the end of 1918, Will Marion Cook organized an orchestra which he called the New York Syncopated Orchestra. Cook scoured the country to find the best musicians possible for his orchestra. In Chicago he engaged a young clarinetist, Sidney Bechet (1897–1949), who would later become a famous jazz musician and vaudeville entertainer. One of his drummers was Buddy Gilmore, widely known for his role in the Nashville Students orchestra of 1905. Will Tyers served as Cook's assistant conductor; George Lattimore, as his business manager; and Tom Fletcher, as an assistant manager, advance agent, and performer. After a four-month tour of the United States, Cook took his forty-one piece orchestra, now called the American Syncopated Orchestra (the Southern Syncopated Orchestra), and nine singers to London and Paris. At the Royal Philharmonic Hall in London the group picked up a loyal fan, the Swiss conductor Ernest Ansermet, who attended every performance and plied the performers with questions backstage after performances. Ansermet wrote a newspaper article praising the orchestra, "the astonishing perfection, the superb taste, and the fervour of its playing," and especially the musicianship and virtuosity of the clarinetist Bechet.

On all of his programs, Cook featured Negro folk music and the music of black composers as well as standard concert works; in a single evening, for example, his group might perform Brahms's Waltzes, his own *Rain Song* or *Exhortation*, R. Nathaniel Dett's *Listen to the Lambs*, W. C. Handy's *Memphis Blues* or *St. Louis Blues*, and spirituals sung *a cappella*. The orchestra's make-up was somewhat unorthodox but in the tradition of Clef Club groups, consisting of violins, mandolins, banjos, guitars, saxophones, trumpets, trombones, bass horn, timpani, pianos, and drums. A highlight of Cook's stay in London was the command performance at Buckingham Palace in August, 1919. Cook took to the Palace about a quarter of his players and arranged special numbers that featured Bechet as a soloist supported by a wind quartet. When King George V was asked which numbers he had liked best, his choice was Bechet's playing of *The Characteristic Blues*. In Paris, Cook's show performed at the Théâtre des Champs-Elysées. When Cook returned to the United States in 1920, most of the orchestra personnel remained, forming small groups that played in the night clubs of London. Late in 1920 the large orchestra was reorganized under the management of Lattimore and the directorship of Egbert Thompson (former assistant to Jim Europe in the 369th Band). The engagements of this group included two months in Paris, at the Apollo Theatre in Montmartre.

Back in the United States, Cook organized a Clef Club Orchestra that served as the core of a touring musical-show company. Two members of the company, singer-actor Paul Robeson and actor-orator Richard B. Harrison, were destined to become famous in the concert world and on the stage.

THE THEATER OWNERS BOOKING ASSOCIATION

The first two decades of the twentieth century were, like the last decade of the nineteenth, golden years for the black man in the field of entertainment. The once-popular minstrel companies were replaced by touring vaudeville companies that gave employment to thousands of singers, actors, and musicians. As we have seen, a dozen or more entertainers and song writers followed spectacular careers in the white entertainment world of New York, London, Paris, and Berlin. Most performers, however, worked under the management of small agencies, of which one—the Theater Owners Booking Association, called T.O.B.A. (sometimes facetiously called "Tough on Black Artists")—provided shows for theaters in small towns and cities of the South and Midwest that were patronized exclusively by black audiences. T.O.B.A. made it possible for young black performers just beginning their careers to find jobs and to develop their potential, while at the same time it assured experienced entertainers of being able to work as long as they wished. Many entertainers who later became famous started out with T.O.B.A., then moved to such white circuits as the Pantages, Loew's, and Keith-Orpheum, which could place them in big theaters and on Broadway. But the most important contribution of T.O.B.A. to the history of Negro music and entertainment was that, like the tenderloin districts of the nation, it provided places where black talent could develop freely at its own pace and in its own direction, unhampered by the demands of commercialism and unconcerned with the standards of white America.

IV

Lift Every Voice

1920-

1924   Opening of the Curtis Institute of Music: Philadelphia, Pa.

1925   Institution of the Simon Guggenheim Foundation Fellowships for improvement in the arts and education; for all Americans, regardless of race.

1926   Establishment of the Schomburg Collection of Negro Literature and History: New York.
       Institution of the William E. Harmon Foundation awards for achievement by an individual Negro.

1927   Institution of the Rodman Wanamaker Musical Composition Prizes for black musicians.

1929   Beginning of the Great Depression.

1931   First performance of the *Afro-American Symphony*, by William Grant Still; first and most enduring of Negro symphonic works: Rochester, N. Y.

1932   Publication of Duke Ellington's *It Don't Mean a Thing If It Ain't Got That Swing;* beginning of the swing era.

1933   Century of Progress Exposition: Chicago, Ill.
       First production on Broadway of a Negro folk opera written by a black composer, Hall Johnson's *Run Little Chillun:* New York.
       First appearance of a black artist with a major white opera company, Caterina Jarboro in *Aïda* with Chicago Opera Company: Chicago, Ill.

1935   Establishment of the Federal Arts Projects of the Works Progress Administration, which gave work to creative artists and performers who were unemployed.
       Inauguration of the annual Berkshire Music Festivals: Stockbridge, Mass.

1936   Organization of the National Negro Congress, consisting of more than 500 Negro organizations.

1937   Organization of the Southern Youth Negro Congress.

1938   Ferdinand "Jelly Roll" Morton recorded the *History of Jazz Series* for the Archives of American Folksong at the Library of Congress (116 record sides).
       Founding of the Southern Conference for Human Welfare.
       First of the "From Spirituals to Swing" concerts at Carnegie Hall: New York.

1939   The Golden Gate International Exposition: San Francisco, Cal.
       The New York World's Fair.

1941–45   World War II.

1941   Beginning of the Minton's Playhouse jazz sessions in Harlem; emergence of the bop style: New York.

1942   Debut of the National Negro Opera Company, directed by Mary Caldwell Dawson: Chicago, Ill.

1949   First production by a major opera company of an opera written by a Negro, *Troubled Island* by William Grant Still at the New York City Opera: New York.

1954   Supreme Court decision overturning legal segregation in public schools in the South.

1955   First appearance of a black artist with the Metropolitan Opera Company, Marian Anderson in Verdi's *Masked Ball:* New York.

Beginning of the Montgomery, Ala., boycott of public buses.

1957   Civil Rights Act passed by Congress.

1958   Institution of the Monterey Jazz Festivals by John Lewis: Monterey, Cal.

1960   First "sit-ins" of black college students protesting discrimination in places of public accomodation: Greensboro, N. C. Beginning of the Negro civil-rights revolution.

1963   The March on Washington "for jobs and freedom": Washington, D. C.

The Century of Negro Progress Exposition (1863–1963): Chicago, Ill.

1965   Debut concert of the Symphony of the New World (with 40 per cent black personnel) at Carnegie Hall: New York.

First of the Duke Ellington sacred jazz concerts in the church: San Francisco, Cal.

1966   Opening of the new Metropolitan Opera House at Lincoln Center, with black singer Leontyne Price in the leading role in *Antony and Cleopatra*, written by white composer Samuel Barber: New York.

1969   Organization of the Society of Black Composers: New York.

Organization of the Afro-American Music Opportunities Association, Inc.: Minneapolis, Minn.

CHAPTER XIII

The Jazz Age

The fusion of blues and ragtime with brass-band and syncopated dance music resulted in the music called jazz, a music that developed its own characteristics. There are numerous theories about the origin of the word "jazz." One to which several authorities subscribe is that the word is somehow related to an itinerant black musician named Jazbo Brown, who was well known in the Mississippi River Valley country. It was said that when Brown played in the honky-tonk cafés, the patrons would shout, "More, Jazbo! More, Jaz, more!" Another theory is that the word can be traced to a sign painter in Chicago who produced about 1910 a sign for the black musician Boisey James stating that "Music will be furnished by Jas.' Band." James, a purveyor of hot music and particularly of the blues, became known as "Old Jas," and the music he played, "Jas's music." Eventually the music was simply called jazz. It is unnecessary to report here all the many and varied theories that have been advanced over the years. James Europe denied, for example, having given an explanation that was attributed to him in the press—that the word jazz represented a corruption of "razz," the name of a Negro band active in New Orleans about 1905. It is noteworthy, however, that all of the theories suggest that the word is to be associated in one way or another with the folk mores of black men, either in the United States or in Africa.

Ironically, the first groups to formally introduce jazz to the public were white orchestras from New Orleans, which had developed there under the influence of Negro groups. In 1915 the Lamb's Club of Chicago hired a white band, under the direction of Tom Brown, that was billed as "Brown's Dixieland Jass Band, Direct from New Orleans, Best Dance Music in Chicago." Two years later an orchestra led by Nick LaRocca, the "Original Dixieland Jazz Band," opened at the Reisenweber Café in New York and made musical history, for during the same year LaRocca's band made the first recordings of jazz music. The Victor Recording Company had offered a recording contract earlier to Freddie Keppard and his Original Creole Band, but it was refused—Keppard was fearful that other trumpet players would "steal his stuff."

In the black tenderloin districts of villages and large cities throughout the nation, Negro ensembles (or "combos") continued to play the kind of music they had been playing for many years, a blues-rag kind of music, most frequently performed by a pianist, drummer, and banjoist or harmonica player or by a lone pianist. Few of the players were aware that their kind of music was invading the dance spots of white America, and there is no evidence that they consistently used the word "jazz" in reference to their music before the 1920s. The leaders of large Negro dance orchestras in such places as New York, Chicago, Denver, Memphis, St. Louis, and Kansas City must have heard about the white jazz groups from New Orleans, but they did not make immediate changes in the names of their orchestras. They were doing quite well, after all, as "syncopated orchestras."

During the last half of the second decade, two phenomena occurred that greatly affected the development of jazz. The first was the wholesale migration, beginning in 1915, of Negroes to cities of the North and West, primarily because of depressed economic conditions in the South, but also because they were beginning to feel that there would never be relief from the unrelenting pressures of discrimination and disfranchisement and from the terrors of lynching there. Since the end of the Civil War there had been more than 3,600 lynchings, most of them in southern states, but some also in the Midwest. Then, with the beginning of the twentieth century, a succession of race riots had swept over the country, and again these were concentrated for the most part in the South. At the same time as black men were moving out of the South, a severe labor shortage was developing in the North, partly as a result of the war. Industry welcomed the black migrants; black men, many for the first time, were able to obtain good jobs—in factories and shipbuilding yards and on the railroads. In the ghettos of the northern cities, night clubs and eating places flourished as never before, and the newcomers demanded "their kind of music" from the entertainers—that is, the blues. The second phenomenon was the mass exodus of tenderloin musicians from New Orleans because of the closing down of Storyville in 1917 by order of the United States Navy. The displaced music makers went "up the river," to Memphis and other river towns, but for the most part to Chicago.

CHARACTERISTICS OF JAZZ

The most salient features of jazz derive directly from the blues. Jazz is a vocally oriented music; its players replace the voice with their instruments, but try to recreate its singing style and blue notes by using scooping, sliding, whining, growling, and falsetto effects. Like the blues, jazz emphasizes individualism. The performer is at the same time the composer, shaping the music into style and form. A traditional melody or harmonic framework may serve as the takeoff point for improvisation, but it is the personality of the player and the way he improvises that produces the music. Like the blues tune, the pre-existent core of musical material used by jazz players is generally short. The length of the jazz piece derives from the repetition of the basic material.

Jazz is primarily an aural kind of music; its written score represents but a skeleton of what actually takes place during a performance. Each performance of the basic material is different, because the players improvise differently each time the music is played. Thus jazz is learned through oral tradition, as is folksong, and those who would learn to play jazz do so by listening to others playing jazz. Finally, jazz uses the call-and-response style of the blues, by employing an antiphonal relationship between two solo instruments or between solo and ensemble.

The influence of ragtime is represented in jazz by the emphasis on syncopation and the presence of the piano in the jazz ensemble. The influence of the brass band reveals itself in the jazz instrumentation, in the roles assigned to each instrument, and in the resulting musical texture. In the classic New Orleans band, for example, three instruments were given melodic roles; the cornet typically played the lead, the clarinet played a counter-melody to the lead melody, and the trombone played the lower voice of the trio. The other instruments—the drums, banjos, guitars, and basses—functioned as the rhythm section. Although pianos were added to jazz bands from the beginning, and often a second cornet as well, the instrumentation remained basically the same as in brass bands. Later, trumpets began to replace cornets and saxophones were added or used in place of clarinets. The addition of saxophones suggests the influence of the syncopated dance orchestra which, as we have seen, used saxophones early in its development.

The brass band had emphasized the ensemble sound, as distinguished from solo music, and this tradition, too, passed over into the performances of the early jazz bands. In many jazz performances of the early 1920s, for example, all of the instruments play throughout the piece, the cornet always retaining the lead melody. In performances that include solo passages, the other instruments typically give firm support, particularly the rhythm section. The ensemble sound of the band was basically polyphonic in nature, not chordal. As many as two or three clearly defined melodies would dominate the texture, and frequently the rhythm instruments furnished little countermelodies.

To summarize, jazz was a new music created from the synthesis of certain elements in the style of its precursors. Its most striking feature was the exotic sound, which was produced not only by the kinds of instruments used in the orchestra, but also from the manner in which these instruments were played. Little attention was paid to "correct" intonation (i.e. playing strictly in tune), for example, or to obtaining exact pitches. Instead, the players glided freely from one tone to another (or through long series of tones in glissandos) and frequently fluctuated the pitches of sustained tones (i.e. used a wide vibrato). Equally striking was the rhythmic intensity of the early jazz music, derived from a solid, driving, four-beats-to-the-measure rhythm coupled with syncopation (accentuation of the weak beats), but governed by controlled tempos and an easy, relaxed approach. The polyphonic texture of the music was a result of "collective improvisation," with each melody player improvising his part in such a way that the parts combined into a balanced, integrated whole. The sound of jazz was in the same tradition as the slaves' singing of spirituals, which to contemporary listeners produced an effect, as we have seen, of "a marvellous complication and variety" of sounds "sung in perfect time."

Jazz developed its own special repertory of melodies and compositions that served as bases for improvisatory elaborations. Among the popular staples of the 1920s were pieces of black composers, such as *Panama* (Will Tyers), *Didn't He Ramble* (Bob Cole and the Johnson brothers), *Original Rags* and *Maple Leaf Rag* (Joplin), the *Beale Street Blues* and the *St. Louis Blues* (Handy); marches and dance pieces, such as drags, stomps, and shuffles; some traditional worksongs, such as *John Henry*, and spirituals, such as *Down by the Riverside;* and above all, blues melodies of all kinds, traditional and composed. Jazz had its own special vocabulary: a *break*, for example, was a brief flurry of notes played by the soloist during a pause in the ensemble playing; a *riff* was a short phrase repeated over and over again by the ensemble; *scat singing* was singing nonsense syllables instead of words; a *sideman* was any member of the orchestra other than the leader.

PIONEER JAZZ ORCHESTRAS IN CHICAGO

It is safe to assume that some orchestras in New Orleans were playing real jazz before the closing of Storyville, but traditionally the history of jazz begins with a few pioneers of New Orleans and their Chicago-based groups—among them, King Oliver and his Creole Jazz Band, whose best period was from 1920 to 1924; Jelly Roll Morton and his Red Hot Peppers, who made a series of recordings during the period 1926–28; trumpeter Louis Armstrong with his Hot Five and Hot Seven, who recorded between 1925 and 1928; and clarinetist Johnny Dodds, who made recordings with several of his groups (the Chicago Foot-warmers, the Washboard Band, the New Orleans Wanderers, the New Orleans Bootblacks) during the late 1920s. Chicago's South Side became the capital of jazz in the 1920s. One year a waggish reporter of the local Negro newspaper, the *Chicago Defender*, observed:

The fire department is thinking of lining 35th Street with asbestos to keep those bands from scorching passers-by with their red-hot jazz music.

The materials of jazz history are phonograph records. It was in 1923 that the first recordings of a Negro band were made—Oliver's Creole Jazz Band, for the Paramount Company in Chicago. Our history may quite properly begin, however, a few years before that time.

KING OLIVER

Joseph "King" Oliver (1885–1938) was the first jazzman from New Orleans to make a permanent impact on Chicago. The details about Oliver's place of birth are vague, but it is certain that he was in New Orleans by the time he was eight or ten years old, and that in 1899 he was playing cornet in a children's brass band. By 1907 Oliver was a member of one of New Orleans' good brass bands, the Melrose. Later he played in the Olympia, Eagle, Onward, and Magnolia Bands; in Kid Ory's band; as well as in lesser-known ensembles. Like most Negro bandsmen of the time, Oliver played his cornet on a part-time basis and worked during the day as a butler. After 1915, Oliver organized his own band, which played for the white college students of Tulane University and for the black patrons of Pete Lala's Café and Café "25." The bandsmen with whom Oliver came into contact were among the best in New Orleans, some of them revered old-timers, others destined to become famous in the future. These men all learned from each other. One of Oliver's young protégés was a talented youngster named Louis Armstrong. Oliver gave Louis an old trumpet on which to practice, the boy's first, and taught him how to play. When the bassist Bill Johnson sent for Oliver in 1918 to play at the Royal Gardens Café in Chicago, he left New Orleans, never to return.

Oliver played in Chicago at the Gardens and at the Dreamland Café. By 1920 he had organized his own band, the Creole Jazz Band, which developed into the finest group of its time. Within two years Oliver sent for Armstrong to join the band. Among his other sidemen at various periods were Johnny Dodd (clarinet), Jimmie Noone (clarinet), Honoré Dutrey (trombone), Bill Johnson (bass), Warren "Baby" Dodds (drum), and Lil Hardin (piano). The recordings made by the band for the Gennett, Paramount, Columbia, and, later, Vocalion recording companies exerted a deep influence upon other jazz bands of the nation, both white and black. And both black and white musicians crowded into the places on Chicago's South Side where Oliver played to hear him in person and to learn from his playing.

Beginning in 1924, however, Oliver's career as a bandleader took a turn for the worse. Some of his best sidemen left the band, including Armstrong; twice the places where he worked were destroyed by fires; a series of tours turned out disastrously; and ill health prevented his playing the trumpet for a while. To be sure, there were some good periods during these years, such as Oliver's sojourn at the Plantation Café in Chicago with his Dixie Syncopators. Several times Oliver made poor decisions—such as the time he turned down an offer to work at the newly opened Cotton Club in New York (a young man from Washington, D. C., Edward Kennedy "Duke" Ellington, accepted that job and stepped up to fame). Oliver spent the last years before his death in Savannah, Georgia, living in poverty and obscurity, but with courage and dignity.

MORTON AND JAZZ

Jelly Roll Morton is regarded as the first true jazz composer; he was the first to write down his jazz arrangements in musical notation, and he was the originator of a large number of the pieces that became staples in the jazz repertory. Morton's arrangement of his own *Jelly Roll Blues* was the first published jazz arrangement in history (1915). In preparing for the Red Hot Peppers' recordings in 1926, Morton carefully planned how each piece would be played, either by writing out the arrangement in advance or by discussing his ideas with the bandsmen so that each would know how his playing should fit into the ensemble (this is called a "head arrangement"). Morton's sidemen included George Mitchell (cornet), Omer Simeon (clarinet), Kid Ory (trombone), John St. Cyr (banjo and guitar), John Lindsay (string bass), and André Hilaire (drums). The resulting recordings have been acclaimed by all authorities on jazz. In an earlier period (1923–24) Morton made some recordings of his piano jazz that are equally valued by connoisseurs and laymen.

Beginning in the 1930s, however, jazz musicians more and more came to regard Morton's style as outdated. His career, like Oliver's, went into a decline during the last years of his life, except for a few glorious weeks in 1938. At that time, Alan Lomax, curator of the Music Division at the Library of Congress, brought Morton to Washington to record his version of the history of jazz for the Archives of American Folksong.

LOUIS ARMSTRONG

When Daniel Louis "Satchmo" Armstrong (b. 1900) arrived at Chicago in 1922 to play second cornet in King Oliver's Creole Jazz Band, he was already an accomplished trumpeter and fully capable of taking over the solo-trumpet role. His music career began when he sang for pennies on the streets of New Orleans with other children. A brief tangle with the law in 1914 (for celebrating New Years Eve by firing his stepfather's gun on the street) sent him to the colored Waifs Home for Boys, just outside New Orleans. There he studied music with Peter Davis (all of the Home's instructors were black) and learned to play instruments, moving up from the tambourine to the lead-instrument cornet. Eventually he became the leader of the Home's brass band, which was often called upon to play for private picnics and to join parades through the streets of New Orleans.

After leaving the Home in 1914 Armstrong worked at a number of daytime jobs, but at nights and on weekends he found opportunities to blow his cornet. His first music job was playing the blues in a honky-tonk in the red-light district. During his free time, Armstrong's favorite occupation was "making the rounds" of the honky-tonks to listen to the blues being played by the district's music makers. Armstrong's talent soon brought him to the attention of King Oliver who, as we have seen, befriended him, helping him to improve his cornet playing and to get music jobs. In addition to working with established bands Louis also organized his own little groups. In 1918 Armstrong took Joe Oliver's place in Kid Ory's band. For a short time during this period he played with Fate Marable's band on an excursion steamer, the *Sydney*, that traveled up and down the Mississippi River. In addition to playing on the boat, the band also played in towns along the river. The period was especially memorable to Armstrong because David Jones, the melophone player, taught him to read music.

By the time Armstrong reached his maturity, Storyville was closed down, but he never forgot its music. In his autobiography, *Satchmo*, he wrote:

> On every corner I could hear music . . . the music I wanted to hear. . . . It was worth my salary—the little I did get— just to go into Storyville. . . . And that man Joe Oliver . . . kept me spellbound with that horn of his. Storyville! With all those glorious trumpets—Joe Oliver, Bunk Johnson—he was in his prime then— Emmanuel Perez, Buddy Petit, Joe Johnson. . . .

To Armstrong, Joe Oliver's playing was the strongest and most creative, but Bunk Johnson's tone was the sweetest. In Armstrong's playing is reflected the best of the great trumpeters who had preceded him and who were his spiritual or actual mentors—Buddy Bolden's fiery, powerful tone, Bunk Johnson's lighter, sweet tone and imaginative phrasing, and King Oliver's delicate but firm style with its inventiveness and wide variety of tone.

Armstrong was the first great jazz soloist and one of jazz's most creative innovators. Over the long years of his career, his genius remained immune to the onslaught of commercialism and to the ascendency of other popular music styles. Thousands were inspired by his playing and tried to emulate it—not only trumpeters, but other instrumentalists who tried to adapt aspects of that style to their own instruments. His special style of singing also attracted imitators. Armstrong emerged as a soloist when he left Oliver's band in 1924 to join a New York band under the leadership of Fletcher Henderson. (We shall return to this point.) He returned to Chicago in 1925, played with a succession of bands, including Erskine Tate's Vendome Theater "Symphony Orchestra," and made recordings with his own Hot Five and Hot Seven groups. It was during these years that Armstrong earned his world-wide reputation. His sidemen for the recordings included Johnny Dodds (clarinet and alto sax), Kid Ory (trombone), Johnny St. Cyr (banjo and guitar), and the pianist Lil Hardin Armstrong (who was now his wife).

Armstrong's first European tour, the first of many, began in 1932 with an engagement at the Palladium in London. Gradually his musical activities were expanded to include, along with personal appearances and recording, appearances on television, at jazz festivals at home and abroad, and in films—for example, *Pennies from Heaven*, *The Glenn Miller Story*, *High Society*, *A Man Called Adam*, and many others, of both American and foreign make. During the 1960s Armstrong increasingly came to represent to the world the spirit of American jazz and its international appeal. He made two good-will tours in 1960, one to Africa under private-industry sponsorship and a second to other parts of the world under the auspices of the State Department.

In 1957 Edward R. Murrow produced a documentary film of Armstrong's travels, entitled *Satchmo the Great*. During the same year a four-volume record set was released, *Satchmo, A Musical Biography*, that included narration and versions of some of his old recordings. A similar collection is the album *The Louis Armstrong Story*. Armstrong published an autobiography, *Satchmo: My Life in New Orleans*, in 1954. A list of Armstrong's recordings (the equivalent of a list of a composer's works in a nonjazz area) is too long to include here.

Jazz specialists generally use the term "classic jazz" in referring to the music produced by the small orchestras of Oliver, Morton, Armstrong, and other black contemporaries. The words "Chicago style" generally apply to the music of some white groups active during the 1920s in Chicago; among them, the Rhythm Kings of New Orleans, Bix Beiderbecke's Wolverine Orchestra, and the Austin Five (of Austin High School). We have already discussed the basic features of classic jazz; its small bands, consisting of a trumpet-clarinet-trombone trio and a piano-bass-drum rhythm section; its emphasis on collective improvisation and polyphonic texture; and its preference for an individualized, expressive approach to the music rather than a "correct," intellectual approach.

But jazz proved to be ever-changing, and even during the 1920s it began to take on a new aspect. Orchestras grew in size, and new instruments were added to the ensemble. With fourteen or more men in a band, it was no longer possible to have collective improvisation or head arrangements. The younger black jazz musicians coming on the scene were more likely to have received their musical training in a college or conservatory than "in the field," as had the pioneers. Entertainment music became for many a full-time profession that brought both financial rewards and social prestige.

THE BIG BANDS

As the nation's music center, New York had attracted black musicians in all areas since the 1890s, but during the 1920s it began to play an increasingly important role in the history of jazz. It was in New York in 1923 that the nation's first "big band" (i.e. of jazz musicians) was organized. The musician credited with starting the big-band movement was Fletcher Henderson (1898–1952), a graduate of Atlanta University, along with his sideman-arranger Don Redman (1900–64), who had been trained at Boston Conservatory of Music and Detroit Conservatory of Music. In New York, Henderson fell heir to the tradition established by James Reese Europe which included exciting music and unorthodox instrumentation, as we have seen, but little of the blues in its style. Henderson had come in close contact with the blues, however, during his first year in New York (1920), when he worked as a house pianist for Handy and Pace's music publishing company, and the next year when his hastily organized band went on tour with blues singer Ethel Waters.

By the time Henderson began an engagement at the exclusive Club Alabam on Forty-fourth Street in 1923, his ten-piece orchestra was playing jazz. Its composition was that of the classic jazz group, except that alto and tenor saxophones were added—reflecting the influence of Clef Club and Harlem honky-tonk ensembles and combos—and a tuba. Obviously, such a large group could not improvise in the New Orleans style. Henderson and, later, Redman made arrangements for the band, alternating solo and ensemble sections, and allowing for soloist improvisation. To be sure, not all of the arrangements were written; often the band used "head arrangements," and sometimes there was sectional improvisation in the finales. Among the special features of the Henderson style were the three-clarinet ensemble (used as a single instrument in counterpoint with a trumpet) and the call-and-response byplay between brasses and reeds. During the period 1924–36 Henderson's band, enlarged to sixteen players, played a great deal for white dances at the big Roseland Ballroom in New York. In its creation of an original style, this band led the way for the big bands that followed, both Negro and white.

The next few years produced a number of Negro big bands, led by such men as William "Chick" Webb (1907–39), Jimmie Lunceford (1902–47), Andy Kirk, (b. 1898), Erskine Hawkins (b. 1914), Cab Calloway (b. 1907), Lucky Millinder (1900–66), Don Redman with McKinney's Cotton Pickers, Luis Russell (1902–63), William "Count" Basie (b. 1904), and Duke Ellington (b. 1899). In the Midwest, Clarence Love's orchestra was popular, especially in Omaha, Nebraska; in Kansas City, Missouri, Bennie Moten (1894–1935) led a big jazz band from about 1922 until his death; in Denver, Colorado, George Morrison (b. 1891) directed one of the best bands in town; and in Los Angeles, the orchestra of Les Hite (1903–62) commanded the attention of the jazz world. Chicago had several active big bands during these years; among them, Erskine Tate's ten-piece orchestra, the Chicago counterpart of Fletcher Henderson's orchestra, and the band of Earl "Fatha" Hines (b. 1905).

Chick Webb was among the first to play at the new Savoy ballroom in Harlem—"the home of happy feet"—where he reigned over the birth of such Negro dances as the lindy-hop" and introduced his singing protégé Ella Fitzgerald to the entertainment world. Lunceford's band was noted for its precision and showmanship and the unique arrangements of Melvin James "Sy" Oliver (b. 1910). Erskine Hawkin's band started out as a college group, the Alabama State Collegians, and made its reputation chiefly at the Savoy. Don Redman's group was the first (and the only Negro band during this period) to play a sponsored radio series ("Chipso," 1932). Les Hite's band, which was "fronted at times by Louis Armstrong, included a talented drummer and vibraphone player named Lionel Hampton. Armstrong also fronted Russell's band from time to time and toured with the band during the years 1935–43. Tate's Vendome Orchestra expanded its repertory to include jazz, but without

ceasing its performance of show music and light classics. John
Kirby (1908–52) was the leader of a small band that was greatly
in vogue during the late 30s. But the two best orchestras for all
time were Basie's and Ellington's.

THE SWING ERA AND
DUKE ELLINGTON

In 1932 Duke Ellington (b. 1899) wrote a song, *It Don't Mean
a Thing If It Ain't Got That Swing*, that provided a label for a
new style of jazz developing among big bands during the 1930s.
Duke was no newcomer to the field of jazz, having written his
first song, *Soda Fountain Rag*, at the age of fourteen and having
organized his first band not too many years later. A native of
Washington, D. C., Ellington showed talent in both music and
art as a high-school student, but decided in favor of music, turning down a scholarship to the Pratt Institute of Fine Arts in
Brooklyn. Until 1922 his five-piece ensemble (trumpet, drums,
banjo, piano, bass or saxophone) played for dances and other
social affairs in Washington and was moderately successful. Then,
with two of his sidemen, Ellington came to New York to join
Wilbur Sweatman's orchestra, became discouraged, and soon
returned to Washington. His group's second trip to New York in
1923 met with better results. Under the leadership of banjoist
Elmer Snowden, the Washingtonians were able to obtain jobs and
finally landed at the Hollywood (later the Kentucky Club) on
Forty-ninth Street and Broadway. There Ellington took over the
leadership and began to weld the group—now expanded to ten
pieces—into a first-rate orchestra.

Duke Ellington had little formal training in music other than
piano lessons. On an informal basis he had long discussions about
compositional techniques with Will Marion Cook, whom he revered as "the master of all the masters of our people," and with
composer-arranger Will Vodery. As a pianist he came in contact with Harlem's active pianists during the time and was particularly influenced by the playing of James P. Johnson, Willie-the-
Lion Smith, Luckey Roberts, and Fats Waller. But Ellington's
ideas were his own and his genius led him to create an orchestra
style marked by rich and daring harmonies, by subtle con-

trastings of colors and timbres, and by an ingenious handling of solo and ensemble relationships. The orchestra became the vehicle through which Ellington expressed his creativity; it came to represent the ideal big "swinging band."

When Ellington's band began its memorable engagement in 1927 at the famed Cotton Club in Harlem, it included two trumpets, trombone, alto saxophone, baritone saxophone, tenor sax (doubling with clarinet), guitar (doubling with banjo), bass, drums, and piano. Later it was enlarged to include three trumpets and two trombones, and in 1932 a third trombone and a fourth saxophone were added. It was during the Cotton Club years that Duke's orchestra began to win distinction for its thorough musicianship and homogeneity. Duke, as the leader, could accept the credit for this, but the contributions of his sidemen were significant. They were brilliant soloists in their own rights; they fitted in well with Duke's temperament; and they remained with him over long periods of time. William Alexander "Sonny" Greer (drums) and Otto "Toby" Hardwicke (alto and bass saxophone) were charter members of the Washingtonians. Other long-timers during this period included Fred Guy (banjo, guitar) and Johnny Hodges (alto saxophone). Trumpeter James "Bubber" Miley, with his "growling" solos, was largely responsible for the "jungle effects" in the orchestra's performances, one of the most distinctive features of the early style. He and trombonist Joseph "Tricky Sam" Nanton became experts in the use of the rubber-plunger mute to give an almost human sound to their playing of trumpet and trombone.

Many of Duke's arrangements were worked out with his sidemen in the true tradition of collective improvisation. Duke would bring to the meeting his musical ideas, and one or another of the bandsmen would make suggestions for changes or additions. Things were tried out on the spot in order to find out whether they worked. Often a composition was changed after it had been performed three or four times, sometimes resulting in an entirely new work. Duke's constantly reiterated statement was, "Good music is music that sounds good." Sometimes other musicians of the orchestra would bring their compositions to "creating sessions" to be worked out by the entire group. In 1939 Billy Strayhorn (1915–67), pianist-composer, joined Duke's orchestra as an arranger and over the years developed into

Duke's musical alter ego. The collaboration between the two men was so close that often neither could identify which part of a musical work was his. Strayhorn was born in Hillsboro, North Carolina, but went to school in Pittsburgh, where he also studied music privately.

By 1970 Duke Ellington had written more than 2,000 compositions, an impressive record equaled by few composers in the history of music. Beginning in the 30s he became known for a long series of popular song successes—among them, *Mood Indigo, Solitude, Sophisticated Lady, In a Sentimental Mood, I Let a Song Go Out of My Heart,* and *I Got It Bad and That Ain't Good.* Strayhorn, too, contributed a number of songs to the band's repertory, including its theme song *Take the A Train.* That Ellington was a composer with serious intentions became evident with his recording of such works as *Black and Tan Fantasy* (1927), *Creole Rhapsody* (1932), *Blue Harlem* (1934), *Reminiscin' in Tempo* (1935) and *Echoes of Harlem* (1935). Ellington wrote his first musical revue, *Chocolate Kiddies,* in 1924; his band made its first film appearance, *Check and Double Check,* in 1930; and in 1933 came the first of many European tours. In January, 1943, Ellington began his annual Carnegie Hall Concerts and presented in the inaugural program his first composition in large dimension, *Black, Brown and Beige.* This began a new period in his career, which will be discussed in a later chapter.

KANSAS CITY AND COUNT BASIE

In 1936 John Hammond, wealthy white jazz enthusiast and critic, heard the playing of a nine-piece band that was broadcasting from the Reno Club in Kansas City, Missouri, and became so excited that he arranged for the Music Corporation of America (MCA) to take over management of the band. The band's leader, William Basie (b. 1904), who was a native of Red Bank, New Jersey, had been active in jazz music in Kansas City since 1928. Basie had studied music as a child with his mother, picking up ragtime on the side in New York from such pianists as Fats Waller, and at a young age began playing professionally with a vaudeville-show company. In 1927 a show with which he was touring became stranded, and Basie found himself without a job in Kansas City, Missouri. For a year he played piano in a movie-theater pit, then joined Walter Page's Blue Devils orchestra. Upon the disbanding of Page's band in 1929, Basie joined the orchestra of Bennie Moten, where he remained until Moten's death and the orchestra's demise in 1935. Soon thereafter Basie formed his own band, featuring the blues singer Jimmy Rushing, and it was this group that Hammond heard playing on a local radio station.

Kansas City in the early 1930s occupied a position in the Southwest similar to that of St. Louis in the 1890s. It had grown wealthy as a trading center, largely because its location at the junction of the Kansas and Missouri Rivers allowed it to serve as a port of call for riverboat traffic, and because it became an important railway junction (connecting East to West, and with direct links to Chicago and St. Louis) and highway intersection point. Money flowed in the city's tenderloin districts, and entertainers flocked there to work. (To be sure, the influence of the so-called Pendergast machine and gangsterdom also contributed to the generally "relaxed" atmosphere of the city.)

The city became a magnet for black musicians: for members of touring bands from the East, Chicago, and the West with a few hours to spare between the changing of trains; for itinerant jazzmen from the South, particularly New Orleans; and for blues singers from urban areas, the Delta regions of Mississippi, and the wide open spaces of Texas, Arkansas, and Oklahoma. Jazzmen met together to match their skills in cutting contests or in interminable jam sessions. A new form of music evolved naturally out of the practical demands of the situation in which the musicians found themselves. All would join in the playing at the beginning of a number, then each would take his turn at improvising on the chorus, and finally they would all play together again to bring the piece of music to a close. The procedure allowed for any number of visitors to participate in the playing, and at the same time allowed the musicians to display their improvisatory skills.

Inevitably the blues became the basic material used in this kind of performance. Its structure was concrete—the standard twelve-bar form and prescribed harmonic patterns—and it was familiar to all jazzmen. Moreover, the basic simplicity of the blues lent itself well to reshaping and elaboration. Blues could be handled to fit any mood; played fast, it generated excitement, and played slowly, it was as melancholy as could be desired. The Kansas City men devised the plan of using riffs as the basis for the opening chorus. The use of these short melodic ideas repeated again and again by the full ensemble, often in unison by the brasses and sometimes by the rhythm section to support solo improvisation, became a distinctive feature of the style. Another innovation emphasized a different approach to the basic beat than had been employed by the jazzmen of New Orleans. Instead of accenting the strong beats of the measure, as in a march, the Kansas City men began stressing all beats equally, thus producing a smoothly flowing beat-rhythm—a "swinging" rhythm.

Blues singers, too, found themselves changing some of their practices in conformity with the Kansas City style. Under the pressure of the driving beat of jazz, the blues became lustier and more powerful. Blues singers were no longer limited to the singing of laments with guitar accompaniment; they could use the same form and text to sing joyfully and with a jazz-orchestra or jazz-piano accompaniment. The "Kaycee" school (K. C., for Kansas City) produced leadership for the jazz movement in its pianists (Sammy Price, Pete Johnson, Mary Lou Williams), in its band instrumentalists (trumpeter Oran "Hot Lips" Page and alto-sax man Lester "Prez" Young), in its singers (Jimmy Rushing, Joe Turner), and its bands (Bennie Moten's, Jesse Stone's, Jay McShann's, Walter Page's, Andy Kirk's). Basie's band stood at the peak of the tradition.

MCA took the Basie band first to Chicago's Grand Terrace Ballroom, then to New York's Roseland Ballroom, and finally to the Famous Door Club on West Fifty-second Street. The place was a little small for Basie's big band, but this did not prevent musicians and jazz connoisseurs from flocking there to listen to its exciting music. At that time the band was composed of three trumpets, two trombones, two alto saxes, two tenor saxes, piano, guitar, bass, and drums. By 1939 a fourth trumpet and a third trombone had been added. Listeners found the band to have

. . . large, robust, and always swinging ensemble sounds, interspersed with numerous fine solos and, of course, the light, infectious piano tinkling of its leader.

Predictably, Basie used riffs in the Kansas City style for full ensemble playing, for antiphonal play between brasses and reeds, and for sectional support of soloists. Head arrangements were more favored than written-out arrangements and as a consequence there was often a great deal of collective improvisation on the spot. The soloists, of course, always improvised. Another innovation of Basie's was to begin the performance of a number with himself at the piano playing the first chorus (instead of using the full orchestra); this enabled him to set just the right tempo and mood for the music.

The Basie band early established itself as an avant-garde group from which other bands borrowed ideas heavily. Drummer Jo Jones, for example, helped to lead drummers to the use of the "high hat" cymbal (i.e. two small cymbals operated by a foot pedal) as a way to maintain the swinging beat. No other orchestra could play the blues as well as Basie's, nor had as good blues singers. The sidemen included some of the chief instrumentalists of the time; among them, Big Ed Lewis (lead trumpet), Walter Page (bass), Freddie Green (guitar), Lester "Prez" Young (alto sax), Dicky Wells (trombone), and Wilbur "Buck" Clayton (trumpet).

Basie's band began to achieve international fame soon after its move to Fifty-second Street. In 1950 Basie found it necessary for economic reasons to disband the large group and tour with a sextet, but he soon organized another big band. Its tours abroad were successful from the beginning (in 1954), as were also its appearances at jazz festivals and in large concert halls of the States. In 1957 Count Basie and his band played a command performance at Buckingham Palace, following in the footsteps of Frank Johnson's Negro Band, which had given a similar performance more than a hundred years earlier in 1838, and of Will Marion Cook's Syncopated Orchestra, which played at the Palace in 1919. Among the best-known record albums of Basie's works are *One O'Clock Jump*, *April in Paris*, *Jumping at the Woodside*, *Blues by Basie*, and *A Night at the Apollo*.

The golden age of big bands came to an end about 1946, brought about by the emergence of new forms of entertainment that replaced dancing (such as bowling and watching TV), the gradual disappearance of big ballrooms, and the changing taste of the public. Undoubtedly, many other factors were involved as well—World War II, for example, and the changing attitude of the jazz musicians themselves toward their patrons, as well as the increasing invasion of commercialism into the world of jazz. The jazz age had produced an imposing array of talent, not only among bandleaders, but also among singers, instrumentalists, song writers, composers, and writer-critics. As early as the 1930s articles and books began to appear in Europe that seriously explored the nature of the new music being created by Negroes in the United States. The origin of jazz was examined, its development discussed, and the contributions of its major figures evaluated. Later would come special magazines devoted to jazz, popularity polls, and jazz festivals. A London magazine, *Melody Maker*, began publishing articles on jazz as early as 1926. In 1934 a publication devoted entirely to jazz, *Down Beat*, was established in the United States. By 1938 recording companies specializing in jazz began to appear on the scene; among them, the Commodore HRS (Hot Record Society) and the Blue Note label. About the same time the first of a steady stream of American books on jazz were published: *American Jazz Music* by Wilder Hobson, and *Jazzman* by Frederic Ramsey and Charles E. Smith. By the end of the 1930s jazz was increasingly being acknowledged as a vital and valid music by American intellectuals—Europeans had accepted jazz much earlier—and jazz critics were ready to single out the "great" leaders, performers, and composers

PRINCIPAL BLACK JAZZMEN AND SINGERS

With few exceptions, there was a great deal of mobility among black jazz performers during the three decades following World War I. Instrumentalists moved from one band to another, soloist organized or "fronted" bands, and some ensemble men moved into the area of solo performance. In discussing performers it is more convenient to associate persons with their instruments than with the orchestras in which they played. Among the most highly regarded trumpeters, after the legendary Oliver, Keppard, and Armstrong, were Bill Coleman (b. 1904), Johnny Dunn (1900-38), Roy Eldridge (b. 1911), Tommy Ladnier (1900-39), Clady "Jabbo" Smith (b. 1908), Joe Smith (1902-37), and Charles Melvin "Cootie" Williams (b. 1908).

We have mentioned already the celebrated clarinetists Jimmie Noone (1895–1944), Johnny Dodds (1892–1940), and Sidney Bechet (1897–1959)—all three players in the New Orleans tradition. Both Noone and Bechet acquired distinguished fans: Noone's playing was acclaimed by the composer Maurice Ravel, who listened to jazz during his visit to Chicago in 1928; and Bechet's performance was lauded, as we have mentioned, by the conductor Ansermet. All three men greatly influenced the playing of the jazz clarinetists who followed them, white and Negro. Other clarinetists who achieved distinction were William "Buster" Bailey (b. 1902), Leon "Barney" Bigard (b. 1906), Edmond Hall (b. 1901), Albert Nicholas (b. 1900), and Omer Victor Simeon (1920–59).

Rated as the three greatest alto saxophonists of the jazz era were Benny Carter (b. 1907), Johnny Hodges (1906–70), and Willie Smith (b. 1908). Another highly rated saxophonist was Hilton Jefferson (b. 1903). To critics, the tenor saxophonist Coleman "Bean" Hawkins (1904–69) was in a class by himself; his style was imitated by most tenors who followed him. Other tenors highly rated during the time were Leon "Chu" Berry (1910–41), Herschel Evans (1909–39), and Lester "Prez" Young (1909–59). It was Sidney Bechet who revealed most thoroughly the resources of the soprano saxophone, although he had developed his style on the clarinet.

With regard to trombonists, the names of Honoré Dutrey (1890–1937) and Edward "Kid" Ory (b. 1886) have been cited. Some consider Jimmy Harrison (1900–31) as one of the first great jazz trombonists. Other decisive figures were Jay C. Higginbotham (b. 1906), Dickie Wells (b. 1909), and Albert Wynn (b. 1907). The jazz-band drummer was at once the most important and often the least conspicuous member of the group. Among the best of the great drummers were three men from New Orleans: Baby Dodds (1898–1959), Alfred "Tubby" Hall (1895–1946), and Arthur James "Zutty" Singleton (b. 1898). Other great drummers were the bandleader Chick Webb, Big Sid Catlett (1910–51), William "Cozy" Cole (b. 1909), and Jo Jones (b. 1911).

The guitar and banjo players rated as superior during the jazz era included, first of all, Johnny St. Cyr (1890–1966) and also Bernard Addison (b. 1905), Teddy Bunn (b. 1909), Albert Aloysius

Casey (b. 1915), Lonnie Johnson (1889–1970), Arthur "Bud" Scott (1890–1949), and Leonard Ware (b. 1909). Although jazz bands rarely used violins, the period nevertheless produced some fine jazz violinists. Eddie South (1904–62) was regarded as having extraordinary talent. Among his gifted contemporaries were Robert Edward "Juice" Wilson (1904–64), Hezekiah Leroy Gordon "Stuff" Smith (b. 1909), and Darnell Howard (b. 1892). Howard also played other instruments in jazz groups. The best bassists of the period in addition to bandleader John Kirby were Jimmie Blanton (1921–42), Wellman Braud (b. 1891), George "Pops" Foster (1892–1969), Al Morgan (b. 1908), and Walter Page (1900–57). With regard to singers, it is often difficult to distinguish among jazz singers, blues singers, popular singers, and folk singers. Certainly the best singers of the 30s who moved in the jazz orbit were Ella Fitzgerald (b. 1918) and Billie "Lady Day" Holiday (1915–59). Other notable singers associated with jazz were Adelaide Hall (b. 1909), Helen Humes (b. 1913), Maxine Sullivan (b. 1911), and Billy Eckstine. Although Bessie Smith was primarily a blues singer, she also sang with jazz orchestras.

Jazz pianists of the period fall into two categories: those who were active with orchestras and those who played independently or with small combos (a subject we will discuss later). The leading figures in the former group were Count Basie, of course; Earl Hines, who had his own band; Mary Lou Williams (b. 1910), who played with Andy Kirk; Teddy Wilson (b. 1912), who attracted national attention when he became the first Negro to tour in an interracial jazz unit; Art Tatum (1910–56) and Cliff Jackson (1902–1970), both of whom were soloists as well as bandsmen; and Teddy Weatherford (1903–45), who spent the last twenty years of his life in the Far East.

BLACK JAZZ COMPOSER–ARRANGERS

In one sense the leading jazz performers were composers as well as soloists; with their improvisations they shaped the basic themes into musical compositions. But some of the jazzmen were responsible also for a large number of the original themes used as basic material; among them, Louis Armstrong, Earl Hines,

Richard Myknee Jones (1889–1945), King Oliver, and Spencer Williams (b. 1889). In a more conventional sense, the jazz composer was the jazz arranger, who built the original theme into a musical composition before bringing it to the band rehearsal. His talent lay in writing the music so that it fitted in with the style of the band and that of the individual soloists. The first bands to use written arrangements were those of Fletcher Henderson, Don Redman (McKinney's Cotton Pickers), and Duke Ellington. The most eminent composer-arrangers were, in addition to those just cited, Benny Carter, Horace Henderson (b. 1904, brother of Fletcher), Alex Hill (1907–37), Jimmy Mundy (b. 1907), Fred Norman (b. 1910), Sy Oliver, Edgar Melvin Sampson (b. 1907), and Mary Lou Williams. Several of these arrangers composed works in the same manner as composers of symphonic music—notably, Duke Ellington.

WHITE MUSICIANS AND JAZZ

Along with the emergence of big Negro bands, a comparable development took place in the white world of jazz. Among the bands most highly regarded by jazz experts—and those least susceptible to commercial concessions—were the bands of Benny Goodman, Tommy Dorsey, Bob Crosby, Artie Shaw, and Glen Gray (Casa Loma Orchestra). Paul Whiteman, originally of Denver, was the leader of the best-known "symphonic jazz" orchestra in New York. Several of the big bands used arrangements written by Negroes. Sy Oliver arranged for the Dorsey band; Jimmy Mundy wrote for Paul Whiteman; Horace Henderson, for Charlie Barnet. Benny Goodman probably used arrangements of black musicians to a greater extent than anyone; at one time or another he employed as arrangers Fletcher Henderson, Horace Henderson, Benny Carter, Edgar Sampson, Fred Norman, and Jimmy Mundy. Bob Crosby occasionally played arrangements adapted from interpretations of major jazz figures such as Louis Armstrong. When Goodman brought pianist Teddy Wilson into his touring jazz trio in 1935, he made jazz history by becoming the first white bandleader to hire a Negro.

Goodman's action (which was inspired by jazz critic John Hammond) was followed by a few token moves in the direction of integration, but it was not until the 1940s that black and white jazz musicians actually began to appear together in public. Among the white bandleaders who most consistently used black singers or instrumentalists were Goodman, Dorsey, Charlie Barnet, and Gene Krupa. Several of the Negro big bands, Duke Ellington's and Count Basie's, began to include whites in the 1950s. To be sure, during the 1940s integrated music ensembles became more common, and in the following decades many of the small combos were mixed racially. On the other hand, the mixing of black and white jazz musicians in recording studios began in the 1920s. Jelly Roll Morton undoubtedly was the first Negro to make recordings with a white band, when he played piano with the New Orleans Rhythm Kings in 1923. Among the black recording groups of the 20s and 30s that included white musicians were those of Louis Armstrong and Fats Waller.

After World War I, leading European composers began to take cognizance of the rich promise and vitality of jazz and to incorporate some aspects of the style in their works. The list of these composers is long and includes the names of such eminent figures as Alban Berg, Frederick Delius, Paul Hindemith, Ernst Krenek, Darius Milhaud, Francis Poulenc, Maurice Ravel, Arnold Schoenberg, Igor Stravinsky, Kurt Weill, and William Walton. These men heard authentic jazz when touring ensembles played in Europe or when they visited the United States; for example, Milhaud, when he visited Harlem in 1920, and Ravel, when he went to Chicago in 1928. Several of these men, of course, eventually settled permanently in the United States. Best known of the works inspired by jazz were Krenek's opera *Jonny spielt auf* (Johnny Strikes Up the Band, 1927), Milhaud's ballet *La Création du monde* (The Creation of the World, 1923), Ravel's Piano Concerto in D (1931), and William Walton's *Façade* (1922). In Krenek's opera, the hero Johnny is a black bandleader from Alabama. Although Stravinsky was among the first of the major composers to use ragtime idioms and to employ elements of jazz in his compositions, it was not until 1946 that he wrote a work entirely in the jazz style, the *Ebony Concerto for Dance Orchestra.*

The jazz age also inspired a number of white American composers to write works employing elements of jazz style. Among the most enduring of the symphonic works have been Aaron

Copland's *Music for the Theater* (1925) and Concerto for Piano and Orchestra (1927); John Alden Carpenter's ballets *Krazy Kat* (1921) and *Skyscrapers* (1926); and George Gershwin's *Rhapsody in Blue* (1924), Concerto in F (1925), and *An American in Paris* (1928). Among Gershwin's piano compositions, the three Preludes in jazz style have won lasting popularity. During the 30s three composers wrote so-called "Negro operas" (i.e. that called for Negro casts), which played an important role in helping to develop black opera singers, by providing them with the opportunity to sing on the stage. Louis Gruenberg's operatic version of Eugene O'Neill's drama *The Emperor Jones* was produced in 1933; Virgil Thomson's opera on a libretto by Gertrude Stein, *Four Saints in Three Acts*, was staged in 1934; and Gershwin's *Porgy and Bess*, based on the play by DuBose and Dorothy Heyward, was produced in 1935.

In 1924 bandleader Paul Whiteman staged a concert at Aeolian Hall in New York called "Experiment in Modern Music," in which he attempted to "make a respectable lady of jazz" by jazzing up the classics and by presenting classical arrangements of jazz. Unfortunately, the audience heard no authentic jazz as played by black jazzmen. On the other hand, the efforts of the wealthy jazz critic John Hammond to bring the music of black folk to the attention of the public were impressive. An enthusiastic devotee of jazz from his adolescence, Hammond provided many links between the Negro world and the white music industry. Among the black musicians he "discovered" and pushed to stardom were Billie Holiday, Count Basie, Teddy Wilson, Charlie Christian, Fletcher Henderson, and the boogie-woogie pianists Albert Ammons, Pete Johnson, and Meade Lux Lewis. For two successive years (1938 and 1939), Hammond produced memorable concerts at Carnegie Hall, "From Spirituals to Swing," where the best performers in all categories of Negro folk music were presented to the public.

BLUES AND SPIRITUALS

It was on August 10, 1920, that for the first time in history a commercial recording was made of a vocal blues by a Negro singer. The singer was Mamie Smith, actually more a singer of popular songs than the blues; her song was *Crazy Blues*, written by the black composer Perry Bradford; the man responsible for the recording was Ralph Peer, the white recording director of the Okeh Recording Company. He had been persuaded by Bradford to let Smith record the song when white Broadway singer Sophie Tucker, who was originally supposed to make the recording, became ill. The response of the black community was immediate—and astonishing to the Okeh officials, for the sale of *Crazy Blues* soon began to break all records, selling at more than 7,500 discs a week. The recording companies suddenly realized the vast potential audience among the black population of the nation for the blues of Negro singers. Within a year or two, companies were selling "race records" to blacks at the rate of more than five million copies annually. The records, made exclusively for the black market, were given special labels or numbers by the recording companies—such as Victor's *Bluebird* label, Columbia's 16000 series, and Decca's 7000 and 8000 series. Beginning about 1922, Paramount in Chicago became one of the most active companies in issuing race records.

The recording companies hired Negro talent scouts to seek out the best singers and instrumentalists available, primarily to record blues. The first black recording singers in the 1920s were all women. The blues they sang were in the classic form and accompanied by the piano or a small jazz combo. Ma Rainey was one of the most influential of the singers and, with justification, was called the "Mother of the Blues." Her singing forged a link between the older rural blues and the classic city blues, for she had been singing blues on her tours with the Rabbit Foot Minstrels many years before she made her first recordings in 1923. Her first accompanying group was the Serenaders, a combo led by the woman pianist Lovie Austin (Cora Calhoun, b. 1887). Included in some of the later groups that accompanied Ma were the celebrated trumpeters Louis Armstrong, Tommy Ladnier, and Joe Smith.

The most renowned blues singer of the time was Bessie Smith (1894–1937), known as the "Empress of the Blues." A protégé of Ma Rainey's, she had traveled for several years with tent shows and carnivals before she was "discovered" by a recording director in an obscure night club in Selma, Alabama. Bessie Smith's style, which combined the emotional fervor of country blues with the vigorous appeal of jazz, made her a special favorite with the Negro public. Her records sold phenomenally well; she was accompanied by the leading jazz artists of the time —Fletcher Henderson and his band, Joe Smith, Louis Armstrong, and the pianist James P. Johnson; and she became a headliner on the vaudeville circuit with her own show, *Harlem Frolics*. During the 1930s she made some recordings of spirituals in her concerts, but these, unfortunately, were unsuccessful. A two-reel film drama, *St. Louis Blues*, made in 1929 reveals the blues singer's great talent, as do also the large number of recordings she made. Her influence was felt by all contemporary blues singers and revealed itself in the singing of many destined for future fame, among them, Billie Holiday and Mahalia Jackson.

Other leading blues singers of the 20s included Ida Cox, Bertha "Chippie" Hill, Sara Martin, Clara Smith, Trixie Smith, Victoria Spivey, and Sippie Wallace. Clara Smith was called "Queen of the Moaners" because of the way she interpreted such songs as *Salty Dog*. Chippie Hill sang in a style similar to Bessie Smith's and, like Bessie, had worked with Ma Rainey. Victoria Spivey was only sixteen when she made her first recording.

A Negro-owned recording company was launched in New York in 1921, Harry Pace's Phonograph Corporation (it was later renamed The Black Swan Phonograph Company). After encountering considerable difficulty in getting a company to press his recordings, Pace finally found the New York Recording Laboratory Company at Port Washington, Wisconsin. The fledgling company made a good start. Black businessman John Nail and sociologist W. E. B. DuBois were on its board of directors; the personnel included Fletcher Henderson as the recording manager and a talented newcomer to New York, William Grant Still, as the music director. Blues singer Ethel Waters gave the company its first big hit with *Down Home Blues* and *O Daddy*. Other recording successes followed. Pace sent Waters and Henderson with his orchestra (then called the Black Swan Jazz Masters) on road tours to advertise the Black Swan label, hiring as troupe manager Lester Walton (later United States minister to Liberia). The Negro company lasted less than two years; it was one of the first casualties of that new invention, radio, which threatened to send all recording companies into bankruptcy. For a brief period during 1927 another Negro-owned recording company, the Black Patti, was operated by J. Mayo Williams, supervisor of race records for the Paramount Company in Chicago. It would be over three decades before the next black recording company would be organized—this one, Berry Gordy's Motown company, to achieve extraordinary success.

By the end of the 1920s the commercial interest in blues singers was shifting from female to male performers, and from classic blues to the more basic, unsophisticated rural blues. The first recording of country blues was made in 1924 by Papa Charlie Jackson, but it was not until about 1927 that extensive recording got under way. Often the recording technicians went out "into the field" to record the singers in their natural environment, taking with them the necessary equipment. One of the best-known rural blues singers of the 20s was Blind Lemon Jefferson (1897–1930), who accompanied himself on the guitar. Jefferson had a decisive influence on the blues singers Huddie "Leadbelly" Ledbetter (1888–1949) and Josh White (1908–68), who were active in a later period and both of whom served as his guide at one time.

A singer of spirituals and other religious songs, Blind Willie Johnson (1899–1949) was noted for his violent, tortured style and his guitar artistry. Big Bill Broonzy (William Lee Conley, 1893–1958), who also played guitar accompaniment, became widely known in the 1930s as a singer in the earthy, primitive tradition. Blind Boy Fuller (Fuller Allen, 1903–40) and Sonny Terry (Saunders Teddell, b. 1911), who was also blind, joined together to make a series of brilliant but moving recordings in the 30s. Terry used the harmonica instead of the more typical guitar. The team also appeared in the "From Spirituals to Swing" concert of 1938 at Carnegie Hall in New York. After Fuller's death, Terry teamed with Walter "Brownie" McGhee (b. 1914), a veteran singer-guitarist-pianist. The legendary Lonnie Johnson made over 700 blues recordings during the 1920s, some accompanied by Louis Armstrong and Duke Ellington.

The Slades, Wilk "Son" Slade and his wife, are credited with having made the first blues recording using jug-band accompaniment (1926). Their Memphis Jug Band consisted of kazoo, harmonica, guitar, and jug. Gus Cannon (b. 1883) of the Mississippi Hill country was another of the early users of the jug band on recordings. Cannon had cut his first recording of blues with banjo accompaniment on cylinders for Victor in 1901. In the intervening years he had traveled widely with medicine shows before he recorded again in 1927 for Victor with his Jug Stompers.

The beginning of the depression in 1929 brought severe consequences for the recording industry, especially with regard to race records. But the making of records for the Negro market never entirely ceased; indeed, before long there appeared a new outlet for race records—the jukeboxes that were being placed in almost every bar, grill, and restaurant of the nation. Rural-blues singers continued to gravitate to the two chief centers of the blues industry, Memphis and Chicago. With more experience, the bluesmen tended to smooth out their rough voices, refine instrumental techniques, and develop more sophisticated repertories. In effect, they became urban- or city-blues singers. The nation's major blues areas, however, still sent the best singers to the recording centers—singers from the Mississippi Delta country, the so-called Territories (Texas, Oklahoma, and adjoining states), the Georgia coastal regions, and the southeastern seaboard states. Inevitably, the bluesmen turned into urban itinerants, traveling the routes of the towns and big cities and coming into contact with jazz ensembles that were increasingly drawing upon blues elements in jazz composition, particularly in Kansas City. Some blues singers moved entirely within the jazz orbit; for example, Jimmy Rushing and Joe Turner, as has been observed, and Jimmy Witherspoon, Wynonie Harris, and the somewhat later Joe Williams of *Every Day* fame.

Over the years black folksingers consistently showed little concern for maintaining a sharp line of distinction between secular and sacred music—for example, between the blues and spirituals—for the two genres shared, as we have seen, many of the same stylistic elements. Often only the text served to distinguish the sound of a spiritual from that of the blues. Most folksingers, whether of blues or spirituals, received their first musical orientation in the Negro church. Blues singers turned easily to the singing of spirituals in recording sessions or in concerts, and occasionally the singer of spirituals took up the profession of blues singer, despite the stigma attached to the latter among churchgoers. Beginning in the twentieth century a new song-type, the "gospel song," was introduced into the Negro church.

GOSPEL SONGS AND THOMAS DORSEY

Just as the Protestant "Second Awakening" movement at the beginning of the nineteenth century had produced its characteristic song, the spiritual, so the Protestant City-Revival Movement of the 1850s created a new song genre, gospel hymnody, that was more relevant to the needs of the common people in the rapidly growing cities. The spiritual was born in the rural setting of the camp meeting, where thousands assembled under the stars amid the blaze of campfires and torch lights to listen to itinerant preachers. The gospel song evolved in urban settings, in huge temporary tents erected for revival meetings by touring evangelists, in football stadiums, and in mammoth tabernacles. The gospel song-makers borrowed the melodies and musical forms of popular songs—i.e. Tin Pan Alley materials—as their antecedents had borrowed folksongs and popular songs a half-century earlier.

When the black people began pouring into the nation's cities during the second decade of the twentieth century, they took their joyful spirituals with them, but found the rural-born music to be unsatisfactory in urban settings and unresponsive to their needs. Consequently, the church singers created a more expressive music to which they applied the term gospel music, but which displayed little resemblance to the traditional gospel songs of the whites. Negro gospel music became essentially the sacred counterpart of the city blues, sung in the same improvisatory tradition with piano, guitar, or instrumental-ensemble accompaniment. The major responsibility for the phenomenal development of Negro gospel music from its beginnings in the 1920s through the succeeding decades lies with one man—Thomas A. Dorsey (b. 1899).

Before he was in his teens, Thomas Dorsey had won a local reputation as a good blues pianist—not without considerable difficulty, however, for there was no piano in the Dorsey home. His father was a country preacher, whose church was situated in a rural area near Atlanta, Georgia. The boy had to walk four miles to a music teacher (and four miles back home), but his determination to learn piano inspired him to make the trip four times a week. Within two years Dorsey was earning money by playing piano for the local Saturday night dances. About 1919 he left Georgia to go North, going first to work in the steel mills of Gary, Indiana. He organized a five-piece dance band there that soon was in great demand for parties in the black communities of Gary and South Chicago. The band's activity gave him practice in making jazz arrangements and also enabled him to earn enough money to study music at the Chicago College of Composition and Arranging. It was during this period that Dorsey began to compose songs.

After joining the Pilgrim Baptist Church of Chicago in 1921, Dorsey turned to the composition of church songs. When the National Baptist Convention met at Pilgrim in the Summer of 1921, one man, A. W. Nix, electrified the convention with his singing of a song, *I Do, Don't You*, composed by C. A. Tindley, the gospel song writer. Dorsey had never before been so moved by a song, not even a blues. He resolved at that moment to write church music that would affect others in a similar way. His first songs revealed his debt to Tindley, who was active during the years 1901–06, but whose music did not become popular in Negro churches until after World War I. The songs were typical tabernacle songs, with little of the emotional fervor that later ones would have. Dorsey's career as a church-song writer was interrupted, however, when he took a job with a band called the Whispering Syncopators. Directed by Will Walker, the band included several players who would later become famous; among them, Les Hite and Lionel Hampton. Later, Dorsey organized a band for the blues singer Ma Rainey and went on tour with her company. During this period he became known as Georgia Tom, a player and composer of blues. Dorsey's marriage brought him back into the church, but he experienced one more period of backsliding when he began a four-year association with the blues singer Hudson "Tampa Red" Whittaker. One of the songs they wrote, *It's Tight Like That*, was so successful that the first royalty statement on the recording brought $2,400.19.

In 1932 Dorsey returned permanently to the church and to the writing of sacred songs. It was not easy to get started. No publisher would take his songs, and when he himself paid for publication, no one would buy the songs. He finally decided to adopt the methods of popular song writers: he would plug the songs, going from church to church to sing for the congregations. Eventually the Dorsey gospel songs caught on and stirred not only Negro churches, but the entire world with their swinging, rocking rhythms and blueslike melodies. By 1970 Dorsey had written more than 400 songs (of which *Precious Lord, Take My Hand* was the most famous), had founded the National Convention of Gospel Singers, and had inspired the organization of hundreds of touring gospel singers, gospel ensembles, and gospel choirs. Gospel songs invaded the theater, the night club, the gambling casino, the jazz festival, and the concert hall. Every small store-front church in the ghetto had its gospel choir; the larger, established Baptist and Methodist churches maintained two or three choirs, one of which inevitably was a gospel choir. By the 1940s the recording industry was discovering that the recordings of gospel singers quickly became "best sellers," particularly those of Sister Rosetta Tharpe, Clara Ward, and Mahalia Jackson.

BLACK JAZZ PIANISTS

Jelly Roll Morton was the father of jazz piano. His piano style represented a synthesis of the chief elements of the blues, of piano ragtime, and of orchestra jazz. An essential part of his performance was improvisation, but he also composed pieces in the same way as jazz composers wrote music for the jazz band. His written piano scores represented only an approximation, however, of the actual sound of his music, which was recognized by his peers to be the best in the nation.

As we have mentioned, the East was noted for its pianists, and after the war Harlem became the center of piano activity. There the pianists were kept busy playing in the tiny cabarets and honky-tonks of the black community and for its innumerable social affairs, particularly the "rent parties." In Harlem, as in other large ghetto areas of northern cities, the only way that many blacks could cope with the problem of paying the excessive rents charged for their apartments was to give parties where "guests" were invited to contribute toward the rent. It was the job of the pianist "to draw people in"—into the barroom or café or the apartment itself—and the vitality and vigor of his playing was his drawing card. The playing of the best pianists could be heard for a considerable distance away. It was very important that a piano should have the correct "barroom" sound; sometimes it would have to be "doctored," by placing newspapers behind the hammers and putting tin on the felts, in order to obtain the effect wanted.

The Harlem pianists were the direct inheritors of the eastern ragtime tradition. They had learned to play by standing at the elbows of the legendary "sharks"; their more recent mentors were Eubie Blake and Abba Labba McLean. Indeed, several of the most noted pianists began their careers as rag pianists in the first part of the twentieth century and only gradually changed their style to adapt to the changing times. The Harlem jazz pianists filled the functions of orchestras until about the mid-1920s, at which time the night spots began struggling to obtain a three- or four-piece ensemble to support the piano. Frequently the label "orchestral style" has been applied to the Harlem piano music of this period: the pianist made the instrument literally roar, using full, fat harmonies in the right hand and a powerful bass in the left hand that empasized the strong beats with low-register octaves or tenths and the weak beats with mid-keyboard chords ("stride piano"). The music reflected the influence of the blues scale in the pianist's use of "blues clusters" (the striking of major and minor thirds or sevenths simultaneously). The pianist's aim was to improvise, to vary and embellish the basic musical material, for which he drew upon several sources —blues, rags, concert piano music, popular songs, instrumental dances and marches, or his own compositions. One of the most celebrated of the pianists, Willie-the-Lion Smith, summarized his aim in this manner:

First I always demonstrate the melody, because they've got to know what I'm playing; then I redecorate it with counterpoint.

WILLIE–THE–LION SMITH

William Henry Joseph Berthol Bonaparte Berthloff Smith (b. 1897) acquired his nickname, Willie-the-Lion, because of his bravery during World War I. His published memoir, *Music on*

My Mind (1964), includes rare, first-hand information about the music of Harlem (and, indeed, of the Negro world) during the first half of the century. Smith was born at Goshen, New York, was educated at Howard University, and studied music privately—at first with his mother, then with a German musician, Hans Steinke, who gave him lessons in music theory. His career followed the typical pattern of black jazz pianists: he began playing professionally at the age of seventeen in Newark, New Jersey, and he worked at various entertainment spots in Atlantic City (a mecca for black entertainers in the East before World War I) and New York before touring Europe as a pianist in 1917. During the war, Smith served with the 350th Infantry.

Afterward, he picked up his career, touring as a soloist, making recordings (sometimes with combos), playing in nightclubs in Harlem, on Fifty-second Street, and, during the 1940s, in Greenwich Village. His tours carried him to Europe several times, to Canada, and to Africa during the 1949–50 season. Like his contemporaries, Smith wrote a great deal of music, but is best known for his piano style, which has been described as having an extraordinary mixture of power and delicacy. The titles of his pieces (*Echoes of Spring, Morning Air, Fingerbuster*) suggest his concern for expressive melody ("charming with graceful contours") and harmony ("rich and unusual"), but fail to reflect his equal concern for powerful and supple basses.

LUCKEY ROBERTS

Charles Luckeyeth "Luckey" Roberts (1895–1968) entered the entertainment world at the age of three, when he took a part in *Uncle Tom's Cabin*. A native of Philadelphia, he settled in New York during the early part of the 1900s, where he studied music with black musicians Eloise Smith and Melville Charlton. Luckey's very full career included touring as a singer, dancer, and pianist in vaudeville companies in the United States and in Europe. From time to time he organized and conducted his own ensembles, maintained a music studio, and played for radio shows.

Roberts is regarded as the founder of the Harlem piano school. His early rags, which served as models for the later piano pieces called "shouts," called for great technical skill. One of his most challenging pieces, *Ripples of the Nile,* was later rewritten in a slow tempo as *Moonlight Cocktail* and became quite popular. In addition to a large number of popular songs and dance pieces, Roberts wrote fourteen musical-comedy scores, and composed several concert works—including *Whistlin' Pete—Miniature Syncopated Rhapsody,* which was played at a Robin Hood Dell concert at Philadelphia. He exerted great influence upon the pianists of his period—including Johnson, Smith, Waller, and later Ellington—and as a society pianist upon wealthy, white jazz enthusiasts. He was a favorite, for example, of the duke of Windsor (then prince of Wales), and helped him to select records for the royal jazz collection.

J. P. JOHNSON

James Price Johnson (1891–1955), born in New Brunswick, New Jersey, studied piano with his mother and privately in New York, where the family moved when he was a youngster. In 1904, when he was little more than a child, he began playing rag piano professionally at a summer resort on Long Island. Later he worked in various places in Manhattan's West-Side Tenderloin district.

The competitive spirit that existed among black pianists of the period led them to practice constantly in order to excel in the frequent cutting contests. Johnson once told an interviewer that he used to practice in the dark in order to develop a firm feeling for the keyboard. During a contest, each pianist would be given a stated number of minutes to demonstrate his skill at improvising on a given theme. Johnson's method for "carving" his rivals (i.e. winning a contest) was to "put tricks in on the breaks" (i.e. to fill in all the pauses of the original melody with elaborate embellishments). Johnson boasted, "I could think of a trick a minute: double glissandos, straight and backhand; glissandos in sixths, and double tremolos." As an adult, Johnson studied piano with a local Italian musician, Bruno Gianinni. He also spent many hours in listening to recordings of European piano compositions, primarily so that he could use "concert effects" in his playing of jazz piano and so that he could "rag" such classics as Grieg's *Peer Gynt* Suite and Rachmaninoff's Prelude in C# minor.

Johnson engaged in a variety of jobs during his long career as a jazz pianist. At one time he fronted a Clef Club band. He played solo piano in various night clubs; toured widely as a soloist, accompanist, and musical director of two shows, Dudley's *Smart Set* and *Plantation Days;* made player-piano rolls and, later, piano recordings; and wrote music scores for several film shorts. Like most pianists of the period, Johnson was a prolific writer, composing most of the music he played but publishing comparatively little. Nevertheless, his publications include a large number of rags, stomps, blues, and popular songs as well as a body of serious works. His first piece was a piano blues, *Mama and Papa Blues* (1914). His *Carolina Shout* became a "test piece" for would-be jazz pianists in the same way that Joplin's *Maple Leaf Rag* had been for ragtimers. Best known of the many popular songs he wrote were *If I Could Be with You, Old-Fashioned Love*, and the *Charleston.*

In later years Johnson gave much time to composing extended works in the tradition of Negro music. Included among his works were *Symphonic Harlem, Symphony in Brown*, Piano Concerto in A♭, and *Symphonic Suite on the "St. Louis Blues."* Best known of his musical-comedy numbers were the songs in *Plantation Days, Keep Shuffling*, and *Runnin' Wild.* His opera *The Organizer* used a libretto by poet Langston Hughes. Most frequently performed of Johnson's larger works has been the *Negro Rhapsody: Yamekraw*, which employs spiritual and blues melodies and some of Johnson's tunes originally written for musical comedies. The work was orchestrated by William Grant Still, and in this form was played a number of times in concerts and on radio and TV programs, such as Williard Robison's "Deep River" radio program and the Firestone TV series. In 1945, an all-Johnson concert was produced at Carnegie Hall. Johnson's influence as a pianist extended to his more celebrated disciples, Waller and Ellington, and to other pianists of the 20s.

FATS WALLER

Thomas "Fats" Waller (1904–43) is regarded by some as representing the summation of the Harlem style and the link between it and modern jazz pianism. Jazz specialist Gunther Schuller has written, for example:

> His real service lay in taking the still somewhat disjunct elements of Johnson's style and unifying them into a single, cohesive jazz conception in which ragtime was still discernible underneath the surface as a source, but no longer overtly active as a separate formative element.

Waller made yet another contribution to the history of jazz: he was the first person to successfully adapt the style of jazz pianism to the pipe organ and the Hammond organ. And yet he played standard concert music equally as well as he played jazz. Son of a New York clergyman, Waller spent his first five years in a home without a piano. He learned to play the harmonium on his own, however, and when he was six (at which time his older brother brought a piano into the house) he was ready to begin piano lessons. When he became older he studied with the white musicians Carl Bohm and Leopold Godowsky. But his interest lay in ragtime piano, which he could hear all around him in Harlem. When he was fifteen, he began playing professionally in cabarets and theaters—particularly at the Lincoln Theater in Harlem, where movies were shown to the accompaniment of music played on a $10,000 Wurlitzer grand organ. He first attracted attention locally by winning a prize in an amateur pianists' contest for his elaboration of J. P. Johnson's *Carolina Shout*. At this time Waller had not met Johnson, but he was later introduced into the circle of the Harlem pianists, and Johnson took over his instruction in the field of jazz piano.

Waller became the most widely known of the Harlem pianists. He toured the United States and Europe as a soloist, an accompanist, and an orchestra pianist (often with his own band). His fame spread when he played a long series of radio broadcasts ("Fats Waller's Rhythm Club") over station WLW in Cincinnati in 1932 and began to record as a pianist, organist, and with his ensembles. Waller was a prolific composer of jazz and popular songs. His first composition, which he called *Boston Blues*, was published as *Squeeze Me* in 1925 (with lyrics by Spencer Williams). Other well-known songs include *Honeysuckle Rose*, *Ain't Misbehaving*, *Keeping Out of Mischief*, and *I'm Gonna Sit Right Down and Write Myself a Letter*.

EARL HINES

Earl "Fatha" Hines (b. 1905) was the Chicago counterpart of the Harlem pianists in the 1920s and 30s. He came from a musical family: his father was a trumpeter in the Eureka Brass Band of Duquesne, Pennsylvania (Hines's birthplace), and his mother was an organist. His pianism first attracted attention when he played in Chicago with Louis Armstrong's Hot Five. Inspired by Armstrong's trumpet playing, Hines developed a piano style in which his right hand played melodic figures similar to those of a trumpet, but *in octaves*, while his left hand provided the firm bass of an orchestral rhythm section. Hines's so-called "trumpet piano" style was widely imitated by other pianists, black and white, of the period. The Hines style has been described as "tormented and passionate," primarily because of his predilection for suddenly introducing passages marked by great melodic and rhythmic complexity into the playing of pieces in conventional jazz style. As has been observed, Hines also earned distinction as an orchestra leader at the Grand Terrace Ballroom in Chicago.

THE BOOGIE–WOOGIE

Mention should be made of the so-called "boogie-woogie" piano style, which became fashionable during this period and apparently originated in Chicago. It was essentially a novel way of playing the blues, with the left hand using an ostinato figure consisting of eight notes to the measure (i.e. repeating the short bass melody again and again throughout the number) and the right hand embellishing the blues melody. The pianist played the bass ostinato at different pitch levels to parallel the basic chord changes of the blues harmony. Jimmy Yancey (1894–1951), who was active as a singer, dancer, and blues pianist, pioneered in the use of the boogie-woogie in the Chicago area in his playing for rent parties before World War I. Other exponents were Clarence "Pinetop" Smith (1904–29), a vaudeville trooper whose *Pine Top Boogie* based on a Yancey ostinato gave the style a name; Meade Lux Lewis (1905–64), who became one of the key figures in the boogie-woogie renaissance of the 30s with his *Honky-Tonk Train Blues;* Pete Johnson (b. 1904), whose vigorous style earned him a reputation as one of the best boogie-woogie pianists; and Albert Ammons (1907–49), an equally effective pianist who formed a three-piano team with Lewis and Johnson in presenting boogie-woogie concerts.

CHAPTER XIV

The Black Renaissance

During the post-World War I period there developed in the United States a new interest in the so-called "Negro problem." White sociologists began investigating the plight of the black man in the South and in the ghettos of the North; white novelists and dramatists became interested in the possibilities of utilizing Negro themes in their works; and, as we have seen, white composers experimented with employing Negro folk music and jazz in composition. Moreover, the white public in general displayed a growing interest in learning more about the black man, and particularly about his arts. Black folk, too, were becoming more interested in learning about themselves. They were becoming increasingly aware that the democracy for which they had fought in Europe did not exist for them in the United States. Furthermore, they were becoming more militant and more articulate in expressing their concern.

On various levels and in diverse ways the black population made known its discontent. There were so many race riots during the Summer of 1919 that writer James Weldon Johnson named it "The Red Summer." The various national Negro organizations embarked on more vigorous programs of action to obtain the rights of citizenship for blacks—such groups, for example, as the NAACP (the National Association for the Advancement of Colored People, organized 1909), the Urban League (the National League on Urban Conditions, established 1911), the National Race Congress, and the National Baptist Convention. In New York the magnetic activist Marcus Garvey succeeded in gaining the support of hundreds of thousands of disenchanted Negroes from all over the country for his "Back to Africa" movement. A general feeling of unrest, defiance, impatience, and even bitterness swept over black communities, and few Negroes were unaffected.

In New York, the nation's business, cultural, and intellectual center—and particularly in Harlem, the undeclared capital of Negro intellecutal life—black artists began to rally their forces. Writers, poets, painters, and musicians joined together to protest in their own way against the quality of life for black folk in the United States. Out of this grew a movement that has been called "The Harlem Renaissance" or "The Black Renaissance" or "The New Negro Movement." It was primarily a literary movement. James Weldon Johnson informally inaugurated the movement with his publication of *Fifty Years and Other Poems in 1917*. (The title poem of the collection referred to the fifty years that had elapsed since the signing of the Emancipation Proclamation, which was supposed to bring first-class citizenship to Negroes.) Other books soon followed—collections of poems, novels, prose—written by Claude McKay, Jean Toomer, Countee Cullen, William S. Braithwaite, Langston Hughes, Jessie Redmond Fauset, Walter White, Johnson, and others. National periodicals published articles about the renaissance movement by such writers as W. E. B. DuBois, George Schuyler, E. Franklin Frazier, Benjamin Brawley, Joel A. Rogers, Arthur Schomburg, and Alain Leroy Locke. Two Negro periodicals, *Crisis* and *Opportunity*, offered prizes to stimulate literary production among black writers and to encourage the younger ones.

Black musicians participated in the movement by turning to the folk music of the race as a source of materials in composition and performance. To be sure, some black composers had been drawing on such materials for a number of years—particularly those who had been associated with the musical nationalism advocated by Dvořák in 1895—but now they became more race conscious than ever. The composers used poems by black poets in their art songs; they exploited the rhythms of Negro dances and the harmonies and melodies of the blues as well as spirituals, and of the newer music called jazz in their composed concert music. Almost without exception black concert artists began to include on their programs the folk and composed music of Negroes, and some artists staged recitals consisting exclusively of Negro music.

Various organizations and individuals offered awards and prizes to black musicians who made significant achievements. In 1914 the NAACP instituted the Spingarn Medal for the Negro who during the period of any one year made the highest achievement in a field of human endeavor. In 1919 the National Association of Negro Musicians was organized "to discover and foster talent, to mold taste, to promote fellowship, and to advocate racial expression." Over the years the Association was to give scholarships to talented singers, hold workshops and seminars for professional musicians, and provide occasions for the performance of works composed by black musicians. In 1925 a black businessman of New York, Casper Holstein, donated substantial sums of money for annual prizes to be given to composers who competed successfully in contests set up by the magazine *Opportunity*. The Rodman Wanamaker Musical Composition Contests for black musicians, established in 1927, offered prizes in several categories: songs, choral works, symphonic works, and solo instrumental pieces. The Harmon Foundation gave awards for both composition and performance. Finally, ambitious musicians could compete, as we shall see, for prizes offered by white organizations and institutions without regard for race or color.

For black concert musicians and composers of art music, the decades of the 20s and 30s were full of paradoxes. Because of the barriers of discrimination, performers generally found it very difficult to launch a career, regardless of how well qualified they were—and yet by 1941 there were three black artists among the ten most highly paid concert artists in the United States, and a fourth was near the top ten. Black composers generally found that the doors of publishing houses were closed to them, and that leading music organizations would not perform their music— but it was during this period that, for the first time in history, major symphony orchestras performed works written by Negroes, major opera companies used black singers in leading roles, Negroes conducted symphony orchestras and radio orchestras, Negroes wrote scores for full-length movie films, and Negroes appeared in drama and ballet productions on Broadway. More than ever before, individual Negroes received recognition for achievement. Successful composers, for example, were given commissions to write additional works and opportunities for performances. Talented students were given fellowships for further study after graduating from the nation's conservatories, often for study abroad. It is noteworthy that young white Americans struggling to get started in musical careers frequently met with some of the same obstacles that black Americans faced—except, of course, for racial discrimination. For them, also, the post-war decades were a time of both uncertainty and promise, primarily because of the changing attitude of the nation toward the arts.

THE GENERAL STATE OF MUSIC IN THE NATION

Since the beginning of the twentieth century, various European schools had begun to challenge the domination of German romanticism and to strike out in new directions toward the establishment either of national schools or of more international music. The United States, at the end of the war, was on the brink of a period of extraordinary development and expansion in the field of music. The movement to increase music-training opportunities for young people, which had begun after the Civil War, gained momentum. Between the years 1921 and 1923, three of the world's finest music schools were established in the East, schools that offered to Americans for the first time the opportunity to study music under the same ideal conditions as in Europe. All three institutions—the Eastman School of Music in Rochester, New York (1921); the Juilliard Graduate School in New York City (1923); and the Curtis Institute of Music in Philadelphia (1923)—opened with generous endowments that allowed them to gather the finest artist-teachers from all over the world for their faculties. Eastman, under the direction of the composer Howard Hanson, became famous for its composition students and for its sponsorship of concerts featuring the works of American composers. Juilliard (which combined with the Institute of Musical Art in 1926) and Curtis became noted for their concert and opera performers. From these schools would come the most celebrated black musicians of the mid-century period.

A second interest of progressive forces among musicians was the improvement of the status of American composers. In 1919 the Society for the Publication of American Music was established. In 1921 two organizations were set up with the primary purpose of providing for the performance of American works and the commissioning of new works: the International Composers' Guild and the League of Composers. The latter soon began the publication of a periodical, *Modern Music*, and arranged for exchange concerts with European organizations. (In 1954 the League of Composers was to merge with the American section of the International Society for Contemporary Music.) Not to be overlooked in the drive for bettering the condition of the American composer were the established concert artists and the directors of leading symphonies and opera companies, whose responsibility it was to insure that the new works of American composers received not only a first performance, but also a second and a third. Fortunately, during this period some of the world's most illustrious and progressive musicians assumed the leadership of the leading orchestras. Leopold Stokowski had gone to the Philadelphia Orchestra in 1912; Serge Koussevitsky became conductor of the Boston Symphony in 1924; and Arturo Toscanini went to the New York Philharmonic in 1926 (which merged in 1928 with the New York Symphony to become the New York Philharmonic-Symphony).

There were yet other sources of encouragement to promising young musicians; for example, the Walter Naumburg Musical Foundation Award in New York, the Guggenheim Foundation Fellowships, and the Metropolitan Opera Auditions. When the Great Depression came at the end of the 1920s, the WPA (Works Progress Administration) came to the rescue of American musicians, providing jobs for them in community music projects and setting up orchestras, choral groups, and chamber-music groups that not only employed musicians but also performed works of American composers.

Americans continued to go abroad for additional study—the composers going now more often to France than to Germany, particularly to the composer-teacher Nadia Boulanger, who had a reputation for developing craftsmanship without destroying a student's individuality. Well-trained singers found opportunities for advancement more plentiful in Europe than in America, especially in opera. Consequently, many began their careers over there. And when they returned to the United States with European credentials, they found it easier to successfully launch American careers.

Black music students and established musicians were greatly affected by the developments taking place in the field of music on both the national level and in the smaller Negro world. The musicians who won distinction during the period spent long years of study and sacrifice in preparation for their careers. They availed themselves of every opportunity for study and for gaining experience, in order to develop poise and self-assurance. The concert artists participated in competitions, sang in church choirs and in local choral organizations, and gave recitals in Negro churches and schools. The composers played in musical-comedy and jazz orchestras, wrote music for radio programs and film shorts, and, like the performers, entered all of the competitions that were open to them.

In addition to the organizations and institutions discussed above that helped struggling black artists to move ahead, there were always the Negro church and the Negro school. The church discovered black talent, fostered its growth by sponsoring recitals, and often paid for advanced study of its talented by raising funds among the members of the congregation. The school, and particularly the Negro college, played a similar role. In several instances, members of Negro college communities raised funds to send a gifted student away for advanced study. Established musicians were given positions in the colleges that allowed them to combine concertizing or composing with teaching, and they were assisted in obtaining grants for advanced study or for composing. The choruses and orchestras of the Negro colleges were invaluable to composer-teachers, of course, as media for testing the effectiveness of their compositions. To a limited extent, the Negro-owned theater also assisted the development of concert musicians, although its greatest contribution was in the field of entertainment music and jazz.

The leading musical figures of the black renaissance displayed their race consciousness in a number of ways. As we have noted, they chose to work with Negro materials in their singing, playing, or composing. Some spoke out publicly against discrimination and other social evils; one or two refused to perform for segregated audiences. The great black artists of the time helped lesser artists to achieve by counseling them, sponsoring recitals, and giving them letters of introduction to white organizations and private individuals who could further their careers. The noted tenor Roland Hayes often lowered his fees so that the poor of his race could hear him sing. Contralto Marian Anderson set up a scholarship fund for young Negro singers. In New York, singer-composer Harry T. Burleigh, who was still active during the years of the black renaissance and was both professionally and economically secure, brought many young singers to the attention of the public.

CONCERT ARTISTS

To the black communities that helped them to rise, the black concert artists who achieved distinction during the black renaissance were more than just talented and successful individuals. They became racial symbols, whose successes were shared vicariously by the great mass of blacks that could never hope to attain similar distinction. Whenever an artist succeeded in breaking down a color barrier, he inspired other talented Negroes to overcome almost insurmountable difficulties in order to emulate him. In a very real sense, he was a trail-blazer; he proved to white America that given the chance black men could sing, play, and compose. He made it easier for those who followed after him to obtain concert management or to get a symphony performed. The first trail-blazer of the new century developed into one of the world's leading tenors during the years 1920 through 1950.

ROLAND HAYES

Roland Hayes (b. 1887) was born on a farm in Curryville, Georgia. The story of his life embodies the "rags to riches" theme, except that Hayes was his own fairy godmother for the most part, and worked very hard to reach the top. He grew up in dire poverty. After the death of his father, the family moved in 1900 to Chattanooga, Tennessee, where Hayes obtained a job working in a sash-weight foundry. His opportunities to obtain an education were limited, but he did sing in the local church choir. When Hayes was about eighteen years old, a young Negro student from Oberlin came to Chattanooga to work for a year in order to accumulate enough money to continue his studies. The student, Arthur Calhoun, heard Hayes sing and impressed upon him the necessity for studying voice. Hayes had not realized that he possessed talent. He observed, "I liked to sing—all of my people do—but I hadn't given it any thought. I just sang because it was as natural to me as breathing." Sometime later Calhoun and Hayes visited in the home of a local white man, who played some recordings of the singing of such celebrated artists as Caruso, Sembrich, and Eames. The music opened the door to a new life for Hayes. Later he told a reporter, "That night I was born again. It was as if a bell had been struck that rang in my heart. And it has never ceased to ring there."

Against the wishes of his mother, Hayes made up his mind to become a singer. The only blacks whom she had known to succeed in music were dance-hall musicians, and "she didn't want any boy of hers to take up that kind of life." Nevertheless, Hayes set out for Oberlin with savings of fifty dollars in his pocket. His plan was to give recitals in Negro churches on the way and thereby increase his funds. Instead, he found his funds depleted, for his expenses ate up the compensation he received. Determined to achieve his goal, he applied for admission at nearby Fisk University. He was admitted to the school and he remained there for four years, the last three on a scholarship. While at Fisk he supported himself by working for a family and by giving local recitals.

He then went to Louisville, obtained a job as a waiter in the select Pendennis Club, and sang every time the opportunity arose. During the year he received a letter from the president of Fisk University, asking him to join the Fisk Jubilee Singers in a concert venture in Boston, with all expenses paid and a small salary. Hayes accepted with alacrity and remained in Boston after the concerts. A white benefactor, Henry H. Putnam, who had heard Hayes sing in Louisville, secured auditions for him with local teachers. As a result, Hayes was offered the option of a scholarship at the New England Conservatory or studying with a private teacher, whom he would have to pay. Hayes chose the latter and began his study with Arthur Hubbard in 1911.

For many years Hayes studied privately while working as a

messenger at the Hancock Life Insurance Company and giving self-managed concerts at Negro churches in order to support himself and his mother, who had joined him in Boston. In 1917 he decided he was ready to confront the musical world. Using the money he had saved over the years he gave a recital at Symphony Hall in Boston, and received press acclaim but little support from the public. Undaunted, he gave a second big concert, which was successful both musically and financially. Then Hayes went to Europe in 1920 where he first studied privately, then gave concerts. His triumphs, which included command performances before the king and queen of England, brought him a world-wide reputation. He returned to the United States in 1923 a celebrity and was able to secure professional management (the Boston Symphony Orchestra Concert Company).

The recital given by Hayes on December 2, 1923, at Boston in Symphony Hall marked the beginning of a long, illustrious career on the concert stages of the world. Sometime later a notice about Hayes would carry the headline, "From Stove Molder to $100,000 a Year," and a critic could observe:

[He] is an artist primarily, and a Negro incidentally . . . the essentially racial quality of his singing is something that exists chiefly in the imaginations of his more romantic hearers. . . . [He] has a beautiful tenor voice, silken smooth in mezzo forte, ringingly vibrant in fortes, and trained to perfect evenness of production in all of its registers.

Other critics wrote about his "meticulous phrasing," "lyric tone," and "mastery of fine nuances in expressive and musical color." He was acclaimed for his perfect command of language in his singing of French, German, and Italian songs, and for his catholic taste in selecting song materials. A 1953 program included, for example, two songs from a fifteenth-century source, the *Lochamer Liederbuch;* songs by a white contemporary composer, Germaine Tailleferre; and spirituals arranged by Negro composers William Grant Still and Edward Boatner.

Hayes had very positive ideas regarding the importance of Negro folk music. He once said to an interviewer:

My people have been very shy about singing their crude little songs before white folks. They thought they would be laughed at —and they were! And so they came to despise their own heritage. . . . If, as I truly believe, there is purpose and plan in my life, it is this: that I shall have my share in rediscovering the qualities we have almost let slip away from us; and that we shall make our special contribution—only a humble one perhaps, but our very own —to human experience.

That Hayes was successful in his desire to make this special contribution was proved again and again. An incident took place in Germany, for example, that tested Hayes's ability to rise above pettiness when his music was involved. When Hayes arrived in Berlin in 1924 to give a recital, he was met with great hostility. An article in the morning newspaper expressed the attitude of the public, "the fear of the calamity of a black man coming into Germany and defiling the great names of music and poetry—a man who at best can only remind us of the cotton fields of Georgia." When Hayes stepped out on the stage that evening he was greeted with a volley of hisses that lasted for over twenty minutes. Hayes stood quietly in the curve of the piano, waiting for the tumult to cease. "Then there was silence," he later wrote, "and that was the most terrifying." Quickly, Hayes rearranged the evening's program in his mind and decided to begin with one of Schubert's most exquisite songs, *Du Bist die Ruh*. His perfect singing of the song, with "finished technic" and yet with sweetness, melted the animosity of the audience entirely. From then on, he was in command.

Many honors were given to Hayes during his long career. He received honorary doctoral degrees from several colleges and universities; among them, Fisk (1932), Ohio Wesleyan (1939), Morehouse (1945), Boston (1948), Howard (1950), Virginia Union (1951), and Temple (1956). In 1924 the NAACP gave him the Spingarn Medal for achievement; in 1949 France gave him the Purple Ribbon "for services to French music"; in 1950 Hayes was appointed to the music faculty of Boston University. Hayes gave a seventy-fifth-birthday concert in 1962 at Carnegie Hall in New York for the benefit of Negro college scholarship funds. The critics responded to his singing with warmth, noting that time had not obliterated the sweetness of his tones nor his mastery of expression.

MARIAN ANDERSON

"The Lady from Philadelphia," Marian Anderson (b. 1902) became the World's leading concert contralto in the twentieth century and the best-known Negro singer in the history of music. She studied music as a child with a Negro teacher, Mary Patterson, who refused to accept a fee, and sang in the choir of the local Union Baptist Church. Encouraged by her family and friends, she began giving recitals in Negro churches, schools, and YMCA halls when barely in her teens. Roland Hayes took an interest in her career and appeared with her in cantatas and oratorios as early as 1916. Her church invested in the future of their gifted young singer by setting up a trust fund to pay for advanced study with the Italian voice teacher Giuseppe Boghetti. In 1924 Anderson's career got off to an auspicious beginning when she won first prize over three hundred contestants in a competition conducted by the New York Philharmonic-Symphony at Lewisohn Stadium. But her recitals at Town Hall in New York and at Witherspoon Hall in Philadelphia received little attention from the press. Upon the advice of her management, Anderson went to Europe to travel and study, drawing upon a Julius Rosenwald Fellowship that she received in 1929.

Marian Anderson's debut recital in Berlin in 1933 was followed by two years of successful concertizing in the leading capitals of Europe. At Salzburg in August, 1935, an event took place which decided her future, when she sang a recital before a gathering of the most eminent musicians in the world. As customary, she sang the conventional Bach and Schubert, and ended the program with a group of Negro spirituals. Vincent Sheean wrote later about the audience's response in his book *Between the Thunder and the Sun* (1943):

At the end of the [last] spiritual, there was no applause at all—a silence instinctive, natural, and intense, so that you were afraid to breathe. What Anderson had done was something outside the limits of classical or romantic music: she frightened us with the conception, in musical terms, of course, but outside the normal limits, of a mighty suffering.[1]

The illustrious Toscanini, who was among those present, declared, "A voice such as this comes once in a hundred years." Similar praise came from the Finnish composer Jan Sibelius. In Paris, Anderson was taken under the expert management of Sol Hurok, and by 1941, she was one of the ten highest-paid concert artists in the United States.

Anderson's career included many notable events, not all of them pleasant. In 1939 the Daughters of the American Revolution in Washington, D. C., refused her permission to sing in Constitution Hall because of her color. Public protest over the incident grew to such proportions that it reached the White House, and Secretary of the Interior Harold Ickes made arrangements for the great contralto to sing in an open-air concert on the steps of the Lincoln Memorial. It was a chilly Easter Sunday morning when Anderson calmly stepped before the microphone and began to sing to the audience of over 75,000 persons overflowing the green in front of the memorial. The occasion was unforgettable for both the singer and those who heard her. Many Americans reacted in protest to the snub given to Marian Anderson. Mrs. Franklin Delano Roosevelt, wife of the president, withdrew her membership from the DAR; leading performers canceled their appearances at Constitution Hall. Anderson's quiet dignity and tremendous talent brought down the color barriers, and Constitution Hall later opened its doors to all without regard to race or color. Anderson herself sang there several times.

In 1939 Marian Anderson received the Spingarn Medal, and in 1940 she was awarded the Bok Medal and $10,000 by Philadelphia for "outstanding citizenship and meritorious achievement." Miss Anderson used the money to establish the Marian Anderson Award for talented but needy young singers. Marian Anderson broke down another color barrier in 1955 when she became the first Negro to appear with the Metropolitan Opera Company; she sang the role of Ulrica in Verdi's *Un Ballo in maschera* (A Masked Ball). In 1957 she traveled 39,000 miles as

[1] Quoted in Lindsay Patterson, ed., "The Negro in Music and Art," in *The International Library of Negro Life and History* (New York, 1967), p. 158.

a good-will ambassador through Asia under the auspices of the State Department and ANTA (the American National Theater and Academy). Other honors and awards include honorary doctorates in music and humane letters, appointment as a delegate to the Thirteenth General Assembly of the United Nations, the Order of African Liberation of the Republic of Liberia, and decorations by the governments of France, Finland, Haiti, Japan, the Philippines, and Sweden.

OTHER ARTISTS

Gifted Paul Robeson (b. 1898), a graduate of Rutgers University, won distinction both as a singer and an actor. An active figure of the black-renaissance movement, he sang in Negro musical comedies of the early 1920s and appeared in plays. When he gave his first recital in 1925 to a packed house at the Greenwich Village Theater in New York, he had had no vocal training, but the success of the concert assured him of a promising career as a baritone. In 1926 Robeson repeated his success in a Town Hall concert. In the following years Robeson performed in plays (notably Shakespeare's *Othello*) and concertized widely in the United States and in Europe. He specialized in singing Negro songs—the folksongs and composed songs of Negroes. After his much-acclaimed appearance in *Show Boat* (1928, 1930, 1932), Robeson added the popular *Old Man River* to his recital repertory. His oft-made comment about his choice of song materials was, "I sing the Negro songs because they suit my voice and suit me." By 1941 Robeson was, along with Anderson, among the top ten concert musicians in the United States.

Another renowned black concert artist of this period was Dorothy Maynor (b. 1910), a soprano whose early musical training was received in her father's Methodist church at Greensboro, North Carolina. Maynor's talent was first discovered by R. Nathaniel Dett at the Hampton Institute, from which she was graduated in 1933. She studied further at the Westminster Choir School in Princeton, New Jersey, and with private teachers. After singing at a concert during the 1939 Berkshire Music Festival, Maynor was warmly praised by Koussevitsky, conductor of the

Boston Symphony; his patronage helped to place her with top management. She concertized extensively in the United States and abroad and appeared with the leading symphony orchestras of the nation. Among the several awards she received for outstanding achievement were the Town Hall Endowment Series Award and the first Alumni Award of Hampton Institute. After retirement, Dorothy Maynor was to share her talent and experience with the children of Harlem by founding the Harlem School of the Arts (1966), offering courses in music theory, performance, drama, painting, and the dance.

For each of the four black singers who achieved world renown during the black-renaissance period there were several who moved on a lower plane, although they possessed much talent and had excellent training. Then, as now, there was room at the top only for a few, and black Americans were well represented among the few. On the other hand, there was a demand, as there always will be, for persons to sing the supporting roles in large opera companies or the leading roles in small companies, to present recitals away from New York, to conduct choruses and instrumental groups in the theater pits, and to teach and coach those aspiring to careers in music.

Todd Duncan (b. 1903), baritone, first attracted the attention of the critics in 1935 when he created the role of Porgy in Gershwin's folk opera *Porgy and Bess*. A graduate of Butler University in Indianapolis, Indiana (1925), and the holder of a Master of Arts degree from Columbia University (1930), Duncan came to the stage with considerable experience in concert singing. In 1934 he had appeared in Mascagni's *Cavalleria Rusticana* in New York; later he was to sing in the stage works *The Sun Never Sets* at the Drury Lane Theatre in London (1938) and *Cabin in the Sky* in New York (1940). Duncan's performance in *Porgy and Bess*, with Anne Brown as Bess, got the opera off to an impressive start. Its first successful run on Broadway of 124 performances was followed by even more successful revivals in 1942 and in 1953. Duncan also toured as a concert singer and appeared with major symphony orchestras. Among the distinctions he received were the Medal of Honor and Merit from Haiti, the Critics Award, and honorary doctorates in music from Valparaiso University and Central States College (Ohio). In 1931 Duncan began a teaching career at Howard University which, however, allowed him to continue with his musical activities.

In 1945 Duncan was responsible for another milestone in the history of Negro music when he became the first black male singer to appear with a major opera company. The company was the New York City Opera under the direction of Laszlo Halasz, and the operas were Leoncavallo's *Pagliacci* and Bizet's *Carmen*. Hungarian-born conductor Halasz is credited with having developed the City Opera into one of the finest in the nation during his directorship (1943–51). His policy of relying on the basic worth of the operas he produced to attract audiences rather than on the fame of established opera stars proved to be advantageous for hopeful Negro aspirants in the field of opera. Halasz was interested in talent without regard to race or color; among the gifted young Negroes that he brought into the company, in addition to Duncan, were Camilla Williams, Lawrence Winters, and Margaret Tynes. Under Halasz's direction the New York City Opera was the first major company, and the only one as of 1970, to produce an opera written by a Negro (a point to which we shall return).

In the field of opera, the coloratura Lillian Evanti made music history in the late 1920s by becoming the first American Negro to sing operatic roles in Europe. A graduate of Howard University, Evanti studied voice abroad and made her operatic debut in *Lakmé* by Delibes with the Nice Opera Company. During her years in Europe she also appeared in Verdi's *La Traviata* and *Rigoletto*, in Donizetti's *Lucia di Lammermoor*, and in Gounod's *Roméo et Juliette*. Upon her return to the United States, Evanti entered the concert field, touring extensively and appearing with symphony orchestras.

In 1933 Caterina Jarboro (b. 1903), a singer from Wilmington, North Carolina, who had studied voice in Paris and Milan, became the first Negro to perform with a major opera company in the United States when she sang the title role of Verdi's opera *Aïda* with the Chicago Opera Company. It was not her first appearance as Aïda, however, for she had sung this and other parts in Europe for three years before returning to the United States. Jarboro made her debut in 1930 as Aïda at the Puccini Opera House in Milan, Italy.

One of the most versatile black concert singers of the period was Jules Bledsoe (1899–1943), a native of Waco, Texas, and a graduate of Bishop College in Marshall, Texas. In 1919 Bledsoe went to New York to prepare for a career in medicine, but was persuaded by friends who heard his fine singing to study voice. His debut recital at Aeolian Hall in 1924 was impressive enough to obtain for him the management of Sol Hurok, one of the giants in the concert-management field. Bledsoe's career included tours of the United States and Europe as a concert baritone, appearances in dramatic works at home and abroad—such as Frank Harling's opera *Deep River* (1926), Gruenberg's opera *The Emperor Jones*, Verdi's *Aïda*, and Jerome Kern's musical comedy *Show Boat*—and appearances with major symphony orchestras singing *The Creation,* an orchestral setting by Louis Gruenberg of James Weldon Johnson's long dramatic poem.

Among other concert artists of the period who won national acclaim were four sopranos. Abbie Mitchell (1884–1960) studied voice with Harry T. Burleigh and Emilia Serrano in New York, and later in Paris with private teachers. Her active career included concert tours and performances in musical comedies, particularly in those directed by her husband, Will Marion Cook. Florence Cole Talbert began her music training at the University of California, then moved to Chicago where she was graduated from Chicago Musical College. She toured extensively in the United States and Europe, winning favorable press notices everywhere for her voice, "which she used with consummate skill." Anne Brown was trained at the Juilliard Institute. Her voice so impressed George Gershwin that he wrote the role of Bess, in his opera *Porgy and Bess,* especially for her. Brown left the stage in 1942 to begin a concert career that included appearances with leading symphony orchestras as well as recitals. Etta Moten was a music and dramatic-arts graduate of the University of Kansas. She sang in musical comedies and stage works (including the part of Bess) and concertized widely.

The instrumentalists of the period included pianist Hazel Harrison, who had begun her career in the first decade of the century (see p. 306); Helen Hagan (1893–1964), a piano graduate of the School of Music at Yale University; pianist A. Augustus Lawson, a graduate of Fisk; and violinist Louis Vaughn Jones (b. 1893), a graduate of the New England Conservatory. Hagan won two awards while at Yale, the Lockwood Scholarship and the Samuels

Simmons Sanford Fellowship, which provided for two year's study abroad. The start of the war forced her to come back to the United States, but she later returned to France where she played for the soldiers. After a debut recital at Aeolian Hall in New York, Hagan concertized widely. Lawson combined playing with teaching at Hartford, Connecticut, where he maintained a studio. Jones studied violin in Paris for two years after completing his service with the armed forces, and remained there for five more years, playing in a jazz orchestra. Upon returning to the United States in 1929, he was active as a concert violinist for two years, then combined playing with teaching at Howard University.

A number of the active musicians combined teaching (either privately or as the faculty member of a Negro college) with performance. The cellist Leonard Jeter (1881–1970) of New York was active for several years as a concert player, although his primary activity was in the field of chamber and orchestral music.

Melville Charlton (b. 1883), organist and composer, graduated from the City College of the City University of New York and received his musical training at the National Conservatory of Music. He first served as an organist at the St. Philip's Episcopal Church; later he served at the religious school of the fashionable Temple Emanu-El and at Union Theological Seminary. In 1915 Charlton was admitted to the American Guild of Organists as an associate member. In addition to winning recognition as an organist, Charlton has composed piano and organ pieces. In 1930 Howard University conferred upon him an honorary doctorate in music.

Kemper Harreld (b. 1885), violinist and music educator, received his musical training at Chicago Musical College and the Stern Conservatory of Music in Berlin, Germany. He was one of the founders of the National Association of Negro Musicians in 1919. Harreld taught in Atlanta, establishing the music department at Morehouse College in 1911 and serving also at Spellman College (beginning 1927). He successfully combined teaching with his activity as a violinist and choral conductor. The concerts of his college choruses and orchestra won national attention for their excellence. As a teacher he inspired many college generations of students to study music and played a role in developing concert artists and a number of music educators who taught in southern Negro colleges. One of his protégés, Mattiwilda Dobbs, became an international figure in the field of opera.

Among the concert artists of the time were two former members of the Hayes Trio, organized in 1917 by Roland Hayes and composed of himself, baritone William Richardson, and pianist William Lawrence. At a later time Lawrence, who was trained at the New England Conservatory of Music and Boston University, served as an accompanist for Hayes in both the United States and in Europe. His highly musical, sympathetic accompaniments received critical acclaim, as did his pianism, for he customarily played a group of solos on Hayes's recitals. Richardson, who studied voice privately in Boston, concertized widely during the 20s and 30s in the United States and the West Indies as a soloist and also as a singer-lecturer in company with Maude Cuney-Hare, pianist-lecturer on Negro music.

PROFESSIONAL CHORUSES

After World War I there developed a widespread interest in choral music, undoubtedly because Americans had gotten into the habit of singing at the many patriotic assemblies and community meetings that had sprouted during the war. On the national level, professional choruses were organized, and choral groups that had been dormant were revived. The performance of oratorios and other large choral works during the concert season gradually became as common as the performance of instrumental works. This renewed interest in choral singing reflected itself also in the black communities of the nation. To be sure, Negroes traditionally were inclined toward group singing, but more for its religious or recreational value than for the possibilities it afforded as a professional calling. The Negro singing groups that toured the country in emulation of the Fisk Jubilee Singers and the Hampton Singers were ensembles, not choruses; rarely did they include more than eight or ten persons. It was during the black renaissance that the professional all-black chorus appeared, for the first time, to take its place on the concert stage along with black soloists, instrumentalists, and ensembles. The pioneering figures in the organizational movement were Hall Johnson and Eva Jessye.

HALL JOHNSON

In 1933 the music critic of the *New York Herald Tribune* noted in his review of a concert by the Hall Johnson Choir that the "clarity of enunciation, not overly-polished, essentially racial quality of tone were further assets in a performance whose apparent artlessness and spontaneity, individual and collective gusto were as marked as in previous appearances" (March 18, 1933). The critic considered it a tribute to the choral director's leadership that the forty-voice choir had been able "to preserve the necessary air of unsophistication" in singing the program of Negro music. To be sure, this was no accident, for Hall Johnson (1888–1970), possessed strong opinions about how Negro folksongs should be sung. He always retained in his memory how the Negroes (many of them ex-slaves) sang during his childhood in Athens, Georgia—in his father's Methodist church, in the fields, along the road, and in the homes as they went about their work. As he recalled it, they "sang with every breath!" It was this kind of sound that he wanted to recreate with his professional group, before the world would have forgotten what a glorious sound it had been. He knew exactly what he wanted to preserve:

> . . . The conscious and intentional *alterations* of *pitch* often made. . . . The unconscious, but amazing and bewildering *counterpoint* produced by so many voices in *individual improvisation.* . . . The *absolute insistence* upon the pulsing, *overall rhythm,* combining many varying subordinate rhythms.

Hall Johnson's musical training was similar to that of other black professional musicians of his time. As a child he studied piano with his older sister, who had been taught by Cousin Jim, the established town musician. No one knew who had taught his mother's cousin, who was the music teacher for most of the young Negroes in town. Johnson's mother, who had been a slave until she was eight years old, possessed a beautiful voice; she and her mother, who lived with the Johnsons, sang at all times—according to Johnson, "whenever they were not talking." Johnson's formal training was acquired in several places—Knox

Institute (Georgia), Atlanta University, Allen University (South Carolina), and the Hahn School of Music—for the father's responsibilities as a presiding elder in the A. M. E. Church and, later, as a college president kept the family on the move. After graduation from college, Johnson attended the University of Pennsylvania, the Institute of Musical Art, and, in later years, the University of Southern California.

When Johnson arrived at New York in 1914, he had done some graduate study and was a violinist. He was soon drawn into the Clef Club orbit, playing with Jim Europe's band. He remained with the band a number of years, including its period of touring with the dancers Vernon and Irene Castle. In 1921 he joined the orchestra of the *Shuffle Along* show, playing first the violin, then the viola. During all these years Johnson was aware that his interest lay in choral music, not orchestral music. Finally in 1925, he gathered together a small band of eight singers who believed, like him, in the necessity for preserving the integrity of the Negro spiritual. By the time of its first recital, the group's number had been increased to twenty.

The Hall Johnson Choir concerts were warmly received by the public and by critics, and the group soon found itself in great demand for concerts and for theater and radio appearances. In 1928 the choir recorded for the RCA Victor Company. Two years later Hall Johnson was appointed choral director for the production of *The Green Pastures*, a drama written by white playwright Marc Connelly and produced on Broadway. Hailed by a New York critic as "one of the loftiest achievements of the American Theater," the play nevertheless presented rather primitive conceptions about the black man's views of the Book of Genesis in the Bible. But it provided jobs for ninety-five black actors and singers and included some challenging roles and much glorious singing. Under Johnson's direction the "Celestial Choir" sang spirituals that he had arranged throughout the play, either off stage or in the orchestra pit.

In 1933 Hall Johnson's folk play, *Run Little Chillun*, was staged on Broadway for a run of 126 performances. The outstanding quality of the play, which was Johnson's first dramatic attempt, was its music, particularly in two spectacular scenes—a revival meeting and a pagan religious orgy. *Run Little Chillun* was revived in 1935 at Los Angeles with notable success. The play represented a milestone in the history of Negro folk opera, in that it was the only one of the successful stage works of the time (i.e. *Four Saints, Porgy and Bess, The Green Pastures, The Emperor Jones*) to be written by a black man. Warner Brothers' decision to film *The Green Pastures* in 1936 took the Hall Johnson Choir to Hollywood. While he was there, Johnson worked with his group in other motion pictures, including *Lost Horizons,* and organized the Negro Festival Chorus of Los Angeles in 1941. Back in New York in 1946 Johnson organized the Festival Chorus of New York City. In 1951 the State Department chose the Hall Johnson Choir to represent the United States at the International Festival of Fine Arts in Berlin. In addition to his folk play, Johnson's works include *Son of Man,* an Easter cantata; *Fi-Yer,* an operetta; *The Green Pastures Spirituals;* and a large number of art songs and spiritual arrangements, the best known of which were *Honor, Honor, Ride On, King Jesus,* and the *Crucifixion.* Hall Johnson received many awards for achievement, including the Holstein Prizes for composition (1925, 1927), the Harmon Award (1931), a citation from the City of New York (1954), and an honorary doctorate in music from the Philadelphia Academy of Music.

EVA JESSYE

Eva Jessye (b. 1895), a native of Coffeyville, Kansas, received her first musical training at Western University (Kansas) and later attended Langston University (Oklahoma). Even as a child Jessye was interested in ensemble singing; she organized her first group, a girls' quartet, at the age of twelve. Although her parents were not trained musicians, they encouraged her interest in music. Her father was somewhat of a local celebrity because of his ability to produce two tones simultaneously (a novel feat accomplished by expert manipulation of the vocal cords) and, consequently, to sing songs consisting of successive thirds instead of the normal single tones. Both parents accepted all kinds of music in the home—roustabout songs and blues as well as spirituals. One of the highlights of her early years was the visit of Will Marion Cook and his musical show to tiny Coffeyville. An emergency arose, and Jessye, although only twelve, was called upon to help copy some music for the use of the orchestra. Cook encouraged the young copyist, whom he called his "little protégé," to continue with her music studies. Through secondary school and college, Jessye concentrated her attention on choral music and music theory, singing in choirs and ensembles. After graduation from college in 1916, she taught music first in the public schools of Oklahoma, then at Morgan College (Maryland). Later in life she studied with Cook and with the white music-theorist Percy Goetschius.

When Jessye went to New York about 1922, she found it difficult as a newcomer to gain a foothold in the music world. Finally, in desperation, she applied for a position as a dietician in a hospital. Her prospective employer, a doctor, came to her humble apartment to interview her, explaining that he could not hire "just anyone" to come into the kitchen of the hospital. He noticed that Jessye had been writing music when he entered and inquired if she were a musician. Upon her affirmative answer, he wanted to know why she was not following her profession. Flippantly Jessye responded, "Because I have to eat." His answer to that came slowly, but firmly, "I don't care what you have to do! Whatever your profession is, if you have been trained in it and you know what you are doing, stick with it and make it pay." Jessye never forgot the man's statement. It marked a turning point in her life and inspired her to become the first Negro woman (and the only one as of 1970) to win international distinction as a director of a professional choral group.

By 1926 Eva Jessye was actively involved in the musical life of the city, appearing regularly with her singers (first named the Original Dixie Jubilee Singers, then the Eva Jessye Choir) on the "Major Bowes Family Radio Hour," the "General Motors Hour," and other radio programs. Her growing reputation led to commissions for organizing ensembles and quartets to sing on special radio programs in New York and in London and in the field of commercial advertisement. In 1929, Jessye was called to Hollywood to train a choir to sing in the King Vidor film *Hallelujah*, which had an all-black cast. Four years later she was asked to be the choral director for the production of Thomson's *Four Saints in Three Acts*. The work was an "artistic as well as dramatic event." The words of the libretto (written by Gertrude Stein) made little surface sense, but the music was melodious and "maintained the mood of solemn nonsense," according to Edith Isaacs, author of *The Negro in the American Theater*. The setting for the staging consisted of oil cloth, gauze, and cellophane; the costumes were made of lace and simulated gold cloth. The lead singer, Edward Matthews, carried off his role of St. Ignatius with just the right "steady, solemnly comic attitude and movement," and every member of the cast shared with him the high honors accorded the performance.

In 1935 Gershwin selected Jessye to serve as choral director for his first production of *Porgy and Bess*. Jessye was to be permanently associated with the Thomson and Gershwin works through all of the Broadway productions and the many revivals in the succeeding years. *Porgy and Bess*, in particular, enjoyed lasting popularity, being produced in twenty-six countries of the world and being revived again and again in the United States, in both its original form and in abridged concert versions. The critics heaped praises on the "big, beautiful voices and the ensemble singing [that] made you want to dance or cry, depending on the purpose," and on the "high quality of musicianship, painstaking discipline, and showmanship." Always singled out for special praise were such choruses as *Oh, I Can't Sit Down*, the picnic song of the folk of Catfish Row; *Gone, Gone, Gone*, a mourning song; *It Ain't Necessarily So*, with Sportin' Life as soloist; the Street Vendors scene; and *Oh, Lawd, I'm on My Way*, the rousing finale.

For Jessye, the ideal size for a professional touring choir was sixteen or twenty singers, all of them soloists who could be featured in the special numbers used to add variety to the program. The singers held jobs from which they could take leaves in order to tour, or they augmented their salaries by working in such other music occupations as teaching and coaching privately or copying music. The repertory staples of the choir were numbers from *Porgy and Bess*, of course, and the folk music and composed music of Negro composers. Jessye's favorite composers were always well represented—Will Marion Cook, J. Rosamond Johnson, Hall Johnson, and John Work. In addition, she herself arranged many of the songs sung by her groups over the years. Jessye's published collections include *My Spirituals* (1927); *The Life of Christ in Negro Spirituals* (1931); *Paradise Lost and Regained*, the John Milton work set in a framework of Negro songs (1934); and *The Chronicle of Job* (1936), a folk drama. Honors given to Eva Jessye include an honorary Master of Arts from Wilberforce University (Ohio) and an honorary doctorate from Allen University (South Carolina).

COMMUNITY ORGANIZATIONS AND COLLEGE GROUPS

In black communities of cities and towns over the country, Negroes continued to sing together in community and church choral societies, and a number of new organizations were started during the 1920s. In Washington, D. C., the Coleridge-Taylor Society, which had been disbanded upon the death of its leaders, was revived in 1921 under the directorship of Roy Wilford Tibbs, an organist and conductor. Tibbs and his pianist-associates, Mary Europe (sister of James Europe) and Van Whitted, all were music teachers at Howard University. Chicago had two well-known groups: the eighty-voice Mundy Choristers was under the direction of James Mundy, a voice teacher and singer; the Choral Study Club was directed by Pedro Tinsley and assisted by pianists Gertrude Jackson Smith and Pelagie Blair. Among other nationally known organizations were the Harry T. Burleigh Association of Terre Haute, Indiana, and the Coleridge-Taylor Society of the state of Washington.

In New Orleans, the United Choirs sponsored periodic songfests for their Negro fellow citizens. In other cities also, community folksong groups were active. But the most vigorous programs of community singing were promoted by a single person, E. Azalia Hackley (d. 1922), a Negro soprano from Philadelphia. After retiring from a concert career, she traveled throughout the country holding "Folksong Festivals," where she taught black communities to sing and appreciate Negro folksongs. During the five years that she conducted the program, she succeeded in visiting all of the leading cities of the nation. In Baltimore, a large community chorus gave concerts in association with the city-sponsored Baltimore City Colored Orchestra under the leadership of W. Llewellyn Wilson. A new organization, the Gilbert Anderson Memorial Symphony Orchestra, came into being during the 1930s in the Philadelphia area as a result of the merger of the Camden Negro Symphony (organized in 1912) and the Philadelphia Anderson Orchestra (organized in 1913). In Boston, it was the Victorian Concert Orchestra, founded and managed by Charles Sullivan, that made a name for itself; in Nebraska the Desdunes Band, led by Dan Desdunes of New Orleans, played for many of the civic events in the state.

With regard to choral music, professional choirs and ensembles dominated the concert world, although concerts by some of the established community organizations were not infrequent. There was a third kind of choral group, however, that more and more became an important part of the concert world beginning in the 1920s: the Negro college choir. As we have seen, the Hampton Institute Choir under R. Nathaniel Dett, its first Negro director, gave concerts in the major churches and concert halls of the nation and toured Europe in 1930. Upon Dett's resignation in 1933, Clarence Cameron White took over direction of the choir, and the group continued its vigorous concert activity. The sixty-voice Fisk University Choir (directed by white musician Ray Francis Brown during the 30s) made national tours annually, as did the Tuskegee Institute Choir under the direction of William L. Dawson, Negro music director at Tuskegee. In 1932 the Tuskegee Choir even included an appearance at New York's Radio City Music Hall on its tour. Among the other Negro institutions that sent out touring choral groups with Negro directors were Morehouse College (Georgia), Howard University (Washington, D. C.), Wilberforce University (Ohio), Virginia State College, Shaw University (North Carolina), and Claflin University (South Carolina). The musical activities of the college groups generally included radio broadcasts as well as recitals, and frequently included appearances at the White House. The Hampton Choir's activity in Paris in 1930 included making recordings for the Pathé Talking-Picture Company.

HARLEM AND THE BLACK RENAISSANCE

Although the renaissance movement was national in its scope, its center was Harlem. The area was both populous and prosperous. The heavy migration of blacks from the South during the war years had brought thousands into Harlem, and this population was augmented by a large influx of black people from the West Indies. The war industries had provided Harlemites with good jobs, so people had money to spend. Musicians fared well under the circumstances, particularly entertainers, but also concert artists. As in the larger world, the smaller world of Harlem maintained a color line. Such exclusive night clubs as the Cotton Club on Lenox Avenue and Connie's Inn on 135th Street catered to whites, although the performers in the shows were all Negroes, and among the special attractions were the jazz bands of Duke Ellington and Cab Calloway. Most of the small night clubs that were frequented by both whites and blacks, or blacks only, were concentrated on 133rd Street between Lenox and Seventh Avenues and nearby.

Edmond's Cellar, where blues singer Ethel Waters obtained her first Harlem club job, was typical of the small clubs patronized by blacks. Its band consisted of a drummer, pianist, and guitarist. The entertainers included singers and dancer-singers, who worked long hours—from nine at night until eight or nine the next morning. Although the entertainers appeared only three or four times during these hours, each appearance lasted for as long as the singer or dancer could keep the attention of the patrons. The patrons in places like Edmond's listened politely to the popular ballads of the day, but most of all they wanted to hear the blues. And for music to dance to, they wanted either lively "hot" music or the slow "gut bucket" kind.

Larger clubs maintained four- or five-piece bands, entertainers, and often singing-and-dancing waiters. The bands, which included saxophones, clarinets, and basses along with the ubiquitous piano, drum, and guitar or banjo, played improvised jazz for the patrons' dancing (few of the players were music readers) and, for the singers, mostly blues, but also ballads requested by patrons. It was the small Harlem club that served as a place where white and black jazz musicians could play together in jam sessions. Whites and blacks also mixed at rent parties, where music was furnished by a drum-piano-saxophone trio, or most often simply by a pianist. The particularly exotic attraction in Harlem was the Savoy Ballroom, built in 1926, where white and black danced to the music of the best jazz bands of the nation. There, one Negro dance after the other was invented—the lindy, black bottom, shimmy, truckin', snake hips, Susie Q—which later moved downtown and into the white world. The Charleston, however, originated in a small night club. James P. Johnson wrote music to go with the dance and introduced it on Broadway in one of his musical comedies, *Runnin' Wild*. Whites joined the black audiences in Harlem's theaters, notably the Lincoln and the Lafayette, to watch Negro vaudeville shows, plays, and musical comedies.

Such books as Carl Van Vechten's *Nigger Heaven* contributed to the growing interest on the part of whites in Harlem. To them it was an exotic place where everywhere there seemed to be gaiety and the sound of good jazz. A small section of Harlem became "a vivid and glorified night spot." Harlem was also, however, the gathering place of the intellectuals, white and black, who sparked the renaissance movement. Some of their adventures were as exotic, in effect, as was the entertainment of Harlem. The black millionairess A'Lelia Walker gave soirées, for example, in her mansion on 136th Street, where Negro intellectuals mixed with white society and came into contact with publishers, critics, and others who helped them in advancing their careers.

It is significant that the Walker mansion, enlarged by the addition of a back-adjoining brownstone building on 135th Street, later became the site of a branch of the New York Public Library that houses the most famous collection of books on the black man in the country. The circulating library of the branch was named the Countee Cullen Branch after the black-renaissance poet; the reference library was called the Schomburg Collection of Negro Literature and History after Arthur Schomburg, who came to New York from Puerto Rico in 1891 at the age of seventeen and amassed a huge collection of books on blacks for his own pleasure. In 1926 the Carnegie Corporation of New York purchased Schomburg's rare collection and presented it to the New York Public Library. Schomburg was appointed the first curator of the collection.

BLACK MUSICAL COMEDIES ON BROADWAY

When *Shuffle Along* opened at the Sixty-third Street Theatre on May 23, 1921, the show made theatrical history. It was the first all-black show to appear on Broadway since the last of the famed Walker and Williams shows more than ten years earlier, and it created a vogue for Negro shows that lasted through the depression years. As we have seen, the musical score of the show was written by Eubie Blake, the lyrics by Noble Sissle, and the book by Flournoy Miller and Aubrey Lyles. It was Jim Europe who brought the four men together to collaborate on a musical which would return Negro shows to Broadway. The show was produced with limited funds, which barely allowed the performers to present two-week runs at the Howard Theatre (Negro) in Washington and the Dunbar Theatre (Negro) in Philadelphia before opening up at the old and previously empty Broadway house. *Shuffle Along* was an immediate success. According to James Weldon Johnson in *Black Manhattan:*

> Within a few weeks *Shuffle Along* made the 63rd Street Theater one of the best-known houses in town and made it necessary for the Traffic Department to declare 63rd Street a one-way thoroughfare.

The glorious singing and exhilarating dancing delighted both critics and audiences. Blake led the orchestra in the pit, which included among its players Hall Johnson, as we have noted, and the oboist William Grant Still (not yet famous at that time). The hit songs of the show set all of New York to humming, then went around the world—such songs as *Shuffle Along, Love Will Find a Way, In Honeysuckle Time, Bandana Days, The Gypsy Blues*, and *I'm Just Wild About Harry*. The latter was revived to become a campaign song for Harry Truman in the 1948 presidential election. *Shuffle Along* brought a "different" kind of musical to Broadway, a Harlem folk show in which no concessions were made to white taste or to theater clichés. It was funny (or sometimes sentimental), fast-moving, and melodious. Several persons in the show later achieved stardom and fame; among them, Josephine Baker, Caterina Jarboro, Florence Mills, and Paul Robeson.

For Eubie Blake the show was the beginning of a new career. The musician, noted all along the eastern seaboard for his rag piano, had aspired to write musical comedies since the time he first heard the operettas of Leslie Stuart, Franz Lehar, and Victor

Herbert in the early 1900s. His first venture, along with lyricist Sissle, into the field of popular music was a song, *It's All Your Fault*, made popular by Sophie Tucker, who had a reputation among black song writers for wanting to give them a helping hand. Encouraged by the reception given to *Shuffle Along*, Blake went on to write scores for other musicals: *The Chocolate Dandies* (1924); *Blackbirds of 1930;* a new edition of *Shuffle Along* (1932); and *Swing It* (1937). Among the memorable songs of these shows were *Dixie Moon, Loving You the Way I Do,* and *Memories of You.* During the period Blake and Sissle also wrote prolifically for shows with white casts; for example, the first song featured by the celebrated white actors Gertrude Lawrence and Noel Coward as a team, *You Were Meant For Me.* In later years Blake and Sissle collaborated on the music for Will Morrissey's *Follies Bergere* and Irvin C. Miller's *Brown-Skin Models of 1954.*

During World War II Blake worked as a musical conductor for the USO Hospital Unit, touring the United States for five years to play for soldiers in USO sponsored shows. After retiring from an active musical career, Blake decided to take up again the study of music and attended New York University, where he completed the Schillinger System of Composition at the age of sixty-six. By this time Blake was a legend in his own lifetime. The honors came swiftly: a 1965 Town Hall concert, "Sissle & Blake," sponsored by ASCAP in honor of their fifty years of contributions to show music; a gala at the Brooklyn Academy of Music in 1965, *Rhythm of America,* starring Blake and Sissle; and the unveiling of a bronze bust of Blake by sculptress Estella Wright in 1967, placed in the Museum of the City of New York.

In addition to the Blake and Sissle musicals, other all-black shows on Broadway were *Put and Take* (1921; music: Perry Bradford, Tim Brymn, Spencer Williams); *Strut Miss Lizzie* (1922; Creamer and Layton); *Liza* (1923; Maceo Pinkard); *Plantation Days* (1923 in London; James P. Johnson); *This and That* (1922; Luckey Roberts); *From Dixie to Broadway* (1924; Will Vodery); *Runnin' Wild* (1924; James P. Johnson); *Rang Tang* (1927; Ford Dabney); *Keep Shuffling* (1928; Fats Waller); *Hot Chocolates* (1929; Fats Waller); and *Brown Buddies* (Joe Jordan). Such productions as Lew Leslie's successive *Blackbirds* shows and *Plantation Revues* involved the collaboration of a number of black song writers. According to Eubie Blake, there were so many all-Negro shows on Broadway during the 1920s that two white song writers wrote a song entitled *Broadway's Getting Darker Every Year*. The depression brought an end to the Negro musical on Broadway; as we have seen, the shows of the 30s that had all-black casts were written by whites, except for Hall Johnson's *Run Little Chillun*.

SPECIAL CONCERTS AND FESTIVALS

The period of the black renaissance witnessed a number of notable concerts in New York, some of which featured concert music of black composers or performers and some, entertainment music. In 1926, for example, the League of Composers presented a concert at Town Hall that included Jules Bledsoe singing a first performance of the Gruenberg setting of Johnson's *The Creation*. That same weekend, the International Composers' Guild included in a concert at Aeolian Hall the première of William Grant Still's symphonic work, *Darker America*. In 1928, a black composer of operas, Lawrence Freeman, produced his opera *Voodoo* at the 52nd Street Theatre.

During the decade of the 30s came the two John Henry Hammond productions at Carnegie Hall, "From Spirituals to Swing." Hammond's first production, which was presented on December 23, 1938, was dedicated to Bessie Smith. It consisted of seven sections: *Spirituals and Holy Roller Hymns*, *Soft Swing*, *Harmonica Playing*, *Blues*, *Boogie-Woogie Piano Playing*, *Early New Orleans Jazz*, and *Swing*. Recordings of African tribal music, made by the H. E. Tracy Expedition to the west coast of Africa, were played as an introduction to the program. The participants included Mitchell's Christian Singers and Sister Rosetta Tharpe singing gospel songs; and boogie-woogie pianists Albert Ammons, Lux Lewis, and Pete Johnson; clarinetist Sidney Bechet with his New Orleans Feetwarmers; blind blues-singer Sonny Terry and his harmonica; and Count Basie with a number of Kansas City bandsmen and blues singers.

A mammoth ASCAP Silver Jubilee Festival held at Carnegie Hall in October, 1939, lasted a week. The second night's concert was given over to Negro music, "from symphony to swing."

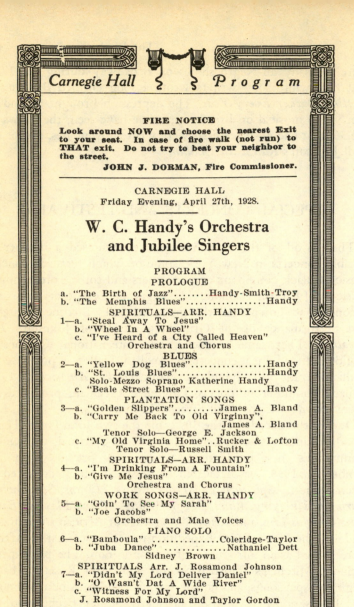

Program of a 1928 Carnegie Hall concert by W. C. Handy. (*Courtesy Mrs. W. C. Handy.*)

Program Continued

CHARACTER SONGS

8—a. "The Unbeliever",
                    Bert Williams-Smith-Bryan
   b. "Wouldn't That Be A Dream",
                              Hogan-Jordan
   Tom Fletcher
   Accompanist, Bernardin Brown

Intermission

Part Two

9—Cake Walk.........Featuring Mme. Robinson
   a. "Dark Town Is Out Tonight",
                          Will Marion Cook
   b. "Exhortation" ....Will Marion Cook
   Male Voices

NEGRO RHAPSODY

10—a. "Yamekraw"............James P. Johnson
   Orchestra
   Piano—Thomas (Fats) Waller

SOPRANO SOLO

11—a. "Spring Had Come" (Hiawatha),
                            Coleridge Taylor
   b. "Hear The Lamb A Cryin'"..H. T. Burleigh
   c. "Joshua Fit De Battle of Jericho",
                       Arr. Lawrence Brown
   Minnie Brown
   Accompanist—Andrades Lindsey

XYLOPHONE SOLO

12—"Maple Leaf Rag"...............Scott Joplin
   W. C. Handy, Jr.

SOPRANO SOLO

13—"Africa" ....Ford Dabney
   Josephine Hall

J. ROSAMOND JOHNSON

14—a. "African Drum Dance" No. 1,
                         J. Rosamond Johnson
   Piano Solo
   b. "Under The Bamboo Tree",
                         J. Rosamond Johnson
   Baritone Solo

JAZZ FINALE

15—a. "Shimmy Like My Sister Kate",
                           Clarence Williams
   Clarence Williams
   b. "I Ain't Got Nobody"....Spencer Williams
   Male Voices
   c. "I'm Feelin' Devilish"......Maceo Pinkard
   Orchestra
   d. "St. Louis Blues"...................Handy
   Organ Solo—Thomas (Fats) Waller
   Orchestra and Chorus

STEINWAY PIANO USED

Management: Robert Clairmont

W. C. Handy wrote in his autobiography about the elaborate preparations made for the performance and the eventful night. Handy, Burleigh, and Rosamond Johnson were appointed to work on securing the best Negro talent of the nation. The concert opened with the singing of Johnson's *Lift Every Voice and Sing* by a 350-voice chorus, accompanied by a symphony orchestra of seventy-five players under the direction of Joe Jordan. The next three numbers on the program were excerpts from symphonies conducted by the composers: *From Harlem* by James P. Johnson, *Sketches of the Deep South* by Charles L. Cooke, and *Afro-American Symphony* by William Grant Still. The second half of the program began with a minstrel show, which featured the popular songs of Negro composers from the days of the minstrel shows to the present, each song writer presenting his own famous compositions to the audience. The finale of the evening offered the chorus and orchestra in Cramer and Layton's song, *Way Down Yonder in New Orleans*, followed by a jazz medley played by the bands of Cab Calloway, Noble Sissle, Louis Armstrong, and Claude Hopkins.

Three great "fairs" took place during the period: the Century of Progress International Exposition at Chicago (1933–34); the Golden Gate International Exposition at San Francisco (1939–40); and the New York World's Fair "The World of Tomorrow" (1939–40). All three events involved black musicians—as consultants for the preparation of special programs, as composers, and as performers. Among the established musicians called upon to contribute either as consultants or composers were Will Marion Cook, Lawrence Freeman, Noble Sissle, Will Vodery, William Grant Still, and W. C. Handy. The Chicago committees gave special emphasis to the Negro pageant *O Sing a New Song* held at Soldiers Field in September, 1934. At San Francisco, the ASCAP-sponsored Festival of American Music held at Treasure Island in September, 1940, included the music of Shelton Brooks, W. C. Handy, and William Grant Still. During the New York World's Fair, Still's music quite literally permeated the air in the area of the main exhibit. Based on his showing in a competition, Still was given a commission by the Fair officials to compose the theme music to be played continuously in the Perisphere for the Theme Exhibit.

THE BLACK ENTERTAINMENT INDUSTRY AND THE FEDERAL ARTS PROJECTS

Despite these events the 1930s ushered in a period of gloom for the majority of black entertainers in the United States. Not all of the blame could be placed on the Great Depression. Two of the most important factors in the gradual disappearance of the once ubiquitous black entertainer were the movie and radio industries. Before the rise of the movie, and the sound film in particular, Americans depended upon the theater for entertainment—there they went to see operas, plays, vaudeville shows, or burlesque, depending upon their tastes. In 1900 there were approximately 5,000 theaters in the nation; by 1940 there were fewer than 200 theaters. It is to be remembered that Negroes owned or operated a large number of theaters, and that there were two or more Negro theaters in such places as New York, Chicago, Philadelphia, Atlanta, and Washington. D. C. Negro stock companies such as the Pekin and Lafayette companies, T.O.B.A., and similiar agencies assured black entertainers steady employment as long as theaters provided the chief source of entertainment for people.

In addition to the vaudeville circuit for touring performers, there were jobs available for local black musicians as theater musicians in accompanying acts of the touring companies and in playing during the showing of the silent movie films. Moreover, the revival of the old minstrel tradition of singing spirituals in the theater created employment for even more musicians. In this period, however, the singers sat in the orchestra pits along with the players and sang their spirituals between the acts of the shows or plays. But T.O.B.A. could not compete with the depression and the growing popularity of the "talkie" movie; it was destroyed by forces beyond the theaters' control. With it went the black entertainer industry.

In 1935 the government established the arts projects of the WPA (Works Progress Administration) to provide employment for the jobless in the fields of music, writing, the theater, and the fine arts. The music unit had as one of its special aims the employing of trained musicians in assignments that would allow them to preserve their skills. Instrumentalists were given assignments in bands and orchestras, singers were placed in choruses and opera groups, music teachers were given classes of children and adults to train. Musicians were also involved in the theater units. And composers of all kinds of music profited—first, because their assignments allowed them the hours necessary for composing; and second, because after their works were completed there were groups available to perform them. There were even jobs for the folksong collectors and persons interested in music research.

The government project was especially beneficial to Negroes. For the first time they were able to participate fully in all of the complex activities involved in stage productions—as actors, writers, directors, technicians, adapters, and producers. In essence, they were provided with the finest kind of apprenticeship for working in the theater arts. Many good things resulted from the program. The theater unit in Chicago produced two works, the *Swing Mikado* (a jazz version of the Gilbert and Sullivan operetta *The Mikado*) and *Swingin' the Dream* (a jazz adaptation of Shakespeare's *A Midsummer Night's Dream*), which created a vogue for "swinging the classics." This led to such later commercial productions as *The Hot Mikado* and *Carmen Jones* (based on Bizet's *Carmen*). The unit in Seattle produced a folk opera, *Natural Man*, based on the legend of John Henry, the "steel drivin' " railroad folk hero (see p. 246). In Los Angeles, Hall Johnson's *Run Little Chillun* was revived and played to enthusiastic audiences for almost a year. At New York, the WPA Theater also produced a musical about John Henry. Another production of the unit was Eubie Blake's *Swing It*.

CHAPTER XV

Composers: From Nationalists
to Experimentalists

After World War I the black composer began to come into his own. Through the 1920s and the depression of the 30s, established composers continued to write music, and new composers appeared on the scene. Most of the music written was performed at least once, and a surprising amount was published. To be sure, a large part of the music was functional, in the sense that it was written for a specific group or a specific occasion. For example, the directors of professional choruses and college choirs often wrote choral works in order to have something "new" to present to their audiences or to use in conjunction with a stage work. Singers arranged spirituals for their own recitals or asked composer-friends to write settings of admired poems for particular concerts. We have already observed how prolific were the composers who also directed orchestras and jazz bands. Even the composers of instrumental concert works wrote, in great part, for the use of their students or friends or themselves.

Black performers frequently found the traditional European repertory to be useless, for one special reason—they were performing primarily for black audiences, and they wanted to be able to communicate with the members of the audiences. Thus the singer sang spirituals or Negro folksongs or settings of poems about Negro life. The pianist or violinist played program music with titles that suggested Negro life and that made obvious use of folklike melodies and rhythms. The dance-music composer utilized boogie-woogie rhythms, the blues, and jazz because black dancers demanded these musical styles. Significantly, the black entertainer or concert artist discovered that when he sang or played for white audiences, they, too, wanted to hear Negro music. To them it was novel, exotic, poignant, moving, exhilarating —it had the very qualities that European music lacked.

THE NATIONALISTS

We have seen that the composers born in the post-Civil War years fall into the category of nationalists; for example, Harry T. Burleigh, Will Marion Cook, Clarence Cameron White, R. Nathaniel Dett, and J. Rosamond Johnson (see Chapter X). These composers were active through the successive decades after World War I, except for Burleigh, who published only one work in the 20s. It will be remembered that Burleigh and Cook were students of Dvořák, and that all of these men were greatly influenced by Dvořák and consequently were committed to the idea of employing the traditional European musical forms—the art song, the symphony, the march, and similar types—as the bases for their nationalist musical ideas. Even Scott Joplin, the "King of Ragtime," began by using march or quadrille forms as the basis for his instrumental compositions. Most of the composers born in the same generation as the pioneers, or in the next two or three generations, followed along similar paths. They used European forms and Negro folk-music idioms; occasionally, they wrote with disregard for the Negro elements.

Harry Lawrence Freeman (1869–1954) became known as a composer of operas. Born in Cleveland, Ohio, he settled permanently in New York. In the early part of the century he worked as a music director for several companies; among them, the Pekin Theatre Company of Chicago and the Cole and Johnson Brothers Company of New York. Five of the fourteen operas he composed between the years 1893 and 1930 were produced in either concert or stage version. His first opera, *The Martyr*, was produced at Denver, Colorado, in 1893; a second performance took place at New York's Carnegie Hall in 1947. Other productions included *The Tryst* in 1911 in New York; *Valdo* in 1906 in Cleveland; *Vendetta* in 1923 at the Lafayette Theater in Harlem; and, as we have seen, *Voodoo* in 1928. *Voodoo* was also performed over WCBS radio in an abridged version the same year. Best known of Freeman's other works were the ballet,

The Zulu King (1934); a symphonic poem, *The Slave;* two cantatas; and numerous songs. In 1930 he received the Harmon Award for excellence in composition.

Florence B. Price (1888–1953), a native of Little Rock, Arkansas, who settled permanently in Chicago, was the first Negro woman to win recognition as a composer. A graduate of the New England Conservatory of Music, where she studied with Chadwick and Converse, Price studied further at Chicago Musical College and the American Conservatory of Music in Chicago. In 1932 she earned the Wanamaker Award for a Symphony in E minor. Her other works include *Symphonic Tone Poem, Concert Overture on Negro Spirituals, Little Negro Dances* for chorus and orchestra, *Negro Folksongs in Counterpoint* for string quartet, and a number of solo concertos, organ works, and chamber music. In 1932 Price played one of her piano concertos with the Chicago Symphony Orchestra under the direction of Frederick Stock at Orchestra Hall in Chicago. Stock also performed her Symphony in E minor on several occasions.

The composer and arranger Charles L. Cooke (1891–1958) was born in Louisville, Kentucky. He was graduated from Chicago Musical College and received his master's and a doctoral degree in music from the same college. At one time Cooke had his own orchestra in Chicago, but he spent most of his career as a staff arranger for music publishing firms in Detroit and for RKO. Later he worked as a staff composer and arranger for Radio City Music Hall. He is best remembered for his musical scores *The Hot Mikado; Cabin in the Sky; Sons o' Fun; Banjo Eyes; Sadie Thompson;* and *Follow the Girls.* Two of his songs were quite popular at one time, *Blame It on the Blues* and *Loving You the Way I Do.* Cooke was also a composer of concert music; his *Sketches of the Deep South* was performed, as has been noted, in one of the ASCAP Silver Jubilee concerts in 1939.

Edward Boatner (b. 1898), singer and composer, concerned himself with the use of Negro folk-music materials from his childhood. Born in New Orleans, son of an itinerant minister, Boatner in his early travels across the country came into close contact with Negro folksinging and the singing of choirs in rural churches. After attending Western University (Kansas), Boatner studied further at the New England Conservatory, the Boston Conservatory, and privately. He taught at Samuel Houston and Wiley Colleges in Texas before opening a music studio in New York after World War I. Boatner's works include: *Freedom Suite* for orchestra and chorus; *Julius Sees Her,* a musical comedy; *Book of 30 Choral Afro-American Spirituals; Sixteen Solo Spirituals;* and a number of songs and spiritual arrangements. Leading concert singers such as Marian Anderson, Harry Burleigh, and Roland Hayes used his songs and spiritual arrangements. Among his best-known vocal pieces were *Oh, What a Beautiful City, Tramping, I Want Jesus to Walk with Me,* and *On Ma Journey.* For excellence in composition Boatner was honored by the National Federation of Music Associations (1919), the National Baptist Convention (1925), and the National Association of Negro Musicians (1964).

John Wesley Work, Jr. (1901–68), music educator and composer, was graduated from Fisk University, received an M.A. from Teachers College of Columbia University, and a B.Mus. from Yale University. Later he won a Julius Rosenwald Fellowship which enabled him to study at the Juilliard Institute for two years. Following in the footsteps of his father, Work headed the music department at Fisk University, and published a collection of folksong arrangements, *American Negro Songs and Spirituals* (1940). He also published articles on the subject of Negro folksong in scholarly journals. His compositions include *The Singers,* a cantata for chorus and orchestra; *Yenvalou,* for strings; *Isaac Watts Contemplates the Cross,* a choral cycle; and a number of piano pieces, songs, and spiritual arrangements. In 1946 his cantata won first prize in a competition sponsored by the Fellowship of American Composers.

J. Harold Brown (b. 1902), organist and composer-arranger, was born in Shellman, Georgia. He received his musical training at Fisk University and earned a master's degree in music theory from Indiana University. Brown's choral works include a collection of spirituals, his first publication (1925); *The African Chief,* a cantata for female voices with concert band accompaniment; *Job,* an oratorio; Kyrie Eleison, for chorus, organ, and strings; and *The Saga of Zip Zan Rinkle,* for chorus. In addition to a string quartet and an orchestral suite, Brown composed numerous works for piano, voice, chorus, and solo instruments. Brown's teaching career included many years in the public schools of midwestern cities, and the directorship of music at Florida

A. & M. College and Southern University (Louisiana). In the 1950s he became director of music at Karamu House and Huntington Playhouse in Cleveland, Ohio. The honors won by Brown for excellence in composition include six National Wanamaker Awards, a Harmon Foundation Award, and a commission from the Citizen's Forum of Indianapolis, Indiana.

WILLIAM DAWSON

William Levi Dawson (b. 1898), composer-arranger, attended Tuskegee Institute and later enrolled at the Horner Institute for Fine Arts in Kansas City, Kansas, where he was graduated with honors in composition. Dawson was also a trombonist, having played with the Chicago Civic Orchestra when he was attending Chicago Musical College and the American Conservatory of Music to pursue further studies in composition and orchestration. In 1927 Dawson received the Master of Arts degree in music from the American Conservatory. A native of Anniston, Alabama, Dawson eventually returned to Tuskegee as the director of music and conductor of the chorus. Under his leadership, the Tuskegee Institute Choir developed into one of the finest college choirs in the country. Dawson won national distinction for his many choral works and arrangements of spirituals and received three Wanamaker Awards (1930, 1931). After his retirement from Tuskegee in 1955, he was sent by the State Department to Spain to train choral groups there.

One of his orchestral works, the *Negro Folk Symphony*, attracted national attention upon its world première in 1934 by the Philadelphia Orchestra under the direction of Leopold Stokowski. A critic of the *New York Times* observed that the Dawson work had "dramatic feeling, a racial sensuousness and directness of melodic speech, and a barbaric turbulence." The *New York World Telegram* commented upon its "imagination, warmth, drama . . . [and] sumptuous orchestration." After returning from a visit to West Africa in 1952, Dawson revised his symphony, infusing it with the spirit of the African rhythms he had heard there. The new version was recorded by Stokowski and his American Symphony Orchestra. The work is in three movements, the first and third of which are in traditional sonata-allegro form, and each has a subtitle: Movement I, *The Bond of*

Africa; Movement II, *Hope in the Night;* Movement III, *O Let Me Shine!* According to the composer, "a link was taken out of a human chain when the first African was taken from the shores of his native land and sent to slavery." Dawson uses a French-horn motive, first heard in the introduction, to symbolically represent the "missing link." The motive appears in each movement, sometimes in full and majestic statement, at other times in transformation. Dawson uses original melodies written in the style of spirituals for the first theme of Movement I and for all themes in Movement II; he quotes actual spirituals for the second theme of Movement I and for all themes in the last movement. Throughout the symphony Dawson handles his musical materials in such a manner as to achieve a programmatic effect—suggesting such scenes as the shout, toiling in the fields, a jubilee, a burial, and the day of freedom. Dawson was directly inspired by Dovřák's views on nationalism in music. His aim was "to write a symphony in the Negro folk idiom, based on authentic folk music but in the same symphonic form used by the composers of the [European] romantic-nationalist school."

MUSIC EDUCATORS

Several of those who published compositions during the 1930s and 40s were more active in the field of music education—as teachers of talented young composers and performers, as leading figures in the organization of musical groups and events, and as representatives and consultants to various national and international music bodies. Oscar Anderson Fuller (b. 1904), singer and composer, was the first Negro to earn a Ph.D. in music in the United States. He received a masters degree in music from the State University of Iowa in 1934 and the doctorate from the same university in 1942 with a major in composition. Fuller taught at Agricultural and Technical College of North Carolina, was head of the music department at Prairie View A. & M. College (Texas), then went to Lincoln University (Missouri) in 1942 to take charge of the music department there. Over the years, several of the many young musicians that he taught or encouraged as students or junior faculty members were to make solid contributions to the field of music; among them, an operatic prima donna, two concert artists, at least one established composer, and three chairmen of college music departments.

Frederick Douglass Hall (b. 1898) organist and music educator, was graduated from Morehouse College and received further musical training at Chicago Musical College, Columbia University, and the Royal College of Music in London. In 1952, Hall earned a doctorate in music from Columbia Teacher's College. His teaching career included the directorship of music at Jackson College (Mississippi), Clark College (Georgia), Alabama A. & M. College, and Dillard University (Louisiana). Hall, a member of the American Guild of Organists, also composed works for voice and piano, chorus, and chorus with orchestra.

Warner Lawson (b. 1903), music educator and pianist, was graduated from Fisk and went to Yale University, where he received the B.Mus. degree in 1929. Before accepting the chairmanship of the music department at Howard University in 1942, he had taught at Agricultural and Technical College (North Carolina) and at Fisk University. Under Lawson's direction, the Howard University Choir developed into one of the nation's outstanding college choral groups; its periodic concerts with the National Symphony Orchestra of Washington, D. C., became celebrated affairs.

Willis Laurence James (b. 1909), composer and musicologist as well as music educator, was graduated from Morehouse College (Georgia) and pursued advanced studies in composition at Chicago Musical College. James won distinction for his research work in the field of Negro folk music, American music, and jazz. His activities included lecturing, serving as a consultant to the Institute of Jazz Studies (New York) and to the American Council of Learned Societies—Library of Congress survey committee on American music. Noah F. Ryder (b. 1914), music educator and composer, attended Hampton Institute and earned the M.Mus. degree from the University of Michigan. He taught in public schools of North Carolina, at Palmer Memorial Institute (North Carolina), and at Winston-Salem Teachers College (North Carolina) before going to Virginia State College as head of the music department at the Norfolk division. Ryder was best known for his choral arrangements of spirituals. His other works include *Five Sketches for Piano* and the *Sea Suite for Male Voices*, one song of which was given a grand prize in the Navy War Writers contest (1944). When Walter Anderson (b.

1915), was appointed as head of the music department at Antioch College (Ohio), few Negroes were holding similar positions in white colleges. Organist and composer, Anderson traveled widely in Europe, representing his college and the State Department in various music assignments.

WILLIAM GRANT STILL, "DEAN OF AFRO–AMERICAN COMPOSERS"

In 1945 Leopold Stokowski wrote of William Grant Still (b. 1895), "Still is one of our greatest American composers." A year later in Helsinki, Finland, a critic described Still's music as "that kind of music which we are accustomed to join characteristically to the word 'American.'" And ten years later, in 1955, a writer observed in *Micro Magazine* (Brussels, Belgium):

> This American composer shows remarkable qualities which place him as one of the very greatest living composers of the New World: a sense of immediate observation; the taste for a rigorous and brilliant orchestration; spontaneity and sincerity characterize his compositions.

In 1970 Still was seventy-five years old, and musical organizations throughout the country celebrated the diamond anniversary of a man whose prolific composing had earned him a lofty and secure niche among American composers for all time. His music had truly become a music of the people. It was performed widely by college groups and civic organizations as well as by professional orchestras; it was heard on college campuses, in community-concert series, on radio and television programs, at festivals, and in the leading concert halls of the nation.

Still was born in Woodville, Mississippi, the son of two teachers. His father, a graduate of Alcorn A. & M. College (Mississippi), was also a cornetist and leader of the local brass band. When Still was three months old his father died, and his mother moved to Little Rock, Arkansas, where she obtained a teaching position in the local high school. As he grew up, the boy was surrounded with music in the home: his grandmother sang hymns and spirituals continuously as she worked about the house; he took violin lessons from a local teacher; and he listened for hours at a time to the recordings of operatic music brought in by his stepfather. Despite his obvious talent in music, Still enrolled in the science program at Wilberforce University under pressure from his mother, who wanted him to become a doctor. It was a useless move. He soon found himself directing the college band, making arrangements for both the band and a string quartet that he organized, and writing his own compositions for performance in recitals. It was during this period that he decided to become a composer. He began to emulate his idol, Samuel Coleridge-Taylor, even to the point of trying to grow a bushy hair style—with little success, for his hair was straight.

After leaving Wilberforce, Still worked at a number of music jobs—playing in dance bands at resorts, playing for vaudeville acts, and working with W. C. Handy's music publishing company in Memphis during the Summer of 1916—and then enrolled at Oberlin, using some money he had received on his twenty-first birthday as a legacy from his father. He was encouraged there in his ambition to become a composer by the theory and composition faculty, particularly when he turned in as a class assignment a setting of Paul Laurence Dunbar's poem *Good Night*.

World War I found Still in the Navy. He had enlisted as a mess attendant, the only job available to a Negro other than that of a steward, but when his superior officers discovered his musical ability he was put to work in the officers' mess playing the violin with a white pianist. In 1919 Still went to New York, but meeting little success in finding a music job, he returned to Oberlin. Later in the same year, Handy sent for Still to come to New York to work in his relocated music-publishing business. This time Still became immersed in the activities of the Negro music world—he worked with Handy in the publishing office, played jazz with the dance orchestras of both Handy and Deacon Johnson, worked as musical director at the Black Swan Phonograph Company, and joined the orchestra of *Shuffle Along* in 1921 as a oboist.

While at the Black Swan, Still learned that the avant-garde French composer Edgard Varèse, who had come to New York in 1916, wanted to teach a talented Negro, without fee, to write in an avant-garde style. Still seized the opportunity, studied with Varèse for two years and developed his compositional skill to a high level. In Boston, where he had gone on tour with the *Shuffle Along* company in 1923, Still came in contact with another leading figure on the American scene—George Chadwick, president of New England Conservatory. Chadwick, too, gave Still a scholarship and taught him the importance of writing "American" music.

Although Still had been composing and arranging music since his early years at Wilberforce, it was not until the 1920s that he began to concentrate on concert works in the larger forms. His first serious works were tentative and experimental; *Darker America* (1924) was, in the composer's mind, "fragmentary, with too much material"; *From the Land of Dreams* (1925), written in the avant-garde style of Varèse, failed to reflect his own creative personality; and *From the Journal of a Wanderer* (1925) he thought contained "too much stunt writing." Notwithstanding Still's reservations, his work was being noticed by critics and New York composers, and in 1925 *From the Land of Dreams* (for three voices and chamber orchestra) received a first performance at a concert of the International Composers' Guild. In 1926, as has been noted, *Darker America* was given a première performance by the Guild. But it was the performance of his *Afro-American Symphony* in 1931 by the Rochester Philharmonic Symphony under Howard Hanson that brought real recognition to Still. This was the first time in history that a major symphony orchestra had played a symphonic work written by a black composer. In 1935 the New York Philharmonic played the symphony's New York première at Carnegie Hall. The symphony became Still's most consistently played work over the next forty years, receiving hundreds of performances in both the United States and abroad.

For a period of about fifteen years, Still wrote primarily in the nationalistic style, drawing his inspiration from all kinds of Negro music—spirituals, worksongs, blues, jazz, and characteristic dances. His *Levee Land* (1926) was written for Florence Mills, the charming diminutive Negro vaudeville star of international fame who died suddenly while still in her twenties. After its performance by the International Composers' Guild, a critic on the *Musical Courier* commented "Four foolish jazz jokes: good, healthy, sane music." Three symphonies composed during this period form a trilogy: *Africa* (1930), the *Afro-American Sym-*

phony, and the Symphony in G minor: *Song of a New Race* (1937). The latter was composed at the request of Stokowski, who introduced the work to the public with his Philadelphia Orchestra. Other works of the period included *From the Black Belt* (1926), a suite for small orchestra; *La Guiablesse* (1927), a ballet with a West Indian plot; *Sahdji* (1930), a ballet with chorus and a narrator who recited African proverbs; *Kaintuck* (1935), for piano and orchestra; *Lenox Avenue* (1937), a ballet suite for orchestra, chorus, and narrator; and a number of lighter works, of which the piano suite *Three Visions* (1935) became best known.

Still worked during these years as an arranger and staff composer for both WCBS and WNBC radio and on a free-lance basis. His initial contacts with potential employers came through Will Vodery, who, as has been pointed out, was one of the first black arranger-composers to gain a secure foothold in the commercial arranging field. Still's arrangements for Donald Vorhees on WCBS led to commissions from such persons as Paul Whiteman, Artie Shaw, and Sophie Tucker. In 1929 Paul Whiteman, who was in California at that time, sent for Still to come there and make orchestrations for "The Old Gold Show"; Still returned to New York in 1930. His work with Williard Robison's "Deep River Hour" on WNBC led to his becoming the first Negro to conduct a white radio orchestra in the nation when he conducted the Deep River orchestra. Still also made orchestrations for musical comedies, including Earl Carroll's *Vanities*, *Runnin' Wild*, and P. J. McVoy's *Americana*. In 1934 he received a Guggenheim Fellowship (later renewed twice) that allowed him to give full time to composing. He moved to Los Angeles, California, and began to compose the kind of music that had been his "first love" since his teen-age days in Little Rock, Arkansas—opera. He had written operas earlier, but had discarded them because of lack of time to work out all of the problems.

Still's first opera, *Blue Steel*, was based on a Negro theme, the conflict between the age-old voodoo and modern materialism, and used Negro folk music to establish the basic moods—jazz being associated with city life, and spirituals with religious scenes. Its hero was Blue Steel, a black worker of Birmingham, Alabama. In March, 1949, the New York City Opera Company under the direction of Laszlo Halasz presented the world première of

Troubled Island, Still's second opera. Its libretto, written by Langston Hughes, outlined the story of the Haitian liberator Jean Jacques Dessalines at the end of the eighteenth century in Haiti. The production marked another "first" for Still: it was the first time that an opera written by a black composer had been produced by a major opera company. However, the leading roles were sung by white singers in blackface make-up.

Still's seventh opera, *Highway No. 1, U. S. A.*, was given its world première in 1963 at the University of Miami's fourth annual Festival of American Music. Fabien Sevitsky, conductor of the University of Miami Symphony Orchestra, directed the production. Verna Arvey, Still's wife, wrote the libretto for the one-act opera, a simple story of the trials of a young couple (white or black) operating a filling station, set against the roar of traffic on a big highway. The work was widely praised by the critics as "an artistic work that is fresh and deeply sincere, and that evokes a genuine emotion." Miami had been the site in 1962 of a première performance for another Still work. *The Peaceful Land*, which won a competition sponsored by the National Federation of Music Clubs and the Aeolian Music Foundation.

Like most modern American composers, Still composed, in addition to traditional concert works, a number of works intended for use in motion pictures, on radio and television, and by schools and colleges. His first full-length music film score was *Pennies from Heaven*. He served as the music adviser for *Stormy Weather* and was responsible for unsigned orchestrations and background music in numerous films, among them *Lost Horizon*. His materials for TV use have been heard as background music for such series as *The Perry Mason Show* and *Gunsmoke*. Still's works for young people include *The Little Song that Wanted to Be a Symphony* (1955); *The Prince and the Mermaid* (1966); *The American Scene: Five Suites for Young Americans* (1968); and a number of songs used in the major school-songbook series. His *Old California* (1941), *Festive Overture* (1944), and *Danzas de Panama* (1948) also have been frequently used in concerts for children.

A list of the composer's concert works, more than one hundred in all, includes thirty works for orchestra, five of them symphonies; three, for concert band; seven operas and four ballets; fourteen works for piano or other solo instruments and small ensembles; and a large number of solo songs and choral works. In 1937 Still published a collection of spiritual arrangements and promised a second volume to be forthcoming in the future. Probably the most celebrated of the choral works was the cantata *And They Lynched Him on a Tree,* for two choruses, contralto solo, narrator, and orchestra, based on a text by a white author, Katherine Garrison Chapin. After its first presentation by the New York Philharmonic-Symphony at the Lewisohn Stadium in 1940, with Negro contralto Louise Burge singing the role of the black mother, the critics praised its "profoundly moving and human character." In spite of his obvious interest in the use of Negro idioms and romantic techniques, Still resists neat classification as a nationalist and traditionalist. Over a long career of more than fifty years as a composer, he wrote everything from popular jazz songs (using the pseudonym Willy M. Grant) to religious motets (for example, *The Voice of the Lord,* a setting of Psalm 29), from avant-garde music in the style of Varèse and impressionistic music (such as *Seven Traceries* for piano) to the jazzy *Lenox Avenue* ballet. In one sense, he is an Americanist, in that he drew upon the nation's folk-music resources as inspiration for many of his works, not only of the Negro, but also of the Indian, Spanish-American, and Anglo-American. With regard to musical style, he displayed in later works an increasing predilection for the conservative approach to composition. Critical responses to the all-Still programs given in several places during the years just prior to the composer's seventy-fifth birthday were unanimous in the agreement that Still's music was "pleasant, easy, graceful music, completely traditional in approach," but that "inside the framework of the conventional . . . [he] exercised originality."

At the age of seventy-five, Still could look back on many awards and honors. We have mentioned already his music for the New York World's Fair in 1939. In 1943, when the League of Composers asked sixteen eminent American composers to write on a patriotic theme associated with the war, Still was included (the only black American) along with the eminent composers John Alden Carpenter, Howard Hanson, Roy Harris, Charles Ives, Walter Piston, Roger Sessions, and others. Still's work, *In Memoriam: The Colored Soldiers Who Died for Democracy,* was given its first performance by Artur Rodzinski and the New

York Philharmonic. In 1945 Still entered a contest sponsored by the Cincinnati Symphony Orchestra, which offered a thousand-dollar war bond to the composer who would create a suitable overture for performance at its celebration of a Golden Jubilee. Of the thirty-nine compositions submitted to the judges (identified only by pseudonyms) Still's *Festive Overture* was chosen the winning entry by a unanimous vote. During his career, the composer won several such contests, and also received commissions from leading symphonies of the nation, from prestigious organizations, and from lesser-known groups as well. His many other honors included a Harmon Award (1927), Rosenwald and Guggenheim Fellowships, and honorary degrees in music from Wilberforce University (M.Mus., 1936), Howard University (D.Mus., 1941), Oberlin College (D.Mus., 1947), and Bates College (D.L., 1954).

THE *AFRO–AMERICAN SYMPHONY*

One reason for listeners' initial and continued attraction to the *Afro-American Symphony* was its modern "American" sound. Still was the first Negro to employ the blues and jazz in a symphonic work; previously, black composers had confined their use of Negro folk idioms in concert works to spirituals, work-songs, and dance songs. Still explained his aim as follows:

> Like so many works which are important to their creators, *The Afro-American Symphony* was forming over a period of years. [It was completed in 1930.] Themes were occurring to me, were duly noted, and an overall form was slowly growing. I knew I wanted to write a symphony; I knew that it had to be an American work; and I wanted to demonstrate how the blues, so often considered a lowly expression, could be elevated to the highest musical level.

It was an ironic twist of fate that the world should receive its first symphonic work written in the jazz and blues style not from William Grant Still, who was firmly grounded in the musical lore of his people, but from the white composer George Gershwin, who had had only superficial contacts with Negro music in his visits to Harlem and to the all-black shows on Broadway. (By a similar quirk, the white Original Dixieland Jazz Band, rather than the black pioneers who created the music, had been the first to receive public acclaim for playing jazz.) White band-leader Paul Whiteman gave a commission to Gershwin in 1924 to compose a jazz symphony for performance in his concert, "Experiments in Modern Music." If Still had received such a commission, the *Afro-American Symphony* would have been per-formed six years earlier, for its music was taking shape in the composer's mind even then.

Still has given to each of the symphony's four movements a subtitle (Moderato assai, *Longings;* Adagio, *Sorrows;* Scherzo, *Humor;* Lento con Risoluzione, *Aspirations*) and a brief pro-gram based on an excerpt from a poem by Paul Laurence Dun-bar. A theme invented in the spirit of a blues melody, first presented after the introduction in the first movement, dominates the entire work.

Ex. XV.1   Blues theme, Still: *Afro-American Sym-phony*

The blues theme is used in later movements in various ways: sometimes a secondary theme derives from it, as in the introduc-tion to the scherzo and in the finale; sometimes the theme itself is stated in a transformed version, as just before the coda in the third movement. The other themes of the symphony, none an actual quotation of a genuine folk melody but rather an invention in the spirit of folksongs, are reminiscent of spirituals, shout songs, jig songs (with banjolike accompaniment), and jazz tunes. Critics found the work to be "straightforward, with no pretense of profundity," and effectively scored. And this is what Still had intended. He wrote, "The harmonies employed in the Symphony are quite conventional except in a few places. The use of this style of harmonization was necessary in order to attain simplicity and to intensify in the music those qualities which enable the hearers to recognize it as Negro music."

ECLECTICS AND EXPERIMENTALISTS

Music historians generally use the term *eclectic* in reference to a composer who draws upon several sources and different styles for his compositional materials and techniques. In the broad sense of the term, William Grant Still is an eclectic, for his music includes many styles and types, although it emphasizes folklorism and the traditional. In a narrower sense, however, the young black composers who emerged during the mid-century years were more eclectic; they refused to be tied down by racial self-consciousness and drew freely upon widely divergent styles and sources in their writing. Some wrote conservatively in the classic forms; others experimented with free forms and exotic materials. The one quality they shared in common was that each believed it important to chart his own course.

Most of these composers, though not all, grew up in black communities and came to know intimately the music of their people, which was now broadened to include along with the traditional spirituals and other folksongs, gospel songs, orchestral and piano jazz, and the ubiquitous blues. The younger musicians also come into contact with bop, rock 'n' roll, and finally soul music—in some instances, participating in the creating of this music. All encountered, sooner or later, the "black experience"— that is, the understanding of what it meant to be a creative black artist in a basically hostile white society—and each coped with it as best he could. Some exploited more thoroughly the African tradition, with its emphasis on functionalism, communication, and purpose; others made the effort to combine African and European traditions into an integrated whole; a few ignored the problem and wrote wholly in the European tradition.

After World War II the status of the black man in the United States gradually improved, and that of the black composer as well, but only to a certain extent. By the 1960s composers born in the North no longer had to go South in search of college teaching jobs or other music occupations, as black musicians often had been forced to do in earlier years. Nevertheless, the black college, along with the black church, continued to nurture the creative artist as well as to serve as his chief patron. On the national level, the champions of black American music were disappearing, and none seemed to be emerging to take their places. There were fewer persons of national and international stature willing to lend a helping hand to blacks, as had singers and instrumentalists in the earlier part of the century—as we have seen, concert-singers Schumann-Heink, McCormack, and Bori; pianist Grainger; violinists Kreisler and Spaulding; and popular singers Sophie Tucker, May Irwin, Marie Cahill, Anna Held, and Lillian Russell. The great patrons of the post-World War I period —among them, Varèse, Chadwick, Koussevitsky, Stock, Stokowski—appeared to be matched by fewer counterparts among the leading figures of the white musical establishment in the mid-century years.

To be sure, there were conspicuous exceptions to the general rule. In Louisville, conductor Robert Whitney developed a reputation as a champion of American music, and included in his international commissioning series at least two young black composers—Ulysses Kay and Hale Smith. Conductor Robert Shaw commissioned several black composers to write works, played the works of others, and in 1969 appointed Thomas J. Anderson as composer-in-residence to the Atlanta Symphony Orchestra—a notable "first" in the history of American music. In Washington, D. C., the National Symphony appointed John Carter as a composer-in-residence. Among the other orchestras that most frequently performed works by black composers were the Baltimore Symphony; the Dallas Symphony, which in 1969 appointed the black associate conductor Paul Freeman; the Minneapolis Symphony; the Nashville Symphony under Thor Johnson; and the University of Miami Symphony under Fabien Sevitzky. In New York, an interracial orchestra was organized in 1965, the Symphony of the New World, with Benjamin Steinberg as director, and it immediately established the policy of commissioning works from black composers. And there were individuals who furthered the cause of Negro music by playing or singing it in their recitals; among them, the violinist Louis Kaufman, who gave première performances of William Grant

Still's *Pastorela* and *Suite*.

John Hammond continued to espouse the cause of the black musician, as he had done since the 1920s. Beginning in the 1960s black concert artists began to include the music of black composers in their recitals more often than they had done earlier. (We shall return to this point in the next chapter.) Black composers more and more found sponsors for their music in white college groups, in white religious groups, and in white community organizations on the city, county, and state level. Organizations such as ASCAP and BMI also functioned as sponsors by offering competitions open to all, regardless of race. Several black composers won prizes in these contests and in similarly sponsored competitions of composers' groups, festival associations, and foundations.

The position of the black composer in the total picture of American music remained relatively the same as it had in previous periods of music history. Two or three composers of concert music in each generation achieved national distinction, following in the course set by Burleigh, Dett, and White at the beginning of the century, by Dawson and Still in a later period, and by Howard Swanson and Ulysses Kay still later. Among the younger composers the names of Hale Smith, Julia Perry, Thomas Jefferson Anderson, and Olly Wilson became known first to those within musical circles and gradually to the music public. At the same time a number of black composers not as well known were active, producing works of merit and contributing to the total creativity of the musical world. In the field of jazz and jazz-related music the black composer dominated, as he had from its beginning. Most jazz composers continued to function primarily as performer-composers, but some also composed in the more conventional sense; among them, John Lewis, David Baker, and Duke Ellington.

Most of these composers were well trained, obtaining instruction and music degrees from the best music schools in the country; most frequently, the Eastman School of Music, the Curtis Institute of Music, the Cleveland Institute of Music, the State University of Iowa, the Juilliard School of Music, and the Manhattan School of Music in New York. Some went abroad for further study, particularly to Nadia Boulanger in Paris and to Luigi Dallapiccola in Florence, Italy. Unfortunately, the scope of this book does not permit discussion of the many black composers of local fame, some of whom may well win national distinction in the future.

HOWARD SWANSON

Howard Swanson (b. 1909) first attracted attention as a composer of promise when contralto Marian Anderson sang one of his songs, *The Negro Speaks of Rivers* (poem by Langston Hughes), in a recital in January, 1950. In the Spring of 1950 several of his songs were selected for performance at a concert of the American Composers' Festival held in New York. In November of the same year his *Short Symphony*, composed in 1948, was given a first performance by the New York Philharmonic under the baton of Dimitri Mitropoulos. The next year, the prestigious New York Critics Circle gave Swanson its award for having composed the best orchestral work played during the 1950–51 season in New York. And Mitropoulos repeated the symphony when the Philharmonic played at the Edinburgh Festival in Scotland in the Summer of 1952. The honors came swiftly, but Swanson had worked hard to reach the level where he stood in 1951.

Born in Atlanta, Georgia, Swanson, moved with his family to Cleveland, Ohio, in 1917. His mother, who was herself a musician, encouraged his early interest in piano, although the family was poor. At the age of twelve Swanson began to study piano; at the age of twenty he entered the Cleveland Institute of Music, where he studied composition with Herbert Elwell. He supported himself during this period by working in the Cleveland post office, first as a mail carrier, then as a clerk. After completing his studies at the institute in 1937, Swanson won a Rosenwald Fellowship that enabled him to go abroad for study. He elected to work with Nadia Boulanger in France, who had played an important role in the training of an earlier generation of white American composers. Returning to the United States in 1939, Swanson worked for a while in the Internal Revenue Service of the Treasury Department in order to earn a living. Then he decided to devote his entire time to composing, regardless of the privation that might result. Among the further honors that came to him were a grant from the Academy of Arts and Letters and a Guggenheim Fellowship.

In addition to the *Short Symphony*, Swanson's orchestral works include an earlier symphony (1948), and Symphony No. 3, which was commissioned by the Symphony Orchestra of the New World and given a première performance in 1970; *Night Music* (1950), Concerto for Orchestra (1954), and Concerto for Piano and Orchestra (1956). In addition he has written smaller works: *Music for Strings* (1952), *Sound Piece for Brass Quintet* (1952), a suite for cello and piano, a piano sonata, four preludes for piano, and a Nocturne for violin and piano. His songs include settings of poems by Carl Sandburg, *Junk Man* and *Still Life;* by Vachel Lindsay, *Ghosts in Love;* by Edwin Markham, *The Valley;* and by Langston Hughes, *Night Song, In the Time of Silver Rain, Joy,* and *Pierrot.* About Swanson's songs one critic has written: "His songs have a delicate elaboration of thought and an intensity of feeling that recall Fauré."

Swanson's best-known work is the *Short Symphony*, in three movements, scored for two flutes, two oboes, two clarinets, two bassoons, two horns, two trumpets, trombone, timpani, and strings. The composer's aim was to achieve in the work the "depth, seriousness, and intensity inherent in a large work." Predominantly neoclassical in texture, but including jazzlike elements in some passages, the work has been praised by critics for its "elegance, sincerity, and grace." The first movement, Allegro moderato, has the outer structure of a sonata-allegro form with exposition, development, and recapitulation (restatement of the exposition material), but deviates markedly from the conventional in its use of a little fugato for the first theme-group. The brief fugato theme is tossed back and forth from winds to strings to brasses:

Ex. XV.2   Fugato theme, Swanson: *Short Symphony*

The second movement, Andante, is in three-part song form (a-b-a), again with an emphasis on call-and-response play between instruments of contrasting timbres (see Example XV.3).

Ex. XV.3   Beginning of the second movement, Swanson: *Short Symphony*

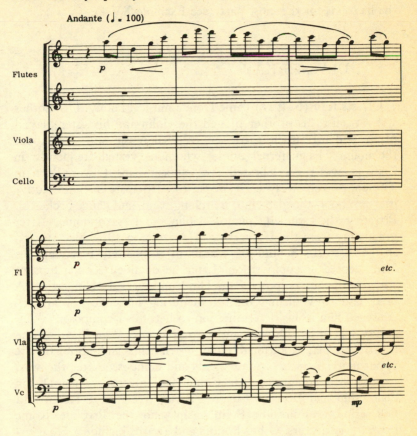

Ex. XV.4   Rondo theme of the last movement, Swanson: *Short Symphony*

The final movement, Allegro giocoso—Andante con moto, is a sonata-rondo. Contrasting sections are different in tempo as well as in musical material. The impudent rondo theme is given to the bassoons for the most part (see Example XV.4).

ULYSSES KAY

Ulysses Kay (b. 1917) came from a musical family. His mother was a pianist; his brother played the violin and his sister played piano; and his father, a barber, enjoyed music and sang about the house. His maternal uncle, whom he visited frequently in Chicago, was the celebrated jazz pioneer King Oliver. Born in Tucson, Arizona, Kay early began to participate in music activities at school—the glee club, marching band, and dance orchestra. Privately he studied piano, violin, and saxophone. After graduating from the University of Arizona in 1938, Kay studied at the Eastman School of Music in Rochester, receiving his M.A. degree in composition. Later he obtained scholarships to study with the composer Paul Hindemith at Yale University. A brief visit to William Grant Still during his college years encouraged him in his determination to become a composer.

Kay served in a Navy band during World War II, where he learned to play additional band instruments and also had the opportunity to make arrangements and compose. After the war, Kay studied composition at Columbia University on a Ditson Fellowship and later in Europe, having received a Rosenwald Fellowship, a Fulbright Scholarship, and the Prix de Rome Prize for two years. Other honors and awards include a Guggenheim Fellowship and honorary doctorates in music from Lincoln University (Pennsylvania, 1963), Bucknell University (Pennsylvania, 1966), Illinois Wesleyan University (1969), and the University of Arizona (1969). Kay was a member of the first group of American composers sent to Russia in 1965 on a cultural-exchange mission by the State Department. He has also traveled in other European countries on musical missions. Before going to teach at the Lehman College of the City University of New York in 1968, Kay worked as music consultant for BMI.

Kay composed prolifically after the performance of his first important work, the overture *Of New Horizons* (1944), by the New York Philharmonic under the direction of Thor Johnson. His catalogue includes twenty works for full orchestra; four works for string orchestra or chamber ensembles; seven, for chorus and orchestra; five, for band; and a number of piano, organ, and choral compositions. One of his two operas, *The Juggler of Our Lady* (1956), received its first performance at Xavier University (Louisiana) in 1962. His works were played widely in the United States, many of them having been commissioned by such organizations as the Koussevitsky Music Foundation, the Louisville Orchestra, the United States Civil War Centennial Committee, the Interracial Fellowship Chorus of New York, the Atlanta Symphony, and various state and country musical associations.

The majority of Kay's works are written in the traditional forms—overtures, concertos, suites, symphonies, quartets, and cantatas. The critics have warmly praised his taut melodic lines, vigorous rhythms, rich polyphony, "vibrant harmonic progressions," and "sonorous instrumentation." Among his best-known works are the film score for *The Quiet One* (1948); *Three Pieces After Blake* (1952); Brass Quartet (1952); *Serenade* for orchestra (1954); *Fantasy Variations* (1963); *Umbrian Scene* (1963); and *Theater Set* (1968).

HALE SMITH

Hale Smith (b. 1925) grew up in Cleveland, Ohio, and attended the Cleveland Institute of Music, where he obtained a B.Mus. degree (1950) and a M.Mus. degree in composition (1952). Smith was one of several black artists nurtured at the celebrated Karamu House in Cleveland, Ohio—where poet Langston Hughes earlier found a receptive audience for his plays and poems. In 1955 Karamu House presented to the public a full program of Smith's music. It was at Karamu also that Smith had the opportunity to write scores for such stage productions as Lorca's *Yerma* and *Blood Wedding*. In 1959 Smith went to New York and began working as a music editor for E. B. Marks Music

Corporation, the Frank Music Corporation, and Sam Fox Music Publishers. In 1968 he was appointed to the teaching staff at C. W. Post College of Long Island University.

Smith has been active both as a composer of concert and school music and as a jazz composer-arranger. Like most young black composers, he gained practical experience by playing in military and jazz bands. His works include *In Memoriam—Beryl Rubinstein* (1953), a setting of poems by Langston Hughes and Russell Atkins for chorus and chamber orchestra; *Epicedial Variations* (1956) for violin and piano; *Contours for Orchestra* (1962); *Orchestral Set* (1962); *Music for Harp and Orchestra* (1967); five works for concert band; two concertos, trumpet and alto saxophone, with band or orchestra; and a number of compositions for solo voice, piano, flute, cello, and chamber ensembles. His scores for films include music for the documentary *Bold New Approach* (1966). Smith's collection of jazz piano pieces for students, *Faces of Jazz* (1968), was welcomed by critics and teachers as "first-rate jazz of great freshness and originality"; it offered excellent material for teaching young intermediate pianists technical and musical problems in a language familiar to students.

Smith's *Contours for Orchestra*, recorded by the Louisville Orchestra, is perhaps his best-known work. Like many modern compositions, it employs serial techniques. Instead of using the major-minor system of keys and scales as a basis for composition, the serial composer uses a *twelve-tone row*, a specific arrangement of the twelve tones of the octave, as the source for the melodic and harmonic patterns in his musical composition (for each work, he devises a different row). If the composer strictly adheres to this method, he will use the twelve tones always in the same order throughout the composition (except for immediate repetitions), but the tones may be used in any octave, high or low. The tone row may be used in four forms: the original; backward (retrograde); upside down (inversion); or upside down and backward simultaneously (retrograde of the inversion). The following example shows Smith's tone row for *Contours* in the four forms:

Ex. XV.5   Tone row, Smith: *Contours*

To be sure, *Contours* hardly impresses upon its listeners that its composer employed certain kinds of compositional techniques. It has the typical sound of contemporary music: it is dissonant and contrapuntal, with unusual orchestral combinations of sounds; and it emphasizes call-and-response relationships between the various instruments. A critic writing in the *Courier-Journal* of Louisville, Kentucky, noted:

> *Contours* opens and closes on a note of protest. The piece makes versatile use of orchestral sonorities, pitting raucous cries from the brass against suave strings, quieting clamorous outbursts from the percussion with the sweet sound of woodwinds. It is a delicately balanced score, virile and persuasive.

Smith himself said of his work:

> Everything derives from a basic tone row and its variants and, though certain rhythmic proportions also derive from it, the idea of this being a serial "sounding" piece was perhaps the farthest thing from my mind. The principal motive (which is first played by the bass clarinet) seems to me to have a definite Latin American flair, and some of the more erotic Brazilian and Afro-Cuban dances were never far from my mind while writing the piece.

Some of the important motives of the work are presented in the following example:

Ex. XV.6   Motives, from Smith: *Contours*

JULIA PERRY

Julia Perry (b. 1927), a native of Akron, Ohio, studied voice, piano, and composition at the Westminster Choir School in Princeton, New Jersey. After receiving her bachelor's and master's degrees from the Choir School, she studied further at Juilliard, at the Berkshire Music Center, and in Europe with Luigi Dallapiccola in Florence and Nadia Boulanger in Paris. While in Europe, Perry organized and conducted a series of concerts, under the sponsorship of the U. S. Information Service, that were acclaimed by the critics. Her best-known works are *Stabat Mater* (1951), for solo voice and string orchestra; *A Short Piece for Orchestra* (1952); *Pastoral* (1959), for flute and strings; and *Homunculus, C. F.* (1969), for soprano and percussionists. Other works include *Episode*, for orchestra; *Seven Contrasts*, for baritone and chamber ensemble; *Fragments of Letters of Saint Catherine*, for solo voice, chorus, and orchestra; two operas, *The Bottle* and *The Cask of Amontillado;* and several works for chamber ensembles and solo instruments. Perry's awards include a Fountainebleau Award and a Boulanger Grand Prix for her Violin Sonata. *The Cask of Amontillado* was given a first performance at Columbia University in 1954.

THOMAS J. ANDERSON

Thomas Jefferson Anderson (b. 1928) was graduated from West Virginia State College (1950), obtained a master's degree in music education from Pennsylvania State College (1951), studied further at the Cincinnati Conservatory of Music, and obtained a doctorate in composition from the State University of Iowa (1958). He studied later at the Aspen School of Music. Before assuming the position of composer-in-residence to the Atlanta Symphony Orchestra in 1969—a position supported by a Rockefeller Foundation grant—Anderson taught at West Virginia State College, at Langston University (Oklahoma) and, beginning in 1963, at Tennessee Agricultural and Industrial College.

Born in Coatesville, Pennsylvania, Anderson received a good start on his musical career from his family, for both parents were teachers and his mother was a musician. As a teen-ager he toured with a jazz orchestra. His music reflects the influence of the jazz tradition and primitive and avant-garde styles as well. His most widely performed works have been *Chamber Symphony* (1968); Squares (1965), "an essay for orchestra"; and *Personals* (1966), a cantata for narrator, chorus, and brass ensemble. Other works include *New Dances* (1960), for orchestra; Symphony in Three Movements (1964); *Five Portraitures of Two People* (1965), for piano duet; *Rotations* (1967), for band; and a number of concertos and works for chamber ensembles. Critical response to the world première of Anderson's *Chamber Symphony* acclaimed its "sensitive use of individual instrumental colors" and the "sometimes pensive, sometimes violent moods" of the work, which was characterized by "constantly shifting melodic and rhythmic patterns." A work commissioned by the Coatesville Area Senior High School, *In Memoriam Zach Walker* (1969), is "very dissonant, but logical," according to the school's band director Donald Suter. "It is strongly influenced by jazz and avant-garde music and based on a twelve-bar blues structure." Zachariah Walker was lynched in Coatesville in 1911. Among the honors received by Anderson have been MacDowell Colony Fellowships (1960–63, 1968); a Copley Foundation Award (1964); and a Fromm Foundation Award (1964).

OTHERS

Margaret Bonds (b. 1913), composer and pianist, earned a master's degree in music from Northwestern University (Illinois) and studied later at Juilliard. Born in Chicago she was encouraged by her mother, an accomplished organist, as a child to develop her talent. Further encouragement came from composer Florence Price and the National Association of Negro Musicians, which gave her a scholarship. Bonds wrote several scores for stage works in addition to concert works. Her best-known compositions are *Migration*, a ballet; *Spiritual Suite for Piano;* Mass in D minor; *Three Dream Portraits;* and of the many songs, *The Ballad of the Brown King* and *The Negro Speaks of Rivers.* Among the awards she won were a Rosenwald Fellowship, a Roy Harris scholarship, and a Wanamaker Award (1932).

George Walker (b. 1922), composer, pianist, and music educator, and a native of Washington. D. C., was graduated from Oberlin College (1941), received an artist diploma in piano and composition from the Curtis Institute of Music (1945), and the Doctor of Musical Arts degree from the Eastman School of Music (1957). After a Town Hall debut in New York in 1945, Walker concertized extensively for several years under the management of National Concert Artists and Columbia Artists. He received a number of grants and awards, which allowed him to study composition for several years with renowned figures in the United States and abroad; for example, a Fulbright Fellowship (1957), a Whitney Fellowship (1958), a Guggenheim Fellowship (1969), and a Rockefeller Foundation Grant (1970). Other awards include the Harvey Gaul Prize (1964), MacDowell Colony Fellowships (1966–69), Bennington Composers Conference Scholarships (1967–68), and grants from the Bok Foundation for concerts in Europe (1963), the American Music League, the University of Colorado, and the Rutgers University Research Council. Walker's first published work was *Gloria in Memoriam*, for chorus and orchestra (1963). His other works include *Address* for orchestra (1959); a symphony; a string quartet; several sonatas for piano and violin, cello, and clarinet; a trombone concerto; a number of piano compositions, including *Spatials* for piano; and ten songs. His *Address* for orchestra has been performed by the Atlanta, Baltimore, and Minneapolis Symphony Orchestras, and the Symphony of the New World. Before going to Rutgers University (New Jersey) to teach in 1969, Walker taught at the New School for Social Research (New York), Smith College (Massachusetts), and the University of Colorado.

Arthur Cunningham (b. 1928), a graduate of Fisk University (1951), earned the M.A. degree in theory and conducting at the Teachers College of Columbia University. He studied further at Juilliard and at the Metropolitan Music School with composer Wallingford Riegger. In addition to following the traditional course of musical studies, Cunningham also studied jazz piano and theory. The first public performance of his music, a program of pieces for solo voices and piano, took place in 1951 at a concert sponsored by the National Association of Negro Musicians in New York. Born in Piermont, New York, Cunningham began writing pieces for his own jazz band when he was in his early teens. In addition to concert works, his output includes jazz works, sacred works, scores for stage works, music manuals, and works for performance by children. Among his most frequently performed works have been his Adagio for String Orchestra and Oboe (1954); *Concentrics* (1968), for orchestra; and the music for *Shango* (1969), a stage work. His other compositions include three works for symphony orchestra; nineteen works for chamber orchestra and chamber ensembles; a ballet for string quartet and jazz quartet; a work for bass voice and orchestra; and a large number of songs, both sacred and secular, for solo voice. His music for stage works include *Ostrich Feathers* (1964), a children's rock musical; *Patsy Patch and Susan's Dream* (1963), a musical for very young children; and a one-act mini rock-opera, *His Natural Grace* (1969).

COMPOSERS BORN IN THE THIRTIES

Black composers born in the 1930s were in an even better position to experiment than had been their predecessors. Almost without exception they were well trained, studying at the best musical institutions in the country, and they received help from various sources—grants from foundations; prizes won in national or international competitions; commissions from various types of organizations, particularly from symphony orchestras and college groups; fellowships and scholarships; and teaching positions that gave them time for composing. For most of the black composers active during the mid-century years, the influence of jazz continued to be a vital one; the majority of the younger composers both played in jazz groups at one time or another and wrote for such groups. Electronic music seemed to be more challenging than serial music for a few, although the employment of twelve-tone techniques continued to have high priority among several.

Few seemed concerned with the writing of "race music" in the sense of deliberately employing Negro musical idioms as an integral part of their individual styles or drawing upon black literary or social themes. This aloofness disappeared, however, after a series of assassinations during the 1960s, which included Medgar Evers in 1963, Malcolm X in 1965, and Nobel Peace Prize winner the Reverend Dr. Martin Luther King, Jr. in 1968. The young composers, in particular, responded to one or more of the tragedies by writing "in memoriam" works.

It would be impossible to name all of the young composers active during the mid-century years. The few men discussed below may be regarded as typical and, perhaps, as the most fortunate in that their music was being performed rather extensively, especially on campuses of Negro and white colleges and by community orchestras and the smaller symphony orchestras of the nation.

OLLY WILSON

The leading figure of the group, Olly W. Wilson (b. 1937), was the winner in the first competition ever devoted to electronic music, the International Electronic Music Competition held at Dartmouth College (New Hampshire) in 1968. Over one hundred entries from electronic studios all over the world were received and judged anonymously by established electronic-music composers Milton Babbitt, Vladimir Ussachevsky, and George Balch Wilson. Of the group of one winner and six finalists, only three were Americans. Wilson, as the winner, received the 1968 Dartmouth Arts Council Prize and, as a by-product, wide recognition of his talent.

To be sure, this was not the first time Wilson had attracted the attention of the music world. A native of St. Louis, his clarinet playing in high-school music organizations won for him a scholarship to Washington University in St. Louis. Although not musicians themselves, Wilson's parents encouraged music study among the children—Olly and three sisters. According to the composer, his father's "was the loudest and best voice in the choir at the First Baptist Church." After graduating from college in 1959, Wilson continued his studies at the University of Illinois, where he received the M.Mus. degree (1960), and at the State University of Iowa, where he earned a Ph.D. in composition (1964) In 1967 he studied electronic music at the Studio for Experimental Music, University of Illinois. As part of his practical experience, Wilson played double bass with symphony orchestras in St. Louis and Cedar Rapids, Iowa, and also with jazz groups. He taught at Florida A. & M. College, West Virginia University (graduate division), and Indiana University, before joining the music faculty of Oberlin.

About the same time that Wilson received notice of his winning the electronic-music prize, a performance of his *Sextet* (1963) by the Atlanta Symphony was being given national publicity. Wilson's works include two for orchestra; five for chamber groups; three ballets; and a number of works for solo voice, chorus, violin, and double bass. Even before he began experimenting with electronic music, Wilson's predilection for unusual combinations of sonorities became evident with such works as *Wry Fragments* (1961), for tenor and percussions; *And Death Shall Have No Dominion* (1963), for tenor and percussions; and *Chanson Innocent* (1965), for contralto and two bassoons. The most widely performed of Wilson's works have been the *Sextet; Three Movements for Orchestra* (1964); and *Cetus* (1967), the prize-winning electronic work.

Electronic music, of which Wilson's *Cetus* is an example, began to attract more and more composers during the 1950s, although it was really not an entirely new development. Actually, the French composer Varèse was a pioneer in the field in the United States, and had experimented with sounds as early as 1934. In Europe after the Second World War, much work was done in France and Germany. To the composer, electronic music offers unlimited resources of pitch, dynamics, texture, and rhythms. A discussion of electronic music is beyond the scope of the present book, but a few generalizations may be made at this point. Sounds, natural or electronic, are recorded on magnetic tape and then transformed electronically into "new" sounds. This may be done in a number of ways—the simplest involving a splicing of the tape, speeding it up or slowing it down, and reversing its direction. In working with the new sounds, the composer manipulates them in much the same way as he does conventional sounds; some sounds are used to provide background accompaniment, and some to function as solo "instruments." A common practice is to combine in a single work both electronically produced sounds and the sounds derived from traditional musical sources. (To be sure, the electronically produced sound may itself have been derived from either a musical instrument or from a nonmusical source.) The completed work is then taped for performance. Not only does electronic music expand the composer's tonal vocabulary; it also allows him to present his work directly to its listeners, bypassing an intermediary, the performer. The composer thus becomes identical with the performer, as happens typically in the field of jazz and folk music. Wilson provided the following explanation for his *Cetus:*

> The title refers to an equatorial constellation whose arch-like configuration was suggested to the composer's mind by the form of the work. This musical structure is the result of an evolutionary process in which basically simple timbres, textural combinations, and rhythmic events become more complex before ultimately returning to simpler relationships. . . .
>
> The compositional process characteristic of the "classical tape studio" (the mutation of a few basic electronic signals by means of filters, signal modifiers, and recording processes) was employed in the realization of this work and was enhanced by means of certain instruments which permit improvisation by synthesized sound. *Cetus* contains passages which were improvised by the composer as well as sections realized by classical tape studio procedures. The master of this work was prepared on a two channel tape. Under the ideal circumstances it should be performed with multiple speakers surrounding the auditor.

COLERIDGE–TAYLOR PERKINSON

Coleridge-Taylor Perkinson (b. 1932) has been associated with new movements in music in both New York and Hollywood. A native New Yorker, he received his bachelor's and master's degrees in composition from the Manhattan School of Music (1953, 1954). Perkinson studied further at the Berkshire Music Center, the Mozarteum, and the Netherland Radio Union Hilversum. When in the early 1960s the Negro Ensemble Company was organized in New York by actor Robert Hooks, Perkinson served as its first composer-in-residence and wrote music for several plays, including Peter Weiss's *Song of the Lusitanian Bogey*, Ray McIver's *God Is a* (*Guess What?*), and Errol Hill's *Man Better Man*. In 1965, when the Symphony of the New World was organized in New York, Perkinson became its first associate conductor. His concerto for Viola and Orchestra (1954) was given its first performance by the orchestra. In addition to concert music, Perkinson has composed music for television and radio programs, documentary films (such as *Crossroads Africa*), ballet groups, and movie films. In 1964 he was commissioned by the Ford Foundation to write a concert piece for black opera star George Shirley, who gave a first performance of the work, *Attitudes*, in a concert at the Metropolitan Museum of Art in New York.

DAVID BAKER

David Baker (b. 1931), heads the jazz studies program at Indiana University, his alma mater. Born in Indianapolis, Indiana, Baker began the study of instruments and theory in high school. After obtaining bachelor's and master's degrees in music education from Indiana, he taught in the public schools of Indianapolis and at Indiana Central College and Lincoln University (Missouri) before going to teach at Indiana University. His practical experience was obtained in both jazz bands and civic and college symphony orchestras. In 1961 he toured Europe as a member of an all-star jazz orchestra organized by Quincy Jones.

Baker's music is functional to the extent that he can have it performed by his large college band or that a large part of it is written upon commission. Moreover, Baker has access to small instrumental ensembles—or can organize them himself—and to choral groups. His output includes sixty works for jazz chamber orchestra or jazz ensemble; a large number of traditional chamber works for string orchestra, string quartet, violin, viola, or cello and piano, and wind chamber groups; a large number of solo piano works and solo songs, some based on texts by black poets; and a number of works for chorus and string orchestra or jazz ensemble. Some of his works resist neat categorization such as, *Reflections* for symphony orchestra and jazz ensemble (commissioned by the Indianapolis Art Council) or *But I Am a Worm* for chorus, jazz ensemble, and string orchestra. *A Summer's Day in 1945* calls for jazz ensemble and tape recorders.

A significant part of Baker's music has been commissioned by various religious groups, such as the Christian Theological Seminary, the Catholic Music Educators Association, and a Luthern church in Bloomington, Indiana. For these organizations and similar ones Baker has written jazz Masses, works for chorus and jazz ensemble, and works that include chorus, jazz ensemble, nonjazz groups, and dancers. *The Beatitudes*, for example, is for chorus, narrator, dancers, and symphony orchestra; a Lutheran Mass is for chorus and jazz ensemble; *Psalm 22* is subtitled *A Modern Jazz Oratorio*. In addition to his music, Baker has written three theory manuals and a book on jazz improvisation, and plans to publish others on the activity of black musicians in the twentieth century.

OTHERS

Noel Da Costa (b. 1930), was taken by his family from his birthplace, Lagos, Nigeria, to the West Indies in early childhood, then to New York at the age of eleven. He received his basic education at Queens College of the City University of New York and at Columbia University, then went to Europe on a Fulbright Grant to study with Luigi Dallapiccola in Florence, Italy. Da Costa has concentrated his attention in the field of chamber music, composing works for chamber orchestra and various unusual combinations of instruments, including *In the Circle* (1969), for four electric guitars, bass, and percussions. Two of Da Costa's works employ texts of black writers: *The Confessional Stone* (1969), for soprano and ten instruments, uses a poem by Owen Dodson; *The Last Judgement* (1970), for women's chorus, narrator, piano, and percussions, uses a poem by James Weldon Johnson.

Frederick Charles Tillis (b. 1930), a native of Galveston, Texas, earned M.A. and Ph.D. degrees in composition at the State University of Iowa. Before his appointment as head of the music department of Kentucky State College in 1967, Tillis directed an Air Force band and taught at Wiley College (Texas) and Grambling College (Louisiana). His first compositions were written for performance by his military band. His recent output includes eleven works for chamber ensembles; five works for concert band or orchestra; a number of works for solo voice, organ, piano, and a suite for unaccompanied viola; several electronic works, including *Three Plus One* (1969), for violin, guitar, clarinet, and tape recorder.

William Fischer (b. 1935) grew up in the Mississippi Delta country and was educated at Xavier University (Louisiana) and Colorado College. He studied further at the Academy of Music in Vienna, Austria. Fischer has worked in the concert field and with jazz groups as a performer, composer-arranger, and musical director. Among the awards he has received as a composer of concert music are commissions from the Rockefeller Foundation, a German State Grant (Deutsches Akademischer Austauschdienst), and a Fulbright Fellowship. His works include several for solo piano, solo viola, solo saxophone, and chamber groups; five for symphony orchestra; two concertos for jazz quintet and symphony orchestra; three operas; several songs, some on texts by black poets; and four electronic pieces. The electronic works generally call for live-tape mixtures; for example, *Batucada Fantastica* (1968), for two tapes and two percussionists; *Gift of Lesbos* (1968), for cello, piano, and tape; and *Time 1* (1966), for saxophone, viola, cello, percussions, and tape.

Two other young black composers whose works are receiving considerable attention are Stephen Chambers (b. 1940) and Wendell Morris Logan (b. 1940). Chambers studied at the Manhattan School of Music, the New School for Social Research, and privately. His works have been played on the "Music in Our Time" concerts held in New York at the YMHA (Young Men's Hebrew Association) under the direction of Max Pollikoff, as well as by college groups and some of the smaller symphony orchestras. Chambers' awards include the Bennington Composers' Conference Scholarships (1964–69) and ASCAP Composers' Awards (1967–69). His most widely performed works have been *Sound Images* (1969), for percussions, brasses, basses, and six female voices, and *Elements* (1967), for strings, flutes, clarinets, piano, glass and bamboo chimes. Logan, a native of Thomson, Georgia, received a master's degree from Southern Illinois University (1964) and a Ph.D. from the State University of Iowa. Prior to assuming his present position at Florida A. & M. College, he taught at Ball State University (Iowa). Logan generally uses traditional forms for his modern musical language and style.

EXPERIMENTS IN CONCERT JAZZ

Duke Ellington was among the first of the jazzmen to write concert jazz in extended forms. During the years 1943–50 he presented annual concerts at Carnegie Hall, each of which included one or more performances of large-form works. The best known are *Black, Brown and Beige; New World a-Coming, Deep South Suite, Such Sweet Thunder* (inspired by Shakespearean vignettes), *A Drum Is a Woman*, and *Far East Suite*. The first-named work became most famous. Subtitled *A Tone Parallel to the History of the Negro in America*, it is a lengthy piece in three movements, employing materials invented in the spirit of worksongs, blues, and spirituals. In 1963, Ellington wrote the music for a show, *My People*, performed at Chicago in the celebration of the "Century of Negro Progress Exposition." (i.e. from 1863, the year of emancipation, to 1963). Ellington also experimented with opera and musical comedy. His opera *Boola* was never completed, but he used some of its material in the suite *Black, Brown and Beige*. His *Beggar's Holiday* (1946) was an adaptation of the eighteenth-century English musical play, *The Beggar's Opera*, by John Gay and John Pepusch.

The occasion of Ellington's seventieth birthday, April 29, 1969, was marked by a gala celebration at the White House in

Washington, D. C. President Nixon presented the nation's highest civilian honor, the Presidential Medal of Freedom, to the composer, and an all-Ellington concert was offered to the guests. Just four years earlier, Ellington had been the subject of a controversy when the Pulitzer Prize advisory committee voted unanimously that he be given an award for long-term achievements, and the Columbia University committee that controlled the award refused to accept the recommendation. Clearly jazzmen and the world agreed with the advisory committee. Ellington's contributions had earned for him a place among the leading figures in the history of American music. His name was synonymous with jazz.

JOHN LEWIS

John Aaron Lewis (b. 1920), pianist-composer, began the study of piano as a child in Albuquerque, New Mexico. At the University of New Mexico, from which he was graduated in 1942, he majored in anthropology, but also studied music. After a stint in the army, Lewis worked with the jazz orchestra of Dizzy Gillespie as a pianist-arranger for a year (1946–47). It was during this period that he composed his first work in extended form, *Toccata for Trumpet and Orchestra*. Lewis continued his music studies at the Manhattan School of Music, earning bachelor's and master's degrees in music. After several years experience in playing with various groups that toured the United States and Australia, Lewis organized in 1952 the group on which he was to concentrate the major part of his attention in the coming years, the Modern Jazz Quartet (piano, vibraphone, bass, and percussion). In 1961, the Quartet appeared in concert with the Cincinnati Symphony Orchestra, the first of many such appearances to follow.

Critics saw in Lewis's works a fusion of jazz and classical elements, but Lewis himself insisted, "Jazz is the focal point for me. I've always been moving in a jazz direction." Nevertheless, he employs such traditional forms as fugues, toccatas, and concerti grossi, and draws upon traditional compositional techniques all the while writing in good jazz style. Some saw a parallel between the approach taken by Lewis in composing music for the Quartet and that taken by Ellington in composing music for his orchestra. Both men are concerned with the vital relationships between improvised solos and written-out ensembles and how the two combine to form a well-balanced musical structure and a well-integrated musical whole.

Lewis's best-known works are *Django* (1954), dedicated to the jazz guitarist Django Reinhardt; a suite, *Fontessa* (1956); *Three Little Feelings,* for brass ensemble; and his film music, particularly for the film *Sait-on Jamais* (*One Never Knows;* released in the United States as *No Sun in Venice,* 1957). Critics singled out Lewis's jazz fugues for special praise; among them, *Concorde,* *Vendôme,* and *Versailles. Three Windows* from the film *Sait-on Jamais* is a sophisticated triple fugue, combining the themes of the hero of the film, the "other man," and an old man, and ending with a coda in which all three themes are heard over an ostinato. Lewis also wrote scores for the films *Odds Against Tomorrow* (1959) and *A Milanese Story* (1962). The Modern Jazz Quartet plays chiefly in concert halls and at festivals in the United States and abroad. Lewis was the organizer of the Monterey Jazz Festival (beginning 1958). In 1962 he formed Orchestra U. S. A., a group whose stated aim was to perform contemporary music of all kinds, jazz and nonjazz. The orchestra was disbanded for economic reasons, but Lewis has persisted in his efforts, and successfully, to combine the Quartet with symphony orchestras in performances.

JAZZ IN THE CHURCH

Just as the eighteenth-century Christians in the United States found inspiration for their lively songs of praise, the spirituals, in the Bible verse Colossians 3:16 (see p. 87), so twentieth-century Americans could also find biblical support for an innovation—the presence of a jazz orchestra in the church. Several psalms exhort worshipers to praise God in His sanctuary with instrumental music, singing, and dancing, but Psalm 150 is most specific:

Praise Him with the sound of the trumpet: Praise Him with the psaltery and harp.

Praise Him with the timbrel and dance: praise Him with stringed
    instruments and organs.
Praise Him upon the loud cymbals: praise Him upon the high sound-
    ing cymbals.
Let everything that hath breath praise the Lord. Praise ye the Lord.

[Psalms 150:3–6]

Although Duke Ellington was not the first to carry jazz into the
church, his sacred jazz concerts (beginning in 1965) contributed
largely to the growing movement for making the music of the
worship service more relevant to the times. The Ellington concert given at New York's Fifth Avenue Presbyterian Church
on December 26, 1965, was recorded. The entire performance
might be viewed in terms of a work divided into several movements, in the same way as a Mass. Ellington composed some of
the numbers especially for the occasion and drew upon earlier
works for other numbers. The opening piece, *In the Beginning
God*, employs full orchestra, choir, and solo voice. Then follow
gospel and spiritual songs *Tell Me It's the Truth, Come Sunday;
The Lord's Prayer;* a saxophone version of *Come Sunday;* two
more spirituals, *Will You Be There, Ain't But the One;* a piano
solo, *New World a-Coming;* and the finale, *David Danced Before the Lord with All His Might,* for orchestra and tap dancer.
Come Sunday and the piano solo were originally performed at
Ellington's 1943 concert; the second pair of spirituals belonged
to his music for the pageant *My People*.

Mary Lou Williams, the former jazz pianist, is another who has
been active in the religious jazz movement. Among her compositions are a jazz hymn in honor of the black saint, St. Martin
de Porres, entitled *Black Christ of the Andes; Anima Christi;* and
Praise the Lord, often used in collaboration with a ballet. Jazz
elements are present in much of the religious music of the
younger composers, and, as has been observed, several of them
have written works wholly in the jazz style.

CHAPTER XVI

The Mid-Century Years

As the United States moved slowly toward its two-hundredth birthday, and the black population toward the celebration of its one hundred years of freedom, there was yet little progress being made with regard to the integration of black Americans into the mainstream of American life. Blacks generally lived in their own communities and continued to develop their own institutions to serve their needs. Of these, religious institutions remained the most powerful; by mid-century, more than five million blacks belonged to all-black denominations. A number of new denominations began to rival the supremacy of the Baptists and Methodists among the common people; for example, the Church of God, Seventh-Day Adventist groups, and Jehovah's Witnesses, as well as several small independent black sects. Some blacks turned away altogether from Christianity to the new Nation of Islam, called the Black Muslims, under the leadership of Elijah Muhammad (formerly Elijah Poole). One of the early dynamic leaders in the Black Muslim movement was Malcolm X, who later broke with the movement and was assassinated in 1965 while presiding over a meeting of his new organization. Ostensibly a religious group, the Black Muslim movement had political and social overtones and attracted thousands of blacks who were alienated from the American way of life. Members of the organization took Muslim names and observed strict laws in diet, dress, and conduct. Large numbers of jazzmen, in particular, also began to embrace orthodox Mohammedanism.

The church continued to support black artists in their projects, whether they concerned concerts, dramas, workshops, or music classes. Other institutions that helped in the sponsoring of music projects were local libraries, YM and YWCA establishments, settlement houses—all of these groups operating under black directors, although receiving some financial support from the white parent organizations. Black fraternal groups began to take a more active part in promoting cultural activities. Blacks organized their own theater companies and community orchestras and choruses. The black press, which had expanded to include more than three hundred newspapers and periodicals by the 1960s, assumed the responsibility for keeping the black population informed of events and people, a task of vital importance since few white newspapers included news about Negroes. A few of the large cities even maintained special radio and television stations that programed news and music solely for black listeners. Thus, the black world became smaller and more self-contained than ever before during the mid-century years.

Beginning in the 1940s, however, barely perceptible changes began to take place with regard to integration. The music called jazz, which had been created by blacks, was gradually coming to represent the only true American music to the world (whether correctly so is another question). Moreover, it had entirely conquered the field of dance and entertainment music; each new idea that came out of black jazz groups was emulated by whites and snatched up by the powerful music industry. Eventually, black and white jazzmen began to play together, thus facilitating the exchange of musical ideas. In the concert world and in opera, too, change began to take place slowly. It was during the 1940s, as we have seen, that Negroes sang with major opera companies for the first time and that the opera of a black composer was first produced by a major company.

THE WAR YEARS

The fourth decade of the century brought World War II. Approximately one million black men and women served in the armed forces, including the newly established WAACs (Women's Army Auxiliary Corps, later Women's Army Corps) and WAVES (Women Accepted for Volunteer Service in the Navy). Although the predictable discrimination occurred in many places, it was not as rampant as during previous wars, and blacks served in many units from which they had been excluded in the past, notably the Air Force and the Marine Corps. Moreover, large numbers of blacks were trained in officer-candidate schools along with whites (except in the Air Corps, which maintained a segregated school).

With regard to musical activities, life was different for both black and white servicemen—and servicewomen—than it had been in past wars. The establishment of the selective-service system obliterated the need for recruiting songs, an important category of war songs in previous times. Servicemen had access to so many outlets for their musical needs that old-fashioned group singing played a relatively minor role. Established concert artists and popular singers as well as musical groups of all types were assembled to tour the United States and overseas, providing entertainment for all units. Moreover, the armed services organized its own bands and glee clubs to entertain at-home bases and to tour. The USO (United Service Organizations, Inc., established in 1941) also sent entertainment groups on tour, including several all-black shows. Nevertheless, servicemen did participate in some group singing and professional song writers turned out a large number of war songs, many of doubtful quality. Among the most popular songs were *White Christmas*, *The White Cliffs of Dover*, *The Last Time I Saw Paris*, *Coming In on a Wing and a Prayer*, *Praise the Lord and Pass the Ammunition*, *Rodger Young*, *We Did It Before*, and *This Is the Army*, *Mister Jones*. Duke Ellington made his contributions with *Don't Get Around Much Anymore* and *Do Nothing Till You Hear from Me* (words to both songs by Bob Russell). The song writers of the nation organized a Music Committee that contacted various branches of the armed services asking for the kinds of songs needed. As a result, each branch had its own songs (some of which became official), as did also the Red Cross, the USO, and the Treasury Department (which used songs in selling war bonds). It will be remembered that in 1943 the League of Composers commissioned war compositions from the country's most outstanding composers of concert music and that William Grant Still's contribution was *In Memoriam: The Colored Soldiers Who Died for Democracy*. A cantata written by the white composer Earl Robinson, *A Ballad for Americans*

(1939), became popular during war times partly because of its patriotic theme, but primarily because of its effective presentation by Paul Robeson in the baritone solo role.

One of the all-black music groups organized during the war years later won fame as De Paur's Infantry Chorus. The group's conductor Leonard De Paur (b. 1915), a native of Summit, New Jersey, served as a choral director for fifteen months in the Air Force's *Winged Victory* show before being assigned to organize a glee club in the 372nd Infantry Regiment. De Paur was a graduate of the University of Colorado, had studied at Juilliard, and had served as the associate choral director of the Hall Johnson Choir in civilian life. His fifty-voice infantry glee club so impressed officialdom that it was detached and sent around to battle areas as a morale booster. De Paur made a point of singing Negro folksongs on his programs as well as the traditional concert works of European and American composers.

THE BLACK REVOLUTION

On December 1, 1955, a black seamstress in Montgomery, Alabama, refused to move to the rear of a bus in order to make available a seat for a white man when ordered to do so by the white bus driver. She later explained, "I was just tired from shopping. My feet hurt." The seamstress, Rosa Parks, was arrested, for in Alabama the law of the state declared that blacks should sit in the back part of a bus. Local leaders called a one-day boycott to protest the arrest and to demand improvement in the conditions for blacks with regard to seating regulations on the city buses and employment of Negroes as bus drivers. The boycott extended to 369 days; it produced a world-renowned leader, the Reverend Dr. Martin Luther King, Jr., who helped to shape a new philosophy for black Americans, that of non-violent resistance, which eventually spread its influence over the entire nation.

World War II, with its emphasis on fighting for "the four freedoms," had created a climate for change to which the growing militancy of blacks made further contribution. Political civic, social, and religious organizations—the NAACP in particular—began to press harder for full equality for the black population. The Korean War, beginning in 1950, brought further progress toward integration, at least for black servicemen and servicewomen. In 1954 the Supreme Court outlawed segregation in the public schools. In 1957 a Civil Rights Act was passed by Congress, the first since 1875. But massive, wide-spread resistance on the part of whites to the extension of civil liberties to blacks—including not only intimidation and persecution, but also murder—convinced many blacks that more drastic steps would have to be taken if the move toward freedom were ever to succeed. At first there was little coordination, however, among the various groups that pressed for change.

On February 1, 1960, four students attending the Agricultural and Technical College of North Carolina, in Greensboro, sat down at the lunch counter of a variety store after completing their shopping. Because they were black, the waitress refused to serve them, but the students sat at the counter until the store closed and returned the next day to repeat the action. Thus began the sit-in movement. Before it was over, blacks and whites had participated in the demonstrations against segregation and dis-crimination that swept the country and that effected a basic change in the availability of public accommodation to blacks for the first time in history.

To be sure, the sit-in movement marked only the beginning of a period of great turmoil and violence for Americans. The national government took a positive stand in the fight to obtain civil rights for blacks. More civil-rights laws were passed and laws already passed were enforced. Some aroused whites took a firm stand against freedom and equality for Negroes. Black organiza-tions closed ranks to fight together in a common cause. A vast army of nonviolent black and white crusaders attacked racism in the United States under the leadership of Martin Luther King and SCLC (the Southern Christian Leadership Conference), John Lewis and SNCC (the Student Nonviolent Coordinating Com-mittee), James Farmer and CORE (the Congress of Racial Equal-ity), the NAACP, and the Urban League. There were mammoth "marches"; from Selma, Alabama, to Montgomery, the capital of the state; on the streets of the nation's capital, Washington, D. C.; through the state of Mississippi; through the streets of Detroit and Chicago. There were bombings and murders—first of ordinary, humble persons, then of student and adult workers in the movement, and finally of leaders in the movement. The hatred and violence reached even into the White House with the assassination of the young president, John F. Kennedy, in November, 1962.

The old spiritual *We Shall Overcome* became the theme song of the movement in the early days.

Ex. XVI.1 *We Shall Overcome*, Traditional

We shall o-ver-come, ___ We shall o-ver-come, We shall o-ver-come some day ___ For I know in my heart It will come true. We shall o-ver-come some day.

On the morning when 10,000 started out from Selma, the people sang about "that great gettin' up morning." There were songfests at night when they camped along the roadside; there were songfests in Washington while the crowds waited for speeches to begin. They sang *Oh, Freedom, Blowing in the Wind,* and other folksongs, but again and again they came back to *We Shall Overcome,* making up hundreds of verses to fit the simple melody.

As the black masses began to realize that nonviolence was powerless against the entrenched racism in the United States, the singing stopped. Instead, there were angry slogans and riots. Only for one day was there singing again—on April 9, 1968, the day of the funeral of the martyred Martin Luther King. The crowds marched through the streets of Atlanta, Georgia, behind the mule-drawn funeral caisson, blacks and whites holding hands and singing *We Shall Overcome.* It was almost as if they thought King's death would set things right. Many songs were heard during the open-air service held after the funeral procession on the grounds of Morehouse College, but the most moving of them was Mahalia Jackson's singing of King's favorite, the gospel song *Precious Lord, Take My Hand.*

King's death left black Americans numb. The different segments of the black population gave vent to their feelings of desolation in varied ways. In the music written by black composers in response to the tragedy there seemed to be an emphasis on the discordant sounds of jazz, twelve-tone, and electronic music. David Baker wrote a jazz cantata, *Black America*, for jazz orchestra, vocal and instrumental ensembles, solo voices, and narrator. Its four movements were named *The Wretched of the Earth (Machinations, Missionaries, Money, Marines); Kaleidoscope; 125th Street* (a reference to Harlem in New York); and *Martyrs: Malcolm, Medgar, Martin*. Olly Wilson wrote *In Memoriam: Martin Luther King, Jr.*, for chorus and electronic sounds. From Frederick Tillis came *Freedom: Memorial to Dr. Martin Luther King*, for chorus. A work written in memory of Dr. King by Carman Moore of New York, *Drum Major*, used sections of King's last speech along with trumpets, trombone, tuba, percussions, and tape.

NEW DEVELOPMENTS IN JAZZ

During the early 1940s several black jazzmen developed the habit of dropping into a Harlem night club, Minton's Playhouse on West 118th Street, after their working hours to play together in jam sessions. Sometimes they met at Clark Monroe's Uptown House nearby. Usually the group included pianist Thelonious Monk, drummer Kenny Clarke, guitarist Charlie Christian, and trumpeter Dizzy Gillespie. The musicians were bored with the sweet insipid sound of commercial jazz; they experimented with creating something more exhilarating. Eventually news of the experimentation drifted throughout the jazz world, and jazzmen began going to Minton's to listen and to "sit in" with the group—some from as far away as Chicago. The jazzmen had no name for their new sound for quite awhile. When a name was applied, it came from those who listened to the music. To them, it sounded as if the music were singing "rebop" or "bebop," and that is what they called the music. Finally, it was called simply "bop."

Each of the jazzmen in the early Minton group had something special to offer. Charlie Christian (1919–42), who had played in Benny Goodman's orchestra (1939–41), brought a new style of guitar playing. He played his electric guitar as if it were a horn, producing long, flowing melodies that were suitable for solos or for melodic lines in ensemble passages. The piano style of Thelonious Sphere Monk (b. 1910) was somber and marked by a subtle use of dynamics; his improvised melodies were highly original, stark, and angular in shape. Kenny Clarke (b. 1914) had played with Teddy Hill's band in 1939–40, then had taken a part of the band to play at Minton's under his leadership. His style of drumming, inspired by the playing of Jo Jones, gave the maintenance of the steady beat to the top cymbal, while using the bass drum to play rhythm patterns or sudden punctuations. At the time of the Minton gatherings, John Birks "Dizzy" Gillespie (b. 1917) was playing in Cab Calloway's orchestra, having previously played with Teddy Hill and Mercer Ellington. Influenced by the style of Roy Eldridge, Gillespie's trumpet playing was driving, powerful, and biting, with short choppy phrases.

Other influential figures in the development of the new music were bass player Jimmy Blanton (1921–42) and tenor saxophone player Lester "Prez" Young (1909–59). Blanton had played with Duke Ellington's band during the years 1939–41. His innovation was to transform the string bass from an instrument that played chiefly notes on the four beats of a measure to a solo instrument that played fluent melodies like the horns, with fast running notes, sharply defined phrases, and ingenious melodic turns. Young instituted the light, "cool" approach to saxophone playing, using a pure tone that avoided vibrato and giving his melodies irregular phrases. In 1942 Charles Christopher "Bird" (or "Yardbird") Parker (1920–55) joined the Minton sessions. Parker's saxophone style derived from the blues, but he freely juxtaposed full, rich tones and thin, shrill ones; smooth, flowing phrases and staccato short motives; on-beat and off-beat accents. Two frequent visitors to Minton's were Earl "Bud" Powell (1924–66), whose fast, highly individual piano style laid its stamp upon the new music, and drummer Max Roach (b. 1925) whose legato, but strongly rhythmical style was widely imitated by other drummers.

In 1943, several of the leaders in the new music played in the band of Earl Hines. There was a nationwide ban on recording, however, so none of the music was preserved for history. The next year a group organized by Billy Eckstine became the first big band to publicly feature the new music and to record it.

Gillespie was the musical director. The sidemen included trumpeters Gillespie, Theodore "Fats" Navarro, Miles Davis, and Kenny Dorham; tenor sax men Gene Ammons, Dexter Gordon, and Eli "Lucky" Thompson; alto saxophonist Charlie Parker; baritone player Leo Parker; pianist John Malachi; bassist Tommy Potter; drummer Art Blakey; and vocalists Sarah Vaughan and Eckstine, who also played trombone. About the mid-40s the new music moved down to West Fifty-second Street between Fifth and Sixth Avenues, where a string of tiny nightclubs welcomed both black and white jazzmen. Gillespie had worked with small groups on "The Street" before joining Eckstine's band in 1944; after leaving Eckstine's band in 1945, he toured with his own band. The next year Parker and Gillespie traveled to the West Coast, to introduce the new music to a rather unreceptive audience.

Bop developed into a music that was characterized by complex polyrhythms; steady but light and subtle beats; exciting dissonant harmonies; new tone colors; and irregular phrases. The old familiar pieces were used as bases for improvisations—such as *Cherokee* or *Stomping at the Savoy*—but frequently the melodies of these pieces were discarded and entirely new melodies erected on the old harmonies. A listener lost his bearings; he could no longer follow the music or anticipate what was to come. Bop players performed brilliantly, eliciting admiration for the display of technical skill and the originality of the improvisations, but one could not dance to the music. Eventually, bop became an esoteric music, a music for listening only, and it lost the interest of those who wanted to dance. Inevitably, there was a reaction against bop from the musicians themselves. So-called "cool jazz" came into vogue, undoubtedly inspired originally by the saxophone playing of Prez Young, but epitomized in the music of a nine-piece group led by trumpeter Miles Davis (b. 1926) during the years 1948–49. Examples of the style were recorded in Davis's album *Birth of the Cool*. The "West Coast Jazz" school that developed during this period, composed of white jazzmen, emphasized the cool style.

It is too soon to appraise the impact upon jazz tradition of the various styles that developed in reaction to cool jazz. Generally here was a "back to the roots" movement (i.e. to blues, spirituals, and gospel songs). Black jazzmen felt that jazz had been drained of its vigor and emotion by an overuse of superficial effects, that jazz should move back to its primary function of communicating directly with listeners. Among the leaders in the "hardbop" or "soul" jazz movement—the jazzmen of the 50s— were bop musician Thelonious Monk, drummer Art Blakey and his Jazz Messengers, pianist Horace Silver, alto saxophonists Julian Edwin "Cannonball" Adderley and Jackie McLean; tenor saxophonist Sonny Rollins; trumpeters Nat Adderley (brother of Cannonball) and Clifford Brown; and organist Jimmy Smith.

THE AVANT–GARDE

At the end of the 1950s came another new movement in jazz, the so-called avant-garde, the leading figure of which turned out to be alto saxophonist Ornette Coleman (b. 1930). A composer as well as instrumentalist—he was the first jazz musician to receive a Guggenheim Fellowship—Coleman's techniques and ideas exerted great influence upon jazzmen in the 60s. Other innovators include pianist Cecil Percival Taylor (b. 1933) and saxophonist John Coltrane (1927–67). The style of Charles Mingus (b. 1922) links the older jazz with the new avant-garde music. Eric Allan Dolphy (1928–64), who played in groups with Mingus, Coltrane, and Coleman, gained recognition for his handling of the bass clarinet as a jazz instrument.

It is impossible, of course, to do more than single out a few of the active jazz musicians of the present time, in addition to those discussed above. Sun Ra and his group, the Solar Arkestra, have appeared at festivals and toured college campuses. His music is rooted in a new black mysticism that includes, incidentally, the use of electronic techniques. Other adherents to the mystical style are saxophonist Albert Ayler (b. 1936) and his brother, trumpeter Don Ayler (b. 1942). Alto saxophonist Marion Brown (b. 1935) and tenor saxophonist Archie Shepp (b. 1937) have won distinction as jazzmen with original ideas. Lionel Hampton (b. 1913), who early won recognition as the first jazzman to use the vibraphone effectively, organized his own group after playing with Benny Goodman during the years 1936–40. He has toured Europe and countries in Asia many times, first with a large band, then during the 60s with a sextet.

Trumpeter Donald Byrd (b. 1932) devotes much time to teaching, at jazz clinics and in colleges. A holder of bachelor's and master's degrees in music, he studied with Nadia Boulanger in France. Pianist-composer Charles Bell, also a teacher, was graduated from Carnegie Institute of Technology (now Carnegie-Mellon University, Pittsburgh). Bell wrote first in the "third stream" style (i.e. an amalgamation of jazz and classical styles), but later moved in the direction of jazz. Pianist Billy Taylor, Jr. (b. 1921) combines lecturing and writing articles with performance. Both Quincy Jones, Jr. (b. 1933) and Oliver Nelson (b. 1932) earned recognition as writers of music scores for films and television programs. Appointed a vice president of Mercury Records in 1964, Jones continued nevertheless his activities as a bandleader, arranger, and composer. After writing his first score for a French film, *The Boy and the Tree,* he wrote for a series of American films including *The Pawnbroker, Mirage, The Slender Thread,* and *Walk, Don't Run.* For television, he composed music for the *Bill Cosby Show* and the theme music for *Ironside.* Nelson was responsible for the music for the television shows *It Takes a Thief* and *Ironside,* and wrote occasionally for *The Name of the Game.* He developed a reputation as a composer of both jazz and concert music. His *Soundpiece for String Quartet and Contralto* (1962) was given a first performance at Lincoln Center in New York; *Soundpiece for Jazz Orchestra* (1964) was performed during "Light Music Week" in Stuttgart, Germany.

With regard to singers and pianists, it is almost impossible to distinguish among exponents of jazz, popular music, folk music, gospel, rhythm and blues, show music, and concert music. Musicians moved easily from one area to another, resisting being categorized as specific types. Certainly to be named among the singers who made significant contributions in the field of jazz during the mid-century years were Dinah Washington (1924–63), Oscar Brown, Jr. (b. 1926), Dakota Staton (b. 1932), Ray Charles (b. 1932), Nina Simone (b. 1933), Nancy Wilson (b. 1937), and Aretha Franklin (b. 1942). Nat "King" Cole (1917–65) moved in the jazz orbit in his early career, as did also Sammy Davis, Jr. (b. 1925) and Lena Horne (b. 1917) from time to time. Ella Fitzgerald continued to reign as queen of the female singers, challenged occasionally by Aretha Franklin, according to some jazz polls. Joe Williams, Jimmy Rushing, Sarah Vaughan, and Billie Holiday (d. 1963) maintained their high rating as jazz singers. The pianists included Dorothy Donegan (b. 1924), Hazel Scott (b. 1920), Erroll Garner (b. 1921), Don Shirley (b. 1927), and Oscar Emmanuel Peterson (b. 1925).

Public interest in jazz increased greatly during the mid-century period. In 1954, the first jazz festival in the United States was held in Newport, Rhode Island. Its success made possible the repetition of the project annually, and helped to pave the way for similar festivals in other parts of the country, such as the Monterey Festival, which was begun under John Lewis's directorship in 1958. A year earlier, Lewis and others had opened the nation's first jazz school at Music Inn in Lenox, Massachusetts, where students could enroll for three-week summer courses. In 1961 white jazz enthusiast Allan Jaffe founded Preservation Hall at New Orleans. In a small bare room, in the best tradition of old Storyville, old-time jazz musicians—both black and white, but chiefly black—were brought together to play for tourists and jazz connoisseurs. Some colleges and universities adopted jazz courses as part of curricula. White producer Norman Granz contributed considerably to the promotion of interest in jazz with his "Jazz at the Philharmonic" concerts, which were first held at the Los Angeles Philharmonic Auditorium in 1944. Granz sent his JATP units on tours throughout the world and sponsored the touring of other groups as well. A distinctive feature of Granz's recordings was that the music of jazz groups was recorded in the concert hall rather than in studios.

RHYTHM AND BLUES; GOSPEL MUSIC

During the 1940s the name given to records made for distribution in black communities was changed from "race" to "rhythm and blues," and by extension the new name was applied to all such music, whether recorded or not. A new wave of blues singers appeared on the scene; a new style of accompaniment evolved with the use of electric guitars and basses. Among the new names were John Lee "Sonny Boy" Williamson, John Lee Hooker, Muddy Waters (McKinley Morganfield), Sam "Lightnin'" Hopkins, and Aaron "T-Bone" Walker—all of them guitarists except Williamson, who played a harmonica. Walker was one of the first bluesmen to use an electric guitar. Bluesman Roosevelt Sykes accompanied his blues on the piano. Muddy Waters recorded blues for the Folk Song Archives of the Library of Congress, as Leadbelly Ledbetter had done earlier. With the decades of the 50s and 60s came Antoine "Fats" Domino, Charles Edward "Chuck" Berry, Otis Redding, Riley "B.B." King, and James Brown. To Brown, the most popular bluesman of the 60s, was given the title "Soul Brother No. 1" by his thousands of fans. Ray Charles and Aretha Franklin belonged as much, or more, to the blues world as to the world of jazz. Although some of the successful blues singers learned their art through the traditional apprentice method, most began their careers in church choirs or with traveling gospel groups, and several were offspring of ministers.

Mahalia Jackson, the nation's leading gospel singer during the mid-century period, took her gospel songs to Newport Jazz Festivals, to concert halls, stadiums, and churches both in the United States and abroad. Other singers of the time were not averse to singing gospel music even in such places as theaters, night clubs, and gambling casinos. Among the best-known singers were "Sister" Rosetta Tharpe, Clara Ward, Sam Cooke, Roberta Martin, and James Cleveland (each of them leader of a group). Song writer and pianist Cleveland instituted an annual week-long gospel show, called the Gospel Music Workshop of America, during the 1960s. Closely related to the gospel concert was the gospel song-play, three of which were performed in New York and in Europe, New Zealand, and Australia during the period: *Black Nativity* and *The Prodigal Son*, written by Langston Hughes, and *Trumpets of the Lord* by Vinette Carroll. Dancer-choreographer Alvin Ailey used gospel music for his troupe's production *Revelations*, which was taken to Europe after its New York performances. Gospel singing followed the same tradition as the blues, with its improvisatory approach, swinging rhythms, and instrumental accompaniment (piano, guitar, or small combo).

The fifth decade of the century witnessed a growing interest on the part of young white Americans in rhythm-and-blues music—much to the surprise of record manufacturers and radio disc jockeys (i.e. the men responsible for selecting and playing recordings on radio programs). Singing groups and blues singers formerly known only to black communities began to command the attention of young whites. Their first knowledge of the black-derived music came through diluted versions produced by such white singers as Elvis Presley, Kay Starr, and Bill Haley. Later the white listeners began to demand the original music— by this time, a synthesis of country blues, city blues, jazz, and gospel music. Among the favorite black singers were groups such as the Ravens, the Drifters, and the Orioles, and individuals such as Willie Mae Thornton, Jackie Wilson, Little Richard, Clyde McPhatter, La Vern Baker, Sam Cooke, and Bo Diddley. The last named was the direct inspiration for Elvis Presley, the leading figure in the white-oriented rock-'n'-roll music, who spent many hours listening to and watching the stage shows produced at the Apollo Theater in Harlem. The songs of the major black singers were concerned chiefly with subjects relevant to teen-agers, but also included "protest songs."

The influence of rhythm and blues became even stronger in the 1960s. Don Heckman, writing in the Summer issue, 1969, of the *Broadcast Music, Inc.* magazine, summarized the matter thus:

> To say that the Beatles were influenced by Chuck Berry, that the Rolling Stones listened carefully to Muddy Waters, that Eric Clapton and Mike Bloomfield know the work of Sonny Boy Williamson, is to state the obvious. The influence of rhythm and blues in the 1960's has come in a series of impressive waves, from the earliest rhythmically primitive Beatles recordings to the recent arrival of albino bluesman Johnny Winters. There is no sign that the influences will diminish, as the recent wave of blues-infused groups —both English and American—makes clear.

For the most part, young black people did not participate in the huge rock-'n'-roll festivals that took place in the United States at the end of the 60s. In black communities rhythm and blues— or perhaps, it should be described as a kind of black rock 'n' roll—remained dominant, with an increasing emphasis on songs that dealt with the "black is beautiful" theme. New singers and new groups joined those who had made names for themselves during the previous decade—particularly the so-called Motown groups, of which the best known were the Supremes (female) and the Temptations (male). In the early part of the decade an ex-production-line worker, Berry Gordy, organized the Motown recording company—the first developed and owned by blacks since the Black Swan Company in 1921. Unlike that ill-fated company, Motown was obviously destined to prosper from the time of its first big success in 1964, a release of a recording by the Supremes. Significantly, Gordy was able to create a broad market for his black-music product, which offered the appeal of popular music without compromising the strength of the Negro element in the music.

THE WORLD OF OPERA

The decade of the 40s inaugurated a new era in the field of opera for blacks. A National Negro Opera Company, organized by Mary Caldwell Dawson, presented Verdi's *Aïda* at the Chicago Opera House in October, 1942, and Verdi's *La Traviata* in Madison Square Garden in New York in March, 1944. The latter opera was also produced by the company in Chicago, Pittsburgh, and Washington, D. C. The leading roles in *La Traviata* were sung by Lillian Evanti, Minto Cato, Edward Boatner, and William Franklin to the acclaim of the press, which also lauded the "solid" choral work of the performance. The major production of the opera company in 1951 was a dramatization of R. Nathaniel Dett's oratorio, *The Ordering of Moses*. In June, 1949, there came the world première of the John Frederick Matheus-Clarence Cameron White opera *Ouanga*, by the Harry T. Burleigh Music Association at South Bend, Indiana. Directed by Josephine Curtis, the production received favorable press notices. In May, 1956, the National Negro Opera Company presented *Ouanga* in concert version with ballet at the Metropolitan Opera House in New York, and later at Carnegie Hall.

All of these productions provided stage experience—not only before the footlights, but also in the orchestra pit and backstage —for hundreds of talented Negroes who would not have been able to obtain the experience in any other way. The periodic productions of Gershwin's *Porgy and Bess* and Thomson's *Four Saints in Three Acts* served in a similar way as a training ground for black operatic talent. The Karamu Theater in Cleveland,

Ohio, was noted for its encouragement of the production of operas and plays that provided opportunities for blacks to perform. In 1949 Zelma George attracted national attention in the title role of *The Medium*, a work of the white composer Gian Carlo Menotti that was presented at Karamu. In 1950 George appeared in the role on Broadway. She also starred in Menotti's *The Consul*, produced at the Cleveland Playhouse, and in a Karamu production of Kurt Weill's *Three-penny Opera*.

As we have seen, it was in 1946 that the New York City Opera Company became the first major opera company to employ black singers as principals. The pioneers were Todd Duncan, singing in Leoncavallo's *Pagliacci* and Bizet's *Carmen;* Camilla Williams, in Puccini's *Madam Butterfly;* and Lawrence Winters, in Verdi's *Rigoletto*. Among those who sang with the New York City Company during the 50s and 60s were Adele Addison, Carol Brice, William Brown, William Dupree, Andrew Frierson, Eugene Holmes, La Vergne Monette, Edward Pierson, Veronica Tyler, and Margaret Tynes. Marian Anderson was the first to sing at the Metropolitan Opera, as has been pointed out, in 1955. McFerrin and Mattiwilda Dobbs followed in the footsteps of Anderson, during the same year. Ten years later black singers were on the rosters of the major opera companies in both the United States and in Europe.

The galaxy of singers at the Metropolitan included Martina Arroyo, Grace Bumbry, Gloria Davy, Reri Grist, Gwendolyn Killebrew, Leontyne Price, George Shirley, Shirley Verrett, and Felicia Weathers. Simon Estes sang with the San Francisco Opera, as did also others listed above. Shirley sang regularly with the Santa Fe Opera in New Mexico; Frierson sang roles with the Philadelphia Lyric Opera Company and the Los Angeles Company; Garnet Brooks sang with the Toronto Opera (Canada). Singers active with European opera companies included Therman Bailey, Annabelle Bernard, Kathleen Crawford, Ellabelle Davis, Charles Holland, Charlotte Holloman, Rhea Jackson, Ella Lee, Leonora Lafayette, Vera Little, Beryl McDaniel, Olive Moorefield, and William Ray. To this list should be added the names of several black artists associated with American companies who also sang periodically in European houses; among them Dobbs, Grist, Price, Shirley, Verrett, Weathers, and Winters.

Young black singers met strenuous competition in bidding for operatic roles, particularly in the United States, but all were superbly equipped to meet the challenge. Most of them studied privately after graduating with degrees in music or music education; most of them had won awards in the various vocal contests held annually in the United States before going on the stage. One of the leading prima donnas of the mid-century years, the "voice of the century," the "girl with the golden voice," was Leontyne Price (b. 1927). A native of Laurel, Mississippi, Price began piano lessons at the age of four. Her interest in music continued through Central State College (formerly Wilberforce) and led to her obtaining a scholarship to Juilliard after her graduation in 1949. Paul Robeson gave a benefit concert to raise additional funds for her musical training, and a local white family in Laurel, the Chisholms, also contributed to her support. Price's performance in a student production of Verdi's *Falstaff* at Juilliard was so impressive that Thomson sought her out for the revival in 1952 of *Four Saints in Three Acts*. Ira Gershwin (brother of George) saw that performance and invited her to sing Bess in a revival of *Porgy and Bess* that ran for two years, including the Broadway production and a tour of Europe sponsored by the State Department.

Price moved from one triumph to another after her tour with *Porgy and Bess*. Leading composers, such as Stravinsky and Samuel Barber, asked her to introduce their songs. In 1955, she became the first Negro to star in an opera on television, Puccini's *Tosca*. She made her professional stage debut with the San Francisco Opera, singing in Poulenc's *Dialogue of the Carmelites*. After a highly successful career in Europe, Price went to the Metropolitan Opera House. Her singing of Leonora in Verdi's *Il Trovatore* at her debut there in January, 1961, brought forth a forty-two minute ovation from the usually staid Metropolitan audience. In 1962 Price was honored by being asked to open the Metropolitan season with Puccini's *Girl of the Golden West*. When the Metropolitan moved to a glamorous new home in the Lincoln Center complex, it was Price who was given the honor of opening the new house with an opera, *Antony and Cleopatra*, written especially for her by white composer Samuel Barber. Further honors received by Price include the Freedom Medal (1964), the nation's highest civilian award, and the Italian Award of Merit (1965) for "contributions made to Italian music."

Metropolitan tenor George Shirley (b. 1934) was the leading male singer among black operatic stars in the 60s. A graduate of Wayne State University (Michigan), with a degree in music education, Shirley first thought of an operatic career during his service in the army when encouraged by his fellow servicemen. After studying privately, he made his operatic debut in 1959 with the Turnau Opera Players of Woodstock, New York, singing in Johann Strauss's *Die Fledermaus*. Then came a series of debut performances with opera companies in Italy—Milan (1960), Florence (1960), Spoleto (1961)—and in the United States with the New England, Santa Fe, New York City, and San Francisco opera companies. Shirley was the winner in several contests before he won first place in the Metropolitan Opera Auditions in 1961 and made his debut there in Mozart's *Così fan tutte*. From that time on, his extremely active career led to a permanent association with the Metropolitan Opera (the first, and only black male as of 1970, to earn such a position) and to guest appearances at leading opera houses and festivals of the world.

SYMPHONY ORCHESTRAS AND
BLACK PERFORMERS

Black instrumentalists and conductors met with markedly less success during the mid-century years than did their counterparts in the world of opera. There were few places for blacks in the leading symphony orchestras at the end of the 1960s: with the New York Philharmonic there was only violinist Sanford Allen; with the Boston Symphony, harpist Ann Hobson; with the Cleveland Orchestra, cellist Donald White; and with the Philadelphia Orchestra, violinist Renard Edwards. Among other orchestras of the nation the black players included violinist Paul Ross, cellist Earl Madison, and pianist Patricia Prattis with the Pittsburgh Symphony; trumpeter Wilmer Wise with the Baltimore Symphony; French-horn player Clarence Cooper with the Milwaukee Symphony; and timpanist Elaine Jones Kaufman among the eight playing with Stokowski's American Symphony.

But there were some reasons for optimism about the future; among them, New York's Symphony of the New World, which included thirty-eight black players among its total of ninety, and the Berkeley Free Orchestra (California). The roster of the Symphony of the New World included black graduates from Eastman, Juilliard, Curtis Institute, Manhattan School of Music, and the New England Conservatory, many of whom had had performed with such prestigious groups as the NBC Orchestra and the Orchestra of America as well as with civic symphony orchestras and jazz groups. The first associate conductor was Coleridge-Taylor Perkinson; the principal players included cellist Kermit Moore, trumpeter Joseph Wilder, oboist Harry Smyles, and pianist Alan Booth. In Chicago there was a training orchestra maintained by the Chicago Symphony that included several blacks. This program, unique among orchestras in the United States, deserved to be emulated by other music organizations.

Interestingly, black conductors seemed to have less difficulty in finding positions than players, although many had to go to Europe to do so. Dean Dixon (b. 1915) was one of the first Negroes in the nation to prepare for the career of conducting symphony orchestras. After an active period of working with community orchestras and appearing as guest conductor with major symphony orchestras, Dixon left the United States, going first to Australia, then taking a permanent position with the Göteborg Symphony in Sweden, and later with the Frankfurt Opera in Germany. Everett Lee, violinist-turned-conductor with a diploma from the Cleveland Institute of Music, settled in Sweden as the conductor of the municipal orchestra in Norrköping, but also maintained a full schedule as a guest conductor in Europe and the United States. When the Newark Symphony (New Jersey) chose Henry Lewis as its conductor in 1968, it was the first time a black man had been appointed to a permanent position as a symphony orchestra conductor in the United States. A year later Paul Freeman (b. 1935), holder of a Ph.D. from the Eastman School of Music, became the associate conductor of the Dallas Symphony Orchestra (Texas) after study in Berlin and much activity as conductor of community groups and guest conductor with European and American symphony orchestras. James DePriest (b. 1936) established himself as one of the nation's fine conductors during the 1960s and appeared in guest slots with leading symphonies all over the world.

CONCERT ARTISTS

The busiest concert artists of the mid-century period seemed to be those singers and instrumentalists who were associated, either permanently or intermittently, with opera companies, symphony orchestras, or colleges and conservatories. Singers Leontyne Price, George Shirley, and Shirley Verret, for example, not only sang operatic roles with companies all over the world, but also appeared as guest artists with symphony orchestras and embarked on annual "sold out" recital tours. Most other black opera singers found similar opportunities to perform on the concert stage. A number of concert artists (and operatic singers as well) came to the stage via such shows as the perennial attraction *Porgy and Bess*, *Four Saints in Three Acts*, *Carmen Jones*, *The Barrier* (a Langston Hughes-Jan Meyerowitz work, 1950, *My Darlin' Aïda* (a musical based on Verdi's opera, 1952), and a *Ballad for Bimshire* (a musical by black composer Irving Burgie, 1963). We have already named several opera singers who sang leading roles in one or more of these shows; among them, Carol Brice, Andrew Frierson, Charles Holland, Olive Moorefield, Leontyne Price, Veronica Tyler, and Margaret Tynes. Among the stars of these shows who won recognition as concert artists were Betty Allen, Muriel Rahn, Rawn Spearman, and William Warfield. Other acclaimed singers of the period include Eugene Holmes, Inez Matthews, John Russell, Kenneth Spencer, Lawrence Watson, and Alan Wentt.

The towering figure among black concert pianists was Andre Watts, who was counted among leading young pianists of the world as the decade of the 60s drew to a close. Other outstanding pianists included Armenta Adams, Allan Booth, Roy Eaton, Natalie Hinderas (a teacher at Temple University in Philadelphia), Eugene Haynes (a teacher at Lincoln University, Missouri), Sylvia Olden Lee, Philippa Duke Schuyler, and Frances Walker (pianist-in-residence at Lincoln University, Pennsylvania). Frances Cole won recognition as a harpsichordist; Kermit Moore, Ron Lipscomb, and Earl Madison, as concert cellists.

MUSIC ASSOCIATIONS AND
MUSIC EDUCATION

With the black revolution there developed a renewed interest among black musicians in acquainting the public with Negro music, in developing talent among black children, and, even more important, in rediscovering their black heritage. In New York in 1968 a group of composers formed the Society of Black Composers, Inc., its stated purpose "to provide a permanent forum for the works and thoughts of black composers, to collect and disseminate information about black composers and their activities, and to enrich the cultural life of the community at large." During its first year, the society presented four major concerts (with the assistance of a large grant from Columbia University), presented radio and television programs, and worked in an advisory capacity with white and black community groups that wanted to use works of black composers in concerts. The music played on the society's concerts ranged in style from the traditional to electronic, and included compositions as far apart in form as excerpts from Bill Lee's jazz opera *Baby Sweets* to Dorothy Rudd Moore's *Moods for Viola and Cello*.

In 1969 the Afro-American Music Opportunities Association, Inc. was founded, with its headquarters in Minneapolis, Minnesota. A nonprofit organization, AAMOA hoped to "contribute to the enrichment of the total musical life of America" by finding a way to cut through the social and economic obstacles preventing black musicians from participating in that musical life. To assist the black executive director, C. Edward Thomas, a board and an advisory council, consisting of eminent figures in the musical world, black and white, were formed. Among other activities, AAMOA published a regular newsletter, sponsored concert-lecture series on black music, and made available a placement service for black performers and teachers. Several of the musicians associated with AAMOA made a special point of featuring the music of black composers on their concerts; among them, pianist Natalie Hinderas, who performed works by contemporary black composers Chambers, Cunningham, Dett, Smith, and Walker in her 1969–70 season of concerts; and Geneva

Southall (research director of AAMOA and pianist-teacher at Grambling College, Louisiana), who emphasized the historical approach in her series of piano lecture-concerts. Two neighborhood schools received nation-wide attention for efforts made to train the young: Dorothy Maynor's School of the Arts at New York and the Elma Lewis School at Boston.

To be sure, various types of white organizations were also active in promoting the cause of black musicians and their music. Several of the nation's leading universities appointed black musicians to their faculties during the decade of the 60s—composers in particular. In New York, the Henry Street Settlement House appointed in 1969 its first black director, Andrew Frierson, to the famed Henry Street Music School. The University of California and the Youth Corps maintained a music institute during the Summer of 1968 at Berkeley, where nineteen young black students were given intensive training in music. In June, 1969, Indiana University held a four-day seminar, "Black Music in College and University Curricula," under the direction of the University's black-music committee—Dominique-Réné de Lerma (chairman), Austin Caswell, and black composer David Baker. Major figures of the music publishing field, eminent black composers and educators, representative college and graduate students participated in panel discussions and lectures on various topics of common concern. The conference was further enriched by the several concerts of music written by contemporary black composers.

More and more during the mid-century years, black musicians became involved in activities other than performing and teaching. Several earned Ph.D. degrees in musicology and ethnomusicology (as distinguished from music, composition, and music education), entering careers as writers about music and teachers in graduate schools. In New York, music critic Nora Holt, one of the founders of the National Association of Negro Musicians, became the only black member of the prestigious New York Music Critics Circle. Holt also conducted programs of concert music on the radio. Among the books and articles on black music that appeared with increasing frequency were studies by black writers John Duncan (Alabama State College), Altona Trent Johns (Virginia State College for Negroes), Douglas Pugh (of the Ford Foundation), Phyl Garland (of *Ebony* magazine), and poet-playwright LeRoi Jones. Also included among publications were reprint editions of earlier basic books on the music of black Americans written by Maude Cuney-Hare, Alain Locke, and the nineteenth-century writer James Monroe Trotter. Some black composers became involved with music publishing companies.

MUSIC FESTIVALS AND COMPETITIONS

Black musicians participated vigorously in the many great music festivals and competitions being held in the United States and in other parts of the world during the mid-century years. Perhaps the oldest of these was the Berkshire Music Festival, established in 1937 in Massachusetts. Black composers and performers on scholarship attended the Summer sessions of the related Berkshire Music Center which opened in 1940, and also the Bennington Composers' Conferences in Vermont. Without exception, contemporary black composers heard their music played at one or more of the many festivals of contemporary music held during the 1960s. George Walker was co-organizer of the New England Festival of Music, held in the Summer of 1967. In New York, the ASCAP Composers' Showcase of 1965 included works by Stephen Chambers. As we have seen, Olly Wilson won first prize in the first world competition in the field of electronic music.

Black performers made an equally impressive showing, appearing as guest artists at all of the big festivals in the United States and in Europe—the Festival of the Two Worlds at Spoleto (Italy), the Glyndebourne Festival (Scotland), and Salzburg Festival (Austria). Most active in this regard were Leontyne Price, George Shirley, and Shirley Verrett. Leontyne Price and Ulysses Kay were members of cultural exchange units visiting Russia: Kay, with a mission of composers sent by the State Department; and Price, with the group of singers from La Scala Opera Company (Milan) in a Russo-Italo Exchange program. At the First World Festival of Negro Arts, in Dakar, Senegal, in 1966, black musicians of the United States were ably represented by Duke Ellington, opera singer Martina Arroya, pianist Armenta Adams, and the Leonard De Paur Chorus.

Black performers increasingly won honors in American and foreign contests, thus encouraging newcomers to enter the competitions. In 1966 basso Simon Estes won prizes in both the Munich International Music Competition and the Tchaikovsky International Vocal Competition, and soprano Veronica Tyler was a co-winner at Moscow. In 1970 Earl Madison included a specially commissioned work—*Eclalette*, for unaccompanied cello, by Arthur Cunningham—as part of his preparation for the Tchaikovsky cello competition at Moscow.

In August, 1969, the National Association of Negro Musicians, Inc. met at St. Louis for its annual convention and also to celebrate its Golden Jubilee anniversary. Honorary chairman of the convention was Marian Anderson; the presiding officer was singer Theodore Charles Stone of Chicago, fourteenth president of the organization. Several concerts were held during the week-long convention: a recital by William Warfield; a performance of Dett's *The Ordering of Moses*, with composer William Dawson as conductor and Jeanette Walters, Carol Brice, John Miles, and John Work as soloists; the show *Sing a New Song* that featured the Barrett Sisters gospel singers, soprano Thelma Waide Brown and pianist-composer Betty Jackson King, the George Hudson Orchestra, and a chorus of one hundred voices directed by Kenneth Billups of St. Louis.

The black musicians who gathered at St. Louis could look back upon fifty years of astonishing developments in the history of black music in the United States. At the time of the founding of the organization, fewer than a dozen black musicians had won national reputations as composers or performers. To be sure, that in itself was no mean accomplishment considering that complete emancipation for the race had not come until 1865. The music of James Bland, Gussie Davis, Scott Joplin, and W. C. Handy was well known in 1918, though many were unaware that black men had composed the music. The names of Harry T. Burleigh, Will Marion Cook, and J. Rosamond Johnson were less familiar to the general public than to the music world, except perhaps in New York. The fame of bandleader Frank Johnson had not lasted the seventy-four years since his death in 1844. Many persons still remembered soprano Black Patti (Sissieretta Jones), however, and most knew of bandleader James Reese Europe. But the jazzmen who were to vitally influence the quality of the world's music were still obscure figures in 1918; the first symphony by a black man had not been written, the operas of blacks had not received critical attention, there were no black singers with opera companies, no instrumentalists, conductors, or associate conductors with symphony orchestras. Few of the founders of NANM can have foreseen the profound changes that would take place during the succeeding years, when black men and women would be counted among the foremost performers of the century and the black man's music would penetrate into obscure places of the world.

Bibliography and Discography

To cite all of the works used in preparation for the present study would be impractical. Consequently, I include in the following notes only the most useful sources of information on the subject, some of which contain bibliographical or other information that can lead interested readers to additional materials. To my knowledge, the present study is the first to appear in print covering the music of black Americans from colonial times to the present. There is available, however, a useful pictorial representation: Langston Hughes and Milton Meltzer, *Black Magic: A Pictorial History of the Negro in American Entertainment* (Englewood Cliffs, N. J., 1967).

There have been numerous books treating certain periods of Negro music history or certain areas of the music. The best of the general studies, although now out of date, is Maude Cuney-Hare, *Negro Musicians and Their Music* (Washington, D. C., 1936). Less comprehensive but also informative is Alain Locke, *The Negro and His Music* (Washington, D. C., 1936; paperback reprint, New York, 1969). Among the general histories of American music that include useful information about the music of black Americans are: John Tasker Howard, *Our American Music: A Comprehensive History from 1620 to the Present* (3rd rev. ed., New York, 1946); John Tasker Howard and George K. Bellows, *A Short History of Music in America* (New York, 1967); Gilbert Chase, *America's Music: From the Pilgrims to the Present* (2nd rev. ed., New York, 1966); and H. Wiley Hitchcock, *Music in the United States: A Historical Introduction* (paperback ed., Englewood Cliffs, N. J., 1969). The outstanding work on the general history of the Negro is John Hope Franklin, *From Slavery to Freedom* (3rd rev. ed., New York, 1967). Its extensive bibliography can be used as a guide to further reading in a number of special areas of Negro history. An extremely useful regional history that includes much of musical interest is Roi Ottley and William Weatherby, *The Negro in New York* (New York, 1967).

The special Negro collections at various libraries contain some kinds of information about black musicians otherwise unobtainable; for example, the Schomburg Collection at the New York Public Library, the Moreland Collection at Howard University (Washington, D. C.), and the Cleveland Hall Collection at the Chicago Public Library. The Philadelphia Library Company and Library of Congress also have valuable holdings. There are few sources for documentary materials on the history of black American music. The present author's collection, *Readings in Black American Music* (New York, 1971), contains materials illustrating this history from the seventeenth century to the present, and there is considerable documentary material in the Hughes and Meltzer pictorial history mentioned above. Volumes dealing with specific periods of history will be cited under chapter bibliographical notes. In some instances, an early edition of a work is listed in preference to a later one because the earlier edition includes references to black music makers that were later dropped.

Within recent years, several companies or associations have issued reprints of primary sources and collections of such materials, thus making available the best possible kind of documentary illustration. Interested readers will want to obtain catalogues from the most active organizations in this field: the Association for the Study of Negro Life and History, *International Library of Negro Life and History* (Washington, D. C.); Arno Press and the *New York Times, The American Negro: His History and Literature* (paperback, New York); Johnson Reprint Company, *The Basic Afro-American Reprint Library* (New York); and the Negro University Press and the New American Library, *Afro-American Studies*, 25 vols. (paperback, New York). Several periodicals include articles on black musicians from time to time: *Ebony, Journal of Negro History, Negro History Bulletin, Journal of the Society for Ethnomusicology, Journal of the American Musicological Society, Notes of the Music Library Association*, and *Musical Quarterly*.

While there is an enormous discography for black American music in the areas of folk, popular, and jazz music, the picture is bleak in regard to recordings of composed art music. The reader is advised to consult the *Schwann Long Playing Record Catalog*, a monthly guide to recordings available at publication time, which may be obtained from record dealers. The catalogue includes among its listings: Composers, Electronic Music, Collections, Operas, Ballets, Musical Shows, Operettas, Films, TV, Jazz, Folk Music, and Popular Music. The semiannual *Schwann Supplementary Catalog* lists imported or unusual recordings that are not listed in the regular monthly catalogue. Composers Recordings, Inc. has been an important source for recordings of art music composed by black composers and undoubtedly will continue to serve a similar function in the future. The catalogue of the Society for the Preservation of the American Musical Heritage, Inc., under the direction of Karl Krueger, includes at least one work by a Negro composer unobtainable elsewhere. With regard to folk music, the Archive of Folk Song at the Library of Congress is an important repository of folk and ethnic music recordings. The Archive issues a catalogue (available from the Superintendent of Documents, U. S. Government Printing Office, Washington, D. C.), and records may be ordered directly from the Recording Laboratory of the Library. Another useful series is that issued by Folkways Records; catalogues may be obtained from Folkways/Scholastics (Englewood Cliffs, New Jersey).

Chapter I   The African Heritage

The most valuable sources of information about African music during the slave-trade period are the writings of men who lived during the time: Thomas Edward Bowdich, *Mission from Cape Coast Castle to Ashantee* (London, 1819; reprint, 3rd ed., 1966); Theodore Canot, *Captain Canot, or Twenty Years of an African Slaver* (New York, 1854; paperback reprint, New York, 1969); Olaudah Equiano, *The New Interesting Narrative of the Life of Olaudah Equiano, or Gustavus Vassa the African. Written by Himself*, 2 vols. (London, 1789); Hugh Clapperton with Denham and Oudney, *Narrative of Travels and Discoveries in Northern and Central Africa* (London, 1826); James Hawkins, *A History of a Voyage to the Coast of Africa* (New York, 1797); Richard Jobson, *The Golden Trade or a Discovery of the River Gambra and the Golden Trade of the Aethiopians. 1620 and 1621* (London, 1623; reprint, New York, 1968); Robert Noris, *Memoirs of the Reign of Bossa Ahadee, King of Dahomy* (London, 1789; reprint, New York, 1968); and Mungo Park, *Travels in the Interior Districts of Africa, Performed Under the Direction and Patronage of the African Association in the Years of 1795, 1796, and 1797, by Mungo Park, Surgeon* (New York, 1800; reprint, London, 1936). Excerpts from some of these sources and other relevant studies are included in the four-volume work of Elizabeth Donnan, ed., *Documents Illustrative of the History of the Slave Trade to America* (Washington, D. C., 1931–35; reprint, New York, 1965).

Among the useful modern studies of West African music are J. H.

Kwabena Nketia, *African Music in Ghana,* African Studies Series No. 11 (Evanston, Ill., 1963); Rose Brandel, *The Music of Central Africa: An Ethnomusicological Study* (The Hague, 1962; paperback ed., New York, 1961); and W. B. Ofuatey-Kodjoe, "The Principles and Techniques of Ntumpan Drumming in Ashanti," in *Columbia Essays in International Affairs* (New York, 1968). Traditional African music is also discussed in Henry Edward Krehbiel, *Afro-American Folksongs* (New York, 1914; reprint, New York, 1962); Bruno Nettl, *Folk and Traditional Music of the Western Continents* (Englewood Cliffs, N. J., 1965; also in paperback); and the previously cited *Negro Musicians and Their Music,* by Maude Cuney-Hare. Among the ethnological studies that discuss the African musical heritage are Melville J. Herskovits, *Myth of the Negro Past* (New York, 1941; paperback reprint, Boston, 1969), and Richard A. Waterman, "African Influences on the Music of the Americas," in *Acculturation in the Americas,* ed. Sol Tax (Chicago, 1952; reprint, New York, 1967). A worthwhile bibliographical study that includes some discussion of materials related to the African slave trade is Dena Epstein, "Slave Music in the United States Before 1860: A Survey of Sources," in *Notes of the Music Library Association,* 20 (Spring and Summer, 1963).

Among the many excellent recordings of traditional West African music, all of which have program notes, are: *Africa South of the Sahara* (Folkways 4503); *Anthology of Music of Black Africa* (Everest 3254); *Baoulé of the Ivory Coast* (Folkways 4476); *Drums of the Yoruba of Nigeria* (Folkways 4441); *Folk Music of Western Congo* (Folkways 4427); *Music of Equatorial Africa* (Folkways 4402); *Music of Ghana* (Folkways 8859); and *Wolof Music of Senegal & the Gambia* (Folkways 4462).

Chapter II   New England and the Middle Colonies

There are no books that specifically discuss the music of black Americans during the colonial period. Important studies on the social and economic life of the time, which provide details about Negroes, are two by Carl Bridenbaugh, *Cities in the Wilderness: Urban Life in America, 1625–1742* (New York, 1939; paperback reprint, New York, 1964) and *Cities in Revolt: Urban Life in America, 1743–1776* (New York, 1955; paperback reprint, New York, 1964). See also Marcus Wilson Jernegan, *Laboring and Dependent Classes in Colonial America, 1607–1783* (Chicago, 1931). Among the sources treating the general quality of life during the time and mentioning incidentally the role of the black man in that way of life are three books by Alice Morse Earle: *Colonial Days in Old New York* (New York, 1862; reprint, Detroit, 1968), *The Sabbath in Puritan New England* (New York, 1896; reprint, Detroit, 1968), and *Customs and Fashions in Old New England* (New York, 1902; reprint, Detroit, 1968); two by John Fanning Watson: *Annals and Occurrences of New York City and State in the Olden Time* (Philadelphia, 1846) and *Annals of Philadelphia*, 2nd rev. ed., 2 vols. (Philadelphia, 1850). Other informative works of this type are Samuel Sewall, *Diary of Samuel Sewall, 1674–1729*, in *Collections of the Massachusetts Historical Society*, Fifth Series, V–VII (1878–82); and Alexander Hamilton, *Hamilton's Itinerarium A. D. 1744*, ed. Albert Bushnell Hart (St. Louis, 1907). The best sources for slave advertisements, of course, are colonial newspapers. At least two indexes are available: Lester J. Cappon and Stella Duff, *Virginia Gazette Index, 1736–1780*, 2 vols. (Williamsburg, 1950), and Hennig Cohen, the *South Carolina Gazette, 1732–1775* (Columbia, S. C., 1953). See also "Eighteenth-Century Slaves as Advertised by their Masters," in the *Journal of Negro History*, 27 (1942).

A valuable modern study is Lorenzo Greene, *The Negro in Colonial New England* (New York, 1942; paperback reprint, New York, 1968), which includes references to local histories that mention black musicians. Some information may also be culled from the following: Joseph Levering, *A History of Bethlehem, Pennsylvania, 1741–1892* (Philadelphia, 1903); Louis Pichierri, *Music in New Hampshire, 1623–1800* (New York, 1960); Helen Wilkinson Reynolds, "The Negro in Dutchess County in the 18th Century," in the *Year Book of the Dutchess County Historical Society*, XXVI (1941); Edmund R. Turner, *The Negro in Pennsylvania: Slavery, Servitude, Freedom, 1639–1861* (Washington, D. C., 1911).

Pinkster Festivals are given special attention in Joel Munsell, *Collections on the History of Albany*, II (Albany, 1867), and James Fenimore Cooper, *Satanstoe* (New York, 1845; paperback ed., Lincoln, Neb., 1962); the Munsell volume includes the material quoted here from Dr. James Eights. In regard to slave dancing in the city of New York, see Thomas F. Devoe, *The Market Book, Containing a Historical Account of the Public Markets in the Cities of New York, Boston, Philadelphia & Brooklyn Etc.*, I (New York, 1862; reprint, New York, 1969). Negro Election Days are discussed in Orville Platt, "Negro Governors," in the *New Haven Historical Society Quarterly*, VI (1900), and Joseph B. Felt, *Annals of Salem* (Salem, Mass., 1845). An excellent study of the New England psalm is Zoltán Haraszti, *The Enigma of the Bay Psalm Book* (Chicago, 1956). The definitive report on psalm singing and missionary work among blacks is Edgar Pennington, "Thomas Brays Associates' Work Among Negroes," in *American Antiquarian Society Proceedings*, New Series, 48 (1938). The Epstein bibliography, "Slave Music in the United States," is useful for this chapter and the next.

Chapter III   The Southern Colonies

The previously mentioned books by Bridenbaugh, *Cities in the Wilderness* and *Cities in Revolt*, contain much of interest relating to the South. Also helpful in depicting the social and cultural life of the period are: Philip Alexander Bruce, *Social Life of Virginia in the Seventeenth Century* (New York, 1907; reprint, New York, 1964); Luboo Keefer, *Baltimore's Music* (Baltimore, 1962); Frank Klingberg, *An Appraisal of the Negro in Colonial South Carolina* (Washington, D. C., 1941); Thad W. Tate, *The Negro in Eighteenth-Century Williamsburg* (paperback ed., Williamsburg, 1965); and J. H. Russell, *The Free Negro in Virginia, 1619–1865* (Baltimore, 1913). Even more informative are three works of the time: Nicholas Cresswell, *The Journal of Nicholas Cresswell, 1774–1777*, ed. Lincoln MacVeagh (New York, 1924; reprint, Port Washington, N. Y., 1968); Philip Vickers Fithian, *Journals and Letters, 1767–1774*, ed. John Roger Williams (Princeton, 1900; reprint, New York, 1969); Hugh Jones, *The Present State of Virginia from Whence Is Inferred a Short View of Maryland and North Carolina* (London, 1724; modern ed. by Richard Morton, Chapel Hill, N. C., 1956). The singing of the slaves is discussed in Benjamin Fawcett, *A Compassionate Address* (Kidderminster, 1775), and Samuel Davies, *Letters from the Rev. Samuel Davies and Others; Shewing the State of Religion in Virginia, S. C., etc. Particularly Among the Negroes* (London, 1761).

Chapter IV   Two Wars and the New Nation

Among the sources that discuss black musicians in the Revolutionary War and the War of 1812 are Herbert Aptheker, *The Negro in the American Revolution* (New York, 1940); Luther P. Jackson, "Virginia Negro Soldiers and Seamen in the American Revolution," in the *Journal of Negro History*, 27 (1942); William C. Nell, *The Colored Patriots of the American Revolution* (Boston, 1855; reprint, New York, 1968); and Laura E. Wilkes, *Missing Pages in American History* (Washington, D. C., 1919). William Carter White, *A History of Military Music in America* (Washington, D. C., 1944) contains information about both black and white military bands. The best accounts of the career of the first black singing master, Newport Gardner, are in George Mason, *Reminiscences of Newport* (Newport, 1884) and John Ferguson, *Memoir of the Life and Character of Rev. Samuel Hopkins, D.D.* (Boston, 1830). Information about Andrew Law and his other Negro student is found in Richard Crawford, *Andrew Law, American Psalmodist* (Evanston, Ill., 1968) and Robert Stevenson, *Protestant Church Music in America,* (New York, 1966). Charles H. Wesley, *Richard Allen, Apostle of Freedom* (Washington, D. C., 1935) gives an excellent account of the life of Allen and the development of the A. M. E. Church. Also to be consulted are Benjamin Tanner, *An Apology for African Methodism* (Baltimore, 1867); George Singleton, *The Romance of African Methodism* (New York, 1952); and Howard D. Gregg, *Richard Allen and Present Day Social Problems* (Nashville, Tenn., n.d.), which includes a reprint of Allen's autobiography. There is also a separate publication of Richard Allen, *The Life Experience and Gospel Labours of the Right Reverend Richard Allen, Written by Himself and Published by His Request* (Philadelphia, 1887; reprint, New York, 1960). A related work of interest is Andrew E. Murray, *Presbyterians and the Negro—A History* (Philadelphia, 1966).

Allen's hymnals are located at the American Antiquarian Society in Worcester, Massachusetts, and are listed, consequently, in the Shaw-Shoemaker Early American Imprints Index. The major libraries of the nation have microcard copies of the *Early American Imprints;* Allen's hymnals are Nos. 38 and 39, Series No. 2, (1801–20). Two eighteenth-century hymnals that may have provided Allen with tunes for his hymnal are: Andrew Adgate, *Philadelphia Harmony . . .* (Philadelphia, 1788) and John McCullock, printer, *The New Jersey Harmony* (Philadelphia, 1797). In regard to other hymn collections of the period see George Pullen Jackson, *White and Negro Spirituals . . .* (New York, 1944), which contains an extensive list of religious song collections published during the years 1709–1943. It does not include, however, the titles of the Allen collections and several other important hymnals of the 1790s. Another useful book is Frank J. Metcalf, compiler, *American Psalmody or Titles of Books Containing Tunes Printed in America from 1721 to 1820* (New York, 1917; reprint, 2nd ed., New York, 1968). The best source of information about Negro religious music at the beginning of the nineteenth century is Don Yoder, *Pennsylvania Spirituals* (Lancaster, Pa., 1961). The definitive book on the hymn is Louis F. Benson, *The English Hymn* (London, 1915; reprint, Richmond, Va., 1962). Among the important books of writers of the period are John F. Watson, *Methodist Error . . .*

(Trenton, N. J., 1819), and the 1818 narrative of the Russian traveler Paul Svinin, *Reis naar Noord-Amerika,* which is translated in Avrahm Yarmolinsky, *Picturesque United States of America: 1811, 1812, 1813* (New York, 1930).

Of the numerous sources of information about Negro singing and nineteenth-century camp meetings, the best is Yoder's *Pennsylvania Spirituals.* See also Fredrika Bremer, *Homes of the New World: Impressions of America,* trans. Mary Howitt, 2 vols. (New York, 1853); Frederick Douglass, *My Bondage and My Freedom,* 2 vols. (New York, 1853; paperback reprint, New York, 1969); Robert Todd, *Methodism of the Peninsula* (Philadelphia, 1886). The books of George Pullen Jackson contain information about camp-meeting spirituals but must be used with great caution, not only because of his bias but because his theories do not take into consideration the existence of Richard Allen's hymnals and the writings of John Watson, Robert Todd, and others of the period. The most informative of Jackson's books are *White Spirituals in the Southern Uplands: The Story of the Fasola Folk, Their Songs, Singins, & Buckwheat Notes* (Chapel Hill, N. C., 1933; paperback reprint, New York, 1965) and *White and Negro Spirituals.* The single best book on "Ethiopian minstrelsy" is Hans Nathan, *Dan Emmett and the Rise of Early Negro Minstrelsy* (Norman, Okla., 1962), which includes an excellent bibliography. See also S. Foster Damon, "The Negro in Early American Songsters," in *Papers of the Bibliographical Society of America,* 26–28 (1932–34), and J. Kennard, "Who Are Our National Poets?" in the *Knickerbocker Magazine,* 26 (1845).

Chapter V   The Ante-Bellum Period: Urban Life

An extensive study of nineteenth-century urban life is Richard Wade, *Slavery in the Cities: The South 1820–1860* (New York, 1964; paperback ed., New York, 1967). There is relevant material about the Philadelphia area in Thomas J. Scharf and Thompson Westcott, *History of Philadelphia: 1609–1884,* II (Philadelphia, 1884); an anonymous monograph, *Sketches of the Higher Classes of Colored Society in Philadelphia. By a Southerner* (Philadelphia, 1841); Benjamin Bacon, *Statistics of the Colored People of Philadelphia* (Philadelphia, 1856); and William Edward Burghardt DuBois, *The Philadelphia Negro: A Social Study* (New York, 1890; paperback reprint, New York, 1967). The New York scene is discussed in Charles Dickens, *Notes on America* (New York, 1842); George G. Foster, *New York by Gas Light* (New York, 1850); George Odell, *Annals of the New York*

Stage, 15 vols. (New York, 1927), III, and the two pamphlets by Simon Snipe (pseud.), *Sports of New York* (New York, 1823, 1824). See also M. A. Harris, *A Negro History Tour of Manhattan* (New York, 1968); Wilson Armistead, *A Tribute for the Negro* (London, 1848); and Daniel Coker, *Journal of Daniel Coker, A Descendant of Africa* (Baltimore, 1820). Data on Negro population is in John Cummings, compiler, *Negro Population in the United States, 1790–1915* (Washington, 1918; reprint, New York, 1968).

The most significant source of information about individual musicians is James M. Trotter, *Music and Some Highly Musical People* (Boston, 1878). See also Russell L. Adams, ed., *Great Negroes: Past and Present* (paperback ed., Chicago, 1969); Benjamin G. Brawley, *The Negro Genius* (New York, 1937; paperback reprint, New York, 1966); Ann Charters, ed., *The Ragtime Songbook* (paperback ed., New York, 1955); Joel Munsell, *Annals of Albany*, IV, IX (Albany, 1871); Wilhelmena Robinson, *Historical Negro Biographies of the International Library of Negro Life and History* (New York, 1967); William Simmons, *Men of Mark: Eminent, Progressive and Rising* (Cleveland, 1887; reprint, New York, 1968); and Marian Hannah Winter, "Juba and American Minstrels," in *Chronicles of the American Dance*, ed. Paul Magriel (New York, 1948). Trotter's book includes the music of several black composers. Among the works that discuss Frank Johnson are Scharf and Westcott, *History of Philadelphia;* Robert Waln (Peter Atall, Esq.), *The Hermit in America on a Visit to Philadelphia* (Philadelphia, 1819); William Carter White, *A History of Military Music in America;* and Richard J. Wolfe, *Secular Music in America, 1801–1825: A Bibliography*, 3 vols. (New York, 1964). Sources with anti-slavery songs or song texts are William Wells Brown, *The Anti-Slavery Harp* (Boston, 1849) and Edwin Hatfield, *Freedom's Lyre* (Boston, 1840).

Music of both northern and southern cities is discussed in William Wells Brown, *My Southern Home* (Boston, 1860) and Peter Neilson, *Recollections of a Six Years Residence in the United States of America* (Glasgow, 1830). Studies dealing especially with the South are Benjamin Henry Boneval Latrobe, *Journal of Latrobe*, ed. J. H. B. Latrobe (New York, 1905; reprint, New York, 1969); Julia Truitt Bishop, "Easter Morn in a Colored Convent," in *Ladies' Home Journal* (April, 1899); George Washington Cable, "The Dance in the Place Congo" and "Creole Slave Songs," in *Century Magazine*, XXXI (1885–86); Henry A. Kmen, *Music in New Orleans: The Formative Years 1791–1841* (Baton Rouge, La., 1966); and Samuel Mordecai, *Richmond in By-Gone Days* (Richmond, Va., 1856). The Cable articles are highly romanticized and must be read with care, for Cable was not an eyewitness to the events he describes. Important ex-slave narratives that discuss music include Alexander Newton, *Out of the Briars* (Philadelphia, 1910); Frederick Douglass, *The Narrative of the Life of Frederick Douglass* (Boston, 1845; enl. ed., New York, 1969); and Solomon Northup, *Twelve Years a Slave. Narrative of Solomon Northup, A Citizen of New York, Kidnapped in Washington City in 1841, and Rescued in 1853 from a Cotton Plantation near the Red River in Louisiana* (Cincinnati, 1853; reprint, New York, 1970). Daniel Payne, *Recollections of Seventy Years* (Nashville, Tenn., 1888; reprint, New York, 1968) is the definitive work on Negro church music; while the white missionary's attitude toward music is revealed in Charles Colcock Jones, *The Religious Instruction of the Negroes in the United States* (Savannah, Ga., 1842).

Chapter VI   The Ante-Bellum Period: Rural Life

The nineteenth-century narratives that discuss music in rural areas include the previously cited books by Bremer, Brown, Douglass, and Northup. To that list should be added: James Battle Avirett, *The Old Plantation . . . 1817–1869* (New York, 1901); George Carleton, *The Suppressed Book About Slavery* (New York, 1864; reprint, New York, 1968); James Hungerford, *The Old Plantation and What I Gathered There in an Autumn Month* [*of 1832*] (New York, 1859); Frances A. Kemble, *Journal of a Residence on a Georgian Plantation in 1838–1839* (New York, 1863; reprint, New York, 1961); R. Q. Mallard, *Plantation Life Before Emancipation* (Richmond, 1892); Lewis Paine, *Six Years in a Georgia Prison* (New York, 1851); George Tucker, *Letters from Virginia*, trans. by F. Lucas (Baltimore, 1816); Isaac Williams, *Sunshine and Shadow of Slave Life* (Michigan, 1885); and an anonymous article, "Manner of Living of the Inhabitants of Virginia," in the *American Museum*, I/3 (1787), pp. 245–48. In *De Bow's Review*, X, XI (June, 1851; October, 1851) are found articles on the management of slaves. Some information about plantation life is given in the introduction to the historic *Slave Songs of the United States*, eds. William Allen, Charles Ware, and Lucy McKim Garrison (New York, 1867; modern paperback ed. with arrangements by Irving Schlein, New York, 1965). Microfilm copies of the Slave Narrative Collection of the Library of Congress are available at several of the nation's major libraries; for example, the Schomburg Collection at New York. Modern works that discuss plantation music include Orland Armstrong, *Old Massa's People* (Indianapolis, 1931) and Newbell Niles Puckett, *Folk Beliefs of the Southern Negro* (North Carolina, 1926).

Chapter VII   The Ante-Bellum Period:
General Character of the Folk Music

The nineteenth-century sources, in addition to the 1867 collection, that contain music are: Mary Frances Armstrong and Helen Ludlow, *Hampton and Its Students . . . with Fifty Cabin and Plantation Songs Arranged by Thomas P. Fenner* (New York, 1874); William E. Barton, *Old Plantation Hymns* (Boston, 1899); Marion Alexander Haskell, "Negro Spirituals," in the *Century Magazine* (August, 1899); James Hungerford, *The Old Plantation;* J. B. T. Marsh, *The Story of the Jubilee Singers, with Their Songs* (Boston, 1880); Henry George Spaulding, "Under the Palmetto," in *Continental Monthly* (August, 1863); and Henry Cleveland Wood, "Negro Camp-Meeting Melodies," in *New England Magazine* (1892). There are also songs in the two Cable articles, "Creole Slave Songs" and "The Dance in the Place Congo." A large number of items in this list are reprinted in Bernard Katz, ed., *The Social Implications of Early Negro Music in the United States* (paperback ed., New York, 1969). The most extensive collection of song texts is Thomas Wentworth Higginson, "Negro Spirituals," in *Atlantic Monthly* (1867), which was later reprinted in his book *Army Life in a Black Regiment* (Boston, 1870; paperback reprint, New York, 1962). See also William W. Brown, *My Southern Home* and *The Negro in the American Rebellion* (Boston, 1880; reprint, New York, 1969) and Lafcadio Hearn, *An American Miscellany, Articles and Stories Now First Collected by Albert Mordell* (New York, 1924).

The sources listed for Chapter VI should be consulted and as well John Lambert, *Travels Through Lower Canada and the United States of North America in the Years 1806, 1807, and 1808,* II (London, 1813) and C. G. Parsons, *Inside View of Slavery: Or a Tour Among the Planters* (Boston, 1855; reprint, New York, 1969). Among previously cited books see Nell, *Colored Patriots;* Nettl, *Folk and Traditional Music;* and Waterman, *African Influences.* The pioneer work on the analysis of slave music is Krehbiel, *Afro-American Folksongs,* and one of the best of the later studies is Harold Courlander, *Negro Folk Music, U. S. A.* (New York, 1963; paperback). See also: William E. B. DuBois, "Of the Sorrow Songs," in *The Souls of Black Folk* (Chicago, 1903; reprint, New York, 1969); Miles Fisher, *Negro Slave Songs in the United States* (Ithaca, N. Y., 1953; paperback ed., New York, 1969), which has an extensive bibliography; Zelma George, "Negro Music in American Life," in J. Davis, ed., *The American Negro Reference Book* (New York, 1966); Bruno Nettl, *Theory and Method in Ethnomusicology* (New York, 1964); Lindsay Patterson, ed., *The Negro in Music and Art* of the *International Library of Negro Life and History* (New York, 1967); and Richard Waterman, "Hot Rhythm in Negro Music," in *Journal of the American Musicological Society*, I (1948).

Twentieth-century collections of Negro folksongs are numerous. Among the most significant are Nicholas Ballanta-Taylor, *Saint Helena Island Spirituals* (New York, 1925); Robert Nathaniel Dett, *Religious Folk-Songs of the Negro As Sung at Hampton Institute* (Hampton, Va., 1927); James Weldon Johnson and J. Rosamond Johnson, *The Book of American Negro Spirituals* and *The Second Book of Negro Spirituals* (New York, 1925, 1926; issued in one paperback volume, New York, 1969); John A. Lomax and Alan Lomax, eds., *Folk Songs: U. S. A.* (New York, 1948); Lydia Parrish, *Slave Songs of the Georgia Sea Islands* (New York, 1942; reprint, 1965); Dorothy Scarborough, *On the Trail of Negro Folk Songs* (Boston, 1925; reprint, 1963); Newman White, *American Negro Folk-Songs* (Cambridge, 1928; reprint; Hatboro, Pa., 1965); John Wesley Work and Frederick J. Work, *Folk Songs of the American Negro* (Nashville, 1907); John Wesley Work, *American Negro Songs and Spirituals* (New York, 1940).

The Epstein bibliography, "Slave Music," has relevancy for this chapter, as does the immense card-catalogue file compiled by Zelma George, *A Bibliographical Index to Negro Music*, which is located at the Moreland Collection, Howard University. Some libraries have a microfilm copy of this index; for example, the New York Public Library. For recordings of Negro folk music, consult the catalogues of the Folkways Records and Service Corporation and the Library of Congress Folksong Archive. The music represented by the following titles includes examples of the several kinds of songs discussed in the text: *Afro-American Spirituals, Work Songs, and Ballads* (Library of Congress AAFS-L3); *Hollers, Work and Church Songs* (Folkways FJ 2801 Vol. 1); *Negro Church Music* (Atlantic Recording 1351); *Negro Religious Songs and Services* (Library of Congress AAFS-L10); *Negro Work Songs and Calls* (Library of Congress AAFS-L8); and *An Introduction to American Negro Folk Music* (Folkways FA 2691).

Chapter VIII   The War Years and Emancipation

The outstanding work on the music of black soldiers in the Civil War is Higginson's *Army Life in a Black Regiment* (mentioned above). A number of other contemporary books discuss music in the army, including: William Wells Brown, *My Southern Home* and *The Negro in the American Rebellion* (both cited earlier); Luis F. Emilio, *A Brave Black Regiment: History of the Fifty-Fourth Regiment of Massachusetts Volunteer Infantry* (Boston, 1891; reprint, New York, 1969); Charles B. Fox, *Record of the Service of the 55th Regiment of Massachusetts Volunteer Infantry* (Cambridge, Mass., 1868); Newton, *Out of the Briars;* and Trotter, *Music and Some Highly Musical People.* Two excellent accounts of life among the contrabands are Elizabeth Hyde Botume, *First Days Amongst the Contrabands* (Boston, 1893; reprint, New York, 1968) and Laura M. Towne, *Letters and Diary . . . 1862–1884* (Cambridge, 1912). Names of army musicians can be obtained from official army records, such as the *Report: Kansas Adjutant General's Office* (Topeka, Kan., 1896). Among modern studies, the most relevant are Dudley T. Cornish, *The Sable Arm: Negro Troops in the Union Army 1861–1865* (New York, 1956; paperback); Benjamin Quarles, *The Negro in the Civil War* (Boston, 1953; paperback ed., 1969); Charles Wesley and Patricia Pomero, *Negro Americans in the Civil War*, in the *International Library of Negro Life and History*, I (1967); Bell Irvin Wiley, *Southern Negroes, 1861–1865* (New York, 1938; paperback ed., New Haven, Conn., 1965).

Few of the several collections of Civil War songs in print include genuine songs of black Americans; the so-called Negro songs in these collections are generally blackface minstrel songs. But a collection such as Paul Glass, *The Spirit of the Sixties* (St. Louis, 1964) is of value in that it includes the songs of the period that were popular among both black and white servicemen, particularly *John Brown's Body*. Similarly, the following recordings are useful: *Ballads of the Civil War* (Folkways, FH 5004) and *Songs of the Civil War* (Folkways FH 5717).

Chapter IX   After the War

Most of the writers mentioned above who discuss Civil War music also touch upon music of the post-war period. Similarly, most of the song collections listed in the bibliography for Chapter VII include after-the-war folksongs. To the list may be added Mary Wheeler, ed., *Steamboatin' Days* (Baton Rouge, La., 1944). It is important to distinguish between collections of genuine folksongs of black Americans and the numerous collections of so-called Negro or Ethiopian songs published during the nineteenth century that contain blackface minstrel songs. Information about black cowboy-musicians appears in Philip Durham and Everett L. Jones, *The Negro Cowboys* (New York, 1965). The best accounts of the Fisk and Hampton singers are given in Armstrong and Ludlow, *Hampton and Its Students;* Marsh, *The Story of the Jubilee Singers* (1880); G. D. Pike, *The Jubilee Singers and Their Campaign for Twenty Thousand Dollars* (Boston, 1873); and Theodore Seward and George White, *Jubilee Songs* (New York, 1884). James M. Trotter, *Music and Some Highly Musical People,* remains the best source of information about black concert artists and ensembles for the period ending ca. 1775. Simmons, *Men of Mark,* includes information not found elsewhere about several men active in the 1880s. See also Peaman Lovingood, *Famous Modern Negro Musicians,* (New York, 1921).

As mentioned in the text, the most important books on black minstrelsy are: Tom Fletcher, *100 Years of the Negro in Show Business* (New York, 1954); W. C. Handy, *Father of the Blues* (New York, 1941; paperback ed., New York, 1970); and Edward B. Marks, *They All Sang: From Tony Pastor to Rudy Vallee* (New York, 1959). Fletcher is poorly organized and has no index, but will be particularly rewarding to the patient reader. Two excellent studies of Bland are John Jay Daly, *A Song in His Heart* (Philadelphia, 1951) and Charles Haywood, *The James A. Bland Album of Outstanding Songs* (New York, 1947). Gussie Davis receives the best treatment in Maxwell F. Marcuse, *Tin Pan Alley in Gaslight* (New York, 1959). End-of-the-century festivals are discussed in various sources already mentioned, including Fletcher, Trotter, and Winter ("Juba and American Minstrels"). Interesting glimpses of black music makers at work during the 1870s are given in Cornelia Adair, *My Diary: August 30th to November 5th, 1874* (Austin, Tex., 1965) and Jacques Offenbach, *Orpheus in America,* trans. Lander MacClintock (Bloomington, Ind., 1957). Music is included in the books on the Jubilee and Hampton singers and in the book by Charles Haywood. Songs of black composers frequently are found in general collections of American songs, such as Margaret Bradford Boni and Norman Lloyd, *The Fireside Book of Favorite American Songs* (New York, 1952). The sound of a twentieth-century Fisk group is recorded in *Fisk Jubilee Singers* (Folkways FA 2372).

Chapter X   The Turn of the Century

For a general understanding of the period and, as well, considerable information about the musical activities of black musicians the best source is James Weldon Johnson, *Black Manhattan* (New York,

1930; paperback ed., 1968). The black composers of Tin Pan Alley are discussed in the previously cited books by Marcuse and Marks; also in Sigmund Spaeth, *A History of Popular Music in America* (New York, 1948); and Isidore Witmark, *The Story of the House of Witmark* (New York, 1939). Attention is given to Negro musical comedies of this period in Edith Isaacs, *The Negro in the American Theatre* (New York, 1947; reprint, 1969); Lindsay Patterson, ed., *Anthology of the American Negro in the Theater,* in the *International Library of Negro Life and History* (New York, 1967); and Cecil Smith, *Musical Comedy in America from the Black Crook Through South Pacific* (New York, 1950; paperback ed., 1961). Of the few books that discuss black musicians in the Spanish-American War, the best are Herschel Cashin, *Under Fire with the Tenth U. S. Cavalry* (Chicago, 1899; reprint, New York, 1969) and William Leckie, *The Buffalo Soldiers: A Narrative of the Negro Cavalry in the West* (Norman, Okla., 1967).

Biographical information about the major musical figures of the first half of the twentieth century may be found in such standard reference books as *Baker's Biographical Dictionary of Musicians, Dictionary of American Biography, Grove's Dictionary of Music and Musicians, Who's Who in America,* and *Who's Who of American Women.* Other basic sources that should be consulted include the three editions of *The ASCAP Biographical Dictionary of Composers, Authors, and Publishers* and Leonard Feather, *The New Edition of the Encyclopedia of Jazz* (New York, 1960) and *The Encyclopedia of Jazz in the Sixties* (New York, 1966). There are many books that are devoted solely to biographical sketches of celebrated Negroes. In so far as music is concerned, the most useful of these are: Adams, *Great Negroes: Past and Present;* Brawley, *The Negro Genius;* Richard Bardolph, *The Negro Vanguard* (New York, 1959; paperback reprint, 1961); Gwendolyn Cherry, Ruby Thomas, and Pauline Willis, *Portraits in Color: The Lives of Colorful Negro Women* (New York, 1962); William C. Handy, *Negro Authors and Composers of the United States* (New York, 1938); Langston Hughes, *Famous Negro Music Makers* (New York, 1955); Ben Richardson, *Great American Negroes* (rev. ed., New York, 1956); Robinson, *Historical Negro Biographies;* Monroe N. Work and Jessie P. Guzman, eds., *The Negro Year Book,* (Tuskegee, Ala., 1912–52); *Tones and Overtones,* Music Department of Alabama State College, 1 (Montgomery, Ala., 1954); *Who's Who of the Colored Race,* ed. Frank Lincoln Mather (Chicago, 1915); *Who's Who in Colored America,* various eds. (Yonkers-on-Hudson, New York, 1927–   ). Two excellent biographical studies are Ellsworth Janifer, "H. T. Burleigh Ten Years Later," in *Phylon,* 21 (1960), pp. 144–54, and W. C. Berwick Sayers, *Samuel Coleridge-Taylor: Musician* (New York, 1915). See also John Duncan, "Negro Composers of Opera," in *The Negro History Bulletin,* XXIX (1965–66); and Julius Mattfeld, *A Handbook of American Operatic Premieres,* Detroit Information Service Bulletin, No. 5 (1963). Readers who have access to a Negro collection (such as the Schomburg Collection in New York City) will find a large amount of information in music scrapbooks and special files.

Chapter XI Precursors of Jazz: Ragtime and Blues

The definitive work on the history of ragtime is Rudi Blesh and Harriet Janis, *They All Played Ragtime* (New York, rev. paperback ed., 1966). See also the previously mentioned Charters, ed., *The Ragtime Songbook,* and Willie-the-Lion Smith with George Hoefer, *Music on My Mind* (New York, 1964). The most important studies of the blues are Samuel Charters, *The Country Blues* (New York, 1959); Charles Keil, *Urban Blues* (Chicago, 1966; paperback); and Paul Oliver, *The Story of the Blues* (New York, 1969; paperback). The thoughts of the black musicians themselves about blues and ragtime are revealed in Nat Shapiro and Nat Hentoff, eds., *Hear Me Talkin' to Ya: The Story of Jazz as Told by the Men Who Made It* (New York, 1955; paperback); Alan Lomax, *Mister Jelly Roll* (New York, 1950; paperback ed., New York, 1956); and Frederick Ramsey, *Been Here and Gone* (New Brunswick, N. J., 1960; paperback reprint, 1969). A poet-writer's feelings about the music of his people is expressed in LeRoi Jones, *Blues People: Negro Music in White America* (paperback ed., New York, 1963). A significant collection of classic studies on the antecedents of jazz and on early jazz is Ralph le Toledano, *Frontiers of Jazz* (rev. 2nd ed., New York, 1962; paperback). See also W. C. Handy, *Unsung Americans Sung* (New York, 1944).

Among the publications that frequently have included significant material are the *American Musical Digest* (New York, 1969–) and *BMI: The Many Worlds of Music,* published periodically by Broadcast Music, Inc. Especially valuable is Don Heckman, "Five Decades of Rhythm and Blues," in *BMI,* Summer Issue, 1969. For laymen, one of the best bibliographies is in William Austin, *Music in the 20th Century* (New York, 1966). For specialists there are Alan P. Merriam, *A Bibliography of Jazz,* compiled with the assistance of Robert J. Benford (Philadelphia, 1954) and Robert George Reisner, ed., *The*

Literature of Jazz: A Selective Bibliography (paperback ed., rev. ed., New York Public Library, 1959). In the two Leonard Feather encyclopedias may be found such information as lists of jazz periodicals, record companies, organizations, and bibliographies. Of the titles cited previously, the following are especially good for ragtime and blues: Fletcher, *100 Years of the Negro in Show Business;* Handy, *Father of the Blues;* Marks, *They All Sang;* Patterson, *The Negro in Music and Art.* Most books on the history of jazz discuss ragtime and blues as antecedents of jazz. Other references in the text are to Booker T. Washington, *Up from Slavery* (Washington, D. C., 1901; paperback reprint, New York, 1965) and to titles cited earlier: Foster, *New York by Gas Light;* Hearn, *An American Miscellany;* Keefer, *Baltimore's Music.*

Many of the standard collections of Negro folksong contain blues (see list for Chapter VII). Handy's best collections are *Blues: An Anthology,* with intro. and notes by Abbe Niles (New York, 1926; reissued as *Negro Spirituals and Songs: A Treasury of the Blues,* with Abbe Niles, New York, 1949). Particularly useful is J. Rosamond Johnson, *Rolling Along in Song* (New York, 1937), which is a veritible history of Negro folksongs, ranging from spirituals and ring shouts to art songs and including jubilees, minstrel songs, prison songs, street cries, worksongs, and blues.

Naturally, very little music from this period is available in recordings, since the big era of recorded music began only after World War I. The superb Folkways *History of Jazz Series* (Folkways FJ 2801–11) does include in Volume 11, however, a performance of Scott Joplin's *Original Rags,* transcribed from the original player-piano roll. Readers who have access to jazz archives may be able to find similar materials. *The Story of Jazz* (Folkways FJ 7312), which, though narrated by Langston Hughes especially for young people, is equally rewarding for adults, includes excerpts from documentary recordings of ragtime and early blues. *The Eighty-Six Years of Eubie Blake* (Columbia C2S-847) contains Eubie's playing of the old standard rags, and the notes that accompany the album provide fascinating glimpses into the past. The Jelly Roll Morton recordings at the Library of Congress are a history of jazz in sound, including examples of blues and rags from the period discussed in the text. Modern recordings of some music of the time are available in *W. C. Handy Blues* (Folkways FG 3540); *Traditional Blues* (Folkways FA 2421–2); and several albums recorded by Knocky Parker: *Old Rags* (Audiophile 49); *Golden Treasury of Ragtime* (Audiophile 89–92); *Piano Works of James Scott* (Audiophile 76–77); and *Piano Works of Scott Joplin* (Audiophile 71–72).

Chapter XII   Precursors of Jazz: Syncopated Dance Orchestras and Brass Bands

Important sources of information about syncopated dance orchestras and brass bands are Rudi Blesh, *Shining Trumpets* (New York, 1946; rev. ed., London, 1958); Samuel B. Charters, *Jazz: A History of the New York Scene* (New York, 1962) and *Jazz: New Orleans 1885–1963* (paperback ed., rev. ed., New York, 1963); Dave Dexter, Jr., *The Jazz Story: From the '90s to the '60s* (New York, 1965; paperback); Gunther Schuller, *Early Jazz: Its Roots and Musical Development* (New York, 1968); and Junius B. Wood, *The Negro in Chicago* (Chicago, 1916). An autobiography that provides insight into the musical practices of this period is Sidney Bechet, *Treat It Gentle*, (New York, 1960). See also titles cited in the bibliography for Chapters X and XI. The best discussions of black American music during World War I are found in Arthur W. Little, *From Harlem to the Rhine* (New York, 1936); John Jacob Niles, *Singing Soldiers* (Detroit, 1926); and Emmett J. Scott, *Official History of the American Negro in the World War* (Washington, D. C., 1919; reprint, New York, 1969).

The sound of James Europe's Society Orchestra is preserved in *History of Jazz: New York Scene 1914–45* (RBF 3). Although no brass-band music of the period was recorded, some idea of its sound can be obtained from listening to the first three volumes of *The Music of New Orleans* (Folkways FA 2461–3).

Chapter XIII   The Jazz Age

The number of books and recordings available for the study of jazz is so enormous that it is not easy to compile a representative list. In addition to the relevant titles cited for Chapters XI and XII and the biographical sources listed for Chapter X, the following are informative: Louis Armstrong, *Satchmo: My Life in New Orleans* (New York, 1964); Eddie Condon and Richard Gehman, *Treasury of Jazz* (New York, 1956); Theodore Cron and Burt Goldblatt, *Portrait of Carnegie Hall* (New York, 1966); Tom Davin, "Conversations with James P. Johnson," in *Jazz Review* (July, 1959); Gene Fernett, *A Thousand Golden Horns* (Midland, Mich., 1966); Charles Fox, *Fats Waller* (London, 1960; paperback ed., New York, 1961);

Richard Hadlock, *Jazz Masters of the Twenties* (New York, 1965); Raymond Horricks, *Count Basie and His Orchestra* (London, 1957); Orrin Keepnews and Bill Grauer, *A Pictorial History of Jazz: People and Places from New Orleans to Modern Jazz* (New York, 1955; rev. ed., 1966); Hughes Panassié, *The Real Jazz,* trans. A. S. Williams (New York, 1942); Hughes Panassié and Madeleine Gauthier, *Guide to Jazz* (Boston, 1956); Frederic Ramsey and Charles E. Smith, *Jazzmen* (rev. ed., London, 1957); Al Rose and Edmond Souchon, *New Orleans Jazz: A Family Album* (Baton Rouge, La., 1967); Winthrop Sargeant, *Jazz: A History* (rev. ed., New York, 1964); George T. Simon, *The Big Bands* (New York, 1967); Marshall Stearns, *The Story of Jazz* (rev. ed., New York, 1962; also in paperback); Barry Ulanov, *Duke Ellington* (New York, 1946) and *A History of Jazz in America* (New York, 1955). Also useful are Virgil Thomson, *The Musical Scene* (New York, 1945; reprint, Westport, Conn., 1968) and Sterling Brown, *The Negro in American Culture: A Research Memorandum* (unpublished typescript in the Schomburg Collection, New York, 1940).

Gospel music is given special attention in Arna Bontemps, "Rock, Church, Rock" in *Common Ground,* (Autumn, 1942; reprinted in Patterson, *The Negro in Music and Art*); Mahalia Jackson, *Movin' on Up: The Mahalia Jackson Story,* with Evan McLeod Wylie (New York, 1968; also in paperback); and John Wesley Work, "Changing Patterns in Negro Folk Songs," in *Journal of American Folklore,* LXII (1949).

Especially valuable for the blues are William Broonzy and Yannick Bruynoghe, *Big Bill Blues* (London, 1955; paperback ed., New York, 1964); Billie Holiday, *Lady Sings the Blues,* with William Dufty (New York, 1956; paperback reprint, 1969); Carman Moore, *Somebody's Angel Child: The Story of Bessie Smith* (New York, 1970); Paul Oliver, *Bessie Smith* (paperback ed., New York, 1961); and Ethel Waters, *His Eye Is on the Sparrow,* with Charles Samuels (New York, 1950; also in paperback). The leading jazz periodicals include *Down Beat, Jazz Review, Billboard* and *Variety.*

Because of the practice among record manufacturers of constantly discontinuing and reissuing titles it is impossible to draw up an enduring list of recommended jazz records. With regard to individual jazzmen or blues and gospel singers the reader is advised to consult the Schwann catalogue. Most likely to be permanent are Folkways albums: the eleven-volume *History of Jazz Series* (FJ 2801–11); the three-volume *Footnotes to Jazz Series* (FJ 2290, 92–93); the six-volume *Leadbelly's Last Sessions* (FA 2941–42CD); and such individual albums as *Blind Willie Johnson* (FG 3585); *Big Bill Broonzy* (FG 3586); *The*

Real Boogie Woogie of Memphis Slim (FG 3524), and James P. Johnson's *Yamekraw* (FJ 2842).

Chapter XIV   The Black Renaissance

Contemporary periodicals and newspapers are indispensable sources
of information about the musical activity of black Americans in the
mid-century years. Developments of the 1920s through the 40s are
described in Taylor Gordon, *Born to Be* (New York, 1929); Isaacs,
The Negro in the American Theater; Johnson, *Black Manhattan;* and
two books edited by Patterson, *The Negro in Music and Art* and
Anthology of the American Negro in the Theater.

There are available full-length biographies or autobiographies for
three outstanding figures of the period: Marian Anderson, *My Lord
What a Morning* (New York, 1956); Shirley Graham, *Paul Robeson:
Citizen of the World* (New York, 1946); McKinley Helm, *Angel Mo'
and Her Son, Roland Hayes* (Boston, 1942); Eslanda Goode Robeson,
Paul Robeson, Negro (New York, 1930); Paul Robeson, *Here I Stand*
(New York, 1958); and Kosti Venanen, *Marian Anderson: A Portrait*
(New York, 1941). In addition to biographical sources cited for
Chapter X, see *Current Biography;* Edwin R. Embree, *Thirteen
Against the Odds* (New York, 1944; reprint, Port Washington, N. Y.,
1968); Mary Mullett, "A World Famous Singer [i.e. Roland Hayes]
Whose Parents Were Slaves," in *The American Magazine* (June,
1925); Alexander Woollcott, *While Rome Burns* (New York, 1934).

For a list of available recordings of individual singers see "Vocal
Collections" in the Schwann regular and supplementary catalogues,
where performers are listed alphabetically. Of the operas or musical
shows discussed in the text, the following are recorded: *Carmen Jones*
(Bizet's music, arranged by Robert Russell Bennett); Gershwin, *Porgy
and Bess;* and Thomson, *Four Saints in Three Acts.*

Chapter XV   Composers: From Nationalists to Experimentalists

Very little has been written about modern black composers. The
standard biographical sources cited for previous chapters may be consulted in addition to the following: Verna Arvey, "William Grant
Still," in *Our Contemporary Composers,* ed. John Tasker Howard
(New York, 1941); Peter Gammond, ed., *Duke Ellington: His Life*

and Music (London, 1958); Madeleine Goss, *Modern Music Makers* (New York, 1952); Edward A. Jones, *A Candle in the Dark* (Valley Forge, Pa., 1967); Claire Reis, *Composers in America* (rev. ed., New York, 1947); and Nicholas Slonimsky, "Ulysses Kay," in *American Composers Alliance*, 7 (1957). Articles in contemporary periodicals and newspapers remain the most important sources of information along with special files and scrapbooks in the Negro or black-studies collections of libraries. An important bibliographical aid is Dominique-René de Lerma, David Baker, and Austin B. Caswell, *Black Music Now: A Source Book on 20th-Century Black-American Music* (Kent State University Press, forthcoming).

Available recordings (with accompanying biographical notes) for composers discussed in the text include: William Dawson, *Negro Folk Symphony* (Decca 710077); Julia Perry, *Homunculus*, C. F. (CRI, i.e. Composers Recordings, Inc., S-252), *Short Piece for Orchestra* (CRI 1451), and *Stabat Mater* (CRI 133); Hale Smith, *Contours for Orchestra* (Louisville 632) and *In Memoriam—Beryl Rubinstein* (CRI S-182); William Grant Still, *Afro-American Symphony* (the Society for the Preservation of the American Musical Heritage, MIA-118—P.O. Box 4244, Grand Central Station, New York, N. Y. 10017); Howard Swanson, *Short Symphony* (CRI S-254), *Night Music* (Decca 3215, 8511) and *Seven Songs* (Desto 6422); Olly Wilson, *Cetus* (Turnabout 34301). Consult the Schwann catalogue for recordings of Duke Ellington, Ulysses Kay, and John Lewis.

Chapter XVI The Mid-Century Years

For a discussion of modern developments in jazz see Phyl Garland, *The Sound of Soul* (paperback ed., Chicago, 1969); Ira Gitler, *Jazz Masters of the Forties* (New York, 1966); Joe Goldberg, *Jazz Masters of the Fifties* (New York, 1965); Max Harrison, *Charlie Parker* (London, 1960; paperback ed., New York, 1961); Lena Horne, *Lena*, with Richard Schickel (New York, 1965); three works of Michael James: *Dizzy Gillespie* (London, 1959; paperback ed., New York), *Miles Davis* (London, 1961), and *Ten Modern Jazzmen* (London, 1960); LeRoi Jones, *Black Music* (paperback ed., New York, 1967); Martin Williams, *Where's the Melody?: A Listener's Introduction to Jazz* (New York, 1966; rev. ed., 1969; also in paperback); and John S. Wilson, *Jazz: The Transition Years, 1940–60* (New York, 1966).

Consult the Schwann catalogue under jazz composer and performer listings for the music of black Americans in the mid-century period. Other relevant recordings are *The De Paur Chorus* (Mercury

90382); *We Shall Overcome: Songs of the Freedom Riders and the Sit-Ins* (Folkways FD 5591); *Freedom Songs: Selma, Alabama* (Folkways FD 5594); *Black Spirituals and Art Songs* (stereo LP album available from Afro-American Music Opportunities Association, Inc., Box 662, Minneapolis, Minnesota, 55440).

Index

Main entries refer, in general, to the musical activities of black Americans, unless indicated otherwise. In many instances works are grouped together, according to musical types, e.g. musical shows, or according to class, e.g. concert halls. Asterisks indicate musical examples. The names of black musicians (but not other black Americans or groups) are entered in boldface.

533